D0744257

Hometown Memories . . .

Lye Soap
and
Sad Irons
Tales from the Good Old Days
in Northwest Missouri
A TREASURY OF 20TH CENTURY MEMORIES

Hometown Memories . . .

Lye Soap
and
Sad Irons
Tales from the Good Old Days
in Northwest Missouri

A TREASURY OF 20TH CENTURY MEMORIES
Compiled and edited by Todd Blair and Karen Garvey

HOMETOWN MEMORIES, LLC
Hickory, North Carolina

Lye Soap and Sad Irons

Publisher: Todd Blair
Lead Editor: Karen Garvey
Design and Graphic Arts Editor: Karen Garvey and Laura Montgomery
Office Services Assistant: Laura Montgomery
Assistant Editors: Jodi Black, Greg Rutz, Monica Black, Heather Garvey, Lisa Hollar, Reashea Montgomery, Brianne Mai, Justin Shelton, and Tiffany Canaday

ISBN 978-1-940376-03-5
Copyright © 2013

Published by

Hometown Memories, LLC
2359 Highway 70 SE, Suite 350
Hickory, NC 28602
(877) 491-8802

Printed in the United States of America

Acknowledgements

To those Northwest Missouri folks (and to those few who "ain't from around here") who took the trouble to write down your memories and mail them in to us, we offer our heartfelt thanks. And we're sure you're grateful to each other, because together, you have created a wonderful book.

To encourage participation, the publisher offered cash awards to the contributors of the most appealing stories. These awards were not based upon writing ability or historical knowledge, but rather upon subject matter and interest. The winners were: Marilou Perris of Albany, OR (grew up in DeKalb County, MO); John W. Hutchcraft of Union Star, MO; John Buhman of St. Joseph, MO; and Phyllis F. Peniston of Chillicothe, MO. We would also like to give honorable mention to the contributions from Maurice W. of Carter of Murfreesboro, TN (grew up in Carroll County, MO) and Wilford Prindle of Bryan, TX (grew up in Daviess County, MO). The cash prizewinner for the book's cover photo goes to Betty J. Clement of Tarkio, MO (grew up in Maryville, MO) (you'll find their names and page numbers in the table of contents). Congratulations! It was extremely difficult to choose these winners because every story and picture in this book had its own special appeal.

Associate Editors

Bonnie Allwood
Carmeta F. Angle
Nancy Belcher
Jean E. Berry
Marie E. Bird
Pauline Blanton
Elaine Flint Bullock
Ed Chamberlin
Ruth Chinn
Philip R. Clark
Beverly Clinkingbeard
Oleda Cooper
V. Cooper
Charles G. Cotton
Virginia R. Cruth
Betty Curtis
Deborah Dilks
Connie Condron Dow
Sylvia M. Eads
Dorothy Essig
Ruthanna Ezzell
Wanda Findley
Velma Francis
Elaine   Grame
Ruby Lamp

Neal Wharton Lawhon
Bernita Lentz
Edmund Miller
Philip K. Moore
Mary A. Morton
Helen Nichols
Raejean Overholtzer
Max Pearl
Bonnie Place
Gene Prindle
Ruth Carol Trotter Proffitt
Mary M. Roach
Mildred D. Roberts
Bettie L. Sawatzky
Betty Smith
Marguerite Smith
Robert L. Smith
Duane Stuart
Betty Walch
Priscilla "Pat" Faulkner Wallace
Lorraine S. Walter
Helen Waters
Juanita Waters
Vada Wooten
Connie Yates

INTRODUCTION

We know that most folks don't bother to read introductions. But we do hope you (at least eventually) get around to reading this one. Here's why:

First, the creation of these books is in its fourth generation after we took over the responsibilities of Hometown Memories Publishing from its founders, Bob Lasley and Sallie Holt. After forty nine books, they said goodbye to enjoy retirement, and each other. Bob and Sallie had a passion for saving these wonderful old tales from the good old days that we can only hope to match. We would love to hear your thoughts on how we are doing.

Second—and far more important—is the who, what, where, when, why and how of this book. Until you're aware of these, you won't fully enjoy and appreciate it.

This is a very unusual kind of history book. It was actually written by 423 Missouri old-timers and not-so-old-timers who remember what life was really like back in the earlier years of the 20th century in Northwest Missouri. These folks come from all walks of life, and by voluntarily sharing their memories (which often include their emotions, as well), they have captured the spirit and character of a time that will never be seen again.

Unlike most history books, this one was written from the viewpoint of people who actually experienced history. They're familiar with the tribulations of the Great Depression; the horrible taste of castor oil; "outdoor" plumbing; party line phones; and countless other experiences unknown to today's generation.

We advertised all over Northwest Missouri to obtain these stories. We sought everyday folks, not experienced authors, and we asked them to simply jot down their memories. Our intention was by no means literary perfection. Most of these folks wrote the way they spoke, and that's exactly what we wanted. To preserve story authenticity, we tried to make only minimal changes to written contributions. We believe that an attempt at correction would damage the book's integrity.

We need to include a few disclaimers: first, many important names are missing in many stories. Several folks revealed the names of their teachers, neighbors, friends, even their pets and livestock, but the identities of parents or other important characters weren't given. Second, many contributors did not identify pictures or make corrections to their first draft copies. We're sure this resulted in many errors (and perhaps lost photographs) but we did the best we could. Third, each contributor accepts full responsibility for his or her submission and for our interpretation of requested changes. Fourth, because some of the submitted photographs were photocopied or "computer printed," their quality may be very poor. And finally, because there was never a charge, "fee," or any other obligation to contributors to have their material included in this book, we do not accept responsibility for any story or other material that was left out, either intentionally or accidentally.

We hope you enjoy this unique book as much as we enjoyed putting it together.

Todd Blair and Karen Garvey
August 2013

TABLE OF CONTENTS

The Table of Contents is listed in alphabetical order by the story contributor's last name.

To search for stories by the contributor's hometown or year of birth, see indexes beginning on page 497.

Linda Milligan	150	Larry Pollard	54
James Mills	243	John Pope	128
Sidney M. Miner	495	Janet M. Preston	320
Maxine Deatherage Monroe	204	Bill Prindle	389
Colonel Philip K. Moore	101	Gene Prindle	354
Jeanie (Garner) Moore	310	Lois Prindle	390
Marian Moore	457	Wilford Prindle	23
Peggy Moore	201	Ruth Carol Trotter Proffitt	207
Marilyn Moran	296	Virginia Province	145
Gary Morris	491	Norman Provow	279
Mary A. Morton	183	Christine K. Punzo	316
Billie Frances Mosley	74	Eunice Rader	377
Frances Berryman Munsterman	146	C. Max Randal	363
Huston E. Myers	97	Connie Rawlings	211
Alice Nathan	286	Betty Reavis	386
Old Bud Neiderhouse	109	Marilyn A. Reed	167
James Nicks	30	Deloris (Tyler)Reeves	322
Buddy Nigh	105	Gladys Reiman	36
Shirley Edwards Otis	275	Katherine M. Rhodes	226
Raejean Overholtzer	103	Joyce Ridge	318
Eileen Oyler	114	Rhonda Riggins	31
Marjorie Packard	482	Alice Rosalie Riley	63
Billie Paden	113	Patricia J. Rix	229
Avis Parman	289	Mary M. Roach	275
Carol Moriarty Parman	69	Dorothy Roberts	245
Doyle H. Parman	307	Margaret McCush Roberts	155
James D. Parman	249	Mildred D. Roberts	166
Emma F. Patterson	376	Reginald Werner Robertson	484
Dorothea Scott Payne	408	Cora Miller Ropp	110
Stan Peery	248	Marjorie J. Roush	404
Patsy Pendergraph	405	Bettie Lee Sawatzky	472
Phyllis F. Peniston	22	Christy D. Schrock	166
Marilou Perris	17	Vincent L. Scott	251
Donna J. Perry	402	Larry Sealey	184
Lois Pauline (Clark) Peterson	313	Ron Searcy	350
Shirley Peterson	399	Marolynn Shafer	387
Rexena Petree	150	Don Shamberger	229
Maxine Pew	386	Robert Shaney	278
Lester E. Pierce	161	Joanna Jackson Shaw	44
Ruth Pierce	197	L' Berta Shelton	240
Kay Jean Pierpoint	394	Juanita Sherwood	38
Geraldene Pittenger	47	Linda Shoots	145
Donna Keever Pitts	260	Ida Mae Shultz	91
Bonnie Place	126	Lettie Siddens	419
L. E. "Drifter" Place	431	Gene Simmons	187

The Tales...

True stories intentionally left just as the contributor wrote them.

Through the Schoolhouse's Eye
By Marilou Perris of Albany, Oregon
Born 1933

Oh me, oh my, it is so lonely here from May 1st–August 31st. I just sit here with my peeling paint, those pesky weeds sprouting up all around my windows, and those corn stalks in the field east of me making noises as the ears grow from silky little nubbins to big fat roasting ears. Sometimes on a Sunday, if I'm lucky, those little Garner girls will wheedle their parents into stopping by on the way home from church to take a few turns on the old merry-go-round in the school yard, or fly for a while on the swings or take some ups and downs on the teeter-totter while the folks read the funnies. But summer isn't much fun for a one-room school like me. My exciting times are the eight months that school is in session.

The folks around here built me nice and sturdy and named me for the Oberg family, which owned the land on which I was constructed. They gave me a nice sloping roof so that the snow in the winter would slide off. They made me with one big room, hence the title "one room school," but I really have a cloakroom, which was a bit perplexing to 1st graders who don't know what a cloak is. There is a shelf for lunch boxes, hooks for coats and jackets, scarves, hats, snow pants, and of course a mat for the muddy boots and overshoes. And if those bigger boys say swear words, they get sent there to think it over.

I have tall windows for ventilation with screen to keep the bees and flies at bay and I love it in fall and spring, the teacher flings open the windows so that the kids can daydream a little about fishing for frogs with a piece of red flannel on a hook. In winter, I get all warmed up when one of the 8th grade boys haul in big loads of coal form the coal shed and helps the teacher, Miss Mary, to stop up the big metal clad stove. The coal shed is good for playing "Andy over the schoolhouse" too.

After the fire building, Miss Mary Dyer has to bank the fire each afternoon before she hikes up the hill to the close place where she boards during the week. Country schoolteachers don't often earn enough to afford a car you know. I sneaked a peek at the check that little Garner girl proudly carried to school in the top of her green lunch box. You see her daddy is the clerk of the school board, so signs the warrants every month. I think she earned $50 per month. All she had to do was to prepare lessons in social studies, health, science, reading, writing, arithmetic, art, and music for all eight grades and prepare the hot lunches with the government surplus foods–powdered eggs, potato soup, powdered milk, cheese, potted meat, supervise recesses, before and after school, and plan school programs to which all the parents were invited.

I wish the outhouses and pony shed were a little closer to me. On second thought, if the outhouses were closer, I wouldn't smell too fragrant. You know on time Barbara Ann and Sue came back to me whispering they found a cigarette butt with lipstick on it and should they tell that Miss Haber smoked? Miss Muriel Haber had two years of St. Joe Junior College behind her, was all of 19 years old. I think she's kind of lonely out here and she really doesn't know much more than the kids. I don't think she will be here more than one year, if that. I was right, after the kids reported about the cigarette to their parents, Miss Haber's days were numbered.

That pony shed has seen a lot of use over the years–all of the Saunders kids rode ponies the 1-¾ miles to school, and sometimes the mud and snow were almost up to the pony's belly. Other children often asked to have a ride at recess and they would ride around and around me. Once the pony bucked and the kid fell off and rolled into my backside. We were both okay.

Inside my walls were four small desks, about 12 big desks, in rows, except for the times when the winds howled and the children were allowed to pull a folding chair up to the stove to keep warm. There was a blackboard in the front of the room and a piano over on the side. One day the teacher asked the kids if anyone played the piano and 1st grader Marilou raised her hand. When the teacher asked who her teacher was, she replied that her mama was. Truth to tell, she had been learning from John Williams beginner music course and her mama had been a music teacher before she married and moved to the farm. The big kids laughed for the teacher wanted someone who could accompany the rhythm band and obviously, that little squirt couldn't do that.

My insides really took a beating the year the class of Richard Lee, Richard Fay, Gerald, and Henry were 7th graders. After several cold and rainy days, when the basketball hoop outdoors was inaccessible, these boys got tired of blind man's bluff, musical chairs, rook, tic-tac-toe, and hangman and wanted to play basketball inside. The weak willed teacher pulled the shades to protect the windows and let them pass and dribble around the desks. A few close calls with the light fixture and books knocked askew were the main problems. Hurrah for spring and baseball!

Well, I graduated a lot of kids out of my little room, but it got harder and harder to get a teacher to put up with this kind of arrangement, so the last teacher, Mrs. Lois Moreland, graduated the last class of 8th graders with the middle Garner girl Sue, in 1949. After that, when the enrollment wasn't up to the average daily attendance of eight students for the eight months, the state aid wasn't available and I was left as I stood in the corner of the cornfield.

The Greene daughter lived in me for several years, transforming my big room into two smaller ones, but in the 1970s I'd been sitting empty and the Ford's bought the land from the state, razed me, and now the ears of corn whisper stories about those hundreds of kids who absorbed knowledge from their books, teachers, my walls, and floors for more than 30 years.

Lightning Strike, Skunked, and Following the Thresher
By John W. Hutchcraft of Union Star, Missouri
Born 1941

I was born in DeKalb County, Missouri and lived my first 9 years about two miles northeast of Union Star, Missouri on the Davis sister's farm. I am the oldest of seven children, five sisters, and one brother.

We had no electricity until I was 8 or 9 years old. Our radio ran by large dry cell battery. On Saturday night, my parents always listened to the Grand Ole Opry from Nashville. My father also liked Gang Busters, Great Gildersleeve, Fibber McGee and Mollie, Duffy's Tavern, and Sam Spade. I learned to tell time, because the Lone Ranger came on radio Monday, Wednesday, and Friday evenings at 6:30 and the Cisco Kid was on Tuesday and Thursday evening at 6:30.

The telephone hung on the wall and had two large dry cell batteries in it, which were changed once a year. We had a party line phone and 10 or more people on the line, with each home having a particular ring. If you wanted to talk to the telephone operator in Union Star, you turned the crank on the side of the phone for one long ring and she would answer.

One evening my parents were out choring and I being about 5 years old, decided to visit with the operator, so I called her. She was not interested in visiting with me, as she had other calls to handle. Sometime later that evening she called my parents and told on me. After my parents finished with me, I knew not to do that again.

I used to get on the stairs, just out of my mother's reach, and mock her while she was on the phone. She would get mad at me.

The phone bill in those days was paid once a year. They called it "central dues," and it amounted to $12.00 a year. The manager of the telephone exchange, Link Graham (a short, jovial man with a cigar he never lit), would bring out new telephone poles each summer. The farmers would get together and replace any broken or rotten poles and cut the brush out of the telephone lines. When it rained, the two steel lines would ground out if they touched wet trees or brush. In bad weather, the switch had to be thrown on the side of the phone or the lightning could come in and blow the phone out. My mom was throwing the switch when lightning struck and it came in and knocked her down when it hit her.

As we had no electricity, my mother had a wringer washing machine with a gas engine to run it. My mother's long hair got caught in the wringer while she was using it to get water out of the clothes. She could not quite reach the release on the wringer to disengage it, so she pulled on her hair to try to stop the engine, but it would not stop running. She finally reached the release and was able to stop it and pull her hair out. She hurt so bad she cried like a baby. Due to my young age, it scared me and I was no help at all.

My father had a faded blue 1930 Model A Ford car. It was a coupe with rumble seat, which I was allowed to sit in, if the weather was warm. I did love to sit back there.

We had no running water or bathtub. We

used an oblong, galvanized tub, which was hung on the back of the house when not in use. Saturday night was bath night and hot water was heated on the wood stove, later a kerosene stove, in teakettles for our bath water. Oh, was that metal tub cold!

In the 1940s and '50s, Wednesday and Saturday nights were "Town Nights," especially Saturday night. In Union Star, there were four grocery stores, 3 produce houses, and two implement dealers who stayed open until 11:00 or 12:00 PM midnight. There were also three gas stations that sold "regular" for 19.9 cent and "ethyl," or (high test) for 21.9 cent per gallon. If there was a "gas war" going on the prices got cheaper. Main street would be parked full of cars. People would be to the show first, and get their feed and groceries later. In summer, there would be many people on the town sidewalks visiting.

Before Union Star built a theatre, we would go to King City on Saturday night to either the Lucille or the Royal Theatre. Union Star built a new movie theatre around 1949 about two doors west of John & Etta Pickard's grocery store. Pete and Toots Gallagher operated the movie theatre for several years. It had first-class projection equipment, and fine movies. The movie would be run twice for those who arrived late.

Some of the special people in my life, besides my parents, were our neighbors that my father traded farm work with at harvest time. They included Alvin and Pearl Lindley, Mr. and Mrs. Oliver Ashler, Floyd and Esther Terry, Ern and Lula Gillip, Charley and Katherine Davis, Orrin and Nellie Aborn, and Charles and Florence Saddler.

Threshing time in July was something a kid looked forward to. There was one threshing machine in the community that belonged to Oscar Angles. He would go from farm to farm to thresh wheat and oats. All the neighbors would congregate at the designated farm on threshing day. It took many hands, and hard work to get the job done, and when you finished at one farm, everyone moved on to the next farm until everyone's wheat or oats were threshed. It took many days to do this. I always knew that we would eat well on threshing day. All the neighbor women would get together and cook while the men were out in the field. Fried chicken, potatoes and gravy, green beans, corn, lots of pies and also iced tea and lemonade in big crocks were the usual fare offered at these gatherings. I was too small to help thresh, but I got to ride on the bundle wagon, which picked up the shocks of grain and hauled them to the thresher. This would have been in the mid-1940s. By the time I was old enough to help, we had an Allis-Chalmers combine.

My father and one of his brothers, Preston, followed the corn harvest one year in the 1930s up into Iowa. Dad said they were paying 3 cent per bushel to shuck corn in Missouri and when they got into Iowa, they were paying 6 cent per bushel to shuck. Dad said, "We thought we had died and gone to heaven." A man could shuck 90 to 100 bushels of corn a day on average. When they followed the harvest in the evening, they would ask a farmer if they could sleep in his barn. If they were not near a barn, they sometimes slept in a haystack provided the weather was good.

Before we got electricity, we had a homemade icebox. Twice a week, my father had to get a 50-pound block of ice to keep it

City Park, just east of town
The Union Star Band in approximately 1907

cold. The catch pan under the icebox had to be emptied every day, as the ice melted.

We always had cats and dogs as pets. One spring when my father was plowing, he hit a nest of skunks. The mother was killed, but the four or five baby skunks were not. The babies did not have their eyes open yet. My father brought them home and put them with a mother cat that recently had lost her kittens. The mother cat adopted the babies and raised them as her kittens. My sister and I played with these skunks until they were grown. As they were not de-scented, we were careful not to hurt them. When they were half-grown, one of them got its paw caught in a rattrap in the chicken house. I, being 5 years old, knew better than to try to get the skunk out of the trap myself, so I talked my mother into getting the skunk out of the trap. Mom got the skunk out of the trap, but she got liberally sprayed in the process. She washed her long, dark hair in milk, tomato juice, and vinegar, but she could not get the smell out of her hair. She finally had to get her haircut.

There were three teachers who were very special to me in school. My 1st and 2nd grade teacher, Miss Ada Stratton, who taught at Union Star for 16 years, was a very kind, sweet person. Mrs. Persis Kennedy Courter taught 3 years at Union Star and was my 6th, 7th, and 8th grade teacher. She cared about her students and made sure they learned. I did not care much for school until I got in her class. Mr. Keith Christie was the high school coach at Union Star from 1958-1960. He was a good Christian man that I will never forget. My senior year, Mr. Christie encouraged me to go out for track, and he made a miler out of me. I

The Hutchcraft Family

was able to qualify for the sectionals and go to Maryville, Missouri to compete. I did not win first place, but it was a good experience.

A Lesson Learned From the Drought
By John Buhman of St. Joseph, Missouri
Born 1910

I was born August 2, 1910 in a farmhouse near Hurlinger, Missouri. My parents were Oscar and Emma Buhman. I was the second of 13 children; there were 10 boys and 3 girls. The attending physician was Dr. Kimberlin of Cosby, Missouri. He came in a horse drawn buggy. When I was two years old, my parents bought an 80-acre farm 2 ½ miles southwest of Clarksdale, Missouri in Dekalb County, near a lake called the Balice Pit. The boys wore overalls; the girls wore dresses made from feed sacks. There were no shorts then. We wore shoes only in cold weather, went barefooted all summer and fall—even to school. We would get new clothes at Christmas or when we started to school in September. We had no toys and with a large family there were lots of hand-me-down clothes with many patches sewn on by our mother.

We started to help out doing chores early in life, working in the fields, cutting weeds, drilling corn with a one-horse drill, shucking corn, plowing with a 16-inch walking plow pulled by three horses. There were no tractors around then, but dad did get a Fordson tractor when I was 16. We would raise corn, wheat, and oats and we would take some of the wheat to mill, have it ground into flour for baking. We raised lots of hogs for our meat and sold some at the market; we had 10 milk cows and had plenty of milk to drink and cream. We used the cream to make butter and we raised lots of chickens. We had a large garden where we raised all kinds of vegetables and planted fruit trees. We dug a large cave to store the fruit, potatoes, and canned fruit. The cave also was used for protection from severe storms. I helped mother do the washing; a Maytag engine ran the machine.

I started to school when I was five years old. I wanted to be with my six-year-old brother, but I was held back the next year on account of my age. We went to Thornton School, which was a one-room schoolhouse with a potbelly stove fired by wood. It was

John R. Buhman and his future wife, Nellie Miller 1935

on a one-acre tract with two outhouses; a day well and a wood shed. There were four boys and one girl in my class; in all eight grades there were maybe 40 students. My favorite teacher was Norabelle Birt. I was not a silly student; maybe a few slaps on the palm of my hand with a ruler and standing in the corner for talking, it was very quiet. I graduated with high honors at the age of 14 and my cousin and I had to go to Maysville, about 20 miles away, to get our diplomas. We rode the one-railcar dummy and got on it at Clarksdale. We wore knee pants for the first time. The two of us bought a package of Camel cigarettes and we each smoked two, but never inhaled them. I took them home and mother found them, did I ever get a good scolding. I have never smoked another cigarette in my life. We had lots of snowstorms while going to school. Once we had at least five feet. It froze and we cut across the fields and walked over the fences. We had 2 ½ miles to school and walked most of the time; we had no snow days.

My favorite radio program was *Fibber McGee and Molly*. We made our own entertainment; we made a croquet diamond, we had our own baseball team, swam in the Balice Pit, went ice-skating, and horseback riding. Saturday night we had free shows in the park in Clarksdale and sometimes my brother and I would ride horseback to town, go to a $0.15 black and white show at the small theater. We would go to the Clark Drug Store, which had five trays of candy on the

counter. We would get a penny's worth of each, which would be a sack full. If we had a nickel left we would get an ice cream cone. We never got an allowance. We never went to St. Joseph until in our teens. Dad purchased a 1918 Dodge Touring car. We had about three miles to church and when there were muddy roads, we would go in the four-seat carriage and snow bobsled with a wagon box on it. To make a little money, we would work in the fields of our many uncles, taking a gallon jug and carrying water to the men who were pitching wheat bundles; maybe make $0.50. We also trapped game and sold the skins and hunted rabbits and squirrels with a 22-rifle.

When I was 19, my brother had a 1924 Ford Touring car; we worked near Des Moines, Iowa and picked corn for two cents a bushel. In the year of 1930, we went to Aurelia, Iowa and picked corn. In 1931 I purchased a 1927 Chevy Sports Coupe with a rumble seat, might have gotten my first kiss in it. I worked for Gary Noble that summer as a hired hand and received $30 per month plus board. I then picked corn for two cents a bushel. When I finished in Iowa, there was corn back home to pick. I worked like this in '32, '33, and '34 for the same wages. I would save enough money in the summer and fall to get me through the winter. I would do chores at the places I stayed on my relative's farm. There was no room at the Buhman's eight-room house because there were 13 children then. While I was home we would set the washtub full of water in the sun to warm it, and then take a bath in the backyard. In the winter we would heat the water in a tank that was attached to the cook stove. We also would heat the water to wash clothes.

The depression in 1929 and the 1934 drought left the farmers without much to live on. The government started the Conservation and Civilian Corp and I joined in July of 1935 with a group of men and we were sent to Leavenworth, Kansas and enlisted there. We were sent to Little Rock, Arkansas and then by truck we went to Ozone, Arkansas. We put up tents to stay in. there were Army officers there in charge. We were building the road and a lot of it was done by pick and shovel. I didn't do that long and worked myself up to Supply Sergeant. We all wore Army fatigues and were paid $30 a month; $25 of it was sent to our folks to help buy feed for the stock. I made

Johnnie Buhman in 1933

it up to $45 for my job. We must have had 200 or more in camp. We also built barracks to live in. In five months, we went to Kanosh, Utah to another camp. I changed jobs to being a cook with the same pay. I was sent with 25 men up the mountain to build damns to hold the melting snow. They brought supplies and food up to us. We made camp and I cooked for the men. There were thousands of boys who joined over the U.S. We built lots of roads, ponds, and dams to hold water; a lesson was learned from the drought. I stayed until April 1936 with an honorable discharge. We came home from Utah in a troop train and I was the cook on the way home. We had phones on the wall and there were about six on the line, they all had a different ring.

Oscar Fisher, my cousin, a memorable buddy, and I ran around in his Whippet car, also with a rumble seat. In the early '30s Oscar would get dates to go to dances at the Frog Hop on the Belt and to Lake Contrary, an entertainment place with a great dance pavilion. We would take turns driving and sitting in the rumble seat with our dates—what fun!

After my nine months in the Conservation and Civilian Corp, the summer of 1936 I worked in the farm fields. I met Nellie Miller when I was picking corn for Neil Fitzgerald near Easton, Missouri. The church sponsored a card party. I was a good Pitch player and we picked partners. I saw a good-looking lady

and I picked her as my partner. She was a good Pitch player and she won the women's first place and I won first place for the men. So I offered to take her home and in a few weeks, they had a box supper at the Spring Hollow School. I was invited so I bought her box supper for $5.00 (two and a half days of picking corn pay) and we ate together. I took her home; this was in 1933. After getting married in November 1936, we farmed for nine years and then moved to St. Joseph in 1945. I went to work for St. Joseph Light and Power as a bus operator. I retired in 1975 as Supervisor of Transportation. We have four children—Jean, John, Sue, and Rosie. Nellie is 95 and I am 102 years old. We have been married 76 years. We still live in the comfort of our own home.

Stay out of the Green Grapes
By Phyllis F. Peniston of Chillicothe, Missouri
Born 1926

It was a blazing hot day in late July in the very early 1930s. Four cousins, ranging in age from five to seven years, were spending the day together while our mothers were helping Aunt Ruth wallpaper her kitchen. It was a country setting. The houses were far apart in this North Central part of Missouri in Ray County farming country.

Depression days were with us, although, at our age, we didn't know we were poor. We were well fed and clothed. We didn't know about designer clothing, if there was such a thing. We wore dresses, made by our mothers, from flowered flour sacks. Barefoot was the style.

Our play activities were games of hide and seek, anti-over the house with a ball, and hop scotch, if we could find a rock to make our game. One of our favorite activities was to run over the top of the cellar, which was a dirt mound over an underground cave. The ceiling of the cellar had a concrete dome and the dirt was rounded over it for insulation. Inside the cellar were bins of freshly dug potatoes from huge gardens. There were rows of jars: pints, quarts, and half-gallons filled with vegetables and meat for winter use. The cellar also served as a shelter for families when the tornadoes came.

Phyllis's aunt, Leslie (Paul) Stark and her cousin, Helen (Stark) Lowrey in the early 1930s

This was the good life we enjoyed at our early age. As we children played that day, the only instructions we had from our mothers was, "Stay out of the green grapes. Do not eat them!" They looked pretty tasty to us, lush green grapes hanging in big clusters on those grape vines. We didn't have time, we thought, for them to turn to that beautiful purple color in late August. So eat, we did. I don't know how our mothers found out about it, but they did. That's where the castor oil came in. We were lined up in a row and given an ample amount of that nasty-tasting stuff. I don't know if it was a preventative for our own good or a punishment for our disobedience.

We all remember it vividly, even today. We laugh, now at ages 86-88, about the day we ate the green grapes.

Practical Joker
By Wilford Prindle of Bryan, Texas

This story took place in northwestern Missouri in Daviess County. My dad is the author of this story. Practical jokes are sometimes dangerous and may even result in tragedy. When I was a freshman in high school, my parents gave up the farm and moved to a different town from where my school was located. I didn't want to transfer to another school near the end of the school year,

and so I elected to stay with my brother. He was married and operated a farm near where we lived. We agreed that I would live with him during the rest of the semester, and then help him with his farming during the summer. It was during this latter period when I played a joke on him which nearly resulted in a disaster.

We were planting corn. He preceded me with a horse drawn, one row lister. I followed closely with a walking drill. We had our work well organized. At the end of the day, when the horses were all in their stalls, he would remove their harnesses and bridles and put halters on them. While he was doing this, I would place grain in their feed boxes and throw hay down from the haymow to fill their mangers. One of the two mares I used to pull the drill could not stand to have her ears touched. My father had owned her for years before my brother got her and she had always been that way. I conceived the idea that it would be very funny to hide in an adjoining stall and, with the help of a long straw, tickle the mare's ear while he was taking off her bridle. The first couple of times she threw her head he just stepped back and asked her what was wrong with her, with a few choice words added in. On the third try, I gave her ear quite a poke. She threw her head as if it was disconnected from her body. It hit my brother in his face and his head hit the stall wall. He fell to his knees as I crouched fearfully in the other stall. Then, I saw him get to his feet. With both hands over his face, he staggered to the stable door. I was afraid that if I immediately followed him, he might suspect that I had something to do with it. Therefore, I ran through the driveway and around the barn. When I reached him, he was still holding his hands over his face and swaying back and forth. Blood was seeping through his fingers and running down his forearm. I pulled down the hand that seemed to have the most blood on it and looked straight into his bloody right eye. The disturbing thing was that the eye was looking through a cut in the eyelid and the lid was completely closed. I was one scared kid. I obtained a towel for him to hold over his face and his wife and I bounced him over eight miles of rough dirt roads to a doctor. After sewing up the cut, the doctor told him that his eye was not damaged. I don't believe I have ever known such relief. However, the doctor wasn't through. He then told him that the eyelid would probably always droop a little. It did! I was always reminded of the incident whenever that slightly narrowed eye was turned in my direction. I never did tell him that it was my fault. To this day, no one knows how it happened but me. Unless this is published, they probably never will.

Suddenly I came to myself and realized the usher was trying to get me on my feet to view the remains for the last time. I couldn't help seeing that tiny, white scar over his right eye. I laid a hand over his folded ones and murmured, "Forgive me, brother," and continued with misty eyes out to my car for the procession to the old cemetery.

My Pony, Button
By Maurice W. Carter of Murfreesboro, Tennessee
Born 1928

I was five years old in the fall of 1933 when Uncle Bill and Uncle Russell returned to Carroll County to escape the devastation the Dust Bowl caused on the family ranch in Stevens County, Kansas. They arrived after dark at our house and insisted I come outside to see what they had brought me. There wasn't much happening in my world during the depth of the Depression, so I jumped up with anticipation. We walked to the edge of the yard, held up a kerosene lantern to see inside a trailer. There, standing in the trailer, was a small white pony! Uncle Russell unloaded the pony; Uncle Bill pulled a saddle out of the car, and strapped it on the pony. He said, "Get on!" Uncle Bill helped me climb into the saddle, and then led the pony around the yard. My uncles had to leave so we put the pony in a stall in the barn. I was too excited to sleep. I rode that pony every day with my mother's supervision. I was an only child and she was overprotective. The winter was too cold to ride often. I named my pony Button.

I thought I would ride my pony to school for the first grade, but no; my mother said I was too little. She had never ending work to do in and around the house, but every day she took me to Bingham school and picked me up every afternoon. It was humiliating. Thirty or more students walked to the one-room school. Only one boy, who was a year older than I,

rode his pony. Despite my constant pleading, Mother didn't change her mind that whole first grade year. The following year, I think my Dad intervened and I rode my pony two miles to the country school. I let the neighbor kids ride as well, and I would drop them off at their homes until I was the last one. One day, as I got out onto the road, something happened. I never knew what it was. One of the kids must have jumped and made a sudden noise because my pony was startled. It jumped about a foot in the air and took off running.

Growing up on the farm, I had heard stories of runaways. Horses or mules would suddenly take off running whether hitched to a wagon or under a saddle. It took time and experience to get the animal under control. I had no experience and was scared out of my wits. I pulled on the reins and yelled, but that only made him run faster. Fence posts and telephone poles along the road flashed by like a picket fence. A quarter mile west from the school, the road to my house turned south, and the road I was on continued straight ahead. My pony never slowed, nor turned, and we thundered on west another quarter mile toward the Miller farm. Button was fading fast, and wanted to end the run; he turned into the driveway. One of the Miller boys was out in the barn lot and undoubtedly heard me yelling. My pony ran right up to Marvin and stopped, heaving and out of breath. Marvin was a kindly soul, and pulled me down from my frozen position in the saddle. We sat down and he started talking to calm me down. He said that horses had a sense about people and could tell your frame of mind. He told me, "You have to show the horse that you are not afraid and that you are the boss."

After Button and I had rested, Marvin put me back in the saddle and sent me home. From that day on, as long as I rode horses, one never misbehaved with me again. When I started third grade in the fall of 1936, I rode my pony every day. One beautiful day in October, I left the last of the student riders and continued on by myself. I was approaching a square corner in the road. All those country roads had square corners, no curves. Brush and trees grew in the fence row, making it a blind corner. I was riding along, singing, right in the middle of the road, not watching a thing. I was thinking I was the only thing on the road for miles. BOOM! I saw it and felt it at the same time. My pony and I and a car had collided! I remember I was lying in the middle of the road and the two women were bending over me, afraid that I was dead. Off to one side was my pony, kicking and thrashing, trying to get up. I can remember thinking that one or more of his legs must have been broken. My left leg was swelling and one of the women cried, "I think his leg is broken." That was the last thing I remember until the next morning. How I got home or any details were a complete blank. I knew I was in my own bed with a huge bulky cast on my left leg. My dad, mother, and Aunt Okla were fussing around. When I was wide awake, my dad told me bluntly that they had shot my pony. Just like that. That was the way it was—a damaged animal was shot, not "put down" as they say now.

I missed all that school year while my leg healed. By spring, I was going strong, ready to take on anything. I got a small horse that summer, but I will never forget Button, my first pony.

An Unusual Horse
By Sherry Clement of Tarkio, Missouri
Born 1945

When I think of my elementary days, there are numerous emotions that flow through my mind. Great times, sad times, fun times and confused times all flow through at the same time. I had some really good friends, special teachers, and it seemed like learning was easy for me. We were eager to learn and try new things, and it was so interesting to hear the older kids lessons as we all were in the same room. If I could get my assignment done I would always try to understand the other lessons that were being taught around me.

Some of my fondest memories were on the way to school. We rode a horse named Joe to school when weather permitted. He was a very friendly kid horse with the patience of Job until he got older. Dad would saddle him and tie a feed sack on the saddle horn so we could place those metal lunch buckets with our noon meal inside. It might be soup in the thermos or sandwiches and miscellaneous items but everyone had the same kinds of lunch so there wasn't any notice of someone having more or less except for one family who often brought onion sandwiches.

Jim, Karen, and Sherry on Joe the horse

We all wore the same kinds of clothes, often leftovers from older siblings so we all felt equal and part of a school family.

Old Joe, as we called him, was an unusual horse. On days that dad needed him to work cattle or something, we would tie the reins around the saddle horn and pat him on the rump and tell him to go home. He would head down the mile and a half to our house and dad would use him all day. When it was time for school to end dad would whistle for Joe to come in from the pasture and dad would put the reins over the saddle horn pat him on the rump and send him to school to pick us up. When we were dismissed he would be out by the door with the reins over the saddle horn waiting for us. Once in a while he would have an ornery streak and my brother Jim would have to run him around the school to settle him down so I could get on. He would step sideways every time I tried to get on. He also could swell his stomach so the saddle girt wasn't as tight as it should be when we tried to step up and the saddle would turn and dump us on the ground, but we loved him and we would get up off the ground and tighten the saddle girt and get back on. We were told that he was an unusual horse in many ways such as he never seemed to be afraid of bridges, road equipment, etc. He didn't spook and jump sideways if we encountered a road grader on the way home. He seemed to change personalities if a man would get on him. He would buck, jump and twist like a bucking bronco.

I remember a few times when we left home late and he would decide to run away with us and we got to school on time after all. He seemed like a human sometimes and could tell what we needed to do. We had some neighbor kids who also rode a horse to school and they would often ride with us. However, their horse was an older horse who wouldn't run no matter how hard you kicked and occasionally the boys would make us girls ride her, and they would run ahead and leave us way behind. One time it was very slick and muddy and they took off running ahead of us and we were so angry at them but we were soon laughing so hard as we saw the third boy fall off into a big mud puddle right in front of us.

We had a neighbor girl who often rode with us to and from school. She and my brother Jim would share the saddle and I would ride on behind the saddle. She had kidney problems and often needed to get off on the ride home to relieve herself. One time that I remember well was when she asked Jim to stop a short distance from her house and he thought she could hold it but she pleaded for him to stop and he refused. The next thing I remember was fluid running down the sides of the saddle and Jim was hollering at her. She quickly let him know that she had asked him to stop.

For some reason we did walk to school occasionally. Usually it was in nice weather but one time it was still pretty cold and we decided to cut across a field that had a stream in it. Of course Jim could step across but I stepped in and my old brown socks that were held up by a garter got soaking wet and were freezing my legs. I finally took them off and they were frozen stiff by the time we got home. It looked like I had a crooked cane in my hand when I walked in the door at home. Sometimes we would walk past a pasture and there was a big bull that walked the fence with us and scared me so badly. We always walked on the opposite side of the road and tried not to look at him but I always trembled when I saw him near the road.

On nice days we could see the clothesline about a half mile from home and we would always fuss over whose turn it was to gather in all the diapers or fold the clothes. We usually took turns gathering the diapers in and the other one would fold and put them away. But we could never remember whose turn it was to do what. We had three little sisters so there were lots of diapers on washday.

One of the special things I remember was putting on plays for the community. We would practice our lines for days. We had to hang up the stage curtains to shut off the front of the room. All the kids would have a part and we could talk the teacher into practice again because someone needed extra practice. I can still recite my first piece: My piece is short and snappy. Hope your Christmas will be happy. All the families in the neighborhood came and brought some snacks to eat after the play. It was a great time of visiting and seeing one another and performing for our parents.

When I became an upper classman I would often hurry and get my assignment done so I could help the younger grades with something. I remember giving a spelling test one time and the word was the abbreviation for pounds. The girl leaned over and said she called that lubbs. We got tickled and laughed for a long while before we could tell everyone what was so funny.

In warm weather we often played softball at recess. Some were good players, some not so good but it didn't seem to matter and recess was always over too soon. In cold weather we had a huge hill out behind the school that was wonderful for sleigh riding. No matter what we were doing we always had to make a trip to the toilet before resuming school. I never liked going in there but there was no other choice. I was one of the lucky ones to have indoor plumbing at home.

I remember one really sad day when we all of a sudden noticed billows of smoke rolling down from the ceiling and soon realized the building was on fire. It was cold so we all grabbed our coats from the cloakroom and ran outside, far away from the building and watched as it slowly burned to the ground. Our parents were notified somehow and they all pulled up to the school to find a bunch of crying kids. I lost a little red jacket in the fire and that was all I could think about.

We didn't go to school for a while but eventually we had school in a neighbor's tenant house. We were in several rooms and didn't have much playground equipment to entertain us. It was hard to adjust to being unable to see all the kids in the same room and we didn't have the old merry-go-round that we sometimes played on. Later an old school house was moved in where the former building had been. It had one big room for class, a washroom, and a cloakroom. It was really pretty nice except it was very cold in the winter months. I remember tearing up large catalogues and folding the pages to stuff between the cracks in the wainscoting. These may have happened from moving the building. We also hung the stage curtains on the north wall to slow down the draft that came through the wall. We often kept our coats and hats on during the day.

These are some of the memories that I had of my country school days and I have often wished I could take my children and grandchildren back for a visit. They would be amazed at the changes that have taken place in the classroom. There are some of the things that are good and some that are not so good.

Neal Carpenter in 2010

A Life Lesson
By Neal Carpenter of Raytown, Missouri
Born 1925

Three young innocent corn fed girls from Stanberry, Missouri and one beautiful, warm spring day; we were looking for adventures and decided to skip school. We only skipped one day per year. We decided to go to Albany, Missouri where my cousin Irene and Frank Groom ran a restaurant. We made our way there and had lunch and started back to Stanberry walking along the highway. We all rode the same school bus and we soon realized if we didn't get a ride we would miss our bus and our parents would know something was up. As luck would have it a car stopped and asked if we would like a ride. It was a young man driving and we knew we should not get in the car, but fear of missing the bus overcame the fear of no ride. We climbed into the back seat and the gentleman asked where we were going. We told him to Stanberry. He inquired if we knew where the Enyart Lumberyard was; of course we knew. He said that was where he was going. Well when he got into town he proceeded on through town toward Maryville, Missouri. Then we were really scared as he pulled off on a country dirt road and stopped. Our hearts skipped a few beats, then he turned himself around toward the back seat and faced

us smiling and said, "I am going to the lumber yard, but wanted to teach you girls a lesson. Don't get in a car with someone you don't know. You lucked out this time." He turned the car around and headed back to town and the lumberyard and let us out. I am presently 88 years old, but have never forgotten the lesson.

Buttons Just Didn't Do Their Jobs
By Virginia Whitmore of Kansas City,
Missouri
Born 1930

I was born in 1930 during The Great Depression, dust storms, and the beginnings of World War II. One of my earliest memories I have is around age two. We lived in the city of Saint Joseph, but I was too young to know if it was a house or an apartment. We had close neighbors and it was during the depression years so city folk were allowed to have gardens and chickens in their yard. Everyone did anything they could to put food on the table. I remember eating very well, about six meals a day. My grandparents lived across the alley and I would go to visit them and of course, they fed me, especially lots of bread and gravy. This, plus meals at home made me a very fat little girl. My father got angry if I did not eat my meal at home when he was there. My grandfather had bought me a high chair at Montgomery Ward or Sears for ten cents.

For my first Christmas, Santa brought a small wooden rocking chair. It was very expensive, almost three dollars. The Christmas tree was very large, but there were very few ornaments. Among them was a small, metal, rite-way jingle bell. I don't believe there were any lights. During these years, I was a very lucky and pampered little girl. I had my hair and dresses like Shirley Temple. Every day I had to endure hours of combing and putting my hair in long curls.

When I was four years old, we moved to a house with acreage. There were trees and flowers, more than you could imagine. Every kind of bird and flower was there. It was a little girl's dream to pick flowers, as many and for as long as you wanted. I made clover chains and hollyhock dolls and brought home fresh bouquets of violets, irises, roses, and daisies every day. My mother became quite ill that year. Her appendix burst and she was in the hospital for several weeks. She was not expected to live. It was July and the temperature stood at one hundred degrees for days on end. There was no air conditioning at the hospital then, or anywhere else for that matter. We had fans, but they could not be used due to mother's high fever from peritonitis. When my mother came home from the hospital, she was unable to do anything for a long time. I would go to her bedside and she would have no appetite, but I was always willing to help her, especially with the cherry pie. My father always liked to eat a big meal at night; he worked very hard. There was always pie for dessert. My mother baked wonderful pies and bread. She made every kind of bread.

The year of 1934 was difficult. During the summer, we had very extreme heat. I know the animals suffered. Many of the chickens smothered and all but one cow was sold. All of the hogs were sold as well. We had a watermelon patch not far from the house and we heard the melons popping open from the heat. It was a good thing I liked watermelon because I ate so many of them. It had been so hot and dry the crops had literally burned up in the fields. So when the winds came, the dust blew and it came rolling across the land. It must have been late August or September when the dust storms came. One particularly bad storm came in the afternoon. The animals had been put in the barn and my mother and father and I stayed in the kitchen with the doors and windows closed. My parents put wet towels and other cloths around the windows to keep out the dust. It was hot and I thought that I would surely choke to death. I couldn't breathe. It got so dark that we lit the kerosene lamps. The storm raged for hours. It seemed like an eternity. The sound it made was so loud that you could not talk, not that we wanted to. If you opened your mouth, you would choke on dust that filtered in, in spite of all the precautions taken.

When winter came, the extreme cold temperatures and snow took over. I remember walking to school when snow had drifted five or six feet alongside the road. I was very small so I would walk on top of the frozen drifts. I made it every day, but I was alone and if I had fallen into the snow that deep, I surely would not be here today. Being a child, I did not realize how dangerous it was. I attended a one-room school with one teacher who taught all eight grades. We had about 14 students in the whole school. One year I contracted scarlet fever and was out of school for a month. Our house was quarantined and I was very sick. There were no antibiotics then and the disease was highly contagious.

During all the bleak times, I believe parents tried to find comfort and cheer for themselves and their children from time to time. One highlight of all was the Fourth of July celebrations. It was always my favorite holiday. My mother would start frying chicken early in the morning and getting things packed for a picnic lunch. We had a Model T Ford and drove to Lake Contrary Amusement park. There was a large wood and grassy area for picnics and the exciting rides in the main areas and a marvelous ballroom for dancing. The large merry-go-round had Denzel hand carved wooden animals that after the park closed, sold for thousands of dollars as collectible antiques. Lake Contrary Park was a fabulous place. It was safe for children to play and ride the boats, Ferris wheel, the big dipper, and merry go round as we chose. We stayed all day and then there were fireworks in the evening! It was my favorite holiday.

When WWII came along the world changed and so did we. My own recollections of World War II were as a young teen. We did our part by collecting paper and scrap metal for the war effort. We lived in the vicinity of Rosecrans Air Field and often had air raid warnings. My mother purchased black out curtains to keep out the lights of the homes so that enemy planes could not locate towns and cities. There was no GPS at that time. My father was an air raid warden who dressed in dark clothing and went around the neighborhood checking if everyone was complying with the no visible lighting regulations. I especially remember riding rickety streetcars or busses (no gasoline) so no one except emergency personnel such as doctors could get gasoline. I was taking a home making class at school and we were learning to cook using powdered eggs and milk because of food rationing. Sugar was rationed and consequently, soft drinks and ice cream had lost its flavor. We were living very frugally, mostly because there was not much you could buy. Ladies silk or nylon stockings and elastic in your underwear were missing. Buttons just didn't do the job very well; I was so embarrassed one day when I popped a button and lost my panties on a downtown street.

The Little Red Fox Named Suzie
By Karen Jones of Skidmore, Missouri
Born 1947

In the mid to late 1950s, my Father Francis Jones was recruited by my Uncle Ora Jones to rid his farm of a marauding red fox. The fox had relentlessly visited my uncle's hen house several times and had killed hens, which were essential to the farm's weekly egg sales. The two determined men lay in wait one night and managed to eliminate the fox.

Upon inspection of their prized kill, the men discovered that the fox was a nursing mother. They back tracked the fox in the snow and found her den of newborns. Not wanting to kill helpless animals, they retrieved and distributed the small balls of fur among various families. My mother Edna Jones was not impressed with my father's sympathy for the little fur ball and made it clear that the responsibility of saving the fox was going to be a family affair. A box with old towels was placed behind the fuel oil stove and our inside dog Trixie immediately adopted the fox which

Karen's father, Francis Jones

had by that time been named Suzie.

Doll bottles were located and raw milk heated to insure Suzie's survival. With my mother's devotion to middle of the night feedings and Trixie's warmth Suzie survived to be a healthy animal with all the comforts of a loving family. Suzie quickly learned that she could jump high, run fast, and avoid the wrath of my mother by hiding under the claw bathtub. Suzie's determination to get on the kitchen table, lick the fresh butter, and hide loose items was her undoing. The battle of wills between my mother and Suzie provided hours of entertainment for the family and my father would excuse Suzie's antics as being "a natural thing for a wild animal." I don't remember exactly what Suzie did to provoke

Suzie the fox

29

my mother, but the fox was unceremoniously banished to the yard where she befriended our outdoor dog Duke, a black cocker spaniel.

Duke taught Suzie how to chase cars, patrol the garden for rabbits, and sniff out moles and mice. The two animals were always together and when Suzie dug herself a den under the snowball bush Duke would sleep on top of it. As Suzie matured, she would venture out and would disappear for days at a time. Her visits home became fewer and then she began to visit only during the night. She would scratch on my parent's bedroom window, accept a bowl of milk with bread, and leave before daylight. Her visits eventually stopped and my father reluctantly cleaned out and filled in her den. The den was full of odd toys, socks, clothes pens, hair rollers, and candy wrappers. Duke continued to sleep under the bush as if he was waiting for her return. Our two-story home on the edge of Skidmore, Missouri held many happy memories of our two dogs and that little red fox named Suzie.

Out Stepped a Hobo
By James Gerry Ferguson of Maryville, Missouri
Born 1948

I was born and raised here and lived most of my life in northwest Missouri and I love it here more than any place I've ever been. Probably the most magical experience I had here was the snowstorms of the early 1960s. In those days, you didn't even think about a previous weather forecast, but rather just dealt with it as it came. I remember my dad getting us four kids out in the car to go to the store the evening the snow began and it was beautiful, sparkling, and pure white. It rose by inches before your eyes. We made our trip with no problems in the '59 Ford.

During that snowstorm, the next morning, dad and I drove uptown and the snow was falling so thick you couldn't see over the intersection. Small town Maryville was where this took place. I'll tell you one more story. In those days, back to the 1950s, the railroad ran through town, where we lived a few blocks from the tracks. One Sunday we had been gone from home all day visiting my grandparents in King City. It was late autumn and getting dark early and so when we got to the house, shortly thereafter it was bedtime. I was the oldest, about nine years old, and my brother and I shared a bed and he was already asleep and I was lying there just looking at the closet door when it opened and out stepped a man. A hobo off the railroad I'm guessing after thinking on it for many years. At the time, I was merely bewildered. I just lay there and he peered around and then backed back into the closet and left it open a crack. I pulled the cover up just under my eyes and watched and right away, he left the closet and exited our bedroom and slipped down the hall. I didn't sound an alarm; I was froze and actually went on to sleep and told my folks about it the next day. I think they thought I'd imagined it or was dreaming, but I wasn't. It actually happened. No harm was done, nothing was missing. I think he found an empty house and was probably after food or money and we came home and he hid because he couldn't get out upon our arrival. It was weird. I remember he had one of those old caps that tie on top and was unshaven with a worse for wear checked coat on.

Gettin' Inverted
By James Nicks of Watson, Missouri
Born 1948

I was raised on a farm in southwest Iowa, ten miles from the Missouri border. That town was Bedford, Iowa.

My story is from the sixth grade. Our teacher was Pauline McCune, Mrs. McCune to our class. We were studying fractions in math, and the word "invert" came up. Mrs. McCune asked the class what that meant. Just about every girl raised their hand to answer and two smart boys did, too. Mrs. McCune looked at all of us, and then she looked at me and said, "Jim, would you please come up here?" so I got out of my desk and went to the front of the class. Mrs. McCune said to all of us, "I'm going to show you what invert means." She then told me to stand in front of her. I wasn't very big in the sixth grade. It happened so fast when she grabbed me and turned me upside down! The whole class was laughing, and I guess I was, too. I never forgot what the word invert meant.

Mrs. Pauline McCune was the best and loveliest teacher I ever met.

Don't Believe Everything You Hear
By Dorothy Donnelli of Platte City, Missouri
Born 1940

I started to school in 1st grade in Fauscett, Missouri. We lived on a farm along Highway 71, a very busy highway at that time. My mother watched my brother and I boarding the bus each morning. I was a thumb sucker and found it a comfort as I entered the big world of education. I did not understand that others might not follow suit with my comforting habit. Consequently after being made fun of and dubbed as a thumb sucker, I stopped, however only at school.

We moved to Colorado for my 2nd grade in hopes of helping my brother's asthma condition. Needless to say, the school in Denver was much larger than the school in Fauscett. I adapted well with help of close family friends that lived in Denver already. Their father was a minister and for a while, we lived in an apartment in the church basement. That proved to be a unique experience in itself – we were never late for church services.

I wore glasses at a very early age due to a lazy eye condition. At the time, the treatment consisted of wearing a black clip-on patch over the affected eye for several hours a day. Being a tomboy, I was forever breaking my glasses or bending them out of shape. My parents were very forgiving. I also got used to being called four-eyes; yes, kids could be hurtful in those days too. One of the pranks I fell for was the promise by some older kids that if I gathered green weeds and plant life and added water and stirred for a long time, it would turn into money. That was a valuable lesson not to believe everything you hear.

One of the funnier incidents of school involved picture day. My mother made most of my clothes and on picture day had hand-smocked a beautiful yellow dress for me to wear. I also had a bright red purse with a long strap on it that I loved to wear. She instructed me not to wear it on picture day and of course, I said I would not. When I arrived at school, I thought it would be a nice compliment to the dress and added it. When pictures came out the evidence was all there; my mother was not happy with me, but as the years passed, it became a funny story to tell from my school days. I finished my school days in Weston, Missouri. We always started the day with a pledge to the flag and in some classes had a reading from the bible. I fondly remember those days.

The Bull Named Buster
By Rhonda Riggins of Chillicothe, Missouri
Born 1949

I grew up on a farm near Jamesport, Missouri, which is Amish country. I was pretty much a tomboy, playing outside, all the time, climbing trees, and hunting rocks. Well, I had these three girl cousins that lived in Illinois who came down for a few days each summer. They always wore frilly dresses and were all "girly." One day I somehow talked them into walking down in our pasture to look for pretty rocks in the creeks. Of course, we had cattle, including a big red bull, named Buster. After we had looked around for a while, we decided to go back to the house, which was quite a ways. About half way there, we could hear Buster and he didn't sound too happy. I looked and saw him coming and I knew we didn't have time to get out of the pasture before he got there, so I told my cousins we have got to climb this tree, which was along a ditch and then wait until the bull leaves. They had never climbed a tree before in their life. They were petrified! I just zipped right up there and finally they all made it whining all the way, afraid they'd tear their dresses or scuff their shoes. We waited for quite a while and Buster left. The girls finally got down from the tree and after more whining, we got back to the house. To this day, that is the one story we all talk about when we all get together.

Always Keep them Laughing
I was born on a farm near Jamesport, Missouri. The evening I was born, there were several aunts and uncles there at the farm. Well someone sent my Uncle Arthur outside to catch a chicken and dress it so they could cook it for lunch the next day. Well, my uncle was so excited about everything that was going on he took out the back door headed for the chicken yard. About midway, there was my mom's clothesline, which he somehow didn't see. He ran smack dab into it, catching him right under the chin, flipping him over it. My Aunt Ruth was watching all of this and she said she laughed so hard, if it had killed him, she still would have been laughing.

That was my introduction my Uncle Arthur, who was always doing things to make people laugh, without actually knowing he was doing it.

Those were the good ole days and today's kids don't know what they missed. Families got together every weekend and did things together, making wonderful memoires to pass along to our children and grandchildren.

Learning to Keep My Word
By Lois Carter of Gallatin, Missouri
Born 1933

As I was born in 1933, I grew up during a good deal of the depression. I was the fourth of five siblings and came along 10 years after my sister. No doubt, I would have been spoiled rotten if it hadn't been for a little brother coming along in 1936. He became my playmate during those growing up years and has stayed one of my closest and dearest friends. When he was about two, we had a female dog that had puppies under the corner of our house. I loved to play with them, but didn't want to crawl back to where they were, so I would cajole him to crawl under and get one for me. A few years later, he would want me to play cowboys and Indians with him and I would promise to do so if he would help me with the dishes. I didn't always follow through with my promise. Once around the house I had played with him, so one day he was so exasperated that he put a shoe brush in a pillowcase and whopped me over the head. At my scream, mother sensed what had happened as he ran out the door. He got a whipping for running from her and I got a lecture on keeping my word. He has forgiven me and we have a good laugh when we recall this episode.

We went to a rural school north of Winston, where all eight grades were taught. During the war years, we did several things at recess to help the war effort. The railroad tracks were not too far away and we would all take a walk down the tracks and pull milkweed pods for the fluff to be used in flight jackets. We would save the foil that came on chewing gum and wrap it in a ball to be salvaged. Eyes were always on the lookout for scrap iron that could be salvaged. The grownups turned these in,

so I never knew just what happened to them. But we were doing our part. My two older brothers were both in the service and mother was very anxious about them. This concern carried over to my brother and me also. We faithfully bought stamps for war bonds and I had some to redeem when my husband and I bought our home in 1961.

My mother had washed laundry on the board until 1939 when dad purchased a Maytag wringer gas-powered washer. One of the bigger boys at school liked to tease me and tell me, "Lois, your dress is dirty" to which I would stomp my foot and tell him, "It is not. My mommy has a new washing machine." We also had a Coleman gasoline iron and mother was scared to death of it, as a neighbor boy had been badly burned when one exploded in his face. The iron did a great job and was quite an improvement over heating the flat irons on the stove. We also had two gasoline lamps. Boy, did we live dangerously! The wicks on these were so delicate after they were lit the first time that a careless finger or shake would render them useless. We also had kerosene lamps to move into the bedrooms. My Saturday job was to clean the chimneys on these and fill them with oil. Chimneys were thin glass so this was done very carefully.

Our family was fortunate that we lived on a farm and dad had a job working at the local coalmine, starting in 1937. Mother and the older ones did the chores and gardening. As far as I knew, we had plenty to eat, though the

Harold and Lois in 1942

32

older ones thought they ate a lot of mackerel. We had three or four cows, sheep, and chickens. During my very young years, there was quite an ice storm and the cows would fall and some had to be destroyed. I always heard the story that my second brother would put on his skates to go pump water for the livestock from a distant well.

We had a party line telephone during the war. I think there were probably 12 to 14 patrons on our line. I remember our number was 94-14. Our ring was one long, one short, and one long. When someone rang another party, all on the line heard it and usually listened in. My brother in the Navy would get rather irate when he would call home and then not be able to hear. As I remember he once spoke up and said, "Would all of you hang up so we could hear?"

I feel I had a very good childhood playing in the creek and climbing trees, we pretended they were our airplanes. We sledded down the hill during the winter. That hill was the lane to our house and had been cindered with the slag from the coalmine helping to make it more passable during bad weather. When I was about 11 we were sledding and I proceeded to make one more run landing on the sled, as we were accustomed to do. My sled runners hit exposed cinders stopping my sled cold but my upper lip hit the braces on the top of my sled. Boy, did that hurt! I of course cried, telling my brother that I had knocked my teeth out. He looked and promptly told me I had not. But, alas, I had broken one of my front incisors off about halfway and the other was damaged on the edge. Money was tight at our house and dentistry was expensive. My mother did manage to find a dentist to do the repairs at an affordable price before I started high school.

We always wanted a horse to ride and when we were small there was an old saddle on the manger in the barn. We spent many hours riding on our horse! Later, we did get a horse, one more than we could handle, and then another that was more docile. After getting experience on the tamer one, we did manage to ride the first. Many a summer day was spent riding around the neighborhood visiting and getting other youngsters to ride with us. Country roads were happy trails for us.

In February of my 8th grade, I had ruptured appendix and spent two weeks in the hospital with penicillin every four hours around the clock, as peritonitis had developed. The country school kids had to go to the county seat to take a test to pass before entering high school. I was not able to return to school until very close to the test time, but my teacher had helped get me ready for it, filling my head with everything she could imagine would be asked. I remember as we started to town for the test she told me, "Lois, I forgot to tell you that Constitution Day is September 17." I don't recall ever needing that bit of information, but still remember and appreciate her dedication to my education. At that time, she would have us learn bible verses as well as the presidents for opening exercises. Oh how times have changed. I was very fortunate to have the family and the raising I did. God has blessed me very much here in northwest Missouri.

Washtub Atop a Water Tower
By Florence Fries of St. Joseph, Missouri
Born 1927

I was raised in a small town during the depression years. In our little town, there wasn't much to do, so we had to find our own fun. We didn't have T.V., games, smartphones, and even a radio, such as the kids have today. In the middle of our town square stood a huge, red, water tower. It was very imposing. It was the first thing to see when you entered town. We kids played around it, on it, and around the bottom. It was our main attraction.

We attended a small country grammar school that had eight grades. We had a man teacher, who was really good, but we had other ideas of him. In those days, teachers were strict. They were allowed to make us mind and if we didn't, we were punished. We were always trying to figure out ways to anger him. We washed our clothes on the washboard and everyone had a big galvanized washtub. They were put away each week until the next washday. His washtub hung on a nail on their back porch. So, one night, when we knew his family would be gone until late, my older sister, a girl friend, and myself snatched his washtub from their porch and carried it over to the water tower. People retired early in our town, so we felt safe that no one would see us. This water tower had a metal ladder that went clear to the top, and there was a long metal rod that ran quite a way up the top of the tower. I was allergic to heights, so I was the lookout and my sister and friend somehow got that washtub to the top and hung it on top of the metal rod. We felt pretty good about it, until we went to school the next day. The teacher was pretty mad. He called the boys up front and demanded to know who had put his washtub up on the tower. They told him they didn't do it and figured out that it was us girls, but the teacher didn't believe them. He said no girls could ever climb that ladder and put that tub up there. We three sat, very innocent, while the teacher told them what would happen if he found out who did it. Those boys were pretty put out, but nobody ever found out who did it, and we felt pretty good that we had put something over on those pesky boys. We carried the secret to the grave, but I'm still here and sometimes, remember some of the very daring things we did.

Back in those days, girls did not do things like that. Most girls anyways. I guess we were a little ahead of women's lib, but it was a forerunner in the right direction.

Moving From One Epidemic to the Next
By Sherry Miller of Trimble, Missouri
Born 1951

I grew up in rural Caldwell County, riding the bus to school each day with my siblings. I remember one afternoon the high school bully was picking on a fellow 1st grader and me. This boy was a real annoyance and we were no match for his sarcasm; however, a petite, but fiery, high school neighbor, Elizabeth Ann came to our defense when she grabbed Larry's ear and threatened to wring it off if he did not stop bothering us. Needless to say, she put the fear in him since he realized that she might pull off his ear if he crossed her again. Also, I remember being excited about watching my older sister get on the bus while I stayed behind and learned my ABC's and how to tell time from our Grandma Hazel (she lived with us since she was a widow and my dad wanted to always see that she was okay). Kindergarten was not mandatory and my siblings and I did not start school until the 1st grade. We got along as well as those who went to half-day Kindergarten.

Sherry, Charlotte, J.C., Doug, and Danny Sloan in 1957

Growing up in the early 1950s, my classmates, and I had to have polio vaccinations. Incentives included getting a tiny red feather pin to wear to show we had the vaccine. Smallpox vaccinations were a must and I remember being taken to the doctor, having my arm scratched and then getting a Band-Aid and being cautioned to not pick at the scab. I was a blessed person and never got either of those dreaded diseases that did cripple and kill some of the kids in neighboring communities.

My husband Jack was not so blessed because when he was 12 years old, he developed systems of what the doctor thought was the flue. Jack was given a shot of penicillin, which did not help. He could not swallow liquids or food. His parents took him to Dr. Spelman at the Smithville Community Hospital in Smithville, Missouri. He examined Jack and told his father to get Jack to General Hospital in Kansas City, Missouri – he said he would call ahead and they would be expecting to see Jack. After Jack and his parents got to the hospital, Jack was given a spinal tap, which determined that Jack had Bulbar Polio. For two weeks, Jack was in an iron lung that breathed for him. He had to stay an additional two weeks at the hospital before he was able to go home. There was an entire wing of the hospital that was filled with Polio patients. While Jack eventually was able to breathe on his own, the polio left

34

him with paralysis of the left side of his face and throat. Due to the lack of experience with this disease, the doctors gave him radiation on his throat hoping this new technology would be beneficial. However, radiation caused Jack to have cancer of the thyroid 10 years later. Consequently, Jack had to have three surgeries when he was in his early '20s. With the thyroid destroyed, Jack had to take thyroid medicine from them on. After all this, Jack feels blessed because some of the youngsters died while he was at the hospital or later when they went home.

My brother Danny Steve and I shared getting the old-fashioned measles, which lasted two long weeks, and then came the chicken pox. It seemed like we got over one epidemic just in time to come down with the next. We even got the mumps. Back then, you were made as comfortable as possible and endured the red spots, itching, fever, etc., and stayed in the house so you did not get worse symptoms or expose the few others who might not have these issues. My brother and I spent most of the time in a bed in the kitchen by the wood stove – talk about the old days.

The first of school was always a big deal since my sister Charlotte and I would each get three new dresses for school. These would be worn two times before being washed since they had to be hung up when we got home from school. Black and white Oxfords with white socks fit the bill for me due to my flat

Jack Miller built this outdoor toilet

feet and our parents thought these shoes were good for everyone's feet. We also got new crayons, a big chief tablet to write on at school, and several pencils, which did, sharper better than some of the pencils now days. For one thing, the pencil graphite was centered in the wood.

A really cool thing happened when I was around five years old. My dad bought a farm north of where we were living at the time. He had it remodeled to have electricity, running water, and inside plumbing, which included a toilet. I am still grateful for these modern conveniences that kids nowadays take for granted. We enjoyed watching "The Lone Ranger" and "Gun Smoke" on our black and white television. In later years, we got color TV and thought we had moved up in society. There were many Saturday nights that we three kids would sit next to our grandma while we watched a scary thriller on TV that involved space creatures, dinosaurs, and one-eyed and other giant monsters. For a special treat, our grandma would give each of us a handful of mixed nuts, which we thoroughly enjoyed.

I remember having the big wooden telephones on the wall. They had to be rung to get the operator and you talked into the mouthpiece and listened with the piece you held to your ear. The neighbor on our line had different numbers of rings, such as three longs, three longs, and a short, three shorts and a long, etc. I no longer remember what our ring combination was. It was not unheard of at all for a neighbor to listen in on another neighbor's call and add to the conversation. Maybe this is why neighbors were closer in the good old days before Facebook. Eventually we got dial phones that were smaller and would fit on a wall or a table. Then came the push button phones that made dialing so much faster. It was a real convenience to have the portable phones that could be carried from one room to another.

My sister and I liked going with our dad, Dan Sloan when he was working in the field. I remember one time he let us ride on the cultivator or disk. At the time, it did not seem risky and we did survive even though we did get really dusty. That afternoon, he introduced us to gooseberries. I can still remember how sour they were and yet he acted like they were a delicacy and something special. To this day,

I still like to have gooseberries in the spring. In fact, I have some planted in the garden so I do not have to worry about mosquitoes and snakes like in the good old days.

Another fond memory involves my sister and a performance she was in during junior high. She got to wear a pinafore and I thought this meant a gingham type of material and discovered years later it was a fancy apron with ruffles and trim. To this day, I still like this type of material and seeing it makes me smile and remember how special I thought my sister was and still is. Thinking and writing these many memories has been a nice reminder of my past and how there were both good and bad things that helped to shape me into appreciating family, electricity, and indoor plumbing.

Walking on the Gumbo Roads
By Gladys Reiman of Helena, Montana
Born 1922

I was just past my fifth birthday when I started 1st grade at Burr Oak country school, about five miles west of Forest City, Missouri. My brothers, sisters, and I walked two miles to school on gumbo roads. During wet weather, the gumbo picked up on our feet so we couldn't get one foot around another. After a couple of steps, we would stop and step on the gumbo cake to pull it off each foot so we could take another step or two.

In the spring of 1930, we moved to a place about a mile from Burr Oak and out of the gumbo. The year of 1934 was a hot, dry summer. The following winter was a mild wet one. In late summer of 1934 the state began work to improve the road, in time making it a gravel road (now Highway 111), but the first stages of improvement left it in such a muddy mess through the mild winter of 1934-1935 that cars could not get over it.

My Brother Jay, then 16, was a senior and I was 12 years old and a sophomore. We walked approximately four miles to Forest City High School. I learned that year to walk at a good pace to keep up with my much faster brother on the way to school. After school, he was long gone and I trudged on by myself. One spring evening I was hardly out of town when a blister developed on my heel and the blister soon broke. I was limping along when

a woman who went to town every day with her two sons in a mule drawn wagon came along. They passed me nearly every evening, but that evening, seeing me limping along, the woman invited me to ride in their wagon. I gratefully climbed in.

I am a strong believer in 4-H. In 1937, when I was 15 and my Sister Mary Alice was 20, we had won a trip to the national 4-H Club congressional in Chicago. We won the state contest as a canned goods judging team; our picture had been in the Kansas City Star. We were celebrities in Forest City, Missouri. The newspaper picture was in the bank window for months.

In 1944, after having taught for three years in a small town in northwest Missouri, a friend and I went to Chicago looking for a place with a little more action. In response to a newspaper ad, we found employment with the Metallurgical Laboratory at the University of Chicago. My job was as a clerk in an inventory unit that kept track of top-secret reports. It turned out that "Metallurgical Laboratory" was a cover name for the Manhattan Project, which developed the atomic bomb. In the building where I worked, I saw such well-known people as Enrico Fermi and Leo Szilard. Fermi conducted the first nuclear chain reaction on the University of Chicago campus in 1942. Szilard had Einstein write the letter to President Roosevelt that led to the development of the atomic bomb. Dropping the bombs has been a controversial subject. They did bring a decisive end to a war in which many more Japanese and Americans would have been killed in an invasion of Japan. I have never known a GI who was not glad to see an end to World War II.

Ground Bread
By Wanda Geyer Findley of Ridgeway, Missouri
Born 1935

One of my fond memories are those trips to Bethany on Saturday to get our groceries. There was mom and dad, four of us kids, and grandma all loaded up in a Model A car, along with eggs to sell. That was in the early '40s and it wasn't easy to buy new tires for the car, so it wasn't unusual to have a flat tire either coming or going to town. We would all unload and dad would take the wheel off, patch the tube, and put the wheel back on. We would load up again and get back on the road.

Mom would give my sister and me ten cents apiece to spend for whatever we wanted. Sometimes it was candy, sometimes a new hair bow. P. M. Places store had a lot to off for a dime.

Mom and grandma would get their groceries and load them in the car with all of us kids. I don't know how they did it.

Mom would get a loaf of bread and bologna and we would all have bologna sandwiches on the way home. For us kids, it was a fun day.

My mother and dad, Gladys and Bill Geyer, played on the sand pile together when they were kids. Later in their teenage years, mom wished for dad to ask her for a date. He had a relative being buried in a cemetery close by and mom decided to walk to the graveside services, hoping dad might ask her for a date. Her smile must have charmed him and she got the date. Of course, it was a horse and buggy date. Months later, they were married and, wanting to cook him something special, she stirred up a batch of yeast bread. After waiting a length of time, she gave up that it wasn't going to raise. Not wanting dad to know about her failure, she took it out and dug a hole in the yard and buried it. The sun was real warm that day and when dad came home from work, he came in and said, "What is that big white thing on the ground?" Her secret was found out and they had many laughs about it through the years. They were married in 1934 and had over 69 years together before dad passed away.

When the chicken pox comes around, I always remember the day I came down with them. I was eight years old. My sister, brother, and I walked to school in a heavy snow. The one-room school had a stove inside a big jacket and on cold mornings, it was real slow to warm the room up. We kids would huddle up around it waiting for it to get warm. This particular morning I kept feeling sicker by the minute as I stood there. I finally told the teacher I was sick and I had to go home. She asked if I thought I could make it by myself. I said, "Yes." I just wanted to get home. I still remember that walk home. When I walked in the door, I started crying and said, "Mom, I'm sick." She put me to bed and piled the covers on to get me warm and I started breaking out all over with chicken pox. In those days, there were no phones and the teacher also walked to school, so nothing to do but walk.

Man-Made Lemon Pie
By Bonnie Keyserling of Odessa, Missouri
Born 1940

Many memories come to my 72 year old mind about rural schools, farm chores, and just things that happened in life. I have chosen one about rural schools after the end of WWII and some of the changes that entered into the lives of men and women, in this case my parents. I remember this as the ''man-made lemon meringue pie.''

Long ago, but not so long that it is forgotten, the rural areas were dotted with one or two room school houses. Several farm families with children gathered together and built a school so their children could be taught grades one through eight. Then the children would be ready to enter high school in town-operated systems.

At least once each year a fundraiser called a pie supper was held. The best pie supper I recall came down in the family as Dad's lemon meringue pie.

In 1945 my father, brothers, and I moved back to the Odessa area from Kansas City and to the reopened Walnut Row School. My parents had worked in defense plants in Kansas City and my mother remained in Kansas City where she still was working in a WWII defense plant. She rode the Greyhound bus to Odessa each Friday and spent the

Some of the students at Walnut Row School in 1946

37

weekend with us.

School had opened the first week of September and the first meeting of all the families was a pie supper on a Friday night. Each wife or young girl with a sweetheart or the prospect of a sweetheart made a pie and decorated the box that held the pie. The boxes were auctioned off. The competition for the most attractive box to auction off and for the highest bid was part of the fun. The winner got to share the pie with the baker.

Our family was motherless and at age six I didn't know how to make a pie. My father believed anything could be accomplished if you read and followed instructions. He wanted our family to be part of the fundraiser and the fun. He decided to make a lemon meringue pie. In those days there were no pre-made crusts or ready-made fillings in the grocery stores. Men seldom if ever cooked back then. The kitchen was for women only.

After a thorough search Dad found in Mother's cookbook a recipe for lemon meringue pie. The day of the pie supper no farming duties were performed. The farmer was in the kitchen cutting lemons and rolling out pie crusts. The actual sequence of events that day are forgotten. I do remember that my brothers and I got to lick the pie filling spoon and give our opinions of the taste.

Since I was the girl in the family I got to draw a few pictures and paste paper doilies on the side of the box while Dad drove to town to pick up Mom at the bus station. She came home about six that Friday and was surprised and pleased that Dad had made a pie so she could take one for the pie supper.

That night we washed behind our ears and headed to the school house. Word spread around that my six foot two inch 280 pound father had made the pie. Smiles and jibes abounded. My father's male friends laughed as they bid up Dad's boxed pie. Normally a spouse or sweetheart bid on the boxes and my mother was turning red with embarrassment. Finally, Dad winked at Mom to let her know to bid. She won the pie and the chance to share the one-of-a-kind man-made lemon pie.

The adults each wanted to taste a bit of the pie. Even Mrs. Miller, the best female pie maker, pronounced the pie was pretty good—for a man.

Grandma's Tidbits
By Juanita Sherwood of Richmond, Missouri
Born 1927

I came to live with Mom and Dad, one brother and four sisters on a little farm on September 4, 1927, in Pollock, Missouri.

Times were hard. My dad whom we called, "Poppy," and Mommy worked very hard to feed us children. We never heard one word about having to do without anything.

Mommy never knew what it was to go to a doctor. The old community doctor came to the house to deliver me. Even before Mommy should have been out of bed, I remember her saying she had to get up and churn butter and make bread.

I went to a country school; all eight grades were in one classroom. My! All the fun we had. We really had to work hard to learn. When recess would come, we would all run out and play ball and all the other games. We all played together, the older ones and the younger ones. All always seemed to be in order. Then the bell would ring, we would all run for the outside toilet and then to the old well pump for a drink of water before getting back to our schoolwork.

Wintertime was worst of all. We always had lots of fun playing in the snow. Most of us were too poor to have a sled, so we got a pie4ce of tin and four or five of us would ride down the hill at the same time. We had so much fun sliding down those hills. Then we would go back into the school and we would hang our coats around the old pot-bellied stove so they would dry for us to wear them home. In those days, there was no cars and buses. If I were real lucky, after school, my brother who had graduated from the eighth grade would come and get me on horseback. We were so poor we didn't try to go on to high school.

We always had a Christmas Program at school and all our parents would come to watch us. All of us students would draw names so each one got a gift. The teacher gave each one of us a sack of candy. On our last day of school, we would have another program and dinner at school and all the parents would come. We had some wonderful times together. We had a picnic in the woods once a year with wieners and marshmallow roast. Each of us girls had a little play boyfriend. We got to run through the woods and play. One Christmas my little boyfriend got mad at me because I didn't buy him a BB gun. We just didn't spend that much money on presents.

I remember taking my lunch to school in a half-gallon syrup bucket. A lot of the time, it was only a butter and jelly sandwich. It was a treat to have peanut butter. I had friends that were twins. They walked to school with me. They had a stepmother who would make sandwiches for their brother, but wouldn't make any for the girls, so mommy would make an extra sandwich for them, so I would trade a sandwich for an apple. The girl's family always had lots of apples all year long, so I was happy to trade with them.

Oh! Yes, we would have a few fights over our belongings when we got ready to go home. We all wore buckle-over shoes and brown jersey gloves, and most kids had the same kind of syrup bucket for our lunch pail. We all got the same kind from the same country store.

I always had three new dresses when school started. My mommy bought the material for them for ten or fifteen cents a yard. One of my sisters gave me a Charley McCarthy pin to wear on my dress. I had a fight with one of the girl at school. She jerked my pin off my dress and stole it. I was very sad. I never had much. I had one doll and I called her Betty. I loved her so much. I would talk to her and play house with her. You see, I was the youngest in my family and I had no one to play with me at home.

I know there was something God wanted me to do. He kept his hand on me all through my life. My mommy wasn't full gospel, but she knew how to pray. Sometimes she would call me in from playing and we would pray together while the rest of the family was working. We had a winding staircase and I always prayed at the bottom step. The old fashioned Methodist prayed on their knees, and that was the way I learned to pray.

I always helped my dad work in the field on the farm and do the farm chores. I learned to milk a cow at a very young age. I remember one time I was putting hay down from the hayloft and I fell out of the loft under the mule's feet. My poppy ran and picked me up and saw that I wasn't hurt. When I would go to the field, I would play in the sand sometimes and make sand castles. I pulled weeds and hoed some too.

When I got older, about nine years old, I would go and cut ice and make a hole in the creek so our cattle could get water. There was an old oak tree on the way to the creek and that is where I would always stop and pray before I went on home.

My Poppy was a great molasses maker. He made them for all the people around. He always made sure we had at least a fifty-gallon barrel full. We made molasses cookies, candy, and cakes. We ate most of it on Mommy's homemade biscuits. We didn't have those nice gas stoves or electric ones. She had to build a fire in the old wood stove. Our house was so cold Mommy had to break the ice in the old water bucket to make the coffee. My Poppy wouldn't let her buy coffee ground. She had to grind the coffee bean and boil it in the old fashion coffee pot. She was a precious mommy, you never heard her complain or grumble how cold it was or how hard she had to work. We all gathered around the breakfast table about 5:30 AM. We all ate at one time. We never stayed in bed like our modern day kids, unless we were sick. The Lord was good to our family, we were never sick, except for childhood diseases. Of course, there weren't doctors and hospitals on every block like there is nowadays.

Mommy always growed red, white, and speckled beans, butter beans, and soup beans. She canned everything she could. She didn't have the nice pressure cookers like are available today. She went out in the yard and built a fire and took her old iron kettle and boiled the food in the jar for one hour. And that was the process of canning. Oh! Yes, back to the fifty-gallon barrel of molasses. Mommy would also have a fifty-gallon barrel of kraut and a fifty-gallon barrel of sour pickles. We all butchered hogs when it was cold weather. My Poppy would salt some of it down and some he would sugar cure it. I have never, ever tasted any pork as good as Poppy cured.

My Poppy also worked mules, they were strong and tough; they never got tired like horses. Sometimes I would drive the mules while he would cultivate corn. I remember it was so hard to keep the mules going in a straight row especially on a hillside. Poppy would keep a sack over the mule's mouth so they wouldn't eat the corn.

Sometimes I would get to go town with Poppy. It was a mile and a half. We all went in the buggy by the mules or sometimes we took the high wheel wagon. I always liked to watch the wheel turn and make tracks in the mud.

When we went to visit out Aunt and Uncle on Sunday, we always went in the buggy or high wheel wagon. We would have such a good time. The kids would play and the men would pitch horseshoes. My Poppy cut hair so he always got the job to cut the men and boys' hair. We all would just sit around and visit for hours. Then it would be our turn to have our Aunt and Uncle over to visit us. So Mommy would run to the chicken house and get a big fat hen, and kill it and we would have chicken with all the trimmings. Mommy would make a big cake. She liked to make an all colored cake, chocolate, red, yellow, and white. They were delicious.

I never will forget the fourth of July. We would all make homemade ice cream and we always had lemonade. Our neighbor made an icehouse and that is where we got our ice, we didn't have a freezer. We used a gallon bucket then sit it down inside a bigger bucket.

Mommy always raised watermelon and cantaloupes in a patch, which we all enjoyed so much. You can see we raised our own treats as well as making our own fun. We just loved going horseback riding in the summer time.

Back to our home, Mommy also had to make her own soap. It was called lye soap. She washed clothes in it on the old washboard. I'm sure as you read this; some of you don't know what I am talking about because of your age. We had P&G bar Soap we used to take our baths. Speaking of our baths, we took our baths behind the old wood heating stove in a number two washtub, the same one we washed our clothes in. We took turns taking our baths. Some would bathe and then go on to bed while the others waited for their turn. Our beds were a straw–tick mattress with a big feather bed and lots of quilts. We couldn't hardly turn over, but with no heat in the house and the wind blowing through the cracks, the heavy quilts felt pretty good. When it was very, very cold we would put a brick on the old wood stove and get it hot, then, we would wrap it in paper and rags and take it to bed with us to keep our feet warm. That was just part of the way we lived.

We heated our flatirons on the old wood cook stove and Mommy and my older sisters would iron our clothes with them. Times were

rough, but we would make molasses taffy and pop, popcorn or make popcorn balls, then we would sit around the old heating stove and talk. It seemed we all had time for each other and enjoyed being with one another. We studied and got all our homework by the old kerosene lamp.

My two older sisters got married. Allie was sixteen and Elva was eighteen. Allie's husband, Ollie worked on the W.P.A. that was some kind of Government job during the Depression. I was really young, but I remember going with them to get some of the good things they passed out for poor people to eat while the Depression was on. They lived in Milan, Missouri. They would ride in the United States Mail truck to visit in Pollock, Missouri. It cost my sister and her husband ten cents to ride the mail truck from Milan. They usually spent a few days with us before returning to their home.

One day something very exciting happened. My sister Allie had a big ten-pound boy. They named him Paul; I called him "Little Paul." As soon as he could talk, he called me "Little E," because he couldn't say Juanita. So, that is the reason my name was "E" until I got older.

I got the3 measles and was so sick, Littler Paul crawled up to my bed and said, "Little E is dead", and in a few days he was all specked with measles.

Sliced Tomatoes, Home Made Bread and Lemonade
By Barbara Taylor Graves of Forsyth, Missouri
Born 1939

I knew when our stepfather began to travel from one neighbor to another it was time to get the wheat cut in the field east of the farmhouse. Neighbors would bring a grain wagon to haul the wheat to the elevator in town. Bundles of wheat straw were dropped over the field and would be placed from 6 to 12 bundles upright to form a shock. One or two bundles were placed across the top in case of rain. The shocks were left in the field usually two weeks or more to dry.

Whoever owned the threshing machine would go from farm to farm huffing and puffing the machine up and down the hills.

Barbara's parents with Dan and Barbara in 1949

My brother and I could hear this machine coming for a mile and we would run back and forth in the yard waiting for it to turn into our driveway.

For several days, my mother would clean the dining room. When extra leaves were put in the big round oak table it stretched across the room and could seat 10 men easily. The large tablecloth was washed, starched, and ironed. My mother and the neighbor women who would come to help would plan the noon meal. Early on the day of threshing women would come to set the table, and fixed dishes of relish, jellies, and fresh churned butter. A trip to the garden would bring radishes, green onions, cucumbers, and cabbage for slaw to the table. Much of the work had to be done ahead such as baking bread, and setting aside dough for dinner rolls. Cakes were baked; cottage cheese had been drained, salted, and ready for the table. Large pots of corn on the cob simmered, potatoes were in boiling water for mashed potatoes, and chicken was being fried in more than one cast iron skillet. A few salads were made ahead. Since we didn't have electricity there were no refrigerators. We had to go to town and buy a 50-pound block of ice to put in the old wooden icebox.

We would save ice for lemonade. My brother and I would help by rolling the lemons back and forth. The juice was mixed with sugar and fresh cold well water. When the men came in from the field they were thirsty. The pitchers of lemonade were handled by a lady who would stand at the table and pour lemonade and ice tea. She would also make sure the dishes of food kept moving around the table, never stopping.

As noon approached my mother would watch toward the field, and when she could no longer hear the threshing machine and the horses were tied up, a bench was set up in the yard close to the well where several washbasins were filled with water. Clean towels, washcloths, and plenty of bar soap along with clean combs were waiting. A bucket of fresh drinking water and a dipper sat waiting for the thirsty farmers.

The kitchen began to bustle with getting rolls from the oven, making milk gravy, chicken was on the platters, and bowls of food were waiting when the men walked into the dining room. The women stayed in the kitchen while the men ate. After they were through and left for the field the women, my brother, and I put clean dishes on the table then we ate. Today small farms are a thing of the past. No more threshing machines, or a crew, and the dinners are all a part of the past.

But I can smell that fried chicken as I finish this story.

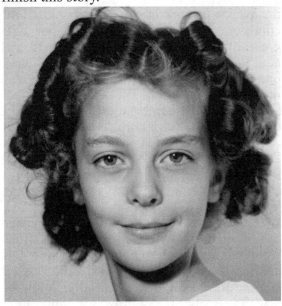

Barbara age 10

The Pre-Primer with Frolic and Do-Funny
By Mary Eulalah Adwell of Tempe, Arizona
Born 1920

I was born in November 1920, and grew up on a farm in Gentry County, Missouri. For several years now, my friends and colleagues have been telling me I should record the highlights of my brief journey called Life. I never really thought that what I would have to say would be of any significance to anyone. After re-thinking the situation, I have decided to write a few things for anyone interested in reading about an era and way of life in America that has passed away. Following are some excerpts.

Montgomery Ward and Sears Roebuck were the two leading mail order catalog companies serving the needs of the people in remote areas and small town America. The heavy thick catalogs were published twice a year: fall-winter and spring-summer. From these "wish books" one could order and fulfill the desires, necessities, and wants of all ages. At one time, Sears Roebuck sold houses that would be delivered and assembled on the site of the buyer's choice. Mom ordered my winter coat and school cap from Sears Roebuck. The order came from Kansas City and I thought that city must be in another state since several days passed before I had the thrill of opening the package very carefully and taking the contents of the package out of the box with great anticipation. Everything "fit to a T," so I could keep the order. I think she ordered Dad's one-piece heavy union suits, too. We call them long johns today. The summer one-piece shorts and shirt combination that Dad wore called B.V.D's. were purchased in Stanberry or Maryville. A familiar summertime question Dad would ask when dressing to go someplace special was, Lelah, where are my B.V.D.'s? I can hear him now. She always had to help him get ready.

Each of us is unique within our being, and has been enriched by the times within which we lived. I'm sure I'm one of a very few that has had an asafetida bag tied around their neck as a preventive for a deadly childhood disease. (Asafetida is a brownish, bitter, foul-smelling resin). When I was very young, before I started school, my mom's cousin passed away while attending nursing school in Osceola, Iowa. As I recall, the cause of death was not determined and, as was the custom, the corpse was kept at home, a practice that would continue until after World War II. This was also the age before babysitters, so children went everywhere with their parents. Naturally, my mom wanted to visit the family.

After we arrived at the home, it seems everyone got "all worked up" because I was there. What could be done to protect me from the mysterious disease? My great aunt, Doll Nelson, had the answer. She called for some asafetida, a cloth, and some string. She fixed

a cloth bag of the "stuff" and tied it around my neck. That was supposed to keep me from all harm. Was that a primitive method? Remember that was several years before any miracle drugs would be available to the citizenry.

On a warm and sunny September day in 1926, I entered McClanahan School. Mom took me in our black Model-T pickup truck over the one-mile plus rolling dirt road I was to travel each day for the rest of my grammar school education. My independent characteristics were already beginning to manifest themselves when I told my mother to go on home and that I would be fine.

At the end of my first day, I remember walking home over that dirt road and following the car tracks and enjoying the earth beneath my feet. I was so happy swinging my dinner bucket vigorously and skipping and walking along that beautiful road decked out with its tall goldenrod, milkweed, and wild roses. Black-eyed Susans were tall and friendly as they nodded in the breeze. My first day of school was over, and I had learned so much. When I reached the top of the hill, where I could see my house and big barn with the windmill below, I saw my mom coming to meet me, waving her greeting. How thrilled I was when I was able to yell to her "I learned to read 'me and we' today"! No reading readiness then: just dive in and read. The green Elson Primer was THE text of the day.

When I was in the fourth or fifth grade, the first pre-primers were used for the first graders. They had a navy blue paper cover with a cute dog and cat pictured in a friendly pose. They were named Frolic and Do-Funny. Oh, how I wanted to go back to first grade so I could use those colorful books! I read the books anyway. Some of the stories in our reading book that I especially liked were "Dog and His Bone", "The Boy Who Cried Wolf," and the one about the old woman who turned into a red-headed woodpecker. At this time, we got several new books about Indians that I read over and over, and I dreamed of becoming an Indian princess and living in a teepee or a pueblo. Just the life for me! Now, how could a girl with Scandinavian blood become an Indian? In my world, it was possible.

After lunch, the teacher would read to us from "Ben Hur" or books from our native son, Mark Twain. Listening to the adventures of Huck and Tom was the best. Classes were called to the front of the room, and students were seated on the recitation bench in front of the teacher's desk. Students at their desks were working on written work and could also listen to the big kids recite. When we were dismissed, the teacher would tell us to put our work in our desk and then followed the dismissal routine: Attention! Hands were placed together on the desk. Tum! Students would tum; put their feet in the aisle. Rise! Students would stand by their desk. Pass! Students were free to go on their way. When I became a teacher, I showed a second grade class that routine and they requested the exercise many times.

When I began school, the seats were large enough for two, and the little kids were paired up with a big kid. So, you see, the "buddy system" isn't new after all. The term seatmate was used, but the idea was the same: big kids helping little kids. In the center of the desktop and to the back was the inkwell and a little groove on either side to put your pencil or straight pen. Everyone had a much cherished pencil box, a Big Chief tablet that cost five cents, and a box of eight basic colored crayons. Before I left elementary school, Crayola had boxes with sixteen different colors. Those crayons were beautiful. Some kids had a jar of paste and a bottle of ink, usually black. I always had both. I think I was in the third grade when the double seats were replaced with single ones. They, too, had an inkwell. The best brand of ink was Script, and the bottle came with a small receptacle near the top that made the ink more accessible for a straight pen and limited the depth in which the pen could be thrust. It kept fingers clean, too. Different pen points were put into the penholder when one needed to write with a wider point.

I always had such a good lunch: fruit or sometimes, stewed tomatoes in a jar and a tasty meat sandwich along with delicious cookies, cake, or pie. Mom made really good deviled eggs, too. What I don't understand is why the kids didn't get sick after their lunches had been on the shelf from early morning until noon. Refrigerators were unheard of. Lunch was always room temperature. I know now some were not as lucky as others. I recall one girl that was living with her aunt and uncle; her family had fallen on hard times. All the girl had in her lunch day after day was two pieces of bread sandwiched together with a mixture of cocoa, sugar, and a little milk to make the mixture spreadable. Halloween was a fun time at school and in the community. We would decorate the room with orange Jack-o-lanterns and orange and black crepe-paper streamers were fastened at the corners and crossed in the middle of the room. Pumpkins were carved and would adorn our porch. On Halloween night, what would happen inside our building? Often times, the big boys would manage to get inside and scatter cattails all over the room. A white fuzz-covered floor would be the greeting for the teacher the next morning. One task that would tax the teacher's patience was getting cattails off a classroom floor. Let me see, sweeping was certainly not the way to solve the problem; no vacuum was available to take up the fuzz. As I recall, rolling up a page of newspaper and setting a match to the paper and holding the flame, very carefully, cautiously, and with little motion, to the fuzzy stuff on the floor was the accepted way to solve the task. Kids loved this activity—playing with fire and getting time off from the books. No one was in a hurry to finish the job. Maybe the job would last all day. Take your time!

The Board of Education was always three men in the district. I know during the Depression $30.00 dollars a month was the usual salary and some teachers were never paid because tax monies didn't come in. After I was married and married women were being hired I had to negotiate for my contract. The argument the board would use was that I should teach for less money since I had a husband to provide for me. That argument didn't "hold water" as far as I was concerned. I always stood firm for the salary equal to others in the Gentry County or maybe $5.00 more per month. I knew I could get a job elsewhere and husband or no husband had nothing to do with my ability to teach. Talk about women's rights. I never did "cave in to the men."

The blackboard and chalk were tools most often used. Making duplicate copies of teaching materials, as we know it today, was a real challenge. Sometimes a hectograph was purchased for the purpose of making duplicate copies. Picture, if you will, two brown wooden trays about 9x13 fastened together so they would fold up like a book. Contained in the trays was a gelatin-like substance that could withstand hot and cold weather. A straight pen and special dark purple ink came with the hectograph. The information intended to be copied was written on regular blank paper. This paper was placed onto the gelatin, the printed side down. This was rubbed and smoothed out and left there for a few minutes until the ink from the print had time to go into the gelatin. The warmth of one's hand helped this process. The original paper was then removed and blank paper was placed very carefully onto the gelatin. This paper was rubbed so there were no bubbles and all of the paper touched the gelatin. This was then peeled off and the process was repeated. It seems to me we could make twenty-five to thirty copies. The hectograph could not be used for several hours, until the ink had time to go to the bottom.

Despite the fact that I grew up during The Depression, my childhood was wonderful and fulfilling. I am fortunate to have spent my youth when and where I did. I was lucky in that there was always money for my education and music lessons.

Lake Contrary Amusement Park
By Joanna Jackson Shaw of St. Joseph,
Missouri
Born 1941

My great-aunt and uncle, Anna and LeForest Ingersoll, operated an amusement park on the south side of St. Joseph, Missouri from 1905-1964. The Ingersoll brothers built many roller coasters across the U.S. Bob had a patent for a part on the coaster that kept the car on the tracks and a patent on the penny weighing machine. He was an expert marksman and held the record on that for many years.

The park in St. Joe was called Lake Contrary Amusement Park. It was built on an Oxbow Lake that was fed from the Missouri River.

In the center of the park was a lagoon. All the rides and concessions were built around the lagoon. A ride called the "Shoot the Chutes" took passengers in a boat to the top of a high ramp where the boat then turned

Lake Contrary Amusement Park

and went down the greased track and into the water. If a person sat in the back of the boat, they most likely got wet.

The park had two wooden roller coasters, The Giant Dipper and the Figure Eight. A big coaster and a small coaster. Bob Ingersoll used to sit in a rocking chair under an old clock on the other side of the coaster tracks where he could see each coaster car as it went by. It was near the office.

The Venetian Ballroom had oak floors and in the center of the ceiling was a mirrored ball that revolved and made rainbows appear on the floor and walls. Around the exterior of the dance floor were rocking chairs for those that didn't want to dance, but wanted to enjoy the music. Many big name bands played in the ballroom and when Anna would walk thru the door, the band always play "Stardust," her favorite song.

The "Fun in the Dark" was a good place to get scared. Cobwebs hit your face; skeletons jumped out and tried to grab you. The car went over many bumps and frightful things appeared.

The merry-go-round had hand-carved Denzel horses and animals with glass eyes and real horsehair tails. Anna went to the factory in Pittsburg and bought the animals. The merry-go-round music could be heard all around the park as the animals went round and round.

The "Old Mill" was a boat ride thru a dark building. The boat would pass different scenery as the water pushed the boat along. I imagine many a young man gave his sweetheart a kiss on that boat ride.

The Penny Arcade was full of pinball machines and machines to test your skills. The Shooting Gallery was where a man could test his shooting abilities. And the "Laugh A Lot" was full of mirrors that made a person look tall, thin, fat, or just plain funny.

The hot dog stand was a good place to get a hot dog, pop, or beer. The ice cream parlor had three flavors of ice cream and some candy bars. Then there was the popcorn stand. In the winter, when the park was closed, Anna would take the big popper to the auditorium where she popped corn for the Policeman's Ball. She gave all the proceeds to the policeman's fund. I was her helper.

Outside of the park was the grove. It was full of trees and picnic tables. Many companies had their picnics in the grove. This was in the days before air conditioning, so the trees helped make the hot, humid summers more bearable.

My aunt said that I could work in the park when I was old enough to count money. I worked selling tickets to many of the rides and worked in the popcorn stand as well as the ice cream parlor. I can remember Fourth of Julys when the midway was so full of people that one could not even see the lagoon. This was the days before television.

In the winter when the park was closed, my parents and I would go visit Bob and Anna on Sundays. There was always singing around the baby grand piano or Bob and Anna working on a quilt. When it came to leave Anna would say, "Go get my purse." It hung on the backside of her bedroom door. She would open the purse and give me all her change. Sometimes I would get $2 or more.

There were lots of poor families that lived around the lake. If Anna knew that a family was having a hard time she would stop the kid as he was walking home from school and tell him that her cook had prepared too much food and would he mind taking some home to his family. She bought many a kid a pair of shoes. Bob and Anna never had any children.

In 1949, there was a huge flood on the Missouri River. Lake Contrary was flooded. The park and their house was under water. Another flood in 1952. Bob died in 1955, some say of a broken heart to see his beautiful park destroyed for the second time. Anna tried to rebuild and operated the park until 1964. She sold the park; everything was auctioned off, and torn down. Today there is a cornfield there.

Anna died in 1973 at the age of 94. Everyone in St. Joseph knew and loved Miss Anna. She and Bob were WONDERFUL PEOPLE, it was a wonderful park, and a wonderful time to have lived.

My Sister and the Dead Snake
By Wilma J. Woods of Kingston, Missouri
Born 1937

We lived on a 75-acre farm off of Highway 13 near Polo, Missouri. We had no running water or electricity in the house. We had a small outhouse a few yards from the house. There was a huge red barn to the left of our house with a large lot. My dad farmed with the team of horses.

There were three of us children: my sister Vivian who was eight years older than I and my little brother Edward who was 18 months younger than I. My sister was so afraid of snakes. Whenever we would hear her screaming, my dad would come running with the hoe if he was nearby. On many occasions, Edward would find little snakes and scare Vivian. He always got into trouble, but that didn't seem to bother him.

It was early fall in the year of 1946. Edward and I had to walk to Highway 13 to catch a bus to go into Polo to school. It was a short walk of about 1/2 a mile. That September morning on the way to Highway 13 Edward spotted a little dead snake. He told me he was going to take it home and scare Vivian. He rolled the snake up real tight and stuck it in his pocket. I told him he was going to be in big trouble when we got home.

On the way home on the bus, Edward told me he had a plan to scare Vivian. Again, I reminded him that he was going to get into trouble. We finished our chores, did our homework, and ate our supper. It was time to go to bed now, and all three of us children slept in the same room. Edward and I had to go to bed first. Vivian since she was 17 got to stay up later. Mom brought the commode in for us to use during the night. This commode was white and shiny. It had a lid with a recessed rim, and a small red knob on top. We climbed into bed and then Edward told me his plan. He had planned on putting the dead snake in the recessed rim as soon as Mom took the kerosene lamp and left the room.

About a half an hour later, we heard Vivian coming down the hall. We covered our heads and tried not to laugh. We heard her set the lamp on the table. The next sounds we heard were the commode lid being lifted followed by an ear splitting scream. The lid sailed across our bed followed by the commode bottom and it went out through the window. Edward started to laugh under the covers. The bedroom door swung open with force and in came our father followed by our mom. The contents of the commode were on the floor and the lid and commode were out the window.

Vivian, in tears, tried to tell Mom and Dad that a snake was on the commode lid. They heard Edward laughing under the covers. A swift hand yanked the covers off of him and he tried telling them that it was just a little dead snake. My dad could not believe the mess in the bedroom. Mom told Edward to find the little dead snake in the mess on the floor and to throw it outside. Dad went to find some boards to nail over the window and Mom and Vivian cleaned the floor.

Edward on the way out of the bedroom began to laugh to himself. I knew he was planning something else with the snake. He came back into the room still smiling and crawled into bed. Moments later a scream down the hall caused all three of us to set up in the bed. I knew that Edward did not throw the snake away. He must have put it in Mom and Dad's bed. Mom came bursting through the door grabbed Edward and he got an awful whipping. Vivian, well, she got the last laugh as Edward came back to bed crying and holding his bottom.

The Luckiest Girl in Missouri
By Janet F. Andes of Liberty, Missouri
Born 1940

This is a true story of the luckiest and best cared for girl in the state of Missouri. The only thing is, I didn't know it at the time.

I was born in March 1940, in a farmhouse near the small town of Brunswick. At the age of 11 months, I caught a bad case of pneumonia and was in a deep coma. It was so bad that my grandma, Myrtle Magruder said, "Put her little shoes away." She called several doctors but only one, a brand new doctor, would come to our farmhouse. He stayed in our farmhouse for three days and nights and used every method and procedure he could think of to get me well. The third day I awoke from the coma and he and everyone in the house clapped and cheered. All our neighbors knew we were poor and probably couldn't pay the doctor, but he was glad that I had recovered

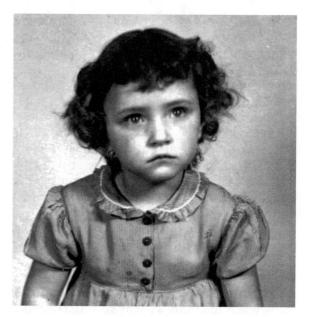

Janet Faye Cook in 1940

and was extremely well fed by my grandma. For him, this was payment enough. Later, this same doctor was called up by the Army and spent three or four years patching up soldiers in World War II.

Apparently, my grandma was so thrilled and grateful by my miracle recovery, she decided to treat me like a "princess," and I never had to do a lick of work for the 13 years that I lived there. We had the best of food such as home cured ham, bacon, fresh beef, chickens, and homegrown fruits and vegetables. In addition, we had a feather bed, wood heat, and a chamber pot under the bed. But I was embarrassed because we were the only ones in the neighborhood who didn't have electricity, running water, and drove an old Model T Ford with a rotted canvas roof. For clothes, I had hand-me-downs and dresses made of feed sacks.

Since I didn't have any chores to do, entertainment was tough. With no other kids around, and not liking dolls, this country girl was forced to keep busy by fishing in the creek, hunting rats with my dog in the neighbor's chicken house, gigging frogs, and playing Cowboys and Indians all alone. I thought, "What a boring life"!

What I didn't know at the time was that while I was feeling sorry for myself, millions of people in Europe and Asia were starving, being killed, and having their homes and cities destroyed in World War II.

I would give anything to talk to my grandma and tell her how wonderful she was to me and thank her and others for keeping me safe, healthy, and "yes" happy! She also taught me how to better handle life's obstacles, get a job, and be kinder to animals.

How Grandpa Cleared the Line

Our family had an old wooden telephone hanging on the wall and a nine party line, which was quite an aggravation. One day my grandpa, Lilburn Magruder really needed to use the phone, but two old ladies had been on the line for what seemed like hours. We had been advised not to interrupt people unless it was a dire emergency. The phone was above the sewing machine, so Grandpa took a chair and got up on the sewing machine and turned his rear to the speaker and ripped out a "big one." The two old ladies stopped in mid-sentence and one said to the other, "Rosie, what on earth was that?" The other said, "I don't know but it sounded a lot like thunder."

While the rest of us were exiting the room to conceal our laughter, Grandpa was patiently waiting for the line to clear and then made his call.

Janet's grandparents Lilburn and Myrtle

The No Bouncing On the Seat Rule
By Geraldene Pittenger of Reynoldsburg, Ohio
Born 1923

I grew up in northwest Missouri, although I reside in Ohio now. One fine spring evening in 1932, when I was nine years old, our family went to Uncle Clarence and Aunt Salina's house for supper. We went in our family carriage, pulled by our mule Tom and favorite workhorse Bill. It had rained the day before and the dirt roads were muddy. Our carriage had three seats. Each seat was wide enough for three people. The seats were leather over padded springs. There was a glass windshield in front of the front seat. We had canvas side curtains, which could be buckled onto the sides of the carriage. We seldom used them because they had only small isinglass windows made out of the mineral mica. We could not see very much out of them and we liked to see everything as we rode along.

After supper that particular evening, my siblings and I had fun playing with our five cousins while our parents visited. Maxine was a year and a half older than me. She and I decided it would be great fun if she came home with us and stayed until church time on Sunday. We asked our parents and right away papa and mama said it would be fine with them. It took Uncle Clarence and Aunt Salina a little longer to decide, but they finally said Maxine could go home with us. Aunt Salina helped Maxine put her Sunday dress, her best socks, and her nightgown into a grocery bag. She was packed and ready to go. Maxine was our guest and I regarded the sides of the seats the best seats in the carriage. I sat in the middle of the middle seat, my brother Calvin sat on the left side, and Maxine sat on the right side. Papa sat on the left side of the front seat and drove the horses. Mama sat on the right side of the front seat and held Dorothy, who was less than a year old and Bernice sat between them. As we rode along, Maxine and I planned the things we would do the next day. We got to laughing and bouncing up and down on the seats; Calvin joined in. Then we got to kind of playfully pushing each other with our elbows, not hard you must understand just gentle little shoves. Papa and mama were talking and did not seem to notice that we were violating the "no bouncing on the seat" rule. Tom and Bill were running, the wind was blowing in our faces and it was wonderful!

We came over the crest of a hill and started down the hill. The team was running really fast now. Then three things happened at exactly the same time - Maxine bounced on the seat, I pushed her with my elbow, and both right wheels of the carriage slipped into a deep rut, pitching Maxine out of the carriage. It really looked like she "flew" out of the carriage. Calvin and I immediately started yelling, "Stop! Papa, stop quick! Maxine fell out! Papa, stop!" Papa yelled "whoa" over and over. That is the command you give horses when you want them to stop. Tom and Bill were smart enough to know that if they slowed too fast, while going down the hill, they would get their legs bruised from the carriage running into them. They ran on until they got to the bottom of the hill. Finally they stopped. Papa handed mama the reins and hopped down to the ground. I started to get out, but papa said in a stern voice, "No! Stay here! Be quiet!" I sat back in my seat, listening to papa's footsteps as he ran up the hill. I was very frightened. I was afraid that if Maxine hit the wheel as she flipped out of the carriage, it might have killed her. Or maybe the carriage wheel ran over her. Or what if she landed on her head and broke her neck? I felt like it was all my fault. I knew we were not supposed to be bouncing on the seats. I had playfully poked her with my elbow. It had never occurred to me that anyone could fall out of a carriage. I said, "Mama, how bad do you think Maxine is hurt? Do you thinks she is dead?" Mama said she did not know and to be quiet. So I sat quietly and prayed. After a while, I heard Maxine and papa talking as they were walking down the hill. She sounded okay. Papa helped her into the carriage. Now, I felt that the middle seat was the choice seat, so I moved over and let her sit in the middle. Papa simply said, "Behave!" When papa said this, it meant that we had better obey all of the rules. But when he said behave, in that seldom used special way, it meant we had better obey all of the rules and also be quiet. Papa took the reins and we started on. We rode in silence. I breathed shallow so I would not even make breathing noises. We three children in the middle seat were so quiet that we looked like wax figures.

Papa stopped by the kitchen door to let us out. We went inside while he went to put the carriage away and take care of Tom and Bill. Mama laid Dorothy in her bed and then came back to the kitchen and lit the lamp. We were astonished to see how Maxine looked. She was covered in mud, from her hair to her shoes. There were only a few places on her face where you could see bits of her skin. She had missed getting hit with the carriage wheel, landed in the soft mud on the edge of the ditch, and rolled down the bank nearly into the water at the bottom of the ditch. The mud was slick and she said she had been afraid she might fall into the water. She had squirmed and clawed her way up the bank to the road. She finally got to her feet just as papa got to her. She was not even bruised, just very muddy. I stood in the kitchen a few moments, staring at her. Mama got a table knife and began scraping some of the thickest parts of the mud off of Maxine's dress. Papa came in and started up the fire in the cook stove. He said it looked like we would need a lot of water. He picked up two big buckets and started toward the well. Mama told me to go take Calvin and Bernice out to the toilet, and then help them get on their nightclothes, put them to bed, and get dressed for bed myself. When I finished those chores and came back to the kitchen, Maxine was clean and just getting into her nightgown. Her shoes were sitting, still covered with mud, on a newspaper. Her muddy clothes were soaking in a bucket of water. Mama sent us to bed.

The next morning when I came downstairs, Maxine's clothes were hanging on a hanger in the kitchen. They were clean, starched, and ironed. I knew that mama had stayed up late to get them washed and got up early in the morning to get them ironed. I also knew that papa had made several trips to the well in order to get enough water. Maxine helped me with my chores. I felt very thankful that she was not hurt. I was especially careful to see that all my chores were properly done. I even volunteered to help with other things, to try to make up for extra work papa and mama had done because Maxine had fallen out of the carriage. I have many memoires of things, which happened during my childhood, as I was growing up on a farm in northwest Missouri during the Great Depression in our country.

48

Life of the Mud Road
By Beverly Clinkingbeard of Westboro,
Missouri
Born 1938

When it comes to the good ole' day's life is remembered with a touch of nostalgia; mud roads are rarely included. In the days of horse drawn buggies and wagons, mud roads were an inconvenience, but travel was still possible. Once the automobile became a must for the family, a pain, subsequently resulting in mud roads disappointed, changed plans, and were decidedly unromantic. As one remembered from days of yore, the old Model A Ford worked best on mud roads because they were higher off the ground and their wheels narrow. But once the modern, low-slung car came along, the less likely you'd get through." Mud holes and steep hills were generally named for the neighbor that lived nearby, such as the Sage Hill and Roach mud hole. Many times a road would be dry, the dust rolling into a cloud from beneath the wheels. All was good until the mud hole. It hadn't dried out yet and was waiting to claim a vehicle. One such place in Atchison County, Missouri was at Long Branch Creek. There was a wooden contraption that served as a bridge. Either end of the bridge was one extension built without banisters. There was a hairpin curve in the road approaching the bridge.

Veda Macrander and her cousin, Zoolene in 1930

First, there was the main road, it made a curve, and the road ran beside the creek, until the tight curve (the hairpin) that enabled the car to cross the bridge. Immediately after crossing, the bridge there was another curve and the road was beside the creek for a ways before going into another curve and onto the regular road. There the driver was faced with cemetery hill. At the creek road, the soil was loamy and black, but the hill at the cemetery was gooey clay. On either end of the bridge's approach was a deep mud hole. More than once children waited with our mother beside the road while our father gained speed, struck the mud hole with enough force to not only get through, but also land on the bridge. We watched with riveted attention and today I shudder to think what could have happened had the car missed the bridge!

For the children who walked mud roads to attend country school, the distance seemed to lengthen when their boots were caked in heavy mud. Popular in our day were the four buckle overshoes and they plowed mud real well. In those days, Saturday nights in town were the highlight of the week. It was a time to sell cream and eggs and replenish the kitchen pantry with foodstuff. A rain could spoil plans quickly, or if already in town, a clap of thunder could send a merchant's customers scrambling for their cars. A friend remembered her father putting chains on their car then adjusting the hood flaps (1930 vintage) to allow air into the engine to help keep it cool. Once school consolidation took place, Willy's Jeep station wagons became "Mud busses." I don't remember the capacity of a station wagon, and I suppose it didn't matter, as we bigger kids held the younger kids and clutched onto them tightly when the vehicle bounced across a mud hole or went into a slide. I will never forget the morning we slid down a hill that had a bridge at the bottom. There were no banisters on the end extensions of the bridge. This day the vehicle gave a lurch and we stopped in the ditch to the side of the bridge approach. We looked down and into the creek. Our driver put the Jeepster in reverse, got some weeds beneath the wheels, and managed to reverse onto the road track! We then took another shot at that bridge and made it! Our driver was a very adept driver. He also smoked every mile, every day. In early spring, there was the freeze thaw factor. In the afternoon, the earth was frozen beneath, but a top layer of the road was thawed and greasy slick. The mud bus would plow through, but come morning it was all frozen again. Slowly the bus would bounce over the horrendous ruts carved the afternoon before.

Medical emergencies were another matter when it came to mud roads. Either the doctor would find a way in or the patient would find a way out. A remembrance of a neighbor that was diagnosed as needing an appendectomy recalled lying on the back seat of their car while her mother steered and her father rode one of the workhorses. The team slowly dragged the car toward a gravel road. They left the team at a neighboring farm at the gravel road and with mud clunking and banging the underside of the car, hurried to the hospital.

Another remembered going to the hospital laying in a wagon. Her husband rode a horse alongside the wagon and the neighbor drove a team of mules. They would call ahead and her father, who lived in another town, was waiting at the gravel road to take her on to the hospital. After the exhausted team had rested, the saddle horse was tied to the wagon and they all plodded back through the mud to home. She also remembered that her husband could never understand why she would choose such a poor time for a health emergency. Another remembrance is when it came to Cupid; a mud road could be the measure of a young swain's interest. If he was willing to leave the car at the gravel road, take off his shoes, and go barefoot or pull on boots and walk to see his ladylove, then you knew it was a mighty serious romance. Just because a road was graveled didn't guarantee passage. Missouri mud is tenacious and at seep holes, the gravel vanished into the mud. These are a few memories of the brawl that could develop between a mud road, a driver, and a vehicle.

Tall Tales and Fish Stories—All True
By C. R. "Bob" Lock of Carrollton, Missouri
Born 1927

Because I was born in July 1927, I wasn't old enough to remember Clara and Harry's wedding in 1929, but I do recall many things that happened while we still lived on the Van Dyke place just west of Marshall (the big two-story brick house where I was born). The house is still there but it is in bad repair.

Our closest neighbors in Marshall were the Ordways. They lived across the pasture north of our house. I was afraid of their big gray geese because they hissed at me. It was at Ordways that Bill got his finger cut off when he and Doodle Ordway were playing turning a pump jack one day. Bill put his hand on a gear and Doodle turned the wheel. Result: Nine fingers left.

Retta still lived at home and would bring me square orange candy wrapped in cellophane. I can still taste how good they were.

We moved to Carrollton in 1933 and Loyola, Bill, and I went to the Calloway School for 21/2 years, then St. Mary's Convent opened again and I started the third grade there. Part of the time Loyola would drive us to school. She was 12 years old. Later we rode the school bus. Mrs. Arch Scott was our teacher at Calloway School. Some of the other kids at Calloway were Sinton and Austin Jones, Bill Smith, Noah Prunty, Audrey Winfrey, and Dink, Teen, and Edna Smith (they were Fuzzy Smith's kids). They lived in a shack down by the river. Fuzzy fished and drank for a living and all of his kids chewed tobacco, except Edna, and she missed school a lot to take care of her mother.

Clyde Robey lived in another, better, cabin on the river. He also fished and drank for a living, but he was "neat." He also was a picture painter and a fantastic liar. He told us that the mosquitoes were so big down by the river that they didn't put screen wire on the windows, they would use woven hog wire fence instead. One year the mosquito hatch was puny, so a big mosquito pushed a puny one through the wire so's he could open the door for the rest to get in. One night he said the mosquitoes were so bad that he slept under an iron kettle. A big old boar mosquito drilled through the kettle so Robey clinched his bill with a hammer he had and the mosquito flew off with the kettle.

Another time he said that he was driving a team and wagon down through the woods when a 'hoop snake came rollin' along. The snake struck at the mule and missed and bit the wagon tongue. They were so poisonous that the wagon tongue swelled up so big that they took it to the sawmill and· sawed it into enough lumber to build a house. When they painted the house, the turpentine in the paint made the swelling go down and it wasn't any bigger than a matchbox.

The fishermen along the river kept the big kerosene lanterns lit to guide the steamboats. There were fishermen living about every 5 miles along the river. One of them was Dave Kuss. He had a nose bigger than Jimmy Durante's. Then there was George Horn, then Robey (he later got a partner named John Gardner who had epileptic fits). Then between Robey and the Waverly bridge lived Luther and Bill Carey. Bill was a "morphodite" (hermaphrodite).

Later in the 1930s, Clara and Harry Sweeney and their family moved to the Herman Bunge farm south of Bowdry. Rosie was only about 2 years younger than I was, and then Betty and Ducky were right behind. Dad named Ducky after Ducky Poo, who was Andy's girlfriend on the radio show "Amos and Andy."

I told Sarah Huff, my granddaughter, that we didn't have television when we were little and she was amazed. She said, "Well, what did you watch?"

One of the best Christmas presents I ever got was an old used red bicycle. It couldn't have been any better if it had been a shiny new Cadillac. Rosie, Betty, Ducky, and probably Raymond all learned to ride on it.

The Sweeney girls were all pretty and very popular. They had boys calling and coming by constantly even though they lived 6 miles from town. It was Rosie's, Betty's and sometimes Ducky's job to milk the cows. To milk cows effectively you had to put your head against the side of the cow while you milked her. So you can imagine, here are Rosie and Betty milking cows at 5 or 5:30 in the afternoon, heads against the smelly cows, hot date at 7. Many fast hair washes, drying, and curling were done in less than desirable conditions with the hot water supply the way it was in those days.

Pat had terrible skin rashes and eczema when she was little. No amount of doctoring her or medication seemed to help. One day one of the doctors suggested that goat's milk might help her, so they tried it and it did help. It took quite a bit of milk, so instead of buying it all from Roy VanTrump, the goat king of Carrollton, Harry started buying some nanny goats and milking them for Pat. To keep the milk supply coming, the nannies had to have babies, so Harry bought some Billy goats, and presto, baby goats. A car would drive in their yard and there would soon be goats on the hood, on the top, and if the windows were open, in the car.

Speaking of goats, sometime in the mid to late 1930s, Swede Wilson brought a Billy goat and two-wheeled cart down to the farm for Bill and me to ride. Now, Swede Wilson was something else. He had a truck and hauled livestock and drank—he drank quite a bit. He was one of a lot of Wilsons in Carroll County. Most of them were not related (he was no relation to Jimmy Wilson, my father-in-law). Anyway, this was a bad goat. When an adult was around, he would behave pretty good, but when just us kids were around him, he would get our goat!

He would really intimidate us, especially me. I was about 6 or 7 years old. He had one long spiraling horn about two feet long; the other had been broken off to about 6 inches long. He had a nice harness and it was fun to ride in the cart as he pulled it. He pulled it a lot better and safer when Dad or Herb or Bert or Ted was around than he did when Bill and I tried it by ourselves. One afternoon I was walking across the barn lot and the goat came up behind me. He twisted his head and put his long horn between my legs then raised up his head and that long horn was in front of me, the short horn behind me and I was in the middle. He was a big strong goat, and I was a small fat boy. He would raise his head so that just my toes would touch the ground and started waltzing me around the barn lot. I started crying and cussing and hollering for Bill. Around and across the lot we would go, he would never get me close enough to the fence to let me grab hold of it. After what seemed like a long time of cussing and crying and hollering for Bill, and humiliation, Bill finally heard me and came running from the barn. When he came past the barn and saw what that goat was doing to me, he lost it. He couldn't have saved me if I had been hurt, which I wasn't—only my pride. He laughed so hard that he got down on his hands and knees because he was so weak with laughter, which only made me madder. With this new

51

distraction, the goat passed me close to the fence and I grabbed a high board and pulled myself off.

I chased Bill and cussed the goat some more but I soon got over it. I never let myself get caught in the open by that goat again. The only satisfaction I ever did get on that goat was one day Herb gave him a gallon of old wine that wasn't very good for drinking anymore but the goat drank it all from a pan and he got drunk and bellowed and staggered around for a while and went to sleep. Then he was O.K. Swede finally took him away.

In about 1936 or 1937, Swede and his wife asked Dad if they could put out a patch of watermelons and cantaloupes on some of our sandy ground down by the river. They planted about 2 acres. When they got ripe, Bill and I would get up at 4:00 a.m. and go help them pick a load of melons. When we came back, Swede would let us keep and sell as many as we could by the roadside in front of our house and let us keep one-third of the money. He would go to Carrollton and park by the square and sell up town. He would sellout about every day. We got 3 cents a pound for them then. That was quite a lot ·of money in those days.

About every summer Sunday afternoon, Dad and the boys, Pappy Duvall and Harry Sweeney, and any other men who happened to be at our house, would load a hoop net and some chicken wire in a wagon or pickup and head for the river where Bowdry Creek entered into the river and was only 2 or 3 feet deep. They would set the hoop net in the creek with the mouth upstream in the creek, then tie the chicken wire to the big hoop at the mouth of the net and stretch the wire netting to each bank. Then everyone would take off their clothes and walk upstream about 400, 500, or 600 yards, then get in the creek and splash and play and get cool and walk down the creek making enough noise and disturbance to chase the fish down the creek and into the net. One hot afternoon they did this and they took me along. I was pretty little and short and wide so they told me, they had an important job for me. They said, "You stay here by the net and don't let any fish get under the wire wings on the net. They went on upstream and had been gone for 20 or 30 minutes and I was kneeling in the mud and water next to the chicken wire wings on the south side of the hoop net, facing the river. Suddenly I felt the wire netting move and felt something between my legs. It pushed farther between my legs and underneath me and I realized a fish had nosed under the wire netting in the mud and just happened to be right under me. So I sat down hard on the fish, mashing him deep into the mud and started to holler for Dad or the boys or somebody. They were on their way back down the creek and heard me hollering and thought that I was hurt bad or drowning or something. As they came running around the bend of the creek through the trees they saw I was just fishing. Ted or Bert jumped in and grabbed that fish out of the mud and held it up. It looked almost as big as I did. We took it home and weighed it. It was a 9 ½ pound buffalo.

The Dude Ranch Drive-In
By Sandy Messner of Maryville, Missouri
Born 1954

"Howdy, howdy there, podner! Welcome to the Dude Ranch Drive-In."

That was the greeting spoken to moviegoers at the Dude Ranch Drive-In theatre in Maryville, Missouri. The drive-in theatre was located on the south edge of town off Highway 71. Many memories were made at the theatre with events including the spectacular July 4th firework display, the sunrise church services held on Sunday mornings at 6:00 a.m., and the unique display of western décor. The theatre was owned and operated by C. E. "Doc" Cook, my grandfather, and Jim Cook, my father. I am the youngest child of that family. Memories and stories of the drive-in days are special to me.

Opened seasonally, workers began in early June to build the set pieces that honored law enforcement, our country, and the western necessities of a shooting gun and a boot with a spinning spur. The wooden set pieces were ten to 15 feet wide and ten to 15 feet tall. They were made with firework lances placed on nails covering the wooden design and a stapled fuse atop each lance. A pulley with guide wires would raise and lower the set piece between two poles. When it was time for the display, the fuse would be lighted. Whether it was the United States flag burning brightly with stars sparkling, the law enforcement star shining brightly, the boot's spinning spur,

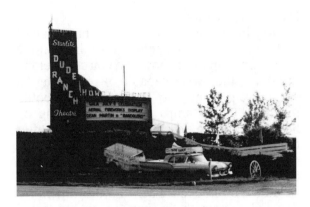

Dude Ranch

or the gun with shooting bullets, hundreds of cars would blare their horns in approval. The aerial display usually lasted an hour. This combination of colorful fireworks was narrated by the owner, Jim Cook. Between these and the set pieces, customers were treated to a one-of-a-kind firework show.

Attendance seemed to grow each year. The drive-in would open on July 4 around 4:00 p.m. and people lined the highway to get their favorite parking spot. There was a playground for the children, a patio with benches and picnic tables, and a concession building called the "Chuck House," where charcoal-grilled hamburgers, hot dogs, popcorn, homemade cake donuts, ice cream novelties, and the usual candy bars and sodas were sold. Also in this building were an antique tack room, the projection booth, an office, and restrooms. The building was made of knotty pine and logs. In the antique tack room was a life-sized horse surrounded with various saddles, blacksmithing tools, oxen shoes, spurs, and autographed photos of western movie stars. The entire building was a showcase for the true western aura that it created.

When the time approached for the movie to begin, my dad welcomed everyone, "Howdy, howdy there podner, welcome to the Dude Ranch Drive-In," and told them about the Chuck House, restrooms, playground, and patio, and proceeded to introduce the featured film. When it was time for the show to begin, he would say, "It's dark enough for a nice, bright picture. The show's in the saddle, so let's let her buck!" And the film would begin to roll. Those spoken words came to be so familiar to the many patrons of the theatre.

Another tradition unique to the drive-in was the Sunday church services held from June thru August. This tradition began in the early 1950s and continued until 1976. Early Sunday morning, a portable pulpit was carried to the rooftop of the concession building, and the Methodist minister would climb a ladder to deliver his sermon into the PA system. If it was too windy or rainy, he would use the office in the Chuck House. Parishioners hung the speakers on the window of their cars to listen to the sermon. Some people in attendance wore Sunday attire, while others chose casual clothes and left the children in their pajamas since they were in the privacy and comfort of their car. An usher walked from car to car to collect the offering. After the services, fellowship took place with donuts and coffee served at the Chuck House.

During the summer months, my younger days were spent playing at the drive-in until I became old enough to join my sisters at work in the box office selling tickets, or at the Chuck House selling concessions. The acreage required a great deal of work. Cleaning up the trash on the grounds from the previous night, placing speakers back on the posts, and cleaning and preparing the concession area for the next night were all duties associated with the business. A donkey, named Pesos, also entertained people, braying loudly as someone approached to pet or feed him. He was allowed to roam in a fenced area around the marquee building.

The employees wore western shirts, cowboy hats, and sometimes wore holstered play guns to fit into the atmosphere. At the time, admission was 50 cents, and children under 12 were admitted free. For the July 4th celebration, admission was 75 cents. One promotion, called "buck night," allowed cars filled with as many people as possible to be admitted for $1. On most Saturdays nights, double features would show.

As with many things of the past, it's sad that this type of entertainment has come and gone. Eventually, the movie theatre industry lost its flare to home movie rentals, and other changes with modern technology. In the early 1970s, the drive-in was closed for commercial developing. Today, when passing the shopping area where Sutherlands and JC Penney stores are located, few know or share in the memories of outdoor church services and the Dude Ranch Drive-In.

53

Pulling a Prank on the Half Rock Liar's Club
By Larry Pollard of Spickard, Missouri
Born 1949

Half Rock, Missouri, was a small town established in 1874 in the southeast corner of Mercer County. At one time, the town consisted of various businesses, two churches, the cemetery, and about 40 homes. Hopper & Son General Store was the hub of the small hamlet where locals could purchase everything they needed to survive. The store also took chickens, eggs, and other homegrown products in by either trade or direct purchase from farmers. There was even a creamery to test and purchase cream.

The original wooden store burned to the ground but because of the importance of the store to the community, it was quickly rebuilt in 1919 and included a second story to accommodate the lodge for IOOF (Independent Order of Odd Fellows) #465. The store was owned by my great-grandfather Tom Hopper and his son Fred Hopper, my grandfather. I mention the importance of the store because it not only sold groceries, feed, fuel, boots, and other farm clothing but it was like a community center for the area.

On Saturday when people would come in from the farms to purchase or trade items they would stay for hours to visit and catch up on the latest gossip. Sometimes people would bring their guitar, fiddle, banjo, and mandolin and have an impromptu jam session. Once in a while, a movie would be shown on the west side of the building. People would bring their folding chairs or blankets and spread out on the grass to enjoy the show. There were many characters in the area and with those characters came pranks and mischief.

When I was around 11 or 12 years old a neighbor boy about my age came up with an idea to have some fun with a few old timers. We referred to those guys as The Liars Club. They would sit on the old long wooden benches in the store and stay for hours to swap stories or actually do nothing. I won't say they were lazy but looking back some of them seemed to have a lot of quit in them. The old crank phone in the store had been replaced with the new modern rotary dial three party phones. As a result of this new technology, our idea came about on how to shake up the Liars Club members.

My buddy and I took the old phone apart and removed the magneto. Depending on the size of a magneto and how fast you could crank the thing, they were capable of producing an AC current from 6 to 110 volts. This could result in 1 to 5 amps current depending on how fast you could crank it. One night after the store closed my buddy and I drove some nails in the long wooden bench leaving part of the head sticking up ever so slightly so it wouldn't be noticed when the old timers sat down. Underneath the bench, we connected wire to the nails and ran the wire into the feed storage room on the other side of the wall right behind the bench. We connected the wires to the magneto and tested it on each other to make sure it would work. The next day as the old timers started coming in and taking their same seat on the bench as they did every day my buddy and I got ready. After 7 or 8 old timers were seated, I gave Jim the sign and he started cranking. After a few seconds, about 5 of the old men jumped and gave out a yell. I remember one of them yelling that he was stung by a bee. Jim and I laughed and as we told some others standing in the store what we did, they laughed too. That was just one of many pranks played on people over the years in that community.

Half Rock wasn't unique to the way of life we experienced there. The state of Missouri and really our whole country had areas just like Half Rock. It was a simple life and most of those towns are just memories now. My wife and I own the whole town now, which consists of 2 houses, one church, and of course the cemetery, which is the only part of town that has grown over the years. The story I have given you is just one of many I have shared with my kids and hopefully those stories will continue to be passed along for generations.

The Stilt-Walking Champion
By Donna Kitterman of Kansas City, Missouri
Born 1944

When World War II was over my daddy and I met for the very first time. I was 14 months old. During the war, my mother and I had been living with her aunt and uncle and their four children. I was already calling my great uncle "daddy" because all the other children did. That soon changed and soon I had a little brother.

We moved into a two-room apartment in Kansas City where my father got a job for the K.C. Power and Light and he worked there for the next 42 years. In this small apartment, mom and dad's bed came down out of the wall at night and my brother and I slept on an Army cot bunk bed in the corner of that same room. We had no car and my dad took a bus to work. My mom would read our grocery list over the phone and soon it was delivered in boxes to our door, imagine that! We went to the apartment basement to wash clothes along with other residents. My little brother loved to stand on a chair and watch the clothes slush in the washer. One day he stuck his hand out and the wringer grabbed it and sucked his arm clear up to his shoulder. Luckily, his bones were so soft they were not broken; there was only a little bruising.

Soon we moved into a small house with an appliance store two blocks away. We would walk there and stand on that street corner for hours watching the television in the window, amazing. A neighbor family got a television and would let my brother and I come over at 4:00 p.m. every weekday to watch *Howdy Dowdy*. After we got a television, my great grandmother would often come to watch *The Ed Sullivan Show*. She would always get dressed up and primp her hair because she really believed that if she could see them, they could see her. She always clapped after each performance.

Back in the early 1950s, when you got sick you could call your doctor and he would come to your house, imagine that! One day I was sick, our doctor came and examined me then took me to the hospital in his car. I had polio and was put into an isolation ward for two or three weeks. I witnessed people in noisy iron lungs, which were sometimes shut down in the night. We all got to know what that meant. It was a terrifying experience for an eight-year-old and my mom and dad could only talk to me from outside the building through a small window. After isolation, I spent another two months in another hospital. During those two months, I became bored and got a little mischievous. Most of that time I was in a large room with eight or nine other children.

One day they served us lunchmeat sandwiches and I did not like them. I convinced all the other kids they didn't like them either and I got in my wheelchair and went around the room putting everyone' sandwiches into their bedpans. Later that evening when the nurse got to about the third child needed to use the bedpan, she looked straight over to me and said, "Donna, did you have anything to do with this?" Everyone laughed and so did she.

When released from the hospital my dad carried me into the house and left my wheelchair on the sidewalk. About an hour later he took me back to my wheelchair, which was now all decorated with balloons, crepe paper, and a banner reading, "Welcome home Donna". Then out jumped all the neighborhood children and they raced me up and down the street and around the block like a parade.

Back in the 1950s, all children played outside a lot, even after dark, imagine that! We played hide and seek in the alley and hid behind trashcans and telephone poles. We all liked to climb trees and I would drive my parents nuts by being high up in a tree with braces on both legs. My father made us wooden stilts with leather straps over the feet and I became the stilt-walking champion. We had contests at night to see who could catch the most lightning bugs in their jar and then we let them go. When we had big snows, my mother would empty the silverware out of the wooden drawer. It was great to make snow blocks in to build our igloo. Most families had a radio flyer and we would have wagon races on the hill at the end of our block. We used our wagon to collect newspapers from our neighborhood for the school paper drive. Our little red wagon also sometimes carried our groceries five blocks home from the store.

Picking Blackberries
By MaryAnn McCurdy of Cameron,
Missouri
Born 1937

My Grandmother, Bessie Mishler, was one of my two favorite people on earth. She spoke often of her memories of her childhood. She was born in 1892. One of her memories that she told my sister and myself was of the good blackberries that she used to pick back

Aunt Sissy in 1935

home on her aunt and uncle's farm in Mount Pleasant, Iowa.

One summer day when my sister and I were staying at grandma's house for the summer, we were told that we were going to have the chance to see that old farm that held so many of grandma's memories. Grandma's brother, Uncle Frank, was coming to take us to Mount Pleasant. Grandma did not have a car, so we walked everywhere we went. We were excited because we were going to go out into those woods that we had heard so much about and pick blackberries ourselves. Grandma told us that it was a long ways drive so we would have to stay overnight too. The day came and we arrived at that farm. It was on a dirt road, a big house, with an upstairs and shutters on the windows; not the kind of shutters I knew, which were for decoration only, no these shutters were closed at night. I remember walking into the old kitchen and it was so different from the kitchens I knew. First of all, it was big, very long, and right in the middle of the kitchen was the biggest table I ever saw. My eyes quickly noticed such large wooden beams running the length of the ceiling and from those large beams hung meat, lots of big pieces of meat. I did not know why anyone would hang meat from the ceiling, but I was told that those pieces of meat had come from the smoke house. At that point, I did learn what a smoke house was and even was allowed to go see where it was and how it looked. I can still see Aunt Sissy's stove. Never had I seen a stove like that, it was big, very big, and black. Aunt Sissy put corncobs in one of those holes on the stove. I could not believe what I was seeing; everything was so

different. I watched as Aunt Sissy opened a big black door of this stove and pulled out the prettiest perfect loaves of golden brown bread that I had ever seen. I remember thinking that I would have liked to have a piece of that bread, but grandma had told us to be careful to "mind our manners." I had high hopes of having a piece of that bread later.

That first day at the farm went so fast, there was so much to see, but soon it was bedtime. I could not understand why we were going to bed when the sun was still going down, but I was told that Uncle Ed and Aunt Sissy were up before the sun. When we went into the room where we were to go to sleep, I was once again, all eyes. It was the biggest bedroom; the floor had planks that were all wood. I had never seen a bed that high and I wondered how one was able to get into it, as it was so high off the floor. Then grandma found this thing that was kind of like stair steps, she moved them up to the side of the bed and then I knew how one was able to get into that bed. Then grandma showed us a pretty white piece that looked like a fancy large flowerpot and she explained to us that if we had to "potty" in the night that this is what we would use, as the bathroom in this house was located behind the house. Well, I decided then and there that I would not have to use that pot all night and I knew I would not ever use that one that

Uncle Charley in 1935

56

grandma said was outside. Suddenly I found myself somewhat afraid at that point, the room was quite dark now as grandma had shut those shutters and she lighted the cutest little kerosene light. Grandma had several of those kinds of lights in her house and we had used them when the electricity was out. Grandma and my sister and myself finally crawled into that big bed and immediately I sunk down into about 10 feather bed, never had I been in a bed with so many feather beds on it. Oh, grandma had feather beds but these were piled so high. Needless to say, I did not wake up all night, but when that rooster started to crow, I began to wake up. It did not take long to head down that stairway where the table was set with eggs, bacon, potatoes, fresh baked bread, and lots of jelly, all homemade of course. I could not understand why there was so much food for breakfast.

After breakfast, we headed out for that blackberry picking. I can't remember going real far, but I do remember getting into tall grass and then we went into the woods and finally the blackberries were spotted and we began to pick, course Peggy and I ate as much as we put into those little buckets. After we filled our buckets, it was time to go home. We took Aunt Sissy and Uncle Ed back to their house and we said our goodbyes and our thank yous. I thought we were headed back to Fort Dodge, Iowa, but I quickly learned that while we were close, we needed to stop and see Uncle Babe and Charley to at least say hello. Well Uncle Babe and Charley were really different. They both had strange mustaches and they lived in a very little house, part of which was still a log house. So we stayed long enough to say our hellos and we headed back home to Fort Dodge, Iowa.

On the way home, my sister got sick and up came the blackberries. Finally, we arrived home at grandmas and we were glad to be there. I will never forget my exposure to blackberry picking, outside potties, mud roads, smoked meats, kerosene lamps, and big feather beds. Uncle Babe and Charley with those big mustaches and their mules. I was about 10 years old and Peggy was about eight. Uncle Ed and Aunt Sissy didn't have a car; they had mules and a buggy. I wish I could have spent more time with them. They were brother and sister. Uncle Babe and Uncle Charley were brothers but I never understood

what they were to each other. They were my grandma's uncles. I never understood more than that, but it is still in my memories and has been for 65 years.

Growing Up During World War II
By J. Peter Thielen of St. Joseph, Missouri
Born 1939

'While I did not grow up in Missouri, my roots are firmly in the Midwest. I was born and raised in Waterloo, Iowa in 1939. Waterloo was not much different, I would guess, than northwest Missouri, particularly during that war period. Like most small towns of the time, it was populated by hard working people who had grown up with an agricultural background. It was a time of great change filled with emotions about family and country. The turmoil of war, of families sending their sons and daughters off to faraway places, a time when our country was poised to do most anything to retain our freedoms.

While I was very young, the war was very real to me. At first, I had no idea as to the causes of the concern that everyone lived with. One of my earliest recollections was when my next-door neighbor, George Dewey, had to go off to the Army. George was a great guy, who always had time to play with us kids. I was crushed the night he came over to say goodbye. I remember that I cried despite my parents trying to keep me from such a childish display of affection. There was no doubt that his leaving signaled a negative happening in my life.

Rationing was something every family knew about. Each family was given a book of tickets, which were used along with money to purchase household items. Without the appropriate ticket, you couldn't buy items even if you had the money. Families and friends worked together, loaning or giving the needed coupons if you didn't have them. Sugar, coffee, and flour were in short supply, there was an Army to feed. Tires and gasoline were needed for the war effort too and almost never available to the general population. Each family with a car (and many did not have cars) would only be able to buy a few gallons of gas a week. Long trips were out. Tires were repaired and re-repaired to make them last as long as possible. I remember looking out my bedroom window once as a car with no tires rumbled down the street on the rims. Recycling was a necessity. Food cans were crushed, put into boxes, and left on the curb for people to pick up. Metal was needed for the war effort. Papers and cardboard were similarly saved for recycling, everyone participated.

My town was pretty big in those days. John Deere had a plant in Waterloo, which had the fifth largest foundry in the world. From my bedroom at night, I could see the flames coming from the copulas of the foundry. There was also a packing plant, Rath Packing, and another manufacturing outfit called Chamberlin's. Situated in the middle of the country, heavy with important industries, Waterloo was a "target" during the war. Deere made the engines for the war machines and most of the metal parts for tanks. Chamberlin, which was located across the street, finished manufacturing the tanks. I can remember driving by and seeing the tanks being loaded on flat cars, ready for shipment to the war. "Blackouts" were scheduled periodically as a precaution against attacks by the Axis nations. Those nights everyone pulled the drapes or curtains to darken all the windows. Lights were turned off. Jeeps, with their lights outs, roamed the city, seeking anyone who violated the blackout. Even the factories were darkened; the city did not exist from the air above. For a little kid, less than five years old, it was a scary time.

A small pendant in the window of a house signaled a family member in the service. It seemed like every family contributed at least one family member to the services. Young men and women were forever leaving for service, some never to be seen again. Troop trains traveled through Waterloo on their way to training bases or assignments. Often people would come out to meet them when they stopped at the downtown station. Young soldiers, off to the war, would hang out the windows as city people reached up to thank them for their efforts. Candy bars and cookies were handed up as a small way of thanking the brave persons off to fight to keep us free.

I remember clearly the day the war ended. I could take you to the exact spot I was standing when it was announced on the radio that the Japanese had surrendered. I am sure I did not realize then all of the ramifications of that announcement. From that day on, many of the things I had grown up with changed. Rationing was stopped, car and gas availability meant that family trips could once more bring happy summer outings, and my neighbor, George Dewey, returned to Waterloo! God bless all those who fought to keep us free!

5 Gallons of Sugar Cookies
By Adalaye Terry-Vaughn of Excelsior Springs, Missouri
Born 1929

Dad (Cliff Terry) and mom (Emma Shelton Terry) were married in New Kirk, Oklahoma on April 26, 1914. My dad was a big man who worked hard all his life. He married my mom when she was 17 years old and he was 25 years old. They had 16 children in all, but only 11 survived. Seven girls and four boys. We had good times and bad, but most of all we had lots of fun. Mom had nine kids in Oklahoma and the other seven were born in Johnson, Kansas. I don't know how they fed all of us. Probably with a little help from the Lord and the rest from friends. They needed all the help they could get.

The first-born was Dorothy Mae. She got the lucky pleasure of being the big sister and helping mom with the other 15 kids. Sort of like a surrogate mother. Then came the twins, Thelma and Velma. They died of whooping cough in 1919. Maudree came next and also died of whooping cough in 1919.

C. D. was the first son, then Delmar, James, and Clarence. Then Gladys the fifth, a

Adalaye's parents, Emma and Cliff Terry

58

daughter, was born.

Then we all moved to Johnson, Kansas. This is where I come into the picture. I was such a cute little thing, the apple of my dad's eye (only kidding). The others will disagree with me. My name is Adalaye. Then came LaDonna, Fannie, and Bonnie. Mom also had another set of twins, Leo and Cleo, who died at birth. But mom wasn't through yet…along came Clara Kay. She is the baby of the family. To this very day, everyone still is trying to boss her around. She just hates it.

After mom had Clara Kay, the doctor said we needed to move from Kansas because of the dust storms, or we would lose mother. The movie "The Grapes of Wrath" during the Depression time describes my families move to Missouri. Dorothy wrote dad about the jobs, green grass, and trees in Missouri. So dad sold what little we had, which wasn't much, and headed east on June 1, 1937. We piled the furniture into the truck and the kids on top. A lady named Clara Mae was helping mom after she had Clara Kay, who was only six weeks old when we left Kansas. She made a five-gallon can of sugar cookies for us to eat on the way. She told us that the cookies should last us all the way to Missouri. She should have known better, we didn't get many sweets, as we were poor. Those cookies were all gone before we got 50 miles away from Johnson, Kansas.

As we made our way to Missouri, it was an exciting trip, as we had never been anywhere! Dad stopped in Dodge City so we could see our first zoo. My brother Clarence was always starting things and I would follow. Of course, I would always get blamed. Clarence and I got in trouble right away. Dad was good at giving his kids a good spanking. That is why we all grew up to be such good kids.

Along the way dad would let us sleep under the truck or anywhere we could spread our beds. Lots of farmers gave us water for dad's truck and his family. They probably said, "I'm glad they are all his and not mine."

It took us over two weeks to get to Topeka. Finally, our truck could go no more and broke down. Dad, Delmar, and Jimmy stayed with the truck to fix it, so they could drive on to Excelsior Springs. Dad bought mom and all us girls bus tickets to Excelsior Springs. Dorothy Mae and her husband lived there.

When we got off the bus on Broadway a

Dorothy Mae, LaDonna, Gladys, and Adalaye in 1929

taxi driver named Bennie Patchen met us at 11 o'clock at night. He would tell us this story until the day he died, "This lady got off the bus with all her children. I thought they were never going to stop getting off that bus.

Dorothy Mae lived in a two-room house. Clarence and C. D. were already in Missouri, as they came with "Sis," as we called Dorothy. Oh what a reunion of children. C. D. and Clarence made all the girls beds outside so they could watch over us. We stayed with "Sis" until dad and the boys came on after they had fixed the truck.

Dad found us a house on North Main Street. That was almost in the colored part of town. Being from Kansas, we had never seen a colored person. Dad always told us NOT to drink coffee or we would turn black. The first colored person I saw was a lady that came to visit mom. When I saw her, my eyes were as big as dollars. I told my mother she sure did drink a lot of coffee. We got settled in and enrolled in the Wyman School.

Every time we caught an illness, we would pass it right down the line, until the whole family had caught it. We never saw a doctor until we were married. Unless it was an emergency, Dad always took care of our ills. By the way, when mom got ready to have her babies, dad would deliver us. By the 16th child, they were getting pretty good at it.

I had enough brothers and sisters to play baseball, hide and seek, ice hockey, or whatever we wanted. We didn't need other kids to play with. When we played ice hockey, we played on frozen creek and used an old tin can as a puck. Our knees and shins were always black and blue when we got done. But we always had a good time.

Everyone had to work. We always has chores to do. He would load us in his truck before dawn to go pick up potatoes in Orrick. Dad and his family had a long row of potatoes to pick up and sack. Then the farmers would come along and pick up the sacks. The farmer would say if he had more like the Terry family to pick up, he could grow a bigger crop. Dad would give us all a dollar (which was a lot of money to us kids) to go to the Saturday night movie. He always made sure he had enough money left to buy food for his family. These are some of the things we would do as a family.

Later mom and dad would get a job in town. Gladys would have to watch us. Gladys would always say, "I'm going to run away from home." Clarence and I gave her a rough time. One time mom and dad came home for lunch and Clarence had poured rainwater on his face and clothes. He told mom and dad we threw it on him. Of course, dad spanked Gladys and I.

Clarence was mad at Gladys and I so when mom and dad went back to work, Gladys and I caught Clarence and put him in the rain barrel head first. We almost drowned him. I often wonder why I took Gladys' side that time instead of being Clarence's buddy. The rain barrel at the corner of the house caught the rainwater for us to wash our hair or whatever else needed washed.

When I think over all the things we did and what we've all have been through, we turned out to be a great family. Anyway, I'm proud of you all and wouldn't have missed it for the world.

Life in St. Joseph, Missouri 1940s-1950s
By Larry Flinchpaugh of St. Joseph, Missouri

I really never thought much about it until I began to write about my childhood experiences, but I now realize what a wonderful, full life I have had growing up in St. Joseph, Missouri. At 73 years old, I can't do all the things I used to do as a youngster, but still have fond memories of my childhood that can never be taken away from me.

St. Joseph was about the right size of town to grow up in, not too big and not too small. If St. Joe didn't have what you wanted, Kansas City was only 50 miles away. The first TV stations were in Kansas City: WDAF Channel 4, KCMO Channel 5, and KMBC Channel 9. St. Joseph's KFEQ, now KQ TV, didn't start broadcasting until about 1953.

I can't really remember when I first heard about a TV, but I do remember daydreaming about it while listening to Captain Midnight, Sergeant Preston of the Yukon, The Green Hornet, and Sky King on the radio. We would all sit on the floor facing the large Zenith radio looking directly into the speaker as if we could see pictures of what was happening. Actually, the pictures painted in our minds by the sounds coming from the radio were as good as a real live picture, maybe even better.

Television was actually invented before WWII but wasn't produced in large numbers until after the war in the 1950s. My family didn't buy one until 1953 because they were fairly expensive. Our first television was a table model Raytheon, costing almost $250. You could buy a nice, used automobile for $250. Before getting a TV of our own, all the

Larry and his sister, Jean in 1943

Larry in 1956

kids in the neighborhood would gather about four o'clock in the afternoon at the Stapleton's house in the 2600 block of Duncan Street to watch the small, 10-inch, round, black and white TV. They had several chairs arranged in the dining room like a small theatre. The TV shows did not start until five o'clock so we would just sit there and stare at the Indian test pattern until the shows started.

The picture was so snowy that all the lights had to be turned off so you could see a picture. The first programs I remember were the *Kukla, Fran and Ollie* puppet show and a comedian and dancer named Pinky Lee. Each afternoon they would show an old theatre movie serial, which would always end with something like a cowboy, tied to a barrel in a mineshaft and then there would be a huge explosion. You had to tune in the next day to see if he really died or somehow miraculously escaped. He always managed to survive. The Howdy Doody show with Buffalo Bob, Clarabell The Clown, Princess Summerfallwinterspring, and Mr. Fluster and Mr. Buster were on the air from 1947 to 1960.

The first TV screens were very small with many being only ten to 12 inches. Someone got the bright idea to mount a large 15-inch magnifier glass on a moveable frame. This would be placed in front of the small screen to magnify it. It worked perfectly, but also magnified all the snow and interference, which tended to cancel out any benefit of a larger screen. Another company had the bright idea of giving you the illusion of a colored TV picture. The dime stores sold a piece of plastic film that had blue at the top, orange in the center, and green at the bottom. You would attach this to the TV screen and you had colored TV for only 69 cents. Well, not actually. It didn't look too bad when watching

a ball game because the sky was blue, the faces were orange, and the field was green. However, other programs looked rather stupid with this color arrangement.

We never even imagined a VCR to record moving pictures. Everyone knew pictures had to be recorded on film and never even dreamed about them being recorded on an electronic tape.

Some people in the 1940s didn't have a telephone and if they did, it was usually a party line phone. Each house shared the line with three or four other people. You had to be careful and try not to dial or talk when another person was talking. I would get in trouble when my mother would catch me listening to someone else's conversation. One would sometimes need to call a person who had no phone by calling the person's neighbor who would then walk to that person's home and ask him to come to the phone.

I didn't think of my family as rich, but we did have all that we needed. Most people had only one car and the wife stayed home. The middle class people could survive at that time with only one parent working. If my mother and I needed to go somewhere, we would ride the bus. If I got sick, the doctor would come to the house. Our house was heated by a large coal furnace in the basement. The Artesian Ice and Coal Company would deliver coal in the winter and ice in the summer for the iceboxes. I think most people in my neighborhood had an electric refrigerator, which, to make it confusing, was also referred to as an icebox. Those with an icebox would place a card in the window that had either 25, 50, 75, or 100 showing at the top of the card. This was an ingenious way of keeping the iceman from making extra trips to the house to ask how much ice you wanted. Children would follow the ice truck to beg for a piece of ice, just for the fun of it.

I remember my dad filling the furnace with coal just before we would go to bed so the house would remain warm all night. Sometimes he would get too much coal in the furnace and the house would get so hot we would have to open the windows in the middle of the winter with snow dripping down the windowsill. There were no thermostats on the coal furnace.

When I was about 16 years old, three of my friends and I discovered a cave in the

61

bluffs above Water Works Road next to the Missouri River. The cave opening was large enough you could have driven a truck into it, except it was full of water. Not wanting the water to deter our exploring, we went back to town and bought four old inner tubes and scrounged up some boards to make a raft. After assembling the crude raft, we began slowly paddling deep into the cave. It started getting scary because the further we got in, the smaller the entrance looked, and our small flashlights weren't helping much. One of my buddies said, "Do you think we are the first to explore this cave?" I replied, after looking at the ceiling of the cave, "I don't think so, there are light wires attached to the ceiling." About that time, the inner tubes separated and the boards fell off our raft. We were splashing around trying to hold on to the tubes, hoping that we would not meet up with any water moccasins in the water. Eventually we floated out the opposite side of the bluff. Later we found out that this had been an old rock quarry. I never told my parents about what a stupid and dangerous thing we had done.

In 1951, the Federal Communication Commission introduced the "Novice" class ham radio license that required the applicant to take a written exam and show proficiency in sending and receiving Morse code at five words per minute. Shortly thereafter, I took the test and passed it, getting my first call letters: WN0RXO. Today, 60 years later, I still have the original call letters, but it is now W0RXO because I had upgraded to a General class license.

The Novice class license only allowed me to communicate by Morse code and, if you wanted to use voice, you had to upgrade to a General class license, which I did a few years later. My first transmitter was built from a kit where all the parts had to be mounted on a metal chassis and then you had to solder wires connecting everything per the schematic diagram provided.

Shortly after getting my ham license, I heard a cricket in my basement that sounded exactly like he was sending a Morse code message. I quickly grabbed a piece of paper and pencil and started writing down the letters. He was chirping so fast I just wrote down the letters as fast as I could and thought I could separate them into words later. Finally, he stopped and I started analyzing the message to see if he had been sending any words. You know maybe God was sending me a message or some alien intelligence was trying to communicate with me through the cricket. I wasn't completely disappointed. As it turned out, the cricket wasn't saying anything intelligent, but he was repeating the same message over and over. Even that I thought was very interesting.

You don't realize at the time how much you have learned from your parents. One morning on a crowded bus, an obviously poor, elderly, black woman got on and there was nowhere for her to sit. Remember those were the days when many ignorant people harbored racial prejudices, not only against the Negroes, but against anyone different from themselves. My mother had me get up and give her my seat. I didn't think much about it at the time, but what a wonderful gift my mother gave me that morning to teach me to respect everyone, no matter their race or station in life. To this day, I have never been burdened with prejudices against any race, rich, or poor, thanks to my loving and caring mother.

In the 1960s, I went to the library to check out a book on genealogy. The librarian directed me to a book section at the rear of the library. Halfway down the aisle, for no apparent reason, I suddenly stopped and turned to my left to see a book directly in front of me. I couldn't believe it. The book was, "The Book of Woodcraft." This was a copy of a book that my father had given me from his childhood library in the 1940s. The book had first been printed in the late 1800s and was the precursor of the Boy Scouts' handbook. How was this possible? I hadn't even thought about this book for years. I was a little shaken until I realized what had just happened. Our senses record everything around us and only those things that have meaning trigger our conscious mind and get our attention. I used this concept later in scanning genealogy census records on a microfiche reader looking for the name "Flinchpaugh." Even though I wasn't consciously reading every name out of hundreds, the name "Flinchpaugh" actually would jump off the screen.

Several years ago, I was studying religion and asked one of our group leaders what was the difference between prayer and meditation? I assumed what I was doing was prayer and what the hippie weirdoes were doing was meditation. She said, "Oh no. Prayer is when you talk to God and meditation is when you listen." This won't mean much to some people, but to me it was one of those "Ah ha" moments. I realized that I had been praying but had not been listening.

Seven years ago when I returned home to St. Joe from California to retire, people would ask, "Why in the world would you move from the excitement in California to Missouri?" I would reply, "For a better quality of life and to be around my friends and relatives that I grew up with."

These Memories Stand Out
By Alice Rosalie Riley of Norborne,
Missouri
Born 1942

My grandma was kind of a "horse whisperer." Grandpa would get mad when he couldn't get his horses to do what he wanted, and Grandma just talked to them and they would do it. Once, she got mad at Grandpa when she wanted to pick some wild strawberries along the side of the road, and he wouldn't stop the team and wagon. She was pregnant with twins at the time, and one of them was born with a birthmark that looked like a strawberry! Grandma always said it was because she got mad at Grandpa. She was also

Alice's Grandpa and Grandma Fitzwater in 1950

a midwife, and once on the way to help with a birth, she said she could reach straight out and touch the snowdrifts, from horseback.

My mama only attended school through eighth grade. She had to wear old hand-me-down men's shoes with cardboard cut to fit inside to cover the holes in the soles. She was still at home when Grandpa bought his first car, a Model A, I think. He drove it home, but having never driven anything but a team and wagon before, he couldn't guide it through the gate. He tried several times and would hit one gatepost or the other. So, Mama ran out, jumped on the running board, and guided the car through the gate. After that, he made her do all the driving!

My daddy grew up helping his dad with his sawmill. He only had a fourth grade education, and then went to work. He always filled out his own long-form farm income taxes! He also worked for other farmers, fourteen hours a day, for a dollar a day. He could fix almost anything and was a good mentor to others. He was given Grandpa's gun because he didn't smoke or drink and he never did!

My parents were each one of thirteen children, Daddy the oldest and Mama the oldest girl. They each lost two siblings as babies, each lost one brother in World War II, and each lost one sister at a young age. They both died at the age of fifty-eight.

My daddy's youngest brother, Norman, (the same age as my brother) and his next youngest, Jack, had a horse they rode down their long lane to shut the gate each night, and then they would fly back to the house. Uncle Jack said one evening it was too dark to see a cow lying right in their path until the only thing to do was jump over her. But just as they were airborne, the cow got up – an explosion of cow, horse, and riders! They all laid there a while. He thought the cow and horse were dead. They finally got up, but the cow always walked kind of crooked. Uncle Norman said he once had a rope around the horse's neck and got it pulled so tight he couldn't get it off. So he ran to the house and got a butcher knife to cut the rope. Grandma came running out, yelling, "No! No!" She thought he was going to kill the horse.

When my mama and daddy married, they were still very poor. They moved a lot because Daddy still worked for different farmers. Before my youngest sister and I were born, they once lived in a two-room house with dirt floors. Mama had only one dress, so on washday, she wore a pinned together old coat lining until she got her one dress washed and dried. Ruthie was the baby at that time, and on the dirt road, their old Model T got stuck in the mud. After trying to free it, Daddy got out to push, looked in the back seat, and Ruthie was passed out. Daddy grabbed her, ran down the road, working her arms and legs, and dipping handfuls of muddy water from the ruts in the road and splashing it in her face to wake her up. It worked. Ruthie also once picked up a little tin can, like we used for drinking cups, that my uncle had set down while filing a kerosene lamp. She drank kerosene!

My brother, William, was sixteen months older than my oldest sister, Betty. He was very shy, but Betty wasn't. So, Mama started them in school together, when Betty was five. Then, as they moved every year with Daddy working for different farmers, the teacher their fifth year taught fifth grade one year and sixth the next, and it was her year for sixth, so that's what she taught them. They moved again the next year, and that teacher said if they had already had sixth, they didn't need fifth, so she put them in seventh. So, Betty graduated from high school barely sixteen.

When I was a baby, during the war, they

Alice's parents, John and Alice Pollard in 1933

gave each member of the family a ration book of stamps. When my youngest sister, Bonnie, was a year old and I sixteen months older, Mama was doing laundry with her old wringer washing machine, went to get something, heard me crying, "Poor baby," and turned to find Bonnie had climbed on the side of the tub, her head bobbing in and out of the water, as I was pulling on her dress tail, but unable to hold her out of the water. She always said I put her up there!

When Bonnie was still little enough to sleep with Mama and Daddy, Betty and Ruthie slept together, and I got to sleep with my best friend and brother, William. He would pick me up, throw me on the bed, and bounce me up and down before we went to sleep. He would take Bonnie and me out to play and pull us around in a little wagon. Once, he turned us over in a mud puddle, while we were wearing new dresses Mama had just made! He'd pull us around on the snow on a sheet of tin with a rope handle. He once built a cart from scraps of wood and old wagon wheels and took us on rides. When I was five, I once spent the whole day outside with him while he worked building us a playhouse with limbs he drove in the ground and put an old carpet around them. He put limbs over the top and covered them with tall grass. That night, the wind came up and blew it down. I loved it but wasn't heartbroken, because I had enjoyed my time with him so much. He made a toy tractor from an eight-inch piece of 2" by 6" board painted green, with a square cut out of one corner, a big head nail for a seat, another for a steering wheel, old wagon wheels on the back, and a spool for front wheels. He made a disc to go with it. The discs cut from a tin can with tin snips and held together with baling wire. We played with them more than he did.

Sometimes I got to visit school before I started (also at five). One winter, I took a pint jar of milk for lunch and placed it in deep snow until lunch. It was like a slushy. Umm, good!

When my daddy's younger brother was killed in the war, Daddy joined the Army, leaving his wife and kiddies, as he called us, in the care of a good friend and neighbor he had worked for a lot. "Uncle" John would take us to town for groceries, the doctor, etc. Daddy was only gone for six months, as he was sent home with a medical discharge because of a hernia and excessively high blood pressure. After he came home, he moved us with a wagon and team of horses and bought the farm where we still live.

We stayed close to the older couple who helped us so much while Daddy was away, Uncle John and Aunt Dessie. Once, Bonnie and I were playing outside, and Uncle John picked us up and took us to their house. We were still small enough that our feet stuck straight out in front of us on sitting in his pickup seat. I looked down and saw streaks of dirt down our legs, the first time I remember realizing we were dirty. We sometimes spent the night. Aunt Dessie would feed us big slices of homemade bread with butter and syrup, and blackberries in little crystal dishes. I think my love of gospel music stems from Mama singing hymns to us and Aunt Dessie playing them on the old piano and organ.

As time passed, Aunt Dessie's memory got bad, and when Uncle John had to go somewhere, he would bring her over to us. Sometimes, she would say she had to go home and start walking down the road. Mama would send one of us to walk with her until we could talk her into coming back. We just watched out for her, as she had done for us so many times. But she could still make that old piano roll!

We usually went to town on Saturday evenings for groceries, etc. We girls shopped with Mama, while Daddy stood on the street corners and talked with the other men in town. So, William got a quarter each week to go to the movie. One day he came running down the stairs, shouting, "Mama, Mama! Look what I've got!" and holding a handful of quarters. Mama had been saving Hy-Klas labels to get Bonnie and me a doll for Christmas but only had enough for one doll. He had saved enough money by not going to the movies to buy the other one, so we each got one! The first Christmas William worked in the city; he brought us a new red wagon full of toys, including a toy typewriter! He was the oldest with four sisters, and he had a nickname for each of us. Betty was "Spet-ma-get," Ruthie was "Rufus-ma-gufus," I, Rosalie, was "Rattle-off-the-lee," and Bonnie was "Bonehead."

Daddy had an old Army Jeep they used on the farm. Once, Bonnie and I had gone to town with Mama and Daddy, and Betty and Ruthie were old enough to stay home alone. They were driving the Jeep around the pear tree. William came to town and told Mama they were driving the Jeep up the pear tree. Once, Betty and Ruthie were in the Jeep, chasing our old bull that had gotten out. They had to stop and get out of the car to get him out of a grove of trees. Then, Ruthie jumped on the trailer hitch and Betty jumped in and took off. It threw Ruthie off. Betty said she saw her flip in the air before she hit the ground. Ruthie said she had always wondered why cartoon characters with a blow to the head always "saw stars," but now she knew!

I have many memories at seventy years old, and now have more with my children and grandchildren. I could probably rattle on and on, but these stand out to me. Of course, I wish some things were different; that I had been a better person, especially. But I'm so glad to know my Jesus, as He is the only way of salvation and seeing loved ones who have gone before again someday. I wish everyone in the world could know Him and accept what He's done for us because, to quote Corrie ten Boom, "The best is yet to come!"

Farm Life
By Donald Vilven of Savannah, Missouri
Born 1933

I was born and raised on a farm in Pott County, Wamego, KS. The farmhouse I was born in was north of town and I remained on that farm until graduation of high school in 1951.

We attended Lion Grade School until we graduated from eighth grade. Delta, my twin along with one brother went to all grades in a one-room schoolhouse. Whenever had snow days we just plowed through the snow to get to the school.

When I graduated in 1951 the draft for the Korean War was really after us young guys. In January 1952 seven of us boys from town went to KC and passed our exam. So they loaded us on a train for San Diego where we went through boot camp. Then we went on 14-day recruit leave. Upon return from leave, we were assigned different ships to report for duty.

My duty station was USS Kermit Roosevelt (ARG-16), which was in the war zone. They took us to the loading dock in San Francisco to a big old merchant ship with soldiers, sailors, and Marines; we had no idea where we were going. After about days at sea, the word got out we were headed for Japan. The merchant ship was filthy and I made up my mind that if I was to serve on that dirty ship I was going over the hill. We got into Sasebo Japan late at night, the boat haul us to the pier. I found the sailors to be real nice. That ship was really clean and nice of course I found out who keep them that way. Spent 22 months on it and got striking rate. I crossed the pond for times. We were back in San Diego when the USS Platto (AO-24) wanted new hands I requested a transfer and got it I spent 22 months. I was released from the Navy with the rate of PN2 that being an administrative and clerical rating.

Baling Hay

We used to have a big team of horses when we baled hay. We had what they called a stationary hay baler. Dad would pull in the field, wet his finger, and stick it up in the air to find out which way the wind was blowing so we didn't get the dust in our faces. Then we took this large team of horses and hooked them to a go-devil. This piece of machinery was large spread machine with long teeth in it that bunched the loose hay and they push it up to the table. Dad always feed the bale and us boys took care of wiring and tying the before they were run out the chamber. One of our neighbors would help with the baling in exchange for work baling his hay. When we went to bale at his place, half of the crew was there, my brother dad and myself. When we did that work, they always had meals at the family who was getting the work done. The bales were stacked in the field and brought in for winter-feeding of animals .That is one of my stories of living on the farm during 1933 to 1952.

Sawing Winter Wood

This story will be about sawing wood for the winter to keep the farm warm. We lived in an old farmhouse that had no insulation for winter. We had a saw that mounted on front of a F20 Farmall tractor. The power of the tractor using a belt and pulley ran the saw. If the log was too big to get on the apron, we used a crosscut saw. We would cut the trees in length so we could get them on the saw platform to saw into smaller chunks. We would cut one

wagon on Saturday and if the weather wasn't too bad, we would try to get another load to stockpile. We hauled wood on Saturday and sometimes on Sunday if the weather forecast was nice that weekend and going to be bad on Sunday. We unloaded the wagon at the woodpile, and then us boys had to keep the wood box in the basement full of dry wood.

We never had electricity until 1942; sometimes I slacked getting the box filled so dad and mom made me do it after dark. We had a lot of coyotes in the woods behind where we lived and cried every night. If you haven't heard one at night, they really can be loud.

Butchering on the Farm

Dad fed a calf until it weighed over 1000 pounds. We had a barn with an opening in the roof so the sunshine would come and help warm the area up, it was called a coop a low. It had big braces running across it. Dad would call up and put the block and tackle solid to the board. He would take the line and run it thru a pulley anchored at the bottom of the post used to brace. Then hook up the tractor. The steer was coaxed so he was directly under the block Dad then shoot the steer, we hooked it on the block and started skinning the steer after that was complete the stomach was removed and all the rest was completed. We then covered the meat with a sheet and let it freeze. We always butchered when the night was going to be in the 30 so the beef would cool out. The next day the meat was brought in and we had a meat saw we cut our own beef up and even made our own hamburger.

We had a big basement under our house where Mother and Dad spent a lot of time Mother was great for canning garden things

I am 80 years old and can remember all the things just like they happened yesterday

One-Room School Days
By Edmund L. Miller of Lee's Summit, Missouri
Born 1939

I started first grade school in 1944 at 5 years of age. I went to school before there was so much to be learned that 9 months were required. We were so tough we had never heard of "Snow Days" so we only had to go through the torture for 8 months each year. Farm kids used to living outside a lot found it hard to start school in the fall when harvest was starting and equally hard to continue in the spring when the creek was running full and the wild onions were shooting up.

My brother, sister, and I walked the ½ mile to our Daviess County District 12 School (Griffith). Probably no one lived more than 2 or 3 miles away so it was really a community school. There were no buses but a few (including teacher Roselle Dowell) did ride horses occasionally. In my earlier years at Griffith, there was part of a horse barn to shelter a couple of horses as needed.

I don't remember my first day of school at Griffith. Probably there wasn't a big fuss with pictures and tears. The one room school did seem big though. We had a concrete front porch on the east side of the building with a space wide enough for all the students to stand to face the flag and pledge allegiance every day the weather permitted. The flag was just a few feet from the porch beside the living well from which we hand pumped our water.

Ed Miller's class at Daviess County District 12 School

In the earliest years, we had a bucket of drinking water on a bench at the back of the room. Later we had a galvanized "Cooler" to run water into our personal cups that hung on nails above the bench holding our lunches. Some country schools furnished hot lunches prepared by volunteer parents. Our school did not.

Farm food was the heart of most lunches. Cold sandwiches including bacon, butter, molasses, fried egg, salt cured ham, fried chicken, crackers/cheese, peanut butter, bologna, Spam, Beenie Weinies. Fried bologna and hot dogs were a treat. Potato chips and bananas were often included. Some had 1/2 pint thermoses for milk, tea, pop. The wise student did not take anything home at night and complain to mother. If you couldn't eat what you brought you had to find someone to trade with. If you threw it away mother would find out!

There were no custodians. Before school opened in the fall, one or more families cleaned out the bugs and mice and pronounced school ready to start. One year my mother was first to open the front door and was stung on the forehead by a hornet. Throughout the year, repairs were done by parents, possibly after discussion at the PTO (Parent Teachers Organization). Fall cleanup was a wipe down of desks and a sweeping of the tongue and groove bare wood flooring using sweeping compound and kitchen brooms. The seats were in rows screwed to boards so an entire row could be moved about. Friday afternoon was special activities time. One activity was moving the seats, sprinkling compound on the floor and wielding brooms. No lawyers were there to tell us child labor was illegal, that brooms could kill, that the union sweepers would strike. The rest of Friday afternoon was contest and fun time.

Coal heated the building my first 3 years. We had coal in a shed near the school. We were 'allowed' to drag huge coal buckets into the building. We also helped carry out the ashes and clinkers. Have you ever seen a red-hot clinker carried down a row of seats and out the door? About my fourth grade, we got an oil-burning stove. We never had fire, tornado, or earthquake drills. In case of fire, we had one bucket of drinking water to extinguish it and one exit door.

Any person who would have messed with a school kid walking home would probably have been mutilated then killed with no charges filed. In some local schools, the boys brought their rifles for hunting to and from school.

Griffith had windows on the south and east sides while we faced west. Electricity was first turned on in 1949. In our one-room, we had four bare 150-watt light bulbs in the ceiling. That year the teacher infuriated some parents because she kept the lights on ALMOST ALL THE TIME.

67

Unknown rider in front of the schoolhouse

Books were my adventure. Our entire resource library was one 30-inch wide cabinet from floor to ceiling. Even the teacher was not sure what it contained. One day we were digging in the shelves and found some phonic (fonix) flip charts. I learned phonics and had fun too. For recreational reading, we had a bookcase of three 36-inch shelves. By fourth grade, I had read everything in the school. One day I had been so engrossed in reading, I neglected to prepare any lessons for the next day. After the teacher finished her fit of yelling at me, she condemned me to miss all classes the next day. Instead of reciting, I had to read all day. The lesson may have been effective but I never forgave what she did to me. My folks were not too happy with either of us. Now in the 2000s my daughter is a reading teacher striving to encourage kids to read!

One Christmas our teacher loaded about 16 of us into her 1936 Ford and drove to Trenton, MO to see the Christmas movie Bambi. I'm pretty sure we did not use seat belts! Current laws would see this teacher punished.

Each fall, to start the year, we would have a big outdoor fire and wiener roast then entertainment inside. My writing was terrible and I was often sloppy. One fall I made the teacher mad by crossing out all my mistakes and drawing all over the page. She put my terrible looking paper on the bulletin board for everyone to see. My parents were embarrassed and then I was sorry!

After the "No class" day and this public embarrassment, I certainly should have qualified for psychiatric repair. However, there was too much work to do to get too depressed. Most of the kids in my school days had the promise if we got spanked at school we got spanked much harder at home and the teacher was always right! I never did get spanked but I probably should have been.

One day the teacher sent my arithmetic paper home for dad to see that I had missed every problem but one. Dad got mad especially when he noticed the one 'right' problem was also wrong. I wasn't a bad student; I just had so many more important things to do instead of homework. Didn't seem to affect my Engineering degree some years later!

About fourth grade, we obtained Book Mobile services. A van like a Frito Lay truck loaded with books came to the school on a regular basis and we were able to walk through it and check out books. I always checked out the maximum. With no television or other electronic media, reading was a window to the outside world. In our house, advertising fliers were even treasured for drawing and making gliders.

We had a bell tower with a rope to ring the day to order. Occasionally the bell rope needed replaced. That seemed such an impossible job to a small child. One time one of the girls was swinging on the flag rope and bent the flagpole. Her dad backed his truck up to the flagpole and repaired the damage. No claims were filed and no attorneys screwed up the repairs. That doesn't sound like today's world does it.

I still believe being cooped up in school hurt freedom loving farm kids worse than it does city kids. We had so many other more interesting things that needed to be done. We did not know what a minority was so we could play anything that did not cause long term damage. Blackman, Red Rover, Hide and Seek, Kick the Can, etc. Our school ground was about one acre and was so sloping we could not really play ball.

In the fall, we had great times making paths through the weeds and grass around the schoolyard. On a hot fall afternoon, the grass smelled so much better than a rubber lined playground. I can hardly believe we didn't get snake bit. I do not believe we even had a first aid kit and of course no phone for an emergency. The only injuries I remember was when I threw a horse weed like a spear and put a splinter in a girl's knee. She lived and I didn't get spanked. One day her brother was riding on my back sledding when we went under a barbed wire fence. I cleared, he didn't.

Our schoolyard had a small ditch that ran through one corner. Much of the year it was dry but any rain soon filled it. This ditch had a lot of rocks. A ditch with running water and rocks needs a dam. I appointed myself chief dam builder and each year we would build and improve on our little dam. One year we out did ourselves and dammed the ditch too well. We had a lot of rain and the water began to rise but the dam held. Mid-afternoon a local father knocked on the door and told us that water was spilling over the road. We engineers had to go un-dam the water immediately. Can you imagine the extreme danger we must have been exposed to?

We had outdoor facilities (privies) known as two holers. The boy's toilet was located in the SW part of the yard and the girls in the NE part. It was not acceptable to fool around the wrong one either. We had finger signals such as one finger requested going for a dipper of water. Two or three fingers indicated a trip to the outhouse. A violently shaking finger suggested great distress and a forthcoming disaster if not allowed.

The schoolyard boundaries were well defined but it was always tempting to wander across the adjacent fences and play in the creek or wander through the brush. One spring day the older boys washed a pan of wild onions and we ate them. The teacher threw a hissy. To this day, I do not see what the problem was but she surely had something in mind.

In my first years, we had daily health inspections. Someone was selected to poll each classmate to see if they brought a hankie, brushed their teeth, combed their hair etc. Some would try to show the inside of a pocket as a hankie and some didn't even have a toothbrush but claimed brushing. The survey was not very scientific.

In those days of hand washing, line drying, and sad irons we only changed clothes when necessary. We often wore the same clothes to school we had worn to do our chores. The coats and overshoes were the same ones too.

These were hung or piled in the corner of the room and became aromatic when the room got warm. As few had raincoats, wet cloth coats were hung around the stove to dry in time to go home.

How do you think we ever survived and grew up to be farmers, doctors, engineers, teachers, bomber pilots, submarine captains with such primitive schools?

My 8th grade graduation from Griffith marked the end of one-room schools in Daviess County, Missouri. We were consolidated into the Gilman City, Harrison County RIV district of Missouri. My Griffith graduating class (2) was quite small but my teachers had done a good job in that one room. Over 50 years later even large districts are struggling to maintain sufficient students to support K-12 schools. What will be next? Perhaps dormitories to spend the week at school returning home for the weekend.

Inner Tubes and Diaries
By Carol Moriarty Parman of Grant City, Missouri

I was born near Twin Lakes, Iowa in Calhoun County in 1938. Dad had a 1928 Chevy that his friends joked about saying "If the engine quits you can put your feet down through the holes in the floorboard and use them for wheels." The first four children were bundled up and driven places in that old car. We went on picnics, fishing and to visit relatives at a distance. I remember the fishing expeditions to "Twin Lakes. The kids would play along the shore and get bloodsuckers between our toes. Dad would use pliers to pull them off our feet. We usually had a fish fry with friends after the day was over.

You never traveled in those days without a patch kit in your vehicle. It contained various sizes of rubber patches, which were glued to holes in the inner tubes of tires. The car was jacked up with a hand jack, the tire removed from the wheel, then the rubber inner tube taken out to find the nail hole. The rubber around the hole was buffed to make a surface that the patch would cling to. Dad would use his knee to stretch the tube flat, buff it, apply glue to the patch, and light it with a match to warm the surface—blow it out and attach the warm patch to the place where the hole was

Bernard Moriarty using a tire pump in 1936

prepared for patching. My brother and I later patched our bicycle tires the same way. They also had inner tubes.

One excursion I remember was taking the family to Clarion, Iowa about a 100-mile drive. It would have been 1948 when I was 10 years old. We never traveled that far and I think we were taking the new baby, Mary to show the relatives on the Corson side of the family. The reason I remember the trip is because I had paper and pencil and I was writing about our 'trip.' It was the first time I was documenting something for the family. Later it was a diary as a teenager and now I am the family historian doing genealogy. Interesting road I have traveled.

Recess Gets Out of Hand

The old rural schools of Calhoun County, Iowa held many opportunities for recreation. It was about 1950 at Lake Creek #7 that I wound up the old Victrola record player while the teacher and older boys were roping off the pillars in the basement to make a boxing ring. She got in the ring for the lively bouts using children's boxing gloves. One of the boys gave the teacher a black eye and that put an end to those games!

While the boxing was going on, I was putting records on the old Victoria. I grabbed the handle and wound it up, gingerly holding the large round needle holder placing the tip of the needle in the right groove of the record and aimed the microphone toward the boxing ring. I wish I could remember the song that was playing! As the box was winding down getting slower and slower, I wound it again and it speeded up making the words go faster and faster. It wound down dragging out the words and music about the time that the boxing match was over and that was a fitting end to the embarrassment suffered by the teacher.

Two seventh and eighth grade boys got in a wrestling-fist fight in one corner of the playground one day. Poor Miss Patty Brush, our teacher that year, was not big enough to break it up. The teacher had to police all these different ages of kids, K-8 at recess, in addition to class-time teaching.

Another way we entertained ourselves was to skate on sidewalk skates on the cement floor in the basement while other children were playing cards in the library corner upstairs. There were door windows in the front of the bookshelves and some older kids cheated by reading the cards in the window of whomever had their back to the library doors. That would cause an uproar at times. I never had a classmate except for third grade when I would get my arithmetic done and the other girl didn't. She would lose recess privileges and I felt sorry for her.

Away from It All
By Mary Waldron Greene of Springfield, Missouri
Born 1948

The House
A very early recollection I have is standing in the doorway of the kitchen of our monstrous

old farmhouse holding on to my dad's striped overalls. The old house was built around the turn of the 20th Century of native lumber. It was fourteen rooms, two and a half stories of pure cold. It was designed and built in the Federal style by a man whose religious beliefs allowed for a future rule and reign of 1,000 years for which he prepared this house. Dad said he could have it back any time. When Mom and Dad first moved there early in 1930, food froze in the bay-type windowsill off the kitchen and bath addition, and the curtains blew, billowing out in the wind even when the windows were closed.

The ceilings were 10 feet tall, the walls lath, and plaster and the floors were poplar. The door locks hadn't worked in years since either my sister or I stuck them full of chewing gum. The exterior doors had either half or full beveled oval glass in them, and the windows had the old weights in the walls with ropes that held the windows in place when they were open. The window and door facings were plain but 6 inches wide and showed years of dings and dents. The plaster in the stairway hall had been painted dark grayish brown with stenciling at the top for a border exactly as it was built in 1909 according to a note on the closet door. The was a 3 foot by 5 foot section of the plaster that had fallen off onto the stairs many years ago that was cleaned up but never repaired, and the pocket sliding doors to the formal living room had long since been removed since they let in too much cold air. The downstairs portion of the stairs had beautiful dark stained bead board paneling, and there was a wonderful hideaway under the stairs and landing that my friends and I spent many a peaceful evening in listening to Elvis's You Saw Me Crying in the Chapel or Are You Lonesome Tonight or some other popular music on the old radio in there until we were probably in our early teens. Once, though, I remember that we got hold of a deck of cards—most likely from my sister–which was not permitted in our house. Of course, we got caught playing some forbidden game like Crazy 8 or Rummy or something and the cards were burned. Well, that was embarrassing.

Heat was always a problem—or rather lack of same. For years we had a wood stove, which gobbled hardwood and made a really hot fire. Dad became concerned about the worthiness of the chimney and bought electric wall heaters to supplement. They ran up the electric bill, so we resorted to a floor furnace. Unfortunately, the water table, even on the tall hill the house was on, was very high, and one night the floor furnace filled up with water. That was the end of it. A Ziegler space heater was the last kind of heat we tried. It burned heating oil and had blowers on it, which made it at least tolerable in most rooms. But, I resolved that the height of luxury would be running around my own house someday in my underwear and being comfortable doing so.

The house was located on a dirt road twenty-two miles from the county seat of Bethany. Now, dirt roads in south Missouri, as I later learned, were considerably different because in wet weather tires only sink to about six inches deep before hitting limestone. In north Missouri there IS no bottom. The only way out in wet weather was leaving the car at the gravel road "over at Harvey's" and taking the 8 N with the carryall box on the back through the pasture to the car or to the school bus. The sod would usually hold enough to allow a few trips in and out before it dissolved into mush.

Chickens

Some families were large and had huge amounts of food to prepare and preserve for the long winter months. Ours was small—just Mom, Dad, and me since my 15-year-older sister had moved to the city when she was but 18. Still, we had several broilers to be killed,

Mary with her parents, Carl and Lurene Waldron in 1952-3

cut up, and either canned or frozen. I remember we would go to the hatchery in the spring, and the trip usually coincided with my dentist's visit. If I was very brave, we would be getting baby chicks afterward. My teeth were straight but not particularly strong without fluoride treatments or chlorine in our well water. The school eventually gave us red tablets to bathe our teeth and help prevent cavities. But one particular dentist's visit involved pulling a baby tooth that fractured into three pieces that had to be dug out. It hurt like everything, but I was brave and got through it, and off to the hatchery we went.

Mom liked the red heavy layers called Rhode Island Reds. They gained fast, laid brown eggs, and weren't so flighty as the leghorns. I, personally, liked the little yellow chicks better, but either was great fun. Mom would prepare a corner of the smokehouse by putting down layers and layers of newspaper, affixing a heat lamp over the area, and standing up either old doors, wagon bed sideboards, or whatever to make a pen. The chicks were vulnerable quite a while to cats, rats, coons, and the like, so we chinked any holes we could find. I would pet, cuddle, and carry them around until Mom was sure I'd wear the fuzz off. I remember sitting in a big living room chair with a couple of them. They'd sometimes try to run under me like they would a mother hen. And, as luck would have it, I lost track of one and jumped up, but too late saw that he had been smashed like a pancake. He wasn't dead, but Mom warned that she was doubtful he'd make a good recovery.

As they grew feathers and became less amenable to being wallered and would flap wings and dash to the far side of the pen at the sight of me, I lost interest. They were moved to the regular chicken house and fattened out.

Our chicken yard would be considered free range by today's standards. Probably 100 feet long by 75 feet wide the yard had plum thickets and mulberry trees that supplied seasonal treats and cedar trees on the north side for a windbreak. The chicken house was an ancient, unpainted two-room structure, one room full of roosts and one room with a wall of nests. It was on the same side of the house as Mom's bedroom, and she could hear any cackles and squawks for help in the stillness of the country nights. On more than one occasion Mom would grab her gun or her axe and head to the chicken house to the rescue. If it was a possum, she would pick up a stick; knock it in the head so that it would "sull" or "play possum" as she called it. She'd grab its tail, carry it to the big flat rock up by the kitchen door, lay it down, and with her axe, dispatch it. Not exactly the PETA way, but back then we did what we had to do.

There would come the day that the broilers reached 2 pounds and ready for slaughter. Some families, like I said, with many mouths to feed, would kill a hundred chickens on a given day, dress them, package them, and can or freeze them. We were lucky and, I thought, pretty affluent since we'd had electricity since I was born, and I was the only one in my entire third grade class to have indoor plumbing. My dad was a plumber, too. (My teacher once asked me what my father did for a living, and I said, "He's an electrician, and he plumbs some." That sounded so funny that I got the giggles and couldn't quit laughing and snorted and spit and the more the teacher looked at me, the more I laughed until my sides ached.) He had also gone to Chicago to an electrician trade school when REA started stringing lines in Harrison County. So, we had a freezer to put these chickens in fairly early on. Some people didn't like the taste of a frozen chicken as much, but we found it quite acceptable.

The actual killing remains a skill that for me remains unperfected. Some used guns, some a board laid on the chicken's head. My mom "rung their necks." The chicken "without its head" would jump around bleeding out, and if you weren't quick, could come after you. I did try—several times, but I think, my circles were too big, and when I dropped the chicken, it's head was very much intact, but the chicken was very dizzy and would stagger away.

Mom didn't like to dress chickens. She felt it was an inefficient waste of her time and that the skin was too full of fat and dirt to be eaten. Nutritionists today seem to bare that out. To dress a chicken you kill it, dip it in scalding water, pull the feathers off, light a rolled up newspaper on fire to singe the hairs that remained, then gut it and cut it up. We skinned the chickens in a flash and the entrails came with the skin, feathers, and hairs. We saved the liver, gizzard, and heart although

Mom had some trouble eating the heart. More of the idea of it, I guess. Now, one of these young birds cooked in lard and Crisco in an iron skillet with white gravy is indeed a culinary delight; there's nothing better in the world.

The Outhouse
By Glen Easter of Princeton, Missouri
Born 1946

In the summer of 1968, my father added on indoor plumbing. He continued to use the old toilet for about a week and then succumbed to the convenience of indoor plumbing. We had running water at the kitchen sink since I was in the 8th grade, but only as cold water. The lack of indoor plumbing was an embarrassment to me as well as a very contentious subject. Prior to that, we had a bucket of water at the sink with a dipper. You drank from the dipper along with everyone else.

Baths were once a week and taken in the middle of the kitchen floor in a number 2 tub. As a child, you thought nothing of it. Everyone swirled around you and it was fun. But as a teenager, it was not fun. In high school, I purposely took showers at school, but there were few of those. In the summer, I took baths in the pond or used the chicken house hydrant, which was pond water. I was cleaner in the summer than during the winter months.

I realized then that my father saw it as an added expense. Not so much the building but the water consumption. We had a cistern that caught roof water and otherwise had to have water hauled to it. When Mom got an automatic washer, Dad began hauling water. We also hauled water during the drought years.

In all fairness to my folks and especially my father, he knew instinctively how to make ends meet. He had only an 8th grade education, but he knew his expenses. But even with that recognized, I seldom brought anyone home from college or otherwise for the lack of indoor plumbing. Later I would realize that many in my high school class did not have indoor plumbing either, but we just did not talk about it. One person of special note was my best childhood friend and classmate; he was in the same boat.

From my earliest memories my sister I were going to college. Not just any college, but to the University of Missouri (at Columbia). I should note that she graduated in 1963 and me in 1968. An education and escape from rural poverty as my folks viewed was extremely important. When we were through college, my father added on the bathroom. When we graduated from college, we owed nothing on our education. We had either worked or our folks had paid our way. Although I have always appreciated the sacrifice of my parents, I have always believed we could have had that bathroom in the fifties and made do.

When rural water finally arrived and we were lucky enough to be an early recipient, my father was more comfortable with indoor plumbing.

The outhouse was located out the back door past the old smoke house and the cave house. When I went to college, I could not understand how my frat brothers could spend thirty minutes on the stool, reading, etc. to take a dump. I soon realized they had indoor plumbing. Their ass had never touched a cold, frosty board in the winter where you got the job done and got the hell back to the house to the oil-heating stove.

In the summer, the toilet would smell but we used quick lime to kill the odor. My father cleaned it out once a year and only he did it. I recall offering to help in college and he said no. At that point, I realized he may not have liked it so much either, but felt it necessary for the time being.

For a boy, peeing was easier. I would make it past the old smoke house and that was far enough. From my studies of ground water since then, it was not, but back then, it was. In the winter, I stepped out into the snow any number of times and peed just outside the door. A few times, I did not make it beyond the front porch. A few times, I left evidence in the form of yellow snow. Early on, we used a slop jar upstairs where we slept. The jar, actually an enamel bucket with fitting lid, would be carried out the next morning. I don't believe the folks used it so much, but as children, my sister and I did. It was also called the honey pot or fruit jar.

Late in the summer of 1968, the outhouse came down and the spot disappeared. Today it is all gone with the old smoke house, cave house, wood house, etc. The cistern was filled with waste lime when we built our new addition in 1994 and is now under the house. I have never missed the outhouse!

Learning to Drive
By Billie Frances Mosley of Kansas City, Kansas
Born 1923

I suppose it was the accident that traumatized me about driving. The year was 1930; My Father had bought a 1929 ford. He taught My Mother to drive in that car. I being 7 years of age took it all in, Mother was very nervous, so therefore I also was nervous. A couple of months after the driving instructions, My Mother, and I were driving up one of the alleys in my hometown, New Boston, Ohio. The alleys were paved, as it was the richest little town in the world, per Ripley's, believe it or not. Wheeling Steel Mill ran the whole length of the town. Having a Mill that large paying tax kept us in the black. As we drove down the Alley, a garbage truck turned the corner in front of Mother, she applied the brakes, but too late, we crashed into the truck. I screamed and began to cry knowing we were being killed. We were two blocks from home, so Mother told me, "go get your Daddy," panicking I went screaming the whole way, yelling, "Mother had a wreck, Mother had a wreck." Daddy came to the rescue and all was fine, but it left its mark on me.

Thru the depression years, we did not have a car, so I was not faced with the pressure of driving. When my husband left for the war, I lived with my parents who had moved to Detroit, MI. I was taking a bus everywhere so Daddy decided to teach me to drive. I was panicked. We got onto a 3-lane road, with very wide turns, I was driving about 30 miles hour. Daddy said, "Turn left." Luckily there was a big turn area, I never cut my speed I just kept turning the wheel. In the midst of it all I screamed, "I can't do this Daddy take the wheel!" I let go of the wheel, lucky daddy had nerves of steel and just sat there. I finally grabbed the wheel back and made the turn. I stopped as soon as I was around the corner, limp and shaken, I did not drive again for 2 years.

We were living in Belton, Texas my husband was still in the army he shared a ride with a fellow solider one day so, I decided to drive our Chrysler to the base and surprise him. The kids were in the back seat, I approached another wide intersection, and a man was hitchhiking standing in the middle if the intersection. I drove to the right of him of course he moved to the right I moved to the left he moved to the left I was screaming, "Stand still!" He finally dove as if He was in a swimming pool and rolled off the high way. "Oh god," I was so relieved I almost passed out the kids said, "Mama you almost hit him," "Oh yes," I said.

Seven years later after my husband came home from WWII, we had then relocated to Kansas City, and we owned a Buick. He told me he was going to leave it home and drive the camper to work. He said I need to learn to drive. "What if I have a wreck," I said. He said, "Tear it up, but drive it." I put the kids in the car, no seat belts; I proceeded to drive to my Brothers home. I did just fine. The Kids didn't make a sound; they knew how scared Mother was. The town still had old tall western curbs, on my way back while turning the corner I cut to close and crushed and rolled the back fender under the car. "Oh Dear," I worried. My husband was wonderful He said we will fix it and you continue to drive and I did. I am now 89 years old; I still drive, even on the interstate. I am so proud of myself I conquered my fears.

A Much Simpler Life Back Then
By Nancy Hope Chitty of Weston, Missouri
Born 1943

My Mother, Father, and I lived on a 110-acre farm NE of Weston in Northern Platte County and my grandparents owned a 130-acre farm on the West side of our property. My father was a tobacco farmer and Weston had the largest tobacco market west of the Mississippi River. Raising tobacco was mostly a four-step process that began in the early spring. My father started tobacco beds, much like starting tomatoes from seeds in March. By mid-May early June, the plants were ready for transplanting in the fields and we had 3 acres to plant. My mother's sister always came and helped pull the plants, then my father drove the tractor and Mom and I sat on the tobacco planter (setter)–the seats were only about 8 inches off the ground and we had to sit with our legs straight while holding the

74

heavy sacks of plants in our laps. The setter had a huge water barrel and a line was run to the 'shovels' that made the furrow. The water was timed with a click and we set a plant with the click so that it was watered at the same time. My Father used a horse and one row cultivator to plow the tender plants. I would get up early and run out to the field for my Father to set me up on the horse to ride. In late summer/early fall, it was time to cut and house the tobacco and was very heavy and hard work. The tall stalks of tobacco were speared on to sticks and hung in big tobacco barns to cure. This became an entire neighborhood effort and all the neighbors pooled their resources and helped each other at harvest time as it took at least four men to work the barn. Even the farm wives got into the action with their huge home-cooked meals. As soon as they finished one neighbor's field, they went on to the next field. In November, the tobacco had cured and was ready to take down and strip the leaves and take to market. Buyers from every tobacco company came to Weston for the sales. When I was very little, my Father carried me around the sale warehouses and would set me up on baskets of tobacco for sale.

We didn't have any indoor plumbing or electricity. My Dad always said, "We have running water–you run out and get it." We had a cistern right outside the kitchen door. The years 1949 and 1950 were what my family called the 'boom' years. While the government had started the Rural Electrification Administration (REA) in the 1930s, we didn't get electricity until 1949. I remember playing

Swamp School
The teacher, Mrs. Sievers is standing in the back

outside until dark then reading books by the coal oil lamp. My mother scrubbed clothes on a washboard and hung them outside to dry. With the coming of electricity, Mom got a wringer washing machine and gone was the old washboard. (I have it hanging in my laundry room now). Crops and cattle were a good cash investment in 1949 and 50 and my Dad bought a 1950 Chevrolet AND a Motorola black and white television. The very first show I saw on television was Gene Autry. My Mother made all of my clothes and a new electric sewing machine made it easier than the old Single treadle machine.

We used crank telephones and were on party lines. Our phone number was 1620 and, since my grandparents lived next door, their phone number was 1630. The first two digits (16) designated the party line and the second two digits represented the number of rings (cranks)–the third digit was the number of "longs' and the fourth was the number of "short" rings. Everyone on the line had to listen to see whose phone was ringing. I recall that my aunt's phone number was 2402 so was on a different party and we had to crank for the operator and have her ring the 2402. If our clocks ran down, I remember that we could call the operator for the time. About the same time that the electricity came to our rural area, we got the rotary dial phones. We still had party lines, but the phones only rang to the party called; but if you picked up the phone to make a call, someone may be using it.

I started first grade In Sept 1949 at Swamp Community School that was located about two miles south of our farm. Swamp was a 2-room school where classes were held in one room and the second room was open

Nancy's daddy, Hope Wright with George Davis Wells
housing tobacco in 1958

for school programs and community events. Miss Katherine Chinn was my first and second grade teacher then she left to take a teaching position is Southern Platte County. Mrs. Carol Sievers taught at Swamp for the next three years. The teachers taught all eight grades with approximately 10-15 children. The country schools were consolidated into the Weston public schools in 1956.

It seemed like a much simpler life back then–hard work without all the luxuries enjoyed today, but it was a time when we never locked a door, left our keys in the car, and trusted everyone. It was a time when a man's word and handshake made a contract without dispute. Those were the 'good ole days'.

Shoebox Slot Machine, Crystal Radios, and Friday Night Fun

By Richard Drozd of St. Joseph, Missouri
Born 1944

When I was 3 or 4 years old, I was playing in my sandbox with a kid named Roger. I have a photo of us in the sandbox. I clearly remember Roger grabbing a toy metal hoe that was lying in the sandbox and he struck me right between my eyes with the hoe. I carried that scar between my eyes for my entire life.

After my mother died, I lived with my grandparents for almost 3 years.

One day my grandmother had gotten her hand stuck in the old wringer on their antique washing machine that was down in the basement. Her entire hand was almost solid black and blue.

My grandmother only purchased laundry detergents that had a free dishcloth or some type of kitchenware inside the box.

Every appliance that my grandparents owned must have been made in the 1920s and 1930s. During the winter, I remember hearing the rumble of coal filling up the coal room in the basement. Their furnace burned coal to produce heat. Their toaster was a small single slice unit made out of metal. After inserting one piece of bread, you would push down on a lever located on one end of the toaster. It would click back up like it was on a wind up mechanical timer. It never produced a perfect piece of toast; my grandma always had to scrape the black off of my toast.

All of the light switches in their house were the kind that had two push buttons, one above the other. One button turned on the light, the other would turn off the light.

My grandmother used a large black iron skillet or a black iron pot to cook dinner.

I long for the taste her goulash just one more time. She made a Czechoslovakian goulash that was out of this world delicious.

When I was only 5 years old, I would ride the Jules Street bus all by myself for a complete loop. When the bus returned to my street, the driver would let me off. I rode the bus quite often and the bus drivers always remembered where I wanted to get off.

My grandfather told me that back in the prohibition era, he used to make his own liquor, and he kept it hidden in a small deep cellar far beneath the basement. He had two wooden kegs in that cellar.

In the 1950s, they used to pay the sales tax with mills. They came in various denominations and colors.

I made my own slot machine out of a shoebox that used the mills as coins. The shoebox had cardboard ledges that caught the mills as you put them into a slot at the top. After so many mills were on the ledges, some would fall off and come out a slot in the bottom of the shoebox. Some of my favorite toys where those that I made myself.

After my Grandfather retired, he had a railroad pass and in the summer when I didn't have to go to school, I occasionally would go with him on the train to Chicago. Riding those old trains were a very memorable occasion. I loved the smell and atmosphere of the old trains. My grandfather always brought along a loaf of Jewish rye bread and a long tube of salami for us to eat on the train. The trains had the best tasting water.

One day, when I was in the 1st grade, I saw a patrol boy beating on his patrol helmet that was placed on a small bank in front of a house next door to the grocery store on Edmond Street. I was extremely curious as to why this kid was banging on his patrol helmet. Just as I bent over to look at his helmet, he grabbed the helmet and ran off. Suddenly, swarms of yellow jackets were coming out of a hole in the ground and I was immediately engulfed in bees. I ran home as fast as I could, screaming and crying all the way home. When my grandmother began removing my clothes, she found bees in my socks, my T-shirt, my jeans and even in my shorts, it was one terrible experience that I will never forget.

One day I was playing with my grandfather's "frog sticker" knife. I accidentally tossed the knife right into a sinkhole right beside a 25-foot tall wall beside Sherwood school.

It was a pretty large hole. When I told my grandfather about me dropping his knife down the hole, he got all upset and shouted his usual "Jez Gosh" plus a few choice words in Czech. He grabbed a hold of me and out to the alley we went so I could show him the hole. He tied a rope around his waist and then handed me an end telling me to hold on it. As I held onto the rope, the old man then went down head first into that large sinkhole and he totally disappeared from my sight. I was absolutely terrified, I was afraid that I would never see my grandfather again. A few minutes later, he was backing out of the sinkhole and he gave me quite a scolding. I never could figure out why my grandfather would risk his life for a $1 knife.

Playing marbles was a common game with the boys in the 1950s. I had a big sack of marbles that I had won from other kids. I don't think any of today's kids would know what to do with a sack of marbles. My favorite marble was the cat eye marble.

In the 1950s, when you bought a 5-cent package of bubble gum, you got a big piece of bubble gum plus you also got a baseball card inside. I collected these baseball cards until I was in the 7th grade. We had a game called "flipping cards" and the winner would get the pile of cards. The other players would flip their cards in turns trying to cover your card in a certain fashion. The first one to do so would win the pile of cards. At one time, I had a grocery sack full of those baseball cards.

Back in the good ole days, we listened to the radio quite often. Unlike today, most people back then didn't own a television and if they did, it displayed only black and white on the screen. Television was brand new luxury item at the time.

I would go over to Mr. Brown's house next door just about every day to listen to his big 1930s vintage Zenith floor model radio. It was a beautiful piece of furniture. I called Mr. Brown using his nickname of Pappy. He could get short wave on this radio as well. Pappy and I would listen to radio shows like Dragnet, The Lone Ranger, The Shadow, Fibber McGee and Molly, and many more for hours on end. Fibber Magee and Molly was my favorite radio show.

From when I was in the 6th grade until I was in high school, I used to make my own crystal radios using a cat hair and a crystal. I remember that the crystals cost me 15 cents.

You tuned the radio by moving the cat hair ever so slightly on top of the crystal.

I strung a copper wire outside as an antenna and one night I listened to music being played on an Oklahoma City radio station. You had to use a set of headphones in order to hear but it was a lot of fun. Of course, there were commercially made radios available but this was more of a hobby and something different, it was something of a challenge.

When I was 6 years old, I saw a kid swinging on a tree branch out over 29th Street. I thought it was neat, just like Tarzan swinging on a vine. After he went home, I thought I would give it a try. I was not wearing any shoes at the time.

Needless to say, the branch broke as I swung outward. When I landed, my right foot landed on a milk bottle that was lying in the gutter, breaking it.

There was a huge gash in the bottom of my foot. A man in a blue car stopped, wrapped my foot in a cloth, asked me where I lived and he drove me home.

When I was dating my wife Pam in the early 1960s, we went to the upper Sherwood School playground one day to fly a kite.

The kite got away and I frantically ran after it at full gallop. I was watching for the kite and I didn't see a bicycle stand that was right in my path, My left shin struck one of the metal posts with full force stopping me dead in my tracks. Never in my life had I ever experienced such a pain. To this day, some 50 years later, I still carry a large round scar on my left shin as remembrance of that terrible experience.

My friend Carroll Vaughn and I decided one day to play hooky from school. It was the very first time either of us had ever played hooky. I had a large closet in my bedroom. Carroll came over after my parents left for work and we set up a Monopoly game in the closet. We hadn't been playing for more than a couple hours when my stepmother had gotten sick at work, returned home, opened my closet door and found us playing Monopoly.

Carroll, Ronnie Long and myself decided to see if we could hit a .22 shell with our BB guns. Ronnie placed a live .22 shell on a concrete block wall in Carroll's back yard and we took turns shooting at it. Ronnie actually hit the bullet and it discharged. The bullet hit Carroll's concrete foundation, ricocheted and hit Ronnie just above of his eye. It was a glancing blow. Needless to say, we didn't do that anymore.

On Saturday mornings, we would ride our bikes downtown. We played the pinball machine in the Greyhound bus station and then would go to the Electric Theater.

For 25 cents, you got a whole day's worth of entertainment. They later raised the price to 50 cents. The theater would show a newsreel, a serial, a cartoon followed by a 3 Stooges flick and 2 full-length movies. We had it made in the 1950s, it's really sad to see how the world has changed since those wonderful days.

We used to have a record hop that was held in Hotel Robidoux downtown. A local radio station held the record hop on Friday nights in the hotel Ballroom, which was located on the second floor of the hotel. It was really a lot of fun.

One Friday night when I was at the hop dancing, the disk jockey played a record called Mexican Hat Rock. Ever so often, the song would have a place where the kids would stomp twice on the floor to the music. I was guilty as anyone. Well, come to find out, the stomping on the floor had knocked some plaster off the ceiling below. The hotel management immediately ceased any future record hops in the hotel. Everyone was very saddened by this happening.

The radio station found another building to hold their record hops. It was located at 10th & Isadore and the building was called The Eagles Lodge. It sure was a great place to go on Friday nights and a lot of fun while it lasted.

Bless Me, Father, for I have Sinned
By Joyce Sherman Comfort of Gladstone, Missouri
Born 1931

Once a month, on Friday, Cathedral Grade School students lined up and walked around

Joyce's sister, Carol, her mother, and Joyce in 1941

the corner to St. Joseph Cathedral Church to go to confession. Before leaving our classroom, we were lead in an examination of conscience by our teacher.

One Friday afternoon I tried and tried to get my teacher's attention to ask to be excused to use the restroom. No matter how many times I waved my hand, Sister Leon looked the other way. Of course, I thought she was ignoring me on purpose.

We knelt in our pews at Sister's direction, waiting to pour out our minor infractions of God's laws, the 10 Commandments, to a priest. He could not see us, nor could we see him. Father Ruggle, our innovative pastor, had replaced the old confessionals with new ones: When a confessor knelt down in the darkened space, a red light lit on the door of the confessional. If no one was inside, a green light signaled the next person in line that the confessional was empty. God's traffic lights! This particular afternoon, I was kneeling on one knee then the other in an effort to control my 10-year-old bladder. Finally, it was my turn to confess my sins. Just as I knelt down and the confessional light changed from green to red, I lost control and liberally sprinkled the kneeling bench. I made the shortest confession of my life, left my puddle behind me, and headed for the opposite end of the church.

Next young confessor was Richard, who had told his classmates since first grade that he was going to be a priest. We called him a sissy because he was quiet and studious. Right after Richard entered the confessional; he bolted

78

out, yelling, "Sister Leon, someone wet their pants in there!" I was cowering in the church lobby, praying Richard didn't know who had committed such a sin (in his eyes, no doubt).

Richard was very close to his mother, but there was no father in the home. When asked about him, the future priest said he had fallen from a bridge he was hired to repair and was killed before Richard was born.

Richard did become a priest and served until his mother died. After her death, he left the priesthood, married, and had a family. He died a few years ago. I often wondered if he remembered kneeling down on a wet confessional kneeling bench when he was hearing children's confessions.

Joyce on her First Communion

Food, Gardens, Subsistence Living
By Betty Walch of Cottonwood, Arizona
Born 1942

Through all my years growing, up until I left home at 17 we ate what we raised and purchased very little other food. As I got older, we purchased more and more.

We always had chickens for eggs and meat. But until I was ten Mom had a mixed group of chickens and raised her own young chicks by letting the hens set on eggs and hatch babies. That was fun, we always had baby chicks. We also had banty chickens, which are a small chicken, and they lay a small egg. The chickens were more or less kept within a pen and had a henhouse, which was closed up each night at dark when the chickens went in to roost. Except the banty chickens, they roosted in trees and the barn. There were always eggs to eat and chickens to cook. Without refrigeration, you just went out and killed a chicken and dressed it when you needed one. Any excess eggs were taken to the feed store in town and sold for grocery money or for the basics. I always had pet chickens and often pet banty chickens that stayed around the house and I named them and played with them. I also had pet ducks, once they were named Winkim, Blimkim and Nod and they would roost on the edge of the slop bucket on the porch and drink out of it and they all eventually fell in and drowned because they couldn't get out. My pet chickens often drowned in the slop bucket also. I remember naming pet chickens after our closest neighbors. They liked to roost on the well curb and poop all over the well curbs and any walkway at the backdoor much to Dad's disgust.

Wells were always right outside the back door at all three farmhouses we lived in while I was growing up. They were a cistern, which means they were hand dug and lined with stones. The water they contained was rainwater that ran off the roof of the house, which was collected in eave troughs and then a pipe took it to the well. This was the method used for drinking water everywhere in rural Missouri at that time including schools and churches. There was no chlorine or sanitized water at that time. Ours always had a concrete foundation around it and then a pump that you pumped water out by hand. A spout had a place to hang the water bucket. Bringing in buckets of water was one of the first chores a child was assigned. Sometimes you had to prime the pump by pouring water down an opening in the top of the pump to get the water started. I pumped a lot of water until I was 17 and left north Missouri. The eave troughs had to have leaves and trash cleaned out of them regularly.

Without running water, all water was bucketed into the house. Finally at the home place where Glen lives we finally had a sink that drained water outside so we did not have to carry out all the used water. A drinking bucket set on a table (usually an enamel table) and a wash pan beside it for hand washing. The dipper in the bucket was used by everyone to get a drink. Water was placed in the washbasin to wash hands and face and then usually just thrown out the back door. If weather was dry, it was saved to water the flowers and garden. Baths were taken once a week in a zinc tub in the middle of the kitchen floor and in front of the heating stove in the winter. Kids first and then adults, all water was carried in and out by hand. In the summer, Dad and Glen went to the pond south of the house to take a bath and swim. That is where Glen learned to swim, in a deep farm pond. As he got older and could swim, Glen went swimming anytime he wanted in the pond, skinny-dipping of course. But in the summer, every night after chores Dad and Glen went to the pond.

Everyone had milk cows and the milk was for personal use. You used it that day or you separated the cream with a hand operated cream separator and then sold the cream that wasn't used by the family at the feed store. You also made butter by churning for the family's use. Dad loved his cream on cereal, pie, fruit, and other things. Excess skim milk after the cream was separated was fed to the chickens and the hogs, along with other table scraps. They were all put in a bucket called the slop bucket. Glen once took a bath in the slop trough from which the chickens ate. He even had his bar of soap with him. He was under age five when he did that. Cream and milk was put in a tub with cool water from the cistern to keep cool for short periods of time or until it could be taken to town to sell. Of course, cows were milked by hand.

Everyone had a big garden and canned lots of fruits and vegetables. Mom's goal was to have 100 quarts of tomato juice, 50 quarts of tomatoes, 100 quarts of green beans, lots of corn, peas, peaches, grape juice and any other vegetables or fruit she had. A big garden was very necessary.

Butchering at home was still done when I was young. Dad and Grandpa Easter butchered the last time the fall before Grandpa died. They butchered hogs. We were living at the Carlisle Farm and had a really good smokehouse with a cave or cellar under it. There was a special room in which hung the cured meat, hams, and bacon. Then you went out and cut off what you needed when you needed it. Sausage, roasts, chops, and unsmoked meat was cooked and canned in a pressure canner. They built a fire

in the front yard and rendered their own lard. The chitlins (pieces of fat with a little meat on them) got crispy and delicious as they cooked the fat into lard. There is nothing like freshly cooked chitlins!

Food preparation without refrigeration was different. Growing up we used very little mayonnaise in the foods we prepared even after we had refrigeration. One recipe I still use today is the slaw. The dressing for the slaw is vinegar and sugar. Vinegar prevents spoilage. Mom made deviled eggs with vinegar and sugar only, no mayo. Dad and I always put vinegar on our green beans and spinach. I think this was done because in early days when they canned without pressure canners they added vinegar to the vegetables and more or less pickled them.

Other foods that were a result of lack of refrigeration were the canned spam and Vienna sausages, which we used in, sack lunches. Another item I remember was fried bologna. If you go to the south, you still see it on menus in restaurants. When the bologna started getting slick, you salvaged it by frying it in a bit of lard. I still like fried bologna.

Another area that was difficult was laundry in the old motorized washing machine and frozen laundry in the winter. When we moved to the Carlisle Farm, we had gotten electricity at the old place where my uncle later built a house. We had no electric appliances except Mom had just gotten a new electric washing machine, which was the kind with the agitator in the middle and the wringer on the top, which was a great improvement over the hand washboard. We still used the wood cook stove at that time. The Carlisle place did not have electricity. The family who was leaving there had a washing machine that had been converted to use gasoline. It had an old lawn mower gasoline engine on it. It had the same agitator tub and wringer on the top. Mom traded her electric washer for the gasoline engine one. We used that washing machine until Glen was in high school.

Dad had built a little lean to screened in back porch onto the home place and the washing machine set there or in the smokehouse. In the summer, it set out under the mulberry tree at the back door, close to the well pump. Laundry done in one of these washer's was always interesting. You heated water and carried it from the stove to wherever the washer was to fill the tub. In addition, with this washer you also had to continue to put gas in the engine. It also started like a lawn mower with a pull cord and you could get it flooded just like a lawn mower! You started with your white clothes first, turned on the washer, and agitated them as long as you wanted. Next, you ran the clothes through the wringer into the zinc bathtub to rinse and then back through the wringer before you took them to the clothesline. Many farmwomen had broken arms or lost fingers from those wringers. There was a release that you could hit. Clothing often got wound around the wringer and you had to release it and unwind the clothing. You used the same water over and over, next doing good coloreds, then towels, and finally the men's work clothes. You might add water along the way but never emptied the tub until you were done. Then the dirty laundry water was used to water the garden if it needed it.

The laundry was hung on an outdoor clothesline. So you chose your day appropriately for good weather in the summer and winter also. In the winter, you hung the laundry out and it froze on the line. Then you brought the frozen laundry in and draped it on furniture around the stove to finish drying.

Glen and I always liked our laundry hung outside with the fresh air smell. I still hang out laundry today and seldom use the dryer.

Laundry Was an All Day Deal
By Sharon Condron Spainhour of
Chillicothe, Missouri
Born 1949

Doing laundry when I was growing up was an exhausting day. First, you wanted a day that was warm enough so the laundry could be washed on the porch. If it was too cold a day, then you had to bring everything into the kitchen in order to wash your clothes. This included bringing in the wringer washing machine plus two rinse tubs. Some of these tubs had legs and some were just tubs that you had to put on chairs. Of course, if you had to do laundry in the kitchen, you also had to be more careful of splashing water on the floor.

Next, you gathered up everyone's clothes and started sorting them into piles. These piles

Sharon's mom, Rosa Condron

were usually whites, good clothes (cottons or what we later called permanent press), work clothes, towels or colored clothes and then the dirty clothes such as muddy chore coats or muddy jeans.

Since everything was washed in the SAME water, you began by washing a load of white clothes first and then worked your way down depending of the color of the clothes or how dirty the article of clothing seemed to be. Dark colored clothes were washed after lighter colored clothes, etc.

Most people had to carry their water a long way for washing clothes but our well was right outside the pantry. The pantry was on the north side of the kitchen and the porch was on the south side of the kitchen. We had running water in the kitchen before many of the other country people we knew got it installed. This made it a little easier for us on washday. We only had cold running water in the kitchen for a long time but that was a luxury compared to going outside to the well to get water. One reason that you used the same water for all the clothes was because it was so hard to carry the water. Another reason was that you had to heat the water for the washing machine. You put it in buckets, pans, and teakettles on the stove to heat so that you could wash the clothes in hot water. About every load, you would have to add more hot water in order for the water in the washing machine to at least stay warm. We only put hot water in the washing machine. The two rinse tubs were filled with cold water. Sometimes your fingers were almost frozen when you were rinsing the clothes.

Finally, after the hot water was in the washing machine and the rinse tubs were full then you could begin your wash. The washing machine had a button you could push in to turn it on. You let the clothes wash as long as you thought it was necessary in order to get them clean. There was a wringer attached to the top of the washing machine. It was on an arm that could also swing around over the rinse tubs. When you decided that the clothes had washed long enough, you stopped the machine and started running each article of clothing through the wringer, if you put too much in the wringer jammed. If you didn't put the clothes in flat, it would pop the buttons off the clothes. My mom would always say, "Be careful and don't get your hand caught in the wringer." I never did but I always thought that would really hurt.

As the clothes went through the wringer, the hot water drained back into the washer and the clothing fell from the wringer into the first rinse tub. After all the clothes from the washing machine had been through the wringer and were in the rinse water, you stirred and swished them around in the rinse tub. Then you could repeat the whole process of running them through the wringer into the final rinse or sometimes we just took them out of the first rinse tub and put them into the second one for a final rinse. In the final rinse tub, you stirred and swished them around again. Granny always put what she called "Bluing" in the rinse water. It was to make the white clothes whiter. It was in a glass bottle and was actually a blue colored liquid. I don't remember my Mom using this; she always used bleach for the white clothes. After the final rinse, we ran them through the wringer again to get as much of the water as possible out of the clothes so they would dry faster. Next, you put them into the clothesbasket to take outside to hang on the clothesline to dry.

The washing machine and the rinse tubs had hoses on the bottom of them so that you could drain the water out when you finished the laundry. This meant that you again carried the same water. If you were lucky, you might have a drain inside to use but most people had to carry it outside in order to get rid of the dirty water. You might use the rinse water on flowers or the garden.

The clotheslines we used to dry the clothes were outside. We actually had two lines. In the back yard, one line started wrapped around a tree. Then it continued to the next tree and wrapped around it. From there it continued to another tree. This was in the shape of an "L." The other line was in the side yard off the kitchen porch. It was a single straight line. (Here we sometimes tied an old mother hen, with her baby chicks, to the clothesline with some bailing twine fastened to her foot. She could then have the whole length of the clothesline to move around.) There was a certain way that you were supposed to hang up the clothes. Shirts, you hung up from the bottom. Towels, washcloths, and diapers could be pinned together so that you would only use one clothespin in order to pin up more articles of clothing. Sometimes if there were many clothes to dry then you would have to find a pole or branch to help hold up the clothesline. If you didn't do this, then the line sagged and your clean clothes would be touching the ground. If you weren't old enough to run the washing machine or wringer, then you would probably get in on hanging up the clothes outside unless you were too short to reach the line. When it came time to get the dry clothes off the line, it didn't matter how short you were. You could pull down on the clothes and snap the clothespins off then let go. The article of clothing would fall off the line and then you could go onto the next article of clothing. Sometimes in the winter, you would hang up the clothes and they would freeze dry. You could take the jeans off the line and they would stand up by themselves! Of course, when you took them into the house and they thawed out, they were still damp and you would have to find somewhere to put them until they finished drying.

After all this was finished, then you brought the clothes into the house either to fold them up or to iron them. Folded clothes for the kids were placed on the stair steps to be taken to your room the next time you went upstairs. This was a good idea but it didn't always happen at least not very quickly. By this time, you were too tired to iron so you sprinkled the clothes. This was done by putting a metal sprinkling top that was fastened on a cork into the top of a glass pop bottle that was filled with water. There were many little holes in the metal top similar to a plant watering can only smaller or similar to a saltshaker with smaller holes. You sprinkled the water on the clothes until they were damp, rolled them up and put the clothes in a plastic bag and put them in the bottom of the refrigerator. This kept the clothes from molding or drying out. Then you could wait until another day when you weren't so tired to iron them. We were so glad when they invented permanent press clothing so you didn't have to iron! Now they are going back to 100% cotton and we have to iron again.

I always said if I got an automatic washer and dryer, I would never complain about doing laundry, and I don't!

Maryville was a Great Place to be a Kid
By Jo Coleman of Gladstone, Missouri
Born 1946

My mother and my three older sisters lived there from the time I was a baby. Mamma hung wallpaper to support us because my dad had "hit the road" shortly after I was born. Living with Mamma was an unforgettable experience. Looking back, I don't think any family had more fun than ours. She knew how to strike the perfect balance between being a strict disciplinarian and a fun mamma.

Downtown Maryville was a thriving metropolis in the fifties. There was always something going on downtown. When I was in the third grade and one of my sisters was in the fifth, the two of us decided that we wanted to do something special for Mamma on Mother's Day. We didn't have any money to buy a gift, but we knew that the downtown merchants always had a "Queen for a Day" contest and the Queen was awarded a gift from each of the participating stores. We decided that we would enter the contest at every store, and we were positive that if we put an entry in every store, our Mamma would be sure to win.

Because we are talking about the fifties, it was no problem for us to venture downtown on our own after school to complete our task. We went into every store on the square and the surrounding streets to pen our entry blanks for the Queen contest. We were methodical about our mission making sure not to miss a store. We went into Haines' Drug Store, Stephenson's Dry Goods, Tobler's Fashions, Time and Gift Jewelers and on to Brown's Shoe Store, JC Penney, Place's Drug Store and on and on around the square. We put an entry in every store that was participating, and when all our entries had been dropped in all the boxes, we walked home. This was our secret. We didn't tell Mamma, and since she was busy hanging paper while we were busy filling out our entry blanks, she was not even suspicious. We were a bit smug about our adventure because we knew Mamma was going to win. So, we waited.

In the next couple of weeks, we just went about our business of going to school and playing after school. Whenever we had occasion to go to town with Mamma, we would fill out another entry form at Safeway Grocery Story or at Holt's Supply or Montgomery Ward, wherever we happened to be. Mamma didn't know that we had marched all around the square putting her name in every entry box.

When the president of the merchant's association called to congratulate Mamma on winning "Queen for a Day" she was amazed, but we weren't. We knew all along that she was going to win!

It turned out to be a very special award. She received free meals at restaurants, a mantle clock, clothes, gift certificates, groceries, an oil change, and many more gifts. Because, like I said earlier, downtown Maryville was a thriving little town back in the fifties. I think it was one of her best Mother's Days. I know it was one that my sister and I will never forget, and we were so proud of ourselves.

The Outhouse Gang
By Herbert Boude of Chillicothe, Missouri
Born 1946

I was born and raised in a North-Central Missouri town. From the early fifties to the early sixties my older brother and I helped our Dad with odd jobs such as hauling junk, brush or belongings. We had one job we both hated.

A lot of the poorer people in our town and neighboring towns had to use outhouses because of no indoor plumbing. We helped Dad clean the toilets (as we called them!). We'd take out the full buckets or tubs and shovel up anything scattered. Then we'd put in clean containers and sprinkle lye around and in the cans to help with odors and such. Then we'd load the full ones in the vehicle (sometimes a pickup, and sometimes a car trunk). We'd ride to the city dump where they had a trench dug for disposal of the payload.

I'm sure you can imagine the lovely fragrance that traveled with us. My brother and I would hold our noses and our very breaths as much as we could. We'd duck and try to hide if we passed any of our friends. But, we always made a little money for the picture show or skating rink.

Well—someone had to do it. Why not us?

A Glimpse of the Past
By Carolyn Sawyers Tulloch of San Jose, California
Born 1932

I have composed parts of this in my head several times with Nodaway News Leader in mind. Each time I consider cancelling my subscription, it publishes something, or information about someone I am interested in. Information about Beulah Sawyers Kroger's 101st and 102nd birthdays, she is my dad's (Scott Sawyers Sr.'s) cousin, a donation made by Laura Belle McGrew and her husband to Northwest Missouri State University (she was my first grade teacher at Knabb County School), the obituary and article about Lester Swaney who gave me horseback riding lessons on Fritz Meirer's 5 gaited mare, a picture of my cousin, Ruth Tebow Burgess, next to a replica of the Tebow House that was on display at the Historical Society Museum, this house was my home away from home when I was a freshman at NWMSTC. These glimpses into friends, relatives, and neighbors who were a part of my own personal history keep me reading.

I was told that I was the only infant in the St. Francis hospital on March 28 of 1932. My guess is that the lack of babies in the hospital at that time was the result of the Depression and the fact that many infants were still being born at home. The hospital along with many of the other buildings that were involved in my growing up have moved to new locations or are completely gone.

I began my schooling at Knabb Country School as a five year old, there was no kindergarten in those days, and I pestered my mother until she allowed me to join my older brother in the one room schoolhouse. In addition to Miss McGrew, I remember Gladys Cook Ritterbush, Hildred Cook, and Marjory Dakin as teachers at the Knabb School. The teachers had to be single and would board with the Knabb/Starks. Penmanship was taught with the Palmer Method and the students, boys and girls alike knitted squares that were sewn together to create blankets as a contribution to the war effort.

The Knabb/Stark family donated the land for the school, in addition to the school house there was a building with two out houses, a barn for the ponies, a storm cellar, a teeter-totter, a coal shed and a well…NO telephone. On cold mornings, Forrest Stark would walk up the hill and start a fire in the potbellied stove.

The school was closed in 1943 and after it closed, the building was used for community gatherings. Now the place that held these buildings and my memories of my early education has returned to farmland and is used for growing crops.

In early December 1938, the original house on my parent's farm caught on fire due to a defective flu on the second floor. Friends, relatives and neighbors all came to try to help put the fire out but were only able to save my mother's piano before the house burned to the ground. There were no fire trucks that came to fight a rural fire.

A temporary structure was raised (again with the help of friends, relatives, and neighbors) and my parents, 3 children and my grandfather were able to move in before Christmas. My grandmother went to live with a sister in Liberty until the new house was finished. This structure eventually became the garage on the property.

The new house was built with the "modern" conveniences of indoor plumbing- bathtubs and toilets, heating and electricity. Our neighbors soon followed suit by adding these to their homes. The dirt/mud roads had graveled surfaces added at about this same time.

The Presbyterian Church that I was baptized in and was married in (not the same day) has moved to a new building. The stained glass windows and the pipe organ were moved to

Carolyn Sawyers on the horse

the new location. I guess you could say they had an organ transplant!

In 1947, the Country Gentleman magazine chose our family to be the first featured in a series of articles that they were doing called Good Farming-Good Living. Our farm was featured because of the innovative farming techniques that my parents were implementing on the farm. After the article was published, we heard from people all over the country, some claiming to be long lost relatives. I even received a marriage proposal from a young man from Steamboat Springs Colorado. He included a listing of all of his assets including his 14 cows.

There was a railroad track that ran through our farm and during the Depression; we would have visits from "hobos." One night my dad heard a knock on the door and thought that it was his friend. He hollered for him to "come on in" and in walked a hobo. My mother always gave these men food and in those years, there were many knocks on our backdoor from weary and hungry men. Now this train track does not carry any trains but has been turned into a hiking trail.

I remember my brother Jim was transporting a container of sorghum that would be added to the livestock feed. During the process of transporting it, the sorghum exploded and covered Jim from head to toe with syrup. Byron Nunnely who was standing nearby said, "Jim, if you will just wait a minute, I'll go get a loaf of bread."

When my younger sister was a preschooler, our Uncle Paul would always bring her licorice when he came to visit. Once when she saw Uncle Paul's car pull into the driveway, she ran out the door yelling, "Uncle Paul, Uncle Paul, did you bring me my liquor?"

The Way It Was in Maryville for Me
The Sears Catalogue was our fancy toilet paper for the outhouse. Our street was a route and we lived on #2. My dresses were made from the sacks that feed came in and rags cut into strips were turned into braided rugs, there was almost nothing we would throw away When I wanted curls in my hair we did our perms at home. When it was rationed, the city cousins came to the country to use our gasoline. We made our own soap, churned our own butter, milked our own cows, and raised our own meat. Pets ate what was left over from the dinner table. We never locked anyone out. I was a water "girl" hitching the pony to the cart taking burlap wrapped crocks of cold well water to the fields. We lived through 90 plus degrees in summers with no air conditioning. I was most inspired by a teacher Mrs. Echart whose standards were high and her heart was opened wide. When I married my husband, we had a shivaree (maybe the last in Maryville.) They pushed me around the courthouse in a fancy wheelbarrow. While things have changed and other things are completely gone. These memories have been fun to re-visit.

Jobs for Young People in a Small Town
By Clark Israel of Kansas City, Missouri

Long before a weekly allowance was popular, eager young people had many chances to earn some spending money or build some savings for college. It may have started with picking up glass pop bottles to be redeemed for two cents each and could progress to shoveling snow, mowing yards, delivering newspapers, shining shoes at the local barbershops and running errands. Two of my best memories centered on the town square: working as a soda "jerk" at a drug store and running the popcorn stand.

Picture a white limestone courthouse surrounded on four sides by an eclectic mix of red brick and concrete block buildings. Movies such as "It's a Wonderful Life" and "Back to the Future" used this image to convey a simpler time. The square in Bethany was such a place.

The stores reflected the needs of the community. The major industry was agriculture. Farming equipment was not as productive as it is today and federal farm subsidies were small. The farmer had to work Monday through Saturday noon. After the Saturday lunch, everyone piled into the car (no seat belts) and headed to town. What they found were three grocery stores, a hardware store, two movie theaters, barbers and beauty shops, the post office, three drug stores, dress shops, clothing stores, a five and dime department store, the library, a meat locker, a music store and a couple of pool halls. After the warning was given to the boys of which places to avoid (i.e. the pool halls), each family member went their own way. The stores stayed open until nine o'clock, long enough to spend your nickels and dimes. The clothing store featured bolts of cloth, patterns, and ready to wear clothing. A baby grand piano greeted patrons at the music store, which featured band instruments and sheet music of the top forty songs. The merchants occasionally held sidewalk sales to attract customers. For a special Easter promotion, a helicopter would drop specially marked Ping-Pong balls to be redeemed at participating stores. A furious game of trading the Ping-Pong balls ensued to get the prize you wanted most. The activity was as close to a stock exchange that you could find outside New York.

I got my first real pay check working as a soda jerk at the drug store.

The drug store was more than sixty years old and included wooden cabinets, a luncheon counter with eight stools, ten small tables with chairs, a comic book stand, a full service pharmacy, and a display of the finest libations in town. The aroma of the store was a delightful mixture of Murphy Oil, horehound drops, the sweet smell of fine cigars, and the remains of aftershave from a broken bottle. The soda "jerk" was a master of mixology. Soft drinks were prepared by mixing the syrup with the carbonated water that came from the soda fountain. A shot of cherry or vanilla syrup completed the deluxe sensation. Milkshakes were handmade, with milk, three scoops of vanilla ice cream and syrup, poured in a metal cup and blended. The mix was then poured into a tall clear glass and topped with whipped cream, another squirt of syrup and a cherry. Using strawberry ice cream resulted in a taste so strong that only the stout of heart could handle. Phosphates required special skill as the drink was topped by a fizz that was produced when the handle on the carbonated water spigot was pushed the opposite direction. A "black on white" was chocolate syrup poured on a big scope of vanilla ice cream and a "white on black" was created by pouring marshmallow syrup on top of chocolate ice cream. The fountain had everything except a banana for a banana split. You had to go to the grocery store next door to buy one and then give it to the soda jerk!

The popcorn stand was my first opportunity to run a franchise business.

The America Legion had a very small hut on the southwest corner of the square. There was room for a large popcorn popper, a table for the change drawer and one person. The plan was simple: purchase the popcorn, oil, and other supplies from the startup money, pop and sell the popcorn, and split the profit. It was a great opportunity to learn the law of supply and demand. Popcorn sold as salvage (split bags) from Prather's tasted just as good as the product from Beavers Market and was half the price. The choice of the proper oil was a little trickier. Prather's also sold lard, which worked, but did not produce the aroma necessary to attract customers. (My apologies to all of those customers who were filled with trans fats, salt, and cholesterol!)

The selection of the paper bags and cardboard boxes was the next major decision. You will sell more bags at 15 cents but a better profit at a quarter. An 8-ounce bag was maybe too little while a 16 oz. bag might more than necessary. Store hours were important. It did no good to start before 6:30 as people were still eating dinner and by 8:45, the traffic died. The size of the crowd varied from week to week. A summer cold snap or rain would cut short the trip for many. The amount of just popped product was critical. Popped corn holds its peak flavor for about 15 minutes and busy people did not wait long to buy an impulse product. Leftover popped corn had no value and cut into your profits. It took about five minutes to prepare a new batch. So what appeared to be the simplest of enterprises was really a fairly complex operation. Imagine what the owners of larger businesses had to do?

While the popcorn stand was hardly the center of community life, it was a special treat at the end of a trip to town. And it provided me a great lesson in the challenges of running a business in the free market system.

Boy, do I Remember the Good Old Days
By Romey Clayton Davis of King City, Missouri

I can still hear mother, "Come on. Get up. Breakfast is ready." Once you got a whiff of that bacon, she did not have to tell you again. One nice thing about back then is when you sat down to eat, you all set down together, and you sat there until everyone was done eating. You could plan your day and talk about things that had happened. You got to know each other. You did not just eat a piece of pizza or hamburger and get on your phone and start texting.

"Mom? I got to call Mary to ask about our lesson. She is on this line, isn't she? Is her ring two long and a short?" Every time I try to call, her old grandmother, what you call her, is telling Albert how many old set-in hens she has set. You could hear everyone's business. Tom called the veterinary about his old cow late last night and someone said there would be men working on the line on Tuesday. Hopefully, we will be able to hear better and daddy won't have to pay out six dollars a year to not be able to hear.

"Dad, what are you doing with the team today?" "I have to help my neighbor grade the road to pay my poll tax."

You got up in the morning, made your bed, got dressed, picked up your pot and out you went to dump it. By the way, that is not a crockpot. If you did not have one, it would not be long until you did because the snow would be six inches deep and the "moon and stars" was 200 feet to the north. I forgot to get the wood in last night. Boy was it dark out there.

After I got cleaned up and it was time to go to school and play Annie over at the schoolhouse. We had a boy that would stop his horse in front of us to make us walk around him as we walked to school. I was not going

Romey Davis with family and friends in 1938

to take any more of that. So I went up on the bank and there it was. An old hen's nest. She won't mind if I take some, but she did not tell me they had been sitting there all summer… let me tell you, we did not have any more trouble.

Sure glad I went to school today. The most wonderful thing happened. I got a kiss! And I almost broke a hamstring. I found out you do not want to introduce your girl to your best friend because they will end up seventy years together. What a blessing.

One time our teacher had to go to his friend's funeral, we school kids got a notion. "How about a picnic?" "That timber over there would be a nice place." The folks did not know about it, but we took our dinners and had ourselves a picnic. Oh, that was fun! We were so happy. Little did we know what was ahead the next morning. How does a teacher find out so quick? And how come I was the first one? Boy, that old board was hot before the last one. The teacher wasn't always like this. We had an ice storm this one time. It got about two to three inches deep and stayed on a good three weeks. Every afternoon our teacher would let school out at noon so we could go coasting up on a big hill north of the school until time to go home.

"Mom, do you know when grandmother is going to get my fatter bed? She picked her geese two weeks ago." "No, not until grandpa threshes his oats so we can get some straw to put in your bed.

In the summer time, it was not so bad. You could always keep up on things in the Sears and Roebuck catalog. Oh, I got a new suit today! It just came my knees so I had to strap it below my knees and put on girl stockings.

Romey and his sister, Lorene

We took Hatticall when your throat is a little sore and I even would grease my chest with some Vick's and put some Liniment on my knee.

Now it is time to go milk the old cow. You did not get milk out of the store. Every day there was the chickens to feed and water. And don't forget the hogs, that's where we get our bacon.

I still have our old head set radio sitting above my desk. It is a 1928 Crowley. Only two could listen at a time. We listened to the shows Lum and Abner, Sky King, Old Maw Perkin and Renso Jone. On the other side of my desk sits old Dancing Dan. In his day, boy could he dance. The saw I cut him out with is there beside him.

As I sit here and think back over the last eighty-nine years, when I was a small boy, we did not have all the nice things we have today but let me tell you, we had love.

Romey's wife, Mary

Mondays are washday. I know what I will have to do now that is washday. I'll have to turn the washer. Wouldn't it be fun to tie a string around it and watch it go around and around? Well, that wasn't too fun. The washer pulled out the stopper and all the water went out into the kitchen.

"Mom, did the mail go today?" "The roads are so muddy." "I'll go see." "Mom, I got a letter from Uncle Sam. He wants me to go get my health checked so I can go with him a on a trip. " She always said he was a grouch, but look what he did.

By the way, I forgot to tell you about our Saturday night baths. You had to go down to the well, sometimes that was a long ways, fetch your water and take it to the house where you would put it on the stove to heat it up before pouring it in the bathtub. You would start with the baby clear up to Dad. Sometimes you had to take several trips to have enough water. If it was hot outside in the summer, you would let the sun heat it up.

Let me tell you about castor oil. It was good for everything. If you hurt your finger or hadn't been to the moon and stars for a day or two, Castor Oil will help.

The 1965 Flood if Smithville, Missouri
By David S. McComas of Independence, Missouri
Born 1948

It had been raining for a week. The ground was soaked with water. It quit raining here and then rained hard up north of us. The stage was set for disaster, for the small town of less than 1,000 souls.

I was 17, living with my father C.B. McComas and stepmother Jessie Pearl nee

Poff on West Brasfield Street, near the southern section of the town. Behind our house, was an empty field, extending about 100 yards or so to the beginning of the bluff called Shannon's Hill that marks the southern edge of the river bottom.

Fearing a flood, which is not uncommon to the area, I went out to my mother's beauty shop near the bridge over the Little Platte River to help her move things up off the floor, in case the water got into the building.

While I was there, a couple of guys from the Army Corps of Engineers came by to talk to us. They said the water might get a foot over the dike, but not more than a foot and a half. They thought it was silly to move the furniture up so high. It turned out they were right about that part. They were a little off however, on how high the water would get.

After finishing at the shop, I walked home and had dinner with the family. We weren't worried. After all, we were quite a distance from the river and while the water had been to the porch before, it did not get into the house. That event was back in 1951, when the whole area was inundated and nearby Kansas City, MO was devastated by the Missouri River. There had been extensive work done on the Missouri River dike system by the Army to ensure that would never happen again.

It was dark before we were notified about how rapidly the water was rising. We drove out to the river to see for ourselves. We went back and started moving furniture up as high as we could. We waited. I was on the front porch when I saw the water coming down Bridge St. I warned my father. He was quiet and grim.

When the water was about 2 feet deep in the street in front of the house, my best friend, Mike Atkins, who was also my cousin, came walking down the street toward the west. We had other cousins near there, closer to the bluff of Shannon's Hill. All I remember him saying was, "You guys are screwed." He continued on.

About 10 pm, I saw water coming up through the boards of the floor. Dad announced we were going to the attic. For a reason I cannot explain, as much as we did to get the furniture higher up, we forgot about our 20 guns in my closet.

We collected my Grandmother, Jessie Pearl's mother and my Aunt Sis who lived very close by.

I am not related to Aunt Sis. Her name was Naomi Anderson. I could write a whole book, just about her and the things she did for me and my sister Marcia. Nobody had greater love for us than she did. Marcia is five years older than I am and I am sure she could tell you more about her than I can. I don't know how we ever came to tag her with the moniker of, "Aunt Sis." She is probably the biggest hero of my life.

About midnight, the lights went out. We had one flashlight. It was made by Rayovac. It was a super duper flashlight, with seven batteries and a sling. It was the flashlight we used to blind frogs with. Dad would be in the bow of the fishing boat, shining the light on the bank until he saw the reflection of frog eyes. Training the light on their eyes, we would head straight into the bank and he would grab them, hand them to me and I would stuff them into a burlap bag. We got about fifty of them one night. That probably wasn't legal.

Since I was a Boy Scout, I was tasked with flashing, "SOS" out of the attic window. "S" and "O" were among the few letters I could remember. It didn't matter. In a situation like that, a flashing light means, "I need help."

It was really dark out. While it had stopped raining, it was still overcast and that meant no moonlight. It was like being on the inside of a coal mine at midnight.

Much later, we learned of a local radio station, sending out a plea for anyone with a boat, to go to Smithville and help with the rescue. I heard, but have no proof that, over thirty private boats were sunk in the effort. I heard of one boat that happened upon a Great Dane caught up in a tangle of barbed wire and logs. They were able to cut him loose and took him to shore. It was difficult, but they got it done without being bitten by the terrified animal.

We heard the engine of a boat. We hailed them. They could hear us, but not see us. They didn't know which direction to go and neither did I. I shined the light of the powerful Rayovac straight up in the air. I shouted for them to look for the beam of light. They saw it and went around the very large and leafy oak tree in our front yard, to nudge up against the roof of our house. As we scrambled aboard, I asked my father whose house was floating by. He said it was our garage. They took us to the base of Shannon's Hill and we got out. Since the boat guys didn't have a flashlight, we gave them ours. They went on to attempt to rescue others. I don't remember their names. I wish I did.

It wasn't easy for the old folks getting up the wet and slippery hill, in pitch-blackness, to the road leading to the new hospital. Thank goodness, it was the new hospital. The old one was downtown, where the water was 12 feet deep. We had ten-foot ceilings in our house and the water was just under the eaves when we escaped. The water went 18 feet over the dike. It was a long trudge up the hill to the hospital. We went in, wandered around a while, talking to other survivors. I went my own way and picked out a part of the floor to sleep on. The floor was covered with people just like me.

When daylight came, I wandered outside. I didn't know what to do. I had never been a refugee before. The Red Cross was there with a food truck. They were selling sandwiches for 35 cents. I didn't have any money. A schoolmate pushed me toward the Salvation Army truck. The guy behind the counter gave me a plain bologna sandwich and asked if I wanted coffee or milk. I was dazed and confused. I didn't know what to say. He didn't ask for money. I finally whimpered, "Milk." He handed over the milk and said to me, "You look cold, here's a blanket." I wandered away, munching on the best sandwich I ever had. The Salvation Army didn't ask for anything. They gave us everything they had, except the truck.

Later, my father found me and we got a ride to someone's house, who had an extra bedroom. They put me in it and I slept like a log.

About a week later, the water went down and the Missouri National Guard came in. There were about eight of them on every street corner. It took a long time to walk anywhere, since every corner had a squad of soldiers who wanted to check your driver's license for a Smithville address.

It was hot and everything and I mean everything, was muddy. I have never been so thirsty for water. Before, I didn't like water, now I craved it. Before, it had to be milk, soda pop, or fruit juice. Now, all I wanted was cool and clean water.

We started cleaning out the house. We pushed mud out with a shovel. The garage was gone but our shed was still there, with tools intact. We had one weird thing. It was one book of the encyclopedia, perched atop a lampshade. The lamp was not where it had been before the water came in. It was on the other side of the room. The doors were closed, to prevent any kind of current through the house. If you can explain that, please let me know.

The local grocery store took the labels off of every can they had, put them in a paper bag and handed them out. They couldn't sell them. You didn't know what you were getting either. It might be beef stew or dog food. It was free, so nobody complained that I know of. The Salvation Army was there for a week, feeding everybody. The Red Cross was gone after the first day.

We started hearing the stories. Like one elderly couple who went to bed like normal, only to be awakened by their adult son. The water was two inches below their mattress. It must have been a shock to wake up like that, in the middle of the night, by somebody with a flashlight and the room is filled with water. Their house went completely under water. They likely would have drowned. One elderly man did. His name was Dub Golden, in his late seventies, I think. He was a nice old guy. Everybody liked him.

We were told of the town drunk, who walked into the water, headed toward downtown. He showed up a week later, still drunk, and unconcerned about the flood.

Several classmates were amazed to find me alive, having been told of my terrible demise. I must of heard of a dozen or so of such deaths, only to find them untrue.

Our next-door neighbor was pumping his basement out and we used the gushing, dirty water to clean the mud off of our guns. Guns and water do not mix well, but this worked to get the mud off. I dried them out the best I could and then applied a liberal dose of gun oil. Most the blue came off of one shotgun barrel, but the others fared very well. Not bad, for being under river water for a week.

A group of eight Mormon men came by. We had enough help, so we directed them to others in need. They would give somebody a day of work and then move on to help another for one day. They worked very hard, for no pay and they brought their own lunch. They did that for a month.

I joined the Navy. My mother told me if I joined the Navy, I wouldn't have to go to Vietnam. I would be clean and dry, three hot meals every day. Guess where they sent me? Yeah, three times. I got muddy and I saw a lot of water. I still have all of my fingers and toes, but my high frequency hearing is gone. It could have been worse.

I'm a Vietnam vet now. We seem to have a reputation for being a little crazy. Proof that I am a little nuts can be found in my attic, where there is an inflatable boat and two large flashlights.

Hobo Stew
By Ida Mae Shultz of Newport, North Carolina
Born 1924

My stories take place when times were hard and it was a struggle for most Americans families to eke out a meager existence. I grew up in the Ferrelview Missouri area, the oldest of seven children. We lived in a two-room house where all of us kids slept in one room. The walls were covered in newspapers and I remember reading the cartoons to my brothers. Many a night we went to sleep laughing at cartoons we read over and over.

We loved to hear our Dad talk about his time as a hobo. Before he met our Mom and settled down, he rode the trains from town to town doing odd jobs. He and other men would gather at night, each contributing whatever food they had earned that day, to a shared pot. They would cook it over a campfire and then sit around and share their "hobo's stew" and their stories. After my Dad settled down, there was many a night a stranger would come knocking on our door for a bite to eat and to relive some good times with my Dad. We kids would peak out from our bedroom door to see who came by and to listen to their funny stories.

When I was in the fifth grade, our class had a contest to see who could place cities in the right places and color a map the best. Coloring was one of my favorite things to do and I had studied my cities over and over. It was a close contest but I won because I had one city, just one city, on the map a smidgeon closer than anyone else. The prize was a new

toothbrush and some toothpaste. I was so excited because I knew exactly what I wanted to do with my prize. I hurried home my Dad's bedside. He was very sick at that time. I held out the toothbrush and toothpaste and told him I won them for him. He gave me his wonderful smile, hugged me, and thanked me. I followed him outside where he drew some water from the well and brushed his teeth. I remember thinking that it made him feel better and that made me happy.

When I was twelve, my father died and everything changed. The responsibility that comes with being the oldest child now seemed overwhelming. My Uncle Henry, who was about my age and like a brother to me, came to help us out. One wintery day, we took the younger kids to play in the snow. He took a metal tub and nailed it on the back of a sled. He was always trying crazy things and he thought this should go really fast. So he gave it the push down the hill and jumped in the tub. But as he jumped, he slipped and ended up head over heels in the tub. He couldn't see a thing as he flew down the hill. By the time he got to the bottom, I was cheering him on but he headed for the trees. He literally had the crap scared out of him and wasn't enjoying hearing me laugh. I never let him live that one down.

That next summer, I was working in the

Ida with her parents, John Henry and Florence about 1926

91

tobacco field of a neighbor to earn money for the family. As we hoed the field, the skies turned dark and the clouds started roiling. The winds picked up and the man in charge told us all to pile in the truck he was taking us to town where he picked us up. As we loaded up, we noticed that the clouds were forming a funnel. We were all scared. He drove very fast the short way to town and I jumped down to run home. I had to warn my Mom and others to get in the cellar. I ran as fast as I could but I felt as if that funnel was chasing me down. I came to a barn and took shelter. I got inside, huddled down in the corner but starting worrying about my family. In a flash, I was out the door and running again. As I got near the house, I started yelling for my Mom to get the kids to the cellar. I rounded the corner of the house and, to my relief; I saw they were just headed down the steps. I ran behind them and we closed the door just in the nick of time. I could feel the door being pulled as we struggled to close and lock it. The noise was frightening and the little ones were scared and crying. It was dark in the cellar so we all huddled together. It seemed like an eternity before the winds finally died down. I crept up the stairs to open the door but my Mom called me back and told me to wait just a few more minutes to be sure. So, we waited again. Then she gave us the go and we all pushed the door open. What a sight. First, we were relieved that our house was still standing. The only damage was the top of the chicken coop was missing, completely gone, no sign of it. The chickens, however, were still sitting on their nests. We were both amazed and thankful because they were a big source of food for us. A neighbor came over to check on us and showed us a piece of straw from the field that was sticking straight out of a tree. Since then I have heard about strange things like that, but thankfully, I

Hereford Grill in 1943

have never been in a tornado again.

We burned coal to stay warm during the winter months. We had our pile of coal not far from our house by a shed. One night when everyone was asleep, I heard a knock on the door. I was afraid and couldn't get up the courage to answer it. Then the person knocked again and for some reason it was clear to me that I needed to answer the door. To my shock, I saw my father standing there pointing toward the shed. There was a lady there with a bucket stealing from our coal pile. I ran out and shouted at her to leave. She looked at me with a forlorn face and said she and her family was cold and needed some coal. I told her to take what she had but not to come back or I would tell all the neighbors. She never came back and I thank my Dad for taking care of us that night. People tell me it couldn't have been real, but I have never doubted what I saw that night.

I dropped out of high school in the tenth grade to help my Mom more and by the time, I was sixteen I moved to Kansas City MO and became a waitress at the Hereford Grill. I had never been many places nor experienced much so this was a frightening and exciting time. It was there I learned so much. I had to serve scallops and I didn't even know what they were. We served seven beautiful, golden scallops on a plate and one day, as I picked up an order the cook overheard me saying I wondered what they tasted like. He laid me one on a napkin and after delivering the plate, I went to the back to eat it. I still remember savoring that first bite. It was like nothing I had ever eaten before. I didn't even know what an ice cream sundae was until I was trained on how to make them. I saved up enough money to buy one of those sundaes. The minute I dug in to the ice cream covered in syrup, whipped cream, and nuts, I was hooked. I still enjoy my ice cream to this day—regularly!

At that time, regulations were strict in the food service business. We always had to have our hair pinned up and wear a hair net. Our uniforms were yellow blouses and pencil skirts (below the knees of course) with brown trim and a brown apron with yellow trim. We were required to wear hose and white shoes. I always took pride in how I looked when I went to work. It meant cleaning and ironing my uniform every night, but I didn't care. I loved my job.

My boss was always looking for new items to serve, so when waffles made their way to the US, he bought a waffle iron. The waffles smelled so good. He ran a test with them and when they were a hit with the customers, he put them on the menu. Every morning he would mix up the batter in the kitchen and the sweet smell of waffles cooking would fill the place. We served them with strawberries and whipped cream on top. They started as a dessert but soon people were eating them for breakfast. The employees were each allowed one free waffle a week. What a treat!

Rebecca's parents Eddie and Elmerjean Berry in 1949

Childhood Chores, Outhouse Spiders, and the Great Pumpkin
By Rebecca Jean (Berry) McGregor of
Atchison, Kansas
Born 1951

I grew up in southwest corner of Buchanan County, almost on the Platte county line; powdery dirt roads in the summer, mud up to your elbows (mine anyway) in the spring as well as fall, and roads slick as glass in winter. But, we were never leery of walking by ourselves nor did our parents give it a seconds thought to let us. We traipsed over wooded areas, mindful of fence lines and gates, fished in the creeks, and explored to our hearts desire; or at least, that of our eldest brother.

Of course, chores were gotten out of the way before any plans were executed. Even though young, we were expected to make our beds. It wouldn't be unusual to be called back into the house from play because the bed had not been given the proper attention; throwing the blankets up over the pillow did not count as having been "made." Playthings were put back in their place before starting anything new. We helped clear the table following a meal, feed, and water the dog, sweep floors, wash windows, dust; Mother made sure that we each were initiated into all the necessities of keeping a home. I remember helping sprinkle down clothes that needed ironing; non-wrinkle clothes were not in the vocabulary as yet, or laundry softener. We used a wringer washer with a rinse tub and the clothes were hung on a clothesline to dry in the breeze. In the summer, all this was done from the porch, and we thought it great fun to help take the clothes off the line. Dad would have mowed the grass beneath the clothesline first while Mom put a pot of ham and beans on the stove to simmer. I can still smell the mixed fragrances that floated upon the summer's breeze of a time so many days ago.

One such day, in particular, stands out in my mind. My little sister needed changing and as Mom had her hands in the washing, I insisted that I could accomplish the task. Practice had been achieved many times with my baby doll. My sister was a year old; I was a motherly three. There was a wooden table on the porch that was used for folding clothes. It would be a nice roomy surface to lay her down on and work; or so I thought! I soon found that to be a more difficult task than changing her diaper. Every time I thought I had her lifted high enough, there was still more of her that wasn't. She was like trying to pick up a slinky from one end! (My short arms and height didn't improve very much over the years; little sister out distanced me by a good two to three inches.) I can still see the odd look on Chery's face with every attempt I made. Mother got so tickled watching my antics, but finally reached over with her long arms and helped conquer the hill, as she would with all of us in the years to come. My early mothering aspirations would find easier fruition seven years down the road when a baby brother would be born, not only on my grandfather's birthday, but also on the day that America watched and listened, as Astronaut John Glenn became the first American to orbit the earth. Many would name their newborns

John Glenn; but Mother and Dad gave Daniel the middle name of Duncan in honor of her father, Elmer E. Duncan.

The very first time that I was allowed to use the electric iron was a momentous occasion. The ironing board was made of heavy blue metal and would adjust to several heights, but it didn't quite have a notch low enough for me. Mother finally adjusted it back to her height and put me upon a chair, handed me Dad's handkerchiefs and watched as I followed her instructions carefully. I felt so grown up and I didn't burn myself once!

We didn't have indoor plumbing until sometime during our grade school years. There was a pitcher pump at the sink for water, baths were accomplished in a round galvanized tub, and an outhouse served our other needs while an indoor pot was utilized during inclement weather and winter. The outhouse was a nice place to go when hiding from your older brother; unfortunately, it was the first place he looked. But it was a dark spider haven that I would have liked to have avoided at all costs because after all, one never knew what might jump up out of that hole and bite you on your you-know-what (All the scary possibilities were given wing in my imagination, but they were first created by my older brother who so loved to embellish and share them with us!)!

One year, as if by magic, a pumpkin patch appeared a little behind and to the right of the outhouse. Of course, we wouldn't have paid any attention to these plants at all if Mom and Dad hadn't remarked that the blossoms that we were seeing would become pumpkins. Some of the seeds that had been thrown out the year before were growing. We watched and guarded that patch all summer, and checked on it every day after school. September came and with it the nicest pumpkin just right for a jack-o-lantern! There was much pleading and begging all through that month; especially on the part of Chuck, my older brother, but the folks kept refusing, stating that it was much too early. Halloween was weeks away and the jack-o-lantern would be all shriveled up if we did it now. My older brother got us in so much trouble over the years. This would be only one of the many follies to come that we had to take part in or perish! He sneaked a large knife out of the kitchen and had us meet him at the pumpkin patch having mapped out his plan thoroughly and convincing us that if WE went

Christmas 1959 having survived the Great Pumpkin Caper

ahead and carved the pumpkin, Mom and Dad would have to let us keep it, and "yada, yada, yada." The great pumpkin, our pride and joy, was set before us. Chuck, welding the knife, suddenly realized that his utensil of choice was probably too large for the cutting of the lid. We were ordered to stay at our posts while he crept back into the house for a second knife. Chery and I sat there looking at each other, and the pumpkin, with scary excitement flowing through our veins. Then it occurred to me. I looked at my sister and said, "You know what? He is never going to let us do any cutting on this pumpkin. He is going to do it all himself with us just watching." That said, I picked up the knife and started cutting the circle for the lid. Just as I was turning the last corner, the knife slipped and came down on my thumb cutting a segment almost off. Chuck arrived to see me trying to hold my thumb together and blood spilling all over the place. He was furious! It was my fault. We were going to get it now, etc., etc., etc. And, of course, he knew what he was talking about. Discipline reined and Mother was none too gentle with the first aid either. It should have been stitched, but it healed and classmates at school had a great time checking on my gory injury every day.

There are so many memories: the wonderful sewing mother did, Dad participating in softball, bowling and building a stock car for racing, stories from my parents and grandparents, and other childhood escapades. Life around the Sugar Creek Christian Church

94

area, which is celebrating its 175th birthday this year, was simple, yet full. Neighbors new each other and helped each other. Everyone worked hard, but took time for socializing. I believe that it was a wonderful time to be growing up, and though there are too many thoughts, memories and stories to tell in such a short space, I hope that you have enjoyed the few that I have shared.

Finding Allen Childers
By Evelyn Anderson of Ankeny, Iowa
Born 1939

While purging my attic, one photo out of thousands of items kept coming back to me. In December 2011, I could no longer ignore the memories it rekindled. I sent an email to the editor of the Cabool, Missouri newspaper to see if I could find Allen Childers, the man in the photo.

Email to Cabool, Missouri Enterprise, late December 2011
Before I was born, my father, Leslie Robison, had a friend from Cabool named Allen Childers. They hunted and trapped together in Northwest Missouri in the 1920s to middle 1930s. They went to coon dog trials together. And won! Though I never met Mr. Childers, my father talked about him so often, mentioning his name and where he was from, that I remember those two details long after my father's death. In the process of scanning old family pictures, I found a photo of Allen Childers and am attaching it in hopes he may still have Cabool relatives who would like a copy. It was taken on my grandparent's farm where my father lived until he was married in 1936. I've also included a matching photo taken of my father.

Email from Enterprise a few hours later
Mr. Childers passed away February 9, 1988, at the age of 74. He was born in McFall, Missouri (I don't know where that is). He was buried at Fairview Cemetery in King City, Missouri. His obituary listed 3 nieces and 5 nephews as his only survivors but did not name any of them. I would be happy to pass this photo and your information on to the Cabool History Society.

Email of my immediate response
Please pass the photo and information to the local Historical Society. Your research

Allen Childers

tells me more than you can imagine. My hometown is King City, Missouri, where Allen Childers is buried. McFall, where Mr. Childers was born, is about 20 miles east of King City.

My father was born in 1905 and grew up on a farm between King City and McFall. Their close proximity probably explains the connection between my father and Allen Childers. They were part of the large cadre of hunters from King City, Berlin, McFall, Pattonsburg, Clarksdale, Fairport and other small communities who met regularly for both economic and social reasons. Selling pelts supplemented their spotty and meager incomes from farming marginal quality land, and provided food and a reason to gather socially.

Hunting was good in the hilly, timbered area where my father lived but the terrain made farming difficult. I remember my father was in the process of clearing timber and stumps from a low, flat patch of ground near the creek, no more than an acre, using log chains attached to a team of horses. The Grand River, several creeks, and sloughs added to the abundance and diversity of the wildlife.

Serious hunters lived in the area. It was not unusual to hunt more than once a week. Every road was a mud road and often travel was limited to walking or riding horseback. No one had a tractor so most of the horses doubled the next day in their primary role of farming. The Rural Electric Administration (REA) had not yet arrived in the area where

Evelyn in 1942-43

we lived.

As a preschool child, I remember wives and children getting together nights while the men and older boys were hunting. We gathered at one home to talk, eat popcorn from corn we grew ourselves, and wait for the men to come home. Kerosene lamps barely lit dark corners in the room. Children played and then slept. This area of Northwest Missouri, though I don't know for sure, seems to have rural Southern roots—the accent and dialect. Tobacco is grown less than 50 miles southwest and the distinctive architecture of curing barns is noticeable. I have always believed many of the early settlers in this area were southern transplants. I still remember the soft lilt in the women's voices in the dim light of the room.

I was an outdoor kid, exploring our hilly farm and that of my grandparents who lived on the adjacent farm. My memories are of searching for signs of wild animals, from their tracks to their nests and burrows, and revisiting each to watch the process that developed. As an only child, going on these outdoor adventures and tending to the farm animals comprised my daily endeavors. I played with my father's hunting dogs, understood his guns, was taught gun safety, met his friends and their families, heard the conversations, and saw many animals, both tame and wild, living and dead.

I am proud of my early life and believe that I reaped the benefits from this close-knit rural lifestyle, which was poor by many standards yet so rich by others. Thank you for helping me understand some of the connections in my memory. I will continue to look for relatives

of Mr. Childers.

Email from Cabool Enterprise week later

Last week I published the photo of Mr. Childers and a bit of our correspondence. Several people have told me how much they enjoyed it. This morning a gentleman called and asked if I could contact you. He said he has some of Mr. Childers' traps and would like to talk to you.

Email to Cabool Enterprise

I talked to him on the phone. He has great stories. Probably someday, I will come to Cabool and talk with him in person. Your help and assistance put this long ago relationship into a modern day "6 degrees of separation" context. How about I buy you dinner when in Cabool? Evelyn

Finding Allen Childeres

Finding Allen Childers would never have happened if I hadn't scanned old family photos and written an accompanying narrative history for my four grandchildren. They are growing up in cosmopolitan Seattle and Calgary in the 21st Century, far removed from my childhood in the early 1940s on a hilly Northwest Missouri farm with no electricity or indoor plumbing. From breakfast until dinnertime, when my mother rang the post-mounted bell, I roamed our hilly farm and my grandparent's adjacent farm. It was a way of life my grandchildren can only imagine. The pictures and narrative might help them understand.

The scanning and writing task took longer than anticipated and become a gift for me also. The pictures were reminiscent of Dorothea Lange's depression and dustbowl photos from years earlier. I am the tousled, barefoot child surrounded by My father's hunting hounds, gazing at the camera.

December 2011 marked over 7 years of sporadic starts and stops to the project, which included sorting items into families of origin and chronologically organizing all the photos and items from my family. There are wills from the early 1800s; ship's passenger lists for passage from Europe to America; war records; county birth, wedding, and death records; and newspaper articles about my mother's and grandmother's rural Ladies Club meetings. These meetings opened with everyone singing My Country 'Tis of Thee and answering roll call. Topics covered burning questions of the day, like "What is my favorite pickle recipe and who gave it to me?" There were 4-H ribbons and my mother's meticulous, hand-written records about her cows and calves, many with nicknames. My father wrote out a homemade scours recipe for calves with diarrhea and kept the local lumberyard calendar from each year he farmed, the pages covered with notes: Cecil Edmondson trucked 30 head hogs to St.Joe—got market high or Planted north 10 in corn.

After my email exchanges in December 2011, I was determined to do a little investigating. I packed a small bag and left the next day for Cabool, Missouri. The hunter who had called asking to be put in touch with me could not meet me until after work so I stopped to thank the Enterprise Editor for her assistance. She suggested that while I waited to talk to the hunter, I visit her retired neighbor, a man who had hunted and trapped all his life. He'd even known Allen Childers. He invited me to his home after I convinced him I was not part of any anti-hunting group. He gave insight into how he hunts and traps, likely similar to how my father did it 80 years ago, and then suggested I visit the local fur trader. At the fur trader's I was given another warm welcome and a tour of his business. Our conversation lasted several hours.

Leaving his business and driving down a country road with dense trees on either side, I glanced to my left and came to a sudden halt. There, partly obscured, sitting at the edge of the woods and watching me, was a coyote. I took it as a good omen. We sat transfixed, just watching each other. Then he turned away and casually sauntered off into the woods. I put the car in gear and drove on, glad to have communed with this beautiful animal.

I finally met the hunter who'd originally called the Enterprise, and we drove to where Allen Childers had lived. He shared larger-than-life stories about his friend Allen, describing him as an affable, good natured, huge barrel-chested man who told stories of outlandish proportion and never met a stranger. My father, in contrast, was friendly but very unassuming and never called attention to himself. My impression was that Allen Childers' life centered around hunting, fishing and trapping, and his friends. As we parted, the hunter held out two small traps that had belonged to Allen Childers. He said they were mementos to pass on to each of my sons—concrete reminders of the friendship between their grandfather and his friend Allen Childers.   I had no idea this story would become so rich in detail when I sent the photo of Allen Childers to the Cabool Enterprise. Everywhere I went in Cabool, the people were warm and generous. They too were connected to the rural tradition of hunting and trapping, just as Allen and my father had been so long ago, and understood how one photo could send me on a search to rediscover my past. Allen Childers was found.

Dedicated to Violet and Leslie Robison, my parents, who gave me the generous gifts of courage and freedom to explore, and inspired in me an awe for nature and a curiosity about the world. And to my amazing sons, who neither hunt nor trap, but have the same gentle demeanor and warmth of my father.

It Happened Just This Way 1939—1948
Andrew County, Savannah, Missouri
By Huston E. Myers of St. Joseph, Missouri
Born 1936

I was born in a four-room farmhouse four miles NE of Savannah, MO during the hottest year in history, the depression, and the latter part of the Dust Bowl on 5-8-1936. I was number 13 of 15 children, all born at home and in the same house. I, my six brothers, and eight sisters all helped with the farm work using horse drawn equipment, hoes, and scythes. All the children had specific chores according to his or her size and age. On Saturdays, our parents often went to town by horse and wagon to sell eggs and cream, coming home with essentials like flour and animal nutrients.

During WWII when foods and fuel were rationed, my Dad and older brothers got lots of experience smoking bee swarms from hollow trees to get their honeycombs. We used honey for our sweetener and Dad traded his sugar rations for flour rations at the grocery store so Mom would have sufficient flour to bake her usual 12 loaves of bread each week. She took great care to protect her bread yeast starter. Mom did her bread baking twice a week with a wood-fired stove. My sisters learned early on how to make scrumptious fried chicken, cream puffs, cakes, and pies made from homegrown fruit.

Huston's parents Selby Myers, Jr. and Elthel Grace Myers in 1948

While my sisters were learning to cook, can vegetables, and mend clothes, the boys and my Dad did the farming and fished for carp, catfish, and buffalo in the 102 River using trammel, hoop and barrel nets. Fish was a main source of meat for our large family, but Dad also kept a live trap for fresh caught fish. The fresh fish were often given to Dr. Myers in exchange for payment of our medical bills.

Our father Selby was born in 1890 and our mother, Ethel Grace in 1896. Life was pretty difficult for them and us kids, but we didn't realize it since it was all we ever knew. Our family was pretty much self-reliant. We raised all of our vegetables, meat, milk, eggs, and grains used for cereal. We burned wood from our forest to heat our house, our wash water, bath water and to cook and can our food. We had no electricity, candles, indoor plumbing, or flashlights.

My Dad and Grandpa built our house in 1914 and during that time, they also dug a water well using a pick and shovel. It was 8 ft. wide and 12 feet deep. The bottom was solid limestone and the sides were rocked from the bottom to the top. All our water was pumped by hand from that well. Dad also dug a storm cave, which doubled as a root cellar and storage for 1500 quarts of canned goods processed by Mom and my sisters. Dad also made sure all our livestock, milk cows, chickens, sheep, hogs, horses, and mules had food and shelter.

Hauling water to the house was mostly the girl's job. It was carried by hand about 100 yards to the house to accommodate all our household needs including drinking water. Without indoor plumbing nighttime visits to the outhouse proved challenging, especially in the dark and cold winters. Mom kept a 2-gallon porcelain coated container for use by the little ones at night that was emptied and cleaned each morning.

My father and brothers did the farming, which was pretty labor intense. They tilled, planted and harvested crops using horses and mules which pulled the single bottom plows, disks, two section harrow, grain binder, mowing machine, dump rake and hay wagon.

After the grains were bundled with string, they were placed in a shock of 6 to 10 bundles, with the grain at the top of the shock to prevent molding and rotting of the grain.

Later when it came time for harvest, the bundles would be gathered onto a wagon and hauled to the thrashing machine. They were then tossed into the throat of the thrashing machine that was powered by a large steam engine. This method of farming left little time to do much else. After a day's work in the fields the boys and dad would take their towels and disappear to the 102 River, a quarter mile away. This conveniently took the place of the daily bath. I often followed along as often as I could get away with it. In the summer, my sisters bathed in two large washtubs behind the chicken house isolated by the dense forest surrounding the area.

I recall when I was small the weather was very dry and it was not uncommon to have dust storms and/or swarms of grasshoppers. Undoubtedly, they were the remainder of severe storms that had occurred in Oklahoma and/or Kansas. When the dust storms came, my mom and sisters would make sure the young kids were in the house and they stuffed dishtowels or clothes around the doors and windows to keep the fine dust out. The dust storms didn't usually last long. The grasshopper invasions stripped the first few rows of the cornfields, but they made good fish bait. Due to the dry weather, well water was scarce so the children would herd the cattle and drive them to the river, about ¾ of a mile, twice a day for watering. I was very young, but tried to go along when I could, especially in the afternoons. I remember watching the cattle wade right into the river to cool off and get a drink and get the bugs off their backs. I was frightened they would drown, but they never did.

98

When I was two my parents made their first purchase of modern technology. They bought a gasoline powered, hand wringer Maytag washing machine, and a Philco-battery powered Philco radio along with a Kerosene Ladden mantel lamp for household light. The new lamp helped the older kids do their homework and the new washing machine eliminated the back breaking job of scrubbing clothes by hand with lye soap on a wash board in tubs of hot water resting on stones over a wood fire. It was a major step forward for my mother and sisters, even though they still had to crank the clothes through the wringer and hang them on three clothes lines 40 feet long, stretched between trees.

My recollection of the new washing machine was that my brothers would daily tease me by placing me into the box the washer came in. I was too small to get out of it they told me they were going to fatten me up and send me to the stockyards with the hogs. Most likely, they wanted to get me out of their hair. In any event I was horrified because I knew the hogs that Dad took to the market never came back home.

Our new radio brought us the daily news as well as episodes of "The Fat Man," "The Shadow", "Sergeant Preston of the Yukon," among others. I also remember being frightened when President Roosevelt, speaking on the radio, told Americans to cover their windows so they wouldn't be seen from the air. He said that the Germans could be flying over America like "Blackbirds in the sky." Little did I know then that was not possible.

Huston's family in 1945

The saddest memory of my youth was when our four year old youngest sister, Janice, was fatally burned one afternoon while all of the other children were at school.

It happened at lunch time when my Dad and older brother had come in from the field for lunch. It was not uncommon for Janice to play in the living room by herself just a few feet away. But on that day, she found some matches normally used to light the pot-bellied stove, used to heat the room and the house. In playing with the matches, she accidently set her long flowing hair and clothes on fire.

We were first sadly shocked that the accident had happened and then saddened further to hear that she had died. Although taken to the hospital she had inhaled the flames and fumes, which burned her lungs. Her extensive body burns were more than she could withstand and in those days, there was little known about treating burn victims. When my brother, Robert was six, he got bit on the foot by a large timber rattler. After the snake bit him, he ran about 50 yards to an older brother, but soon became ill and lost consciousness off and on. Dad hurriedly went to a neighbor to call for help. He eventually got hold of Sheriff Bruns who quickly came the four miles to take my brother to Dr. Myers' office in Savannah. The Dr. said the only chance Robert had was to get anti venom that was new and only available in Kansas City, which was 70 miles away. Sheriff Bruns got assistance from Sgt. Inman of the Highway Patrol to go to Kansas City to pick up the anti-venom and deliver it to Dr. Myers' office. By the time the anti-venom was administered to Robert, he was unconscious and his leg had more than doubled in size and had turned black. Dr. Myers gave our family little hope Robert would make it through the night but he did regain consciousness and began to show improvement. It took him several months to recover and recently celebrated his 82nd birthday. The snake however did not survive.

With the exception of my youngest sister, all my siblings walked 2 miles each way to attend Dewitt School, a one room school house located 2 miles east of Savannah, MO. Although those siblings attending Savannah high school had to walk 4 miles each way, two of them had perfect attendance during their 12 years of school.

When I was in the 4th grade, I and another

Seven sons of Selby and Grace Myers

student were asked to take the waste basket out to the burn pit and burn the waste paper. This was in early fall when summer weeds and grasses had grown to sizable heights and made it difficult to run and play. When I and my class mate realized the dead grass would burn as well as the paper, we proceeded to ignite the grass and weeds. In just a few minutes, the fire quickly spread and was threatening our schoolhouse. The older students and neighbors beat the fire out. Our punishment for starting the fire was to stay in 15 recesses and copy dictionary pages. I would have rather had a paddling.

Teaching in a one room school house presented many challenges. Some teachers had to walk the two miles from Savannah to DeWitt School, often in inclement weather. Very few cars were available due to metal shortages and auto production stoppages during WWII. While transportation was a huge challenge for our teachers, they faced the additional problem of teaching all 8 grades in one room. We in lower grades often learned from listening to discussions in higher grades. Sometimes classes were combined and occasionally students skipped grade levels.

By 1943, two of my brothers were inducted into the US Army. In 1948, our family moved to Iowa and things got better rather quickly. We had more uniform heat and hot water in the house because we then burned coal. In addition to having electric lights in the house and barn, we now had a corn picker pulled by a tractor and we had a crank telephone in the house. These were all welcome changes although we still attended a one room school house. When I started high school, I had the advantage of being picked up by a school

bus. It is little wonder that my older siblings thought I had it pretty easy.

Your Cake Is Burning
By John A. Dillingham of Kansas City, Missouri
Born 1939

In the early 1950s, in the newly annexed areas of Kansas City North, those of us living on farms, with your neighbors a quarter- to half-mile apart, we were on party telephone lines, maybe with six families.

One day I wanted to call the young lady "next door," both of us being in middle or early high school.

Two elderly (probably in their 40s) ladies were talking about their newest, tried recipe—in fact, one had something at the moment being cooked in the stove oven. She was describing every morbid detail.

After trying patiently, and every ten minutes lifting the receiver to find they were still talking, I broke in on their conversation to say, "I think your cake is burning in the oven. I can really smell it!"

They immediately hung up and I got to call my neighbor.

Flood Memories
By Helen Patricia Fountain of St. Joseph, Missouri
Born 1934

I will always remember the flood of 1952. It was my senior year in high school. My family lived about two blocks from the Missouri River. The new highway access now stretches over the area where all our homes once stood.

My brothers and I went to the river daily to see the rising water and to watch the scores of soldiers working to hold back the flooding waters. The National Guard was called in to assist in the many hours of hard labor needed to accomplish the task. We lived near the then thriving Muchenberger Recreation Center. The National Guard was stationed there at the center. This meant our basketball games, table tennis, etc. was put on hold.

Everyone in the neighborhood got to know many of the soldiers and were grateful they were striving to save our homes. On Sunday

100

afternoons, after church services, my family would invite a few of the soldiers to stop in for a visit. I had the opportunity to help pass the time by playing a few tunes on the piano and we would all have a sing-a-long. They truly appreciated the family's hospitality!

After it was all over, everyone in the neighborhood was indeed surprised to see how the flooding had actually changed the direction of "The Mighty Mo" in St. Joe and surrounding areas.

I also have fond memories of playing the pipe organ at my Catholic Holy Rosary School and church for weddings and other gatherings.

Growing Up In Trenton
By Mary Foland Holt of Trenton, Missouri
Born 1937

When I was a little girl growing up in Trenton, I lived on W. 13th Court, which was about seven blocks from uptown. We walked to Davis Food Store for mom. It was between the big Baptist Church and Kress.

We loved going to the movies, which cost ten cents to attend a Saturday matinee. This consisted of a cartoon movie and a serial, which continued each week, a western with Roy Rogers, Gene Autry, Hopalong Cassidy, or some other exciting western star.

On the way to the movie, we would stop at the corner of 9th and Main at the little popcorn shop, owned and operated by an older couple by the name of Garner. They had wonderful, small, white popcorn for a nickel a bag. It was delicious!

We would meet our friends at the movie and have a fun Saturday afternoon and then walk back home. We didn't have to be afraid on the streets of our small town, back in the '40s and early '50s. What a great life we had growing up in Trenton, Missouri. I wouldn't trade it for all the money in the world.

I also loved to put on my metal skates (clamped to my shoes and tightened with a key) and skate three blocks to my cousin, Vera's house. We would skate together on the sidewalks in front of her house on Crowder Road.

I only lived a few blocks from Jewitt Norris Library. (Oh, how I loved our library, and still do.) I spent a lot of time at the library and then would take my books home, throw a blanket under a shade tree in our front yard, and read for hours. What wonderful books I read as a child growing up in Trenton, Missouri. One time a bird left his calling card on top of my head as I was reading. It didn't discourage me from reading in the yard.

The B-25 from Rosecrans
By Colonel Philip K. Moore of Pleasant Hill, Missouri
Born 1937

My family lived on a farm about two miles west of Amity, Missouri. Mid-morning, Thursday, July 15, 1943, my mother had cleaned me up to go to town and put the about six-year-old, who was prone to get dirty, in the car to stay until my younger brother was cleaned up for town. There was the most terrible roar I had ever heard, my mother came running and shoved my brother into the car and went to the barn where my father was. A B-25 bomber from Rosecrans Field had crashed into the field approximately 200 yards beyond the barn. It was a terrible crash because the plane was just in pieces and the bodies of the five airmen were as broken up as the plane. At my age, I wasn't allowed to go near the site until it was cleaned up. What I remember were the hundreds of people who came to the crash site in the weeks and years to come. We had a pasture next to the road and, on Sundays, it would be filled with cars. A large flatbed came and picked up the engines and had to cut through the fences because our gates were too small or not straight enough. I was told that it took six two-and-a-half-ton trucks to carry the rest of the plane off and I did see them pass our house. We found parts for years. My main find was a two-and-a-half-foot length of aluminum pipe that I used for years as my rabbit hunting stick when my cousins, brother, and I went hunting.

My parents spent many hours showing people around. Many were to have sons or they themselves were in WW II in the years to come. But at the time, this was as close as they came to the war. Families of the airmen continued to come for a few years and I could tell that my dad shared their pain. We always wondered what efforts the pilot had to make to clear our farmstead.

In the years since I have spent 30 years as an Army officer, never wanting to be a pilot, and remembering the day every time I flew.

My Brother, the Barber
By Lyle M. Harrison of Gilman City, Missouri
Born 1946

I lived with my grandmother, or I guess she lived with me, my brother, and my mom and dad until she died on March 1, 1959.

She told a story or two that sounded pretty good to a young boy.

The first one was her dad used to run a chuck wagon. She said they had a cook stove in the front of the wagon and the young cowboys liked to crawl back under the wagon and look through a crack in the bottom of the wagon box up her and her sister's dress. She said they wore them old long dresses back then.

The cowboys were laying back under the wagon, looking up their dresses. "M" was what they called her sister. "M" walked up to the stove, got a teakettle full of boiling water, walked along the crack pouring boiling water. She said six cowboys came out from under the wagon, yelling and hollering.

This is another one she told. A man was in prison, who was some of her relation. I don't remember who.

He made saddles. He made one every other day. He told the jail keeper, if you will get me a fifth of whiskey, I'll make a saddle the next day. He did. The next day he went back to a saddle every other day. The jail keeper told him, "You made a saddle in one day when I gave you the whiskey. You can do that from now on."

This one is the best. My grandmother's brother would come once a year to our house to visit his sister, which was my grandmother.

I was around 11 years old when this happened. He came into the living room around 9 o'clock in the morning. Here's his exact words, the best I can remember. My grandmother's name was Carrie. Everyone called her "Cad." He said, "Cad, I got up, eat breakfast, drank a little coffee, had to go to the toilet. Got about halfway there and an old, red rooster started fighting me." We had an old, red rooster that stood around waiting for you to go to the outhouse, and then he'd start fightin' you. "I fought him to the outhouse, got inside, and slammed the door."

"I was setting there looking at the catalog and my piles kept twitching. In a little bit I spread my legs apart, looked between them, there was an old hen pecking my ass." He said, "I tore a couple of pages out of the catalog, wiped, pulled my pants up, opened the door. There was the old, red rooster. Had to fight him halfway back to the house. I'm about ready to go home."

He drove a streetcar in Omaha, Nebraska.

That really happened over 50 years ago and it's still funny.

Mom made chicken and noodles out of the old, red rooster not too long after that.

We milked by hand in the summertime out in the barn lot. Just walk up to an old cow, give her two or three ears of corn broke into three or four times in an old dishpan, sit down, start milking. I was sitting there milking. I heard, "Get up." Looked around, dad was setting there on his milk stool, which was a stick of wood with a board nailed on one end and an old cow was setting on his lap. She got up as soon as she got rested up.

When I was growing up nobody complained about not having what they wanted to eat, or they didn't say, "I don't like that," because you ate what you grew. You just set down and eat. I still love cornbread and beans, cow salve, clabber cheese, only ours was homemade. Fried chicken, mashed taters, just common food.

My toys were about all homemade. A button with a string run through it and you pulled both ends, the bottom whirled around. Pop guns made of elderberry limbs, willow whistles, corn stalk fiddler, darts made of cedar shingles, tops made of spools thread come on.

When we got electric lights, dad turned the lights on; you could see every dirty place in the house.

A neighbor came over one day and told my dad to come over Saturday night and watch television. We went. There was two or three other families there. They all had kids. We had cornbread and beans for supper and ate them while watching the new TV. Later on, we all ate popcorn. We watched "Gunsmoke," "Rin Tin Tin," "The Pendulum Swings."

We watched until the test screen come on at midnight. Then everybody went home.

The neighbor that had the new TV, had a divan that the seat was wore out on, so he went to the sawmill and got two boards cut the right length stuck between the arms and the bottom and you sat on the boards.

When I was 12 or 13 years old, a neighbor came over and ask me if I would want to work once in a while. He ran a maintainer for the township and they were building King Roads and I would make 50 cents an hour or somewhere around $5 a day, rippin' out fence, piling roots and brush, rollin' up wire. I said, "Sure." I had poison ivy all summer.

I made enough money to buy an electric welder that I still have and it still works. Most of all, I made enough money to buy my school clothes. Dad went to Trenton. I went into Hurshes, bought five shirts for $1 apiece. They were on sale, five pair of jeans, don't remember the price. I went across the street to Wards and bought a pair of new slippers with a new material called neoprene for soles about a quarter-inch thick. Dad told me to take them back, they wasn't any good. Then tops wore out, the soles were still good. They cost $12, high priced back then, over a day's work.

I went to a one-room school by the name of Battle Creek.

My brother sat behind the neighbor girl. I seen him cutting her hair with his round-nosed scissors. That evening her dad brought her over to model so dad could see what a good barber my brother was. Dad wasn't impressed. She was bald headed on the back of her head. Every school day the rest of the year we would walk out the door, dad would ask my brother if he was going to open his barbershop that day.

This is a speck of my life. Dad made my childhood the happiest years of my life.

Nomadic Childhood
By Delores Sloan of Maryville, Missouri
Born 1928

My mom and dad were married in New Market, Iowa on June 1920. Their first two children were born in Clearmont, Missouri. But dad never stayed in one place very long. Number three was born in Clarinda, Iowa, number four and number five were born in Shenandoah, Iowa. (I was number four.) I started school in Centertown, Missouri. But number six was soon born in Jefferson City, number seven in Trenton, Missouri. One year the last three were in three different schools in one school year. Although I had most of my schooling in Jefferson City, I had to finish my 11th grade by correspondence from Jefferson City, and graduated in Clearmont, Missouri (a class of eight!).

The oldest two quit school in their 12th year—unable to keep up. The rest of us hung in there and graduated. I'm happy to say we all turned out to be solid citizens—none inherited the "nomad" features of our dad.

Two retired military men, three state employees (retired), one as a Missouri Highway Patrolman. We couldn't put down roots as children, but certainly did when we matured!

Delores Sloan's family in 1968

Snapping Turtle, Yum!
By Raejean Overholtzer of Carrollton, Missouri
Born 1953

When I was growing up as a child there was no welfare from any government agency or church help for young families who were struggling in Iowa or Missouri. Everyone in my family had to pitch in and use their talents to do their part. At the age of three, I learned how to fish in northwest Iowa in E. Okoboji, Little and Big Spirit, and Diamond Lake. It was my job to catch the fish because my parents could not afford to buy a fishing license and I did not need one. Little did I know, til much later, that I filled each of my grandparents' and our freezer over each year from our few hours' fishing trips each weekend. About this time, I also learned to help in the garden, planting and harvesting vegetables and flowers. Later my brother at age three also learned how to do these duties. I eventually had less of the work! At my age of five, great-uncle Frank Adams, who owned a couple of tourist cabins and cleaned fish for a living, showed me how to clean fish alive. Why alive? You don't get the smell or fish taste to the meat. The process is very quick! Since we only got one television channel that was littered with interference (snow), we spent a lot of our time outside. Life was simple back when I was growing up because you had to do everything yourself as choices were limited to maybe two choices—do it or not do it. Use your own resources because there were not many resources to use. Stores were stocked with basics only—not everything you ever dreamed of to choose from. We were considered poor by the community, but we thought we were rich because we had family, food, and a roof over our heads!

On Christmas Eve in 1960 we moved to Liberty, Clay County, Missouri next to Highway 69 on the west side of the highway and town that was then very rural. It was a daring move because neither of my parents had a job. Our food supply slowly went down. Again, my brother and I began our next training lessons. There were no ponds or lakes around us. We had grown up with guns in our home, at the relatives, and at friends' homes. We were taught, when crawling, to respect the guns and everyone else's property—that meant keep your hands off! If you could not do that then you got a good, hard swat on the butt. Let me tell you—you minded real quick and hopefully a person did not get too many of these swats ever again, because they hurt! I was the age of seven when we started shooting a 22 rifle. We were taught all aspects of the gun and to never, ever point a gun at a person. After much practice, we were let loose on our own. We brought home small game and learned to butcher it all too. We, the kids, owned our first guns at the end of that year. Even though money was tight, we picked up every glass pop bottle we could find to get them to get an allowance. We even learned about walnut trees and other fruit trees on when to harvest their fruits, but also how to prune them. These exercises made us grow up quicker because

it built more responsibility and advanced our character. We had a special talent of finding big snapping turtles, which we did not shoot. We picked them up by their tails and carried them home. It was a challenge! They had to be carried as far away from us as possible so they would not bite us. They were big and our muscles were developing and not so big. We did a lot of dropping them and picking them back up and moving on again and again. When we got them home, we placed them in a large, metal tub (our swimming pool) with water and baking soda to clean out the mud, and topped with a screen and tire in the garage. We fed them fish and fruit to keep their weight. Then after a week, dad and us kids would butcher our prize snapping turtle and we would get our swimming pool back. In school, I was known by my classmates since third grade as the "good girl" who could climb trees, hit, catch, and run the best in baseball, and who owned a gun. Little did I know at the time, the boys were very jealous of my outside abilities til years afterwards. I looked at it as their loss!

Our chores were always busy work to do because after a year or two we each got a horse and we had a few dogs. Since we moved to horse country and every farm had at least one or many horses and sometimes large mules. There were also local horse shows everywhere. We rode our horses in the ditches or along the road to and from the events that we rode in pleasure and racing events. About this time, also we were in a 4-H club where I learned to make my own clothes. It was helpful from grade school through high school. We both took cooking and woodworking classes and made some really neat stuff to eat and save for future homes! We had three television channels at this time, but it went on and off the air at certain times and programming was very limited. When we moved to Missouri, we saw a lot of "blue negroes." The "blue negroes" were people who had not intermarried and their skin was a royal, sky blue that radiated over their black color, which I hardly ever see any more. I must say, their skin color was absolutely beautiful! I did not like the government's standard of dividing us into white or Negro (that is what the word was used when I was young for black) because as children of GOD we were taught to treat each person with the same respect that we wanted back. There would be a lot less tension in this world if the government would get rid of their standard of dividing us by "race." At school, we were segregated for quite some time. There was a double standard here too! We could not have a Negro in our class, but we could have China Slaughter as our school crossing guard. My first day of school was embarrassing to me because I gave him my class exchange gift. All the kids brought personal gifts for him, in front and after me—besides their class exchange gift. We finally got it straightened out, but was I ever red-faced. China was a real JEWEL though! He knew all of us kids by name and kept up with each one of us in and out of school. I think I was in seventh grade when the Negroes finally made it to our school. I had great friends that were Negro and we did not care about the outspoken differences. We even lived through the unsettling riots in Kansas City without wavering in Liberty. I was proud of our community! Because I was a second generation American, my family roots were originally from Germany, Norway, and Scotland. None of my family before me had finished high school except my mom, so college was never mentioned. Even though we lived in a college town, I did not know what it was til I was in high school. Even my freshman high school counselor did not explain it to me. He asked what I wanted to do and at that point, I had no idea. His narrow-minded remark was, "Then you probably will be barefoot and pregnant!" Looking back that was disappointing advice to say to a student, because he really grounded me to be caught in his sights as poor and untrainable! Well, I ended up working at William Jewell College in my sophomore, junior, and senior high school years after school and on weekends. I was mentored by the college's first lady and one of my best friends, Virginia Field. She gave me the best advice, "Go to college, if you can, and keep learning even after that—knowledge is power!" It was in my plan with GOD that I took her advice. The week before college started, I signed up, and then later graduated a few times. As usual on everything I have done, I paid my own way without help from others! I look at life as a continued path of learning, if you just stop and pay attention. You can keep expanding your knowledge by learning more about the topics you are interested in. I have done a lot of this in all kinds of side classes from many different sources.

I can even remember the lack of population in our area. But when Highway 69, a smaller, four-lane highway, got expanded to Interstate 35 (I-35), it gobbled up more land for the new four lanes. We lost half of our front yard, play area, and pasture for the new expansion. At the corner of 69 and Barry Road was a huge hill that had to be knocked down on the southwest corner for the new get off (exit to go east or west). They used the hill as fill for the exits and to build up the road for the bridge that went over the interstate. Soon we were moving the country in freight by truck and getting more cars. Note: I even watched the trolley cars leave in downtown Kansas City because Ford and General Motors threatened to move out if everyone did not have a car. So then, I saw buses come because some people just could not afford a car or could drive, but needed to move around the city. What a vicious circle of get rid of, build something new, then have to build something else, then get rid of it of something again, to be back where something started originally in the name called "PROGRESS"! If people or governments had what we had to live with, then it would have been built for the ages because our resources and money was so tight. It has been a waste of resources and money to see things not planned out for a longer period of time—going over and over again in the name of progress.

Shingle Ball
By Buddy Nigh of St. Joseph, Missouri
Born 1936

I was born on a farm eight miles northwest of Spickard, Missouri in 1936. I was about five years old when this happened. Dad was putting a new roof on the barn. He tore off the old shingles. My brother and I found a new game with the old shingles. We tossed them in a well to hear the water splash; we were really having a good time until dad arrived on the scene. My dad was very strict; both of us knew we were in big trouble. Dad tied a rope around our ankles and dropped us into the well. We did that until the well was clean. My mom was having a fit all the time we were cleaning up our mess. That was the last time we put shingles in a well.

This is about my school days through grade eight. My brother, Jack, and I were in

105

Buddy's 8th grade class in 1949-50

the same grade school. School was two miles from where we lived. For our first year of school dad bought us a Shetland pony. The first day we rode her to school didn't go very well. She went to the first corner from the house and stopped. One of us held the reins and the other one threw rocks at her. She still would not go around the corner. Dad was watching all of this happening. Needless to say, he had a way of getting her to go around the corner. She was a fast learner. No more trouble getting her to go around the corner.

One cold day we took our sled to school. We told our sister, Judy, to stick her tongue on the metal. It peeled some skin off her tongue. She told dad what we did. I bet you can guess our punishment. Our sister, Judy, followed her brothers everywhere. One time she wanted to go swimming with us. We didn't want her tagging along, so we filled her long hair with dirt. She told on us again and another whipping received.

In the 1940s, my mom and grandma belonged to a ladies' club. One rainy day, the ladies walked across the pasture to our house. Each lady brought a covered dish for lunch. They had to go over an electric fence next to the barn. Dad always turned the fence off before they arrived. My brother and I came up with a funny plan. We would let them start over the fence and then turn it on. One of us was the lookout and the other was by the switch. It was quite a sight to see. The women were screaming and food was flying everywhere. My brother and I were really enjoying the scene until dad walked in the barn. All the noise got his attention and he knew who caused it. You can guess what happened after that.

I have told a lot of people if today's children had parents like mine, this would be a better world. Dad was very firm, but he always had time for us.

They bought us a little pool table for Christmas. We played on the linoleum around the table, mom was not pleased about that, but dad told her she would get a new one when the kids were gone. He told her they are only little once, so let them have fun. We lived on a farm where there was no running water, electricity, or inside bathroom. In the winter, we took a bath in a tub behind the warm morning heating stove. I was 14 before we had electricity. I didn't have an inside bathroom or running water until we were married in 1956.

My mother was a hard working woman. In the 1950s, she held Stanley parties in people's homes. Her working helped dad feed and buy clothes for the family. I used to help her set up the displays. After that, I had to set and listen to her sales pitch. I knew the product very well. That is probably why most of my working like I was a salesman for Sears.

When my brother and I were nine or ten, we smoked corn silks in the barn. We told our five-year-old sister if she watched for mom and dad, we would let her smoke some. I just talked to her on the phone and she let me know we did not let her smoke the corn silks.

My first eight years of education was in a one-room schoolhouse. One teacher taught all eight grades. It was called the Nigh School. It was about two miles south of Modena, Missouri. I always had very good teachers. They were Myrtle Slover, Norma Gannon, Ethel Stewart, and Harold Elliott. Winters were very severe in the 1940s and 1950s. I remember ice-skating to school for the quarter exams. Dad had to feed the livestock on one winter day wearing a pair of ice skates. Each school day began with the Lord's Prayer and pledge of allegiance to the flag. I still believe each school day should begin like that. Every Friday we had a spelling bee or ciphering contest. One year we had a ciphering match with the Modena school. Our drinking water was a well with a hand pump. We had a metal cup hanging on a chain. All the kids drank from it. Coal was our source of heat. The teacher arrived early, so it would be warm. It was heated by adding coal to a stove. I have some pictures of the school and students. I wish my three children could have shared our good times down on the farm.

Ralph Bahler
By Julia Hautzenroeder of St. Joseph,
Missouri
Born 1919

Ralph Wayne Bahler, born 12 September 1918, died 2nd March 2004. Ralph was the second son of Ernest G. Bahler (Yank) and Wilhelmia Rosina Lenz Bahler (Minnie).

Ralph was born in a log house built in 1842 on Bahler Hill. He was born on the day his father registered at Richville School House for World War II. When I met Ralph in November 1944, he had brown, curly hair and 5 foot 6 inches tall. Ralph weighed 180 pounds with the physique like Charles Atlas.

He was a Corporal in the U.S. Army in Camphowz Texas. He came to a campus party with 14 other service men.

Ralph played the piano all evening. Songs: "Isle of Capri," popular songs of the day. We had food, games, and singing. Come time for curfew and lights out. Ralph remained and removed his coat, rolled up his sleeves, and went to the kitchen and wash dishes. I kept him busy, dishes for 18 women students and faculty sponsors and the other men.

I was a senior student of North Texas State College, Denton, Texas. Major in Home Economics. I had just a few hours to gain my bachelor degree.

We became acquainted, dated with permission of Ralph's commanding officer, Captain Anderson, and my parents. We were

married 22 of July 1945 in the little chapel in the woods on the campus of Texas Women's College, Denton, Texas.

Ralph completed his enlistment 31 January 1946, was terminated at Jefferson Barracks, St. Louis, Missouri.

We crossed the state in a 1939 Dodge sedan to Oregon, Missouri.

After 82 happy years, five children, he passed and was buried in Maple Grove Cemetery, Oregon, Missouri.

E.G. Ralph, and Minnie Bahler in 1943

Times Gone By
By Pauline Blanton of Hiawatha, Kansas
Born 1935

Where to start? Back to when I was a small child? Seems the best place to begin. I was born in rural Hiawatha, Kansas, the second child of my parents. I must have been an ornery child. I was too young to remember, but my mom told me I chased my older sister around with dead baby chicks just because she would scream and run away. I remember taking my sister's rag doll (her Christmas present) up into a tree because I was mad at her. It rained that night and ruined the doll. Needless to say, mom made me give mine to her.

Our winters were filled with snow piled up high. I have seen pictures of mom standing by the clothesline hanging up diapers with drifts of snow everywhere. My sister and I dressed

Ralph in 1942

107

up warmly to "help" her, or just to play.

Dad and, I am guessing, his brothers, grandpa, and maybe neighbors made sorghum. Mary and I got to ride the horses as they went round and round stirring the hot, gooey molasses. Which was then poured into containers to cool. One time Mary leaned over to smell and fell face first into the mess.

When I was around four years old, Dad was shelling corn with the hand corn sheller. The sheller had a pulley on it that kept the gears going. I would lean over and hand him ears of corn. The wind blew my hair into the gears and my head was pulled into it. I had to have 16 stitches put in. I remember dad driving like a crazy man with mom holding a washbasin under me and wiping blood from my face. It was a good thing one of the aunts had come to stay after mom had given birth to yet another sister. I could remember the smell of ether for years after that incident. That was the "anesthetic" used during the time. I remember lying on a cot with a heat lamp on the injured site to promote healing.

Mary and I used to love playing in the water trough on hot days. We always had to be watchful of the bull coming up for a drink, and many times had to scramble for safety. One year, bumblebees had made a nest under the trough, and we had disturbed them with our playing. We tried to get away from them, but Mary was stung 12 times. Needless to say, we no longer wanted to play in the pasture.

We attended a one-room school house along with the neighboring families and, yes, we had to walk two miles to school, but I don't remember it being "all up hill." With so few kids to teach, we could advance a year in less than a year's time. Mary did the second and third in the same year and I did the first and second. Not too long after, dad bought a house and some acreage in the town of Hiawatha. He went from farming to carpentry and made a living for the family that had grown to six children. They had lost one between me and another sister years before. Yet again, we walked to school, though not as far. On bitter cold days, dad would drive us to school.

Fast forward to later in my life as the issue between blacks and whites became evident in our lives. We grew up with colored children in the neighborhood and we had no idea there was such a thing as prejudice. However, I know the white children were allowed to swim in the local water spot for six days, but the blacks only got one day a week, after the water was all dirty and murky before it was drained for another week. Makes me feel like a real heel knowing people didn't treat them better. Also, they were not allowed in the restaurants. They could go to the back door and order food, but had to take it with them. The schools were segregated, but as children, we had no idea how they were discriminated against. By the time I was in my teens, I found out it had caught up with the colored boys across the street when they started calling us "white trash." I was so hurt the first time one of them called me that, I called him a "nigger." Hope God forgave me for that one.

When I was a young teen, I got married, and started having my own family. When I was at home, we had electricity, a floor furnace, and running water. However, I soon found out not all homes did. We cooked on a wood-burning stove, read by coal oil lamps, heated the houses with a coal or wood-burning stove, and had to go outside to the shanty to use the toilet. What a difference my life became. We moved quite a bit. Most of the homes had electricity, but none had running water. We lived for 45 years in one home. The longest of any and we had electricity, but for many years burned wood for heat. Natural gas came many years later and we put in a furnace. My husband had managed to put a toilet in the house. Up til then, we used an outdoor toilet. After he got the toilet put in, he knocked down the outhouse. There were rats galore running around. I spent one day sitting on the porch shooting rats with a shotgun. If they moved, I gave them another taste. My husband counted 12 dead rats when he came home from work. Try though he may, he never could get the well to pump water into the house. The water had become unfit to drink, so we hauled water from town to cook with and he drew water from the well and we used it to do laundry and flush the toilet. It wasn't until my dad passed and we bought my childhood home that we got to have water come out of a faucet after 50 years without.

Like my folks, we lost a young baby, but we too had six children. The baby died from "acute flu pneumonia" at the age of two and one-half months. We later lost a 49-year-old daughter to breast cancer. My husband didn't have an education, but he managed to keep his family fed. He had dreams of having his own business 'cause he wasn't one to go looking for work. The Lord provides though, and work came looking for him. He worked for the rock quarry and the water works plant in St. Joe, Missouri, a cement company, the city water/lights department and at a salvage yard in Hiawatha, Kansas. He tried his hand as owner of a salvage yard when that business closed, and he had his own trash route with two employees. Bad health caused him to retire early and he died from lung cancer two years after we moved to town.

As a youngster, during World War II, I remember when evening came, before the lights could be turned on, we had to draw the shades. If the town was darkened, the enemy couldn't see where to drop a bomb. Things had to be rationed, sugar, for one, and gasoline. If you didn't have the "stamps" you didn't get to purchase either item. Before refrigerators became a commodity, we purchased ice from an ice truck for the icebox. We had a really nice iceman that would break off chunks of ice for the kids in the neighborhood. The nicer you were the bigger chunk you got. Some of the greedier kids weren't as lucky. When oleo came out, it came as a package of all white, but had a yellow button in the middle of it that you broke and worked it in the white cube to make it look like butter. The neighbor kids were either ignorant of this fact, or just lazy, but it always looked like they spread lard on their bread.

Fast forward to today and I am comfortable with life and appreciate the luxuries we have now but did without growing up.

The Haunted Timber
By Old Bud Neiderhouse of Oregon, Missouri
Born 1940

Circa 1954, early spring, Forest City, Missouri. John Fitz's Sinclair gas station. Oh, by the way, regular, 12.9 cents a gallon; hi-test, 14.9 cents; coffee, ten cents. Thus, the scene is set. Old Bud Neiderhouse, age 14 years, workin' after school and weekends there. Henry B., local area farmer, shuffled into the station and sat down in the pale green, steel lawn chair and looked at proprietor John

Old Bud Neiderhouse

F. and addressed him. "Why say, now, John, you heard of anyone a-findin' any mushrooms yet?"

"Wal, they found some little white one out in th' bottom. I figure some big morels might be down on th' bluff at Nina (pronounced Nīnēē) Foxe's timber.

At this "Hēēn-rī" said, "That's it! I'm a-goin' down there right now!!" An' he left.

I waited on several customers, approximately 30 minutes elapsed, and Henry returned, shuffling at a high rate of speed. Once more, he took his seat in the old lawn chair and looked at John with a strange look on his face. He acted as if he wanted to tell John something, but could not bring hisself to speak! Finally, he said, "John, there's sumthin' dang wrong down thar in 'Ninee' Foxe's timber."

John, "What seems to be the trouble?"

Henry replied, "Wal, I hadn't walked very fur when a voice called out to me. They said, "Hello." I hollered back to 'em, "Howdy to ye. Say, are you boys a-findin' eny mushrooms?" They didn't answer….Oh, they's up thar in th' brush—I cain't see 'em, an' they's probly hard-of-heerin'. Then I seen some toadstools an' kept on walkin' till all of a sudden 'they' called out agin! An' this time 'they' wuz plum across th' timber—ahead of me—an' 'The Voice' cum frum up on high, an' it didn't even sound human! I got the horriblest feelin'. They wuz eyeballs a-seein' me that I cud not see. It wuz plum awful. I got the hell out-a-there, an' I wudn't go back fer money, marbles, or chalk! No way!" And then he left.

I looked at Tom an' Crawferd. They looked at me an' John. "It sounds like a 'hant' to me!" said Crawferd. Tom said, "It's probably a 'haunted timber'." An' we all allowed as we thought so too! Several minutes passed. Then, here come Leonard and Archie, the Hindersun brothers. Leonard was carrying a fishin' dip net (bale 'n war), wired to the end of a ten foot cane fishin' pole.

I said, "Where on Earth is you boys headed with a rig such as that?" Leonard said, "Oh, maw's ol' poll-parrot eescaped an' we think she's roostin' down in 'Ninee' Foxe's timber." Oh, my land sakes. At this point the "mystery" was solved!

Tom was killed in a car wreck not long after. Only 14 years old. I loved him as a brother, an' if I can make it to Heaven, when I cross over I hope to see him again, and all my old pals. And my folks. And our best pal, Lord Jesus Christ!

Moving to the Jamesport Area
By Cora Miller Ropp of Jamesport, Missouri
Born 1940

It was the month of February 1957 when our family of nine moved from Fishersville, Virginia to Jamesport, Missouri. Our belongings were loaded on a boxcar at Fishersville, Virginia train station and brought by rail to Sherwood Crossing where it was unloaded onto wagons pulled by a team of horses. Driving the two miles thru mud to the farm dad had bought.

This was thru the winter thaw, very muddy and foggy. Mother and us seven children came to Trenton, Missouri via Amtrak train. The realtor, W. E. Bray, meeting us at the train and taking us out to our new neighbor's for the night. After breakfast, the neighbors took us to the farm. Soon wagonloads were driving in the lane and unloaded at the house. It was a bustle all day. The cows and horses were taken to the barn. At noon, the neighbor ladies had food set out in the kitchen. All helpers had plenty to eat.

After lunch, the ladies helped mom organize the house and got all the beds ready for the night. The canned food was packed in a box wagon and oats poured over the jars to keep jars from breaking. Those jars were all carried to the cave or storm cellar as some may have called it.

After a good night's sleep in my own bed, I wanted to go out and see what this new farm looked like. To my surprise, as I stepped on the outer porch it was so foggy I could not see farther than the yard. But to my delight, a cardinal was singing his welcome song in one of the treetops.

The red cardinal was the state bird of Virginia and I always admired it. Now coming to Missouri, the cardinal was the first bird I hear. Later, I learned the cardinal was also the state bird of Missouri.

The house having three bedrooms, bath, living room with fireplace, large kitchen and pantry, plus two small screened-in porches. The 306 acres had a barn, hen house, 100+ was tillable across the road. A nice fishing pond across the road. A creek run through the farm on south side of the road. Lots of walnut timber. We children would spend lots of time playing along the creek.

There were trees along both sides of the lane with lots of iris planted in between the trees. Dad replanted a lot of iris along the fencerows along the road. There were flowerbeds in every corner possible. An elderly couple had lived there before we did and the lady must have had a knack with flowers.

Dad and the boys were cutting wood in the timber and cut a tree down that had two little squirrels inside. These were brought to the house for pets. I don't remember how long we had them, but they were cute and full of life.

At that time, we milked eight cows. Separated the cream. After it was cooled, we poured it into a five-gallon cream can. At the end of each week, A. G. Martin (a trucker) came by to pick up the can of cream. It was sent to Kansas City. That was our grocery money for the week. In order to keep the cream from getting a sour smell, mom had fixed a muslin cover to strip over the cream can with elastic on the edge so it would stay tight.

One day when we were gone to church, coming home we found both pet squirrels drowned in the cream can. Oh no! There goes our grocery money for next week!

During the summer, one afternoon I decided to go fishing in the pond. To my surprise, I caught a three-pound bass.

One year the walnuts were very plentiful. This was in the days before we were able to sell walnuts. That year the boys picked them up and run them thru a corn sheller, then laying them out in the brooder house. That winter sister, Laura, and I cracked and picked walnuts until we had done 16 bushels. Friends and neighbors got walnuts to use also.

There was one spot in the creek that had a stony ledge. At times when I just wanted to be alone and quiet, I'd go down to my favorite spot where I could sit on the ledge with my feet in the water. It was time well spent.

We had a paint horse, which we called Betty. She was a safe driver and we all liked her. She was used many times in the open buggy.

One summer day I went down to the cave to get some canned goods. Here I found a copperhead snake laying on top of the peach jars. I went outside and got me a hoe, carried the cool, live snake outside, threw it on the ground and hollered at mom to come and look at this snake. We looked at it, deciding what kind it was. She asks, "Is it dead?" I says, "No." The snake did not wiggle because she was still cool from the temperature of the cave. Mom took the hoe and made short end to the snake.

Another time I was walking barefooted along the walk and saw a short, thick snake behind some hollyhocks. I got a hoe and killed it. It was a rattlesnake.

The outhouse must not be missed. After a meal and at dishwashing time it was a busy place. At night, we set the chamber pot into the bathroom. All family members used the pot during the night. It was a girl's chore to keep the pot emptied and rinsed, turned upside down during the day. At night, it was taken inside again. We had no running water in the bathroom.

Wringer washers is what we used to do our weekly laundry. All little children were cautioned to keep their hand out of the wringer, and us older ones were to always shut the wringer off when not in use. Most of our clothes were homemade.

In the summer of 1960 mom and sister, Laura, decided to go to the south part of the farm to pick blackberries. This was across the creek up on a hill was a large blackberry patch. They decided to hitch Betty to the open buggy and drive back. It would have been too long a walk for mom, let alone hoping to bring berries back. So driving back and unhitching Betty and tying Betty elsewhere away from the buggy.

Mom and Laura started picking these big, luscious blackberries. All at once, it dawned on them that they are out here in the wilds, far away from the buildings. What if a bobcat should show up? What would we do? As they were discussing what to do, "Gr-r-r. He-e-e." They looked at each other. Did you hear that? They were two scared women. Pretty soon, they heard the sound again. This time it was too close for comfort. It did not take the two women long to run for the buggy. But, but where is Betty? She was tied on the other side of the patch. They were still standing on the buggy when, of all things, here comes brother Jr. just laughing to see them standing on the buggy.

Exploits in NW Missouri
By Pastor Richard Eisenberg of St. Joseph, Missouri
Born 1943

Back in 1948, at age five, I was having a good time in Borger, Texas when one day my family loaded up in the car. There was dad, mother, and we four siblings. I was told we were going to northwest Missouri. No one asked my opinion or gave me time to think about it, but I didn't have steady work, so I decided to tag along. We drove into Kansas City as I was waking up and everywhere I looked, up and down the sidewalks, there were so many trees I thought we were going through a forest. In parts of Texas, you could drive a long way between trees.

Northwest Missouri had trees everywhere. Fad was an ironworker and said he wanted to trade the home in Kansas City for some farmland further north. We wound up in Oregon, Missouri living in a house one block from the school. We had a cherry tree, peach tree, plum tree, and a grapevine in the backyard and lots of peony bushes and flowers.

My brother was five years older, and one sister three years older, and my youngest sister was one year younger than me. Everybody was bigger than me, even my younger sister. She was taller and I was so skinny dad made me eat extra ice cream to fatten up.

We had a huge garden on the south side of the house and dad rented a garden four times bigger on the block just west. Being an ironworker, dad was gone for weeks at a time and my older brother, who was six foot three early in life, told me I was in charge of the garden.

My grandmother came and spent a few weeks with us one summer. One sunny day a man came and brought a team of workhorses, hooked them up to a plow, and started plowing up the garden closest to the house. One of those horses was named Daisy. It seems Daisy had a mind of her own and the man started using some words dad used when he was really upset. Well, my grandmother surprised us all by getting up and storming out the back door. I had never seen her so mad. The problem was that the man working the team of horses was questioning the ancestry of his horse named Daisy. Well, you need to know that as it happened my grandmother's name was Daisy. Mother's mouth fell open when she went out to see what the shouting was all about. After grandmother realized the horse's name was Daisy and the owner of the team stopped laughing and apologized, everything settled down.

Bob, Zona Marie, Dick, and Elizabeth

My mother picked one of the hottest days in that hot summer to send me to the big garden to pick green beans. A friend of mine stopped by as I was getting ready to go to the garden and came up with a great idea, "Dick, let's hitch a ride over to Forest City and go swimming at the 40-foot hole." The 40-foot hole was the best swimming hole and left beautiful white sand on the north side. Someone built a diving board extending out over water that was so clear you could see fish swimming several feet deep as plain as you could see fish in a fish bowl. Well, I thought the whole situation over and came up with a foolproof plan that King Solomon would have

been impressed with. I took a large grocery box, put two large pillows in the bottom and, with my friend's help, we picked enough green beans to cover those pillows and fill that huge grocery box full of green beans. Of course, we went swimming and had a great time.

By the way, I wouldn't recommend grade school kids or teens hitchhiking like we did back then. In those days, the churches were left unlocked and most of the homes the same. Well, we had a great time swimming and when we got back home, I was so tired after I ate dinner I watched a little TV and went to bed. However, I absolutely forgot about the box of green beans with two large pillows until I went to bed and noticed my pillows were gone and it was too late. Too late to go to the garden and pick enough green beans to replace two large pillows. Yes, your sins will find you out.

The closest I came to not living through the summer was one day when I was trying out my slingshot that was made of a choice branch with a "Y" shape and two large strips of rubber, cut out from an old inner tube. My mastery of this weapon was something to see. We had a huge yard and my older brother had his shirt off while he was cutting grass with the old style lawn mower where the power came from the power of my brother's legs and arms. I was getting very confident of my aim and decided to shoot a stone over my brother's head as he was quite a ways off, walking away. He will never know, right? That day I learned to never use a flat coal cinder in a slingshot. My aim was perfect but that coal cinder had dropped in flight ten feet lower than a smooth stone would have. Oh my, right in the bare back. I couldn't outrun him of course, if he caught me, sure death. I ran to the house like a shot, mother was cooking beans in the pressure cooker and threw both hands up and hollered, "What is going on?" I headed straight for the stairs and ran into the

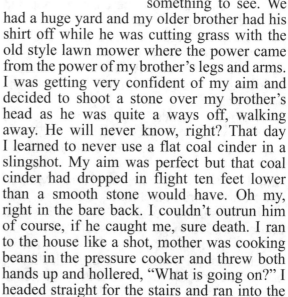

bedroom my brother and I shared. I slammed the door and fastened the bolt lock and ran to the window. I knew the door wouldn't stop him, so I opened the window. Took my bed sheet and tied it to the bedpost. Climbed out and was hanging out the window. BAM! The door busted open and I dropped to the ground using the sheet.

I have fond memories of many exploits, like in the winter on the north side of our house, back when it used to snow heavily in northwest Missouri. We had the most popular hill in town for sleigh riding. Kids came from all over the area and we had great times.

While in grade school I worked for a hog farmer on Sundays from one o'clock to 7 p.m. Among other things, I cleaned 32 brooding houses and learned to respect the power of a mother sow hog. One day I left one of her piglets in the unit and felt safe because I closed and locked the door. When she heard her piglet squeal the next thing I knew, she busted through that door like it was nothing. Even with rubber boots on, I jumped out of that roof door like I was shot out of a cannon.

The job paid me $3 for six hours of work. But in those days I could go to the local movie on Saturday night and buy popcorn for only 25 cents. The good news is I lived through these exploits in northwest Missouri and am able to write and tell you about it!

Making Apple Butter
By Sylva Bowman of Savannah, Missouri
Born 1923

The 1st Saturday in November is the Annual Lords Acre Day Sale. It is to raise money for improvements to the church, also to aid financially for the year.

Lord's Guild made apple butter one year. We had permission from local orchard growers to pick up apples under the trees to make cider and some to peel to put with the cooked down cider. We used a cider press to make the cider; we had several dozen gallons of cider. It was kept in a cool place until time to make apple butter.

The day started early. We had a large copper kettle that was placed on an iron stand. We poured all of the cider into the kettle, lit a fire under it, to begin heating the cider to a boiling. We boiled it down about halfway, and then started adding the peeled and sliced apples and as they cooked, we continued adding more apples till the mixture was very thick. While this was cooking, it had to be stirred continually to keep from burning. They had a long pole with a paddle on the end to stir with. This usually took most of the day. When thickened, we ladled it into jars and sealed them, to be sold later at the sale.

First Love
By Billie Paden of St. Joseph, Missouri
Born 1920

I grew up in Missouri, sorta. I was born in Missouri, Dearborn, Missouri. My daddy Loyd Harrison Bailey and mama Georgia Melvina Sims transplanted me to Alamo, Texas when I was a ripe five years old, along with my beloved grandpa, Wm. Houston Sims and Grandma Sims, Grace Victoria Walters Sims. The night before leaving we visited my grandpa, Cyrus Bailey from 9th and Charles in St. Joseph, right behind the post office in St. Joseph. The affection dad bore his parents says we probably were with grandma and Grandpa Bailey, says we spent longer at the Bailey residence than 4th night. Anyway, the memory of Grandpa Bailey's vest is what drags me back. That night I was playing in grandpas' vest and I was not returning it so I could take it to Texas. No girl. I made such a loud scream that no one knew what to do with me; I think my dad was seriously tempted to spank me. Something he never did but once in his life. Grandpa said, "Oh let her alone. I don't care if she takes that old brown thing to Texas!" "No, we're not going to let her think she can have her way by kicking and screaming." So I guess we left for Dearborn and the great state of Texas without the old brown vest. Not to return until I was in the 4th grade.

At that time, Texas had 11 grades and Missouri had 12. Which meant when you returned in 4th grade, you were immediately transferred to 5th grade. If this situation was reversed and you went south, you were put back a grade. So to make a story short, I was elevated two grades. We went to stay in Dearborn. It was promotion time and I was promoted to 6th grade. My Grandpa Sims had returned and started another restaurant. Mama went back to working for Grandma Sims, her mama.

My favorite teacher was Frances Wilkerson in Dearborn. She had a short, very handsome son starting high school that all the girls were crazy about. He was a little old for me. Tommy was a best friend with a handsome, huge, football player who I did fall for. But of course, he treated me like a Tommy's little sister. Now I can barely remember his name. Oh yes, John Robert, but last name? That I cannot remember.

In Dearborn, I graduated from grade school, 8th grade, in 1934 when dad carted us to Alamo, Texas again. It was sooner this time when Grandma Sims welcomed me again. While I was in Texas, one of my Missouri school friends wrote me and told me J.K. had found there were other girls in Dearborn High. I wrote back, "That's ok; I'll take him back when I get back in Dearborn." And I did, I think.

I went to a reunion in Dearborn about 50 years later and saw these old school mates again. I did not know him and he did not know me either. He had to ask. Now Jack Gabbert knew me! Later I got tired waiting for him to notice me so I stood by him waiting by his side to get a word in. Without noticing, he was carrying on a long conversation with someone. He reached out and took hold of my arm and said to the man, "And I want you to meet my first girl, and the first girl I ever kissed." I didn't want to lose track of him, but wonders of wonders he died after I had been married 37 years. We had both been married. He had worked in London, been married and lived in Texas. I had raised five kids and been divorced before I could make contact with him, he died. And here I am still here at 93.

I have many more memories of Missouri. I am still here in St. Joseph. Why does God still have me here? I do not know. My oldest daughter lives in Texas and she is 71. She and Jack have four children. The oldest child lives in Oklahoma and the youngest in Florida. I have five children, Steve died at 56. I am a Christian; I have 13 grandchildren and one great grandchild. Getting older everyday using a lovely wheel chair. All my children are belonging to Jesus. They are all healthy and strong.

My Pets
By Eileen Oyler of St. Joseph, Missouri
Born 1929

I've had pets from cows to chickens. My pet cow was a Jersey Guernsey mix at milking time I would call her by name and she would come in. one night I was milking and a neighbor man showed up. He started laughing because I was talking to the cow. I told him I always talk to her. All of my animals know their name and come to them. One time we had a red rooster. He hung around the back door. I would go out and say do the buck and wing ruffes. He'd drop a wing and run in a circle. We've had so many dogs dropped on us. I had two dogs that would chase me about a half mile when I would go out. They would wait for me to come back. I would stop and pick them up; it made their day to ride home. Somebody shot one of them last week. Now I have an Australian Sheppard that was dropped. She is an albino, one eye, and can't see well out of the other. I have to keep her in the house so she won't get run over. I told my daughter I was willing her to her so she would have a home. Another pet we had was a white ferret. She slept under the refrigerator. People would come to see her. I would holler, "Rat Fink," about five minutes and she would come out. One day she got outside, when I found her, she was curled up with the dog, both asleep. I live by myself; my dogs and cat keep me company.

Working in the Good Days
By Rick Mason of Trenton, Missouri

I was born and raised in Trenton, Missouri. I left Trenton in 1969 and I returned in 2008. I ended a marriage after 37 years and changed a dream. I have loved only one lady I dated in high school for one year. I am now retired single and have many memories of Trenton. Trenton is now going in the wrong direction in my thinking. I was big in bowling. I finished grade school and junior college from the same building. I graduated high school in 1965 and junior college in 1968. I worked for Joe Farris for cars at MFA gas station. Full service was the norm, put air in the tires, check the oil under the hood, and clean the windshield on all autos. You always asked all drivers what if they wanted full service. Most cars cut oil checks and windshield cleaning. Fuel was 29 cents. I pumped many gallons at 19 cents. Trenton had JC Penny, Wards, Steins, Smiths & Howards. You could get good clothing then. Bowling 45 a game shoe rental was f15 cents. I carried higher bowling average in town while I was in high school. I was young, some men were okay with it, and some were not. We had Joes IGA A&P beside a small food stores. Trenton was a great small town. The railroad left in the 1980s due to poor leadership of the union. Big company people worked as did my mother, all of her adult life. My mother passed at the age of 50, my father at the age of 43, and my grandmother at the age of 88. My grandmother worked at Hypower Café for 22 years. She made pies seven days a week. Hypower Café had great food. I started to work at nine years of age carrying papers.

Father Christmas
By Melissa Kimball of Weston, Missouri
Born 1953

An important memory for me involves Weston's own Father Christmas, Tom Hooper, of Leavenworth, Kansas.

My sister-in-law had stated when she first had children that she wanted no Santa photos. She wanted the children to know about Christmas and Jesus.

They came to visit and she saw Father Christmas and wanted Aaron's photo with him. Later they came after having Bethany and they got her photo with Father Christmas.

She was amazed to hear Weston still has the same Father Christmas. I have photos of Father Christmas with myself and our two dogs at the time and my husband and our two dogs. Since then we have lost our one dog, Hobo, due to age.

Weston's had the same Father Christmas for 25 years; I believe this to be correct.

Here at Weston lots of businesses have come and gone but the Town Mouse has been here since before I moved here in 1987.

Sebus Hardware downtown has been there even longer as well as Missouri Bluffs. McCormick distillery was giving tours for years until about 1989 of the distillery east of Weston. When they had to stop these tours,

they opened a shop in town on Main Street.

Snow Creek ski area opened I believe in 1986 and still operate with changes such as now they snow board as well as ski. It is just north of Weston.

The Weston hotel has been restored since I moved here in 1987. I believe it has been going about the last ten years. In 1987, the Main Street was gravel in Weston Missouri. Since 1987, two bridges downtown have been replaced.

Other than downtown the Depot since before I moved in '87 to date, the Hull Lumber from before '87 to date.

Melissa with Father Christmas

My Roots
By Keith Stanton of Savannah, Missouri
Born 1925

Mother made our clothes and then kept them patched and our socks darned, clean, and ironed. If we had a car early on, I can't remember it. The first car I can remember was a '34 Chevy, sometime well after 1934. Pop worked with Uncle Claude Roberts and Guy Phillips selling some kind of farm feed supplies for a short time after we moved to Savannah. He then worked for Bob Kneal in the Ford garage, where Reynolds Body Shop is now. Then he went to work for Whitchurch Hardware store and worked there until he had his heart attack in the late '40s. He worked from 7 a.m. to 7 p.m., five days a week, then from 7a.m. to 11 p.m. on Saturday. He received $7.00 a week for this for a number of years and was glad to get it. There was no paid vacation, hospital insurance, and the other good things we have today.

Mother baked cupcakes and sold them to people around town. She put them in old suit boxes and I delivered them. I remember one time taking some to Mrs. Brandow, that lived about a black and a half west of the school, as I started up to her house I stubbed my toe and dropped them, spilling them all over the ground. I didn't think anyone had seen me so I picked them up and took them to the door. Mrs. Brandow took them and did not say a word about me dropping them. She had seen me and later told mother about it, and thought it was funny. Mother did not feel that way about it as I found out. Mr. Brandow had a blacksmith shop and made things for the farmers to use.

In 1935 mother had a breast and underarm cancer removed at Dr. Nichols San, here in Savannah. The method for removal was to put some kind of acid on the area and it literally burned the area treated until the tissue affected was removed, needless to say, this was a very severe treatment. As I recall, mother was in the center for six weeks or more and then it took over a year to heal. It did prove to be successful, as she never had a reoccurrence. Josie Swagert worked for us about a year keeping house. As I recall she was not the best cook in the world, but she could fry eggplant. Mother was in the hospital in Maryville in 1941 for a complete hysterectomy. Dr. Long did the surgery. She was very ill from this and it was touch and go for a while as to whether she was going to make it or not. I remember riding up with Dr. Long one evening to see her and on the way home, when we got to the four-mile curve he went straight on down the dirt road. I did not know he was asleep.

When I got big enough I started mowing yards with a push mower and a hand trimmer. In 1941, I started working in the North Side café for Jenny Franks. I worked after school and Saturdays for a year or so. I remember one evening a bum had ridden in to Savannah on the rails and came in and asked how much I would charge him for a bowl of hot water. I told him nothing and got it. As I watched, he took the ketchup from the table and put some in the water, and then he took the sugar jar and added sugar to it. He then took a newspaper from under his coat and unwrapped some crackers and had tomato soup. I also gave him a cup of coffee and told him I might need to know how to do this sometime and it would be worth the cup of coffee.

Another time a couple came in that were in town for someone to have treatment at the cancer center. They were acting somewhat strange and I asked them what was bothering them. They wanted to know what kind of town this was, as they had seen a bunch of men with beards running around shooting shotguns into the air. This was the year of the 100th anniversary of Andrew County and the men were growing beards for that. Periodically they shot pigeons to keep them from having too many around the square.

One night Myrtle and Press Shaffer were in at closing time and after they left I saw they had left a big sack setting by the stove that heated the place. It was very cold that night and we had a good fire going to keep the place warm. I looked in the sack and found it had a big 10-pound tub of lard in it. I took it out and put it in the refrigerator and went on home. The next morning when I arrived Press was waiting for me. He was sure the lard had melted and ran out all over the floor and I would be mad.

After I left the North Side Café I went to work after school and Saturday for Julius and Geo Schmitt in their grocery store on the north side of the square. One of my jobs was to wash the weenies with vinegar water so they wouldn't be slick. They had a loft in the back of the store with tin around it so rats couldn't get into the flour, pepper, sugar, tea, and other things stored in it. Julius' office was under one end of it. He had a big electric fan setting out in the hallway blowing into his office. One day he had sent me up to sack pepper, I thought it would be fun to see what he would do if some pepper got into his office, so I threw a small scoop over the side into the fan. When he recovered from his sneezing fit he came out told me to stop sacking until he was out of the office. One day I went up to sack tea that was in a big open box. Julius' cat had been using it for a litter box, so I went down and told him about the mess. He came up, looked at it, took one chunk and hit it on the side of the box and told me to shake off all I could and go ahead and sack it. Julius and Geo loved to play, and more times than not about closing time they would start in. they thought it was great fun to throw something across the store and hit someone with it. I don't remember anyone getting hurt too badly.

They had a mild mannered young deliveryman, by the name of Toie Wampler that delivered the orders that peopled called in to their homes. One day he came back real red faced from his route. After much prompting it seemed at one stop when he went in the young son asked him to come into the bedroom as he had something to show him, when they went in the boy went to the closet door and opened it and there stood the older sister in her birthday suit. She had heard him coming just as she was getting out of her bath and had ran in to hide. Working for the Schmitt Grocery was a real learning experience.

I left there and went to work for Ernest Dray in his drug store on the south side of the square. I worked there until I got out of high school. One morning right after I opened up a man came in and wanted to buy a half pint of whiskey. Of course, I was not 21 and you were suppose to be before you sold liquor. He couldn't make up his mind what brand he wanted, but after so much time he bought one. He then told me he was a liquor inspector and I was under arrest for selling while I was underage. I told him I would have to call Mr. Dray, who lived upstairs, as I was there by myself. Mr. Dray arrived shortly with Harry Latham the local P.A. Mr. Latham told the man to go on down the road, as anyone ought to know it was wartime and Mr. Dray could not find anyone of age to work and he had given his okay for me to sell. That was the last time I ever heard from them.

It was only a matter of time until I would be drafted for WWII, so I left the drug store and got a job at one of the packinghouses in St. Joseph. They put me to work hauling meat on a cart out of cold storage, where it was 20 below zero, out to a rail car where it was over 90. I didn't feel my health would stand that so I quit.

Mother was very disappointed when I was born, as she had planned to have a bouncing baby girl who she would name Rosemary. She told me a number of times as I was growing up, "She did not have to have me," she always stopped short of saying, if she would have known I would be a boy I would not have been born. I always had that feeling. She and pop got married when they were 17 and I think she was sorry she married so young. While they always seemed to get along okay, I feel she felt somehow she should have married a rich man, I mean rich in money, as Pop was rich in ways money could not buy. The folks always belonged to the Christian Church. The night I was baptized it was raining and the dressing room we changed in had a bad leak in the roof and I always said I was sprinkled and dunked both the same night. I still to this day do not have strong religious convictions. After we married and the kids started coming I joined the Catholic Church where Leola belonged.

When I still lived up on the highway, I remember playing with Ed Hayward; mother never felt I should play with him, as his family was not good enough. He now has his Doctorates degree in Pharmacy. One day we were playing horse. We put a rope around our waist and the other was driving and I started to jump across a rain filled ditch when Ed said, "Whoa" and pulled on the rope and I fell in the ditch and got my clothes wet and dirty.

One day we noticed an almost solid string of cars going by on the highway headed north. We did not know why but later found out they were lynching a black man on top of a schoolhouse southwest of Maryville. This was a sad day for all of mankind when a thing like this can happen.

We moved from the house on the highway to a house at 700 W. Main in Savannah. I do not remember the house having plumbing in it at the time we moved in, but it did before we left there. One time Uncle Claude and Aunt Jessie came over from Kansas to stay all night. The attic was floored and I had moved my bed up there to have a room all of my own. I had got a bunch of Alph Landon signs for President and put them up there and took Uncle Claude to see them and he would not stay in the same house with them and they went on and stayed somewhere else that night.

The Conductor
By Carolyn Abbott of Kansas City, Missouri
Born 1927

It was the summer of 1933 when our family took a train from Kansas City to Colorado Springs for our annual vacation. I was six years old and nothing could be more thrilling, I thought, than this overnight journey.

Carolyn and her older sister, Janet

When bedtime came, I was much too excited to sleep. Finally, at perhaps 2:00 AM, I slipped out of my berth and wandered down the aisle. Everyone was asleep, or so it seemed, until suddenly a conductor appeared before me. He smiled and asked what I was doing up at this time of night. I replied that I was too excited to sleep, because I loved riding on that train so much. "Well," he asked, "would you like to see the engine?"

Of course, I wanted to! So when we came to a curve, he took me to a small connecting car and held me up to the glassless window, where I could lean out a bit and see that beautiful engine in the bright moonlight, coming around the bend. Soon, though, I lost sight of it, whereupon he told me some wonderful stories about trains.

By then the train was coming to a stop. He asked if I'd like to get off for a few minutes and of course, I said, "Yes." So we stepped off, stood on solid ground for a while, and then got back on. He took me to my berth and helped me get settled. He told me "goodnight, get to sleep now." I hope I thanked him and said goodnight.

What a kind, caring man he was. He made that night pure magic for a little girl! It's too bad, but I don't think anything like that could or would happen now. But perhaps I am wrong about that. I hope so!

Why Were We Spared?
By Walter Maris of Savannah, Missouri
Born 1936

In 1945 my dad, home on furlough from the Pacific theater of WWII, moved us into a small rural town, Gentry, as mother had signed to teach the first four grades of the school. Gentry had not progressed very far out of the depression. Our residential streets were dirt and the main street a poor gravel, which was reduced each spring to no more than a hog wallow base with the coming of the spring thaw. There were only two or three homes that had inside plumbing so outhouses were a part of the scenery. However, that landscape was altered each year at Halloween. There had been a long time practice of tipping over outhouses as a Halloween trick without the treat. There were a few years according to local tradition where older guys would haul the outhouses into Main Street and then line 15-20 of them up in a row. While the young guys no doubt had some hilarious and adventurous encounters, it did create a hardship for some of the victims who had no way to get their outhouse back without hiring, sometimes volunteered, a farmer with tractor to return the outhouse to the premises. While we lived there, we did witness that many outhouses including our own were tipped over each year, but only a few were dragged to Main Street.

The population signs on the north and south side of town on Highway 169 declared 196 residents lived in Gentry and it was not changed the entire eight years we lived there. The old-timers who set out on the benches in front of our lone grocery store didn't agree with that figure even a little bit, declaring our town would not make 150 even if we were to count the dogs. The old-timers would put in several hours a day on those benches, swapping stories, sometimes arguing, and ever so often needing a refill for chewing pleasure they would cut off a chaw of their tobacco plug, frequently stepping out to the ditch to spit.

The standard of living would probably be considered rather poor according to today's standards but we were mostly all in the same condition. People worked hard for what they had and would join together to help those who were sick or injured. No one went without food or shelter. The town had a few tough type guys, but generally, when there was a fight it was among their own. There were two churches in the town and each Sunday morning they would toll the bells to invite people to services. The best clothes we had were worn on Sunday and then put away for the week. The top clothes for many of the men was the newest and cleanest pair of overalls they owned and often worn with a white shirt.

One year, I believe in '48 or '49, we experienced a natural disaster, which would test the mettle of our whole area. One spring day during recess, we were playing softball when an ominous looking cloud came up in the west creating a weird like stillness as it hovered over for a while. It slowly moved to the northeast and about an hour later, we heard that the town of Worth, just three to four miles north of us had been struck by a mighty tornado. The storm totally wiped out the town leaving only a few large trees with all the limbs broken off and the bark peeled from the trunks. Thirteen of the 125 residents were killed. For the whole next week one could walk across 169 through backed up traffic, inching along as the sightseers came from all around to view the devastation.

Many people in our town had friends and relatives in the destroyed town. This caused us to ponder why we were spared while our sister town was devastated. Some folks were angry with God, asking how a loving God could allow this tragedy. However, in the midst of the pain and suffering our churches began quietly and effectively ministering to those who were hurting. They opened up their homes to those left homeless; some provided food and clothing; others provided a shoulder to lean on or to cry on.

People helping each other made a lasting impression on me and my three siblings. We establishing enduring lifetime friends while in that little rural town and some 60 years later we still have contact with a number of them. We consider our friendships the main reward of rural experience.

Grandmother's Routine
By Nancy Gloth of Kansas City, Missouri
Born 1946

My grandmother was Ina Hook Booher; (born July 6, 1900 and died February 4, 1974) grandmother was a housewife who had a regular routine. Monday was grandmother's washday. Grandmother took great pride that her whites were whiter than any other housewife's. Grandmother made her own lye soap from beef tallow and 20-mule team borax. Grandmother may have had a secret, because her lye soap was white as snow.

Nancy's grandparents, Ina Hook and John Booher 1960

The sheets were hung on the front lines to hide what was on the back lines.

Tuesday was grandmother's day to iron. Grandmother ironed everything, sheets, pillowcases, kitchen towels, handkerchiefs, and overalls.

Wednesday was grandmother's day to mend and patch fixing every rip and tear. Grandmother had a button jar filled with all color, shapes, and sizes of buttons. Grandmother could match any lost or missing button.

Thursday was grandmother's day to do as she pleased. Grandmother might visit with family, or friends, or she might do odd chores or go to town.

Friday was grandmother's day to clean. Grandmother's house was always neat and clean. Grandmother's living room was used only to entertain company. I was not allowed to go in it as a child.

Saturday was grandmother's day to bake. Grandmother baked three pies and one-cake and ice box cookies. Grandmother's pies were the best and pretty as a picture. Grandmother seemed to favor brown sugar for her cakes, and her icebox cookies would melt in your mouth. Her big glass cookie jar was always full. Grandmother did not believe in afternoon snacks. I had a hard time getting to that cookie jar without getting caught.

I have tried to make the icebox cookies but they are not the same. Maybe grandmother had a secret.

Sunday would find grandmother in church. Grandmother always had a big Sunday dinner. Sunday afternoon grandmother loved to sit on the front porch. When evening came, the Lawrence Welk show was one of grandmother's favorites.

My Early Years on the Farm
By Tom Stegman of Lathrop, Missouri
Born 1936

In the spring of 1946, my family bought and moved to a 160-acre farm. I was nine years old the eldest of three boys. Our old place was 60 acres so the new place looked like quite a challenge.

My father said we would all have to work hard to make it a success. At that time, we farmed with horses, so it fell my lot to learn to do field work with a team of horses. We broke the ground with breaking plows, one riding, and one walking plow. Then disc to make seedbed and planted corn, beans, and milo with two horses, two row riding planter. I ran disc and my dad the planter. It seemed quite a feat for a 9 to 10 year old boy to handle a 4-horse team on an 8-foot disc.

I was kept out of school during the planting and harvest seasons. My brother 2 years younger than me brought my work home so I could study at night.

Our house didn't have central heat or air conditioning. In the winter, we took turns changing clothes next to the wood heating stove, and baths in a galvanized washtub behind it. My mother cooked on a Home Comfort wood stove in the kitchen. In summer we opened the windows to let in air and bathed in the same tub in screened in back porch.

We had a large garden, which we all had to keep weeded. When the garden crops matured, we gathered and canned to store for winter use.

Tom's father, Vernon with a neighbor in 1940

We butchered our own meat, had chickens for meat and eggs. We also had a large herd of milk cows, which we milked by hand. We churned our own butter, made cottage cheese and sold milk and cream.

Looking back it seems like a hard life, but we were happy and had a lot of love.

In 1951, my father bought his first Ford tractor. It was small compared to tractors of today, but took the place of two men and eight horses with time to spare.

Memories
By Roger Hunt of Pocahontas, Iowa
Born 1933

My parents and I moved here in 1937, and lived with my grandmother, aunt, and uncle. We moved several times and never had running water, always an outhouse.

We took a bath in a collapsible rubber tub. Coca-Cola, six pack small bottles given away, left on our doorstep. I remember sliding down the curved sidewalk in front of the school, and running around Main Street on Saturday nights. I learned to ride a bicycle. I remember playing cops and robbers outside and trading comic books. We had rubber band gunfights in a barn west of school. My family didn't have a reliable car. We went to Fort Dodge two or three times a year and took the bus. It stayed at the hotel in the morning and returned in the evening.

I remember shooting pigeons off the old Methodist church. I had a dog named Tinto. I missed the Korean War. I watched the building of gym in 1953. In the early '40s, there was a tornado southwest of town, it brought lots of rain. I went to school the next day floating on a plank under the railroad bridge.

WWII, we got into football games by bringing scrap metal, used grease, even toothpaste tubes for the war effort.

I remember lying on a wooden bridge over creek north of town and watching minnows swim by.

Listening to the radio was a favorite past time, One Man's Family, Ma Perkins, Amos and Andy, The Lone Ranger, and the Guiding Light.

I remember picking milk weed pods to make things for the war effort.

I remember riding on the railroad tracks with Kenny M. do not touch the steering wheel once you get on the tracks.

Go to church run home to change clothes, go to Hwy 4, and hitch hiked to Rockwell City to the stock car races and then hitch hiked home and only got stuck without a ride once. Hitchhiking 1,000 miles in the state with my buddy, 5 or 6 trips. Going to my uncle's farm for a few days in summer to be with my cousins. Met my wife to be in 1959. She came here to teach school. We were married in 1961.

Our Parents Knew Before We Got Home
By Clara Soverns of Kansas, Kansas

I have lived in Kansas all my life. I was born at the old Bell Memorial hospital, which is now the Kansas University Medical Center.

We lived three blocks from the hospital. There was about four blocks all the kids could roam. Everybody watched over us. If we did something wrong or got in trouble our parents knew before we got home.

My uncle had an old icehouse in the middle of our block. That was fun but cold to watch them make ice.

Our school was at the end of one block. I had two of my dad's teachers.

We had two mom and pop grocery stores. One was across from the school, and the other at the end of that block. Us kids would buy penny candy, and pop after school.

My grandmother would take me to Macy's to talk to Santa at Christmas. We would ride the bus and while waiting she would hold me and wrap her coat around me. I would peek out back up against her legs to keep warm.

My mother was a good cook. She made us a dish she called Spaghetti Red and it was great the next day too. We had toast and she would pour warm milk over it.

I was married at fourteen and had my first son. We have a large family now. We have grandkids and great-grandkids. We had three daughters, and two sons. We also have now four cats and one dog.

Our kids are gone and have families of their own, but they take care of dad and mom.

I can remember taking a bath in the old tin tubs. Put it near that old potbelly stove. We use to put bread on that stove to toast.

My dad was teaching me to skate one day in our back alley and he broke his wrist. We had old iron skates with a key.

In the winter my dad would take us sledding down the old hill to Southwest Blvd. My brother and I would lie on top of his back.

My mother and her sister my aunt use to take us kids down to Turkey Creek to catch crawdads. My mom would cook them. That was great. My aunts would take lots of outdoor showers with me. Turn that cold hose on, it was fun!

Never Will Forget
By Lois Jones of Chillicothe, Missouri
Born 1938

The day on the family farm starts through rain, snow, ice, or mud the chores have to be done. Sometimes it's hard to greet the day with a smile realizing the work to do. We lived in a two-story house heated with a wood stove. On cold nights we would heat bricks on the stove wrap them in newspaper and take them to bed to keep our feet warm. Dad farmed with horses to make the best of the land. It was a few years before electricity was available.

My parents did not have it easy in the thirties on the farm making a living and starting a family. I remember my folks saying as a wedding gift her folks gave them a milk cow with a calf. We always had plenty of milk to cook with making everything possible to use the milk, biscuits and gravy, custards, soups, cottage cheese, and butter. As a small child growing up we all had jobs to do, feed the chickens, gather the eggs, slop the hogs, and keep the wood box full for the cooking stove. The job that took the longest was churning the cream to make butter, and then we got to drink the buttermilk. There was always plenty of food on the table to eat, sometimes not what you liked but you ate it anyway.

Summertime the folks had a large garden. When the vegetables were ready, everyone helped to prepare them for canning. We had fruit trees so canned apples and peaches in the fall. The neighbors would come help when the folks butchered two to three hogs at a time. The meat was cured and hung in the cellar, canned, or hung in a well to keep cool.

We would often during the summertime take a bath in a creek that runs through the backside of the farm.

I never will forget the one room schoolhouse. The teacher would come early to clean and get the room warm from a potbelly wood stove in the back of the room. She would ride her horse most of the time. The outhouse did not bother us because we had the same at home.

My sister age 6 and I was 5 years old walked a mile to school. Our mother fixed us each a lunch in a metal lunch box every day. Sometimes we would have an egg sandwich on homemade bread, or a biscuit and always a cookie or piece of cake.

Girls wore dresses that were made of flour sacks, wintertime we wore long cotton socks fastened to a homemade contraption to hold up the socks. We had snow pants to keep warm walking to school but took them off when we got to school. Students all drank out of a tin cup that hung on the well pump or out of a bucket in back of the room all using the same metal dipper. There were two girls and one boy in my class.

Games we played at recess were marbles, drop the handkerchief or ring around the rosie. My parents rented until 1944 when they bought a farm a few miles away so we moved in the spring of 1944. We now lived in a school district where we were bused to school in a small town.

I could not tell time when I started at the new school. The teacher sent me with another student that knew how to tell time to help me. I really had trouble it was hard for me but finally I got it figured out.

Saturday evenings the family would go into a small town, parents would buy their few groceries for the week. Summer time they had a silent movie in the park.

Sundays everything was closed and every Sunday the folks took us to Sunday school and church. If the businesses closed on Sunday today, there would be more attending church instead of shopping.

If the kids of today had a job to look forward to instead of watching TV or riding around in a vehicle thinking of trouble to get in to.

We always had home cooked meals and the family would all set down at once to the table to eat. Sundays after church, we usually had extra family members for dinner plus a dessert. The children all learn to cook at an early age.

My sister and I would help do dishes we would line up wooden kitchen chairs from cabinet to cupboard to put dishes away.

I married a farmer in the sixties and he drowned in a boating accident leaving me with four young children to raise by myself. I managed to stay on the farm and children all graduated from High School. I am still on the farm and have a garden every year.

Remember a smile does not cost anything and has no value to anyone until it is given away.

Perfectly Fit Dresses
By Neva Everly of Bethany, Missouri
Born 1926

I grew up in the great depression era. Jobs, money, and food were scarce. All people were poor or not wealthy, not like the great difference between the really wealthy and the middle class or poor people of today.

Most people made their own clothes. At the beginning of the school year I would choose three designs of cotton material from the catalog, my mother would order enough of each one to make me three school dresses. She usually made her own pattern but the dresses always fit perfectly. Everything had to be washed, starched, and ironed, no permanent press. Some of the boys came to school barefooted until it became cold or snowed. Child-like I thought they just liked going barefooted, now I know they didn't have shoes until it was necessary.

We played games like house, where the tallest children were always the parents, hide and seek, tag, hop-scotch, drop the handkerchief, and ring around the rosie. Girls had paper dolls, the dolls were cut from the newspaper, and the next copies had clothes that would fit. Also, you could buy paper dolls in books. We also roller skated where there was a sidewalk.

Food wasn't too plentiful, so some people ate rabbit, squirrel, and picked dandelion greens to cook for a vegetable.

Most children had the red measles, German measles, chicken pox, and mumps.

We were vaccinated for small pox. The most feared disease was polio, which crippled many children and adults, and was fatal to

The first and second grade class in Gilman City, MO in 1932

many. At that time, they weren't certain how it was contracted. It was a wonderful day when the vaccine was discovered.

Since small towns and rural areas had no running water we had outhouses, or privies, as we called them. For toilet tissue, we used Sears catalogs, some people used corncobs.

We also had feather bed mattresses. Ticking was filled with goose or chicken feathers. We had to shake the feather bed each morning and smooth it out. Some people had straw mattresses.

I Should Have Been the Hero
By Gene Steinmeyer of Maryville, Missouri

The sign just outside the city limits said, Clatonia – Population 220. Now, 40 years later, the sign signals growth of 70 people, to 290. It's not a growth though, just a different time. Forty years ago, most the residents were second and third generation citizens of the Clatonia area. Families raised their kids, the school thrived with students from the town and country, and retired farmers moved to town to be close to their grandchildren.

I had finally made it to double digits in age. At 12 years old, school was finally out. I had to do my required chores, like mow lawns, pull weeds, or hang clothes outside on the line. That was the most demeaning chore since a gorgeous high school cheerleader, who was my neighbor, spent most of her summer lying outside working on her tan. She only seemed to notice me when I was doing the outside laundry. Embarrassing!

If I was dedicated, I could finish those chores well before lunch. The rest of the day was spent with my passion, baseball. I usually

received $1.50 for mowing a lawn. That meant 15 packs of Topps baseball cards with five cards per pack. It also had a hard stick of bubble gum that usually was thrown to a stray dog.

After lunch meant a meeting with a few good friends to play baseball in one of two pastures that happen to be situated right in the middle of the town. They were affectionately called Dandelion Park and Cow Pie Park. One was covered with yellow flower weeds and the other was covered with you know what.

After a quick supper, it usually meant little league baseball practice at the high school baseball diamond. A father volunteered to coach us and we felt like major leaguers. Our team was just average and the coaching was below average. It didn't matter as long as a bat, glove, and almost white ball were involved.

If summer days got too hot for a long game, Bobby, who was equally nerdy about baseball cards and I would play a baseball card game Bobby had invented. We would put together a roster, keep statistics, and play with our heroes on baseball cards for hours. Some obscure players became our favorite. Virgil Trucks was my favorite pitcher. Smokey Burgess, a catcher and pitch hitter, was Bobby's go to player. I still loved the famous players best. My hero was Mickey Mantle. I loved the Yankees and sold my soul to get the entire starting line-up. I even had Hector Lopez, the forgotten Yankee outfielder. The other two outfielders were Mantle and Roger Maris, who broke Babe Ruth's home run record. I thought life was complete when I traded for Whitey Ford, even if the card was scarred from being clothes pinned to Bobby's bicycle spokes.

I don't know who thought it up, but one of the older kids decided Clatonia should have their own World Series. Every kid was contacted, even the bookworms. That's as close to a computer nerd as there was 40 years ago. It might seem impossible, but 18 kids from Clatonia, population 220, were recruited to play in the baseball classic. The game was played in a vacant lot next to Cow Pie Park. The only real hazards were a junked 1952 Chevy in left field and an uphill slope in right field. Also, there wasn't much grass, but it didn't matter.

My brother, Roger, was 19 months younger

than me. He hadn't hit his growth spurt. It was easy for me to pick on him when I was in a bad mood. I considered myself the superior athlete to Roger in every phase of the game of baseball. I had more power, was slightly quicker, and definitely knew the game better. I lived baseball. However, we needed Roger to fill out the 18-player roster. The teams were divided amazingly equal. Everyone knows that the real World Series is the best of a seven game series. Seven dates were scheduled, lineups were nailed to a nearby tree, and the fall classic, played during a very hot July in Clatonia, was underway.

Through six games, each team had won three games. I had played pretty well and my younger brother had done very little to improve my image of his baseball skills. Then it was time for game seven. I'm sure the players from each team had trouble sleeping the night before. I know I snuck out of bed to listen to the end of a television western, Sugarfoot. I loved television, even if it was black and white and we only got three channels on a clear day.

Just like the entire series, the game was tight. The game went into the bottom of the ninth tied. My brother and I played on the home team, so we had a chance to win the game. We got a runner on third with one out, but the ninth place hitter, Roger, my brother was scheduled to hit. Roger could barely make contact, so I didn't feel good about his chances. I was wrong. He tapped the ball to the second baseman. Everyone who has any knowledge of baseball is aware you have to hold the runner at third and throw out the runner at first. Every self-respecting baseball fan knows that. Bobby Richardson, the Yankees second baseman, had taught me that. The Clatonia youth playing second base that day had no such knowledge. He ignored the runner at third as he bolted for home with the winning run. Instead, he threw Roger out at first. What an idiot. We had won the game on a fielder's choice. We had won the Clatonia World Series. Then the unthinkable happened. My teammates carried Roger off the field on their shoulder. He was the hero. He had driven in the winning run with a tap and an idiot. Roger didn't even know the definition of a fielder's choice. I had dreamed of being that guy on everyone's shoulders. Now my nerdy little brother will be forever remembered as

the hero of the Clatonia World Series. It wasn't fair, just like the homer Bill Mazeroski hit in the bottom of the ninth to beat my Yankees in 1960. At least that hit went over the wall.

We Wore Out the Grass
By Helen Walters of St. Joseph, Missouri
Born 1947

Reminds me of the time when my brothers and sisters, there were six of us, were playing in the backyard when mom and dad were gone. I think they went to the store. We lived up on a hill and our backyard was a nice big hill. Well one day, we were not very old; we went down our backyard and went sliding down. When we wore out the grass it didn't slide very well so one of us went into the house and got moms box of Tide soap and used the whole box. Now that was a lot better, we could slide much better. We were so dirty with mud and grass all over us you could not tell who was who, and we were having so much fun we didn't hear mom and dad come home. We were in trouble. Dad shouted about the yard with all the grass gone. Mom was mad about her new box of Tide. Lucky we didn't get a whipping, but we were grounded. Mom got the water hose and hosed us all down outside, made us strip down and go take a bath. In the wintertime, we had our own hill to sleigh ride.

Mary, Olga, Helen, and Mike in 1950-1960

Socialism and Democracy
By Ed Coles of Cameron, Missouri
Born 1937

Sometimes I feel like writing things down to remember and to remind me from time to time what is really important. This is one of those times. There is much talk that we are moving in the direction of socialism, our latest elections prove to some degree that socialism is more a part of our nation than the original purpose the founding fathers intended. From a personal view, it seems to me that socialism and democracy are incompatible. I often heard early in life that our nation was the land of opportunity, granted we had some major growing to do since the time of my youth. However, the land of opportunity was more a concept than a plan to implement.

I have been reading some books about the history of our nation and the leaders that have been involved in the creation of this nation. George Washington was a one of a kind type of leader. From George I get the idea that the two things he really held dear in his leadership role was the idea that personal liberty was to be valued. After all, one of his greatest accomplishments was that he always did things his way. His leadership proved that liberty was not possible without responsibility. George left Mount Vernon, his home, which he dearly loved, for eight years, to lead the army. The point I want to make is that George not only believed that liberty and responsibility was important to democratic rule, but that it was essential.

Another leader that I have been enthralled by is Abraham Lincoln. Probably we enjoy our way of life today because of the efforts of Abraham Lincoln. From Abraham, I learned that one must prioritize. In all of his efforts the one effort that was made clear was that, he wanted to preserve the union. He said the union will stand, and it did. The cost to our nation was huge, I learned, when we visited Springfield, Illinois, at the Lincoln Library, as many as 1,300,000 people lost their lives in the Civil War.

Our history books are filled with great leaders, we need to include Harry Truman too. He used the atom bomb to end the Great War of the last century. It has been said we were going to win that war anyway, but the bomb and its use would make clear that no country could go to war without there being some lasting consequences. Hooray for Harry.

What I am trying to say is that socialism and democracy are not compatible. I learned in college something to the effect that socialism was designed to represent that from each in accordance with his ability and to each according to his need. Democracy was to be reflected as follows: From each in accordance with his ability and to each in accordance to his ability. With that concept in mind, socialism does not lend itself well to the idea that we live in the land of opportunity. I think it unwise to punish those who seem to prosper in our country and make incomes more uniform. It seems only wise to understand that from each in accordance with his ability and to each in accordance with his ability, can we have the upward mobility and personal aspirations that have always been a part of who and what we are and who and what we represent.

I want to end with one final thought. My son told me that there are personal mission statements. These seem to be developed for more upwardly motivated folks. For our country, I like to think of our constitution as our national mission statement. It tells us how we can do things and even guarantees certain freedoms. It seems to me that our country changed our national mission statement when they decided we should operate with the concept of separation between church and state. That, perhaps, was not a bad thing, except that it gave the power to control our religion to the state. It is no longer just us, the state that will decide who, when, where, and if the free exercise of religion can take place. To me that was a major infringement upon our personal liberty. Even Honest Abe said, "Government must guard from being too intrusive into our personal liberty that it can no longer react in times of great emergencies." I am of the opinion that our constitution can be something perpetual in nature, but it must not have powers that make our way of life unbalanced. What I am trying to say is that some things need to belong to the folks and the issue of religion is one of those.

Really, I am trying to end this; however, I need to end it with one final thought. When our government decided to infringe upon our personal liberty, it was only a small thing to move into our personal responsibilities. Health care comes under the scope of personal liberty, no one should tell someone else what to take in the way of medicines or prescribe pills that one would not want to take. Finances for health care comes under the scope of personal responsibility. What I am trying to suggest is that our way of life and health care must be personal. When the government gets into health care we move even more so in the direction of socialism.

I need to add one final thought about personal responsibility that addresses the minimum wage. That to me is government's way of getting involved in small businesses. My thinking is that we need smaller government not a bigger more involved government. Perhaps, if I were to be in charge, I would add to our road map, our constitution, and to add one final amendment. It could say, "The right to worship shall belong to and be vested in the people of the United States."

I think it only proper to support my thoughts. I have a degree in Sociology from MSSU, Missouri Southern State University. It seems only natural when we make changes to our road map there will be consequences. The world will generally follow us in what we do. Today the world is awash in debt. They call it sovereign debt. It could be that the world has taken over too much of the folk's personal liberty as well as their personal responsibility.

My First Job, Date, and Marriage
By Bonnie Place of Gallatin, Missouri
Born 1926

Summer was here, the last day of school walking home I past the cafeteria "Jerry Anns." There was a sign in the window "Help wanted." I went in and was walking on air when I got the job. I went home and told my mom and dad I had a summer job, they were neither one very happy, and my dad said no way was I working and waiting on tables. I said, "Well I would think you would rather I be working than running the streets like all my friends." His remark was, "What made you think you would be running the streets!" After much pleading, I got to keep my job.

I met my first boyfriend there. I was only allowed to date on Saturday afternoon. My first date, we decided to walk a couple of blocks and then take a bus to the movie to

Bonnie's husband, J. B. Place

the Missouri theater in downtown St. Joseph. When we got on the bus there sat my mother and sister, we went to the back so we could get off first. I was really upset with them. When we bought our tickets, guess who was in line, my mother and sister. Went upstairs to sit and watch the movie. After the movie, we had ice cream and a coke and as we were leaving the drug store, my heel on my shoe broke. We went to the shoe repair shop and while sitting there who walk in? You guessed it, my mother and my sister. I cried myself to sleep for several nights. We moved to the country

Bonnie Brown

126

that fall and I went to a different school and it was too far for me to keep my job.

My dad bought St. Josephs livestock auctions. The next few years were busy for everyone in my family. WWII was declared and everyone in our country wanted to do whatever we could do to help. I went to town and tried to join the women services. I was only 16, but was tall for my age. They told me I had to have my parents' consent, like that was going to happen.

The next year a friend and I started helping at the U.S.O. you were not allowed to date any of the young men that came in just serve them and visit with them. They could not take you home. We both worked there and I went to dances at Rosecrans Field, well chaperoned. Those dances were held at the officers club. I met a young man there I had seen at the U.S.O. that summer. I was staying in town with my grandparents and I came home from work one evening and on my grandparents front porch visiting with them was my future husband. He had found out from my friend where I lived. I was working a Hirsch Department store at the corner of 8th and Edmond downtown St. Joseph. We were married that next fall. Talk about learning about life, being married so young. My dad said I could never come home if I married this young man. But I was always welcome with open arms.

A Pet Coyote
By Kay Gibson of Watson, Missouri
Born 1943

Watson, Missouri is in the utmost corner of northwest Missouri. It's almost a ghost town now, but oh the memories of my youth there. I was born during WWII. My dad already had one girl and he needed a boy to help him with the farming. But since a new baby allotted an additional 25 pounds of sugar and flour, he kept me. He made a farmer out of me and I helped him farm all of his life.

Dad put me out in the fields at an early age. I cut my teeth on the drawbar of a tractor. At 14, I learned how to drive the tractor. I tilled the soil, rolled the newly planted corn, and cultivated corn. Back then, we cut weeds by hand instead of using chemicals. My dad raised an excess of everything. He planted eight acres of watermelons and we hoed them.

Our school was a small school. I not only knew everyone in my class, but I knew everyone in school. I loved school and never wanted to miss a day. We played basketball and couldn't miss a game. We walked a ½ mile on a dirt road to catch the bus that only came the highway. Many cold nights after the games, we walked in from that road to the house. In the summertime, on Mondays when my mom washed, we would water down the dirt road in front of the house to keep the dust from blowing on the damp clothes hanging on the line.

When I was little, Watson had a doctor who was also a state representative. Dr. Gray sang "Jimmy Crack Corn" to me while he gave me shots. Watson had shows on the lawn when I was young and sometimes we got to go to town to see them. We had a bandstand in the park and one time, we had a hula-hoop contest, and no, I didn't win. At one time, Watson had several stores, a couple banks, and a doctor's office. All that is gone now. We don't even have a gas station anymore. It was the last thing to go.

A couple of our favorite pets were a pet coyote and a pet badger. The baby coyote came to our house due to a flood and he stayed at the house during the day, but went up into the hills at night. Due to his killing chickens and baby pigs, we gave him to the conservation department and they made movies with him. We had a baby brother by then and we didn't want any harm to come to him. The badger we had when I was 16. He was so tiny when we got him; I used an eyedropper to feed him. I had my driver's license and he liked to ride in the car with me. He hid under the seats and would surprise my friends by poking his head out on occasion. He loved soda pop and ice cream. He too ended up with the conservation department because his tunnels were undermining our shed and house. Along the bluff where we lived, about 10 feet down, there were rows of rock that stuck out of the side of the hill. Snakes loved to sun there. Our coyote loved to kill them. When my sister and I saw our first "spreading viper" snake, we were certain we had encountered a cobra.

We didn't have a milkman. My sister and I would walk up to my grandma's house each day and bring home the milk for the next day. My mother made our clothes. She could look at a pretty dress that we had admired in a book or a store and she could make one similar. We lived at the foot of the Loess Hills. We roamed those hills. I doubt my mom knew where we were half of the time. When my sister and I were teens, we decided to sleep out on top of the hill. We carried our blankets and sandwiches up to the top. Then we went and visited an aunt who lived a couple hilltops over. When we returned, a varmint had eaten our sandwiches. We had flashlights and decided it would be funny for one of us to stand with a sheet over us while the other shined the light on us when a car would come down the highway. The car stopped and then took off, roaring its pipes all the way to Watson. We thought we knew who it was, but we never mentioned it, and he never did either. One night, a car drove as close to the hill as it could get and shone its lights on us. Our parents didn't know we did this, and though it was fun then, I'd be scare to try it now. We were never bored. We gathered eggs and fed the pigs every evening after school. We ironed and did dishes. We helped dad in the fields. Dad made work fun and I still enjoy working outside. We led very sheltered lives in our little corner of the world, and though things have changed, I intend to live in this area until I die.

"696"
By John Pope of Little Rock, Arkansas
Born 1925

I was born on a farm in Dekalb County, Missouri. We soon moved to a farm in Nodaway County near Maryville. I started school in a one-room country schoolhouse and my first teacher was my mother. Midway through my third grade year we moved to Maryville. My mother lost her teaching job, and with the depression years, it was difficult to make it on the farm.

Maryville had one Taxicab Company. It was the "502." My folks decided to start another cab company and somehow they did. The telephone number and name was the "696." With the help of other relatives living in Maryville they made a living.

One exciting thing that happened to me during our first year in Maryville was my winning a Shetland pony. The city fathers had sold tickets for a pony to be given away at Christmas. The drawing was held on the

The pony won by John at Christmas in 1933

courthouse lawn near the old bandstand. I can still see myself leading that pony down the East Second Street to where my grandparents lived. There was quite a number of town kids trailing along behind.

I spent many hours riding in the cab on calls, and soon knew where every street and business in Maryville was. Not too many people owned cars during the 1930s. Much of the cab company's business was to and from the college. You would pick up or drop off your fares mainly at two locations at the college. One the east door of the Administration Building and two the Women's Residence Hall, at that time those two buildings and the Gym made up the college campus.

My family lived above a jewelry store on Main Street, Highway US 71, between 4th and 5th Streets. The apartment was also the office for "696." Two other young boys lived within two blocks of where I lived and soon the three boys became friends and spent quite a lot of time playing together. One friend I will call P.H., the other friend I will call R.L. The father of P.H. ran a small hamburger joint called the Bearcat Inn. It was very popular with the college crowd, especially with the football players. I can recall seeing many big guys going in and out of the Inn. P.H. and his family lived in a house next door to the Bearcat Inn on the west. The second friend R.L. lived with his family in a house on the northeast corner of west 4th and Fillmore Street. R.L.'s father was in business in Maryville. The square block where these houses were located had much open ground, which made a good place to play for the boys.

During the period we lived close we had many good times. However nothing stays the same. P.H. and his family moved out of Maryville to a small town to the east. I saw P.H. only once after he moved. P.H. died at an early age.

R.L. and family moved to a larger home farther west in Maryville. We continued to see each other some, but slowly drifted apart. We have however seen each other at Maryville High School class reunions through the years.

R.L. and J.P. are still alive and in their late '80s.

J.P.'s family moved to Minnesota, but J.P. finished High School in Maryville staying with his grandparents. J.P. also obtained a B.S. degree from N.W.M.S.H.

R.L. obtained a Dr. Degree from Ohio State, and later was employed by a large Oil Company. He became one of the top executives before he retired.

As I Remember It
By Ramona Fuenfhausen of Liberty, Missouri
Born 1934

I was born March 25, 1934, the youngest of three daughters of Roy and Snowma Fleming. We lived on a farm near the Shoal Creek area somewhere south of Breckenridge, Missouri. I recall going to visit Butch and Juanita Skinner in a buggy drawn by a horse. I recall while we were there we were very shy and would be very quiet and wish we could play her player piano, and occasionally she would open it up and play it for us and I thought that was a beautiful sound.

Once in a while, we would go on down the road to Juanita's mom and dad's house that would have been Horse and Genevive Bryant. I thought they had a beautiful house and very elegant furniture. It was probably just ordinary but you must keep in mind we were very poor and did not have much furniture.

I did not think of myself as desperately poor as we lived pretty much like all of the other people we knew. We had no phone, or electricity, the radio was battery, my mother made our clothes out of feed sacks, and we walked a mile through fields to a one-room country school. Our lighting was kerosene lamps, our heat was wood stove and mothers stove in the kitchen was also wood.

I also recall going to Butch and Juanita's and going out into the cane field where they had a mule tied to the thing that went around and stirred the cane as it was being cooked down. Dad and Butch would gather in the cane and get it into the pot and Juanita and mom would keep the fire and mule going, what great times they must have been, even though I was not aware of it at the time. What hard work for the adults living in those times. The cane was made in the following manner: The mill was a series of cogs, where someone had to feed the stalks a few at a time. A single horse was led round and round to make the cogs turn. This was often a child's job. As the juice was extracted, it was strained into a barrel. The pan for boiling was set over a deep pit where a suitable fire was made and kept going as long as it took to boil off a batch of molasses. The juice was transferred to the pan and a careful watch began. Skimming off the foam and stoking the fire was a constant three to four hour vigil. When it was just right, it was poured into one-half or one gallon jars or buckets for our own use.

Mom and Juanita were like sisters and did many things together. Juanita called mom "Snow." I can still hear her coming in the door before daylight at our house with a washtub and a sharp paring knife in her hand and talking very fast and sort of loud and laughing a lot and telling mom that they must get busy as they had a lot of work to do.

That work would be to pick tomatoes, corn or some other vegetable from the huge garden, often times the three of us were delegated to pick the produce. They would spend the day pickling, peeling, cutting, cooking, and canning whatever the vegetable(s) for the day was ripe and ready for harvest. They did all this on a wood kitchen stove.

The water supply was a sink with a hand pump that you had to prime, priming was the act of pouring a little water in the top of the pump while you pumped the handle really hard until water started coming out. We did not drink that water as it was cistern water, cistern water is that water collected in a well mostly from the runoff of the water into the downspouts on the house. Our drinking water was from another well a short distance from the house with a big pump on it and we had a bucket that we pumped full and took it to the kitchen and it sat by the small pump.

Mom and dad raised and prepared all of our food such as vegetables and meat. We may have been poor but we always had plenty of food on the table and clothes to wear even if they were made from boxes of clothes Aunt Dorothy, would mail to us from Oregon. All of our other clothes were made from feed sacks. In those days, the feed came in pretty printed cotton material. Mom would go with dad to the feed store to buy the feed in order to get the printed sacks she wanted. Since there would only be no more than two yards of material in a sack, she would need more than one sack of the same color for dresses for herself and us girls, as we grew bigger.

Mother did not have many patterns to use to make our dresses most of the time she would see a picture of a dress she liked and then design her own pattern.

I remember mom making homemade cheese. She had her own cheese press in the basement, which she and dad put together. I also remember coming home from school, Turkey Creek, and being so hungry and

The Fleming family in 1937

cold and mom would have made homemade cinnamon rolls and bread and when you opened the door, the smell was wonderful. In the early days of living on the farm, she cooked on a wood stove, as there was no electricity out in the country at that time. We moved back to the farm when I was about 16 or 17, the REA (Rural Electric Association) had gone through the country, and then all of us country folk were able to have electricity.

We moved to what we always referred to as the "Dale Place" north of Breckenridge when I was about 5 years old and that is where I started to school in a little one-room schoolhouse in the country known as the "Reed School." I have a picture of Reed Church, as the school is gone. My grandpa Cicero Fleming had taught at that very same school. He was oft times sent to the Country Schools to keep the young men in line as sometimes they would go to the country school until they

were sixteen even if the school only went to eighth grade as the law was that a child could not drop out of school legally until he or she was sixteen. Consequently, some of the boys would get pretty good size and get to be a little more than some of the female teachers could handle. Cicero was a very small man but was written up in the Paxton Annals as "A well known educator and strong disciplinarian."

The first car I can remember us owning was one that dad bought from Butch and Juanita. It had belonged to Juanita's son Byrle Copple, he was in the service, and they were selling his car for him. He was in WWII. His brother, Richard Copple's tooth prints were in the dash of the car as he was in it and was in a wreck and that is how the prints got there. My dad did not have to go to the war as he was a farmer, but they were afraid he might have to go if it lasted.

As WWII dragged on a lot of exempt people were drafted. In the evening, after dinner we would sit around the big cabinet style battery operated radio and listen to the news of the war. Dad's favorite was Gabriel Heatter. I remember sitting on my dad's lap while we all listened to the news and we were expected to be real quiet, as he did not want to miss anything.

We moved to our farm south of Breckenridge when I was in about the second or third grade. My folks had scraped enough together to buy a 180 acre farm.

We all had chores. Barbara and Naomi had to help milk the cows. I was too young so my job was to feed the chickens and gather the eggs. If you have never taken eggs from underneath an old sitting hen you have not lived.

In the winter, Naomi and I were responsible for gathering in the wood every day for the stoves. In the summer, they would send us to the cornfield with a hoe and have us chopping cocklebur and warned us not to chop down any of the new corn stalks. We were also given a small can with a small amount of

Ramona's family in 1944-45

kerosene and told to go pick potato bugs off of the potato plants in the garden. We mowed the yard with one of those old hand pushed mowers and sometimes we would use a rope and one would push while the other pulled from the front.

A real joy would be when the hogs would get out of their pens and go into the cornfields. It usually would be discovered pretty early in the morning and dad would call us all downstairs and we would head to the field to try and find the hogs in the corn, which was usually much taller than the hogs. You could hear them but never find them. I hated those darn hogs! Boy they were good to eat when dad butchered them.

We lived there until I was in the fifth grade and my folks rented the farm out and bought the restaurant in Breckenridge. We moved into town and lived above the restaurant. I hated that time of my life because mom would have to get up really early and go downstairs to start the cooking for the day and I always felt so lonely. I then started to Breckenridge School in the 6th grade. I never took the 5th grade, I took 6th grade twice, during that period of time for some reason or another they decided it would benefit somebody to skip 4th graders to 6th grade then the next year they would go back to the 5th grade. They also skipped 6th graders to 8th grade then the following year they would go back and take 7th grade, so my sister Naomi went from 7th grade into high school. It made the rest of her years of school a little complicated.

After the folks sold the restaurant, they decided to open a drug store and it had a teen town in the back. I was not allowed to go into teen town as they told me I was too young.

Naomi spent a lot of time there. Barb had to help work as a clerk.

Dad went to work for Frank Trager building bridges. We moved to the "Pond" house a block over from Main Street on the black top. We lived there several years. Mom worked for the dry goods store. Byrle Copple worked for dad, as dad was the foreman on the job. Clastine ran a beauty shop. Sammie Sue "Henry" Heavner and I were best friends and spent a lot of time together. She would stay at our house when there was a ball game to go to. We were both on the basketball team. I was #16 and played guard, and fouled out of almost every game I played. I was also a cheerleader and the drum majorette of the band.

We moved back to the farm when I was about a senior in high school. When I graduated from high school, I went to work for the Hamilton Shoe Factory for the summer. I rode to work with Nancy Skinner. She was Butch Skinner's niece. In September, I quit the factory and went to Kansas City, Missouri to go to Kansas City secretarial school.

Boyhood Memories
By Delbert Beechy of Bloomfield, Iowa

Memories of a childhood are probably the most vivid and cherished of anytime in our lives. I remember very well when I was 7 years old. Dad and mom, with 10 children, moved from Topeka, Indiana to western Grundy County, Missouri close to Jamesport in 1958. With one semi load of belongings, we only got within 3 miles of our destination. We met mud head on. So things were loaded on wagons and with teams and a neighbor with a ton truck, we made it the rest of the way. This was very different from flat, paved Indiana.

We are of the Amish faith and we attended church regularly. We had church in our homes.

There was hard work from the very start. We went to Gee School, a one-room country school when I was in the 1st and 2nd grade. The first morning dad drove the scholars with a two-seated buggy and one horse. We encountered mud and hills, would you believe. We thought the school was just a little ways east of us. After driving three miles dad stopped at a T road, by a house, to ask where the school was. Well, said the man, it's

131

another three quarters of a mile south. So we had almost four miles to school. We walked the distance many times. In muddy weather, our boots got so heavy and wide that we had to shake them off before going on.

We had birthday parties and box suppers. One day after a birthday party, mom came and picked us up with the two-seated buggy and two horses. About one half mile from home a balloon burst and one horse makes a jerk, breaking a single tree, where the tug was fastened. The tongue came out of the neck yolk in front and stuck in the ground. The tongue broke and the buggy came to a screeching halt. In a few seconds, the two horses were headed lickety split toward home. In no time flat, they were over the hill a quarter of a mile away.

I don't remember who stopped the horses, but there were some anxious moments until we all got home, safe and sound. I remember an older man in the community who used to say it was worth $25 to see horses running away! But that is truly a matter of opinion.

We had no bathroom and just one outside two holer. Sometimes this was a very busy place for a family of twelve, and yes, the Sears and Montgomery Ward catalogs became very useful in these privies. Money was scarce to buy anything from these catalogs, but they could be utilized for other purposes! Cheaper than toilet paper!

With no bathroom we'd fix a place in the living room with a big tub of water for our weekly bath. Of course we draped some sheets around us, and with water being scarce we would use the same water several times. We had running water, run and get it!

But dad had three ponds and in the good ol' summer time us boys, there were seven of us at the time we moved, spent many hours swimming. Over the noon hour or in the evening. Our well often went dry those first years and swimming was serious business. Even for Saturday evening baths. Our longer hair sometimes became very hard to comb because of pond water. After a long day in the warm sun we were glad to skinny dip in the pond. We had no time or money for swimming trunks. We would run out on the diving board and down we went headfirst. Wow, was it ever cold at the bottom.

Dad had a sawmill and us boys all worked there at one time or another. This helped build strong backs and muscles. Sawmilling is good work for a man with a lot of boys.

We usually had a lot of threshing to do, oats and wheat. I always liked to help pitch bundles or run the bundle wagon. The old threshing machine was a marvelous thing. Sometimes the shocks, as they were called, with oats and wheat bundles, stood in the field for at least three weeks. This gave snakes a chance to hang out under the shock. Several times we found big old rattlesnakes underneath. Sometimes there was a nest of young ones. We had a dog named Shep that was a very good snake dog. If he got the chance he would grab an old rattler about four inches behind the head and literally shake the dickens out of it.

I also remember very well how we would sometimes encounter huge black snakes six or seven feet long. Sometimes they would be up in the rafters of an old barn where they ate sparrow and pigeon eggs. There were large round bumps in the snakes where you could see they had swallowed whole pigeon eggs.

Dad started raising turkey's right after our move. We had 2,000 in a flock and we usually had two flocks. We'd put them in pens of chicken wire and steel posts about a half-acre in size. About once a week we'd move them to a new pen or down the field. There were feeders to move, fountains, and shelters. I drove many a steel post and pulled them out a week or two later. We hauled feed to these big birds with a team and wagon. We loaded and unloaded with scoop shovels and muscle and sweat. There were bins in our granary with corn and concentrate (protein) in separate bins. One boy got in one bin and another in another bin. We'd scoop so many scoops of corn and so many of concentrate. This way it was mixed by the time it was loaded. Sometimes two or three loads a day.

They had to be fed rain or shine. Sometimes the mud got halfway to the horses knees. We had a wagon with a tank that we hauled water with. Several loads a day and extra on Saturday to last till Monday morning. No work on Sunday.

Sometimes on moonlit nights something would make the turkeys stampede. They would crowd against the fence until the posts would break or bend. Then they'd crawl over each other and on to the outside where they were free. The next morning we had turkeys almost in our front yard. We had no choice but to chase them back. Sometimes a quarter mile. One of us would go ahead with a load of feed or water, and the rest would chase them with a long stick with a red flag on the end. They were afraid of red. It took a lot of sticks.

In the fall of the year we'd load them out on big semis. Here again we loaded by hand. Planks were fixed on the side of the trucks where men stood. We had a crew of men and we caught them by hand and hoisted them up to the men on the plank. Some of the big toms weighed 30 pounds!

In wet weather we had to run them up in the yard by the house to load and the trucks stayed on the road. Sometimes this was about a quarter of a mile. The weak ones would get down in the mud and eventually couldn't move. With their wings in the mud they would flop and flop and if you were close, you were bound to get plastered with mud! With a flock of 2,000 turkeys it was no small task to run them up the farm lane to the yard.

Like I said the weak ones would get down and the ones behind would trample right over them. If we saw them in time we would catch them and put them over the fence and later we'd butcher them. We always had neighbors helping us and we'd give them one of those turkeys for pay!

Now this mud would get sticky with manure mixed in and by the time the job was done we would look like black people. It took more than pond water to get us clean.

This turkey manure was potent stuff and that's how we built up the soil. We raised good crops without chemical fertilizer. But it made weeds grow too and several fields had a mat of cockleburs in the corn. We boys had the "fun" job of pulling those burs by hand! But that was better than pesticides, which were about unknown at that time.

Several things stand out in memory of the late 1950s, the first years we lived there. We had a neighbor, Thelma Atkinson, that was a widow lady that lived back in a dead end road, and she had an old telephone hanging on the wall that had a crank you used to dial. There were party lines where just a few neighbors used the same line. I remember some eavesdropping would be done and you had to wait to make a call until your neighbor would get done talking.

I've mentioned how muddy it would get

at times, but we also had some very dry years, and also grasshoppers. But mostly good memories remain etched in my mind and I wouldn't trade them for anything.

Growing Up in Gilman City
By Joyce Ann Coffman of Ames, Iowa
Born 1950

I grew up in a small town, Gilman City, Missouri, located in north central Missouri just 38 miles from the Iowa line. I graduated from Harrison County R-IV school just like my dad, Everett, Jr. in 1932 and my Aunt Elaine Lawrence in 1936. After my dad's discharge from the army in 1945, he and his sister, Elaine, built and operated the Lawrence Service Station located on Highway 146 from 1946-1976 first as a DX affiliate and later as Texaco.

In those days, the customers drove up to the gas pump over a cord that rang a bell. Attendants went out to pump the gas, wash the windshield and windows, and check the oil, all a part of the daily job whether it was raining, snowing, very hot or cold. They didn't even receive tips! Lawrence Service also owned a transport to haul fuel from Kansas City. There was also a farm delivery truck for fuel oil deliveries to farmers and in-town customers.

My grandfather, Everett, Sr., and wife Myrtle, moved to Gilman in 1913 where he was a foreman of a bridge crew on the QO & KC railroad. That railroad line followed along

Lawrence Service Station
Everett Lawrence, Jr. and Charlie Tourney

Everett, Jessie May, and Elaine

highway 146 so Gilman was a bustling city in the mid-1900s. Everett, Sr., quit the railroad and in 1915 opened the first independent service station in Gilman, the Gilman Oil Company. He sponsored a 25-piece band, Foxy Entertainers, who performed on the radio station in Shenandoah, Iowa.

Elaine, Auntie, as I called her, drove me to and from school every day. On the way home, we stopped where she and granny, Myrtle, lived that is now named Broadway Street. Granny always had a slice of homemade cake or pie waiting for me to devour, what a treat!

My mom Jessie May, was a conservative hard-working lady. My dad was quite busy at the station so the chores around our house and property were left to mom. She did not have an automatic washer till 1994. We had a wringer washing machine and the wringer part quit working first. So mom squeezed and wrung clothes by hand. There were two rinse tubs used to get the soap out after washing. Clothes were hung outside on the lines even in cold temperatures so frozen stiff clothes were brought inside later. The Firestone refrigerator was still working till 1999 when I thought she needed to update. Actually, my concern was for her defrosting the freezer and carrying hot water to accomplish that.

On December 22, 1961, there was a terrible snowstorm; I was in 6th grade. My mom and auntie went to Gallatin to the bank that morning. They had a slow, dangerous drive on K Highway back to Gilman. My mom guided by locating the tops of fence posts. School had not been dismissed and it was too dangerous to send out buses by then. This was the day of our Christmas Party at school; we even had a

tree in our classroom. I was very disappointed to miss the party because mom and auntie got back to town and came directly to the school for me. Many kids were stranded in the school building or sheltered at downtown businesses or homes in town. Some kids did not make it home for Christmas.

Christmas for my family started Christmas Eve, waiting for my dad to close the filling station early, around 7:00 pm, which always seemed to be a long time. We usually had tuna salad sandwiches, chips, and date pudding with whip. These are days prior to Cool Whip- we took a package of Dream Whip, milk, and a beater to make the whipped topping. Christmas Eve would usually be at our house and Christmas Day dinner at granny/auntie's for many years. I don't remember going through mountains of newspaper ads to pick out what I wanted for Christmas. We didn't hear about Black Friday and the race of stores to open at early morning hours.

I'm very proud of growing up in Gilman City, the upbringing by my family and the small school education I received which have all shaped me into the person I am today.

Just Country Kids
By Virgil "Junior" Lee Johnson, Jr. of
Richmond, Missouri
Born 1946

I was born in 1946 in Breckenridge, Missouri at home. My mother died when I was 4 years old. I have been told it was pneumonia and also I have been told it was from cancer. I was never positive which one. My father took us to my maternal grandparents, the Harpers, and then disappeared. I had 3 sisters at the time. They were 9 years, 8 years, and 15 months old.

When my grandparents got guardianship of us 4 kids, they were old enough that they were able to draw a check, which back then they referred to as old age assistance. They got welfare because of having us as well. With both incomes, they received about $140 a month.

In 1952, my grandparents bought a 40-acre farm in Carroll County, Missouri. It had a 3-room house on it where they lived with their grown son, Elwood, me, my 3 sisters, and my grandmother's father, eight of us in a three-room house. The house had no running water, electricity, or indoor bathroom. They cooked and heated the house with wood and we used kerosene lamps for lights. Later grandma's sister also lived with us about a year after we moved to that farm. Later when we got electricity and our first TV, I remember great grandpa Logan would be playing his fiddle. We kids would turn up the TV so we could hear it better. Great grandpa Logan would just play his fiddle that much louder.

They always grew a big garden and canned their vegetables. We had hogs, chickens, and cows so we had eggs, milk, butter, and butchered whenever we needed meat. We seldom shopped in town except for staples like flour, coffee, salt, sugar etc… Grandma made our bread, and the best noodles you ever put into your mouth. My uncle hunted small game, and whenever I got older, I had a single shot .22-caliber rifle so I was able to bring home squirrels and rabbits to eat as well. My dogs were keen at letting me know where those squirrels were hiding. If they barked at the base of a tree, you could bet there was a squirrel up there.

My grandpa and Uncle Elwood dug a cellar where we stored our potatoes and canned goods. They dug it with shovels, eight feet deep and twelve by eight feet inside. It was lined with poles they cut and it had old barn wood for a roof, covered with dirt.

My grandpa was ¾ Indian so he knew how to farm and take care of the land and his animals. He and my uncle farmed the 40 acres with a team of gray draft horses named Pet and Bird. Those horses looked like elephants standing up on the hill, they were huge, but grandpa could get them to do most anything he needed them to do. To take care of animals, my grandpa always planted oats for the horses to eat as well as timothy hay. The cows got red clover hay and corn. The corn was picked by hand and thrown into a wagon pulled by the horses. We stored the corn, still on the cob, in a room built onto the side of the barn. After we took the corn off for animal food, we used the cobs as fire starters in our wood stoves.

We had a water well in the yard about a hundred feet deep, but we didn't use that one for water. We used it as our refrigerator. We would put milk in a gallon lard bucket with a lid on it and lower it down by its handle on a rope just above the water line. It kept the milk really good and cold.

There was a small creek that ran through the farm. It provided a great swimming hole and in the winter, we could ice skate for hundreds of yards before we had to turn around to go back. I also spent countless hours collecting American Indian artifacts there. I would cut small trees and use a piece of string to make a bow and used dried horseweeds for arrows. My sisters and I would climb up a small Hickory tree and bend it over. One of us would hang on while the rest would jump off. The tree would spring back up and give us a wild ride, if you could hang on. Another game we played was we would find an old tire and coil up in it. The others would roll it around the yard. But now I can't even be on a swing without getting dizzy. My country basketball goal was a white wall cover off an old car tire nailed to the barn. Grandpa actually bought me a store bought basketball.

We had a radio that was battery operated. Grandma liked to listen to The Grand Ole Opry and the Roy Rogers program. The battery for the radio was six volt and bigger than a loaf of bread. A copper wire was attached to the radio and the wire was ran out the window. That was attached to a copper rod that was driven into the ground. When the battery got weak, we would get a little more use out of it by pouring water on the copper rod where it was driven into the ground.

My grandma had a Maytag washing machine with a gas engine on it. Since we didn't have a water supply in the house for it, my grandpa made a sled with a barrel on it. We would pull the sled to the creek with the horses and fill the barrel with water for the washing machine. Then she would wash the clothes on the porch and hang the clothes over the garden fence.

In the winter, we had feather beds to sleep in. The wood stove would sometimes burn out during the night and when you got up the house was so cold that the water in the wash pan would be frozen. Your first thought was to get a fire started quickly and get back in that feather bed until the fire in the wood stove warmed up the room.

My grandparents who raised me had no education but were determined to see that my sisters and I graduated from high school. My uncle Elwood, my grandparent's oldest son never went to school or got married. He stayed home all his life and helped his parents farm the land and helped take care of us as well. We never attended much church be we were raised in a Christian environment. I remember my grandmother washing dishes at the wood stove, so the water would stay hot, singing The Old Rugged Cross and all the other old familiar hymns. Later we had neighbors that would come get us and take us to church as they went. When I was 12 years old me and my sisters were all baptized in a pond on November 2. It was definitely cold!

One Halloween my friend Randy and I were riding around the small town of Tina near where we lived. We were in our young teens so my grandmother's nephew, Bob, was driving us. We were doing harmless pranks, nothing serious, like putting hay bales and chicken crates in the street. Main Street was and still is gravel.

The next day some of the town's people would go clean it up. We would always volunteer to help but they never knew it was us that had done it. This particular Halloween the Carroll County deputy sheriff came to town. Bob and I took off in the car so that we wouldn't be caught. We weren't sure where Randy went. Later we asked him where he went. He said he hid out in the outhouse behind the general store. He heard the deputy coming so he climbed down into the two-holer toilet and braced himself with his arms and legs underneath the side with a lid. When the deputy opened the door and didn't find anyone, he left. Randy waited a few minutes then climbed out and began to walk home.

My uncle Lewis lived about a mile from us. He had a TV before we did, one of very few around back then. He raised a crop of navy soup beans one year. He pulled the plants and filled a room in his house floor to ceiling. He would allow people to come watch TV only if they shelled beans while they were there.

My grandkids don't believe me whenever I tell them I actually did walk up hill both ways to school when I was in the first grade. Down the hill from home to a creek half way to school then up the hill the rest of the way to school...reversed on the way home. The total distance was approximately half a mile altogether.

At Christmas time, we always went to the woods and cut a cedar tree. We decorated it with paper cutouts and stringed popcorn. We didn't have money for gifts so they were almost always homemade. Sometimes the church would bring a fruit basket with a small gift for the four of us kids. I remember a die cast metal car one year and a football another year.

In those days, we had everything we needed and we didn't need money to buy it. Most of the kids that we went to school with didn't have much either so there wasn't kids making fun of us. We were all just country kids.

I graduated from Tina-Avalon High School in 1964. I got married to Marilyn Hockett in September of 1965. On Christmas Eve of 1965, I got my draft notice to go to the Army. I took that draft notice to Independence, Missouri to a Navy recruiter and told him that I wanted to join the Navy instead. I left for boot camp in May of 1966. I went to boot camp in San Diego as well as commissary school there. That's where our first-born son, Larry, was born. After commissary school, I got orders to go to Pearl Harbor Hawaii for two years. The Navy flew me to Hawaii and Marilyn and Larry returned to Missouri. She saved up money and flew to Hawaii in January 1967. We were there together only 3 months, six months for me altogether, whenever the Navy decided to send me back to California to be stationed on a ship. We had to borrow money from some Navy friend's parents in order to get Marilyn and Larry back to California.

I served during the Vietnam War but I was stationed aboard a vessel that wasn't allowed in the war zone. I was one of the "Plank Members" of the USS Samuel Gompers AD-37. We were the first seamen assigned to her. We would go out to sea 6 months at a time, and then go back to the states for 6 months. I made 2 West Pac tours visiting the ports of

Virgil "Junior," Hellen Grace, Carolyn Sue, and Pearl Marie in 2012

136

Pearl Harbor, Japan, Hong Kong, Singapore, Taiwan, Guam, and the Philippines.

Whenever our ship would go to sea, Marilyn and Larry would go back to Missouri and stay with Marilyn's parents in Tina, Missouri. When the ship would return to the states, they would come back to California to be with me. We lived in several places in and around San Diego during those times. We also lived in Bremerton, Washington twice for a short while whenever the ship would need repairs at the shipyard there.

Grandma Cavender in 1948

Saturday Evening May 1945
By Carolyn Cavender Lloyd Buck of
Lawson, Missouri
Born 1940

In late September of 1940, a baby girl was born to a farm family of northwest Missouri. They named me Carolyn. Actually, I was born in Kansas City, that being the nearest hospital for our area.

I came home to live with my parents and three big sisters, Juanita 15, Helen 14, and Jo Ann who was 8. Helen helped my mom a lot with my care. When I started to crawl, they found that I was unable to see well, and felt with my hands where I was going. They took me to a well-known eye specialist, Dr. Lamoine, in Kansas City. They discovered that I was born with congenital cataracts where as a white spot covers the pupil of the eye. When I was 2 years old, they did surgery to scatter the cataracts. I can remember the bandages that covered my eyes. With thick glasses, I was able to see fairly well, the left eye with more vision than the right. I misplaced my glasses a few times and had the whole family searching for them. Dr. Lamoine was a very good doctor. He would show me bright and pretty pictures and would drop coins on the floor for me to find. He was my doctor for many years.

I can remember a few things about my childhood. My dad and uncles farmed their own and rented ground. They had workhorses, mules, cattle, pigs, sheep, and chickens. Dad always drove a pick-up truck. We lived in an old farmhouse. We had a big wood cook stove in the kitchen and a kerosene cook stove too. My mom would use them to make

wonderful meals including vegetable soup and asparagus soup, too. We had a heating stove and beds in the next room. In the front room was a davenport and a dresser with my clothes. Every chance I got I would throw all of my clothes out onto the floor. I was always getting in trouble for wading through mud puddles with my little white high top shoes.

We did not have electricity or indoor plumbing, so we used coal oil lamps and made trips out back to the outhouse. On wash day water had to be carried from a well a good ways from the house. A fire was built under a big black kettle and clothes were boiled and then scrubbed on the washboard. We rinsed them with two rinses, one with bluing in the water, and then hung them on the line to dry. Homemade lye soap was used to clean the clothes.

Carolyn's parents Florence and Charles Cavender with Carolyn in 1945

My dad hunted and trapped to sell the furs for Christmas money. He had a fox fur made into a wrap for our mom. I was afraid of it. When the road graders would come by our house, I would hide under the bed.

On a Saturday evening in May of 1945, mom started to build a fire in the wood cook stove to cook supper. She had always told Jo Ann and me to get to the door in case of a fire. Jo Ann had been cleaning our shoes, as most Saturdays after supper; we would go to town for groceries and to visit with friends. Our older sisters had graduated and went to Kansas City to find jobs and stay with relatives. Mom poured kerosene in the stove to start the fire, but there must have been coals she didn't see. There was an explosion and fire shot across the floor. Jo Ann was so frightened she threw our shoes back into the kitchen and ran. We all got out safely, but mom went back in to get her purse, when she did, her clothes caught fire. She rolled on the ground to put out the fire but was burnt terribly. Our dad had been in the field working when he saw the smoke and came running as quick as he could. Neighbors came to help, and the ambulance came to take mom to the hospital.

We had an elderly great aunt that lived just up the road from us and Jo Ann and I went to stay with her that night. Mom told her to take care of her babies. I could look out her window and see the embers of our house

glowing in the night. I was so scared and upset. Our mom never came home from the hospital. Three days later, her blood vessels collapsed and she died from the severe burns covering her body. She was only 40 years old. Storeowners in town and neighbors gave us clothes and many things to help out after the fire.

All of my sisters attended country school and graduated from Lathrop High School. Jo Ann went to town school when she started 6th grade. I was the only one of us who didn't get to go to country school. I started 1st grade in the fall of 1945. The only living grandparent we had was our grandma on our dad's side of the family. She lived in Lathrop and dad decided that we would spend the school year living with her. Grandma was good to us and took good care of us, but she was one who liked to go visit her children. Jo Ann and I decided that we would rather be in the country with our dad and elderly aunt, so we moved back to the farm. Our Great-aunt Lora was 82 years old.

I want to say that I had wonderful teachers who understood my visual problems and put me in the front row and worked with me. I wish I had room in the story to tell about each of them. I graduated in the class of 1958. I also want to say that I loved all of my sisters dearly but my sister Jo Ann has been like a mom and a sister to me, as well as a best friend. We have been blessed to have each other all these years.

Tales of My Mother and Father's Life
By Juanita Phillips Gibson of Pharr, Texas
Born 1927

My mother, Gladys M. Stanley Phillips, lived to be 100 plus 6 ½ months of age, November 12, 1905 to May 6, November 12, 1905 to May 6, 2006. Her parents were Luther and Caroline Stanley of rural Eagleville-Ridgeway area. She was the youngest of the 5 daughters. She graduated from Ridgeway High School and went one year of college at N.E. Teachers College at Kirksville, Missouri. Her older sister, Blanche, taught for over 50 years in schools in Harrison, County. My mother began her first year of teaching in a school north of Cainsville on the east side of Grand River in a little one-room school

Carolyn's dad and his girls in 1955

138

Juanita's mother, Gladys Phillips in 1938

named Surprise. My dad met her there at one of the Box Supper events they had. He started courting her and after school was out, she moved back to her home south of Eagleville. He went by horse and buggy as that was the only way to travel in those days over the many hills. He said when he left her home late in the evening he would tie the reins to the buggy and tell the horse to head home across 20 miles of roads. In an hour or so they would be home. There were a few cars but none that would go over the back roads like horses could.

My parents were married that November 24, 1926. My father had been married before and had a 5 ½ year old son. When they went to get married in Maryville, Missouri they took his son, Paul and mother's sister, Blanche with them. My mother raised Paul as her son from the day my parents were married. She was a devoted mother if ever there was one. Settling in the old farmhouse that had been the Phillips family home for many years was, I am sure, very hard for her at the young age of 20. They had no electricity until 1947.

They had no washing machine, so all the clothes were washed by hand in a tub of warm water and a scrub board. Then hung outside to dry or hung behind the stove in the wintertime. Meals had to be cooked and ready at noon. That was when dad would be in from the fields to eat. She never knew how many people she could count on for a meal. Sometimes dad had a hired hand or maybe someone would stop by to visit, and dad would say, "Come on in." Mother always had plenty of food on the table.

Mother was an independent woman. If

dad was busy in the fields and she wanted something done...she did it herself. I remember when she wanted to make a bathroom in the house. She partitioned off a space in the kitchen and had a sink and bathtub put in there. Then she took part of a small bedroom that was connected to that area and partitioned it off for the toilet stool. She hired someone to dig a drain out into the chicken yard. Then dad hooked up a gasoline motor to the pump from the well outside of the house so we finally had some running water in the house. I don't know how she did it with taking care of 5 children, cooking, and laundry by hand, gardening, canning, patching clothes, and keeping a large house clean. Somehow she found time to patch clothes, make me dresses out of my aunt's clothes, and a few dozen other things.

Mother always took us to the small country church north of our home every Sunday for Sunday school. She was involved with a group of ladies that sewed and quilted. She was also involved in all our 4-H projects. How she did it, I don't know!

I have fond memories of staying with mother's parents Luther and Caroline Stanley, and also my two single aunts that lived with them. During the summer months we would spend some time with them in the old two-story house with an attic. Grandma had a huge

Juanita's father, Nort Phillips in 1938

flowerbed with a big fishpond at the edge of it. In summer there were always several of the huge gold and red goldfish in the pond. In the winter they kept them in the cellar in big tubs till spring. They also had a cistern near the house and they kept a rope and a bucket in which they lowered milk and butter down into the well to keep it cool. Guess it was cooler there than in the cellar.

Grandpa farmed with a team of horses on poor hilly soil. It was hard to make a living on that poor land. In the old garage sat an old model T car. It wouldn't run but we children spent hours traveling all over the world, sitting there in that old car. What memories we had. Up in the attic were old clothes and shoes my aunts had and we would play "dress-up" for hours.

Grandma always had pots of flowers and ferns in the house. I remember the old fern stand with the fern leaves that would touch the floor. When my aunt Blanche moved to a care center she asked what would you like to have? I said, "The old fern stand." My husband refinished and it still has a special place in my living room.

I remember a trip my family took to the Lake of the Ozarks. My mother always did the driving, I hardly remember my dad driving if mother was along. Anyway, I can remember dad saying, "Now mother, we can't go any faster than 35 miles an hour." It was a trip from 7 miles south of the Iowa line to the Arkansas border. Loved my mother dearly, she was truly a special woman.

My dad, Nort O. Phillips, lived to be 100 plus six months of age, August 7, 1892 to February 1, 1993. His parents were Charles and Amanda Phillips. Amanda died in 1921. Grandpa Charles lived till December 1934. I do remember him when I was very small. I have heard many stories of what my dad and his brother did when they were young. Nort was the youngest of 5 sons. His parents and my dad and brothers moved to the Akron community in 1900 north of Cainsville, Missouri. My dad lived on part of the land until he retired in 1957. Grandpa Charlie as he was called was a horse and mule trader. His almost uncanny knowledge of horses and mules attracted a buyer of national renown and through this man's influence Charlie was sent to New York City where he studied firsthand the buying and selling of horses and mules.

He and his sons, including my dad, had many acres of corn crops, which were tended by a long string of mules, and my dad continued to use mules until many years later. He finally bought a John Deere tractor to replace some of the mules.

My dad saw more changes in this world than any other generation will ever see…the first car, first airplane, first man to walk on the moon, and the first spacewalk. He told us about buying the first Model T car in the community, the first horse drawn hay baler, the first two-row corn planter, and grain binder. Then came the thrashing machines. Each summer the thrashing machine crews would harvest the oats and wheat that had been bundled and hauled to be thrashed. While the men were harvesting the grain, the ladies were preparing a huge lunch for them. The men loved to eat at our house at noon, as mother was one of the best cooks in the community. I was always helping her and the other ladies as much as I could, but when I got a chance I would jump on the pony we had and take jugs of water to the men in the field.

During the depression my dad had a hired man to help him because of his poor health. I remember him saying he paid him $1 per day, 7 days a week, and gave him milk, eggs, meat, and other vegetables. We always had at least 6 to 8 Jersey cows to milk every morning and night by hand. The milk was brought to the house and run through a hand cranked cream separator. I was responsible for washing the separator, which was a job I did not like. The cream was put into 5-gallon cans and taken to town to sell so we could buy groceries. We churned our own butter, made cottage cheese from the milk and the rest of the separated milk was fed to the hogs.

Our house was always heated by coal, as there was a coalmine in Cainsville. My dad said they would take a team and wagon and haul coal from the mine and in winter it was by bobsled. By the time I was small it was hauled to our farm by truck. When I got old enough it was my job to get the coal buckets full by evening. That was one of my chores and if I didn't get it done by dark, I had to take a lantern with me. The house was heated by coal, stove in the front room and the cook stove in the kitchen. The rest of the house was cold in the wintertime. The kitchen stove was used year around to cook, make bread, and can all the vegetables from the garden and the meat that had been butchered. There was no air conditioning.

Dad always helped us with our 4-H projects. I always raised beef calves to show, my brother raised sheep as his projects. Dad had a good eye as to what would make a good 4-H calf. I won many ribbons with my calves that I showed. Dad had sheep that were bred to make good 4-H projects for my brother. His herd of sheep was known for averaging 2 lambs to almost every ewe.

Dad's love for horses led him to raise five gaited saddle horses. He had a couple he took to shows. He kept a stallion and raised colts from retired five gaited saddle mares. We were always riding them in parades in the area. We also had a Shetland pony to ride and he had a mind of his own. Sometimes we rode him to school when it was real muddy and sometimes he would balk and not cross the small white bridge just north of our house. We'd have to go back home and get dad to ride him across the bridge, as the pony knew better than to balk with him, then the pony would be ok for a while. Every once in a while the pony would brace all four feet and lower his head and off we would go…tumbling to the ground in front of him. Dad would have to punish him and then he would be ok until the next time. We never lacked things to do. Dad always had projects for us. He was always willing to teach us.

I have heard him tell stories of when he and his brothers were young…at Halloween, how they would swipe a buggy and take the wheels off and put it back together on top of the schoolhouse. He was a very interesting man to talk with and quite intelligent for someone with a 6th grade education. He was still very sharp minded even at the age of 100...that was my dad.

The Phillips family in 1986

Electricity Comes to the Farm
By Connie Dow of Chillicothe, Missouri
Born 1947

On December 12, 1955, the lights were turned on in our family farmhouse two miles west of Blue Mound, Missouri. I was 8 ½ years old before we had electricity. I remember reading by our kerosene lamp that sat on the library table and the shadows in the room if you moved away from the circle of light created by the lamp. We would spend some time reading or my mom might be doing some sewing at the end of day. Our days started when the sun came up and bedtime came early.

Although I remember a little about that time long ago, I only have a vague memory of an icebox on the porch, I decided to call my aunt Reva Agnes Condron, age 87, my dad's sister, to see what she could tell me about iceboxes during the past. We discussed how before ice boxes there were icehouses where people dug holes in the ground and filled them with sawdust and blocks of ice from the pond. Aunt Ag remembered her mother, my grandma Ruby Perry Condron, telling about when she and granddad Kirby were courting in the early 1920's he brought her apples in the winter as a treat! The family had an orchard and the apples had been stored in the icehouse in the fall and packed in sawdust to be used later.

Aunt Ag remembered that when she was growing up Mr. Evans, the iceman had a route and would bring a block of ice each day to their farmhouse to put into the icebox. She said that Roy Wright, who ran the station, a small store a few miles away to the southeast, also ran an ice route. She said that her mother used to put butter and milk in buckets in the well north of the house to keep them from spoiling. During WWII, people had oleo and it was like lard and had some yellow coloring that you blended into it to make it look like butter.

When Aunt Ag was growing up in the 1930's sometimes in the summer her dad, Kirby Condron, would let her take the car up to Avalon on Saturday to get a block of ice to make homemade ice cream with a wooden hand-cranked freezer. "We had to make two freezers because there were so many of us." Kirby and Ruby Condron had eight children,

Lissie, Leona, Patricia, and Reva in the 1930s

my dad, Jack, was the oldest and Reva Agnes was born a year and a half later.

Aunt Ag told me that, Grandma Lissie, dad's stepmother and her Aunt Leona both had an Icy-Ball before electricity. It was a type of refrigerator that ran on kerosene.

As we talked we decided that there wasn't such a great need for cold storage back then since we had milk twice a day from our dairy herd and fresh eggs each day and chickens to butcher when we needed them. We canned vegetables from our large garden and fruit from trees and vines. We didn't really have leftovers with such large families. We butchered a hog in the fall and the meat was stored at Avalon in a freezer locker when I was growing up.

On the farm where I lived, there was a cellar, a dirt floored space underneath the kitchen. We reached the cellar by a door that you raised up from the porch floor to reveal concrete steps leading into the cellar. Here we stored all our canned goods, tomatoes and tomato juice, relish, green beans, pickles from our garden, grape juice, and jellies. There were gunnysacks of potatoes and boxes of apples, squash, turnips, and onions.

We had a pantry just off the kitchen on the north and it wasn't heated so in the winter it was a huge icebox. We kept lard there and it was a place to cool pies and cakes. Ag told me that grandma Lissie, the generation before, used to cook on a kerosene stove in the pantry in the summer to keep the heat out of the kitchen.

I enjoyed visiting with Aunt Ag and we both agreed that when electricity came to

our farmhouses many things changed for the better.

Raising Chickens

Growing up on the family farm we raised lots of animals, cattle, sheep, hogs and chickens, to feed our family of seven, which included my mom and dad, Rosa and Ralph Condron, and my siblings, Sharon, Dan, Robert, Lori, and myself.

In the spring, my mom would order chickens by mail. The mailman would deliver a large, flat box, about 36 inches X 36 inches and about 8 inches tall, which contained 100 baby chickens. The box had a divider, so that about 25 chicks were in each section. My dad would drive up to meet the mailman, bring the box down to the house and then the fun began. We spread some newspapers out in the yard under the large walnut tree where it was shaded. Then we sprinkled chicken feed on the paper. We filled a mason jar with water, and turned it over a glass chicken waterer. My mom, my sister, and I would take each chicken out individually and dip their beak in the water so they would start drinking. Then they would start eating the chickenfeed. We counted the chickens and we were sometimes surprised to find a chicken with different colored feathers. Sometimes there were dead chickens, but not too often.

We had to be careful and keep the dogs and cats away, or they would eat the chickens. Finally, the chickens were cooled off, were eating and drinking and could be put in the

Sharon, Patricia, and Connie in 1954

142

brooder house, a small shed by the gate. The shed had been cleaned out and fresh straw put down. The chickens looked so small when we first put them in the brooder house, but after a few weeks, they began to grow white feathers and fill up the space. It was my job to feed and water them every day, but I'm sure my mother checked up to make sure I did it correctly.

When the chickens were old enough to be butchered, it was an ordeal. The pullets, female chickens, were kept to be layers for our egg supply, but the roosters were killed. First, we kids would use a wire hook to catch the chicken by the leg, hand it to my dad and he would pull its head off. We would do about five at a time. It was great fun to watch the chickens jumping around without their heads for a few minutes before they collapsed.

Then we would get a chicken and take it to my mom, who had a bucket of boiling water ready to scald the chicken, which caused the feathers to be easier to pluck. After dunking them in hot water, it was the kid's work to pick off all the feathers. When the chicken was clean, mom would singe the chicken over a flame on the stove. Then in it went, into a tub of water, where mom would cut open the chicken and take out the entrails.

The liver, heart, and gizzard were saved and the rest discarded. The gizzard was really hard to clean because it had small rocks and sand in it to help the chicken digest food. My mom always thought the heart was a treat after it was fried in hot grease, so she usually ate that part.

My dad said when he was young; the chicken feet were cleaned and saved, and fried with the rest of the chicken. He had to eat the feet a few times when there were many people for supper. Thank goodness, my mom never followed that tradition.

After the chicken was cleaned, it was put into another tub of clean water and cut into pieces. The pieces were put in a metal dishpan, washed again, and then packaged in a large plastic bag and put into the freezer. With about 100 chickens in the freezer, we were ready for winter.

Of course, on the day we dressed chickens, we also ate chicken for lunch. Somehow, that fried chicken wasn't quite as tasty as the chicken dinners we had in the winter. Little kids were given the chicken legs, while older kids got the thighs and men ate the white meat and women were stuck with the back and wings or other leftovers like the neck.

We would have mashed potatoes and gravy with the fried chicken. Mom would make a large batch of biscuits and serve fresh lettuce and green peas from the garden, sliced tomatoes, and green onions made the meal perfect. I really get hungry sometimes for the taste of large, ripe, red tomatoes and wilted lettuce straight from the garden with hot crispy fried chicken!

Collecting For the War Effort
By Nancy R. Belcher of St. Joseph, Missouri
Born 1931

When I was in about the 4th or 5th grade of McKinley School, we were dismissed early one day to go collect scrap metal for the war.

Two of my friends (Dorothy and Helen), and I collected several pieces, which included an old metal toilet. I remember we had one of those kind in our enclosed back porch. We had a load in our wagon, but managed to get it up the hill on a Swift Avenue and over to school.

When the day was over, there was a big pile of scrap metal on our playground. All the hard work was worth it, though.

Lost In the Fog
By Robert Stinson of St. Joseph, Missouri
Born 1931

When the superintendent of schools decided that the district supervisors should have principal certificates, it created problems for all of us who were supervisors. Me of course, did as he suggested and made arrangements with the state college local to help get the required courses for certification as principals.

One dark evening in February, as we were leaving the college, the weather suddenly changed and we headed for home in the thickest, heaviest fog we had ever seen! Creeping along the highway, we spotted two red lights ahead of us, and lined up behind the vehicle and stayed behind him! We went for several miles trailing him, when suddenly the lights (red) stopped and of course, so did we! We were concerned and hoped for the best. Were we sitting on the highway, did we turn off, or what. Before we could panic, a man appeared at the side window and quite pleasantly said, "Hi fellows, what can I do for you? You see, you're in my garage!"

My Brother's Rotten Experience
By Darlene Y. Terry of St. Joseph, Missouri
Born 1936

When I was very young my parents took my brother and I to my uncle's farm on weekends, we enjoyed going and looked forward to playing with our cousins. We were playing hide-and-seek and my brother was IT. I hid on top of the chicken coup. I could hear my brother below, so I moved back a little and felt my foot hit something, and then my brother yelled. It seemed there was a bucket of rotten eggs on the roof, and when I moved my foot, I knocked them off on top of my brother. They smelled so terrible that I vomited on the roof. My mother made him use a hose to wash off. She put his clothes in the trunk of the car and made him ride on the fender of the car all the way home. He was so mad he told my mother that I did it on purpose. Needless to say, I got spanked! It was worth it, because to this day my cousins and I have a good laugh about it. My brother only scowls.

We were poor during the Depression, but now we are rich with memories.

My Dad, a Man of Integrity
By Louise Wilkerson Cummins of Stanberry, Missouri
Born 1934

It was back in the Depression days when Dr. Paul Forgraves, a revered physician was practicing in St. Joseph, Missouri. He was pacing the halls of the hospital one night a bit impatiently, waiting for an emergency coming in, and it was my dad bringing my very sick sister in for an appendectomy. When Dr. Forgraves saw who it was, he said, "I'd do anything for this man." It seems he had treated my sister once before and had to pay the bill. My dad sent $5.00 a month until it was paid. Dr. Forgraves later wrote in a letter to us that "he" could count on the fingers of one hand, the number of people who had done such a thing.

All this; from my dad, who worked 16 years for $60 a month and no vacations. There were six of us children, and with a garden, a cow kept on the edge of town for milk and butter, a mother who baked all of our bread and with an occasional hog butchered, we got along.

Later on when an emergency arose, we would either sell the cow or the car to pay for it. Many years, without a car, my dad walked to work.

We had the greatest of parents who cared for their children above all else and who believed strongly in education. I wouldn't want to go back to those days, but of the six, I still live in this town surrounded by relatives and friends, and I cherish that.

No Milk, The Udder Truth
By Patty Stevens of Chillicothe, Missouri
Born 1937

When I was young, I tried to milk a cow and could not figure out how to get the milk to come out. My father came out and said, "What are you doing." I said, "I am trying to get the milk to come out, but it won't come out."

When I was in grade school, they would wash your mouth out with soap, if they say a bad word in the school.

When I was young, I used to go to the Saturday night movies at the older Ben Bold Theatre and the old Grand Theatre. That was "the good old days."

School and Skunk Don't Mix Too Well
By Wilbur T. Hill of Liberty, Missouri
Born 1923

I recall an incident in my life that occurred in 1937 on my way to grade school when in the eighth grade. We lived about one mile and a half from the country grade school on a farm. Instead of walking the road, I went through a timber area that was between our house and the school. I had set steel traps and box traps in the timber area, and would check on them to and from school. The usual catch in the box traps were rabbits and other critters in the steel trap. I would skin them and sell their hides for 15 cents per hide, and the rabbits we would eat.

One morning I found a skunk in one of

the steel traps and he was still alive, and he showered me with his protective odor. I went on to school, which was a one-room school with the heater in the left rear corner, and my desk was next to it. About 30 minutes after school started, our teacher Mr. Howard, came to my desk and said, "Wilbur, I think it best if you go home."

When my mother saw me coming, she came out of the house to greet me, and when she got near to me she said, "Do not go into the house." She then brought me a change of clothes and I changed in the chicken house, and then buried my clothes in a straw stack and after a week, the odor was all gone from my clothes. They were then washed and was as good as new. Of course, I then took a bath and returned to school the next day.

The critters caught in the traps included rabbits and other small animals. I would skin them and sell the hides for .15 each. We would eat the rabbits. I never caught another skunk.

Virginia's father

Country Specialty House, The Privy
By Virginia Province of Olathe, Kansas
Born 1918

I spent all my growing up years on the same farm in N.W. Missouri, 15 miles S.W. of Maryville, Missouri, 18 years in all, on the same farm, which I sold about 10 years ago. Currently I'm living in Olathe, Kansas with my daughter. I'm now 94 years of age, a retired schoolteacher. I continue to receive the Maryville Daily Forum that had your request for N.W. Missouri Hometown Memories articles.

How I remember the one small room specialty house located across the back yard by the brooder house for young chickens. I only visited this outside privy when Mother Nature demanded that I really had no other choice. The architecture and interior rough, raw rafters had evidence that the building was not designed to encourage callers to linger, but rather to attend to pertinent business and leave.

On the cold, blustery winter days, with me it was just any old way to get inside of that house and out again, wishing all the time that I had a better place to go. In the summer seasons, I opened the door with caution for fear of being welcomed by a wasp or even a snake.

We had three round holes from which to choose, and I being of small stature, chose the smallest always. Once situated in the little hole, I would start thumbing through the preseason Sears or Montgomery Ward catalogue for a suitable page. This little bit of pleasure was sometimes a difficult task, if rain had soaked the wish book, or snow had sifted through the shanty cracks and ruined the best pages. The black and white pages were my favorite for usage. The colored pages were too slick.

In later years, I learned from my mother that my father never did pursue the accommodations of the specialty house. He found his pleasurable moments for relief, while seated on a wagon tongue behind the barn. Oh well, it was for each his own way in those days, no plumbing to worry about.

Saturday Shopping Girl
By Linda Shoots of St. Joseph, Missouri
Born 1949

In the early 1960s, I was a young girl around 11 or 12. I was the oldest child at home, so my mom, not being able to go to town anymore because of health reasons, would send me. On the first Saturday of the month, she would send me on the bus to town to do some shopping for her. I would always put on my best cotton dress, patent leather shoes, and even wear a hat sometimes.

We lived on Marie St. in the South end, so I would have to walk up to the "Valley" on King Hill to catch my first bus. Then, it would take me to the junction where I caught the bus going to town. I could hardly wait! This was one chore I always loved to do. I'd get off the bus at the United Department Store, get out my shopping list and away I'd go from one store to another. I loved to browse and see the beautiful things in the stores. It made me feel so grown up. I loved going into Mattinglys, the Dixie Shop, Penney's, Grant's, The Three Sisters Store, and Woolworths. I'd dream about working in one of those great stores someday and eventually at 16, I went to work at Grant's and later the Dixie Shop. But, before going back home, I would always go to Kresges (The Dime Store).

We never had much money, but Mom always let me go there to get a piece of pie with ice cream. It was so good! I loved all those stores and to this day, I wish that they'd come back.

Downtown was a work of art—a safe place to walk, even as a child growing up, and as for me and my husband of 41 years, we still remember walking hand in hand, window shopping, for something that was fun to do. So, to all the Christmas bell ringers—to the man with the monkey and balloons, and all the Apple Blossom Parades, I say to you, "Thanks for the memories from this Saturday shopping girl!

Square Dances, Oh, What Fun
By Wardie B. Hines of Gower, Missouri
Born 1916

Since I was born in 1916, I am now 96 years old. I am almost helpless, but with a little help, am able to stay in my own home and fortunately have kept my mind. I well remember things we did in our teens. One that stands out in my mind was the square dances we used to have. It was about all the entertainment we had then. Since our parents worked hard all week to eke out a living, we had the dances on a Saturday night. The

young boys would get on their horses and go around the neighborhood announcing that the dance would be at our house that Saturday night. Most of the older homes had several rooms, so we would clear out the adjoining rooms so eight couples could dance at once; four couples to each room, with the musicians consisting of a fiddler and guitar seated between the rooms. Each young boy or man would ask a young girl or woman to be his partner for that set. Twenty-five cent was charged to each male for the evening, and the money was given to the musicians. A caller was assigned to each room to announce the steps. These dances would sometimes last until the wee morning hours, stopping to have refreshments at midnight. These refreshments were usually lunchmeat sandwiches and coffee. One of the most prosperous families served Jello with bananas on it. The first Jello I had ever tasted, and thought it was the most delicious thing I ever tasted. A lot of years later I wrote to the Jello Company and asked them when Jello was first made, and they said in the early 1920s.

Most families had smaller children and brought them all; put them on the bed or pallet when they got sleepy. I don't know why these were called square- dances; we always had waltzes between times. These were in the sort of Depression years, and entertainment was scarce.

Can you imagine how the young people of today with all the modern things they have to do, would laugh at this, but I remember these years as simple, but good times with good neighbors, good friends, and good fun.

Thank God for Long Hair
By Frances Berryman Munsterman of
Weston, Missouri
Born 1949

I've lived in Platte County all my life. I grew up as a tenant farmer's daughter. That simply means if you could farm for the landlord or landowner, then you got to live in the house, use of a barn for livestock, chicken house and so on. You rode the school bus to and from school. You did chores around the farm before and after school. There was very little school activities. With six children and two adults, there was never any extra money for anything.

I was nine or ten the year we moved to Jim Hornback back farm. We had a 4-room house, a big outhouse, a big yard, and a chicken house. There was a rail fence around the yard.

My mom and step-dad worked on the farm in tobacco row crops, hay, whatever would bring a dollar at harvest. We always had chickens and eggs, and sometimes a calf, if the landlord worked out a deal with my parents, or even a milk cow. I was much too young to know all the details of what it took to secure this sort of a deal.

I remember carrying water from the spring and emptying it in a caldron to heat for wash water for washing clothes. We hung clothes on an outside clothesline, winter and summer. We carried wood for the winter and cool spring mornings for the wood burning stove, which Mom cooked on and heated water for dishes and baths in a round galvanized tub that we carried water from the spring for in the summer. We all had to do our own share around the house and farm if it was time to harvest the hay. This was the best time ever! Cause it was the time when my oldest brother and the neighborhood boys, 12 to 18 years old, all got together and hauled hay for all the neighboring farms. After the day was done, that's when the family would go to the neighborhood swimming hole. (Salem Hole) we called it. It was just down the road from Dice Store, a country store, and the Salem Church. It was quite a stream, clear and at the end of the stream, was a deep hole. We never did find out how deep it was, but I nearly drowned in that hole.

My sister and I were walking hand in hand along a rock wall under the water. I was out in front, and to my surprise, and almost demise, I slipped off the wall. Down, down, down I went and I didn't know how to swim.

So, as the story goes that's been told through the years, my mom was up top by the creek, my step-dad was up there too. My mom saw my long (very long hair) floating on top of the water and pushed my step-dad into the deep hole. And it seemed like forever, and up and out the water, I came. Thank God for long hair.

We still went to this wonderful place with picnics and friends about every Sunday. It truly was a wonderful time in all, we cherished childhood.

I'm 63 years old now this took place in 1958. There were a lot of good times. We were poor, but you know what, everyone was in the same boat. We worked hard and had a great life. We never wanted much and boy was that a good thing, cause there never was much, but I wouldn't trade it for anything.

This took place in a small rural area in Weston, Missouri. The landscape has changed and the country store is out of business, but still standing, and the church is still there and alive. Houses grew up around Salem Hole. It makes you wonder if anyone else ever found the beautiful little clear stream that played such a wonderful part in all my family's lives, (A fond memory!)

A Friend I Won't Forget
By Paula A. Gibson of St. Joseph, Missouri
Born 1944

I was five years old when I started kindergarten. I was very bashful and scared to death to start school. I was the oldest of four girls and we lived right across from high school. My mom sent me to school the first day. I was scared and I cried. I wouldn't go in school. While I was standing there, Mom kept telling me to go in; she couldn't leave the house because she had my baby sister to stay

Paula and her sister, Shirley in 1950

with.

Well, here comes a high school girl, and she asked me what was wrong. I told her I was scared to go in the school. She talked to me and calmed me down and told me everything would be OK. I finally went in, and she went on her way.

I found out years later that she lived next door to my in-laws. She invited me to come over and visit. We became close and we even canned green beans together. I will never forget her, because she was so nice to me, and it so happens, her name was Paula, just like mine.

Twin Brothers, Off To War
By Lawrence J. Jones of Raytown, Missouri, Born 1924

I have attached a letter from my twin brother, Leonard, written to our mother and dad while he was stationed in Germany during WWII.

Leonard and I, along with a brother Orville lived on a farm 6 miles south of Cowgill, Missouri. Our parents were Felix and Blanche Jones. Orville had a draft deferment from WWII, but Leonard and I were drafted at 18 and shipped over-seas–ETO-November 1944, (Battle of the Bulge!), Discharged, February 1946.

Leonard expired in 2007, and I too am running out of double digits, (88 years old). He was 20 years old at time of this forgoing letter.

May 19, 1945, in Germany,

Dearest Mom and Dad, Hurrah! No more censoring of our letters. Law got back about 2 days ago. He spent one day in Paris before going to London for 7 days, then on his way back he spent 3 days in Paris. He really had a furlough.

We are now in Altena, Germany, a small town of about 18,000. We're trying to get the railroad in shape from Siegen to Dortmund. Those two towns are on the map. We're about half way between them. We don't know how long we will be here, but supposedly until the road is ready.

We haven't been any further east than Laasphe, Germany, the place just before this. The last place we were in combat was in the Ruhr Pocket, so we never did get to the Elbe River, or very deep in Germany.

Since we're in the British sector for occupying, we probably will move further east and south into the U. S.'s sector, that is, if were slated to be occupational troops. Right now, the rumor is that we are, but you know about rumors. The worst time we had was in the Belgium Bulge last winter. We did get to no man's land, there once laying mines. Since were in Headquarters section, that usually isn't our job (being radio operators), but one night we were needed, so about 12 of us were drafted to go. The platoons, because of casualties, etc. were getting short-handed. We were very lucky when it came to casualties. We did get close to the front often though, since the radio was on the jeep with the C.O. We had another exciting night, the night we crossed the Rhine, also in Southern France, at Rhineberg, near Cormar.

The Ruhr Pocket wasn't so bad. We were always in shelling distance and some hit very close. We were fired at once by a sniper. The bullet passed between Lawrence and I, hitting a brick wall close by, (Some fun!)

One house by the Rhine that we had left about an hour before was hit by an 88 shell bomb in the part of the house we were in completely demolishing it. It's a good thing we had left.

The night we crossed the Rhine, Law, and I were in a foxhole close to the banks of the Rhine with a radio set. They didn't cross where we were at, but the shelling was terrific. It was going out, thank heavens.

Will have to wait until we get home before we can tell you all we'd like to.

We came over on the Aquitania. We were on board a day or so before we left N.Y. harbor. We landed in a bay near Glasgow, Scotland. We got off at Greenoch, Scotland. We then traveled by train to a place near New Castle Emlyn, Wales. We lived in some buildings right outside Vilindie, Wales.

We left England at Portland, where we climbed on L.S.T. boats. We traveled across the channel, up the Seine, to Rouens, France. From there we traveled by trucks, after spending the first week in pup tents on a wet field in France. We traveled then up to the Bulge by way of Charleroi, Belgium. Our first day of combat was Christmas Day. The day before, we saw some of our planes shot down.

If we had been in the infantry, we would

have had it a lot worse. Those boys really deserve all of the credit they can get.

We've collected about 100 pistols from kids here in Altena. Two of our fellows got shot accidently today, by pistols. We have turned them all in to the Supply Sgt. I saw one of the boys right after he was shot through the chest. He was taken to the hospital. He was in quite a serious condition. The other fellow was shot through the hand.

There's not much for us to do now. The platoons are seeing that civilians work OK while in Headquarters section. We've been doing a little typing, watching the phone, and odd jobs.

Whenever we change locations, we have to put in a phone, that means, string phone wire.

We got a letter from Aunt Bill today. She was excited about going home. Day before yesterday I drove a civilian for quite a distance looking at R.R. Stations.

I said. "We're about half way between Dortmund and Siegen, but I guess we're closer to Dortmund.

I think I shall hit the hay soon, Lots of Love and Kisses. Leonard

I'm sending some pictures. I would like to get some pictures of some bombed buildings. I wish you could see some of these cities. I haven't seen many, but there's really nothing left. They might as well build someplace else. Law Saw Aachen and Cologne on his trip.

Dad Hammered a Man's Leg
By Pat Stamper of Kearney, Missouri
Born 1953

My dad's blacksmith shop in Utica, Missouri was the favorite meeting place for all the old town loafers and farmers back in the '50s. I heard many stories when I was growing up as a young boy. Some were funny and some frightening. Some of the things I saw were pretty scary, too. One in particular stands out.

An old man in Utica had a wooden leg. His name was Claude Sprague, a.k.a. Toes. One hot, dry summer day, Claude came to the shop asking my dad to repair his wooden leg. The wood had split due to the hot, dry summer weather.

My dad cut out a piece of tin from an old oil can and was nailing it onto Toe's wooden leg, above the knee, to keep the wood from splitting. A salesman drove by going to the brick plant and witnessed what appeared to him as my dad hammering on someone's leg. He turned the car around immediately, got out, and ran up to the shop. He said, "I just drove by and it looked like you were hammering on that guy's leg!" Dad said, "Well, I was. I was nailing on a piece of tin where his leg had split." Toes then pulled his pants leg up and showed the salesman my dad's patch job. Everyone had a good laugh, including the salesman, who had a great story to tell for the rest of his life.

Going to School with the Chicken Pox
By Doris Griffin of Trenton, Missouri
Born 1921

I grew up in the rural community near Spickard, Missouri during the Depression, and my parents struggled to get the bills all paid. But we had plenty of food.

I attended the same one room school all eight years and had several different teachers. One thing I remember was the chicken pox breakout. One of the families let their children come to school. We were all exposed, and most of us got them. But I didn't miss any school, as the teacher let us come since we all were exposed. We even had the Christmas program during that time. How times have changed! The first school bus I rode was a pickup truck with a box frame and seat on each side. There wasn't room for more than ten students.

For many years, my parents lived one fourth of a mile from the Rock Island Railroad tracks, and many times hobos would come to our house wanting food. My mother would feed them if they would do some work, like cut wood and pile it or help feed the livestock.

The trains would start a fire sometimes along the rails, and it would spread to our land. We would fight it with wet burlap sacks soaked in water. One Thanksgiving day a fire spread to our cornfield, and it really come close to the barn before they stopped it. There were no fire districts back then.

I have many memories of days gone by, but how things have changed!

Flower Girls of the Forties
By Rexena Petree of Lawson, Missouri
Born 1934

In our small town of Elmira, located in Ray County, Missouri, it was a custom to have flower girls at funerals. This was in the forties, so the custom no longer exists.

Myself, and two of my pre-teen friends were chosen. It was quite an honor. We wore our prettiest dresses, then lined up at the back of the church, where the funeral director handed each of us a flower wreath. We then, marched up the isles, placed them on stands near the casket, then took our seats.

We had three churches in our small town, so we were honored to be asked to participate often.

Rexena's grandma, Clara Williams and her sister, Aunt Myra Phillips in the 1940s

Friday Night Card Parties, so Much Fun
By Linda Milligan of Gilman City, Missouri
Born 1943

In the late 1960s, we purchased farmland and moved to Harrison County. Our neighborhood was a close-knit group. We took turns having a Pitch card party every other Friday night. The party began with lots of visiting.

I think we drew cards or numbers to determine whether players started at the high, middle high, middle low or low table. Partner players that collected thirty-one points, advanced to the next highest table for the next round. If we had an uneven number of players show up, we played "call for your partner." Each player kept track of their own points, and the highest two moved up.

The host furnished soft drinks, plates, cups, silverware, and prizes. The prizes were awarded to high score man and woman, low score man and woman and door prize by drawing. A player could take home candy, handkerchiefs, batteries, salt and peppershakers, potholders and the like.

After the games, we ate salads and snack food that everyone bought, which when put together, made a meal—and we visited some more.

"Butch"
By Warren James of Stanberry, Missouri
Born 1926

When I was a boy of about 12 years, I lived with my parents and brother on a farm about six miles southeast of Stanberry, Missouri.

Each spring we would get 200 baby chicks and it was my job to take care of them until they were grown.

One spring my mother and I were taking the chicks out of the boxes, when we discovered one that was deformed. My mother was going to dispose of it, but I told her I would take care of it. I named him "Butch." His beak, instead of the top part laying on top of the bottom, it was crossed; also he only had one eye. In order to feed him, I had to set him in a bucket of feed, because of his one eye. When he pecked at something, he would miss it by about an inch. Butch became quite a pet and when I stepped out the back door and called his name, he would come running to be picked up. He also had other problems. For some reason he grew no feathers except for a ring of them around his neck. This resulted in him having quite, a sunburn. He never got as big as the others, maybe about a pound.

"Butch" came to a sad end. We had constructed a creep pen where the smaller chickens could get to their feed while keeping the grown chickens out. One day an old hen got in somehow, and I threw a rock at her and missed, and hit "Butch." He laid around a couple of days and died. I buried him in a corner of the yard.

The Great Coon Hunting Expedition
By John D. Eggleston, Sr. of Maysville,
Missouri
Born 1916

It was on a cold November night in 1938 that three of my hunting buddies, Cottey Thompson, Bruce Pittsenbarger, and Lawrence (Ziggy) Pittsenbarger, and I decided to load up our dogs and head out to the Lost Creek area to hunt for coons. Our transportation, supplied by the Pittsenbarger boys, was an old spring wagon pulled by their trusty mules, Joker and Jem.

We reached our destination and released our dogs to begin their hunt. We hunted for hours, and due to cold and fatigue, finally decided to give up and head home. It took some time to gather everyone and their dogs to begin the walk back to the wagon. We were relieved when we saw the rise just ahead that blocked our view of Joker and Jem. As we topped the rise, relief was no longer an issue, as it appeared that the mules had started home without us.

Already cold and tired, we weren't thrilled with the prospect of walking five miles to get home. As we walked, we discovered there was some wildlife out that night, but we kept a wide berth between us and the black kitty with the white stripe down his back. A couple of miles into the walk, we approached Rube Gilbert's land and were thrilled to see Joker and Jem had stopped to graze Rube's filed for a midnight snack.

When I was finally home and tucked in my warm bed, I had to laugh at the events of the night. Now, nearly seventy-five years later, it still brings a smile to my face when I think of it.

As Busy as Bees
By Brenda Bennett of Dodge City, Kansas
Born 1959

When my brothers and I were kids, we were always in search of ways to make money. We collected empty pop bottles and took them to the store. My oldest brother and I fed the neighbor's sheep. I also helped the neighbor's wife clean her house and helped my grandma do her spring-cleaning. But the most exciting, and maybe a little dangerous, was killing bees in my dad's combine. My dad told us if we killed the bees, he would give us fifty cents a bee, thinking this would only cost him a few dollars. So my two brothers and I took the challenge.

I was armed with a broom, my oldest brother had a board, and my younger brother had a corn knife. Our plan of attack was to bang on the side of the combine and then start swatting the bees with our weapons of mass destruction. The first bang produced several bees. We started swinging. To our dad's surprise, we were killing the bees. After we killed the bees flying around, we would bang on the combine again, and the whole thing would start over.

My oldest brother started yelling and ran into the house, brushing at his head. He had a bee in his hair. So I took my broom and brushed at his head. As he was jumping and yelling, he jumped on the bee and killed it. We started arguing about who killed the bee, so Mom settled it by saying we had to split the fifty cents on that bee.

When we came out of the house, my younger brother was screaming, running, and waving his arms in the air, while Dad was following him. Dad was swinging the corn knife, trying to swat the bee that was chasing him. My grandparents drove up the driveway at the time and saw this. They thought my dad had lost his mind by chasing my brother. They didn't see the bee.

At the end of the bee killing, we went up to our dad for payment. He gave me $9.25. My oldest brother got $5.75, and my younger brother got $2.00. He did more running than swatting. My dad couldn't believe that we had stuck to killing those bees, but I think he was more surprised that it cost him almost $20.00. I guess you could say my brothers and I were as "busy as bees" on that job.

At Twelve Years Old, I Was Queen for a Day
By Connie S. Merriott of St. Joseph,
Missouri
Born 1942

I grew up in South St. Joe, in the 1940s to 1960s. I was born in 1942.

I remember my mom having 'stamps' to buy shoes or clothes after the war.

We had an icebox and whenever the iceman came around in his wagon—, which had a rubber curtain on the back, instead of, a door and he had a rubber mat on his back. He would grab 'blocks' of ice with a large tong and put it over his shoulder onto the rubber mat and carry it into our house and put it into the ice box. My brother and I would follow him back to the ice truck and he would give us a sliver of ice wrapped up in a newspaper, like a cone. We would go off, very happy, licking the ice (no flavor), like it was such a treat.

I remember my mom taking me through a 'walk tunnel' under the railroad tracks by Hoof & Horn Restaurant. The tunnel allowed workers from the stockyards and Swift & Company and Armer's to get to work without having to cross railroad tracks or wait for trains. They filled the tunnel and closed it in 1950s or early '60s.

We girls were not allowed to wear jeans or long pants to school, so when it got really cold outside, we wore them under our skirts and took them off when we got to school and just put them in our locker. I had about a ½-hour walk, to and from school.

I remember trolleys in the junction in South St. Joe, and using plastic, green, or red tokens to ride them.

I would rush home every day from grade school so I could watch (On our first TV) Howdy-Duddy and Clarabell and Pinky Lee and also Kate Smith (She always sang, "When the Moon Comes Over the Mountain). She was a fairly large woman.

Back in (1953-1955) Hosea Grade School moved into a new school. I remember helping Mrs. Beal move things from the old school to the new school, about ½ blocks away. That year, 1954, they chose a "Queen" to represent the new school in the Apple Blossom Parade. I was chosen and got to ride on a float. I felt so lucky to represent Hosea.

Going Home
By William H. Davis of St. Johns, Florida
Born 1914

This story is part of a life history written by my father, William H. "Henry" Davis, who lived on a farm near Eagleville, Missouri. After attending and graduating from Maryville Teacher's College and teaching at Barnard

William's grandparents, James "Jim" Hiram and Penelope Trammell Davis in 1942-44

and in South Carolina, he worked at Bolles Military School in Jacksonville, Florida for ten years. This story is about going home for Christmas and would apply to the years of 1942 to 1944.

Going Home
The Greyhound bus headed north on Highway 169 and stopped at a crossroad which was adjacent to the yard of Anna Canaday's farm. This road, which leads to the west, is about one and a half miles south of Eagleville, Missouri. I got off the bus and it moved off to the north, its lights disappearing in the darkness. The time was about 8:00pm.

It was cold, and a light snow covered the ground. I was dressed more suitable for a Florida winter. I had on a felt hat and a light trench coat over my suit. I had bought light overshoes in Kansas City. I picked up the suitcase and started walking the one and a half miles to the farm of my parents. The dirt road had been badly rutted and now, being

William's parents, William H. "Henry" and his wife Betty Todd Davis in 1946

152

frozen, walking was difficult. It was about one hundred yards to the first corner turning south. Another one hundred yards took me to the corner, which turned to the west. It was a straight walk then on the frozen road to my home.

Walking over the road reminded me that a hedgerow once lived on the road on my right hand as I walked to the west. I remembered that Charley Marks had pulled the hedge trees out with his old one cylinder tractor. I soon neared the farmhouse of Billy Raines. Billie and Nettie had been our neighbors for many years. Billie had been my Sunday school teacher at the Christian Church in Eagleville. I crossed the bridge of Shain Creek, which was named after Tom Shain. It was about one hundred yards to the steep hill approaching my home. This one hundred yard strip of road was often under water during the spring flooding.

I began the climb up the road towards my farmhouse home. I was nearly home now, so I hurried. I was near the top now and could see the lamp light. I knocked on the door, and there waited Mom and Dad (Jim and Nellie Davis.) I was home for Christmas.

We Weathered the Storm but Spent the Night in the Car
By Vada Wooten of Maryville, Missouri
Born 1930

My parents lived on a farm on the Andrew-Nodaway County Road in Northwest Missouri. About nine miles east of their farm was a small town, Bolckow.

Every Saturday night in the summer, there was a free movie on the town square. The road into Bolckow was on the west side of the square, and went around the square. There were businesses on the three other sides and streets leading to the residential areas. The road on the east side of the square went into the country to the other towns and farms east, north and south.

My parents had several milk cows and lots of hens. They had a separator in a shed close to the house, and the milk was poured in a bowl on top of the separator and a crank was turned which separated the milk from the cream. The milk flowed through a spout into a bucket, and another spout the cream flowed through

into another bucket. The milk and cream was kept in the cave to keep it cool. There wasn't any electricity in the country in the early years before WWII in N.W. Missouri. After the eggs were gathered from the henhouse, they were kept in the cave too.

On Saturday night, we went to Bolckow and took the cream and eggs to get the groceries that we needed, to the lady behind the counter, and she put the groceries in a paper sack, because the other people did the same thing. In the meantime, my parents, my brother and I, and the other customers went to the park to watch a free movie. The park had lots of foot wide boards placed on large tree stumps in several rows, which filled the park. At one end of the park was a large movie screen, and at the opposite end of the park, behind the rows of seats was a small building with the movie camera in it. The movie didn't start till after dark, which was after 8 PM. The park benches were full of people and anyone getting to town late, stood around the edge of the park to watch the movie. Some people brought folding chairs to set on.

One Saturday night, a rainstorm in the southwest was getting closer to town; lightning and the wind was getting stronger. My parents decided it was time to go home. Mother went in to the grocery store for the bag of groceries. We got in the car, and by that time, it was raining. We started home, the last four miles was dirt road, which was really muddy by the time we got there. Dad was having trouble keeping the car on the road. The mud was really thick. We started down a long hill and the car slid off the side of the road into the ditch, which was too deep to drive out of. So, there we set rest of the night and it was raining all night. Next morning, Dad walked three miles in the mud to home and bought back a team of horses to pull the car out of the ditch, and the horses pulled the car home with us in it.

I was spending the afternoon with Grandma while my mother drove to town to buy groceries. Grandma told me about the Gypsies traveling through the country in their covered wagon, pulled by a team of horses.

Grandpa and Grandma was married in 1890, and moved to a farm. Grandma had a large vegetable garden and lots of fruit trees. She canned vegetables and fruit in glass jars; also had a pumpkin patch and potato patch.

Late summer, when the potatoes were dug and pumpkins ripe, they were stored in the cave, the potatoes were kept in large gunnysacks, and with the canning finished, there would be enough food to last to the next fall.

Grandpa had several acres of corn, wheat, oats, and hay; all were stored in big wooden bends, except the hay. It was stored on the second floor of the barn.

One day, first year they married in late summer, Grandpa was working in the field behind the barn and their neighbor across the road was working in his field too. The neighbor could see the road from the hill he was on, and noticed a covered wagon pulled by a team of horses coming down the road. He knew it was Gypsies, and he hid behind some bushes to watch. The Gypsies stopped on the road, at the foot of the hill behind Grandpa's house and a couple of women wearing dresses with long skirts, and two men got out of the wagon and walked into the timbers behind Grandpa's house.. On the other side of the timber, my grandparent's henhouse and cave was located near the yard fence, and a third man walked up the hill and around the house and knocked on the kitchen door. Grandma went to the door, the man asked for food. Grandma walked across the kitchen into a storeroom and brought food back to the man. He stood there talking with Grandma for several minutes. After a while, a wagon drove by the house and stopped. The man left and got in the wagon and they drove off.

After the Gypsies were down the road, out of sight, the neighbor that was watching from his field went to Grandpa's house. By that time, Grandpa had come in from the field. Grandma told him she had gave food to a man. Grandpa scolded her for leaving the door open and unlocked while she got the food. The neighbor told my grandparent's he saw the men and women come out of the timber carrying bags, and each man pulled a pumpkin from the big overalls they were wearing, and put them in the covered wagon, and the women pulled chickens out of their shirts and put them in the wagon. The Gypsey women's skirts were double, sewn together at the hem, and had slits in the sides where they had stuffed the chickens. They also carried baskets. Grandma went to the henhouse to gather the eggs and there were only a few eggs and she noticed a lot of chickens were

missing. Grandpa saw the cave door was open, so he went outside to close it, decided to look in the cave first and found that a lot of the jars of vegetables and fruit that Grandma had canned, were gone. Also, two big bags of potatoes and pumpkins were gone too. The Gypsies had helped themselves to a lot of food.

WWII, December 7, 1941…Early morning, sun up, breakfast over, Dad put on his coat, went out on the back porch to put on his over boots to go to the barn to feed the hogs and horses and milk the cows. The telephone rang. Mom answered it, her older sister calling. Mom listened, said, "Good-by," hung up and rushed out to the back porch to tell dad what her sister said.

He took off his over boots, came inside, went to the living room, turned on the battery operated radio with the volume low and set in front of it with his ear close to the radio, with his hand over the other ear. Mom wouldn't let me or my brother go in the living room. We had to stay in the kitchen. Mom called her younger sister, ask her if she was listening to the radio; she wasn't. Mom told her sister Pearl Harbor had been bombed by the Japanese, now I knew what was wrong.

As the war processed, President Roosevelt talked on the radio often, and my brother and I were allowed to listen. The president suggested people plant larger vegetable gardens and the people living in big cities put large flowerpots on their outside porches and patios, and fill the pots with potting soil and plant tomato plants and vegetable seed, if they had yard space, to plant vegetable seed. Also, the streets in the big cities had a wide strip of grass between the two lanes of traffic. People were asked to plant gardens in between the two lanes to help feed the people. Also, when people ate in café's the president said not to leave any food on their plates and to take a piece of bread and wipe up any liquid on the plate and eat it. Everyone was allotted food stamps and gasoline stamps to buy gas for their cars and trucks. Also, there was fear of enemy planes getting past the lookout towers. The president asked people to buy dark colored window blinds and dark colored curtains and hang them over the windows and windowpanes in outside doors. Also, the lamps to be placed on opposite side of the room from the windows, also the streetlights and neon lights were to be off in the towns and cities.

Living on a farm, my brother and I had chores to do after we walked home from school, gather the eggs from the hens nest in the henhouse carry wood from the woodpile and put it on the closed in back porch for the wood stoves, and fill the lamps with kerosene. People living in N.W. Missouri didn't have electricity.

After we ate supper, we were allowed to walk to the next farm and play with the neighbor kids. We usually took a flashlight or kerosene lantern. During the war, we weren't allowed to use a light, if a plane flew over, there was a fear it might be an enemy plane and we would be shot, so we could only go on the clear nights and during the fall moon; so we could see.

One Saturday, while we were sitting at the table eating dinner, our parents were discussing the war. I was only eleven, my brother nine and a half years. Our parents were married ten years before they decided to have children. I spoke up and said, "If I was older, I would enlist in the Army for women." My brother said he would enlist in the Army, too. Mom and Dad stopped talking and looked at each other; never said another word. I was afraid I was in trouble, I felt like sliding out of my chair and sitting under the table.

A card company made a deck of cards with pictures of airplanes from other countries. Mom bought a deck and my brother and I took turns showing each other the pictures. We soon were able to identify each country's symbols. When an airplane flew over the house, it was our duty to go outside, check the symbol on the bottom of the wings; make sure it was a US emblem.

The president also announced, when a can of fruit or vegetables was opened, not to throw away the can. We were to cut the ends out, smash the can flat, put the pieces in a cardboard box, and return them to the grocery store to be picked up by the food delivery truck. The cans were taken to factories, where they were melted and used to make things needed by the military.

Since my brother and I weren't old enough to enlist, it was our duty to fix the cans, put them in a box and take them to the grocery store and hand the box to the clerk at the grocery store, when our parents went shopping.

Gutsy Maggie
By Margaret McCush Roberts of St. Joseph, Missouri
Born 1941

Very early in the morning of Sunday, October 26, 1941 in Savannah, Missouri, my dad and my two brothers were up, dressed, and ready to go duck hunting. Dad went in to check on Mom before they left. Mom said she didn't think they should go. In fact, she thought Dad should send one of the boys to Dr. Steidley's house to tell him the baby was coming. That's when I made my entrance into the world.

Then, the problem was to find a name for me. Dad said that since Mom named the other three kids, Bill, Jack, and Marilyn, he should get to name me. Mom agreed, but hoped he didn't do what most of his family did and name me after one of his relatives. Three days after my birth, Dr. Steidley told Dad if he didn't find a name for me that day, he was going to name me himself. Dad was looking out the window, racking his brain for a good name, but nothing came to mind. Just then, our two neighbors, Margaret Smith and her sister, Ann Smith, were coming over to have a look at me. Dad said, "That's it – Margaret Ann." So that is how I got my name.

Mom liked the name and no relative that she could think of was named Margaret, so all was well with the world. Later, an uncle

Margaret McCush in 1942

155

stopped by and told the folks that Great Aunt Maggie was thrilled to have me named after her. Mom turned very pale, and her mouth and eyes became the size of saucers.

Now, Great Aunt Maggie wasn't an ordinary aunt. She lived in a little house that hadn't seen any paint, inside or out, in at least fifty years. It was way up in the hills of Amazonia, Missouri, where the snakes outnumbered the people five to one. Great Aunt Maggie made her own clothes, which must have been taken from patterns of the 1800s, with many petticoats. She also made her sunbonnets, with ruffled bills and neck protectors.

One day, she was bitten by a snake, and it got its fangs caught in her petticoat. She ran around the yard, screaming like a banshee, with the snake flying behind her. Finally, she spotted a garden hoe and whacked the snake. She then went into the house, and with a pocketknife, cut an X mark in each fang mark, and then spit chewing tobacco into the cuts. Everyone said it was lucky she was chewing that day instead of smoking her corncob pipe, or she might have died.

Mom always made sure that everyone who mattered knew I was not named after Great Aunt Maggie, but I like to think that I was. I believe her life would have made a great TV series, something like the *Grizzly Adams* show, only perhaps called *Gutsy Maggie*.

Ganns Hill My Home, My Past
By Glennrose Gann Steward of St Joseph, Missouri
Born 1934

Our family lived at Halls, Missouri, up on the bluffs, in the woods.

When I was five, we moved to St Joseph. Mom and Dad bought a 3-bedroom house for $500.00. The house was on Morris Avenue, the first street, West of King Hill where the big water tank and the flag where.

There were nine kids, two boys, and seven girls. We went to McKinley Grade, seven blocks away, counting the short cuts, Benton High School, also seven blocks away.

We were outdoor kids. I would make Mom mad on purpose, so she would run me out of the house, where I wanted to be.

The big grey water tank was the reservoir

for the South side. The flag was put there at a later time. I was eight years old at that time.

We had a path to follow from the road to the house, Dad later, put cement steps in.

We had an outhouse and a spring for water. The water was pure and I believe the chemicals (natural) are the reason we are all healthy.

There was four houses on our street. The street was one block long, dead end, with a circle turn-a-round. Each house had spring water. There was a wagon track that ran across the back of the property. A large rock jutted from the bank. A small basin was at the base of the rock. Spring water flowed from below the rock, filling the basin. It was said, people in the area hauled water from the basin, also early on; the Indians used it also.

We kids knew every rock, every tree, and every path on the hill. We were cowboys and Indians, Tarzan and Jane, whatever our imagination took us.

I got married, left the hill after a fashion. I bought the land below the hill, all of Morris Avenue. A landslide took the home place, fire took the end houses. I built a two-story house on the end spot. Only two homes remain.

The hill, we called it Ganns Hill, that is our name. It is home to me, and always will be. I could tell some good stories about the hill and the people.

Most of the people from the hill are all gone except my siblings. One sister passed away a few years ago. We are in our seventies and eighties now. People go upon the hill to see the vast views from high up. The big tank is gone, replaced by two larger ones on the East side. A rail is in place to keep people off the face of the hill.

Each year before the poison ivy comes up, I walk the hill, checking it out and remembering times past.

My home, my past "Posy"

A Day of Disaster
By Jean Farthing of St. Joseph, Missouri
Born 1945

It was easy enough for my girlfriends and I to ditch school that spring day in 1961. We were sophomores, 16 years old, and each of us deeply in love. Our guys picked us up in a 1949 Plymouth, and we were off for a day of

156

fun.

The day started off at a local park, for a morning of walking and talking. Someone came up with the idea of driving to Kansas for a couple of six-packs. We lived in St. Joseph, which is in Northwest Missouri, and about 15 minutes from the Missouri/Kansas border. Drinking age in Kansas at the time was 18, and all three guys were old enough to drink. Beer was $1.00 a six-pack and gasoline about 30 cents a gallon.

We took the old highway, which went through the south of town passed the stockyards, over a long bridge and into Elwood, Kansas. The radio in the old Plymouth was playing tunes by a new rock star, Elvis Presley. We all sang, "Love me Tender" along with Elvis. We pooled our cash and had enough money for two six-packs (Budweiser, of course) and $3.00 of gas. Beer was purchased and the guys quickly consumed it in a park in Kansas.

On the drive back to St. Joseph, we were going way too fast, when the driver suddenly lost control. The car flew off the highway and rolled (according to witnesses) at least two times. All six of us crawled out of the car, dazed but not hurt. The stench was horrific! We were literally covered in cow manure. We had landed in the stockyards, in mounds of manure. Police and ambulances appeared out of nowhere. The smell of manure must have overrode the smell of alcohol, as the driver never got a ticket that day.

Ambulances took all six of us to St. Joseph Catholic Hospital emergency room to be checked. My day of disaster was compounded, as the emergency nurse on duty turned out to be my mother. As the ambulance unloaded us, the look on her face told me I would probably be grounded for life. I will always remember a short, little nun running through the emergency room with a large bottle of room spray, holding her nose as she went.

It took more than one bath that night to even begin to feel clean and get rid of the horrible smell. All of my clothes had to be thrown away. The next morning all three girls were stiff and sore, but went to school at the insistence of our parents. In those days, there were very few valid reasons to miss school. The Plymouth could not be salvaged. Damage to the vehicle was minimal, thanks to the soft manure, but there was no way to get the smell out of the upholstery.

One month later, on a Memorial Day weekend, I married the driver of the Plymouth and returned to high school on that Tuesday, eventually graduating in 1963. As the pastor was joining us, I had to remove my engagement ring to place the wedding band on. I noticed a small speck of cow manure was still lodged in the small diamond. In retrospect, that was an omen foretelling the future. That teenage marriage, however, is another story…

Never Rope a Cream Can
By Ethel Ann Williams of Darlington,
Missouri
Born 1942

I was born June 14, 1942. As I think back on my childhood years and growing up as the oldest of six children, three girls and three boys, there were a lot of special memories, some good and some not so good. We grew up on a farm, eight miles west of Carrollton, Missouri.

We arose every morning at 5:30 and milked cows and separated the milk with an electric separator. We put the cream in five-gallon cream cans.

We did all these chores before we got on the school bus. Sometimes the bus driver would just back up the bus at our house and turn the engine off and wait on us. Sometimes he waited as long as fifteen minutes. But he wouldn't wait on any of the rest of the kids on the bus.

One particular time, when we had finished separating the milk and had the cream in

Ethel's parents, Harold and Margaret in 1960

157

Hauling hay

five-gallon cream cans, it was on a Saturday morning. So we didn't have to go to school. We didn't have to hurry and get ready for school. It was time for the Huckster man who came after the cream to come and get it. My brother, Glen Ray, was roping the five gallon can full of cream. Our mother had just told him to stop or he would turn it over. Then she went out to the washhouse to start the washing, and of course, Glen Ray roped the cream can one more time and tipped it over in the kitchen floor. Mind you, this was five gallons of cream on the kitchen floor.

Our mother came back in and saw what had happened. She never said a curse word that we knew of. She looked at Glen Ray, and she said, "Gosh a mighty dam," and started scooping up cream from the floor. She got it up just in time for the Huckster man to pick it up. Mother mopped the floor three times, and it was still slick. She is 77 years old now and we tease her now about her cussing problem.

Our father loved us very much, but he was very strict with us. He taught us all to be honest, hardworking; never quitting anything we started until it was finished. We all turned out pretty fair. There is a beautician, a teacher counselor, two farmers, a C.P.A., and a western storeowner. Daddy taught all the boys to hunt and fish. They all love to still do this. Mom taught the girls to cook and sew. All the girls can cook, but needless to say, the oldest one never did learn to sew very good at all. Our mother still lives in the same farm. Our dad passed away in 1979.

I have many happy memories. We all worked together, and we all played together, too. We all went to church together as a family. I wish today people would take more time to do things as a family and enjoy each other and love each other and their neighbors like they did back in the '50s and '60s.

I'm Part Wolf and Part Bridge
By Alma Simpson of Bethany, Missouri
Born 1920

I am Alma Jane Bridge Simpson, born to Hubert and Helen Wolf Bridge on March 16, 1920 on a farm around Mt. Moriah, Missouri. I had an older brother and a younger brother and sister. When I was born, the doctor asked my brother what he was going to call his little sister, and he said Alma. That's because a neighbor gave him a little kitten and that was the lady's name. So I guess I am part wolf and part bridge.

We always lived on the farm, so we grew up knowing how to work and entertain ourselves. We moved ever so often, but we was always between Ridgeway and Eagleville.

Yes, I remember school days real well. We lived one-half to three-fourth of a mile and walked to a one-room school. Dad would take us with a sled and horse if the snow was real deep. In the late '20s and early '30s, we had some bad storms. One year, we had 32 children in our school. To support the school, we would have plays and have box suppers. We kids would fix boxes decorated and have food in them. We would auction them off. Whoever bought them is who we ate with. We had fun. I had to go to school early. I got my diploma on the 20th of May in 1933. Alva L. Allen was the County Superintendent.

I did fishing and hunting both with my older brother after school. We changed our clothes, got a hot slice of homemade bread and butter, and off we would go to the creek to fish. The swimming was done in the creek, too, or at the Brooklyn Falls. We went hunting in winter when it came a big snow. My brother and I would go rabbit hunting. I would tromp the brush piles and scare the rabbits out, and he would knock them in the head with a stick. We did a lot of trapping for coon and skunk. One time, we came home smelling so bad we had to take a bath in the smokehouse.

After I graduated from the eighth grade, I always helped Dad in the fields. I planted corn with our pony and I drilled behind my dad. One time at the end of the day, Dad had us stop and fish under a rock. There was a big, blue catfish under the rock. The rock had a hole on both sides of it. Dad asked me if I would get in the water and stop up one hole with my two hands. I was in the water about to my shoulders. I put my hands in the hole, and the fish bit my hands, but I stayed with it until Dad got the fish. My mother was mad and said, "Don't do that anymore." But we had fish for supper.

Our pets were dogs and cats. We also had pet calves or sheep that we had to feed on bottles.

Depression times were hard. We grew a garden and canned. We picked berries, gooseberries, raspberries, and blackberries.

I remember the outhouse and chamber pots very well. They were very cold to sit on when it was snowing and the wind was blowing. Castor oil was a weekend thing we had to do. It was not very funny.

The first car was an old Model T that we had to crank. Then later, we got a Chevy. We always lived on mud roads. Before cars, we always went in the wagon.

We didn't have a telephone until about 1929. We finally got a radio after the phone. On Saturday nights, when the *Grand Old Opry* came on, Dad would call up the neighbor and tell him it was on and leave the receiver down, and they would listen, too.

We had to do things the hard way. I learned to milk cows and shuck corn in wintertime by hand with a shucking pep. I was hit in the head by someone every once in a while. I grew up knowing what work was, because I had chores to do.

We didn't get into too much mischief. We weren't bad. We just got in a fight every once in a while.

The neighbors all helped one another in their thrashing. They went from one neighbor to the other with the old thrashing machines.

I learned to dance with my dad. Neighbors took turns, once a week by clearing a room to dance in. We had three who played the music. We had fun.

I could go one and on, but I am going to quit. I just finished my 93rd birthday, so I am tired!

Syrup Buckets, Clean Gardens, and Lessons Learned
By Martha Burks of Amazonia, Missouri
Born 1932

My parents were Horace and Jennie Perry. We had no car. Daddy always took us to town in a horse and buggy. We lived in a two-room house with no electricity and a cook stove. They always had a big garden, and Mommy canned a lot from our garden for winter. She would always say, "It will taste good when the snow flies."

One of my first memories was of a spring evening when I was about four years old. I was with my daddy, who was milking our cow, when out of the darkness two little lights were coming over the hill. It scared me. I thought something was going to get me. I ran into the house to Mommy. Imagine my fear when those two lights came into our driveway! What a relief it was to discover that it was my daddy's brother, and he was driving a CAR, something that there were not a lot of around at that time.

One day out of the blue, Daddy took me to the neighbor's. Daddy said, "I will be back after you in a while." Later in the day, when we were home, Daddy picked me up and took me into the bedroom and said, "Look what Mommy has," as I looked at the wrinkly little baby. I said, "Well, where did she get that?" Daddy took me to the kitchen where there was a white flour sack with a face drawn on it. Daddy said, "She came in that!" In those days, new mothers had to stay in bed for a few days, so my Aunt Lilly came and stayed with us to help around the house and with me. Later in life, my aunt told me she had to pop my bottom, as I was making too much noise! I did not get many spanking growing up. We had to sit on a chair for a while. That was hard as a little kid, to sit still.

It was springtime and school was about out for the summer. Another girl and I both went for a visit one day, as we were supposed to

Martha's parents Horace and Jenny Perry with their children

159

start school in the fall. I remember taking my lunch in a Karo Syrup bucket. When I opened it for lunch, it was a fried egg sandwich. It smelled really good! I am sure I had cookies, too.

When school started in the fall, a girl named Harriett and I were the only two in the first grade. Harriett and I walked from the same direction to school, so we tried to meet at the same time so we could walk to school together. The following year, there were several students waking with us to school. My daddy had always said, "Don't get in a car with someone you do not know." One morning, a car came along and everyone else got in the car except me. I didn't know them, although some with us did. I started walking the rest of the way to school by myself, until a big black bull came over to the fence and bawled at me. Then I ran the rest of the way to school. Daddy later told me that if everyone else rode and knew them it was okay to ride, too. I do wish he had made that clear before that morning. In reality, it was probably more dangerous walking by myself.

The country school only had ten to twelve students in all eight grades. Our school supplies were a Big Chief tablet, two pencils, and a box of crayons. The water was carried in a bucket form a well outside and had a dipper. We all used the same dipper. There was no electricity or heat. The teacher would come early to school and build a fire in the wood stove. On occasion, the teacher would bring a kettle of hot soup and keep it on the wood stove until noon, and then we all received a bowl of hot soup. What a real treat on cold days.

One time, Daddy staked out a corner of garden, one for me and one for my sister. When it came time to hoe, he gave us each a little hoe and said, "See which one of you can get your garden the cleanest." My sister hoed down everything that was green. She did not know a bean from a weed. Well, hers *was* the cleanest.

My parents always taught us right from wrong. One day, I went to play with our neighbor kids. The little boy had a whole lot of pretty pop bottle caps. I didn't think he needed them all so I put some in my pocket and brought them home. Mommy asked me where I got them, and I said, "He wouldn't give them to me, so I took them." Well, Mom switched me back up the hill to his house to give them back to him. I learned my lesson good that day, never to take something that didn't belong to me.

Hard Times Dad Sold Hogs For 2 Cents a Pound
By Velma Francis of Bethany, Missouri
Born 1921

Memories of my first school year, was when I was 6 years old. I went to a country school, (Victor) in North Harrison County. It was a one-room building with a cloakroom, one for girls, and one for boys, to hang up their coats and put their overshoes in. One teacher taught all 8 grades, reading, writing, arithmetic, spelling, health, language, geography, history, and art. School took up at 8:30 with pledge to the flag and doing some exercises. We had a large stone jar on a table for our drinking water. Each kid had a folding cup to drink out of. We had an outhouse in the corner of the schoolyard. It was a small building with a bench made with two round holes cut out for you to set on and do your job. It was mighty cold in the wintertime. At recess, we played Andy-Over, Bushman, Ball, Marbles, and Hopscotch.

My first movie was at Blythedale, Missouri. It was a silent movie. It was outside and we sat on boards. The next movie was a talkie. It was great! I think I was 8 or 9 years old then. The first movie theatre I went to was at Cainsville, Missouri. I remember seeing Gene Autry, Roy Rogers, and Shirley Temple. It was a dime to see the show.

My first experience with a phone was the old crank phone on the wall. It was a party line; you had two long and a short for your number. Everybody on the line could hear you.

The Depression years were very hard. It was so hot and dry. The grasshoppers and cinch bugs were really bad. We had to get up early in the morning when the dew was on to spread poison bran on the edge of the fields to keep them from eating up the crop. We had to carry water for drinking and house use, nearly a mile away. Cows ate leaves off the trees. I remember my dad selling hogs for 2 cents a pound. We had no electricity and the house was so hot we had to sleep outside sometimes.

Velma at age 9

We had lots of chores to do. We had to carry in wood for the heating stove and pick up chips to start the fire in the kitchen Range that was used to cook on. We carried in the water for the night and also, we had to empty the chamber pot and we all hated this job.

We made the most of our toys. Sleds were made from old boards and they worked pretty good. We used old wheels for our wagon that was also made from old boards. We had stick horses, our fishing poles were made from tree limbs and we used twine string, and wire for hooks. We caught lots of crawdads while fishing in the pond.

My mother made most of my clothes. She made dresses, underskirts, and bloomers. She even made our mittens in the wintertime.

When we went to Grandma's (Shain's) house, we had to go in the team and wagon. We had no car at that time. We covered up with blankets and Mom heated rocks to put in the wagon to keep us warm. It was several miles to her farmhouse. Those were really rough times, but I'm glad now that I seen that kind of living. Kids, now days couldn't survive. I've seen many changes in my time of living, some good, some not so good.

Crank and Holler Phones
By Lester E. Pierce of Stanberry, Missouri
Born 1923

My Granddad on my mother's side was a farmer, thresher, lumber sawyer and ran a gristmill, never using steam, but the old portable one-lung engines, and later a 16-30 Rumely. He maintained a telephone line, probably as long as the community got a system. I speak of the 1930s when the fourteen-gauge line was hung on the poles he cut on the farm, and kept the brush cut five miles to the village. I was born in 23', so wasn't too old or stout to dig holes to set a new pole or climb out of the wagon to do a repair. Grandpa had a tractor run back, and crippled him, so I did most of the work.

The uncles loaded up three barrels and a smaller one, and tools and we headed out. At that time all the fuel oil and gasoline for starting and for other Standard Oil products of Indiana, were on the wagon on the way home. Usually we had the phone line operating and checked at the central office, but it was a full day of work.

The old battery powered phone hung on the wall, and during the storms, it was supposed to be disconnected, but I have seen a strong arc of fire. The brush would grow up yearly, and had to be kept down as well as possible. During a rainstorm, the line being bare, would ground out, or nearly so. Later, when the neighborhood line was used, it was the intent that the users would work the line. When the phone rang everyone on the line would "listen in," so it often was noticed that one phone would have run down batteries, so long before many present day users were born, the telephone was a different experience.

The One-Room School—this day and age, the schoolroom is crowded if more than fifteen students are in a class. We read stories of fifty or more scholars in one-room schools before our time. We count faces in pictures that appear the whole community attended. Now, consider, the only modern article was the blackboard, no electricity, plumbing or even personal use of drinking cups, a privy in each corner of the yard and usually a well in the one acre school yard.

There sat eight grades of kids, and years ago, some were eighteen years old. Now, let's consider what took place in the little room.

Generally, one class sat up front, and the rest were studying their lessons, but was that so bad? While one class were reciting, the others in the room were listening, so over the years this served a double purpose. At hand are schoolbooks of a couple or three generation back. Take these to present day schools, and teachers would be lost.

As to the disciplining, the one room school of fifty or sixty or so many scholars, their many different stories, but kids went to school to learn. Discipline at school, often was carried further at home. Now, we read daily of disciplinary problems being attacked and the school administration are practically fired or jailed. So ask the question of the old time primitive type of learning, being so, back in ancient times. The only answer is, MODERN!

Seventy Years Later…..I've learned that time don't erase memories or even speed them up or slow them down. The mention of names of those of memories; is but a part of remembering. As yet, I am not required to be licensed to reminisce. I have learned that what appeared to be fact hasn't always been right. Supposition can be a factor, as follows.

I attended a farm meeting a few days back, and at the intermission, a fellow sitting at a table in front of me turned around and said, "I am Dean Showen, I read your item in the paper." Well, it's not unusual to be reminded; I do write "Pierce's Pennings." I said, "I went to high school with an Eldon Showen and always supposed he got me in trouble." Immediately, he said, "I know the story, my uncle told many times about turning the sparrows out in the school." Now, all these years I was supposing Eldon was, let's say, the culprit. Dang! That was around 1940, so with a bit of finger counting, that was seventy years ago. Puzzle solved!

Now, the story has to be told. One morning Superintendent L.A. Zeliff rapped me on the leg and directed me to get a stepladder from the janitor, and get rid of the birds. Several barnyard sparrows were flying down the hall to the far window.

Now, I don't exactly recall, but I think a window was opened. Apparently, accordingly to Dean, Eldon had said to open a window to let the birds out. Maybe that was the connection that Eldon was present and Dean had said Eldon had said to open a window. The weather wasn't good outside, but now I can settle my thoughts.

Halloween Applied…Back around 1930, before I started to Spessard School, a story was told that the teacher boarded in the Rector Price home. She hung the school keys behind the door as she returned each day. This one morning after Halloween, she unlocked the door as usual, and there sat a wagon with box, all set up. There was an open just inside the double doors, and in front of the jacketed old Cannon stove.

The young teacher ran a half mile to tell Rec all the windows and doors was locked and nothing else bothered, except for the wagon. The story goes, that son John was present, so Rec had it all figured out. He told John to get the boys that had put the wagon in, to get it out and set it up outside.

Times Have Changed—I attended the Spessard when Franklin D. Roosevelt went into office March 4, 1933. I tended cattle beyond the school and often carried as model 1906 Winchester, as I hunted and trapped. After tending the cattle, I took a shortcut back to school. I just sat the old Winchester in the corner of the cloakroom with all the clothing, overshoes, and dinner buckets for the day. Come time to go home, I picked the old rifle up and went home. Now 2013, the old school is gone. What a different atmosphere we find, as society is broken.

Tinker Had the Rabies
By Norma Jean (Benson) Medlin of
Ridgeway, Missouri
Born 1935

I was born in Unionville, Missouri to Frue and Gladys Benson, on July 29, 1935. It was a very warm day, and the doctor came to the house to help my mother deliver me. He came in, checked Mom and said, "When you are ready, wake me up, and he laid down on the Divan. I was the baby of the family of six children, four girls, and two boys.

At the age of four my father died, being sick for some time with his heart. My mother, having no money, paid the expenses by cleaning the funeral home every week.

We had no car, so we walked everywhere we went. The only way out of town was by car or train that came in every day, or walking.

My neighbor across the street from us felt

Clinton and Norma Medlin in 1953

sorry for me for Daddy dying. He milked a cow or two and delivered it by a pull wagon around the neighborhood. He would come over and say, "If you want to go with me, be sure your face is clean." His wife sewed clothes for people.

Our neighbor across the street and down ½ blocks, their name was Marton, and their son Bob, was a friend of my brother Jim. They each had a dog. One evening we heard a noise in our screened in back porch. Skippy, Jim's dog was out there. A dog had got in and fighting Skippy—Jim ran out, grabbed Skippy, and jumped in the house. The mean dog went across the street and grabbed Tinker. The two boys took the dogs to the vet, tied them in a barn for two weeks, and in two weeks our dog was OK. Tinker had the rabies. The doctor sent Tinker's head in to be checked. Jim, Bob and I, buried the rest of Tinker. Jim shot his gun above the grave and I sang a hymn.

Norma's brother, Jim Benson in 1950-51

We had a park one block away from our house. The kids could go up there in the evening. There was a lady that came in and watched us play and sometimes played with us. The park closed at night at 9:00 PM and we kids went home.

I took my first train ride when I was 10 years old. The train went as far as Laclede. We had to get on another one. The other train went to Kansas City—we waited over two hours in Kansas City to get on a train going to Tulsa, Oklahoma.

The winters were bad. We walked to school and back. Sometime they turned school out early.

My brother Jim got a job when he was twelve at the Unionville Paper. The owner gave him a bike built-for- two. He would take me on it, but I had to peddle.

I graduated in 1953—got married 2 weeks later—we will be celebrating our 60th wedding anniversary in May.

We didn't have any money to take a Honeymoon on, so for our first night together we flipped a coin: heads for me to stay at Mom's and tails to go to his folks farm. My husband won.

That weekend, the neighborhood friends of ours, came out to the farm to Chivaree us. We had candy for them. They tried to catch my husband to throw him in the pond. He ran to the house, told me to stay in the house; he ran out the back door and jumped a fence. He got away by getting to the main road. His brother-in-law was there with his car, and he got away from his friends.

Country School is the Best
By Eileen Schaeffer Dozier of Lowry City, Missouri
Born 1938

I went to Highland Country School, southeast of Oregon, Missouri in Holt County. Highland School is still standing. Faye Markt was our teacher in my fifth, sixth, seventh, and eighth grades. Students that I can remember were Bob McAfee; Gary Derr; Willard and Lewis Fansher; Jimmie, Deanna, and Betty LaHue; Kathleen, Harvey, and Darlene Noble; Mary Fansher; Alfred, Edna, and Marion Hufford; Cecil, Maxine, and Kenny Miller;

Charles and Earl Cromer; and Jim, Eileen, Philip, and Kenneth Shaeffer. After the eighth grade, we went to Oregon High School.

In the spring on Friday afternoons if weather permitted, we would play other country schools in baseball. We had a nice ball diamond, swings, and a merry-go-round. Sometimes while outdoors for recess playing baseball, a highway patrolman would stop and watch us play and give us some pointers.

We had a flagpole where we saluted the flag each morning, and we always had prayer. We had spelling bees and arithmetic at the blackboard. We always had diagrams in English on the blackboard, too. We had current events, art, civics, music, history, language, health, reading, and geography. We always stood up front to give book reports. We always had poems to learn. Our school had an up-to-date library. A county nurse would come and keep us up to date on our shots, etc.

We always had programs on Halloween, Thanksgiving, and Christmas. During the winter at community meetings, our parents would play cards, and we children would go sledding. We had a nice hill south of the school. The Dudecks brothers came over and played their trombones for us at one meeting.

Also, our teacher taught us to square dance. Faye played the piano. So we always learned the new songs that came out back then.

We always had plenty to do, and our teacher made school a lot of fun. Also, we would take turns bringing soup or hot chocolate to school for everyone to have something hot to go with their lunches. We had a hot plate so no one went without lunch. Also, we took turns doing the dishes.

That was back in the good old days and some of the students are gone now. But thank God for memories.

After my brother, Jim, started high school, Philip, Kenneth, and I rode our pony to school when the weather was bad. We had about three miles to go and at the halfway point was a spring where the pony always stopped to get a drink. She stayed in the stable at school during the day. This one cold, rainy November day, Kenneth wanted to hold the reins. He said we never let him drive. So we did. He was in front. At the spring, the pony put her head down to drink, and oh yes, Kenneth went in headfirst. Phil and I got off and put the

wet boy on, and I put Philip on to help keep Kenneth warm. Yep, I had to lead the pony home. I would walk a little ways, and then I had to kick to get the mud off my boots. That was the only time Kenneth held the reins.

One day in January, 1950, a sergeant came to our school and passed out New Testament Bibles from the Gideons. We appreciated that. I still have mine. It is a little worn but it is still holding together.

Teacher would have a pail of water for us to put our hands in to thaw them out after the long walk to school. Hands would be awfully cold after walking to school a long distance, even if we were wearing gloves and packing books and lunch. Some children would cry.

One Sunday afternoon after church, Philip and I rode the workhorses with no saddles. He went around this big pond. My horse was splashing and swimming and I came near to falling off. I don't know how deep the pond was but it scared Philip.

Another time, Philip and I jumped over the rock wall at one end of our yard, and we saw this snake lying on a rock with maybe six inches of the snake sticking out. I picked up a short stick and poked it and it rattled. When Dad came home, he tore up the wall and killed a big diamondback rattler.

We always had water in the creek to play in on hot summer days.

We would go to town on Saturday nights and get groceries, visit, and maybe go to a movie. We would go home and listen to the *Grand Old Opry,* providing the battery didn't run down. We kids would ride in the back of the pickup on the wagon seat.

We would sleep with the windows open and in June when it rained, we could hear the corn growing.

We always raised big gardens and canned everything we could. So we had plenty to eat in the wintertime.

We always set traps. One morning, my cousin, Bonnie, who was staying with me, and I went out to check this one trap. We had a big animal and tried to pull it out of the hole, but after a while, it pulled off its toes and got back down the hole. It was a good thing it did, because we found out it was a badger. It kept hissing at us.

In the wintertime, on Saturday nights, we would have apples, popcorn, and fudge, which we made. We would have neighbors over. We kids liked to play hide and seek and who seen the ghost tonight. One night, Mom and another woman came out with sheets on and scared us. We had no light pole, so it was dark.

We liked to play handy over, where we would throw a baseball over the school building to the other side. We would choose up sides. This one time, we had a new baseball and of course, a fire in the stove. Yes, I threw this ball. After a while, the other side came around and wanted to know when we were going to throw the ball. I threw it and it went down the chimney. I felt bad, because it was our new ball. This was at the Benton Country School.

We learned a lot at the country schools. I was glad I went to the country schools instead of in town.

Pat Farris

4-H and Teaching Have Been Great
By Patricia Farris of Gower, Missouri
Born 1933

I was born in 1933 in Hamilton, Missouri. For a time, my parents rented farms. They decided to take the big step and buy a farm at Dearborn, Missouri in about 1943. By the time we moved to our own farm, there were four children, three girls and a boy.

Being the oldest, I was a tomboy. I spent most of the time outside, helping my dad. Dad taught me how to drive the tractor, mow hay, plow, bale hay, etc. When I was old enough I joined 4-H Club. Then the jobs became more varied.

I broke an American Saddlebred colt to ride. Twin Springs Chief was truly my horse. Two of my friends and I used to take our horses for trail rides through the countryside. It was a good way to build our friendships, as well as good training for the horses. People can't really do that this day and age.

4-H taught me even more. I raised "show" steers. I took them to fairs all around northwest Missouri. Did you ever see a ten or eleven year old girl giving a 1,200-pound steer a bath? Needless to say, I was as wet and soapy as the steer. But I did very well in showing my animals.

I did a lot of projects in 4-H. My mother was my leader. I had to rip out many a seam and redo it correctly. I still have the first thing I made. It was an apron made out of a flour sack, printed with ships, planes, etc. Some place in that time frame World War II was finishing up.

I attended 4-H camp, where I learned to square dance, played games, competed in contests, and had my first boyfriend, who just happened to be the lifeguard.

The most embarrassed I ever was was when I was mowing hay. I had a red handkerchief around my hair and was wearing cut-off jeans and a sleeveless denim top. Plus I was covered with dust and dirt. A car came across the field and pulled up alongside the mower. Of course, I stopped, and a high school boy got out of the car. He came out to ask me for a date! All I can say is I do clean up nicely.

Along with all of the farming and 4-H projects, there was high school. There were the usual studies, basketball, speech and drama, cheerleading, orchestra and band, plus the contests that went with these things. Putting on plays was my "cup of tea." We took them to the county, district, and state contests. This stayed with me through college and teaching. I can't tell how many times I've used speech and drama in my teaching. Children loved it as a much as I.

I went away to college for two and a half years and began teaching at age 19. At that particular time, one could teach with a 60-hour certificate if one continued working on a degree. I had a class of fifth graders. There were 36 of them. Some of the boys were taller than I. Two thousand ten was their 50th year out of high school, and I helped them celebrate it.

I had a wonderful basis for a long, great career of teaching. I have been retired for twelve years from that career that lasted nearly 40 years. I now live in the town I started teaching in. I do see a lot of familiar faces. They could be children or even grandchildren of those I taught. "Do you think?"

We Waxed the Floor with Our Sock Feet and Were Taught to Be Happy With What We Had
By Mildred D. Roberts of St. Joseph, Missouri
Born 1933

I was born during the Depression years of the '30s. Things like sugar, flour, and gas were rationed. Stamps were issued for a certain amount, so you were careful not to waste anything. My folks would butcher a hog in the fall, and other times my Dad would kill a rabbit or squirrel, which was fried. No one ever said, "I don't like that." We never went to bed hungry, but we were thankful for everything.

We lived in the hills of Halls, Missouri, walked about two miles to school—no buses! We had two rooms, in school—the big and little room. Our drinking water was drawn from a well and put into a large crock, no indoor plumbing—in the heat or cold, it was outside.

Each morning we raised the flag and said the "Pledge of Allegiance." We also had a book for every subject, and used them. There were no 'I-pods, they hadn't been invented yet, and we didn't even have electricity. I was 17 before the rural electric ran lines from town. We had several coal-oil lamps.

Laundry was done on a board. We had to carry the water from the well at the bottom of the hill. Clothes were hung on a line to dry. They were always starched, which was made from flour and water—cooked until it was clear—then thinned with water. They were hung on the line till dry, then brought in, sprinkled with water—then rolled—to be ironed the next day.

Irons were made of heavy metal, then, heated on the wood stove. You would need at least three irons, as they cooled pretty quickly, so you kept reheating them.

While Mother ironed, my job was to scrub the living room floor, which was linoleum. Then, after it was dry, we waxed it with a heavy paste wax. We let that dry, then put sox on our feet, and slid over the floor to shine it. My sister was 7 years younger than me, so she could help with that. After several bumps and falls, it looked pretty good.

We liked to help around the house, as there were no toys, like today. We had jacks; which is a ball and about 10 metal pieces –you picked one of the pieces after throwing the ball. Outside, we jumped rope, threw the ball over the house, with someone on the other side. We played hide& seek, and baseball if neighbor kids stopped by.

In the wintertime, which there was always lots of snow, we slid down the hills. We didn't have sleds, so we used a piece of tin or the scoop-shovel. There were no insulated clothes and overshoes were just one piece of rubber with four buckles. If we didn't have gloves, we put socks on our hands. We stayed out as long as we could, then went in, and stood behind the wood stove to dry.

We don't have weather now, like we did in my younger days. Then, it would snow the early part of November and we hardly saw the ground until March. It was freeze and thaw—then, more snow.

We only went to town on Saturdays, then, to church on Sunday. My dad worked on the railroad, so he was gone every day--and there was no going any place in the evenings.

In summertime, we stayed outside till dark. To fight the bugs and flies—my dad would burn some rags to make smoke. How we must have smelled! Yes, we were poor, but happy. We were taught to be happy with what we had—material things weren't important.

I Survived Six Weeks of Solid Ice and "Black Sunday"
By Christy D. Schrock of Jamesport, Missouri
Born 1926

I feel privileged to be part of this Northwest Missouri History Book. I am 86 years old and lived the first 38 years of my life at Yoder, Kansas, nearly 300 miles west of my home here at Jamesport, Missouri.

The stories that I have to write about reached to some extent to this area, but were perhaps more severe at my home in Kansas.

On the evening of January 6, 1936, we had a light freezing rain falling, but at 9 PM, this turned to a fast falling sleet. This pounded on our metal roof, noisily, all night. By morning, the weather was quiet at 15 degrees. We had a white world of sleet of 6 inches deep. This was frozen solid, like ice on a pond.

This ice caused many, many problems for livestock men. Cattle got down, disabling some with broken bones or out of joint. Some tied gunnysacks on their feet for footing. Horses were shod with sharpened iron spikes on their shoes. This ice did not go away soon, but stayed on for 6 weeks. Yes, this was a bad storm for older people and livestock men, but here is the other side of the story, what fun on the ice for 6 weeks.

A few days after it came, I learned to manage ice skates. I went to a one-room school 1 ½ mile from home, so skates took me to school for 6 weeks. These memories and of many other ice games we had in those 6 weeks, I will never forget. Older boys and men on a saddled horse pulled skaters. Cars also went in large fields and pulled skaters. The water content of this storm produced a bumper wheat crop that year.

I do remember a little of the Great Depression, along with drought conditions in the early 1930's causing the dust storms of Western Kansas, bringing on the name of the Dust Bowl for that area. The Southwest winds carrying the Western Kansas dust into our area, and on further east. In about 33 or 34 of these dust storms were quite common.

We had no light in our school, and during one of these storms, it got so dark that school let out at noon. The teacher was afraid of us getting lost going home, so he took us home in his Model-A Ford. This happened three days in one week. Otherwise, school was never dismissed because of a dust storm.

I also remember April 14, 1935. This being Palm Sunday, my parents decided to attend a neighboring church. The day started in perfect, clear as a bell, not a breath of air, and springtime temperatures. My older brother and I were left at home, but having permission to walk 1 mile across the field and spend the afternoon with the neighbor children (our friends). The day went on, and 4 o'clock found us upstairs with a card game. Suddenly, someone looked out the window and exclaimed, "There is a very black cloud back in the west. It is going to rain or storm." Brother and I immediately decided to go home.

Coming out of the house, the storm had hit; no rain, but dust and 25 mile an hour wind. It turned dark, visibility was 50 feet or less, and the air so full of dust, it nearly chocked us. We followed the fence going home, so we would not get lost. I do not remember the length of this storm. This storm was one of many, but the worst one in history and the Kansas History books lists this day as "Black Sunday."

The farming methods of the Western plains did not reduce the Kansas winds, but it did stop the dust, and the plains are no more called (The Dust Bowl), but is now (2013) part of (The Bread Basket of the Nation).

Jesse James Brother, Frank, Spent the Night
By Marilyn A. Reed of Kearney, Missouri
Born 1927

I was born and raised on the family farm north of Kearney, Missouri. My forefathers came here from Kentucky in 1828.

I remember at a very young age, probably the early 1930s, playing in the old stone Wilson house near Watkins Mill, where my uncle lived at the time. He liked foxhounds and liked foxhunting. The old Wilson house

Marilyn and her father, Robert G. Reed in 1942

has been disassembled and taken to Hodge Park. My uncle's father raised horses, and one time Frank James, Jesse James' brother, came to see about a horse and stayed the night. My uncle said he was scared, because Frank James slept with his pistol under his pillow. I don't know if he bought a horse.

One time at a gathering in Excelsior Springs, I won first prize at a baby contest. I still have the picture.

The ladies in our neighborhood formed a club they called the "Keepers Club." They had regular meetings on Wednesday each month. They would discuss various things, talk about what they were doing, and have some good things to eat. I got to go with my mother, which I enjoyed.

I started school in first grade at Kearney. Later I convinced my daddy to let me change to Muddy Fork School, since it was a short walk. I remember the school was very cold in the winter since it was heated with a wood stove. Later, I changed back to Kearney Schools and I was able to ride the school bus. This ride home on the school bus was a long trip, as I was the last one to get off. We had a horse named Punk that I sometimes rode to school. I rode down 33 Highway, then gravel, to the railroad track to Kearney. I would get off and the horse would come back home by itself. I would then walk the rest of the way to school. When my class graduated from High School in 1946, there were just seven girls in it. The three boys had all enlisted in World War II.

I helped my daddy around the farm. He fixed a wooden seat next to his cultivator, and I rode with him plowing corn. When he worked, he would work nights at Lake City Arsenal during the war. I did the milking for him.

I joined 4-H, and had several projects like sewing, canning, gardening, and livestock. I won many ribbons for my work at the State Fair. I also won a trip to the Chicago 4-H Convention. I still have the scrapbook.

During the hot, dry Depression years, water was scarce and we had no electricity for pumps. The shallow hand dug wells failed often and we had to haul water from Kearney. I remember Daddy worked for REA, to sign up people for rural electrification. It was a treat when we turned on our first electric light in 1939. The co-op is now Platte Clay Electric

Co-Op. Their home office is in Kearney.

In spite of many things being rationed, we looked forward to the spirited basketball tournaments. It was a treat to go to Mathew's Drug Store in Kearney for ice cream or a coke.

I raised sheep for wool and saved the money to go to Cosmetology School. During High School, I would attend on Saturdays and then attended full time after graduation. I rode the train from Kearney to Kansas City and then took the bus to Cosmetology School. When I received my license, I went to work at a shop in North Kansas City. By chance, I did my husband's mother's hair and she introduced me to her son. May 1, 1949 we were married at the Baptist Church in North Kansas City. We spent our honeymoon in Colorado, and have lived happily ever after in Kearney, Missouri.

Honesty and Truthfulness are Important
By Rowena Smith of Columbia, Missouri
Born 1938

It was a very hot day in June 1938 when my parents brought me home from the hospital. The doctor told my mother to only put me in a diaper. It was a cloth diaper with no rubber pants. I proved to be a problem, because my mother's milk didn't agree with me, and I cried a lot. My dad was a farmer. I believe he was a tenant farmer, as he worked on another man's farm. After trying several formulas and buying ingredients that were really not affordable, my dad, out of frustration, went out and milked a cow. He filled my bottle with warm milk from a Jersey, rich with cream. That was what I was raised on. For the first few years of my life, I would only drink milk that was half cream.

Around Christmas, 1947, we were getting ready to go to my fraternal grandparent's house. I was very excited because the old car we had had a rumble seat. I hadn't been allowed to ride in it yet, because of the weather and such. But I was going to ride in it because it was such a beautiful day.

The washtub was put in the living room close to the stove, and we were taking turns washing up while listening to the radio. While I was standing there with little or no clothes on, the man on the radio said something; "Oh, look what she's doing! Wonder what she'll put on?" Well, I was convinced that man on the radio could see me and my lack of clothes. My parents, being the voice of reason, convinced me he couldn't and we resumed getting ready to go. I got my rumble seat ride. What fun!

Christmas at school was an all-school affair. Parents sat on bleachers and kids ran around, excited that Santa was coming there that night. I went back to where my mother and dad were sitting, but my dad wasn't there, and mom had his felt hat in her lap. When I asked where he was, Mom said the restroom. When my name was finally called to come get my candy from Santa, I looked at Santa's hands and got so excited I almost jumped up and down and gave away the secret. Those were my dad's hands that were handing out my gift. My dad was Santa! I think that was the year I got my bicycle, but knowing who Santa was took first place. However, I was very glad to get a bicycle.

In January of that following year, as my mother was braiding my long hair, my mother remarked that Grandma wasn't up yet and that she'd better check on her. She left, and when she came back, she had my coat. She told me to go to the neighbor's house. Grandma had most likely died soon after she went to bed. My pet dog that she always said she didn't like but would protect from the bully hounds in town that killed anything they caught, after her death was found lying in her bed on her pillow. He missed her as much as we did.

The following year, I attended a country school for a few months, and then we moved to a larger town. I was able to graduate from the new school eight years later.

My first day at the new school was really scary, because although I had gone to three other schools, they were much smaller. Also, I was extremely shy, and although I always had friends, I was not out going and didn't have any self-confidence. The girls at this new school were mostly business peoples' children. They were also some of the nicest and friendliest that I'd ever met. They never did anything without including me. Sometime in the next couple of years, I developed some confidence, thank to my friends.

During my junior high years, I had a wonderful teacher. Of course, no one liked her at the time. She was scary to the new students because she expected our very best

and didn't hesitate to let us and the rest of the class know when we failed her expectations. One of her favorite sayings was "caught with your pants down." Another was when she saw a student yawn, "stifle that yawn." Then she would move the student to an open window to sit until they woke up. We also had homework every night. She also taught us to do research, write papers, read books and write reports, write skits on the books and perform the skits, made sure we knew how to dance, how to do introductions, and so many more things besides the 3 R's. She also taught me to never give credit where credit isn't due. I really learned a lot in those two years, including being able to stand up for myself.

My high school years stand out, as my principal taught me more about being truthful. My father was called Honest George, so I already knew about honesty and truthfulness. Posters in our school that claimed false promises were torn down. I'd like to do that today many times. My principal also believed in good sportsmanship, not only for athletes but also for the cheering crowd. I found games lacking in sportsmanship later with booing and fighting. I wonder what happened? Are honesty, truth, and sportsmanship still in the dictionary? It is unfortunate that teachers do not have the right to discipline anymore. We need more teachers and principals like mine.

Pine Flavored Potatoes Not the Best, but We Had to Eat Them Anyway
By Ruby Hawkins of Braymer, Missouri
Born 1939

One of my earliest memories is of cod liver oil. We had to take it every day. It was horrible and I couldn't get the fishy taste out of my mouth. One day, after much fighting to get my brother and I to take it, my mother said, "It's not that bad, Daddy will take it too." We watched Daddy take a big dose. He promptly threw it up. We never had to take it again.

We lived in the country in a three-room house with no electricity and a well with a bucket. Eventually, there were eight of us in that little house. I had five brothers and sisters. There were so many of us that, occasionally, my father would leave one of us in town. Once someone ran out in front of the car and

169

yelled, "Efton," you left one of the kids back there." When we stopped the car, I could see my eight year old brother Randall, trying to catch up. He could have probably caught up with us, that old Model-A barely crawled.

On another occasion, Dad left the three year old, Judy. We didn't miss her until suppertime. We had all scattered when we got home, some were playing down on the creek; others were building a playhouse in the cornfield that surrounded our house. When we found out that she was gone, my father didn't want to go get her until morning. She had never been away at night and we knew she was crying. My mother couldn't drive, but my twelve year old brother Roy, could. He drove to town and brought her home. She had cried the entire time that she had been left at my uncle's house.

We were so poor, we ate whatever the boys could catch. We ate squirrels, rabbits, raccoons, and groundhogs. There were no deer in the area then. If the so-called wolf had come to our door, we would have ate him.

A man came to the door and told dad that a freight car had burned. It was loaded with potatoes, and he could have all he wanted. We thought this was great. Dad brought home a huge load of those potatoes. What we didn't know, was that the pine box car had flavored every one of those potatoes. Food was so scarce, we had to eat them. We had pine mashed potatoes, pine fried potatoes, and pine potato soup. I sure was glad to see the end of those.

My mother boiled the coffee grounds over and over, and fried the potato peelings. She boiled wieners and put dumplings in them because there wasn't enough wieners to go around. The dumplings were pink.

Mom made our clothes out of feed sacks that my uncle would bring. It took two of the same kind to make me a dress. She thought I didn't look good in red, so she told him to never bring red. I was five when I caught him going out the door, and I whispered, "Bring me red." When he came again, he brought me two red flowered feed sacks. I knew I would finally get a red dress, because she wouldn't waste them. She sewed on a treadle sewing machine and made her own patterns. If she saw it, she could copy it. She once made me a dress just like the one in a magazine advertising Tide detergent. The dress was hanging on a clothes line.

During the '40s and '50s, Gypsies roamed around the country. We were used to Hobos and Tramps, and we shared what we had with them. We were warned about Gypsies. There were all sorts of stories about them. I don't know how much was true.

One day my mother decided to get some things out of the attic. To get to the attic, we put a kitchen chair on the table, and pushed a panel in the ceiling to one side. She very rarely ever took any of us with her, but that day she pulled us all up, even three month old baby Sue. We sat on the rafters, careful not to step through the ceiling. While she sorted boxes, I sat with the baby on my lap. The baby was asleep, with sunlight from a crack, shining on her face. We heard a car door slam, and voices. We knew no one would be coming until Dad came in the evening. We sat very still and Mom pulled the panel shut, leaving just a slit to see down below. I looked down into our kitchen. I saw a lot of dark skinned men and one woman. She had long dark hair, and was wearing a long, bright green dress. I saw the bracelets on her arm shine as she went through the cupboards and drawers. We sat on the rafters, too scared to breath. To this day, I don't know how six children kept so quiet, and what if the baby had woke up? Some say they kidnapped babies. I wonder what they thought the chair was on the table for. There wasn't much to find in a house as poor as ours, and they were soon on their way.

My mother told my twelve year old brother that if anything ever happened to put the kids under the bed.

One day a man came to the door. He said he was selling magazines. Mom told him that she wasn't interested, and tried to shut the door. He got very aggressive and shoved her backwards. My brother put us all under the bed, even the baby. There wasn't much room there. I heard my mother hit the floor, then a lot of yelling and cussing. My father had come home and grabbed the butcher knife, our only weapon. The man ran, but we heard that they caught him, after attacking another woman.

We never got much for Christmas, my little brother used to say, "How come when we get poorer, Santa gets poorer?'

Cousin Paul was an only child, and he got a lot of toys, so we would visit him to play with his. Back then, a lot of boys got chemistry sets for Christmas, Cousin Paul got one. One day while we were playing, he brought it out; lots of bottles and vials of stuff. His mother had just made us a pitcher of Kool-Aid and set it on the porch. We poured all the stuff in the Kool-Aid and drank it; never had any ill effects from that.

From an early age, I remember sitting in front of our old battery radio listening to the Grand Ole Opry with my father. Everyone else had gone to bed, just the light from the little dial in the dark. I felt like I was right there at the Ryman with Hank Snow, Ernest Tubb, Roy Acuff, Carl Smith, and the Carters. Hank Williams was my favorite. When he died in 1953, I was devastated.

When we were teenagers, the highlight of the summer was the Fair at Toit Park. You could lose your parents and have a lot of fun. One particular Stage Show was sponsored by the R. B. Rice Sausage Company. Their star performer was, Little Cora Rice. She was 13, but looked older. We had seen her on TV. She was very pretty, and all the boys were madly in love with her, including my older brother. She even gave him a picture, taken at the photo booth. He's gone now, but I still have it. I was so jealous of her. I tried to find fault with her. I told him that her arms were too long, she was short wasted, her smile was too big, and her hair too curly, but in my heart, I wanted to look just like her. I wonder where she is now.

We wore our jeans rolled up, just below our knees. We preferred boy's jeans, not girls, they just fit better. Girl's jeans had three cornered pockets with a pearl snap on them, no pockets on the back. My brother Roy had just gotten new jeans, and we were the same size. I had new jeans too, but with that pearl on the pocket. He had worked all week putting up hay. I knew he would come home and get ready for Saturday night. I put his jeans on and left him mine. I made sure I was gone early. I knew we would all end up on our little Main Street. I just had to stay out of his sight. I saw him later, at a distance, instead of his shirt tucked in; it hung down, covering those pearl snaps. I hurried home and got in bed, knowing he wouldn't beat me and disturb the others, and by morning, he would have cooled off.

Now, I wish I had been a better sister, because he took care of me.

Memories of Mercer County, Missouri
By Ruth Chinn of Kansas City, Kansas
Born 1912

Grandpa and Grandma Hamilton

On a farm near Topsy, Missouri on February 22, 1912, there was a huge black cloud in the western sky, and a new baby girl named Lennis Ruth Hamilton was born. My grandmother Hamilton nicknamed me Little Snowflake, saying that I was the only snowflake that didn't melt in the Great Blizzard of 1912. The shutters on the house clattered, and the howling wind encircled the whole house and blew snow through the cracks under the doors. My family said that it was the worst storm in fifty years. The snow drifted to the top of most of the farm buildings, and the men had to shovel a tunnel to the barn.

When I was six years old, I came close to death during the 1918 flu pandemic. The flu was very painful, and I had a high fever. We lived in a one-room cottage, and neighbors would bring wood for the fire, but they would not come in for fear of catching the flu. My grandmother Hamilton came over to care for me and asked what I wanted to eat. I said, "Fresh grapes," but that was an impossible request in the middle of winter out in the country. Grandma had brought a jar of pickles, she cut them up in tiny bites, and I ate them. At eleven o'clock that night, I remember my fever breaking, and I got up out of bed as if nothing had ever happened! Almost every family lost someone from the flu, and it was not possible to bury the people because the ground was so frozen. They took all the bodies to a big barn and stored them until spring. My father helped dig the graves, and they had a huge funeral. The preacher talked a long time, and I saw tears running down my father's face. I went over and hugged my father's leg until the service was over. Death was new to me, and I didn't realize until later that he had lost many of his friends.

We were only allowed in Grandma Hamilton's parlor on special occasions. The shades were usually kept drawn to keep the carpet from fading. The carpet was made from strips of braided material and nailed to the floor. We were allowed to eat an apple in there because it wouldn't spill on the carpet! We would set on the floor while Grandma played the organ and Grandpa played the violin. We would sing the old hymns and have a grand time! Grandpa made several violins from wood sent from Germany.

Grandpa and Grandma Hamilton had a big, green parrot named Polly. When Polly was out of his cage, he would hide behind the front door and yell, "Help, help!" We taught Polly to sing the hymn *Right in the Corner Where You Are*. Polly would sing this hymn and then go, "Ha, ha, ha," and he even took a bow after his performance! Polly also learned to say, "Maw, let the hogs out," which he repeated over and over until he about drove us all crazy. One day, Grandma had heard enough, and she took a pencil and wacked him. Polly shut up but wasn't one bit happy about it and started mumbling. After that, when we wanted Polly to hush up, all we had to do was lay the pencil down by the cage. We could carry Polly all over the house on a pillow, but I would not dare touch him for fear of being bitten! Polly entertained our family for twenty-five years and another family for twenty-five more years.

Lennis Ruth Hamilton Chenn

My Parents and Cousins

At a very young age, I was always taken with my parents to the country dances in people's homes on Saturday nights. They would clear one room and roll up the rug for dancing to fiddle music. I would get tired and fall asleep on a pile of coats. I was picked up and carried to the buggy or wagon, and we bounced home late at night. My father called the square dances with his musical voice. My mother played the piano and never missed a note. They all played by ear.

When I was about six years old, my father had a new car with large spokes in the wheels. We liked to ride with the top down on the dusty roads and over the rickety bridges. One day, I was riding in the back seat with my cousin, Wilma. We were swinging our arms free as we went over a high bridge. Wilma had let loose of the safety bar and bounced so high that she came down on the door handle and caught her dress tail on it. The door flew open and Wilma was upside down, swinging out over the river when we crossed the bridge. Boy was Wilma screaming! Dad stopped the car and tossed Wilma back into the seat and slammed the door. Dad didn't say a thing. During the rest of the trip, Wilma and I sat very still with our eyes wide open and held on tight to the safety bar.

When we were young, we had very few toys to play with but most farmers had big, huge ropes. We loved to jump rope with them, and I learned to turn two ropes. My friends learned that with perfect timing, they could jump in between the two ropes. This was quite an accomplishment, and they would line up to give it their best try. With a rope in each hand, I would turn the ropes and count one, two, three, and four. I would never let my count get off, and I would turn the heavy ropes until my shoulders hurt.

My favorite cousin, Cliff, and I loved to go to the branch or creek. The clear water ran over the rocks, and it was a shady and cool place to play. We would dig in the sand banks, building room after room for our castles or dream houses. After the rains came, our magic dreams were washed away the next day we would start all over again.

One summer, Cliff and I started picking the dry gypsum pods, which looked exactly like a pill. I secretly wanted to be a nurse and here was my chance. We lined up some cousins under the shade of the apple tree, and they pretended to be sick. I fed them the gypsum seeds to cure them, and Cliff took about twice as many as the other cousins. Of course, I didn't take any since I thought I was the nurse. That night, Cliff woke up violently sick and was out of his head. Grandma forced him to drink strong salt water, which made him vomit. Cliff almost died that night and that was the end of my nursing career!

Married Life

In the summer, all the farmers helped each other put up hay and I had to cook dinner for twelve men who came to help my husband, Glenn. As the men left for the field, they told me to have a big meal ready by noon. Later, a terrible thought crossed my mind: Glenn had forgotten to kill the chickens I planned to cook for dinner! I was horrified at the thought of killing a chicken. How could I kill six of my pet chickens, who would follow me and even sit on my lap? Finally, in fright I decided I would try. I went to the wire coop and took one out. It started to sing a song of some sort and put its head against my arm. I walked around quite a while trying to get enough courage to kill it. I picked up the axe and went to the chopping block. I stretched out its neck, and that darn chicken stared me right in my eyes. I let it go and off he went, squawking in much fright! I had watched my mother-in-law wrap her hand around a chicken's neck and give it a quick swing and swing it until its head was severed. I had to kill those five chickens, so I did one with a fast twirl, but the next one slipped out of my hand and tried to get away. I was desperate, with only five chickens. So I ran fast, snatched it up, and finished the job. Finally, I finished killing them all and felt faint. Next, I ran into the house and brought out a tea kettle of boiling water. I placed two chickens in a big bucket, dowsed them with boiling water, and turned them until all the feathers were soaked. Then I began plucking the hot feathers until they were bare. I kept this up until all five were clean. I took them inside and pumped cold water over them until they were cool. I must say that I cut up some of the chickens and tore the rest apart! I sawed the firewood, and then fired up the stove to start frying the chickens. It must have been 110 degrees and sweat was running down my forehead. In between the frying, I made cottage cheese from the milk in the cellar, placed the soup beans on the cooler side of the stove, and made ice tea, biscuits, and gravy. I had a mountain of food on the table when the men arrived. I glanced at Glenn, and I saw a sign of pride and approval on his face.

When I was young, I stepped on a nail and my father-in-law treated it by heating up some coals and holding my foot over the hot coals. He said that if he could get my foot to bleed, it would purify itself. After a while, my foot started to bleed and it worked! It healed perfectly, and I was able to walk and run again.

My husband's father bought three farms and planned to give them to his children. Thing went pretty well for several years, until the market broke in 1929 and Roosevelt closed the banks. The bankers demanded payment and Grandpa Mann couldn't pay. Grandma Mann maneuvered $900.00 out of the farm foreclosures and found a fourteen room, two story house in Jamesport, Missouri for $1,200.00. How could she pay for the extra $300.00? Grandma would not give up, and she looked up the company that was installing lights through northwest Missouri. She offered to board all of their men at a reasonable rate and here came seventeen men. The Depression took away the jobs and eventually, one at a time, seventeen of us lived in the big, white house along with the boarders. My husband and I moved around, following jobs, and each time, we came back to Grandma Mann's house to live.

Kind, Helpful, Poor Country Folk
By Marian Campbell of Trenton, Missouri
Born 1926

I was born in 1926 in north central Missouri and grew up during the Depression. My birth was at the family home, where my mother was born 25 years before. Her father had built the house just a year before she was born. It was a simple, five-room house, with two bedrooms and no closets, no bathroom, no water system, and no electricity. We did have a telephone, the old-fashioned kind that hung on the wall. It was a good thing we had one, because it was needed to call the doctor. We were five miles from our little town of Laredo, where our doctor lived. It was the first of March, when often times the "spring thaw" has begun. Dr. E. J. Mairs got stuck in the mud road on his way out to the farm and

173

Marian Pollock in 1927

had to walk on in. My grandmother was there to assist in my delivery.

My sister, Evelyn, was two and a half years older than I was. We had over two miles to go to our country school, so our father bought a tiny Shetland pony, Fannie, for her to ride when she started to school. When I started, he traded Fannie for a bigger one to hold both of us. That was Daisy. As we grew, he got a larger pony, Prince, and also bought a little two-wheel cart to hitch the pony to. That outfit attracted a lot of attention at school.

When my sister started to high school in Laredo, Dad bought a nice riding horse, Beauty, for her. We sold the pony, and I walked to country school with the neighbor kids. In the years following, roads were graveled and school busses took us to high school in town.

Our little country school, Bethel, had many good patrons, teachers, and bright students. My grandparents lived across the road from the school, and many of the single lady teachers boarded there. My grandmother was a good cook and a very kind person. It was an ideal place for the girls, who had just graduated from Trenton Junior College and were on their first job. The Pews were the only ones in the district that had electricity. A Delco set of batteries in the basement provided lights in every room, a radio, a refrigerator, and power to pump water into a

small reservoir. The kitchen sink had a faucet and a drain, but no hot water. And there was no bathroom. During the 1936 Presidential campaign, neighbors would gather there to hear the candidates' speeches and to hear the results on Election Night.

Alf Landon, the Republican candidate, was going to make a stop in Trenton, our county seat, on a certain date. Our teacher, Harry Craig, wanted to take his pupils to see him. My grandfather and a neighbor provided cars to take us to the Rock Island Depot for this event. Campaign buttons were thrown out to the large crowd. I didn't catch one, but I already had an Alf Landon button. I also had an FDR one! While we were in town, we visited the Republican Times newspaper office, Swift and Co., and the Coco Cola Bottling Co.

We didn't have much for entertainment in the 1930s. The radios were good for ballgames, boxing, and afternoon soap operas. Church and school activities were an outlet for the young folks. We were 17 miles from Trenton, where the parks, swimming pool, and movies were. In the early '30s, we girls never went to Trenton, only to get coats and shoes. Mother made our dresses out of feed sacks or made over from our aunt's dresses. We had mail delivery every day, but we couldn't afford the newspaper. Magazine salesmen would take

Marian and Evelyn riding Daisy

174

a nice hen or two for a year's subscription to Successful Farming, so we had that and Wallace Farmer.

It was hot. We had no fans or refrigeration. We did have a good cave that kept milk sweet and food from spoiling.

One morning, my mother forgot to have Dad kill a chicken before he went to the field. That was to be our dinner. So when the mailman came by, she asked him to kill it. He was glad to oblige. Years later, she learned to do it herself. We were all just kind, helpful, poor country folk. People today wonder how we survived!

The "Good Old Days" Were Hard
By Mary Ann Willis of King City, Missouri
Born 1930

I, Mary Anne Eiberger Willis, was born 1-8-1930 at home on a farm. I had a father, mother, three brothers, and one sister. We were all five about two years apart in age, so we had a lot of fun playing together. I had an uncle, aunt, and cousins who lived a mile from us, and we played with them often.

We lived about two and a half miles from a country school where we attended for eight grades. We had to walk or ride a pony to school. There were about 23 children in all eight grades, with one teacher teaching them. The teacher roomed with one of the neighbors near school. One teacher rode a horse to school, also. At one time, there were five horses tied up by the school that the children rode. My father made us a cart that our pony would pull, so we rode in the cart part of the time. One other family had a cart, also. It was a one-room schoolhouse on a dirt road, also. There were no electricity, no lights, and no running water. The teacher had to start the fire every morning with coal and wood to warm the schoolhouse. Also, she had to pump the drinking water from a well nearby, bring in a bucketful for the children to drink. There were two outhouses, one for the girls and one for the boys.

The girls wore homemade dresses made from feed and flour sacks, prints and solids. The boys always wore bib overalls. In the winter, everyone wore long legged underwear and long stockings. Also, we wore overshoes, as we had a lot of snow and also dirt roads. We were really cold when we got to school. We took our lunch in a lunch bucket.

When we got home, we had our chores to do. We had to pump water for livestock and get in wood and corncobs for Mother to cook with in the kitchen stove. Also, it kept the house warm, mainly in the kitchen. That was the main room we lived in. We never had electricity until I was in high school. So we never had a refrigerator or icebox.

We did our butchering of hogs and beef in the coldest part of winter, so we could have fresh meat to eat all winter. My uncle helped butcher, and one time they butchered five hogs in one day. We had a building called the smokehouse where the meat was kept, and Mother would get meat out there all winter. She also canned meat and fried meat, and then put it in big two and three gallon crock containers and put lard on the top over the meat, and we ate that in the summer time. She would also clean casings from the hog, and they would grind a lot of meat for sausage, stuff it in the casings, and smoke it. We would also have to render the fat off the meat in a big black kettle outside to get lard to use. We had a lot of it, and it lasted until the next winter when we butchered. It made wonderful piecrusts and fried chicken.

For pets, we had cats, one dog, some rabbits, pet lambs, and also some pet pigs we would help to raise because the sows would have too many pigs. My dad would give us the piglets to raise, and when we sold them, we would get the money.

We lived ten miles from town, so we never got to go to movies on Saturday night. We had a battery-powered radio, but my parents used it mainly to hear the weather forecast and get the markets. Once in a while, we could listen

Mary Ann and her brothers

175

to *Amos and Andy* or *Fibber McGee and Molly* for entertainment.

My brother was in the Korean War. In the Depression years during World War II. everything was rationed. We used stamps issued to us every month for things we bought like gas, rubber, and groceries, etc. I remember sugar was scarce, so my mother made sweet pickles using saccharin for sweetener. We had our own chickens for meat and eggs. With no refrigerator, Mother had to dress the chicken in the morning that we would have it for dinner, as there was no cold place to keep meat except in cold weather. We had milk cows to milk, so we had our own milk, cream, and butter then. So there weren't many groceries we had to buy. With plenty of milk and cream, we had a lot of homemade ice cream of a wintertime, as we had ice from the tanks and ponds.

We had a wringer washing machine that we had to turn by hand, and also a washboard to use. Our telephone was a hand ringer type on a rural line, which we had a number that was ours. Ours was 2930, which was three long rings. It was a party line, with about six other neighbors. We could listen to our neighbors talking if we wanted to be nosey!

My grandparents on both sides of the family came from Germany. They passed away before I was born, but my parents could speak German, and we learned some.

Swimming pools weren't around years ago. We went barefoot all summer, so we would go wading in some creeks and shallow ponds some. Of a winter with a lot of snow, we went sled riding a lot. We had some big hills to go down.

Some people say the good old days, but I would say they were very hard to live in and something we would never forget and never wish back.

The R.O.T.C. Competition
By Stephen B. Givens of Easton, Missouri
Born 1949

I can honestly state that those years spent at home with my family were the best, with the best memories of my life. Of those, my high school years were the best. I had such admiration for my sisters that I chose to attend the same high school as they did. Even though I was at least six years younger than both of my sisters, they were never embarrassed or

R.O.T.C. Drum and Bugle Corp.

ashamed to be with or take me along with them. The high school we attended in St. Joseph, Missouri was Lafayette.

Our sophomore year, all the boys were required to take R.O.T.C. I dreaded it at the time, but it turned out that I excelled in it. I received several honors and awards, but by the year's end, I was a 2nd Lieutenant. Although I could perform all the necessary marching and rifle code of arms, the school reinstated a Drum and Bugle Corps, which the district had not had for years. Since I played percussion in the school band, I enrolled as a snare drummer. Ours was the only unit like it in town. We practiced long and hard, and our efforts paid off, as we were asked to march in parades, exhibitions, and our annual R.O.T.C. Revue.

I enjoyed all aspects of the R.O.T.C. program, so I signed up for my junior year. The commander of the Drum and Bugle Corps had graduated at the end of the year. I was asked to take over as commander and accepted it with honor. Although there were new members, a good number returned from the previous year. In addition to the marching events the Corps participated in, for the first year we were also present and marched in an exhibition on the football field at the University of Missouri in Columbia and in Leavenworth, Kansas, on the parade grounds of their only military school. This year turned out to be even better than the first. I ended the year as a Captain.

I again signed up for my third and final year as a senior. In addition to the continuing responsibility as commander of the Drum and Bugle Corps, I was also designated Battalion Commander. Each battalion staff officer was assigned a sponsor officer to accompany them during certain activities and events. The sponsor officers were female and had the same rank as the staff member to whom they were assigned. Each high school was considered a Battalion. St. Joseph had three public high schools, each with the R.O.T.C. program, and the combined schools were considered a Brigade. Being a high school senior was exciting alone, but also being the Battalion commander, the Commander of the Drum and Bugle Corps, and the anticipation of my upcoming marriage that following summer made it not only the best year of high school, but the best year of my life.

Each year, the stage to showcase the activities of the R.O.T.C. during that year was the Annual R.O.T.C. Revue. I had the Drum and Bugle Corps practicing hard for our exhibition and as the Battalion Commander, I was a candidate for the Brigade Commander. One of the three Battalion Commanders would receive this prestigious honor. In preparation, I had to give speeches, take written tests, and go before the heads of the R.O.T.C. program in St. Joseph, regular Army Majors Venn and Parker. By the time of the Revue, I had attained the rank of Lt. Colonel. My parents, future in-laws, and many other friends and family attended the Revue to support me. The Drum and Bugle Corps performed flawlessly. I received several medals and my sabre, but my school didn't win any competitions (rifle assembly, best drilled squad, or best drilled cadet). The previous year, the Battalion Commander from our school had received the Brigade Commander; therefore, I felt I had no chance of receiving it. The final activity of the Revue was the naming of the Brigade staff. As Major Venn gave his opening remarks before the naming of staff, I thought back to when my parents drug me to one of these R.O.T.C. Revues. My older sister, Sandy, was the sponsor officer to the then Battalion Commander of Lafayette when he was named Brigade Commander. She was as excited as he. Major Venn announced the Brigade Commander as Lt. Colonel Steve...and then he stopped. He then informed all in attendance that the three Battalion Commanders had first names of Steve. He then finished his naming of the Brigade Commander as Lt. Colonel Steve Givens, my name. Our entire section jumped to their feet and began applauding, grabbed me by my arm and pulled I got up

and took the position as Brigade Commander while the remaining staff was named. I then knew how my sister felt some six years earlier. The next week at school, I was congratulated by students, teachers, office personnel, and even the principal. There was even an announcement made over the PA system during morning announcements. My rank was raised to full Colonel and I attended the two other high schools during their Federal Inspections. This is a memory I hold dear to me. I relive it over and over again.

Working Hard for a Good Life
By Juanita Waters of Williamsburg,
Kentucky
Born 1930

Being born in 1930 definitely makes me a senior citizen, and I do remember the drought and hot weather of the thirties. With no electricity, we had to endure the heat. However, my mom, Anna (Crockett) Rodenberg could think of ways to help, such as putting our bedclothes in a deep cellar and leaving them until bedtime. By then, they were cool. Then she would put them back on the bed quickly, which was pretty comforting to lie down on.

Fun in those days was playing with cousins who lived close. Family reunions at home were always great, and talk about good cooks! With my family, two brothers, and

Juanita's mom, Anna (Crockett) Rodenberg

my parents, there was always plenty of food. My parents were both from large families and were always ready to help others when necessary.

In '39, we were in town on Saturday night, as usual. That's when we sold eggs and cream for grocery money. Once a year, at Easter we would have "store bought" cereal for breakfast. My aunt, uncle, and their two daughters would spend the weekend with us, and that's when my dad and Uncle Ogle would see who could eat more eggs, of which we always had plenty. And of course, we always had home cured ham. What a meal!

One Saturday night while we were in town, our house burned, and we lost everything except for my fox terrier, Maggie. The first neighbor to see the fire knew I had a dog, so he opened a door, and Maggie ran out. We found her at my Aunt Ruth and Charley Rodenberg's house the next day. It seems there is always something funny that happens during a tragedy like this. That night, one of the stores in town was having a sale on pocketknives, and when my younger brother was told our house was on fire, he said, "I know, but where can I find those ten cent pocketknives?"

Each Saturday night, we were given one penny, and I always knew where I was going to spend mine. At the candy counter in Miss Hoffman's variety store. I would buy a one-cent pack of gum, which tasted like chewing flavored cardboard, but I always made it last a week.

Having no insurance on the house that burned posed a problem, but my parents had enough money to buy an old house from a neighbor. With a lot of help from friends, relatives, and neighbors, the old house was torn down and a so-called new home was built which is still standing. That was probably the start of my dad's heart problems, which took his life in 1942 at the age of 39. There wasn't much time for grieving, since it was left to Mom, my two brothers, and me to pay for the farm.

There were many jobs involved, such as stripping cane to make molasses to sell in the fall. My Aunt Ruth and Uncle Charley came early every morning to help out. At 4:00am, Mom would start a fire in the furnace, and this is how the cane juice was made into molasses. Actually, it was an interesting process, which made a sweet, syrup-like product that was

Juanita Rodenberg's family in 1940

really very healthy.

Many different jobs were done for not much money, but it all helped out. My first job was when I was in the sixth grade. We lived two and a half miles from school, so I would leave at 6:00am. I would have a fire started and have the one room school warm by the time our teacher, Mrs. Hoffman, got there. For this, I was paid $1.50 a month, and yes, it helped. My brother, Bubby, and I sheared sheep all around the Norborne area. I caught the sheep, he sheared them, and then I would tie the wool, which we would both put in large burlap sacks when we were done for the day. Another job was carrying water to the men in the threshing crew. My mother would wrap gallon glass jugs in burlap sacks so they could be soaked with cold well water before being filled, hung on the saddle horn and carried to each wagon in the field. I had a well-trained pony, but I'm sure most of the water would be warm before I could get it to the men. At age 14, I would detassel corn with a crew in the summer time and the pay was much more.

To me, school was always great. While in grade school, there were usually about 15 students with all eight grades being taught. One neighborhood boy and I were in school together for 12 years. He was the only one I knew when I started high school in Norborne. However, friends were easily made, even though my dresses were made from feed sacks. No one seemed to notice. The kids were great, and I still keep in touch with a few of them, but so many have passed on.

In '47, I went to a house dance with my brother, met a young man who had served three years in the Marines, and the "love bug" took over. Two years later, we were married at the Baptist Church in Norborne. Twenty years later, we were parents to three boys, and then along came three girls. We were so fortunate, because they have all been hard workers and done well. The grandkids are following in their footsteps. There's seldom a day passes that my husband, who was on his way to the South Pacific at age 17 in World War II, is not spoken of because of the comical things he would say or do. In '87, he had a severe stroke, which paralyzed his right side and took most of his speech. For 23 years, he fought a long, hard battle against the stroke, and later years, cancer. Our kids were always here when I needed them. Pop, as most people called him, and I had 61 years together. There was never much money, but the many friends were more than anyone needed to be happy.

I just can't end this story without praising my mom, whose maiden name was Crockett, a distant relative of Davy. Being from a family of 10, times were not easy. She began teaching at age 18 in a one room school and had 54 students in all eight grades. At age 22, she married Jim Rodenberg, a hard-working, very kind, and honest farmer. When he died, at age 39 from heart trouble, she carried on, and when I graduated high school and could stay home and keep house and drive her where she needed to go, Mom started college and once again started teaching. At 63, she graduated from Missouri Valley College at Marshall, Missouri. Many young lives were touched by Mrs. Rodenberg, who retired from teaching at age 75. At age 89, her life was taken by cancer, and I really missed calling her every Saturday and the letter we would get every Wednesday. What a great lady!

I am 83 and have never owned a computer. I write a lot of letters and send many cards, hoping to keep the "lost art" of writing going. A stroke three years ago has hampered my lifestyle; however, I was so fortunate, because only my balance, left side, and energy have been affected.

Finger Curls, Trollies, and Flour Sack Dresses
By Dixie Lee Leffler Wilkinson of St. Joseph, Missouri
Born 1941

My name is Dixie Lee. I was born in 1941 to Dick and Dorothy Leffler in St. Joseph, Missouri. There were eight kids in all. When we moved to 14th Street around 1944 or 1945, we didn't have much money. Before that, we lived on 18th Street, and my dad came home from the war. I remember we were happy.

My sister and I used to dress up. She was two years older than me, and we had a brother two years older than her. They were close and played together. Myrtle and I used to dress up in high heels, long dresses, and hats with our dolls and go over to the playground at Everett School. The door is still there and these big steps.

Mom cleaned houses for people. People brought their clothes and sheets and curtains for Mom to wash and starch. The doilies were really big. She would wash, starch, and iron them so that they stood up real stiff and ruffled. The curtains she washed and stretched on stretchers made of wood. She also worked in a factory called HD Lee Work Clothes for years.

Myrtle and I went to Everett, catty-corner from our house. It was the big school on the corner of 14th and Olive. The principal's name was Mr. Bishop. It just took us a minute to get there. We'd come home for lunch. Mom would make our bread. Everyone said they could smell it a block away. We'd have cocoa and bread and butter at noon. We also had inkwells in our desks that we dipped our ink pens in.

On days that Mom was home, she'd finger wave my hair for me and my girlfriend. She did this by wetting my hair, combing it one way, putting her fingers there, and combing it the opposite way. Then Mom would repeat, moving her fingers to the next wave, and down to the end of my hair around my neck. When my hair dried, she would comb it and it stayed wavy until it was washed again. When my hair was longer, we used to curl our hair on rags or wires from the coffee bags, 8 O'clock Coffee. It made our hair real kinky.

We didn't like school. My sister and I were very shy, but we had a lot of friends. There was a school up on St. Joe Avenue called Krug School. That's where they sent my brother. They said he had to go to school there because he could not read. He wasn't taught to read. All he learned at Krug School was a trade. This was from early years of school.

We had what was called an icebox. It was wooden. It had a small compartment that was small and held a square of ice that we bought from the iceman. We'd put out a special yellow rectangle sign so he'd know we needed ice. He drove a little ice truck that had a special tool that knocked into the ice, and he'd carry it in the house and put it in our icebox. We would get into the back of his little ice truck and deliver our chunk of ice with his ice forceps. We would grab a chunk of ice off the ground or out of his truck.

It was such a peaceful time. We didn't have fans or air conditioners, so sometimes we slept outside on our front porch. We never locked our doors. We didn't have to. I remember ever so often, someone would come to the house. My dad would cut the man's hair, maybe give him a shave, and feed him, and he'd be on his way.

There are names I remember from back then, just different people that Myrtle and I used to make fun of and talk about. One was crazy Sara Indian Wahso, and this cold black man who had a mole above his lips. His voice was so deep you think it come from his wooden leg. His name was Hooks. We were scared to death of him. He lived in a real dark little shack through the alley off of Messanie Street, behind what was at that time a cathedral where nuns lived. It was always dark and depressing up there, but Hooks's little shack was up behind there. It was 15th. When ole man Hooks talked, he roared. But when he walked by our house, Myrtle and I would run up to him and follow him sometimes to the school grounds, and we would sit and talk. He told us that he had a wooden leg and a rubber toe. We'd tease him about it, and he showed us his leg. It was brown and shiny. He walked with a limp. There was a trash man who picked up

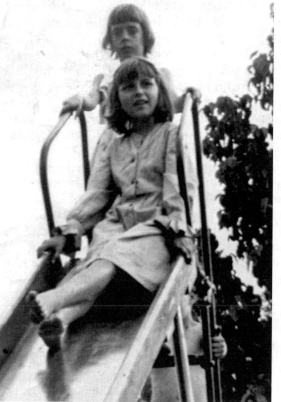

Dixie and her friend in 1951

the trash. He had a white horse and pulled a wooden cart.

Summer was wonderful. No air conditioners running, no power mowers, no TVs, just radios. I remember baseball games on most radios. My dad listened to *Inner Sanctum, Amos and Andy, The Lone Ranger, Gunsmoke, Canadian Mounted Police*, and *The Shadow*. There was an ice cream shop on 15th Street.

Our neighbors on 14th lived on the corner, and we lived next door. There were Fred, Victor, and Louis. They were all old when we were neighbors, but we used to visit them, and the father used to say he used to play with or hang out with Jessie James when they were young. You see, we just lived up the street and around the corner from Jessie's house. Louie Roudolf was an old man, and he used to go out in his front yard, throw a quarter down, and pick it up and say, "Look what I found." He and his brothers owned the Roudolf's Drug Store up on 19th Street. All of this was in the '40s and '50s.

The Navel Reserves, in the '50s, had these big, aluminum huts where the Navy used to hold their meetings and do their marches and drills. We were so lucky. I was a young teen and so was Myrtle, but on Tuesday nights, when the guys were up there having their drills, we would pretty up and go up there across the street onto the lot. We would watch them through the window. They'd flirt with us, and we with them. Boy was it fun. Sometimes they'd say something to naughty to us. Sometimes they marched on the playground. It was just down the bank and steps from them. There were two big cannons in the front of the building and across the street was Everett

Hill, where we could see over the land.

In the summer time, too, we used to all gather on the corner under the streetlight, all the kids in the neighborhood and from around. We'd play hide and seek, tag, red rover red rover, or girl chase boy. There were no drugs, just good times, and clean fun.

We didn't have a car when we were growing up, so if we wanted to go anywhere it was by streetcars or buses that ran or trollies. Sometimes the trolley would come loose or something and the bus driver had to get out and put things up there back on track.

Myrtle and I used to walk from one end of St. Joe to the other. We would walk just to walk, usually toward the south end from 14th Street. I remember as we walked, we'd come across people we thought needed our help. Always, they were old women. One in particular was an old woman who lived in a little ole shack. Her skin was rough, dry, and black from not getting to wash. She had a coal stove in her little place, and her hands and face were black from that. So we helped her clean her little place and brushed her head. That made her happy and us, too. If we got bored, that's what we did. We visited the nursing homes around St. Joe, too. They weren't what they are now. Green Acres was nice, but one nursing home was shabby and dirty. Down on 18th Street off Mitchell Avenue was a real poor area where the railroad tracks ran through, and there were many little shacks down there. That's where the little old lady lived. We weren't allowed down to 6th Street. My dad said he'd better never catch us down there because it was a bad part of town. There was a train depot and a lot of bars and red light places. My dad was a switchman on the railroad.

We didn't live on welfare, but people were always giving us bags of clothes. So we were always getting to try on clothes. Mom made a lot of our dresses out of flour sacks. Flour came in big bags that was really pretty material. Mom made our bread, so we went through a lot of flour. We wore dresses, not jeans, or slacks in the early '50s. Also, there was a see-through package that had a white substance with an orange bead in the middle. We squeezed the bag and the bead until it all blended and made the oleo yellow.

St. Joe was such a wonderful town. It always has been, and it has so much history behind, overlooked, and undiscovered. A person could have a really interesting life just exploring its history. That's what my son is doing from the riverbeds to the cliffs.

Good ole days!

Poking at Bumblebees and Crossing Troll Bridges
By Dean Fitzgerald of Columbia, Missouri
Born 1928

I went to first through fourth grade at Soloman School. In first grade, my teacher was Edgar Chamberlin. He was sixteen or seventeen years old. There had been an old underground cellar three to four feet from the middle of the school. A nest of bumblebees had moved there. As a six year old, my classmates and I used long sticks to prod them into action, and then we ran as fast as we could. But often one of us would get stung. Edgar decided we had had enough, so he made us stay inside, and then he took a long pole with a gunnysack tied on it. He put a bit of kerosene on the sack, lit it, and poked the nest. As the bees flew into the flame, they lost their wings. Thus, he destroyed the nest.

Edgar drove a 1929 Model A Coupe that had a steam whistle on the exhaust, and we begged him to blow it for us. Often he would, and he even let us crawl under the car and see how it worked.

There were four six year old boys in the school, and I was one of them. We kept Edgar pretty busy. He tore pages from a coloring book to keep us busy. One day, he gave me one with a top and directions to paint it striped. I looked through my colors and found none with stripes. So I told Edgar this, and he explained how to solve my problem. They were ok, but much later I realized how weird I had been.

It was about ½ mile from Grandpa's house to school. After a three or four foot snowfall, the roads would be closed, and I would walk home from school. Walking home on closed roads was just too easy, and I had fun. Once, I climbed up on the snow bank on the side of the road. I was having a great time until I broke through, and the snow was two or three feet over my head. Before I could worry or fear, my dad looked in the hole and pulled me out. He made me walk on the road. That was a real bummer then.

Before school ended, we moved a ten acre plot with a house and barn. I was to complete the years at Soloman though it was about a mile walk to school across a huge creek bridge. We had just read The Troll Under the Bridge. So I'd sneak up to the bridge every morning and listen and listen. If I heard nothing, I would run furiously across the bridge, and strangely, I'd always make it.

A Happy Life on the Farm
By Elaine Flint Bullock of Bethany, Missouri
Born 1932

The childhood that I had on our farm was quite different from my life today.

My great-great-grandparents had given land next to our farm for a church and a cemetery. Many folks came to church in horse drawn carriages. Some people had cars. The Antioch Cemetery is still there, but the church is gone.

Our drinking water came from a cistern. Water ran down a pipe from the roof into the cistern. Once we had a dead snake in the cistern, but we drank the water anyway, after my father got the snake out.

The outhouse had *Sears Catalogs* for toilet paper. In the coldest weather, we used a large can in the house. Our only heat was one wood burning stove for the whole house. The bedrooms were so cold that we had to have several quilts over us each night.

On Saturday nights when we needed to get clean, we put a large tub by the stove. The whole family took turns using this one tub of water.

Each family on our telephone line had a different ring. Everyone could hear all the rings. Everyone could listen in to the conversations, too. Sometimes neighbors would just talk to each other.

Even though I was young, I had to help with the chores. I fed each horse several ears of corn each day and also gave them some hay. I had a cow named Brownie. She let me ride her from the pasture into the barn to be milked. As young as I was, I milked her. I gathered the eggs each day. Sometimes an old hen who didn't want me to take her eggs would peck me. One year, we had a mean old rooster who would chase me out of the chicken yard.

Farm life was very pleasant, and our family was very happy.

The Jeep in the Chicken House
By Mrs. Howard Jackson of Easton, Missouri

Every spring, my mother, sisters, and I made lye soap to use as a laundry soap. We would grate it and put it in the washes. What beautiful white clothes it would make!

One spring day, we took our old, used grease and lye, put it in an iron kettle, and literally cooked it. Then we took it off and put it in containers to harden.

After we had finished, my parents had to leave. My sisters and I promised we would come back in the evening and slice it before it got too hard to do so. Later that evening, my sister who lived nearby came by for us in a little topless Jeep.

My daughter and I climbed in the back, and my sister and my ten year old son were in the front. She asked him if he would like to drive. "Of course!" he said.

Down the road we went, laughing and having a gay old time until we got to the folks' house. They had a slightly sloping driveway. My son's legs were too short to apply the brakes properly, and we went right through the back of their chicken house.

Well, we went ahead and sliced the soap, dreading to have to tell what had happened. The next morning we went down to our parents' house and told them. They had not even seen it as yet. They laughed and said they were going to demolish it anyway and this helped to get it started. Whew, what a relief it was!

The Evening Our Old Outhouse Burned to the Ground

In the spring of 1959, my husband and I just purchased our home. There were no bathroom facilities, only the old outhouse. Living on a windy hill, in the fall I lined the inside with old feed sacks to keep out the chill of winter.

One spring day in the process of redecorating, I was on a stepladder in the upstairs hallway patching cracks. I heard our daughter yell something about fire. I climbed down and ran down the stairs. As I went through the kitchen, my husband was going through the day's mail and I said, "Cheryl yelled fire." We ran out of the house to see the old outhouse in flames. Our 9 year old had dropped one of his gloves down the hole. He couldn't see to retrieve it, so he lit a match. The old feed sacks were quick to ignite and burned very rapidly.

Being early in the evening, the farmers were all coming in from their chores. They saw the blaze and thought it was our house. Like most farmers, they came to offer their assistance. Pretty shortly, our lawn was full of on-lookers.

Heard laughing going out the driveway, one young man asked Dad, "Do you know what that was?" Someone wanted to know if we were going to punish him. His father replied, "I think he has been punished enough."

Sitting on a nearby hill, he was wringing his hands and watching the goings on, scared half to death!

Always Mind Your Parents
By Edna Goodknight of Princeton, Missouri
Born 1926

I was born in 1926. I have written my own autobiography and tell many stories to my grandchildren. This is one story that should teach children that it is best to mind their parents.

My parents lived on Highway 65, south of Princeton, and this occurred in probably the early thirties. There were always a lot of transit men walking the highway to try and find work. We called them tramps. They would come to the house asking for food. Mother would always cook something for them and give them coffee, but she would never let them in the house.

On this day, a man's car broke down, and he asked if he could leave an old trunk on the front porch until he could return for it. Mother was particular about her house and yard. She said no, but he could leave it in the smokehouse in the back. Both of our parents told my sister and me not to bother it. My sister was five years older than I was. Later she said, "Let's go see what's in that old trunk. The folks will not know we're out there."

A few days later, she became very sick, and when Mother took her to the doctor, he

thought she had food poisoning. Then I took sick, and they thought we were going to die. As they did in those days, the neighbors came in to help the folks, and they had the doctor come to the house. He said we had scarlet fever. He let the neighbors go home, and he quarantined us. All the children at school were vaccinated. We were very sick for some time. In fact, my sister's heart was affected.

Several weeks later, the old man returned for his trunk, and while visiting with Daddy, he said his wife had died from scarlet fever. That was what we had seen in the old trunk: dirty old bedclothes. Always mind your parents.

Button Underwear
By Mary A. Morton of Cameron, Missouri
Born 1934

I have seven brothers and sisters. We were all born and raised on the farm.

Our mother always raised chickens. So when she went to the feed store, she made sure all her sacks matched. That way she would have enough material for dresses and underpants. She didn't use elastic but buttons for the panties.

I was in the third grade, and my teacher was Shirley Whisler. One day she caught me eating candy in class. So she took me to the

Mary, her brother, Junior, and sister, Louise

183

bathroom to spank me. When she raised my dress, I was so embarrassed that she saw my flowered panties.

The schoolhouse was for grades from first to twelfth. It is no longer in Mt. Moriah, MO. It was torn down several years ago. Dad got some of the bricks.

My Strongest Memory
By Larry Sealey of King City, Missouri
Born 1941

I was born on November 6, 1941, one month before Pearl Harbor. We lived at that time on a rented farm northeast of King City. Four of us children were born there at home.

Somewhere around 1945 or 1946, we were having a bad thunderstorm and sometime in the night, the folks heard a plane go over the house real low. The next morning, a sheriff's car and a military car came up our mud road. The plane had crashed into a big hill in the Wakemath 440, a large pasture west of us. The pilot and co-pilot were both killed.

I started to Shepard School in the first grade, at five years of age. As March 1st was moving day, Dad had rented another farm, and we moved to the Hughes place on Hammer Branch Creek. I then went to Karr School, which was two miles from home. We either walked to school or drove the horse and buggy.

My strongest memory was of our roads being mud, and we had no electricity. A car came by our home one night fighting the mud, and we didn't know who they were.

We had a neighbor about a mile across country named Mary Hammer. After the '30s, some people didn't trust banks, and Mary was one of them. She kept her money at home in cans and so forth. A lot of it was old gold certificates and silver certificates. The car that went by that night had two or three men in it.

Several days later, Mrs. Hammer was found beat to death, lying in her cattle pen. The men had beaten her with her crutches. Her money was stolen. The police caught them in Stanberry, trying to spend some of the old money.

My two older brothers and I walked over to her old house about a year later to explore. When we got into her house, a shutter upstairs banged with the wind. We thought it was a

Marilyn, Jim, Jerry, and Larry in 1946

ghost and ran for it. Jim and Jerry lodged in the window and by the time I got out of the house, they were a quarter of a mile ahead.

Back then, we took care of our own phone line and ours broke. Dad told Mom not to ring it until we got home. The telephone wire was real springy and us boys pulled one end and Dad pulled the other. Just as Dad was tying it, someone rang from the other end. Dad forgot his Sunday school lessons right there. Needless to say, we had to go get the wire again.

We lived there for about two years, and then we moved again on the first of March to a farm Dad had bought. We were then in the Ford City School until it closed, and then we went to King City School.

Mom, and all the women of that time, had it hard, but they never complained. In many ways, they were tougher than the men.

We had an old wooden radio that we could play on Saturday nights. We listened to *Amos and Andy*, *The Shadow*, *The Romance of Helen Trent*, *The Cisco Kid*, plus *The Grand Ole Opry*.

The Squawking in the Three Holer
By Judith A. Wood of Plattsburg, Missouri
Born 1942

I was born in 1942, and I guess times were hard, but I don't remember all of that. Mom canned everything she could grow and whatever the neighbors had left over. One of her greatest joys was to take the family down into the cellar to see the jars all lined up on the full shelves. The red tomatoes, green beans and pickles, yellow corn and fruit, pickled beets, peas, and the purple grape juice all made a beautiful display. The potato bin was filled, and we were ready for the winter.

Mom made me pick grapes, and the big black and yellow spiders would scare me. I was afraid they would jump on me. My brother and I would swipe a saltshaker and go out and lie in the garden and eat ripe tomatoes where Mom couldn't see us. Dad would pull up a turnip, wipe it off on his overalls, peal it right there in the patch, and we would eat it. They were so sweet and good.

On butchering day, Dad would build a fire under a steel barrel of water and get it good and hot. A hog was killed and tied to a rope, which ran through a pulley in the hayloft. The rope was tied to a single tree behind a horse, and it was my job to guide the horse up and back to raise and lower the hog into the barrel to be scalded. The men would then scrape off the hair. The animal was processed, and the hide with the fat on it was rendered in a big black kettle over an open fire. The lard was used for cooking and lye soap. We kids ate some of the cracklins, and Dad saved some for his coonhounds.

We burned wood for heat in the winter. My brother and I were responsible for keeping the woodpile on the back porch stocked. If we were lucky and it snowed, we could pile it on our sled and haul it to the house instead of having to carry it. Dad would cut the wood and split it in the fall, so he wouldn't have to wade in the deep snow later. I often ended up on one end of the crosscut saw on some of the bigger logs. My brother and I also had to pick up corncobs out of the pig lot for kindling to start the fire should it go out overnight.

We had an old fat cow pony named Catus. I had a pet raccoon named Sandy.

There was always work to do but we still found time to run and play. Summer was terrific. We ran and played from the time we got up until dark. We played in the ditches, the ponds, the pastures, and the brooder house after Mom moved the baby chickens to the big chicken house. The barn was also available when the cows were in the pastures.

Once, while playing in the brooder house, we were experimenting with items we had taken from the kitchen. We learned that if you mix baking soda, aspirin, and vinegar and put a cork on the bottle real quick, you can blow the cork quite a distance. Mom never found out about that.

We all loved to play in a large, deep ditch with a lot of trees on both sides. We called this our big jungle. The fence line up the hill was our little jungle, because it didn't have as many trees. My older sister, Charlene, would swing on the grapevines and yell like Tarzan. She was my hero.

Once in a while, I would talk my brother into playing dress-up and dolls with me, but most of the time we were playing cowboys and Indians. We would run all over the pastures. Sometimes we had old brooms with twine tied through them for reins. We built a tree house in the windmill instead of a tree.

One time my brother got some chewing tobacco, and we snuck off to the little jungle to see what chewing tobacco was all about. We didn't know you were supposed to spit, so we swallowed the tobacco juice. Talk about being sick! Mom never found out about that either.

Our outhouse was a ways from the house, and we girls did not like to go out there by ourselves at night. Luckily, it was a three holer, so we could go together. One night, as we all sat down pretty much at the same time, something started flopping around and squawking under us. We all screamed bloody murder and ran out the door at once. We ran all the way to the house. Later we learned that a hen had gotten down in there, and we had greatly disturbed her.

In the winter, we had the chamber pot so we didn't have to go outside in the cold. Also in the winter, we bathed in a washtub behind the heating stove in the kitchen.

Mom was very good at making do with what we had. The printed chicken feed sacks ended up as dresses. She always made sure to sort through the sacks to get enough of the same print to make a dress. Hand-me-down clothes were always welcome at our house, too.

In order to keep our clothes clean, we would carry water from the well, heat it on the stove in a big tub, and then dip it into the wringer washer. Mom also had a tub of hot bleach water and a tub of cold water to rinse the colored clothing in. She would use a broomstick to fish the clothes out of the hot water and get them up to the wringer. I thought it was so much fun the first time she let me run clothes through the wringer. Even in the winter, Mom would hang clothes on the line and let them freeze dry. I later used a wringer washer myself for a while after I got married. There is a lot of pride in seeing a line full of bleached, white diapers waving in the breeze.

Every washday, because so much work was involved in the carrying of the water and the washing and hanging of the clothes, Mom would cook a big pot of beans for the evening meal. It was the original one dish meal. I still love cornbread and beans with chopped onions and a splash of vinegar.

We usually got two pairs of shoes a year, one winter and one summer. Last year's sandals were worn as play shoes so the new ones could be kept for good, such as going to town on Saturday.

One summer, I was wearing last years' sandals, which were too short for me, and my toes hung over the edge of the shoe. I jumped off the porch, and cut the bottom of my big toe off on a piece of glass. Mother used kerosene to stop the bleeding, put some sulfa drug she had on hand on the wound, and wrapped a clean rag around it. She told me to go play, which I did. We were miles from a doctor, so Mom took care of pretty much everything that happened to us.

With all the outdoor activity and homegrown food, we were all pretty healthy as I remember. One of Mom's favorite remedies was cod liver oil. We all had to pass by her with mouths open as she ladled a tablespoon of warm cod liver oil and poured it down our throats. Vicks Vapor Rub and a warm cloth usually broke up a chest cold, and various kinds of poultices were used to draw out splinters and infections. The Watkins man and the Raleigh man also supplied various salves and potions. As a treat, we could buy root beer syrup from the Raleigh man and make our own root beer.

We truly walked a mile and a half in deep snow to catch the school bus at the highway. If the roads were dry, the bus would come by the house, but in snow or mud, we had to walk to catch it. We would be so cold we would cry and the tears would freeze on our faces, but Mom always had homemade hot chocolate and homemade bread waiting for us.

If Dad knew a big snow was coming, he would park the car out on the main road. We would then have a ride in a horse drawn wagon up through the pasture to get to the road where the car was parked when we went to town on Saturday for groceries. We lived on an east to west road, and it always drifted full. It sure was great for sled riding down the hill, though. Dad's old car would always die on Main Street and I would hide on the floorboard so no one would see me.

Speaking of homemade bread, I used to be so embarrassed when I had to take homemade bread and fried country ham in my school lunch. The other kids had white bread and bologna. What I wouldn't give for some sugar cured country ham and a loaf of homemade bread now.

We had a wall phone with the party line that all the women would get on at once and talk. They would also listen in on each other's calls. We didn't have a TV until I was in the sixth or seventh grade, so we always listened to *The Shadow*, the Friday night fights, and *Amos and Andy* and all the good old shows. A Saturday night movie was fifteen cents.

Mom's first refrigerator had a motor on top. Our old farmhouse was burned after we moved because the owner said it was haunted. I was always afraid to stay in it alone as a child, so maybe it was.

Dating at the Frog op Ballroom
By M. Patricia Luckenbill of Plattsburg, Missouri
Born 1934

I had a wonderful time growing up in Dearborn, MO, population 391. Daddy took our one car to work every day of the week, so we walked everywhere to school, for groceries with my little red wagon, to get fifty pounds of ice for our icebox, to church, etc. We had no telephone or television, only a radio. I took my calls from my neighbor, the Doctor of Dearborn. Any calls I made out I made at the pay phone.

We went to free shows (movies) put on by the merchants of Dearborn. I had a used boys' bike and my roller skates. I played basketball with the neighbor kids with a basketball goal tacked on above a garage door. I played high school girls basketball, and we won 21 first place trophies in two years. We were good! I was a forward, and we played ½ court.

I wasn't allowed to date until I turned sixteen years old. And I never went steady, and I kept a record of all the boys I dated in a Big Chief tablet. I dated one hundred and fifty boys during my dating years before I married. My curfew for dates was midnight. I loved to go on dates and meet other good-looking boys at the Frog Hop Ballroom in St. Joseph, MO. We dressed up like movie stars in high heels and hose with garter belts. Big Bands would come for the dances every Saturday night. On Sunday nights, I could go to eat out and to a movie in St. Joseph, MO. I was only allowed to date on Saturday nights and Sunday nights, because of going to school and having homework during the week.

At the Frog Hop Ballroom, the big bands were like Glenn Miller, Benny Goodwin, Ralf Flanagan, Lawrence Welk, Ray Auborn, Danny Kaye, and many more big names. They had popcorn bowls and big bottles of 7Up to go with bring your own bottles and big tall, strong bouncers at the doors. I never got in trouble, and I didn't drink. I wasn't old enough, but some of my dates would drink a little. If I had gotten in trouble, my folks would have grounded me for one month.

I married my sweetheart from Plattsburg, MO in January 1953. He had just gotten home from thirteen months in Korea.

M. Patricia Luckenbill in 1952

Thankful for My Education and Training
By Gene Simmons of Cameron, Missouri
Born 1926

My early memories go back to farm days on a one hundred and thirty acre farm eight miles northeast of Kansas City, MO.

I attended a one room, rural school. It was heated by a large stove. I had several teachers, but my favorite was a male teacher who coached our softball team. We played other school teams in the area.

A farmer had land and an apple orchard, which adjoined our schoolyard. I remember going over and stealing eating apples. I rode an old riding horse that sometimes stumbled. I later had a small Shetland pony, which I rode to school and which would occasionally decide to run off. One day, she ran off with me and a neighbor girl riding, throwing us off.

In those days, we took lunch to school. We used small metal lunch pails, taking sandwiches and fruit. I remember that in those grade school days, we boys would hurry and finish our lunch before the teacher and then wait outside. When he came outside, we would snowball him! I guess we were just being ornery.

I remember that in those early years of grade school, we occasionally had community meetings at night, where we students put on the program. I had a guitar, which I would play and sing. I now would say I was horrible.

In my grade school days in the thirties, money was scarce, and I looked for ways to make some money. Our farm had some rough land with timber, which was shelter for wild life. So, in winter I would trap skunks, civets, and possums and sell their hides for money. As I remember, skunk hides paid one dollar. I would set five or six traps and check them early in the morning before school. On mornings when I got some skunks, I would carry quite a strong odor to school, much to the dislike of other students!

Also, to make money in the summer, I would use my Shetland pony and carry drinking water to the local threshing crews. Men would gather the grain bundles onto rack wagons and take them to the nearby threshing machine. This was all hot work, and the only refreshment was my drinking water from two jugs I hauled from the saddle on my pony. I received one dollar per day and would follow the threshing machine from farm to farm, for a total of around six to seven farms. However, I did not go on a farm unless asked by the landowner. I kept the water jugs wrapped in burlap, so as not to get hot from the summer sun.

Of course, the aforementioned methods were ways I had of making some money, in addition to my selling some fat hogs, sheep, and some wool. These monies were placed in a small bank account for later use in paying for college. I remember keeping some of the money in a small cloth purse prior to taking it to the bank for deposit.

A neighbor's farm had an old swimming pond, which I and the neighbor boys used. I had not learned to swim, and Mother disliked me going there to swim. One of those neighbor boys would later be drafted into the Army and lose a leg and an arm in Germany. Boy, could he ever run before going into the Army!

Also in those days, we had skating parties in the winter at a nearby Kelly Hill. This was a steep road where we gathered, with a covered bridge at the bottom where we took shelter and had refreshments. We each had our sleds and enjoyed sledding down that hill.

I also remember in those early farm years in the summer, we would go to the outside cellar when a storm would come up. We never got blown away, but it sure seemed like we would. We had no basement but used the storm cellar.

Also, in the winter when the weather was bad, we had a cousin who lived across the road and who would come over and would play cards. We called the card game "pitch."

My cousin's father, my grandfather's brother, fed hogs at a certain time each day. He used ground oats and water, making what we called slop. The hogs really liked it and they would squeal their heads off when eating it. Of course, later when I became educated, we fed our hogs corn, tankage, and linseed oil meal, which we thought was better.

My grandmother lived a short distance from our house on the same farm. Because she was afraid to be alone, I would have to go to pick her up so she could stay overnight at our house. This was after Grandfather had passed away. I never knew my great-grandfather, who had come to our area around 1850 from Illinois. I remember that one reason my grandmother was afraid at night

was that a neighbor family had a son who was not "right" which meant he had some mental problems. He was kept on a chain, but he had gotten loose once and gone to the neighbor's house and scared them. Later, he was placed in a mental facility.

In my very early years, in the thirties, we travelled by horse and buggy. Then later we traveled by motor cars, Model T cars, Model A cars, and then by Ford V-8s. In the early thirties, we had a two-door green Model A car and then a two-door black Ford V-8. After staying a week with an older brother who operated a filling station, my parents picked me up one night in a new Ford V-8, and boy was that something! That sure was some car, but it would not plow through mud roads like the old narrow wheel Model T cars. Later, when I went to college, I commuted in an old 1929 Model A car.

After completing grade school, I walked one mile to catch the school bus to King City, Missouri. eight miles away to attend high school, which I fully enjoyed. I took general courses like English, Math, business, and vocational agriculture, which I enjoyed the most. I had home agriculture projects like hogs, sheep, etc. My favorite high school teacher was the agriculture instructor, who showed me the ropes and took me to adjoining states to buy breeding swine stock. I built up a herd of hogs of good quality and was disappointed when I went to the Army and later saw how my dad let the quality go down. But I did not realize how his heart was not in it like mine had been.

One day I remember we were having shop in agriculture and testing cream with a hand driven machine. I was turning the tester with a cream sample mixed with acid, and I turned it so fast that it blew up, spewing acid in the face of a classmate. We all thought he was hurt, but it turned out ok.

When they were ready for market, I took market weight fat hogs up to Stanberry to sell to a commission firm. Although not connected, I remember having an early date at the Stanberry Park one 4th of July with an attractive girl. The 4th of July annual celebrations were a big event in the early days. I remember they would always have the best wrestlers from St. Joe, which was quite an event!

Also, we sometimes took fat hogs to the

St. Joseph market, but never more than twelve to fifteen at a time, which was two to three litters, more or less. I also remember going down to the St. Joseph market with an older brother who ran a country store. We took hogs to market and upon return brought a load of fresh vegetables, bananas, oranges, etc. We always stopped at the market square to get the vegetables in St. Joseph.

Also in those early days, we did not have running water toilets, so in the summer, we had wooden outhouses and for toilet paper, we used *Montgomery Ward Catalogues*. However, they were not as good as regular toilet paper. In the wintertime, we used metal chamber pots, which we took outside to empty.

We took castor oil when we were sick. It was enough to make one sick in itself.

Party line phones also were the only type of phones in our rural area. Each party had their own ring and our ring when calling us was three long rings followed by one short ring. When calling out, we turned a crank on the side of the large wall mounted phone box. And of course, one could listen in on the line to another party when they were talking.

Saturday night baths were taken in large, round metal tubs. Washing machines were large and round, with attached hand driven wringers.

As to Saturday night movies, this was a real treat. I used to go to them with my dad. Dad would generally sleep through them! They were always a double movie with one city type movie and one western. After the movie, I would get two hot dogs (what a treat) to eat on the way home. Dad and I would go to the movies while Mother would do her shopping. We could do these things after picking up the weekly cream and egg money at the poultry house, those items first being delivered to the poultry house when we arrived in town.

We first got an icebox after years of not having one when we got a share in a local icehouse, where ice was put up in the winter for use in the summer. We would get large chunks of ice in the summer and haul them home and place them in the icebox. That was a real treat!

Also in those early years, we had a small brooder house, which I converted to a carpenter shop in which I spent long hours making small wooden toys. One I remember

Gene Simmons in 1975

was a model of a bomber, which I still have! I even had a sign on the outside calling it Simmons Carpenter Shop.

I had an older brother who was my dad's favorite. He could get by with anything, such as mischievous things. He only went two years to a local high school. We did not get along, and I think it was due to Dad's favoritism.

I graduated at the top of my high school class but did not receive any scholarships. My financial help for college was to come later from Army service, which followed from immediate entry into service after high school. As it turned out, I graduated high school in May and after my 18th birthday in July, 1944 I was drafted and sent to Camp Robinson near Little Rock, Arkansas. After seventeen weeks of basic infantry training, I was sent to Germany.

My mother passed away while I was in the service, after being in poor health. She had always been my best support, having gone to college herself when young. She believed in the education of one's self. My dad had only gone to eighth grade elementary school, with no college.

I was thankful to be able to come back home from service and graduate from the University of Missouri in Agriculture

Economics. I taught agriculture to veterans upon graduation, and then worked in the MO Agriculture Extension Service and later the Federal Land Bank. I then became a real estate broker, and then a State certified Real Estate Appraiser. I retired five years ago. I purchased 320 acres of cropland, which I now lease out for a living income. Upon reflection on my life, I am thankful for the training and education I have received and look forward to a few more years!

Santa Let Me Down
By Connie Yates of Burlington Junction, Missouri
Born 1929

I was six years old in November of 1935. Living in the Depression years was very hard, although I didn't realize it until much later. In 1935, being an only child and as young as I was, I didn't have enough experience to know the difference between having nothing and having plenty. My father had lost his job at Larabee Mills. By the time I was six, we had already moved five times, probably because we weren't able to pay the rent. At age six, we lived in an upstairs one room and shared a bathroom with about ten others who also lived in the house.

The one room contained a bed, a small table, and two chairs. I sat on an upended box. Our icebox was an orange crate placed on its side in a raised window, with the window pulled down on it to hold the crate in place. My mother tacked a piece of oilcloth over the front to help hold the cold inside the crate and keep the outside cold from coming into the room. It didn't work very well, because everything, such as milk, lettuce, lunchmeat, and whatever else was in the crate froze, and it also chilled the room.

It was December, and I was looking forward to having Santa Claus bring me a new doll. We were a religious family, and it seemed we were at church every time the doors were open. I well knew the Christmas story of Christ's birth and it had its place at church, but Santa Claus was another totally different part of Christmas. I didn't remember too many Christmases, but this one was uppermost in my mind. Santa was going to bring me a new doll. I had asked him for it when I saw him at the Woolworth's Dime Store downtown.

My mother sat me down and explained that she and my dad had to pay for the gifts that Santa brought, and this year they had no money to pay for anything at all. Apparently, she had contacted a group of people that were helping provide gifts for needy children and had turned in my name. For on Christmas morning, I had a gift all wrapped up. It didn't really appear to be a doll, but I had a present from Santa! I also had a crudely sewn net stocking that held an apple, an orange, a banana, and various nuts and hard candies. I was so excited to find a gift wrapped for me from Santa. He had come after all! The world was a wonderful place at that moment. I eagerly unwrapped the present and found that it was a Boy Scout Handbook. Of all the stupid gifts, I got a Boy Scout Handbook, and I wasn't even a boy.

The Santa I believed in wouldn't have done this to me, and I immediately told all my little friends on the block that there was NO Santa. He would not have treated me this way! I think all the mothers on the block hated me, and for some unknown reason, I didn't play with the other kids for a while. My mother tried to brush it off, but it did no good. Like I said, times were hard, and believe it or not, they got harder as we went along. I grew up with more Christmases that weren't much better.

After I married and had children, times were much better in the '50s. Christmases were still religious events in our lives, but Santa always came and brought the children gifts. They didn't get everything they asked for, but they got their favorite requested gift.

To this day, I could just skip Christmas as just another day. The children are grown, married, and have families of their own to provide for. My husband and I just sit and watch TV or read a book; nothing special. Back in those dark days, my husband remembers receiving a pocket comb as his only gift one Christmas.

Santa is a magical person who makes a child's outlook on life one of happiness, pleasure, contentment, and joy. The religious aspect of Christmas makes a child understand how the Babe in the manger brought love, peace, tranquility, hope, and humility to their lives for the present and also for the rest of their lives, if they lived the kind of life Jesus portrayed for them.

Even though Santa ruined my early Christmas in 1935, I was not the only one that this same kind of happening occurred to. Even today in a land of relative plenty, I imagine there are many children who don't get a gift from Santa that they want or are pleased with. Happy memories? Sad memories? Memories of hope for the future.

Jim and Lula's Fruit and Vegetable Stand
By Max Field of Kansas City, Missouri
Born 1934

My father and mother, Jim and Lula Field, owned a fruit and vegetable stand on Highway 59 north of Oregon, MO. It was a labor intensive living. Cultivation, planting, watering, weeding, harvesting, maintaining tools, and selling products at nearby towns were all part of the job. My brother, Morris Gene, and I helped before and after school and in the summer. Every spring, Dad would borrow $200.00 for seed on a handshake with the bank president, Roy Hornecker.

The stand was a social gathering spot when watermelon was ripe. Cold watermelon was sold by the slice and eaten at picnic tables by the creek. Rinds were tossed over the bank for the cow to eat.

There was a rope swing that let us swing out over the water and back to the creek bank. Once, a lady from town wanted to try it out. I still remember her skirt flaring out like a parachute when she lost her grip and went into the water.

Field's Vegetable Stand

Lula and Jim Field

The stand was about halfway between Kansas City and Omaha. The wrestlers who were on TV each week would stop for a break as they traveled for live matches in both locations. On TV, they would appear to be huge enemies, but they would be friendly at the vegetable stand and ride together all the way. I remember Bob Geigel was one of the wrestlers.

It was a great place for my friend, Jerry Turnbill, and me to play. We would build a small dam of dirt and make a pool of water. We rode our bikes for miles and hunted for ducks and squirrels. One day, my brother put a stick of dynamite in the creek bank and set it off. The noise beat us back to the house, and he received a spanking from Dad.

During World War II, gas rationing cut down on travel to the market. Dad went to work in the bomber plant in Kansas City, and the family moved to Parkville for a few years. After the war, Dad dug a basement and built a kitchen onto the house. The well pump provided running water in the house for the first time. Then the farm was taken by eminent domain when Interstate 29 was built. It was difficult to give it up.

Many people remember their visits to the fruit and vegetable stand. Dad was a local character. He had signs all around that showed his sense of humor and opinions. He was a joke and storyteller. He also wrote a weather column for the newspaper that contained editorials and observations as much as the statistics of weather.

191

Kerosene Cures, Bull Snakes, and Corn Shuck Ticks

By Pearl L. Heck of Princeton, Missouri
Born 1927

My mother and dad were married in 1918. They had a baby every two years until they had seven children. They farmed on rental land. The older kids rode a horse to school. The horse's name was Dollie. She had a mate named Pet. When the kids got to school, they turned Dollie loose, and she came back home. One day, the neighbor man wanted to ride Dollie to visit my dad, but he could not catch her. The family had a big collie dog. Dad trained him. He would say, "Way back," and the dog would go out and round up the cattle in the evening.

My dad got sick and the doctor thought it was TB. They kept him away from our home because they were afraid us kids would get it. It turned out to be cancer of the throat. He was sent to Sunny Slope, a sanatorium. After he passed away, it left my mother with seven kids and no income.

We sold our farm equipment and stock and moved to a different county so we could get help. Our help was $30.00 per month, and we paid $5.00 rent for a small trailer with no plumbing or electricity. We lived there for a couple of years. Then we moved to the country, where we still had no plumbing or electricity.

We walked two miles to a one-room school. The teachers could not be married. One winter we walked over the fences because the snow was so deep and hard. This was in the thirties.

We tried to help ourselves. We raised potatoes and other vegetables. One night, my two older sisters heard noises and looked out the window upstairs. Two men took our wash boiler and filled it with our potatoes. I guess they were poorer than we were.

After three years there, our older brother came down with scarlet fever. We were quarantined all winter. We would not have survived if our neighbor man had not helped us. He brought us fuel and food. We kids had dug a pretty deep hole in our back yard, and snow had filled it in. When the man brought coal, one of his horses fell in the hole. We had to unharness him, and he got out. I still feel bad about that.

The next summer, our brother went to work for a farmer. He made room and board and so much a month. He worked all summer for no pay. My mother went to collect some.

Our mother's mother, our grandmother, worked for the same guy. She came to our home sick with diabetes and dropsy. She was bedfast. Mother cared for her until she died. She stayed with us all summer. Then she went to live with a son for the winter, and then she came back to us in the spring. She died not long after returning.

This guy started courting our mother. Soon they married, and we moved to his farm. The very first night, my younger brother and I were taken to the barn. There were five cows that needed to be milked. We learned fast that from then on that was our chore, morning and night. Then we separated the milk from the cream. The cream stayed with the house. The skim milk went to the pigs and the chickens. We had no refrigerator, so warm milk wasn't very tasty.

We used to climb in the corncrib. Up high in a window was a bird's nest. One day, we went to get the eggs out of the nest, and a big bull snake came crawling out. That put an end to the bird's nest.

I knew a lady who took big bull snakes and put them around her neck. She said that when she was a girl in North Dakota, they lived in a sod house. Snakes would fall from the ceiling onto her bed. She learned not to be afraid.

On our stepfather's farm, we lost a big sow. No neighbors saw her. So my stepfather decided to track her. After a long trail, he tracked her to our neighbors' barn. She was shut up in a pen inside it. That ended that friendship. After that, the neighbors' collie dog came to our place. He was shot. I don't know what happened to his body.

We had a team of horses. One was spotted and one was white. Their names were Bird and Silver. Both of the mares came up one morning with a baby colt each. That was a wonderful sight. Bird died in the stock field in the fall. I wanted to go skin her to make a pair of chaps. Our mother said no. I dreamed of those chaps for a long time.

We had a team of mules, too. Their names were Spike and Rood. One day, they were on the road with a wagon. Spike just dropped dead. I guess he had a heart attack. We got to stay home from school, we were so upset. Animals were our best friends then.

We had a lady country doctor. One evening, she was going home from a call in her horse and buggy. A guy jumped out of the side road and grabbed her horse. She pulled out her .45 and told him to let go of that horse. He saw the gun and did, and she went on her way.

One winter, I wanted to go sled riding. I needed warm pants. My mother had a big fuzzy coat that had belonged to her mother, who had passed. She had been a big woman. I wanted to cut up that coat and make a pair of snow pants. After begging for quite a while, Mother gave in. I cut and sewed the coat on a treadle machine. I wore them that night to go sled riding. I was eight or nine years old. That was my first try at sewing.

We used to put socks on our hands for mittens.

One time, our mother had a good fire in the old cook stove. We always left the oven door down to help warm the house. My little brother was about five years old. He didn't have any pants on, and he sat on the hot oven door. He blistered his bottom.

My younger brother and I had to stay out of school to saw wood and to pick corn. One time, a rabbit jumped out in front of our team and scared them. They jumped and ran off, upsetting the load of corn. We had to get help to upright the wagon and pick up all the corn.

One winter I had a bad croup. I wasn't getting any air in my lungs. My mother took a spoon of sugar, took the wick out of the lamp, dropped one drop of kerosene on the sugar, and gave it to me to take. I swallowed it. It cut the crud out of my neck with no side effects.

Sometimes, we didn't have oil for our lamps. Mom would put a rag in a saucer and put grease or lard on the rag. She would light it, and that was our light a lot of times. It lasted for hours. It was better than the dark.

One time in school, a sixth grade boy drew a picture on the board. He wrote "teacher" under the picture. Boy, the man teacher took a three-inch board and put the boy over his desk. That boy really got a beating on the hind end. It scared the rest of us to death.

We had this neighbor who hatched her own baby chickens. If they weren't perfect, she cut off their heads with a pair of scissors and dropped them in her kitchen stove with a fire going in it.

One time there was head lice in school. The boy who sat in front of me had them. I could see them running up and down his neck. We got them, but not for long. Our mother combed them all out of our hair. My sister had really tight, curly hair. They were the hardest to get out of her hair.

We slept on big corn shuck ticks. When we would thresh, we would empty our ticks and put in fresh shucks. It made a pretty good bed. The ticks were made out of pillow ticking.

Everything went to the cellar. It stayed cooler in there. It was a good place to go for a storm, too. Every home had one.

One time, our folks went to town and left us kids at home. My brother and I went to the hen house and got one dozen eggs. We took them to our little country store. We got fourteen cents per dozen. We bought candy. Mom never missed the eggs.

Mom washed clothes on the washboard and hung them out. In the winter, we'd bring in the underwear and overalls, and they'd be frozen stiff. We would stand them up until they thawed out, and then hang them up to dry. Everyone wore long underwear.

We would pick big tomato worms off of the tomatoes and potatoes. We'd make a big mound of dirt, lay the worms on it, and slap them with a board.

My brother and his wife rented a farm from this couple. The couple would come to visit for several days at a time. They lived quite a ways away. The Mrs. would get up in the morning and sit on a pot in the middle of their living room, having coffee, for a half an hour at a time. They had an outside toilet. I don't know who took it out.

From Brooklyn to Venice
By Ed Chamberlin of Ridgeway, Missouri
Born 1943

I was born in 1943, during World War II. I spent the first ten years of my childhood on a farm in the Brooklyn community. We didn't have electricity or indoor plumbing. We cooked and heated the house with wood. We had horses, cows, hogs, and chickens on our farm. My sister's and my jobs were to feed the chickens and hogs, gather the eggs, and carry the wood in.

Ed with his friends in 1954

The town of Brooklyn consisted of a general store, a blacksmith shop, a telephone switchboard, a church, a schoolhouse, and eight houses.

Spike Pollock, the blacksmith, was a tall, thin man who smoked a crooked stem pipe and could fix almost anything. The old timers around Brooklyn always said if Spike couldn't fix it, it couldn't be fixed.

Bud and Beula Fitzgerald ran the general store. Bud was one of my childhood heroes. He was always happy and full of fun. He was a practical joker and was always pulling something on someone.

There were horseshoe pegs set up behind the store, and when the weather was nice, the old men in the community would gather out back and pitch horseshoes. When it was cold or rainy, they would sit inside around the woodstove and play cards. A bottle of pop cost a nickel, bubblegum was a penny for a piece, and candy bars were a nickel.

There was a country school every square mile. We lived right in the middle; the Pibern School was one mile north and the Eureka School was one mile south.

I started school in the 1949/1950 school year at Eureka. Grades one through eight were all taught in these little one-room schoolhouses. There was a total of nine kids in school my first grade year. I went to school there until the middle of my fifth grade year, walking to school most of the time. Sometimes I rode my horse or my bicycle. The road was dirt, so in wet weather, we waked the shortcut through the timber.

In the fall of 1953, my dad did the only impulsive thing he ever did in his whole life. Thinking perhaps that the grass really was greener on the other side of the fence, he sold his cattle and team of horses, bought a new Chevrolet car, and we moved to Venice, California. Up until that time, I had never been more than ten miles from home. I had never seen a body of water more than one hundred feet across, and I had never seen a black person.

We arrived in Venice around noon on New Year's Day, 1954. We rented a small house close to Venice Beach. Dad went to work for his uncle, and Mom enrolled me in school.

School was a lot different in California than it was in Missouri. There were about five times as many kids in my fifth grade class as there were in my whole school back in Missouri. That first day of school, the class bully chased me home. The second day, he did it again. The third day at recess, I challenged him on the playground. He was quite a bit bigger than me, but all the farm chores and walking to school back in Missouri paid off. I was stronger and faster than he was, and I whipped his butt. The teacher sent us both to the principal's office. The principal gave us both a couple of swats with his paddle. From then on, I didn't have any more problems at school.

Summer in Venice was like living in a fairy tale for a ten year old farm kid. My new friends and I would go to the Santa Monica Amusement Park to ride the rides and play the games. We would go to play at Venice Beach and swim in the ocean or ride our bikes or

Ed and his friend, Roger Clemm in 1954

194

roller skate on the sidewalk. Life was good.

After eight months in California, Dad decided he'd had enough of the rat race of living in the city, and we moved back to the farm. When we got back home, we found everything just the way we had left it. This would be quite amazing in this day and age, as we hadn't even locked the house. But that is just the way it was in the 1950s. Those really were the good old days.

The Battle Between Brother and Sister
By Beverly L. Gibbons of Tarkio, Missouri

In the mid '50s, we were living and working on a farm in Northwest Missouri. We had a son born March 1950 and a daughter in October 1954. She was getting to be pretty active and big. Brother and she had spent the afternoon wrestling in the house. Of course, due to age and size, it was vexing her and so she stopped, arms on hips and announced, "Let's go outside. Mom you don't want blood all over the living room," meaning she was really letting big brother know she meant business about winning the battle between them.

We still talk about the day she thought she was big and mean enough to whip big brother.

Adventures on the Farm
By Linda Wilson Mangels of Kansas City, Missouri
Born 1956

I was raised on a farm, and I wish everyone was! We raised Hereford cattle, wheat, and alfalfa. We butchered our own meat. We raised a garden and canned our food. We had a potato field that was so large! Grandfather plowed the field to turn the potatoes to the top of the soil. We all carried sacks on our backs to pick up potatoes and carry them back to the cellar. We had apple trees, so much cooking and canning had to be done. We had grape vines, so we made and canned jelly. We had a plum tree and gooseberry bushes. We children didn't like to harvest these, nor eat them, but on the farm, you do your chores. We had a mulberry tree, and it was a huge, mature tree. As children, we would go through the pasture to eat the ripe berries. Our parent had told us to stay out of those mulberries, and not to eat the mulberries. They would ask us, "Did you eat the mulberries?" We exclaimed back to them, "No; oh no!" However, the proof was stained on our faces and hands! We also had paw paw trees, whose fruit is an acquired taste. We gathered morel mushrooms in the spring. We fished at the pond in the summer. We would chase the cows out of the pond on hot summer days so we could swim. We would ice skate on the pond in winter before we used the axe to break the ice so the cattle could drink. We learned to sew our own clothes. If times get tough, it will be good to know these things.

My favorite part of growing up was the trips to Kansas City. The stockyards were still open back then, and we sold our cattle there. We shopped at Wards and Sears. The stores were huge and beautiful. I remember every time we went to Sears, there was a man out front selling tamales. What a treat to get fast food! When I grew up and married, I left the farm and moved to Kansas City. We still visit the farm when we want to ride horses or fish in the pond. I will always have these great memories.

Muddy Creek Bottom
By Carl Spillman of St. Joseph, Missouri
Born 1940

I grew up five miles east of Denver, Worth County, Missouri. The roads were mud and we had no electricity until the REA built lines. Then they applied rock to the roads in the summer of 1948.

We lived halfway down a long hill to "Muddy Creek Bottom." Ike and Cora Hensley lived down across the bridge, up a lane, over a low water stream.

How modern they were with a pitcher pump in the kitchen sink.

We had to carry water 250 yards up the hill. Ike drove the model T in the summer; but winter, it was stored on blocks in the car shed. He would drive the buckboard, pulled by the big white draft horse team, wearing his sheepskin coat and furry cap, on the road to Denver with produce, (cream and eggs) to sell.

It was not uncommon to see teams in Denver in those days of late 1940s or early 1950s.

Popeye
By Carole McClellan of St. Joseph, Missouri
Born 1936

"Popeye," the name given to my grandfather's clubhouse on the river in the 1920s, was where family gathered in the summer for picnics.

There was no electricity, heat, or water in the two-storied frame house. We used kerosene lanterns, pumped water from a well, and brought huge blocks of ice to keep food cold in an "icebox." The bathroom facility was an "out-house" affectionately given the name "blow-me-down," a phrase used in the "Popeye" cartoons!

A weeded lot in the back of the property had to be cleared before the game "cork-ball or bottle-caps" could be played. It was played like baseball with a narrow bat. Across the gravel road, we swam in the muddy river, and paddled a canoe, filled with cousins so it barely floated. Hiking to the single railroad trestle bridge, we'd walk across it never thinking what we'd do if a train had come. A cable hanging from this bridge, gave us the chance to take turns swinging on it and dropping into the water below, without ever checking the depth.

One big room in the upstairs of the house held four double beds and a baby crib. One of the younger cousins slept in the crib and three in the double bed. Others slept on the living room floor or on the screened "L"-shaped porch.

Always hot and dusty, we had fun sunning on a blanket, picking clover and tying it into chains, reading comic books, doing acrobatic poses, and telling tales on the porch swing. A small wooden dock near the water's edge

Some of Carole's family members at "Popeye" Club House in about 1950

collapsed with my brother and me on it as we kicked our feet. Thankfully, our mother reached down to pull us out!

A Good Place for the Children
By Catherine Henley of Plattsburg, Missouri

Let's think back in time to the 1890s. The location was a neighborhood just a few blocks from the Union Station in Kansas City, Missouri. A man owned a grocery store with living quarters above the store. He had a horse-drawn wagon with a canvas canopy top. The sign on the wagon simply stated "A. Schmitt Groceries and Meats." He would rise very early two or three days each week and drive the short distance to the city market north of the Union Station. There he would purchase farm fresh fruits, vegetables, and produce for his customers and neighbors. This man and his wife were my grandparents.

In the early years of their marriage, they lived above the store. They had two little girls and another child on the way. Now the time had come for them to move to a home with more living space and a yard for the children to play in. They found just the property they needed only a couple blocks from the store at 24th and Cherry Streets. It had a nice two-story Victorian style with a wraparound porch on the south and east, a large yard on the north with lots of sweet clovers, and wonderful shade trees. At the back of the property was a barn with a stall for his wagons. There was also a chicken house. He was able to sell the eggs and chickens to his customers. The south city limits for Kansas City then was at 31st Street. Grandmother told Grandfather this would be a very good place for the children. He bought the property, and that winter, my father was born in that house. They raised their family there.

As time went on, the children, their spouses, the nine grandchildren, and other relatives and friends would gather there on Sundays to eat dinner and visit for the day. The grownups played croquet and pinochle, and sometimes the men and some of the boys pitched horseshoes. The children played games, and many times would pick clover and make chains with them. We decorated Grandmother's porch beautifully with chains of clover, made wreaths for our heads, garlands to wear around our necks, and anything else we could think of that needed "beautifying."

When Grandfather passed away, Grandmother decided that it was "too much house" for her. At first, she rented it out. Later on, she sold it. Today, more than a century later, that neighborhood is famous for Crown Center, its outdoor ice-skating rink, and Hallmark Cards. The property where the grocery store was is now occupied by Truman Medical Center. Where Grandmother and Grandfather's home was is now where Children's Mercy Hospital is now. Grandmother was so right, and still is, when she said, "It's a very good place for the children!"

Life on the Farm as an Only Girl
By Ruth Pierce of Hamilton, Missouri
Born 1939

I was born in a small town called Bonanza. It was there in the 1800s and early 1900s. My dad was a farmer and Mom was a city girl, but she adapted to farm life. She was an only child and Dad was one of 12 children. I had three older brothers, which I always wanted to follow around. They didn't like me to. We lived in a three-room house with no electricity or running water. We had a back house, but Mom would have a pot inside at night. We had all the animals—cows, horses, chickens, and pigs. All the vegetables and meat back then was raised on the farm. Oh my! There has been no better smoked and cured ham! Mother could make the best bread I have ever had. I've tried and tried to make it like her and cannot. I don't think I knew what bought bread was back then. Mom would sell eggs and cream for feed. She picked out the feed sacks to use the material to make my dresses out of. One time we were going to Cowgill to sell the eggs and cream and my brothers and I were all in the wagon. I sat on a box, and they kept pulling me up. Mom would say, "Let her sit there!" I felt like a yoyo! Come to find out, the eggs were in that box! They were certainly scrambled after that!

I went to a one-room school called Baker Hill. There was no running water or lunches. The teacher would put a pot of beans for us sometimes. I wouldn't always keep up with my brother. It was cold. My one-armed brother would put a belt around my waist; I don't think my feet hit the ground the entire way there! We lived next to Shoal Creek, and I think it flooded every year. We sold out there and moved to Mirable. We had three bedrooms there; I had one and the boys had the other. One time I cleaned their room and moved the bed. I heard a big boom one night. They had jumped for the bed and it wasn't there. I was laughing, but not them!

When I went to school in Mirable, it was a lot bigger. There still was no inside bathroom and the outhouse was about a football field's distance away. We had an icebox but didn't get too much ice. The closest was in Hamilton, about 20 miles away. We would put milk in a jar and lower it in the well to keep cool. Dad had a racehorse and did good at it. He made enough to buy school shoes and supplies. We would have one pair, so we went barefoot most of the time. A cousin from town would come and spend a week with us. I made her take off her shoes. If I didn't wear shoes, the she didn't either. Her feet were tough after a day or two. We was always on a horse with no saddle. One time my brother god Dad's out from upstairs and put it on the gray mare. I was on the other one. He got spurs from somewhere and jabbed her with them. She bucked him right off and tore the saddle up. We nailed it back together and put it back. I still laugh about that. Life was hard back then, but we weren't in the house watching TV or playing video games. We made our own fun and we were healthier then. We got lots of fresh air.

The Little Girl and Her Doll
By Helen M. Brock of St. Joseph, Missouri

All little girls want dolls, right? Right. But what kind of dolls do they want? At four years of age, such niceties of conversation were not part of my makeup. All I knew was that I wanted a doll, and I made sure that my dad and grandma knew I wanted a doll. No, they didn't ask either. Come Christmas morning, there were two doll-sized packages under the Christmas tree. Oh, joy! Wow! Zipadee-doo-dah! Then, I opened the first package. There was a burgundy, plastic boy doll that wound up with a key and walked in a circle like a kid who had polio and wore braces. No blond curls, no brown braids, *nothing* like I was expecting. So, of course, I went from the "thrill of victory" to the "agony of defeat in the matter of a few seconds. What I didn't' know at that time was that my dad had had to order that doll all the way from Chicago. There was a second package waiting for me. My grandma had handcrafted a sailor doll for me from parts she had obtained over two years. Paddy became a treasured companion for many years, and I wish I could have passed him on to my children, but he perished in a house fire.

Helen and her doll, Paddy

Winter Triumph in a Simpler Time

Winter, in my estimation, is the best of all the seasons of the year. With it comes cool temperatures and snow! Perched on the highest hill in town, I was the mistress of all I surveyed. With my trusty steed, Bluebell, the blue sled (none of those garish red sleds for me) I took off running. The newly waxed, metal runners gleamed in the sunshine. I still remember the satisfying "whomp" when my tummy met the boards, the skillful maneuvering necessary to gain speed, and the schuss of the runners. Then I would gain speed right past the first block, gain more speed, and then "thump" on the railroad tracks. Could I make it? Did I have enough speed? If I did, I could make it to the town cemetery and I would be the queen of the hill! It was the acme of all the children's aspirations— even the boys. Could I do it? My legs were pumping, my heart was racing, and I just kept telling myself, "I think I can; I think I can; I think I can." I started slowing; slowing, and

then I gained a final burst of speed and steered to the left where the snow was still pristine. Success was mine! Bluebell Brock and Helen, victorious, trudged home to hot chocolate with Grandma. Of course, I had to provide an explanation as to why my boots, coat, hair, and pretty much all of my clothes were filled with snow. But, it was worth it! After all, I am 70 now and I still smile over that feat!

The Old Blackboard
By Ermel Joslin and Kelsi of Maryville, Missouri
Born 1932

When I was young, I went to a country school called Liberty. I started school in 1937. I was 5 years old. Each day I had to walk 2 miles to and from school. In the winter, we wore long old cotton hose, coats, hats, scarves, mittens, and overshoes. The snow would be so high that you couldn't see the fencepost. It would be so cold the school had an old wood stove, that by the time I got warmed up, it would be time to go home.

We just had one teacher. (Most teachers were Woman) She taught eight grades. We had Reading, Arithmetic (which today is known as math), Science, Geography, History, and Health. We played Ball, and Darebase. In Darebase, you would have a team and would chase the others back, and if you caught one, you would get a mark for your team.

At school, if someone got in trouble, the teachers would spank them. They used rulers, sticks, and belts. They did it if someone got caught cheating and swearing. If someone talked back, they would make the person stand in a corner. We used the old blackboards (aka chalkboards); we would do a lot of arithmetic and spelling problems at the old blackboard. After school, they would beat the erasers together to get the chalk dust out of them. We took our own lunches to school. We had peanut butter sandwiches.

December the 7, 1941 was Pearl Harbor. That was the start of the World War II. They talked about Germany and Hitler. They called Hitler "The Furer." He was just awful. He killed them Jews you know. 1941 when the war started, sugar was shortened, and Sugar stamps were issued.

I would gather eggs from the chickens

Mother raised. I also churned a lot of butter. After we churned the butter, we took it to the cellar to keep it cool. We didn't have refrigerators back then. We had an old tub and washboard. Mama scrubbed our clothes one day each week. They would put the water on the stove, and boil the Clothes to get out the germs. We had an old wood stove. We cooked on it at the house, (it was a Warm-Morning Stove.) We sold cream. You milked the cows and cream would naturally form on top of the milk and you'd skim it off. Daddy plowed the fields with a team of horses. Daddy didn't get a John Deere tractor until he bought one in about 1944. Mother raised a big garden. She would can tomatoes, green beans, peas, and corn. We had lots of pie and cake. You didn't buy groceries; you would just buy flour and coffee. Well that's about all.

Outhouse, Wringer Washer, and Saturday Night Baths...
By Arthur T. Enss of Norborne, Missouri
Born 1939

I was born in 1939, from my earliest memory we always had an outhouse. My first home was a basement house, and we lived down in a hollow electricity but no running water. Our outhouses were always two holers; we could not always afford store bought toilet paper so we used the pages of the Sears and Roebuck or Montgomery Ward's catalogue. The soft pages were used first and the slick pages were a last resort, sometimes we were lucky enough to find or get hold of an outdated phone book, which had all soft pages. The worst part of the outside toilet was in the summer, the wasp, bees, spiders and odor, in the winter the cold seats and cold winds blowing around your bare bottom plus sometimes you had to clear snow off the seat that had blown in through the cracks in the wood, but it kept the odor down, as well as all the bugs.

Favorite pet
I was very young and a friend of my dad gave him a Chow Chow puppy, my family named the puppy Teddy (so named because he looked like a Teddy Bear) he had a full fluffy red coat and black tongue. My grandfather always teased us that the dog was eating coal.

Teddy was a pure bread Chow, the man that gave my dad the dag owed my dad a favor for some work he had done for him. Teddy grew into a very protective guard dog of the family. Where we lived was very isolated in the hollow there was one other family that lived down the hollow. Teddy looked after all of us, but was defensive of my brothers, sister, and myself. If mom ever wanted to punish or whip us she had to take us into the house because Teddy would not let her whip any of us kids. We lived about a mile and half from school by road, but one half mile as the crow flies. Teddy walked us to school each day and then came back home. From our house, you could hear the school bell ring; he learned which bell meant school was dismissed for the day. Teddy would get up off the porch and trot off to meet us and walk us back home. When we walked to the store, he always went along, if a strange dog came out barking at us Teddy never paid much attention to small dogs, but if the dog was his size and wanted to fight then the fight was on. I do not remember Teddy ever losing a dogfight; some were draws and had to be broken up. The only fight he ever lost was with an automobile, Teddy was struck in the top of his head, it did not kill him but it did cause severe problems and he started going mad. My dad had to put him down which was very hard on everyone. We buried him in the yard, I never had another dog or pet as wonderful as Teddy

Critters
When we lived down in the hollow we raised chickens and had a couple of ducks, we kept them in a wire coop. One sunnier day a duck got loose my brothers and I was trying to catch it, the duck went under the overhang of the basement house roof my brothers were nine and ten years older and were too big to get under the overhang. I was four or five years old so they talked me into crawling under the overhang on my hands and knees to chase the duck out the other end, half way through the craw I came in contact with a large wasp nest, because it was summer I was wearing only shorts and of course the wasp started stinging me. My brothers were able to pull me out and started killing and knocking the wasp off of me. They took me in the house where my mom washed me down with baking soda water, then made a paste with red dirt and vinegar and put a blob on each sting, this helped to reduce the

pain and swelling. I had to lie down and rest, that was the worst encounter I ever had with critters.

Wringer Washer

My mom washed cloths with a wringer washer from my early years as well as on a scrub board until I left home to join the Army. We had no running water; we caught rainwater in a rain barrel this was mostly for cooking and washing our face and hands. On wash day my brothers had to walk down the hill to the cistern which was filled from an underground spring, they would carry two five gallon buckets of water each back up the hill to fill big pots so my mom could heat water on a kerosene cook stove, this hot water was poured into the washer, more was gathered for rinse tubs. I wanted to help so I carried a one-gallon syrup can of water. I probable spilt more water than I carried. The rinse tubs were placed alongside the washer the rinse tubs were on legs with casters, after washing the cloths they would be run through the wringers into the first cold water rinse tub, she would swing the wringer head over the cold water tubs and run the cloths into the second tub and then into a cloth basket to be taken outside to be hung on the cloth line to dry no mater winter or summer.

The wringers were motor driven there was a lever on the wringer head which allowed the operator to engage the wringers for forward or reverse motion or stop. There was an emergency release bar at the top of the rollers so if your hands got caught you could use your wrist to hit the bar and it would pop open the rollers so you could get your hands out. After the washing was done, you would wheel the washer and or the rinse tubs to the back door and release the drain hose from the side of the tub and allow the water to drain out the back door onto the ground. That was pretty much a full day for my mom.

Saturday Matinee

This was a very special time for me; my family did not have much money, so for my mom to give my sister and I thirty or fifty cents to see a movie was not always easy. The movie on Saturday was only fifteen cents per person and if we were lucky enough to get a quarter each we could buy candy or popcorn. Sometimes my sister would let me have her extra ten cents so I could have both candy and popcorn. I was only seven years old and my sister was

seven years older. The walk to the movies was about two miles, back then you could let your kids walk to the movies or store and not be worried about their safety. There was always a continued serial prior to the main movie; the serials were fifteen-minute monster or space. The main movies were mostly westerns, my favorite stars were Roy Rogers, Hopalong Cassady (William Boyd), Lash Larue (cannot remember the actors name,), and Gene Autry. My sister would never let me sit with her; she always sat with her girlfriends and flirted with the boys.

Saturday night bath

When we lived in the hollow, we lived next the Standard Oil refinery and they wanted to expand so we were bought out and forced to move. My dad used the money to purchase a vacant lot and he and my brothers built a concrete blockhouse, we had running water and electricity but was not hooked up to the sewer, so again we did not have a bathroom inside the house. We took our baths in a round metal tub, there were five of us in the family, mom, sister, two brothers, and myself, my dad was not home much so he hardly took a bath at home. We would bring in the round tub from the cold so it could warm up, we were lucky enough to have a hot water heater so we did not have to heat the water on the stove. We did not have partitions in the house except for mom and dad's room, so we would put table chairs around the tub and hang blankets on them for privacy. My sister would bathe first more hot water was added and mom would bathe next, some of the dirty water was dipped out and more hot water was added for whoever was next until everyone who needed a bath had bathed and all baths were completed and yes they were usually on Saturday night. The rest of the week, we used a wash pan to clean up.

Chamber Pots

All the years we had outhouses we also had chamber pots, late at night no one wanted to have to truck out in the dark or cold with a flashlight to go to the bathroom, so you used the pot. We only did number one in the pot if you needed to do more you went to the outhouse. In the morning the pot would have to be taken out to the outhouse and be emptied, we never had an inside toilet or bathtub until I was ten Years old.

Family Radio Shows

The radio was our primary source of

entertainment, when I came home from school I would listen to favorite shows. Batman, Superman, The Green Hornet, and The Lone Ranger. We listened to Fibber Magee and Molly, Amos and Andy and Sundays the Who-done-its crime shows, the best was The Shadow (La Mont Cranston) the Shadow Knows.

Party Line Phone

When we got our first telephone, it was quite the thing to have a phone in our house. We were on what they called a party line, which meant more than one household could talk on the same line or listen in on your conversation. Each household was assigned a certain number of rings so they would know if the call was for them. The phone came in one color only (BLACK). I do not remember what the phones were made of but I do Know they were very heavy and the material was very hard, there was no dial if you wanted to make a call you picked up the receiver and with the other hand pressed the plunger up and down and the operator would answer and you would tell her what prefix and number and she would ring the phone of the person you wanted. Each prefix was a certain name and then the number such as (Glendale 555) I do not remember our prefix and number. There could be as many as six households or as little as one other on the party line depending on how many wanted a phone. Sometimes you would get someone on your party line that liked to talk a lot and if you needed to use the phone, you could not as long as someone else was on the line. The only way was to pick up the receiver and ask the person on the line if they would please get off the line because you needed to make a call, sometimes that worked and sometimes it did not, it was quite an experience being on a party line, believe me it was no party, HA HA.

Ovaltine
By Peggy Moore of Overland Park, Kansas
Born 1934

In the mid-1940s, I lived in Pattonsburg, Missouri in Daviess County. My parents had only a battery-operated radio to listen to. There was no electricity on the farm yet. These radios had two batteries to operate them. One was the size of a car battery and the other was a smaller one. The radio was to

Ovaltine Decorder Whistle

be used for market news. After school each day, I listened to one of my favorite programs, which was whatever was on that particular evening—Sky King, Captain Midnight, Lone Ranger, etc. I guess I was lucky to have this time slot. These programs always had an offer to entice children. They required a box top or label and a dime or quarter to mail in with it. This one particular offer needed an Ovaltine label and a dime or quarter; I can't remember which. This was to order a decoder/whistle. Upon receipt of my decoder, I would listen each evening for the message to decode. The catch was (with my parents) was that in order to get the Ovaltine label, I had to drink the Ovaltine. Believe you me, I never forgot Ovaltine! I still have my decoder.

Catholic Picnic
By Betty O'Connor Curtis of Cameron, Missouri
Born 1924

During some of the depression years, St Munchins Catholic Church had an annual picnic to supplement the finances. Some of the parishioners living in town couldn't find jobs; others had low paying jobs and a lot of the farm families were having a hard time surviving because of the dry weather and low prices. It was held in the Korneman Grove, a beautiful timber pasture about four miles south of Cameron on Highway 69.

The ladies served a delicious fried chicken dinner with potato salad, green beans, sliced tomatoes, other relishes, cake, and ice tea. The ladies donated and fried the chickens, only the meaty pieces at home, and also from their gardens contributed the vegetables and other foods. They continually fried more chickens on kerosene stoves in a tent on the grounds. My Grandma Josie Quell was in charge of some of these dinners, and was assisted by all the ladies of the church. The high schoolers and other young people served and cleared the tables. Grandma's right hand helper was her black friend, Janie Wilson. Janie often helped Grandma with cooking and dishwashing when she had a big family or other church dinners. Then when Janies's church had possum suppers and their fundraisers Grandma went to help her. Janie always wore a long white stiffly starched apron and helped other families in town with their entertaining. Food was kept in a screened tent. They served until the food supply was exhausted. I can't recall for sure but I think they charged one dollar for the meal. As my folks didn't have the money for us to eat, Mother fixed us a picnic of the bony pieces of chicken and all the trimmings. We ate on a blanket under the shade tree by the car.

A temporary stage was set up by the men for entertainment and speakers in the afternoon. Games of a carnival type—bingo, turtle races, throwing hoops over bottles, a fishpond, and other games of chance with small prizes for the winners. They had stands where they sold ice-cold pop of various flavors. Also, Chapman's Dairy brought out their ice cream truck and sold ice cream bars dipped in chocolate and peanuts. We really enjoyed the soda pop and ice cream, as we did not ordinarily have these at home.

Another drawing card to the picnic was the raffle for a new 1933 Chevrolet car furnished by the local dealer at cost somewhere around $500. Tickets were sold at ten cents each as near as I can recall. A member of St. Munchins, John Sigrist, won the car. Early that morning his wife, Catherine, had given birth to their third daughter, Marguerite. On the way home, we stopped a minute for my Mother, Marie O'Connor, to make a short visit to see the new baby and congratulate them. Catherine's mother, Catherine Quell Muenker and my mother's grandfather, Joseph Quell were brother and sister, and they had come to America from Germany.

At the picnic in 1934 there were several politicians speaking, and among them Harry S. Truman. I remember seeing him arrive in a neatly pressed white suit and white hat sitting squarely on his head. A friend, Jewell Sloan of Cameron and near my age, related to me he was also there that day and he remembers, Truman's daughter Margaret, about twelve years old had two white Scottish Terrier dogs on a leash with blankets on their backs saying, "Vote for Truman." He made a speech campaigning for U. S. Senator, and won the election that fall. Later he became President of the United States when Franklin Roosevelt died in office. I have always been proud to have seen and heard him in person.

It was a lot of work for the men and women of the church, but as a youngster, it was a lot of fun to play games with your friends, and we were always looking forward to next year.

Back When Neighbors Helped Each Other
By Dorothy Lou Grable of Agency, Missouri
Born 1918

I am a 94 year old lady and live alone with lots of help from my family. I live on a farm that has been in our family since it was homesteaded by my great-grandparents. I have fond memories of my childhood. I feel fortunate that I can remember it, though I can't brag about my short-term memory! My thoughts turn to a one-room school that I attended. The teacher taught all eight grades and did the janitorial work as well. I think her salary was 50 dollars a month. One lady teacher boarded with us and became one of our best friends. After she married and moved away, they came back often and stayed several days with us. Box suppers were held often at school. The girls and ladies would decorate a box and fill it with food. The boy or man who bought it would eat with the female who made it. Sometimes we would have a contest to select the most popular girl, or maybe the ugliest man. That certainly created a lot of fun! People paid a small amount for each vote.

It is with sadness that I think about the town of Agency, Missouri, which was about a fourth of a mile from where I live. It was such a thriving town with every kind of business that was necessary to make a good town. At one time, we had three doctors, maybe four. There was a busy train depot with two trains that came each day. We were blessed with the largest stirrup factory in the world, which employed many people. It is hard to describe the famous Agency picnics. They were held annually on the last weekend of July in a beautiful grove on the northeast corner of Agency. Such huge crowds were there. On election years, politics flowed freely. One year, the special guest was Harry Truman. When all of the floods came along, all of the businesses had to leave. There is nothing left except memories, but we are thankful for the three churches, post office, tire shop, car repair shop, grocery store, and deli that relocated out of the flood area. Many new houses have been built out of the flood area, also.

When I was young, we had no electricity or indoor plumbing. My mother washed using a washboard and hung the wash out on a clothes line no matter what the temperature was. I thought it was fun to turn the wringer. It was considered a luxury when we finally got electricity and a bathroom! I can't begin to describe the Depression of the mid-1930s. It was almost impossible to get money enough to live on. My parents worked so hard. They always milked cows and sold milk, butter, cream, and eggs. My mother canned everything she could. My father could usually make a living on the farm, but he had to get a job, which paid $100.00 per month. That would buy a lot, though, as everything was so cheap. For an example, bread was a dime a loaf back then. Not many charities, food kitchens, or help of any kind was available. I often think about how neighbors helped each other when I was young. On butchering day or during the harvest season, there was always plenty of help. I remember seeing a wagonload of men with scoop shovels going to a home where there was a death. They scooped the deep snow out of the lane so that cars could get through. Another example of a good neighbor was when one of our neighbors called my mother early one morning and told her not to let me start walking to school. She had seen a strange appearing man walking down the road. We found out later that he had escaped from the state hospital. These are just a few of the many acts of kindness that I remember.

It is impossible to write about the many changes that have taken place in the past 80 years! I'd like to mention just a few changes, though. Very few farmers in this area raise wheat now. The farmers have machinery now that will plant a field in a few hours that took several weeks back then. A car could be purchased back then for $750.00. Sadly, I don't know many of my neighbors now, and we used to know everyone in a wide radius. Some of the changes are great, and some are not so great. However, of course I am classed as being "old-fashioned!"

Saturday Night Life
By Norma Edson of Richmond, Missouri
Born 1932

There are many stories I could share about Bethany the county seat of Harrison County. My 12 years of school were all spent there. The Baptist church was my church home, but that isn't any different than many others. The different part will come a little later and it involves my sister and me. Our dad worked at the Bethany Oil Company for several years. King City Cream Station was also a part of this business. Then, Highway 69 changed its route through Bethany and Bethany Oil moved out to new highway; the business where Dad had worked became King City Cream Station. The original building was greatly enlarged and the two buildings were connected. The business also did poultry, eggs, and feeds. A man and his family moved to Bethany from King City to become a part of the operation.

On Saturday nights in Bethany, two movie houses were open. Stores didn't close on Saturday. They stayed open till after the movies were over. Farmers came into town on Saturdays to do their "trading." They would bring their eggs and cream in and return later to pick up their cream can or their egg crate (or both). People sat in their cars around the square and visited. The young people walked around the square after the movie. Sometimes they would go to one of the four drug stores around the square or stop at the popcorn stand on the corner by Penny's Store. After the movie was over, my sister and I would go to the cream station. Mother also worked there on Saturdays, so we couldn't go home. Some Saturdays there was a person to stay with Sis

Front of the new addition to the King City Cream Station 1943-1944

and me so we would be home, but on some Saturday nights, we stayed at the cream station.

This is the unique part: Sis and I would crawl up on those feed sacks and sleep. Sleep, that is, until the farm wife would come in to choose the feed in the sacks she wanted. "Clarence, I want this sack here, and this one here, and here is the third." Dad would move sacks so the lady could have the feed in the sacks she wanted. This was during the World War II days and material was scarce. It took three feed sacks to make a dress for the women. Clothes were made from these sacks. Scrapes from the sacks (or worn out clothes) were used for quilt pieces. After people were finished with their business, it was time to close up shop for the weekend. Money had to be counted, and it had to tally to the penny. I remember one Saturday night when it was almost two o'clock before they tallied. Then it was time to go home. Our family had no car at this time, so we walked home. That wasn't too bad in warm weather, but was sure cold in winter. During the week, the men usually rode a bicycle to work and went home for the noon meal. These are the memories of my Saturday night life!

The Frog Hop
By Maxine Deatherage Monroe of St. Joseph, Missouri
Born 1922

It was the late '30s and early '40s as two barely grown up girls went to ask their Dad if he would take them to the Frog Hop. We lived out in the country and the beautiful Frog Hop Ballroom was about 20 miles away in the town of St Joseph Mo. We had a large family and barely enough to eat and the luxury of going to town was reserved for important things like grocery shopping or cattle buying, certainly not to go dancing. With gas for our old car at twenty-five cents a gallon, we shouldn't ask for that privilege, but we were also very determined young ladies and at 16 and 17 years old, the Frog Hop was THE place to be. We secretly hoped that we would get good enough at dancing that we could become instructors and get in free on class night. That would save fifty cents and buy more gas.

So we joined forces and followed our Mothers instruction for getting supper on the table, all the while coaxing our Dad to relent and take us to town. All he could say was, "Now you girls know we can't afford to spend money on gas and we certainly can't afford the fifty cents more to get us in the door of our beloved Frog Hop." With copious tears, theatrics, and promises to do more chores we kept wearing Dad down. Until he finally threw up his hands and said, "OK but this is the last time." Well we grinned at each other in triumph but also knew it would be the same scenario come Friday and just maybe we would have dates for Saturday night. That sometimes presented a problem because we both had to have dates so we would be together!

We hurriedly got dressed in our finest, got on our dancing shoes and we were off to town in our old 35 Chevy! Dad let us out at the door reminding us to be as pretty on the inside as we looked on the outside. We heard this each time we went out! Oh how happy we were dancing the night away with our friends. Then the evening was over and Betty and I would dash up the hill behind the Frog Hop to wake our Dad up. He had slept in the car while we danced to save the precious gas.

We were full of happy chatter on the way home but Dad fussed about having to get back up in a few short hours to go to his job at the packinghouse. I realize how fortunate we were to have a Dad that would allow us to enjoy our youth!

Yes, we got to be dance instructors on Thursday nights and if we talked hard enough, we were lucky and went again on Friday nights. We were luckier still if we got to double date on Saturday nights to dance to the Big Band sounds of Jimmy and Tommy Dorsey, Glen Miller Cab Calloway, Harry James, and many others. What wonderful memories as we jitter bugged the Nights away. They are still fresh and precious memories to me at the age 90 years. My advice to the young people today is make happy memories while you can.

A Memorable Teacher and Schoolhouse
By Imogene Clark of Osborn, Missouri

The year was 1946 when I started first grade at the Garden Prairie School in DeKalb County. It was about seven miles north of Cameron, Missouri. This was a one-room school, and included grades one through eight. There were three students in my first grade class, and 25 students total at the school. Our teacher, Miss Addie, was the typical old maid. She wore long dresses with the high neck, her hair was always pulled back in a bun on the back of her neck, and she wore her glasses on the end of her nose. She ruled with a ruler, and even used it several times, when necessary. She rode a horse to school each day, and during the winter, if the weather was bad, we did not have school. I lived just a quarter of a mile up the road, so I walked to school each day. I remember the old coal stove, the coal shed, (with the older students taking turns to bring in the coal for the fire), and the water pump at the front door. Each student had their own tin cup to use for a drink from the well. I also remember he coat/lunch room, the individual desks with the lift up top, the wall chalkboard, and the floor to ceiling bookshelves that were packed full of books. I learned to read with *Dick and Jane and Spot*, and loved the spelling bee every Friday. There was a basement, and we did use it when there was a storm in the area. The one holer stood out behind the building. No, we did not use the Sears and Roebuck catalog; we had real toilet paper.

There was a large tree beside the school, and in the spring, we enjoyed our lunch under the tree from our metal lunch boxes. I still have my green metal lunch box, and have enjoyed showing it to my grandkids some 60 years later. Winter activities included, fox, and geese, snowball fights, building large snowmen, and just playing in the snow. Parties were always fun, especially on Valentine Day when everyone (yes, even the boys) had to decorate a valentine box with a lunch inside. Prizes were awarded to the prettiest and fanciest ones. We dressed in our finest for the Christmas program, and all the parents attended.

Imogene Walker, Lois Hahn, and Bill Swords
Three first graders at Garden Prairie School

Refreshments were served after the program.

In 1962, I got married, and we decided to have our rehearsal dinner at Garden Prairie. We cleaned up the inside for the food and set up tables in the big front yard for the rehearsal dinner. It was a beautiful June evening, and a special memory for me. In 2012, we celebrated our 50th anniversary, and I went back to Garden Prairie for a walk down memory lane. The building still stands; the outside is deteriorating, paint is chipped off, windows are broken out, boards are falling off the front, the front door stands open, and tall grass grows in the front yard. Inside, vandals have totally destroyed everything. The piano and bookshelves have been demolished, there is graffiti written all over the chalkboard, and the stove, and desks are all gone. Yes, tears came to my eyes as I stood there and remembered everything. I am a retired teacher, and spent 41 years teaching kindergarten. As I stood there, I thought to myself, "This is where it all started." Thanks for the memories Miss Addie and Garden Prairie!

The Village I Grew Up In
By John Delameter of Kansas City, Missouri
Born 1943

I grew up on a large farm south of Princeton, Missouri in Mercer County. I was the ninth of 11 siblings. I attended a one-room schoolhouse throughout my first six years. I remember going through the Sears and Roebuck catalog with my mom and picking out new clothes and supplies. Of the things

I remember most about this order was a red plaid book satchel and a black lunch pail. I was very disappointed when the order came because they substituted the black pail for the blue one that I wanted. Well the big day finally arrived and our mom drove me and one of my older brothers, Derald, and sister, Twylia, to school. As we stepped in the room, the teacher, Miss Susan Alma Warden, spotted me and came back. She picked me up, took me to the front of the room, and gave me a big ole kiss right there in front of everyone. As a five year old little boy who still believed that girls had cooties, I was mortified. After that, I was ready to go back home with my mom. This was Miss Warden's first day of teaching, so we both had a lot to learn. Back then, if a teacher attended college during the summer, they could teach during the winter, and then go back to college during the summer until they got there teaching certificate. All anyone wanted to play at recess and noon was baseball. I hated the game, so one Friday afternoon on our way back inside, I hid the ball in some bushes, thinking that would put an end to the "ole ball game." Well, it did put an end to it until someone found it. Then, my little reprieve from baseball was over.

For several years, we attended the Antioch Baptist Church that was also in the country. It was also just one room and a path. I loved going there and singing. I really loved Vacation Bible School and Revival meetings that lasted two weeks. As far as I know, this building still stands. I still go back there to visit from time to time. The first memory that comes to mind when I walk down memory lane there is the bible school lessons under a hickory tree with sugar cookies and grape Kool-Aid.

When I was nine, I started going to the church camp "Grand Oaks Assembly." That was the highlight of my summer. It was on those ole camp grounds that I heard a lot of character lessons about God. To this day, I still remember some of them. It was at this camp that I accepted Jesus as my personal Lord and Savior. When I was 12 years old, I guess I had decided that girls did not have cooties after all, because that was where I got my first kiss. Her name was Linda. I still remember floating back to my dorm room, just knowing I had found the "woman of my dreams." However, she didn't turn out to be!

In May of 1955 my younger brother Jerry and I were building a tree house and he cut the limb off that I was standing on. I fell and broke my arm. When the local newspaper editor learned of this, she had my mom bring us to town with the ax and took our picture. We made the front page news.

In the early '50s, we got electricity, and my mom bought a strand of electric lights for the tree (all it consisted of was eight lights) and a red cellophane wreath with a red light in it. She also bought the most beautiful blond headed angel for the top of the tree that I have ever seen. I still have that angel and she tops my tree nearly every Christmas. We also got an electric washing machine at that time. Now, I was used to the old noisy engine machine. This one had to be vented, so she had some kind of a pipe that they ran out the open window in both the winter and the summer. When Mom filled it with water and pulled the red knob on it, I could not hear it running and thought it wasn't working. Of course, I found out later that it was a quiet washing machine!

One day, my brother Jerry and I were playing in and by the crick. We had divided up the land, and his had this beautiful birch tree on it. He decided that he was going to cut it down. Well, me being a tree lover, I traded him all my land for a small spot of land under the tree. The last time I was down there, the tree was fully grown and is now a beautiful tree. I want to visit there this summer and look up my tree again and see how well she has weathered her life.

When my sister Jo started taking home economics in High school, I always loved it when they baked because she would bring home goodies for us to eat. She is still a great cook and I always enjoy staying with her and having coffee and goodies on her side porch overlooking a big red barn. I can honestly say that I am still a good ole country boy! I played the Tuba in the band and loved marching at football games and in the parades. We always had a homecoming parade, and in the summer we played summer concerts on the bandstand on the Princeton Square. Here are a few of my favorite things from my childhood: the smell of the dirt from a freshly plowed field, playing in the creek in the warm water, picking lilacs and wild flowers and taking them to my mom, and "helping" my dad build things. I loved working with wood projects with him, but was not real crazy about working in the shop where there was grease and oil to get dirty from.

When one of the farmers had crops to harvest ECT, all the other farmers would go help get it done. Then, in a day or so, they would go on to another farmer's home to help with theirs. The wife of the farmer fixed a big meal at noon for everyone, and they would say that they were having hands for dinner. She always brought cold drinks and a sweet snack out to the field in the middle of the afternoon.

One day, my brother Jerry and Dad came home from Princeton. Jerry told me that there was a store in town that had what they called a television in it. He said that people were all gathered around to see it. He said that it was like listening to the radio, but that he could see the people that were doing the talking. Later, my Sister Lea and her husband Loren Hickman bought one. We would go there on Saturday nights and watch Jackie Gleason and Wrestling with Bob on channel two in St. Joseph.

Hillary Clinton said in her book that "Every child needs a village to grow up in." Looking back, I see that I had a wonderful village of people to help guide me to adulthood. I shall always be indebted to all of them. Thank you from the bottom of my heart. You are all a gift from God!

Smoldering Rubble
By Ruth Carol Trotter Proffitt of Springfield, Missouri
Born 1941

It was a cold day in January with a blanket of snow on the ground. I was only 6 years old when the family drove to another town for a doctor's appointment. This town was 30 miles from where we lived in the country. On the return trip home, my parents noticed smoke coming from the southwest. Mother and dad started guessing where it might be and what it was. My brother insisted that it was located where our house stood. We all kept a watchful eye on this horrendous inferno, and the closer we got to our small home town of Norborne (located two and one-half miles from our farm) it soon became clear that it was indeed our house that was burning. Upon arrival, there was only a corner of smoldering rubble that remained of the two story home that my grandfather had built. It was late in the

Wetherholt School

afternoon and we were in total shock. All that remained of our personal possessions were the clothes on our back and the car we were riding in.

We had wonderful neighbors that took us in that night and provided a hot meal and warm bed for us to sleep in. This being 65 years ago, I can vaguely remember all the details; however, it left a memory that I'll never forget.

Back to our neighbors, they held a shower for us in the one room Wetherholt School that was about a mile from our home place, where I attended until rural schools were consolidated. A neighbor let us move into a vacant house that had been empty for several years. It was just across the road from the home place and we lived there until warm weather, then we moved back across the road. The barn loft became our bedroom, the garage was our uncle's bedroom, and the smoke house became the kitchen. All this happened while our new home was being built. It was quite a summer trying to sleep in that hot hayloft. I well remember going with my sister and brother to the barn to retire for the night and when my brother opened the barn door, there was a pair of feet headed up the ladder to the loft. Well, as you can imagine, the door was quickly shut and my siblings both took off running. Being much smaller than my sister and brother, I fell down and started screaming for help. They did come back to get me and we made it safely back to the smoke house. I suppose it is a good thing that age helps one to forget some details.

My mother gave me the beautiful green Depression glass dishes that were given to us at the shower, which are on display in my china cabinet and are now a collector's item.

Things that happened during this time of overcoming tragedy taught me a great lesson that will never be forgotten. First of all, that our neighbors were the finest people anyone could ever ask for. They have all passed away but their memory lingers on in my mind.

Blizzard
By Joseph E. Sullenger of Darlington, Missouri
Born 1951

Life in the country in northwest Missouri could be really tough at times. Late in 1963, I was in the seventh grade. The classroom was on the second floor of the Albany high school building and had windows facing west. Around 9 AM, snowflakes begin to fall. The snowfall kept getting heavier and the teacher was called to the door by the principal. After a short discussion, she returned to the classroom and announced that school would be let out at 1 PM, as the owner of the school buses was afraid that any later then that, the buses wouldn't be able to navigate the roads. The school bus owner actually wanted to leave earlier then one o'clock. The principal argued that he couldn't count the day as a full day of school if he let out any earlier.

The bus owner agreed to the time with the warning that the buses would leave at one PM sharp, not a minute later. If the kids weren't on those buses, they would be left. The teachers made allowances to give the kids time to get their things together and make it to their bus. Many children didn't take the warning serious enough and were left behind. At one o'clock sharp, the buses left. I made it to my bus but many were left behind and town families took them in until their parents could retrieve them.

Traveling by school bus, it normally took 45 minutes to get from the school to the road intersection where I was let off. I don't remember how long it took that afternoon but it was considerably longer because we slid off the road and became stuck 3 times. Farmers who lived along the main roads were out and about with their tractors pulling stuck vehicles out of the grader ditches. The last time we became stuck before my younger brother, a neighbor kid, and I were let off the bus was a mile or so up the road. A neighboring farmer pulled us out and followed the bus to our stop.

At that intersection there was a small building where we left our overshoes. That building was real handy for us as it provided a place to get out of the rain and snow and a place to keep our overshoes. From that building to my home was approximately three quarters of a mile down a dirt road. The family car was parked by that building so I knew dad had prepared to be snowbound. During snowstorms, the roads would often be blocked until the township road grader with a snowplow could open them. That might take up to a week sometimes. The main highways were taken care of by the state and they would be first to be cleared. We three kids put on our overshoes and bundled up as best we could and prepared for a long, cold walk home. The farmer on his tractor told us to climb on his tractor and come to his house, as he wasn't going to let us try and walk home in this storm. We quickly agreed and climbed on the back of that tractor. He lived a short ways away.

The fire in his heating stove sure felt good. After a while the snowfall abated, however the wind was still ferocious. The farmer's wife had called our parents to let them know where we were. Since the snow had quit falling, it was decided that we could go on. Between my home and the farmers home was a bridge across a creek. The farmer said he would walk with us to the bridge. His wife insisted we put on more clothes and she found a few old coats to lend us. We walked to the bridge where the neighbor wished us well and then returned to his home. A short distance from the bridge the road started up a steep hill. The road had high banks on either side going up that hill. The drifting snow blowing across the top of those banks created a tunnel of snow. I'll never forget the sound of the wind whistling across the top of that tunnel as we walked up the hill. Once home, I went into the living room where we had a wood heating stove. Lying on the floor next to the stove was the magneto from an old tractor my dad owned. That tractor hadn't been used in a while. It had steel lugged wheels on the back and rubber tires in front. Originally, it had rubber tires front and back. Dad had bought those steel wheels some years earlier and put them on. He only used the tractor when the going got tough. The next morning he took the magneto, now dried out, and put it back on the tractor. The tractor was started with a hand crank and after a short while of fussing with it, the tractor started.

With that tractor, he was able to haul hay from the stack to the cattle. After a few days, we knew the highway had been cleaned of snow, so we ventured out on that tractor to the car. The snow was deep and packed and the rubber tires on the front of that tractor would lift up on top of the snow whereas the steel wheels on the back just cut through the snow. Many times dad would have to stop and backup to get the front tires back down in the snow so that the tractor wouldn't tip over backward. It was rough going. Once we got to the car, we were able to go to town and buy essential groceries. We didn't require a lot as my parents raised most of what we lived on. There was a neighbor who live a mile or so on past our home that needed a prescription refilled and that was the main reason we ventured out. We picked the prescription up from the pharmacy and once back home I started out on foot for the neighbor's home to deliver it. I was to meet the neighbor's daughter halfway and give it to her to take back home. Wading snow waist deep in places made for a very tiring trek. When I met the neighbor girl, we both lay down on the snow and rested exchanging a few pleasantries before returning.

If memory serves me correctly, many of those children stuck in town missed being home for Christmas. Fortunately, blizzards such as that one seldom occur.

Telephones...

Until the early 1960s, our telephone was a wooden rectangular box with hardware attached. It was mounted on the wall of our living room. It had two small hemispherical bells attached at the top and below that was a mouthpiece you talked into. The earpiece hung on the side on a hook. You had to hold that earpiece to your ear with one hand. On the other side of that box was a little crank handle. When you turned that little crank, it made everyone's phone ring as long as you cranked. The phone system was a party line. When your phone rang, so did everybody else's.

You had to know what your phone number sounded like to know if the call was for you. As a youngster, I never could figure out what the code was. When I started school, the first grade teacher asked all of us students to go home and get our phone number. Return the

next day and give it to her. That evening I asked my mother what our phone number was and she replied, "Two shorts and a long." The next day the teacher started asking each student what his or her phone number was. Of course, all the town kids gave her a series of numbers. When she got to me, I replied, "Two shorts and a long." The teacher chuckled and said that she needed the phone number." I kind of got belligerent about it and said, "I don't know about any number, my mother said it was two shorts and a long." The teacher then told me to go home and ask for the number. That teacher was on the same phone system we were on so she understood what the problem was. That night I asked my mother about it and she laughed. Then she explained that she should have known better. She then told me that our phone number was 3309. Somehow, that equated to two short and one long ring. If you were a snoop, you could pick up your earpiece when the phone rang and listen to the neighbors talk. I heard of a few neighbors who didn't think twice about cutting into a conversation and asking questions if they didn't understand what you said. That phone exchange had a switchboard office in a little building in the nearby village of Darlington, MO. The operator lived there. If you wanted to make a long distance call, you had to go to that switchboard office and have the operator dial it for you. She would then connect the call to a phone in the hallway and you could talk to whom you were calling on that phone. About 1962 someone looked into our phone exchange's license to operate and discovered that the license had expired a few years earlier. The community then decided to join a phone exchange system that served neighboring communities. Of course, that system used modern dial telephones.

The old wall crank telephones used a bare steel wire mounted on poles to connect everyone. The new dial system used a buried multi-strand cable. It was quite exciting to see that cable buried in the community. The equipment used to bury the cable consisted of an Allis Chalmers HD-11 crawler tractor hooked to a cable plow. The cable plow had a large knife blade that cut down into the earth about three feet. The blade was hollow and the new phone cable, stored on a large wooden spool, was fed down through that blade. There was a smaller bulldozer hooked to the front of that HD-11 to assist in pulling and turning the whole apparatus. That smaller bulldozer also cleared brush and dug crossings across ditches. My dad and I were watching that rig go past our home. My dad had made his living for several years with an older Allis Chalmers crawler tractor. He looked at me and said, "You know how they came up with the 11 for the model number?" Of course I didn't. He then told me that is what that tractor weighs, 11 tons.

Many in the community kept their old wall crank telephones connected between them so they could gossip on their private line. Everyone else disconnected their old phones and reclaimed the wire.

Mary's family of nine in a four-room house

To Missouri by Covered Wagon
By Mary Weldon of Kidder, Missouri
Born 1932

In 1925, Carl and Lillie Harris, their two-year old daughter Ethel, two Grandpas, and a friend packed their belongings in covered wagons and headed from Nebraska to Breckenridge, Missouri. This is where Carl's sister lived. They did odd jobs and traded horses for a place to stay at night. 21 days later, they arrived in Breckenridge. Dad worked on the railroad, did farm work, broke horses, and did basically anything to make a living. The family moved several times, and seven more children were born. The last move was when Dad bought the 80-acre farm in Liberty Township on Lake Viking mud road for $1,700. He made a $100 payment on the house each year. We had a four-room house, a barn, and an outhouse. The last child was born there in 1943, making nine children. Ethel had already gotten married. Her husband was overseas in the Navy, so she came back home with her son for a few months. Dad went to work for Ed Froman.

I remember one time Dean, ten, Wayne, nine, and I, twelve, took the horses and wagon to cut wood with a crosscut saw. We got the horses going pretty fast and Wayne was sitting on the side of the wagon. Well, we felt a big bump and heard a loud yell. Wayne got run over with the wheel! He got up and brushed off; he wasn't hurt. We didn't tell Mom for a while, but Wayne couldn't keep quiet. We got scolded good for running the horses.

Six of us attended Liberty Center School, walking or riding Old Lady, our special horse, one and a half miles to school. We would ride three at a time. She shied at little things and sometimes we got thrown off. She would run straight to the barn. We did a lot of extra walking. She was very gentle otherwise. We could pile on as many kids as there was room, with Wayne standing on her heels and holding her tail. She never made a bobble. We had no saddle and we tied her to the coal shed until school was out.

Our school served as a church, with a different denomination each Sunday. Sometimes in winter, we followed the base of a big ditch to within a quarter mile of school. Sometimes we stopped at Mrs. Lightfoot's to warm frostbitten fingers. Mom kept busy making mittens out of clothing from a community box. She made all of our clothes or mended existing ones. Our entertainment was radio: *Hopalong Cassidy, Dark Shadows, Yukon King,* etc. were our favorites. We made stilts out of poles. We rolled in old tires and we always had marbles. We were fascinated by tumblebugs. We went to the free shows in Altamont and Winston. The sun heated our bath water on Saturdays. Other times we rigged up a shower; it never lasted very long.

There were times Mom caught the train at Gallatin to Nebraska to see her folks. She usually took the baby and second smallest with her, leaving Bea and I (Mary) to help Dad and control the other boys. What a job! One time Bea and I canned dill pickles with the directions of the Kromeck girls. There are 13 members of the family that have served in the Armed Forces. Our Harris family dates back to 1864 in Daviess County. Our great-great-grandpa, Hiram Harris, is buried in the Centerary Cemetery. The folks are gone along with two brothers and one sister. We hold a Harris Reunion each August at the home place where Brother Dean lives and maintains. He and Jerry still do some farming in Daviess County. What a fun life! We had a lot of hard times, but it has made each of us strong people.

The Day Dad got Struck by Lightning
By Connie Rawlings of Platte City, Missouri
Born 1943

I would like to share a personal childhood memory of an event, which was quite newsworthy at the time in my rural community in northern Plate County, Missouri. In the 1950s, my father, Cecil "Tiny" Miller, was struck by lightning and survived to tell the tale. I was 12 years of age, and the event was indelibly imprinted on my mind. My family was living on our farm west of Camden Point, Missouri in June of 1955. My uncle resided on a great uncle's farm adjoining my maternal grandparents' farm west of Dearborn, Missouri. My father and my uncle sometimes assisted each other with farm duties.

On a warm summer day, my father and my uncle were "putting up hay" on the uncle's farm west of Dearborn. My uncle was using a tractor baling the hay and my father was pulling a hay rake with a 1940s Willy jeep (which I fondly called "Nellie Belle" from an old TV show). I had gone with my father that day to visit with my aunt while the "haying" was being completed. In the afternoon, storm clouds approached rather quickly and the lightning and thunder were reminders that everyone should take cover. My aunt and I discussed the fact that my father and uncle should be coming to the house. We waited and waited, but they never arrived. Instead, as I was watching the road for them, I saw an ambulance travel along the road and turn into the driveway of my grandparents' home, which was visible from my uncle's house. It was apparent that something terrible had happened. I can still remember the overwhelming fear that I experienced at that moment.

As the story unfolded, I learned that my father and uncle were in the process of leaving the hayfield. My uncle had parked his machinery, and my father was in the process of unhooking the rake from the Jeep so they could use the Jeep for transportation back to the house. That is when the lightning hit. My father had his hand on the metal rake, which served as the conductor for the lightning. The strike obviously knocked him to the ground and rendered him unconscious. My uncle, who was not struck, saw my father on the ground. It had started to rain very, very hard, and my uncle felt he could not leave my father to go for assistance. On the other hand, my father was a large gentleman and my uncle wasn't sure how he was going to move him. Apparently, the adrenaline kicked in. He lowered the tailgate of the Jeep and wrestled my father up enough to get him in the back of the vehicle. As we would later learn, that move probably saved my father's life, as it was determined the movement acted as artificial resuscitation and my father's breathing returned. My father would later say he must have gone to Heaven or Hell for a short time.

My uncle drove to my grandparents' home, and an ambulance and the local doctor were called. Amazingly, my father was not taken to the hospital. In the 1950s, medical precautions were not the same as today. My father had been paralyzed and burned, but had regained consciousness and was aware of his surroundings. The current of the strike had passed out the top of his head, burning the side of his face. It was weeks before a comb could be used in his hair. Of course, by the time he could comb it, it was "kinked" beyond belief. The paralysis finally left. He remained in bed at my grandparents' home for a few days, and then returned to our own home.

The next day after the event, my uncle, a cousin, and myself returned to the hayfield. We were trying to see if we could locate my father's cap. We found it approximately 60 feet from the rake. It was referred to as an "engineer's" cap, having eight triangular pieces of material sewed together to a center point. All eight seams had been ripped and blown outwardly, an indicator the strike went out the top of his head. I still have the cap. It is a good illustration to be used in sharing the story with my grandchildren. My father had no recollection of being hit by the lightning. He thought, since he was paralyzed, he had suffered a stroke. It was quite a "shock" for him to learn he had been the victim of a lightning strike. It was a horrible experience and served as reminder of the perils of being a farmer working in the great outdoors.

Farm/School Life in the 1950s
By Timothy D. Duncan of Orrick, Missouri
Born 1949

I was born on February 26, 1949 to James O. Duncan and Laura M. Duncan-Lauck at Excelsior Springs Hospital. I had an older brother named Jimmy. In 1953, I had a sister born. Her name was Pamela Mae. Pam died in 2009 after fighting cancer for five years. We lived on a farm about seven miles north of Orrick, Missouri. Dad had 80acres that he had bought from his grandparents. We had cattle, chickens, and hogs. At one time, we raised three little pigs on our front porch and in the house. We named them Inky, Pinky, and Stinky.

We had a two-hole outhouse for going to the bathroom. We went to the bathroom at night in a pot. It sure was cold out there in the winter. In the summertime, we would just go in the backyard. I remember that Mom and Dad had friends come by. I went to the bathroom in the backyard, and then stuck my nose in the door and said, "Dad! Come and look at this big turd that I just crapped!" I was probably about four years old. We had no running water, just an old well, and a cistern. We did baths in a big round tub. In the summer, we did baths outside. In the winter, we did them in the kitchen. At that time, we had no TV, just a radio. I don't remember when we got our first TV. It was a few years later before we got a color TV. We had only one TV for the whole family. Now, I have five. With Dad working a job at Percy Kent Bag Company in Kansas City and trying to farm, we had to do the chores. I learned very young how to milk a cow. I probably haven't done that since I was just out of high school. I think I could still do it, though. Some things you never forget how to do. In the 1950s, the Russians sent something into outer space. It was called Sputnick. We got a little brown and white dog and named him Sputnick. We called him Sput for short. At the same time, we had a big white rooster. The dog and the rooster had some real battles. Our yard was fenced, and all we had to do was step outside and holler, "Here, Rooster!" and here he would come. If we kids ever got out of the yard, we would get flogged by that rooster.

In 1955, I started school in a two-room schoolhouse. Only one room was used. The school was called Wallace. There were about 28 to 30 kids in all eight grades. There were

Tim's sister, Pam with Tim in the checkered shirt

four in my class. We had one teacher for all eight grades. Luckily, we only lived about a quarter mile from school and walked almost every day. Others lived farther away and rode horses to school. Later, after first grade, we got a horse and named him Old Boy. That was our summer fun, all three of us riding that old horse. We had no saddle, so we just rode bareback. Back then, the school year was only eight months. In April, me and my brother would jump in the pond with a skim of ice on it. It was kind of cold, but we didn't mind at that age. As a fifth grader, our school was consolidated and I went to a school called Elk Horn R-7 until I started high school. I went to high school at Orrick High school and graduated in 1967. As a sophomore, I met my first love, Carroll Merriman. We went together about a year and a half and broke up before our senior year. We had some really memorable times.

On January 24, 1967, the clock stopped at 12:52—our school was struck by a tornado. It was a very warm January day with temperatures around 75 to 80 degrees. I was sitting in study hall, and the wind and rain started. I closed the window, and the window blew out in my face. I ran across the hall into the boys bathroom.

212

Things were flying down the hallway. We lost two students that day. The next day, the temperature was 30 degrees and frozen.

I got married in 1972, but it didn't last but two years. We divorced and didn't have any kids. I got married again in 1978 to Candy Roberts. We have two kids and two grandkids. We're still married. As for Carroll, my first sweetheart, we met in 2012 and talked over old times and how many classmates we've lost. She is married as well and has two kids and two grandkids.

Life is Something
By Dr. Harold E. Hayden of Worth, Missouri
Born 1932

Many times I have stated, "Life is something" and the longer I live, the more I believe it. When I was born in 1932, the odds of my becoming a Doctor of Veterinary Medicine seemed remote. Several obstacles were involved. By the time I reached high school age my parents, Will and Nettie (McCarty) Hayden, lived on six miles of mud roads, therefore transportation to school was difficult. I was the youngest of twelve children so extra funds for education were not available and if scholarships were in existence, I was not aware of them. Unlike some young men, I didn't have a car of my own. Also, the Korean War was looming, so my number could be called up at any time. BUT—the answers to some of these adversities was thusly.

Since two of my siblings had not finished high school because of the mud roads, I was encouraged to stay with my sister and husband, Pauline and Orville Bailey of rural Maryville, MO. I helped with their dairy operation and still caught the school bus, which traveled a short distance from their home on a graveled road. My expenses for school was earned by farming on the shares with my parents in addition to my being engaged in trapping and selling furs.

My parents let me use their car for dating (one girl) and when I went to the University of Missouri I either hitch-hiked or got a ride with other students who were attending also. As to the draft situation, I received a college deferment and since I was interested in a profession, which was sorely needed, in our area, the board co-operated although I would be eligible for service until I was thirty-five years old, if needed. Some of my relatives

were concerned because I wanted to marry while I was in college but it all worked out great as my wife, Wanda Pierson Hayden worked for the university when she joined me in Columbia.

I also held down several part-time jobs. When I graduated in 1958, we settled at Barnard, MO. and unknown to us, several people thought we wouldn't have enough business to stay. After forty-four years in practice, time proved that there had been a definite need. In addition to my being willing to work, the state of Missouri had begun the Brucellosis eradication program, which required all breeding cattle to be tested, and then Tuberculosis testing started. While neither of these programs was profitable for me, it afforded me the opportunity to meet many folks in the area and if they felt I was competent, they would call me for their other work.

At first, our neighbor, Delbert Icke, liked to ride with me and show me where people lived but it wasn't long until he told me that I knew more people than he did. One of the most helpful items in my business was a two-way radio, which kept me in contact with my home-office.

My clientele area covered quite a distance and in some cases overlapped other veterinarian's territory. If one could map out the farms that I visited it would encompass the towns of Bolckow, Conception, Conception Jct., Graham, Guilford, King City, Maitland, Rea, Rosendale, Savannah, Stanberry, to south of Maryville, and of course, the Barnard area. Every day tested the knowledge of what I had been taught or had learned from experience. For me, it was all interesting. Although I received several bumps and bruises, I never suffered any broken bones but I did spend many long days and nights to complete my schedule. Since days were filled with calls on large animals, nighttime was when we performed pet care concerns.

When I retired in 2002, rural life was changing dramatically. Whereas a farm family had formerly been self-sufficient with their own meat, butter, eggs, and garden supplies raised on their acreages, the era of larger farm implements and trying economic times promoted the plowing up of pasturelands for grain crops and a lot of farm wives had to find jobs to help keep the farm afloat. Smaller farms were gobbled up by larger operations, corporate hog farms moved in and the government offered tempting programs to reduce the cultivation and use of certain types of land. In time, it all lead to fewer farms being occupied and the regular farm family population has dwindled. Now, people seek places to build homes on small rural acreages to escape the crime and congestion of cities but they must commute to their work instead of stepping out the back door. The values and opinions of farmers/ranchers are becoming less important in our political scene so where will it all end? No earthly being can know but I still say, "Life is something."

Neal's Adventures and Accomplishments
By Neal R. Dawson of Kansas City, Missouri
Born 1920

Neal R. Dawson, retired Maysville Postmaster, had a job making TNT at Weldon Springs Ordnance Factory when he volunteered for the engineering branch of the United States Army. He was inducted on 24 August 1943 at Jefferson Barracks in St. Louis, Missouri. During his service in World War II, his journey went through Camp Claiborne, Louisiana on the way to Camp Sutton, North Carolina to fill-in for the engineers. After that, he sailed from New York and landed in Greenock, Scotland. He and his comrades had charge of the docks at Liverpool before the invasions. In Utah Beach, he manned a ball and crane and helped tear down Monteberg after it had been shelled. Using a portable rock crusher, he made gravel for the roads from the ruins of the buildings. The weather was turning cold and drizzly. From Cherbough to St. Lo, he ran gasoline pipes along the side of the road, guarded them, and pumped gas through them. In Couville France, the second platoon built a stockade for 250 prisoners and guarded and fed them. It was rainy for almost 40 days. They constantly waded in knee-deep mud and muck.

The Raising of the Flag

He arrived at the Battle of the Bulge on 21 December 1944, and for 19 days, he wired all the bridges on the Meuse River in the cold and snow in preparation for demolition. They hauled in the 101st Airborne into Bastone since they could not fly in due to the weather. They were drawing rations from ships for 50,000 troops at Camp "Lucky Strike," a German airstrip in France. February 14, 1945, they found him north of Marseille, France, where they oversaw the making of 10,000 cement blocks a day. They were building the "Stepping Stone to Tokyo." Supply buildings and mess halls to house GIS were being processed for reassignment to the Pacific. It covered ten square miles and was a city complete within itself.

He was able to spend V.E. Day, May 9, 1945, with his brother, Lt. J.F. Dawson, who was stationed in Marseille at the Ordnance Depot. After that, he passed through the Panama Canal and laid anchor at Mogg Mogg. This was when the first atomic bomb was dropped on Japan. His final stop was in Korea. He was on detached duty with the 1108 Combat Group, an engineers' combat group, for about a month. On 8 January 1946, he was discharged after serving two years, four months, and 25 days. He had actually heard Axis Sally on Tiger Rag and Tokyo Rose in Okinawa urging the troops to give up. They said that they would take care of the GIs. This was just a blatant attempt to demoralize the Americans. While at Buckner Bay in Okinawa, he was in two typhoons, one of which claimed 600 lives. As a guest of a co-worker from the days at Weldon Springs, he was aboard a sub-chaser when it happened. During his service, his awards included the Army Commendation Medal, Good Conduct Medal, American Campaign Medal, European Theatre of Operation

214

Neal R. Dawson at the Memorial

Medal, and three Bronze Stars for the France, Rhineland, and Ardennes battles and campaigns. He also received many ribbons. In following years, he flew Class A flights all over the world with the Army and National Guard. He spent 1,000 hours in the air, including flights to Europe, the Virgin Islands, Easter Island, Azores, Spain, Bermuda, Iceland, Goose Bay, Labrador, and Santiago Chile. In 1989, he flew into the Panama Canal, placing buoys to help monitor El Niño.

Neal had applied for the Honor Flight about a year before the trip actually occurred. About a week before the flight, 51 participants went to Kansas City to meet other veterans who would be on the flight. They enjoyed a wonderful meal together. His account of the trip mirrored Bob's, and he noted that they departed at about 6:00 A.M. from KCI. They were back to Maysville about 10:00 that night. They received two sack lunches and a constant supply of drinking water. Since he sometimes depended on a wheelchair to get around, they provided wheelchairs and put them in the baggage compartments of the buses. He appreciated Bob pushing him around most of the day. There was a crowd of people there to greet them at every stop, thanking them for their service. A large crowd was even waiting when they returned to KCI that evening.

He enjoyed the experience, revisiting some of the sites he had seen before in Washington D.C. He also saw some new ones. He has been to Bastogne on a World War II tour, and has seen the World War II memorials and visited Munich and other sites. These were all a source of great pride. Neal repeatedly says that he has had a good life and that he is grateful for a good wife, Evonne, with whom he will celebrate their 69th anniversary on October 11. He is also grateful good children and grandchildren. He has traveled the world over, is an avid golfer. He had a hole-in-one at age 86! Neal grew up in Grant City with his grandmother after his mother died when he was 12. He has been a postmaster, a licensed embalmer and funeral director, and a realtor. The accounts of his lifetime of service are proof of the richness of his life.

Standley's Branch...A Place for Boys
By Ken White of Stockton, Missouri
Born 1929

Standley Branch is a stream that you wouldn't find in any history book, unless it get a line or two in the history of Carrollton, Missouri, but like the mighty Missouri and Mississippi Rivers, it too has stories to be told and this is one of them.

The slow moving waters of this small creek, barely three feet wide in many places, was for a number of years the gathering place for neighborhood boys to play while learning about the world as they grew up. I was one of them and Standley Branch holds memories of adventure, danger, thrills, fun, and play. Born within a stone's throw of the creek, I had a daily association with the creek for many years. A railroad track passed over the creek in several places near our home. Earlier boxcars carried grain to flourmills up the track and several trestles crossed over the stream. One of these was a gathering spot for young boys to meet for a planning session or play.

The stream contained everything from crawfish to broken glass. It's a wonder any of us survived wading barefoot among rusty tin cans, broken bottles, barbed wire, and snakes. We did and most of us lived to tell about it.

Some of the memories include; times when, if things weren't going too well at home or school, I could always pick up a tree branch, a piece of string, some bacon and head for the creek to catch crawfish. As I sat watching the line for a crawdad to pick up the bait I would watch water bugs scoot over the dingy water, see a turtle swim by or just listen

215

to the crickets talking and soon the problem I thought I had earlier was gone.

After a heavy rain, the creek offered another form of entertainment. Johnny Benjamin and I would stand on the bridge over the rising water and watch for bottles to float by and try to hit them with rocks. There was a never ending supply of rocks because we were on a gravel road so we had our choice of sizes to throw. If we missed a big bottle, we could run to the next bridge and intercept it there. Few, if any, made it to Wakenda Creek where Standley Branch ended.

Sometimes we would get worldly, write a note, put it in a bottle, and slip it into the creek. We knew the creek flowed into Wakenda Creek, then into the Missouri River and on to the Mississippi River then into the Gulf of Mexico so who knows? Someone along the way might find it. I guess my love for fishing started at the creek. I found a few deeper holes in the creek where a few catfish and perch lived. I would get some bait and could catch a few fish. It didn't matter there were still outhouses along the creek and some people even used the creek for a dumping spot. I would bring my catch and my mother would clean and cook the fish.

The creek was close to highway 65 at the time and the Great Depression was just ending. I remember seeing tramps and bumps walking down the road looking for anything useful. Once in a while one would stop and see if they could do some work for my parents in exchange for food. My mother would usually fix them something to eat and trade it for some work.

The creek was a great place in the summer. I could keep cool in the shade by the water, or sometimes jump into the almost clear water along with other neighborhood boys.

Summertime wasn't the only season that I enjoyed the stream. In winter, when the water was frozen, we would get a group together; Johnny, Gene Sherwood, Joe, and Jackie barrier, Tommy Findley, myself and anyone else that wanted to start an ice hockey game. We used a small tin can for the puck and as for sticks; we would pick out any sort of wood that resembled a hockey stick. Many shins were cut and pants ruined in the games, but no one was really the worse for it.

Once I had a humdinger of a fight on the creek. Two brothers started a fight with me;

I pushed one of them into the water that was about three inches deep. He started shouting, "I can't swim and help I'm drowning." Then his brother got into the act so I pushed him in as well. I left them both sitting in the water crying.

Other memories of my youth along the creek included some hunting. After school I would pick up my single shot 12 gauge shotgun, head south on the creek where rabbits, doves, and even ducks could be found. Although I never bagged very many, it was, I guess, the start of my love for hunting. Even today, when I drive by Standley Branch, I look over at the places where I used to do all the things many years ago and see the places where I fished, hunted, swam, waded and played and wondered if boys still use the creek as a place to do all the things I did. I hope so.

Coal Oil Lamps to Read By
By Betty Henderson of Cameron, Missouri
Born 1924

During the early 1930s, my dad bought a 60-acre farm near Savannah, MO. It was rather cheap due to the depression. The big two-story house was very old and the kitchen was leaky and floor slanted so we only used it for storage. We used the big dining room the most and it had a large iron range that we used for cooking and heat. We took baths in a galvanized tub close by the range. There was no electricity, plumbing, or phone. We had coal oil lamps to read by.

I was aged 8 to 11 during our time on the farm. My chores were to carry water from the pump, go drive up the milk cow from the pasture, weed the garden, etc. My best friend was my collie dog, Bum. We were always together.

In summer, we kept some food in the cave to keep it cool. I made many trips up and down for Mom. The only time we had ice for our icebox was when my older siblings would come to visit and bring it from town.

I walked to a one-room school in the country. There were about 18 pupils up to eighth grade. All the boys wore overalls and had bare feet until frost. The girls wore feed sack dresses.

My Dad worked in Chicago on the railroad part of the time to get a little extra money, since the farm was not a moneymaker. Mom and I tried to carry on the work, but she could not drive the old cars. They had to be cranked to start the engine and one time my Dad broke his wrist doing this.

Once, when Dad was gone, the cow stuck her head in the barbed wire fence and got a little hole in her ear. It had hit an artery and a little stream of blood was spurting up about 6" high. She would shake her head and splatter blood all over. Mom told me to run down the hill about three blocks to where Old Lafe lived and get him to help. He came and mixed together some cobwebs and soot to put on the wound. It worked! Old Lafe lived in a little shack down by the creek. He and his wife had had 13 children and his youngest girl was retarded. They said she had fallen out of the highchair on her head. She was my playmate.

Lafe had a big white handlebar mustache and was noted for his tales. We had big trees in our front yard and Lafe showed us where big strips of bark were missing. He said that had happened in a bad storm and lightning struck there.

Dad had several old cars since they kept breaking down. One was a blue panel laundry truck, which he called "The Blue Streak." It only cost $15. Going to town, we had to cross the 102 River. A big hill was there and Dad would turn off the ignition and coast down the hill to "save gas." The problem was getting up the hill. Sometimes Mom and I had to get out and push to help it get to the top.

Winter was hard on us. We moved the big range into a smaller room, closed the upstairs bedrooms and Mom and Dad slept in

Betty and her dearest dog, Bum in 1931

a small downstairs bedroom. I slept on a cot. Sometimes my grandma lived with us. She had been in a wheel chair for 30 years due to a stroke. She did not go to bed but sat in her chair dozing. One night was very cold and she sat by the fire putting in a stick of wood once in a while so it would not go out. We had left a cup of water on the high shelf of the range and by morning, it had ice on it. We told this story for years.

Another cold winter I woke up one morning and there was a newborn calf by my cot. Dad had found it and wrapped it in an old blanket. The tips of its ears and part of its tail were frozen. It lived and we named it Frosty.

Once we had a big snowstorm with high drifts. Dad could barely make it out to do chores. It was cold a long time and was not melting. I was bored staying inside and had begged my Mom to go out to play but she said it was too cold. Finally, I made little notes reading, "I want to go OUT" and stuck and pinned them all over the room. Mom relented and made me wear so many clothes I could hardly waddle. At least I got to play with my dog in the snow.

Dirt Roads and Mud
By Wanda Pierson Hayden of Worth,
Missouri
Born 1936

While some folks consider living in a rural community a disadvantage, I personally feel that good values and morals were part of farm life in early Nodaway County. Both my parents, Lee and Louie (Garner) Pierson, were raised in large families on rented land. In 1935 during depression years, their marriage started out by "working by the month" for Sheridan and Sadie Graves, about one mile north of Quitman, MO. I was delivered there on Halloween evening 1936, by Dr. Carlos Cossins of Burlington Jct., who, incidentally neglected to register my birth. Since we had no car, our neighbor Fred Miller took my dad through mud to get the doctor while Millie Miller stayed with my mom.

In the four and one half years we lived there, my experience with animals varied from raising baby chicks in an upstairs room to playing with bucket calves in our front yard. When I was about three, I nearly scared my mother to death by wandering into a lot with sows and baby pigs. I was an only child so I looked forward to having company. One time, our landlord's grandson, Rex Plummer, came with his family and when he tired of me bothering him, he grabbed the back of my neck and growled, "Amscray" (pig-Latin for scram).

Before I started school, we had lived on several farms--the Harold and Elsie Gray place southwest of Clearmont, the Harry Mutz place one mile north of Burlington Junction and finally the Joe and Nannie Workman farm three-fourths mile northeast of Workman Chapel. This was close to where my parents had grown up and dated by going to church where there were as many as 150 young people attending. During my first through fifth grade school years, I went to Lone Valley (nicknamed Monkey Run) where my dad had received all of his education. My teachers were young ladies who received a one-year teaching certificate following high school. They usually boarded with local families. In consecutive order, my teachers were the Misses Evanell Walker, Wanda Lee Grace, Virginia Clark, Betty Egger, and Georgia "Patsy" Henry. Being a teacher in schools without electricity or plumbing was quite a challenge but we were all used to the absence of those conveniences.

Students took turns carrying in cobs and coal as well as water from the well, sweeping oiled floors with a compound, washing the blackboard and beating erasers. Our library books were stored in one, five-shelved glass enclosed cabinet so extra reading was limited. Everyone brought a sack lunch and though we nearly froze to death, classes were rarely canceled due to weather. During the 1943-44 term, our school went about with a team of horses and wagon to collect scrap metal for the WWII effort. We also collected milkweed pods to make life vests for the military sailors.

Games that I remember playing at recess were Handy Over, Blind Man's Bluff, Mother May I?, Hide and Seek, Rover Come over, Tag, and of course, Fox and Geese when it snowed. In nice weather, we chose up sides for baseball if we had enough students. Several times a year there were community meetings with programs put on by the children or sometimes the parents, dividing up in the men's group or the women's group. There were always refreshments, which made it extra special.

On a personal level, family entertainment involved visiting with relatives or neighbors with whom you exchanged fieldwork. Card playing of Pitch, Pinochle, or Rummy provided an exciting pass-time for adults and this produced lots of merriment for hours. Many enjoyed Canasta when that was introduced. My dad enjoyed sports, especially boxing and baseball. Each community had competing teams, playing in any level area available. Following church Sunday afternoons would find families watching the men do their best to win. My dad was catcher for the "Toad Hollar" team and my maternal grandfather, Pearl Garner, and Uncle Ross Garner were with the "Gully Jumpers."

Radio (battery operated before electricity) aired news, market reports, and even professional baseball games. I hurried to get my evening chores done so I could listen to my favorite show, then later we would listen to "Fibber McGee and Molly." In the early 1950s, we had our first experience with television. Our neighbor, Everett Carmichael, had purchased one and on a dark, rainy evening, my parents and I walked a half mile through thick timber guided by lantern light to watch a special championship boxing match. The reception was very poor.

In 1944, we bought 80 acres from Purl and Ludy Pence, which was in the same district, but I had to walk farther—a half mile through pasture and another three-fourths on dirt road. Gravel roads were scarce and it seemed to always be muddy. About this same time, I started taking piano lessons from Mrs. Lester (Bonnie) Ringold, a farm wife. Her fee was $1.00 for an hour lesson and I continued with her for six years.

Many times, I thought her eight-day clock must be ticking too slow. One day when I arrived for lessons, their garage was smoldering and several cars were there. While eating breakfast they had heard a car honking but thought it was on a nearby road. Their auto had shorted in some way and destructed along with the garage.

Lone Valley closed in 1947 due to a lack of students but I had enjoyed having a classmate since fourth grade when Lincoln Hurst moved to our district. The fall of 1947, I started going to Sunrise School about one and one-half miles on dirt roads and now I had two classmates, Wilbur Hornbuckle and Barbara Carmichael. Mrs. Jesse (Flossie) Tanner was the teacher.

In March 1948, we purchased another farm south and west of Workman Chapel to an area known as "Toad Hollar." While many say they lived just on the edge of such a place, I claim full citizenship to this unmarked area. Switching schools was difficult but now I had three classmates, Kathlyn Taylor, Ronnie Howard, and Lincoln Hurst. We lived in the Mt. Vernon district but it had closed several years earlier and consolidated with Ireland. It was now four miles to school so the district hired George Kunkel to transport several of us in his car. Thankfully, it was a graveled road except for a quarter mile I had to walk if it rained. Other children who were packed in was Gary Weir, Ruth and Gary Kunkel, Lincoln Hurst, and Shirley and Dorothy Davidson. Until the end of school in 1948, we picked up Betty Jenson, too. Mrs. J. Vernon (Aileena) Taylor was the teacher and here we had electricity with a good heating stove. This building is still standing although it was converted into a home many years ago. The other schools I attended have been destroyed for many, many years. When I graduated from Ireland in 1950, my parents had moved back to the Pence place so from March until school was out I boarded with a wonderful older couple, Sam and Araminta Taylor. They were so good to me and she was an excellent cook.

I often wonder if my presence in their home was a comfort or if it had stirred up old emotions as they had lost their only child, Rebecca, when she was about my age. She had been a schoolmate to my mother. As graduation neared, we eighth graders were the only pupils present for a day of extensive testing to see if we were eligible to attend high school. We all passed and our ceremony was held at the Wilcox, MO. Methodist Church in conjunction with the rural school there who had only one graduate, Irene Johnson. Each one of us had to perform something for the program and Kathlyn Taylor and I played a piano duet, "Tea for Two." I have a list comprising of forty-nine children with whom I attended country grade school during my eight years.

Some I have seen through the years, others moved on and still others are no longer living. I would like to mention, too, that there was freedom in our schools to express patriotism and faith. Each day started by giving the Pledge of Allegiance to our United States flag and early on I remember having an art project that included The Lord's Prayer. In the late '40s, our school was visited by a husband-wife team who sang "This Is My Father's World." I was fascinated because the husband played an accordion, something I had never seen.

If I've mentioned dirt roads and mud a lot it is because those conditions governed folks' coming and going in rural daily life of yesteryear. My high school years involved lots of mud, too, but that's another story.

The Icebox and the Earthquake
By Nancy Ann Webster of St. Joseph, Missouri
Born 1938

I was born October 4, 1938, on a farm, in Caldwell County, near Cowgill, Missouri, to Dorothy and Wesley Diment. Through the years, I have seen a lot of changes in the way we live.

The drought and depression made it difficult to find work in the 1930 and early 1940s. My parents, me, Daddy's parents, Robert and Maud, his brother, Glen, and sister, Lucille, her husband, Orville, and children headed to California and were able to get construction jobs in 1941.

We rented cabins in a court since we had to move with new construction jobs. A court would be somewhat like a motel except each cabin was a separate building with a small yard space. Our cabin had a big bed, table and chairs, one comfy chair, sink and cabinet,

Nancy with her parents, Dorothy and Wesley Diment in 1942

cook stove, and a very small bathroom, and an icebox. The bathroom had a stool that you had to pour water in it to flush it. Our relatives all lived in cabins near us.

I was fascinated with the icebox! It was about four feet tall and about 18 inches square and flat on top. It had two compartments. The top one was where the large square of ice was kept and the bottom compartment was where the food was kept. A man delivered ice on certain days; it was in large squares that just fit inside the icebox. He would take it out of his refrigerated little truck with big sharp ice tongs and bring it into your house and place it in your icebox, after you paid him. There were no refrigerators in homes yet. I was sure that it would be fun to climb on top of that icebox and sit there and feel big. My Mother told me that I would fall and get hurt. I was four yrs. old and quite sure that I would be just fine! My Mother was in the bathroom taking a shower, so I moved a chair to the cabinet next to the icebox and climbed up and sat on top of the icebox! I was feeling like king of the world when we had an earthquake! Everything in the room shook including the icebox and me! I was sure God was punishing me for not minding my Mother! Mother came running out of the bathroom, grabbed me off the icebox, hugged me, than swatted my behind for not minding! I wasn't quite as fascinated with the icebox after that earthquake!

Nancy in 1943

I remember going to the Pacific Ocean for the first time. It was the biggest thing I'd ever seen! Daddy put me on his back and went into the ocean water! It was so fun and exciting! Daddy was big and strong and I knew he would never let anything hurt me so I wasn't afraid.

My parents saved up enough money to come back to Missouri and buy a farm and to be near my maternal grandma before my brother was born.

I went to a little one-room school for my first grade and part of my second grade. There were several one-room schools. Many children had to walk to school so the schools. I would have had to walk alone so Daddy usually took me to school in the horse and buggy. Mother packed me a big lunch in my lunch bucket. I didn't eat it all so every day Daddy ate the rest of my lunch on the way home as he drove the horse and buggy. Mother thought I ate it all. Both of them were happy so I never told Mother that I didn't eat it all!

We made our own soap out of hog fat, cut into small squares, and lye cooked in a big heavy black pot out doors for a long time. It was poured into a shallow pan, let get hard then cut into squares. Then you had soap to wash your clothes and use for your bath.

My Mother used flat irons to iron the clothes. A flat iron had a detachable handle. She had three or four flat irons that were heated on the wood cook stove. When one iron became too cold to iron, she put the cold one on the stove to heat again and put the handle on a hot iron to continue ironing.

The wood burning cook stove that we used to cook our food was a bit tricky to keep the temperature just right, especially if a cake was in the oven. It was a pretty stove, with white enamel on the whole outside. Mother would take waxed paper and polish the tops of the burners and warmer space until it shined, while it was still warm, after she finished cooking the food. On rare occasions, we bought a loaf of bread at the store. The bread sack was made from a waxed paper. She saved these sacks and used them for polishing the stove. Each sack could be used several times before the wax was all gone. My Mother wanted everything to be as pretty and clean as it could be!

Daddy worked hard but he liked to do fun things too. He liked to play music with friends, fish, and go 'coon' hunting with the hound dogs. I never grew tired of hearing Daddy play his guitar and sing and tell funny stories. He could take a simple story of something that had happened and make it exciting or funny! I think my Mother got her joy from watching Daddy have fun! They adored each other!

Most of the farm children's clothes were homemade. My grandma Diment and my Mother would take a brown sheet of paper and draw a pattern on it, cut it out, lay it on the fabric and cut out the pieces for the dress.

During World War 2 everything was used, nothing wasted. Sugar, gas, and car tires were rationed, each family was allotted a certain amount and no more. We got a ration book that had stamps. We all saved and tried to help the government not go into debt with all the war expenses.

When I was in second grade just before harvest time we had lots and lots of rain and the little creek running through our farm became a huge creek and flooded our crops. The water came up to our house but the foundation was high enough that it couldn't come into our house. It washed away all of our corn crop, garden, and the fruit orchard that my parents had just planted that spring. I remember walking on the dry mud left by the flood in our yard and enjoying the crunchy sound until I remembered how sad Mother and Daddy were, and then I cried. We sold our livestock and moved to town and Daddy once again got construction work to earn more money to buy farmland that was on higher ground so we wouldn't lose everything again! We kept the low farmland; it grew wonderful corn crops when it didn't get flooded.

We moved to Cowgill. There was a train depot there and it was a busy, thriving small town. In a town nearby, they had free movies every Saturday night. They had a big screen outside and we brought blankets and sat on them on the grassy lawn to watch the movie! No refreshments were sold so you brought you own snacks.

I had a vivid imagination and was easily entertained as were most children in those days. I had several dolls and spent long hours playing with them. A limb off a tree made a fine stick horse that was one thing my little brother could do with me. He had a wagon that we played with a lot. One spring I watched Orioles build a nest in the big shade tree while I played with my dolls under it. I was fascinated with how they could build a nest that hung down under the branch and look like a sack! Later I watched them feed their baby birds. Laying on blanket studying the stars and clouds making up stories about them was a fun thing to do. We had a battery radio that gave us hours of entertainment. After school, sitting on a blanket under a shade tree, I would listen to "The Lone Ranger," "Baby Snooks," "Terry and The Pirates," "Fibber Magee and Molly," "Amos and Andy," and music. On Saturday night, the whole family listened to the "Grand Ole Opry." I also loved to read books and comic books.

We later bought a piece of land large enough to plant lots of crops, on high ground. Daddy built us a new house on top of a hill. He was a good carpenter and a hard worker. He loved to build things and grow things.

We didn't have indoor plumbing while I was living at home. My grandparents didn't buy toilet paper so we used the Sears catalog in their outhouse, my cousins and I fought over the soft green pages of the catalog! I had lots of cousins and we got together about every Sunday at Grandma Miller's house. We older cousins would lock the younger cousins out and tell secrets in the outhouse! I have several times told one of my younger cousins that I was so sorry about how we treated her when we were kids!

I had several pets down through the years. I always loved animals. Grandpa Miller gave me a little lamb before the flood. I called her Patsy. Daddy was ready to cut her tail off short, telling me that all sheep have their tails cut short so they will be healthier. I cried and cried and begged him to leave it long so he did. A cow stepped on it and pulled one-half of her tail off! When we moved to town we sold her, again I cried. I also had a pet chicken (that we sold when we moved to town). I would pet her and talk to her while she sat on her nest. She would run to me in the chicken yard. One day she laid an egg in my hand! I was so excited! I later (at our new farm) had a little pet pig, I named her Darling. I would take her something to eat, stand by the fence, and call her name. She would run to me just as fast as her little legs would carry her! A big boar hog got jealous of her and hurt her so badly that she died. I was so sad! Daddy brought home a stray kitten that was about starved. I nursed him back to health and named him Tinker.

Tinker died of old age.

I got married as soon as I graduated from high school. We didn't have indoor plumbing in our first home. We had electricity so we had a refrigerator and a television set. We still had to heat water in a teakettle or pan on the stove to have hot water. We had to carry water and fill the washing machine and heat it with a little water proof heater submerged in the washer. Years later when we bought an automatic washer, I nearly cried to waste so much water that still looked clean! I loved the dryer though!

We didn't know about "going green" but our old generation was certainly conservative with everything we used! We worked hard for everything we got! We were willing to help others and were generous with what we had! Seems like more people were honest and kind during those days!

School Days and Big Storms
By Bonnie D. Harville of Robertsdale,
Alabama
Born 1932

I was born in 1932 in Stanberry, Missouri. My Dad, Roy D. Duley, was an engineer and superintendent of the Stanberry light and power plant from 1929 to 1947. He was responsible for most, if not all, the improvements in city services during those years. When you read about those in the tri-county news history columns, please remember to give him credit. My mother, Mary Myrtle (Fletcher) Duley, was the farmer of the family. She sold eggs, butter, chicken "fryers," and garden produce locally. I've delivered many a bottle of milk around the neighborhood. I had two older brothers, Roy Jr, known as Delford, and Clyde, better known as Abe. Both served in the Army in World War II. We were a "two stars in the window" family.

We lived on a couple of acres outside town but within city limits. I can't remember which direction, but if you know Stanberry, the road crossed the Wabash Railroad tracks, Wildcat Creek (on what was at the time the "White Bridge") and went on out past Art Brooke's farm, the Johnson place, Claude David's place and the old Grantham place (where we moved to later on) towards the Star Schoolhouse. We had cows, pigs, chickens,

geese, guineas, and gardens. In fact, according to the popular children's song in the 1930's and 1940's, "Playmate," I had it all—dolls and a playhouse, apple trees to climb, rainwater barrels to holler in, a cellar door to slide down, and more. Mom didn't let me go anywhere else to play, but I never lacked for playmates. I had two tire swings, a cellar cab "hump" to coast down in a Western Flyer wagon, and a really nice sand pile, thanks to generous neighbors, Jim and Ernest Stuart, who hauled sand for a living back then. It seemed the neighbor kids always played at our house. In our apple orchard were a couple of tractors to drive, two or three old car skeletons to use as "forts" in "rubber gun fights," plus, best of all there was a real old-time threshing machine and the Hart-Parr tractor which once operated it. Those were relics of the 1920s when my Dad and others of the "Duley clan" ran a threshing crew at harvest time in Missouri, Kansas and other states. Those big machines were excellent for playing "war" during World War II. There was a neighborhood "dump ditch" for treasure hunting and a hayloft equipped with a hay hook rope—an early zip line, if you will. We could ride on from one end of the hayloft to the other and then drop off on a bed of sweet smelling hay.

I started to Stanberry Public School at age seven, and my favorite teacher was Miss Mona Frances Brown, who taught a group of us third grade girls to tap dance for the annual school "Operetta." We idolized her.

Bonnie's parents, Roy and Mary Duley with Roy, Bonnie, and Clyde in the 1950s

Bonnie at age 2

Later, we heard she lost her job because she was seen out dancing. Dancing, at that time, was "not the thing to do" for teachers. These were, indeed, "olden times." When I was in the fifth grade, my folks moved out of town to the old Grantham place so Mom could keep more cows, sheep, and Daddy's hogs. I had to switch to Star School, a one-room school with grades one through eight. During grades five through six I shared with others the chores of gathering wood or coal for the black heater in the corner, carrying out ashes, and lugging in the water bucket from the well. The school was on top of a hill, and on snowy days, we could bring sleds. At recess or after lunch (which we carried in a syrup bucket), we'd sail down the hill on our sleds. I actually got my first kiss on one of those exciting rides. "Run, Sheep, Run," "Farmer in the Dell", "Fox and Goose" and "Send" were favorite recess games, and on the fourth Friday of the month, a local school team came to play softball. Competition was fierce, especially with Crosswhite School. On other Fridays, we either had a spelling bee, a ciphering match, or perhaps our least favorite, "current events." This was when we had to recite something from "The Weekly Reader" in front of all classes. I went back to town school for grades seven through eight.

Who could forget summer Saturday nights? Mom and Dad, relaxed on a park bench, would be proudly listening as both my brothers played in the SHS band. I'd probably be with a bunch of kids around the old Civil War cannon until the music started, then I would run to Dad, beg for a nickel, go buy a "tutti fruity" ice cream cone, then join the kids "licking and skipping" around the old bandstand. I guess my childhood in Missouri was safe and simple, but one thing I hated was stormy weather. Thunder & lightning (especially lightning), made me scrooch up shivering in some corner (still does, as a matter of fact). One day, my mom sat me down and told me this story, which, she thought, made me so fearful of storms.

The annual Fourth of July celebration became Stanberry's most anticipated day of the year. My Dad was secretary and treasurer of the local volunteer fire department. That group of town fathers sponsored a celebration, which included a Ferris wheel, glider, 2 merry-go-rounds, and even a stage show. However, sometimes, July's weather didn't cooperate. According to Mom's story, folks woke up to heat, humidity and a threatening sky on the Fourth of July in 1932, but of course, the show must go on. Mom, who was seven months pregnant with me, walked the mile in to town towing two excited little boys by the hands. She headed for the power plant where Dad worked, and told the boys to go across the street to the park where everything was, but to hurry back to the plant if the weather got bad.

Well, it got really bad. When the boys ran back, Dad shoved a heavy cash box that was holding all the money the VFD had taken in into Mom's hands, and then hurried her and the boys into the tiny scale house in front of the plant. A tornado hit Stanberry that day. The power went out, trees were falling, and folks from the park were running everywhere, she said. Dad was busy in the plant, of course, but a group of men, all strangers to Mom, approached the scale house and shoved her, (hugging that box of money with a frightened little boy hanging on each leg) into the very back corner. She said she had never been so scared in her life. She didn't know anyone around her, the storm was howling, as were the boys, and there she was, alone, with the VFD's moneybox. Now, this tale has a happy ending, of course, but she said she reckoned her experience during that day of terrible lightning and thunder must have affected me in the womb, somehow. Dad and my brothers told other stories about

223

the day, but I don't think anyone else now living knew this particular story but me.

Ranch and Military Life
By William R. Clark of Belton, Missouri
Born 1933

According to my birth certificate, I was born at home at 0730 on May 4, 1933. I was the second oldest in my family. We lived on Ranch 5, which my Dad and Uncle worked and managed. It was located southeast of Tarkio, in Atchison County Mo, and owned by the Northwestern Insurance Co. It consisted of approximately 1,200 acres. My Dad later purchased 804 acres from that company. Ranch operation was a combination of grain/ hay crop and animal raising. Cattle and hogs that were raised were later shipped to stockyards in St. Joseph and Kansas City, Missouri. My Grandpa, Grandma, and Uncle lived in the "big house" which also served as the Ranch 5 Headquarters. It was also used to feed and provide a place to sleep for the hired crew. This is where I spent most of the summer and fall prior to starting grade school. The "little house" was about 300 feet from the big house, where grandma kept her "nice things." In between the two houses were two smoke houses where the black ranch cook had his sleeping quarters and personal items. Ranch 5 Headquarters was at the end of a dusty, dirty, muddy road, depending upon the seasons. It was very hot in the summer and very cold in the winter. Our family house was located a half mile north of the headquarters. This is where we lived until I finished sixth grade.

My Grandma made homemade bread using Fleishman's Yeast. It was put in the top compartment of the wood stove to rise prior to baking. We ate it with homemade butter and a slice of onion. It was not bad! I helped my uncle get slivers of wood for coal fires in the forge. The forge heat was used to form horse and mule shoes. The hoofs were first trimmed, and then horseshoes were fitted, formed, and nailed. The nails were then clenched after lopping off the excess length. Turning the hand crank on the forge had to be done just right for proper forming and fitting. Near the forge was a foot-pedal-operated grindstone for sharpening mower sickle bars, corn knives

and scythes, etc. I helped grandma heat water in a large, black, open kettle on a wood fire. The kettle was also used to render out cracklings when butchering and to make lye soap and lard. Grandma eventually got an old one-cylinder Maytag washer. Sometime in the early '40s, my mom acquired a two cylinder Maytag. These Maytag engines had flexible exhaust pipes that had to be put outside while operating. Both had foot-operated crank peddles. While my Grandpa was teaching me to whittle, I cut the knuckle on my left hand about an inch long and to the bone, leaving a scar. There was a lot of blood. Grandma got out the coal oil, washed my hand good and wrapped it in a clean white rag. Colored cloth was never used because it contained dye that could cause problems later on.

I remember one occasion before I started school a trainload of cattle was shipped in by railroad and unloaded on a street a short distance from Main Street in Craig, Missouri. These cattle came from rangeland in New Mexico and Arizona and were driven from the railroad to the ranch on horseback. Prior to settling in and getting on full feed, a veterinarian was brought in for vaccination, castration and dehorning, as needed. A branding fire was built on the ground just outside of a corral with a squeeze chute to hold cattle for this purpose. Prior to releasing, they were branded with the number "5" on the left rear quarter, which was burned into the hide. Hair branding was not used because hair growing out of the brand would disappear, along with proof of ownership. I sometimes walked the road to the Headquarters after dark. The shipped-in cattle would run up alongside the fenced line on the high banks on each side of the road, knowing something was in the road. I was told this is a trait of nearly all wild cattle. I later found out how they would react to anyone or anything caught in any open area—especially feed lots! We moved the cattle on country roads with saddle horses. When coming to a bridge, the cattle would not cross, as it had steel banisters about four feet high on both sides. We put down straw on the wood flooring, and the cows and steer finally crossed by the driving and pushing from the saddle horses. The big Hereford bull was a different story altogether. He refused to cross. Eventually, he crossed by being dragged by a big saddle horse named Rowdy, which we purchased in Valentine, Nebraska in 1938. This was something to see. The bull had all legs forward refusing to walk. Rowdy just spread on all fours and dragged the Hereford across. The bull kept tossing his head and rolling his eyes. He had both ends in operation—bellowing and leaving deposits behind! This was the same bull who enjoyed scratching his back on a live electric fence! Today, the only thing left of the Ranch 5 Headquarters area is a remnant of what used to be the weight and scale house. The big house, little house, barns, implement sheds, silos, grain bins, fences and corrals are gone. This entire area is now growing either soybeans or corn.

I started grade school in September 1939. We walked to a one-room country school (South York) one mile to school for the first four years, then two after we moved to another house. We sometimes rode in a high-wheel wagon used for corn picking, with the back or bump board removed and pulled by large workhorses. One time we used a high, two-wheel seeding cart with the chain removed. It was pulled by a team of work mules over the worst road in the county. I sometimes entertained the other kids by walking on the bridge banister located about eight feet above the bridge bed and 20 feet to the creek below. When snowdrifts plugged the roads, the big "V" plows opened roads to only one lane, leaving at least eight inches of snow on the ground. Originally, we recited the pledge to the flag with our right arm extended forward and raised above our heads, with the palm turned down; later, we put our palm up. Eventually, we put our right hand over our heart. It was due to the Nazi salute in Germany under Adolf Hitler. I remember coming home from school and seeing a copy of *Look* or *Life* magazine on the table. The front cover was of German Soldiers fighting in Poland. Over the years, I've repeatedly seen that front cover picture.

We had school plays a couple of times a year. Each of us had assigned parts to recite or act out. At the Christmas play, parents brought in food. One time, our family of six traversed the two-mile mud road in a 1929 Model-A Ford that had a rumble seat. Mom and Dad were in the front seat and kids in the rumble seat. This old Ford had the front spring leaf broken and was supported by two or three 2x4s nailed together. The muffler had long since been dragged off due to the deep ruts in the roads.

The exhaust pipe came straight off the engine, about a foot. With my dad driving in low gear, full throttle, you could hear us coming two miles away! By the time I started high school in 1946, we still had the Model-A and a new 1946 bright yellow Willy's Jeep my brother and I used to travel the eleven miles to school. Sometimes the front axle was out on the Jeep, and even with chains on only the rear drive, it was no match for the Model-A with chains.

In the eighth grade, our school went to Tarkio High school to compete in area track meets. Our training and what practice we had, was on a dirt road at a crossroad at the bottom of the hill from the schoolhouse. In order to compete, our teacher marked off the distance she thought we would be running. I wore bib overalls and lace up work shoes with hooks at the top. The town kids practiced on oval track wearing track shoes and running shorts. I still believe I won; however, we were running on their turf that day. In high school, I was in FFA. For my project, I raised and fed out two Black Angus steers. They brought top dollar at the local market on show day.

On June 2, 1949, at approximately 7:45, just after sundown, a tornado hit and completely destroyed our family home and all farm buildings. The surrounding damage was massive. My Dad and I finally got all family members into the fruit cellar. All had serious injuries. I had multiple bruises and imbedded particles in my body. A neighbor who lived one mile from us came walking up the road saying his house had been blown away. He didn't know the status of his family members. We were both stunned. We walked a mile north to the next neighbor to get help. We eventually got to town and help. The worst injured of our family members were taken to Shenandoah, Iowa to the Hand Hospital. Three days later, my younger sister died from injuries sustained in the tornado.

In November of 1950, I was classified 1-A by the draft board, so I volunteered for service. Four of us local guys went to the recruiting offices located in the post office building in St. Joe. In order of their locations, the Army recruiting office was first, Marine Corps second, Navy third, and Air force fourth. They all asked the same questions. "When can you leave?" and "Do you have a birth certificate?" I was the only one without a birth certificate, and told them it blew away

SSgt. William R. Clark

was assigned to the 414 FTR Wing, Oxnard, AFB, California. I reenlisted at Oxnard and was assigned to Grandview, AFB, Mo. (in 1957, the base was renamed Richards-Gebaur AFB in honor of a deceased Airman killed in action in World War I and an Airman killed in the Korean war). I served in three capacities at RGAFB: Active duty, Civil service and DOD, totaling 42 years of service.

Golden Moments of my Youth
By Katherine M. Rhodes of St. Joseph,
Missouri
Born 1941

As told to me by my Mother, Luella Inscho Wood, I made my debut as she watched the sunrise through the skylight overhead in the delivery room at Mercy Hospital in St. Joseph, Missouri. According to her rendition, I was the only baby in the nursery and was coddled and spoiled by the staff during our brief stay there. Some of my fondest memories of early childhood are reflections in my mind of living on Garden Street, in St. Joseph, Missouri. It was here my sister, Eva, was born at home, and the following year my sister, Jessie, was born. Mother made it to the hospital this time. We three sisters enjoyed many hours of playful frolic in those early years as we grew. We spent many spring and summer days playing house under the branches of the young tender trees which nature had planted in the backyard of our Garden Street home. In our imagination world, it could be anything we chose. I cherish the many snapshots taken of us three sisters.

My sisters and I took many walks up the street to visit our maternal grandparents and Aunt Phyllis, who was a delightful playmate also, being only a few years older than me. During the war years our Aunt Ruth and Cousin Gayle resided with our grandparents, Gayle was a fun and loving playmate as well. We would take walks all year long. My mother has often told us about bundling us up in our snow pants, coats, and hats for our winter walks to see Grandma, only to carry our wraps home rather than wearing them home. I am sure we were not aware of the cold air, as we were always dressed warmly, long heavy stockings, high top shoes, and, of course, warm winter dresses.

in a recent tornado. I was refused by all until we got to the AF recruiter; he told me "I'll have you one in three days." I wound up in the USAF. We traveled on a troop train for three days and nights until we arrived in San Antonio, Texas for five weeks of boot camp at Lackland Air Force Base. After graduating, I was assigned to Headquarters 8AF, Carswell AFB, Fort Worth Texas. The next assignment was at 42 Bomb Wing, Limestone AFB, Maine, followed by Army engineering school in Fort Belvoir, Virginia. By graduating first in my class of 43 students, I had my choice of bases: Korea, Okinawa, or Greenland. I refused these assignments, and was assigned to 27th Aviation Squadron, Bergstrom AFB, Austin, Texas. Within ten days, the squadron received orders to Korea. I guess this was what they called the Texas two-step! Going from Oakland, California to Yokohama, Japan took 23 days with MSTS on a two stack twin prop ship, the USS General A. E. Anderson with five thousand troops. Fourteen months later on a Single Stack MSTS transport, the President Jackson, we sailed into pier 91 through the Strait of Juan de Fuca at Port Angeles. The return trip took 17 days with 1700 troops on board to Seattle, Washington; apparently, some of the GIs bought a one way ticket. Following the Korean assignment, I

One of my most cherished memories while visiting my Grandmother, Maude Inscho, is how I loved to watch her make pies. I would listen to her humming and singing as she rolled the dough out to put it in the pie tins. She would then fill them with fruit, and then pop them in the oven. I can almost smell the pleasant aroma of fruit and spices now. I have inherited or mimicked this practice throughout my life as well, and often think about her and those early days as I sing and hum.

While living here on Garden Street, World War II was declared. In November 1943, our Father, Marvin Victor Wood, left us in the care of our mother as he went off to fight the war in Germany. He served in the Army until October 1945. While he was away, his photo occupied a space on the library table in the living room of our home. This was so we could see his face every day. Ration stamps were issued for various staples and other items. They were as precious as a treasure might be, and Mother kept ours safely on top of the kitchen cabinet.

It was during our tenor on Garden Street when I was old enough to start my school

Katherine's mother, Luella Woods holding Jessica with Katherine and Eva in 1945

days. I was enrolled in kindergarten at Hyde Elementary in September 1945 and walked to school with the neighbor children each day. I remember being "excused" from the story time circle. The teacher had joined the circle with an armload of books. I whispered to my classmate, "She is crazy if she thinks she can read all of those books." I was put at a table on the other side of the room. I was made to lay my head down on the table. Needless to say, this left an impression in my mind. I was never disrespectful to my teachers after that incident.

Our family welcomed a new member in September 1946. At last, a brother! He was named Marvin Wood Jr. (Sonny). Soon after his arrival, we moved to Rosecrans Fields, into an apartment that had served as military barracks during the war. I was enrolled in the first grade at Washington Elementary in St. Joseph. I remember playing on the asphalt with other children who also lived in those apartments. One night, across the way near the boiler building (where we three sisters could see from our bedroom window), we saw the sky light up with the flames and smoke from a fire at the boiler building.

The Missouri River flooded, covering the street. We traveled to downtown St. Joseph in the spring of 1947. Shortly afterward, my family would move once more to a six-room house on Highway 71 south of Faucett, Missouri. I was enrolled at Faucett School to complete my first grade. I completed the remainder of my school days and graduated from Faucett High School with the Class of 1959 in the same building. Many friendships were developed throughout those years, and I am pleased and blessed with so many long-lasting friendships from those golden school days.

There was no electricity and no plumbing in the house. Our water came from a well, and our toilet consisted of a wooden two-seat outhouse, located a good distance from the house. Our light was provided by oil lamps and lanterns; cooking and heating was provided by wood and coal when we first moved there. Eventually we owned a battery-powered radio. After a few years, Daddy had one room wired for electricity. He also got bottle gas for

227

cooking, and eventually for heating. Laundry was done by hand in large washtubs, the water for laundry being heated on the cook stove. After the installation of electricity, Mother had a huge green twin Dexter washing machine and a small electric heater for heating the water that Eva, Jessie, and I often carried from the well, bucket by bucket, to fill the machine tubs and the rinse tubs as needed for laundry, drinking, and cooking.

I walked to and from the crossroads, known as Taos Road, to board the school bus each morning and return home each afternoon. Our dog, Boots, would accompany me for many mornings and wait until I returned home. One morning, he was hit by a car as he was crossing the highway to go back to the house. I cannot remember for sure, but probably by second or third grade, the bus route changed, and we were picked up in front of the house. Mother would walk with us along Taos Road on many occasions in spring and summer. She sometimes went to visit our neighbors and friends Mary Finney and her family to the west or Marie Habluetzel to the east. Homer "Shome" Finney and Warner Habluetzel were farmers in the community, and were often in the fields. She would also visit Bea Rose on the highway south of us. When visiting at the Finney farm, we played with the Finney children, Mary Ellen, Bill, John, and Dorothy. While we were playing, our mother had a nice visit with their mother. Sometimes pony rides would be part of the day's activities. After a wonderful lunch together, we would start our journey home to be there in time to prepare supper for Daddy. Eva, Jessie, Sonny, and I were privileged to stay with the Finney Family in the spring of 1949 while Mother was in the hospital for the birth of our sister Ruth Ellen.

Some Sundays we would walk to church at Taos, following Taos Road beyond the Finney Lane, and then westward to the crossroads. The building on the Southeast corner, now the home of Bob and Bonnie Lee Robinson, had been a grocery store owned and operated by my maternal grandparents Maude and Hayden Inscho, and Bea (Grandpa's sister) and Bill Parker. Across the road on the southwest corner on the Round Tree Farm owned by Austell (W.A.) Landis, was a small house, a weather-boarded log cabin. It was here that my aunts, Ruth, Alma, Esther, and Ruby lived. It is also, where mother was born. It is believed that the cabin was built in the 1830s. In the early 1950s, the weatherboarding was removed and the cabin was razed by Carl and Robert Robinson. The logs were tagged and numbered to be taken to the Patee Museum for reconstruction at a later date; however, the logs became infested with insects and had to be destroyed. On the northwest corner was a large old store building which now had been converted into a home where Carl and Adele Robinson live.

One Sunday morning, we three sisters walked to Sunday school without Mother. As we were strolling and skipping along, a car pulled up beside us. The man asked us if we knew where the Berming-Halleck Cumberland Presbyterian Church was located. I replied "No." Then, the gentleman asked where we were going and I told him to Sunday school, He offered us a ride and we directed him the aforementioned corner and turning north up the road to the church where we were going to Sunday school. To our amazement, this was the church where he needed to be. He was the preacher, H.C. Reeves, coming for his first time to preach at our church. We had Sunday school every Sunday with a preaching service only on the first Sunday of each month. The preacher was always invited to a church member's home after services for dinner before returning to his home in Cameron, Missouri. Our family took our turn for having the preacher for dinner in the years of service that followed. Some Sundays, Daddy would drive us to the church and pick us up afterward. Sometimes, we would ride home in the rumble seat of our neighbors' car. Their names were John and Bea Rose, and they lived south of us on Highway 71. We took many afternoon walks to visit Bea Rose in the summer months. She would almost always make a pitcher of fresh-squeezed lemonade for us to enjoy.

Throughout the years that we lived on Highway 71, our family would continue to grow with a sister, Vanita in 1950, a brother, Hayden in 1952, in 1954 a sister, Donna Jo. Donna Jo's time with us was very brief, as her time on earth was very brief. In 1955 another sister, Mildred was born, and in 1957, a brother, Andy. In 1959 after graduating from high school, I took a summer job at Noma Lites in St. Joseph, which lasted only a few weeks. I then procured employment with Townsend and Walls on the hosiery counter. This was until I departed from my home for admission at St. Luke's Hospital School of Nursing to pursue my career as a registered nurse. I spent three years at St. Luke's. I graduated in 1962 and passed the Missouri State Nurses exam, thereby obtaining my RN license.

In 1960, once again, our family increased with another sister, Elizabeth. Soon after her arrival, my parents moved the family once more into a more modern home, which they purchased, in Willowbrook. In 1963, our family increased with the youngest of our siblings, a sister Penny. The family has also increased during this time with the addition of three grandchildren for my parents. In 1958 my niece, Manda Kay Donaldson was born, in 1960 my nephew, Tom Donaldson, and in 1961 my niece, Melinda Donaldson. This was only the beginning of a grand legacy for my parents.

Springtime, summertime, and fall and winter holidays are full of many fond memories when grandparents, aunts, uncles, cousins, friends would gather for dinner and playtime fun. Sometimes it would be Mother's family, sometimes Fathers, and sometimes just friends. It was often at our home or the homes of others, No matter whom, or how many, the joys and treasures of family and friends were cherished and nourished by my parents. This left a legacy of love and faith for their ancestors to embrace and promote.

Sundays with Grandma
By Patricia J. Rix of Plattsburg, Missouri
Born 1931

In 1941, my dad was called to the Marines, so as a ten year old; I went to my grandmother's farm in Illinois. She was a housekeeper and cook for an older crippled but active farmer. He was a rough ole fella, but he had a big heart, a big laugh, and ruled! On Sundays, my grandma and I would go to church. The biggest part of Sunday was helping my 250 pound grandma put on her corset! I had her to breathe in and out to hook it up in the back. We couldn't help but start laughing. Sometimes we laughed so hard that we would cry! I always looked forward to Sundays. I still laugh when I think about it!

Farming and School Days
By Don Shamberger of Maryville, Missouri
Born 1936

My mother told me I was born in the worst year of the century. January was the coldest on record, with temperatures below zero and heavy snow. People could not get to the timber to cut firewood, so they cut trees in the yard. July had record heat with several days above 100, and record droughts causing the dust bowl. It was in the middle of the great depression, with crops almost worthless, if you had any to sell. The year was 1936. I was born in November in the house that I would call home for the next 24 years. I joined a family with an older brother and a grandfather. My dad's mother died when he was eight years old, and my grandfather (who everyone called Pa) had raised my father and a brother.

When I was five years old, I started my education at the Morgan country one-room school in the fall of 1942, and attended for the next four years. I had no other first grade classmates. My brother Dale and neighbor boy Vern Inman would come by and we would travel the mile and a quarter to school. I don't remember how many other students attended, maybe six or eight. The building had a closed porch where we would leave our coats, overshoes, and lunch. There was a basement were the wood furnace was located with a grate in the floor for the heat to come up. Dad's cousin, Artie Snowberger, lived a quarter of a mile south of the school. He would come up and start the fire on cold winter days. Artie and his wife, Alma, provided room and board for Miss Thompson, my teacher for my first four years. There was no electricity, and if any event was held at night, (such as the annual Christmas program), a large Aladdin kerosene lantern was used for light. Everyone also had a tin cup, which was used for drinking water. The water was pumped from the well ten feet east of the front door. The boys' toilet was in the southwest corner of the schoolyard next to a shed. The shed was used to tie the horses in winter or rainy weather. The girl's toilet was to the north. Next to the road, under the trees, was a rail to tie the horses when the weather was nice. The roads were dirt, sometimes mud when it rained. We walked, rode horses or ponies, bicycles, and sleds when the snow was on the ground. The pony

I rode was "Wilkie." He was named after Wendell Wilkie, who had run for president against Franklin D. Roosevelt in 1940. He was a dumb Shetland pony, who had one gait—a slow walk. I don't remember missing school because of rain, snow, or muddy roads.

I remember on a winter day after it had snowed, we had taken our sleds to school. During our lunch hour, we were sledding on a hill north of the school. We were probably a quarter of a mile north of the school having a great time. Miss Thompson, came out on the porch, and was ringing her bell, signifying lunchtime was over. The older boys said, "Pretend you don't see her. We can keep on sledding." After a short time, up the road our teacher came with her heavy coat on, ringing the bell. This time there was no way to ignore her. I think it was a while before we got to go sledding during recess or the noon hour.

I really don't remember the Japanese attack on Pearl Harbor when it occurred on December 7, 1941. I know I had a fear that my dad would have to go to war. My mother would tell me he was too old. The most memories I had was the rationing of gas and rubber tires. Other items were also difficult to buy. Dad had his name at several implement dealers, as he was trying to buy a tractor. I believe he finally got an H Farmall in 1944 at Pumpkin Center. I remember the large olive drab planes carrying troops and supplies in a V formation, flying so low I could see their turning propellers. I could hear the roar as they approached. I would run out in the yard and look up they passed over. We went out in the fields in the fall and gathered milkweed pods. We placed

Dale and Don with Wilkie the horse

them in net sacks that people would get when purchasing oranges and grapefruits at stores. We tied the sacks of pods on the fence around the school so the wind and sun would continue to dry them. They were used by the air force to make parachutes. I remember going around the community with somebody in a wagon pulled with horses, picking up scrap iron to be used by the Army. Bill Snowberger, My second cousin was to graduate from high school in 1943 or '44. They were drafting boys as soon as they graduated. Bill wanted to go in the Navy, so he quit school a month before he was to graduate so he could enlist in the Navy.

When I was in the second or third grade, I had been having some ear and throat problems. Mom had taken me to Dr. Wallace Findley in Graham. He said I needed my tonsils removed. My parents took me to his office in Graham one morning. I laid down, and Dr. Findley administered the ether to put me out. He then proceeded to remove my tonsils. He needed no receptionist, no nurse, and no assistant of any kind. After my tonsils were removed, Mom took me to his residence, which was a block or two south of his office. We stayed until evening, and went back to his office where he prescribed some ice cream at Fred Mowry's drug store across the intersection. I'm guessing the entire bill was less than $5.00. It has lasted just fine for 70 years.

One of my early jobs was water boy for the threshing crew. I used my pony, Wilkie, to deliver water in a gallon crock jug with a corncob stopper. It was usually covered with a water-soaked burlap sack to keep the water cool. The crew usually consisted of the man who had the machine and his helper, who was called the grease monkey. Two or three wagons, which were used to deliver the shocked grain to the machine. Three or four additional men were used to throw the bundles on the wagons. A couple of wagons were needed to haul the oats or wheat to the granary where it was scooped off. A spike scooper was an additional man needed at the granary to help with the unloading. If they could find anyone stupid enough, they would have a straw stacker. A crew would be 12 to 14 men, plus two or three women to cook dinner. The men would wash up outside in a wash pan. All of this labor was needed for probably seven to 15 acres of oats and wheat. If the yield was 30 bushels to an acre, that would be 200 to 450 bushels of grain.

I do remember one of the last times we threshed at home. I was water boy, and we were finishing up at our place in early afternoon and were moving to Fred Barr's, which was two and a half miles northeast. As the bundle wagons would finish unloading, they would move up the road. As the crew was diminishing, I decided it was time for me to start up the road. Wilkie was moving slow. As members of the crew would finish their tasks, they passed me. A kick in the flanks got little results. I was about halfway there when I could hear the roar of the tractor pulling the threshing machine in the distance. Everyone else had passed me, and now the threshing machine was gaining on me. A half mile from the next field, around went the threshing machine. When I got to the new field, the threshing machine was set up and the first bundle wagon was unloading. How embarrassing! It must have been traumatic to have such a vivid memory 70 years later!

Another summer job was riding Andy the horse to pull loose hay up in the barn loft. In earlier years, loose hay was loaded on hayracks and moved to the barn. Most of the years, I would ride the horse and pull up the hay, and Dale and Vern Inman would bring hay into the barn from the field with a tractor and a wooden forked contraption that was attached to the front of the tractor. It was called a buck rack. They would leave a pile of hay in front of the barn. A man would set the hayfork into the hay and yell "Okay!" A one and half inch hay rope ran through a series of pulleys that were attached to my horse on one end and the hayfork on the other. As I proceeded riding my horse away from the barn, the hay on the other end would go up into the barn. It would hit the track at the peak of the barn and proceed into the barn. Someone in the barn would yell "tripper!" and a man on the ground would pull the trip rope. The hayfork would release its load, and the hay would fall into the loft below. The men would then move the hay around the barn with forks. I would turn Andy around and go back to the barn and wait for the fork to return to the ground.

In the spring of 1945 I had returned home from the Morgan school and was in the house eating my after school snack. That was when my mother heard on the radio that President Roosevelt had died. I ran to the barn where my father and Pa were grinding corn for the dairy cows to tell them the news. The fall of 1946, Dale and I started attending Graham Elementary School. I was in the fifth grade, which was combined with the sixth grade. Our teacher was Frances Hayzlett. On the first few days of the school year that fall, we went three quarters of a mile to meet the so-called bus. The bus, driven by Charlie Dicken, was a pickup with a stock rack covered by a tarp. It had wooden benches along each side. The bus would stop, Charlie would get out and remove the wooden stock rack end-gate, the student would get in, the end gate would be replaced, and we would proceed to school. This was only temporary, as they were converting a panel truck to a school bus. The panel truck was orange with benches along the sides of the windowless rear compartment. Our driver was Milford Sweat, the high school principal, and history and industrial arts teacher. The only oil road was route A, between Pumpkin Center and Graham, the rest were dirt, mud when it rained or the spring thaws occurred. We were some of the earlier riders to get on, with the route meandering the area three to four miles north of route A, back to the west six miles to Graham. When it was muddy, we were often late. After the war, the King Bill was passed, which provided assistance in graveling farm to market roads in Missouri. Farmers contributed money for gravel roads that went by their homes. These contributions added to state-funded money provided many miles of gravel roads. While not all roads were graveled, most homes would be close to a gravel road. We were awarded a real bus, driven by Alan Wright. While it wouldn't pass today's inspection, we never had an accident.

Legendary Horse Trainers from Parnell
By JoElla (DeFreece) Gilbert of King City, Missouri
Born 1938

JoElla's grandfather, Joe Prather in 1938

When I was a child growing up in Parnell, a small town located in the corner of Nodaway County northeast of Maryville, Missouri, we had an elementary and high school, two churches, and around 15 businesses. There was one family that lived in the west part of town, which everyone referred to as being very wealthy. That was the family of Ben A. Jones, his wife Etta, a son Horace (Jimmie), and daughter Pauline. They lived in a four-story brick house that was tall enough to need an elevator. They had adjourning houses for their hired hands, plus big barns, including the first round barn in Northwest, Missouri. One of their large barns held the stable for their horses and a racetrack. This was all surrounded by white board fencing. In addition to their large home in Parnell, the Jones' also owned many acres of land where they raised black cattle and many thoroughbred horses. Mr. Jones was also employed by Calumet Farms of Lexington, Kentucky as a horse trainer. When his son, Jimmie, graduated from high school, he joined him while his daughter, Pauline, moved to Springfield, Missouri.

Once the family members had left the house, Mrs. Jones (Etta) was left behind to care for the home place. Mrs. Jones was a little lady with a soft voice. She always wore dresses and lace tie high heels. Since she was left alone, Mrs. Jones had a German police dog for her protection and several employees to help her take care of the farm. My grandfather, Joe Prather, was hired to care for the horses and had his own living quarters in the tack room. Each horse had its own stall where they could be fed and cared for. When the horses were old enough, they would be shipped to Calumet Farms for racing or breeding purposes. My sister, Marilyn (DeFreece) Runde, was hired to help out around the house, and when I was 12, I was asked to help, too. My jobs included

doing the regular housework, washing the eight-foot windows, cleaning the venetian blinds in the office, dusting the winding staircase, and washing the beautiful china and crystal. The hardest job was polishing all the silver trophies and plaques that were scattered throughout the home. The wages were small, but working after school and throughout the summer I earned what I thought was a big check. Luckily, when I arrived for work, she had her rather large protective dog on the screened-in back porch, and before entering, I always made sure that he was there.

While cleaning at Mrs. Jones' I got to see and experience several different things. I got to see Mrs. Jones dressed up in her fancy hat and fur wrap or coat to go shopping in the big cities such as St. Joseph or Kansas City. I would see the chauffeur get the Cadillac out of the garage and drive up to the front of the big, beautiful home. Mrs. Jones would always ride in the back, and at my age, I never knew

JoElla's father, Henry DeFreece and family in 1936

232

why. This was a spectacular sight to see from someone like myself. When Mr. Jones and his son would come for a visit, they would fly into the Kansas City airport and the chauffeur would bring them to Parnell. Mrs. Jones and her help would cover the dining room table with her fancy tablecloths and napkins. She would get out her fine china and silver for serving, and she would have the help prepare several fancy dishes for the men. While the men were home, they would discuss business and then leave again for Kentucky. When the men were away, Mrs. Jones would find time to relax in her own special room. Where she would sit and read or do needle pointing while listening to the radio. However, she definitely missed her men while they were gone.

Another very vivid memory I have of the Jones' was in 1948. The Jones' were entering one of their horses, Citation, in the Kentucky Derby. My father, Henry DeFreece, and seven of the local men decided they wanted to go. My father, who had thirteen children, decided it was too expensive to fly, and so the eight men decided to take my father's stock truck. On Sunday, the week before the race, the seven local men came to our home. They raised the stock racks on the truck, threw a tarp over the top, and stocked it with several bales of straw for bedding, coolers, blankets and a change of clothes. On Monday morning, the men kissed their families goodbye and headed to Louisville, Kentucky, which was 625 miles away. When the men got home, they had great news to tell. Citation had won the Kentucky Derby! They also told us kids to go comb through the loose straw on the truck where there was probably some loose change. We found $5.15, and to us that was even better news. The men continued to talk about their trip for months.

As the years continued, the Jones' trained many more derby winners. Two of them, Whirlway and Citation, went on to win Triple Crowns. After retiring, Jimmie returned to Parnell where he lived until his death in 2001 at the age of 94. Jimmie Jones also became a member of the National Museum of Racing Hall of Fame and was inducted into Missouri Sports Hall of Fame in 1996. Today Parnell has closed its school and most of its businesses, but the beautiful home of the Jones' has been sold and restored. It is still standing in the west part of town. The Jones' turned their wealth into millions. The Jimmie Jones estate gave millions of dollars back to Nodaway County, and it is an honor that in a small way, I got to see the experiences of the Jones'.

JoElla's grandfather, Joe Prather

Life on the Farm in the 1930s
By Jessie Marie (Long) Jones-Smith of
Maryville, Missouri
Born 1931

As a little girl born in 1931, it didn't even dawn on me that we were living during the Depression. Not once did I ever hear my parents or anyone complain that we were poor or that we were living in "hard times." We lived a simple life and certainly didn't have much, but neither did anyone else. It was just our way of life.

It was in the roaring twenties that my dad, Oliver W. Long, and my mother, Mildred M. (Goff) Long were married in the fall of 1923. My dad had graduated from the Stanberry Normal College and my mother was attending the Maryville Conservatory of Music. She was an accomplished piano player, among many other talents. My dad owned the mill in Mound City, Missouri, and they first lived on the mill property in Mound City; however, the mill burned down and they moved east of Graham, Missouri. My grandma, Mary Long, had purchased the farm that was located about seven miles southeast of Graham. They all lived together in the large two-story house up on the top of the hill. It was about a mile west of the Bethany Christian Church. It was in this home that all five of us girls were born: Mary, Fanny, Jessie, Olive, and Belva. My name is Jessie and I was the middle child. We three older girls were all very close and were always working together on some big project.

In the mid-30s, our cousin, Edward Miles, and our uncle, Theodore Goff, came to live with us. As young men, they did most all of the farm work, as our father was busy working with real estate and settling farm estates. Also around that time, the tractor was beginning to replace the teams of horses. My father started the Long Implement Company in Maitland selling Allis-Chalmers tractors. His nephews, Solomon Christian IV, and Elva Christian, became his partners, and it then became the Long and Christian Implement Company. In later years after the Long family moved away to Quitman, MO, it was renamed to the Christian Brothers Implement Company.

Our family was very self-sufficient in spite of the fact that there was no electricity, no running water, or inside plumbing. We did have a cistern beside the house that caught all the rainwater through the downspouts from the roof whenever it rained. We also had a pitcher pump inside the house that we could pump the water in from the cistern. We burned kerosene lamps that furnished our light after dark.

The Long family portrait taken in 1935

There was timber on the farm, so we had plenty of firewood for the kitchen cook stove and for the wood heating stoves to keep us warm in the wintertime. We girls helped carry in the wood as soon as we were big enough to carry the pieces of cut wood. Of course, everybody in our neighborhood had their outhouse with the Sears catalog hung on a wire! We bought very few groceries from town—50-pound bags of flour and sugar, plus yeast, coffee and spices were the main items. We had a large round cave just north of the house with wide double doors and steps to get down into the cave area. Inside this cave were rows and rows of shelves. These shelves were full of canned fruit and vegetables from our big garden and the fruit trees. In one area were large bins full of our homegrown potatoes and apples. There were also onions hanging from the ceiling. After the fall harvest, our cave was full of enough food to last all winter.

In the fall when the weather started to get cooler, it was time to select a pig to slaughter. This was a big event, with even the neighbors coming to help. They would cut off the hams, the shoulders, and the slabs of bacon. These were all heavily seasoned down with salt and spices and hung in the smokehouse to cure. Some of the meat was cut up and my mother would put it into half-gallon jars for processing. It was then stored in the cave. The rest of the meat was ground up into sausage with seasonings and stuffed into casings. She would then put them into the jars for processing and storage as well. Nothing went to waste. After the fat was trimmed from the meat, it was made into lard by boiling it in a big black kettle over a hot fire. This lard was used for cooking and baking. Our milk cow furnished us with all the milk, cream, and butter we needed. My mother knew how to make the best cottage cheese from the milk that would clabber. We had lots of chickens each year, so we also had plenty of eggs and fried chicken. It was up to us girls to gather the eggs each evening from the henhouse and to make sure the chickens were fed and watered. The Watkins man had a horse and enclosed wagon and would travel through the country selling his products, liniment, ointments, spices, and even vanilla. There was a chicken coop fastened to the back of the wagon. If people didn't have enough money, he would accept some chickens in exchange. My family and all the neighbors were faithful church people. Everybody worked long and hard, but when Sunday came around, the Bethany Christian Church was full of worshippers. People came in from all over the neighborhood by car, horse and wagon, or some just walked.

As I mentioned before, my mother was very skillful. When we three older girls were real small, she crocheted each of us little white dresses with a big bow tied on the shoulder. She also made all of our dresses from the colorful patterned flour and feed

234

sacks. If there was enough material, she would also make matching bloomers and a bonnet. In the evenings after the work was all done, we would all sit around in the living room and listen to her play the piano or join in singing together. We girls all took music lessons on the piano from our neighbor lady. It was my big dream to someday be able to play the piano just like my mother. I still have my mother's sheet music and love to sit and play the piano every chance I get.

We learned how to work at a very young age, but don't be mistaken, we also knew how to have a good time! We had a large front yard full of trees and bluegrass. In the spring, nobody in our neighborhood would mow their yards until after the bluegrass went to seed, so we would play hide-and-go-seek in the tall grass and behind the trees. Many a playhouse was built by throwing a large blanket over the clothesline! In the wintertime, we would build snow houses with two or three rooms in the huge drifts of snow out by the roadside. There wasn't much traffic, especially when the roads drifted full. At Christmastime, we always had a homegrown evergreen tree cut from the pasture. We girls would decorate it with long chains of cut colored rows of paper from our notebooks and with long strings of popcorn. On Christmas morning, we would wake up early and Santa would always bring us just one gift, but how we cherished that gift! We usually got a new doll or some precious toy. Our little stockings were hung and they would always be filled with peanuts and candy and a large orange sticking out of the top.

Whether it was spring, summer, fall, or winter, we three older girls were old enough to be really curious and quite adventurous. Living in the country had so many interesting and wonderful opportunities. There were no televisions, computers, cell phones, or fancy toys like we have today; however, we did have big dreams and vivid imaginations! Here is one of our big projects that I do want to share with you. It was getting late in the summertime. We had heard the men talking about building a pond so the livestock could have more water, and maybe they could use it to go swimming, too. We girls started talking about this and Fanny exclaimed, "Let's make our own little pond!" Mary answered by saying, "Where would we get any water to put in it?" I jumped up and answered, "I know!

Jessie's father, Oliver W. Long in the early 1930s

When our mother does the washing, we'll be anxious to empty the water for her. Don't worry! She'll let us. You know we generally empty the water out behind the chicken house, so she won't know the difference." The field back there had been the potato patch, and the ground was still soft and just perfect for this. What a great idea! Feeling as though everything would turn out just wonderful, we got busy. After much hard work, our little pond was finally finished. When we asked our mother if we could help empty the wash water, she was very delighted about us wanting to work. The first few buckets of water didn't stay in the little pond very long, but it finally got so the water would stay in longer. The next morning we ran outside to see our pond. We were so disappointed and thought we surely did something wrong, as the water was all gone. On the next washday, we tried it again with the same results. We had such a big dream of how much fun we would have wading and playing in the water; however, we decided it just wasn't worth all the work and effort.

Since we had several family members as neighbors, quite often we would have large family gatherings on Sunday afternoons. These were memorial times, and we got to know all of our aunts, uncles, and cousins in the area. Living in the neighborhood in the big house with so much family close by made this the ideal place to grow up as a

235

young girl. It was truly a learning experience. In later years, I learned that we had been living through the Depression; however, with the love and faith within our family and friends, we just did what had to be done and was thankful for all our blessings.

In January of 1940, I became nine years old. It was in March that my family moved to our new home south of Quitman, Missouri. My grandma Long, Cousin Edward, and Uncle Theodore all moved with us. When World War II began on December 7, 1941, Edward was now old enough for the draft and left to serve in the United States Army. We quickly made new friends and Quitman was now our new home.

School District No. 4
By Archie Claycomb of Blythedale, Missouri
Born 1921

I was born and raised in Harrison County, Clay Twp. Akron Community, and went to school at Akron School District No. 4. The schoolhouse, like most of the country schools, sat on one acre of land with the building probably 15 feet by 20 feet. The Akron store was right north of it. Across the road was the Blacksmith shop. Up the road a short distance was the Presbyterian Church and down the road ½ mile was the Methodist Church. The schoolhouse was not big enough to hold all the people, so the school programs were held at the churches. There were seven one-room districts in Clay Twp; three on the east side of Grand River and four on the west side of the river with 8 to 30 students in each district at that time. The school year was eight months long, beginning in August and we were out the first of April. School was held Monday through Friday, regardless of the weather. Classes started at 9:00 a.m. and lasted until 4:00 p.m. There was a 15-minute recess twice a day and a one-hour lunch period. The kids all walked to school or rode a pony. The school district was about three square miles. No had had much over two miles to walk. We didn't have much in the way of playground equipment. We would mainly play baseball – kids brought their jump ropes, marbles, and jacks. One teacher taught all eight grades and did the janitorial work. I had the same teacher the last four years and we played baseball all school year chose up sides and

played. Students went to the front of the room to recite. The younger children learned a lot by hearing the older ones recite. I started to school in the fall of 1927 at Akron District No. 4, there were 37 students ranging in age form 5 to 18. At that time there were 29 homes in the district. Some had three generations living together. When the school closed in the spring of 1953, they had nine students and only 21 houses.

Daily Inspections
By Donna Wilcox of Cameron, Missouri
Born 1936

I went to a one-room school from the last part of my 2nd grade through my 8th grade. We had a cloakroom where we hung our coats. There was a shelf where we put our dinner buckets; many times, we traded lunches. Our day always started out with reciting the pledge of allegiance to the flag. Then we had inspection to see if our hands and fingernails were clean, if our ears were clean, and if we had brushed our teeth. One teacher taught all eight grades. Because of this, the 3rd and 4th, 5th and 6th, and 7th and 8th grades alternated from one year to the next. At recess, we played many games on the playground. We played softball, dare base, Mother May I, and Ante Over along with other games. There were also swings, teeter-totters, and the bars. My sister and I walked 1-¼ miles to school in all kinds of weather. I remember many times gathering around the big coal stove to warm our hands and feet. We had outdoor toilets. Our drinking water came from a well. Students took turns bringing drinking water and everyone drank from the same dipper. When school took up after lunch, the teacher read to us from books for 30 minutes. We all enjoyed this very much. Many times through the years, we had school programs where we sang songs as a group, small groups, and solos. We also had plays. Some of the times, this took place during Halloween, Christmas, and the last day of school. We had one family who seemed to bring in the childhood diseases. We experienced the seven-year itch and head lice. On the last day of school, we always got to go to the woods for a picnic and games. When I was in the 8th grade, my teacher was only five years older than me. In country schools, teachers only had to have so many college hours in order to teach.

One day after school, I was riding home with my teacher. The school was two miles from my home. She got not more than a quarter of a mile from school when I saw my little sister, who was only four years old, coming down the road. She said she was just coming to meet me. Needless to say, my mother was frantically looking for her. This little sister was quite a little songbird from the time she was two years old. She would perform at some of the school programs. I especially remember her singing "Roly Poly" at a program. She went on to get her Master's Degree in Music and taught for many years. Another thing I remember was having spelling and arithmetic matches. This was on Friday afternoons.

Tales of a Share Croppers Kid
By Virginia Golden of Dearborn, Missouri
Born 1937

I was born into a sharecropper's family and the first thing I can remember was when my brother Jack was born. My siblings were older than me and were sent over to my grandparent's home, but I was only two, so I wasn't. I was in one bedroom while mom was having Jack in the other. I remember sitting on the bed crying and once in a while dad would come in and say, "Skump, everything will be alright."

Of course, we moved a lot, as we were sharecroppers. We didn't have a lot of money, so we had to make our own kind of fun. The first thing when we moved into a new home was draw the horseshoe magnet on a string around the house and all around picking up nails then picking up glass to as we were all barefoot in the summer.

Mom always made fun of us children. She would take us on nature walks and tell us about the trees, flowers, and birds. One place we lived had a creek running through it with flat rocks like stair steps running with water. We would take bread and butter sandwiches and on hot summer days we would sit on the step rocks in the shallow water and just observe nature. There was an old ground hog that would come out if we were quiet and forage for something to eat buds would fly

in and light not too far from us. All kinds of flowers grew along the banks of the creek.

The place where I started school we had to walk ¾ of a mile down a mud road or dirt if it was dry. My older sister took me the first day, dressed in my flour sack dress, which meant mom made our dresses out of flour sacks, which were pretty prints. Mom would give dad a small piece of the sack that she wanted to make sure she got another sack of the same design. I think it took only two to make me a dress, as I wasn't very big.

My folks worked in the fields and in the barn as they raised tobacco, and Jack and I went along. We played under the wagon and made mud pies to when in the field. When they stripped the tobacco, we would play on one end of the bench or under it. Mom would make soup on the stove in the stripping room and we would eat there too. Then mom would make a pallet one end of the bench and Jack and I would take our naps. This is how the years went until I was in the beginning of high school and then my dad got a job and we moved to town, so ended my sharecropping days.

Life of a Mechanic
By Ronald Lathrop of St. Joseph, Missouri
Born 1943

Our dad loved cars. Most of the time we could afford only one used car that was shared by the family. The one I remember most was the 1955 Oldsmobile, four-door hardtop, with the model name of "88 Oldsmobile," blue and white, in and out. It was so huge my mother had to sit on a pillow to be able to see over the steering wheel. I was the only boy in the family, and the youngest, dad helped me buy a used 1954 Buick convertible my senior year of high school. This made my sisters jealous, but they got jealous about many things. One of the best memories was taking the car, going fast, running it into the ground. I told people I bought it from a woman named Dyna Flow; that was the name of its transmission.

Our dad was a good part time mechanic. He knew about the old cars from growing up in the depression. My dad and I would work on that Buick together. We fixed the brakes, carburetor, and other basic maintenance. Major things were fixed by a professional,

Ronald with his mother, Lillian Lathrop

which we never claimed to be. Dad's first car also had a crank in front that one person had to turn while the other person started the car. The throttle was a mystery to me, but I know it had to work correctly also. Some of the other features of the cars were running boards on the side to help the passengers into the car. The front windshield opened with a crank to let airflow through. There were also small side windows that let in air. There could be a shade over the front windshield to protect from the sun.

There was no air conditioning until the 1960s. Some lucky people had air coolers that hang on the side of the passenger window. Our Holiday 1955 Oldsmobile Coup was plush. We were one of the lucky people enjoying cool air conditioning in the summer. The "88 Oldsmobile, I remember most and carry the fondest memories of me and my dad, the mechanic.

We Would Roll Our Own Cigarettes
By Lou Anna Williams of Dearborn,
Missouri
Born 1922

In 1936, during the Great Depression, my father lost his mind and killed my mother and then him. This left my brother and I orphans. He lived with Uncle Arch and Aunt Laura and I lived with Uncle Bob and Aunt Rose Stelder;

we had no money. Later I went to Lathrop, Missouri to live with the Coleman family. She wasn't well and I helped around the house. They sent me to school in Converse, Missouri where I graduated from the 8th grade. I came back to Dearborn with my aunt and uncle and went to school at Edgerton, Missouri and then to Dearborn School.

I quit school when I was a sophomore and I married Virgil Williams - I was 16 years old and he was 19 years old. We had no place to live. We lived with his Brother Leon and wife Velta. Finally, in 1941 I got my estate money of $250. We bought Lot 11 in Dearborn, Missouri from Morris and Sarah Pitluck. At that time, this part of town was known as Little Italy. We had four boys – Vernon, Marion, Billy, and Larry. They were all raised at home. My husband was drafted in to World War II. The commodity truck came once a month. We got mostly staples, which we were very thankful for. I had to have stamps to buy sugar, cigarettes, and gas. My husband returned from the war after two years. There were no jobs. Finally, Halferty Brothers built the big grain elevator that stood at Z Highway and Commercial. My husband and boys helped build them. Then my husband was hired to work there. Times were getting a little better. He worked there for 26 years. I ran the telephone office in Dearborn until it turned to dial in 1954. We bought Lot 34 at Lake of the Ozarks in the 1960's. We all enjoyed going to the lake – boating, fishing, skiing, and relaxing for years. We then bought Lot 12 next to our house at Lot 11 and remodeled it. We moved in it in 1964, Vernon and Twyla Farris Williams moved us in our newly remodeled home while we were at work and Larry Williams helped them.

We had a wind up Victrola and a record of Whistlers Mothers, which was played often. My husband worked at Halferty Mill and elevator; they would get chicken feed in printed sacks, which I got and made shirts for the boys to wear. Sometimes if farmers didn't want the little chickens, we would get them. We once had 300 leghorn chickens. We had a Model A Ford with a rumble seat. We were very proud of it. We also had a parakeet we called Tweety; he could talk. Lee Lamar and my husband ran the old icehouse in Dearborn. They delivered ice to people around Dearborn. When we all had iceboxes, we put pans under them to catch the water. It sat by Dick Lamar's garage; the Buildex Plant in new market formerly Carter Waters and Haydite Plant. My Grandfather Joseph Stalder and Sarah, his wife, owned all the land from New Market, probably two miles below the Buildex Plant at that time where I was raised. They lost the farm and we had to move when Carter Waters bought it so we moved on Z Highway close to Edgerton, Missouri. One of my grandchildren, Bobby Williams, works at Buildex.

I went to Cox School on old Highway 71 close to what was Sunset Inn-tavern. It was a one-room schoolhouse. Then I went to Boydston, which was a one-room school as well. There were no buses - we walked to school. In winter, ice was saved from ponds and horses pulled it to the icehouse where it was covered with straw, also a smoke house. When we butchered the meat, we cured and hung it in the smoke house. Neighbor kids and I would sleigh ride and ice skate in winter on the hills and ponds. The Chicago great trains ran through Dearborn for years. They would throw our mail off as the train went by and mail going out was hung on a pale and the engineer would grab it with a hook. Ray Griggs was depot agent. When we wanted to go to the big city of St. Joseph, we would walk from Dearborn to Highway 371 and catch a greyhound bus at the White Castle run by Paul Blacketer.

My kids would make cars out of a thread spool and rubber bands and they played with big weed sticks for guns. Eventually we got skip leaders for them for Christmas. They were very happy to have a good toy. I stayed with my Aunt Lizzie and Uncle Eule a lot. They had 13 kids. Us kids would get dry tobacco leaves from the patch and roll cigarettes with newspapers and smoke. I took castor oil and gave my kids castor oil. They didn't like it, but they took it anyway. It was supposed to cure everything. We listened to *Lum and Abner, Amos and Andy, The Shadow*, and many more stories on the radio. I had a wringer washer for years. The depression years were terrible. There was no work and no money. We couldn't pay last month's rent of $6.00 to Florence George, so we painted her house for her. The foxhunt once was a big event. There were carnival rides, booths, music, and food. Dogs were put in a barn type building until night and you could hear them barking all night when they were hunting. I still live in the same house with my two cats Shadow and Hobo. I am able to do most anything.

I Always Have to Sit In the Front Seat
By Bonnie Livingston of Platte City,
Missouri
Born 1932

I was born June 9, 1932 at Trimble, Missouri; it was during the Great Depression at home. Two years later a brother was added to the family, Donald Pulliam. I grew up in the northern area of Clinton County and across the road was the county line of Platte County. Mom and dad farmed over 60-acres of farmland with a team of horses and used horse drawn cultivators, mowers, rakes, and discs. All of our food products were raised on the farm. We had a garden and all the food was canned and stored in the cellar for the winter supply. We had one apple tree and lots of rhubarb out of the garden. Mom would order the seeds for the garden from early May Seed magazine. I loved the rhubarb on toast or biscuits for breakfast and fried apples and applesauce.

We purchased baby chickens from a hatchery that were delivered by the postmaster. When it came time to dress the chicken's mom would build a fire under the big black kettle and heated the water to a temperature to scald and pull the feathers. She would plan on killing 25 at a time. Consequently, we had fried chicken and gravy with biscuits for breakfast a lot of days. However, I had a problem eating the chicken after killing them the day. When dad wasn't trying to till the ground to plant seeds, he also hauled livestock to the markets in Kansas City and St. Joseph for neighbors and family members. He would tell mom, "If you all want to ride along, we need to leave in about 20 minutes." That meant she took a washcloth and our faces were scrubbed on the trip. We always stopped at the exit of the stockyards and there was a vendor selling bananas, 10-pounds for $1.00. So we would eat them on the way home and I still love them.

When it came harvest time, mom would drive the truck for the grain to haul it to storage. She would prepare food for the workers at harvest and it was my duty to see that the food was ready to go on the table and see that the table was set when the men came in for lunch. That is when I had to learn to cook.

My dresses were made out of printed feed sacks. The chicken feed sacks were very pretty when made up in a school dress. When I entered the 1st grade, the school did not have school buses. A Packard that held six or seven students from my area rode in it to school. I was the youngest one in the group, so I always got to ride in the front seat; it made all the other kids jealous. I had a habit when getting home from school of always kicking my shoes off and putting on my house slippers. Well I had many a dream of rushing to the bus and still had my house slippers on how embarrassing. What a treat to try and remember the things that have happened in your past, but what a joy we can still remember.

The Rebellious Child in the Corner
By L'Berta Shelton of Pinehurst, North Carolina
Born 1926

When I was in the 1st grade, we were in a one-room schoolhouse. My older sisters and brother walked through a timber about 1-½ miles. There were two neighbor boys that walked part of the way to their home. One evening on our way home, the boys saw a nest up in a tree and decided to see what was in it. One climbed up the tree and found a black snake. They decided to pop its head off by taking hold of the tail. The snake slipped out of their hands and wrapped around my ankles. My older brother said, "Hurry and get that snake off of her." I used to have convulsions and my sister thought I might have another one. There was no immediate danger, but this left me fearing snakes up in to my adult life. Many years after I was married, we were driving back into our driveway; there were two big black snakes, which crossed in front of our car to a tree. I insisted my husband run over them, but his response was, "I wouldn't because they are good to eat mice." That was until they started to affect his birds that was a different story. For years, any snake that would slither in front of me always made me

The New Hope School in 1939

stop and freeze in my tracts. However when our child came along I tried to curb my fear for her sake.

We had a country store that money were saved to be able to buy peanut butter, sugar, flour, salt, baking powder, and vanilla. From some of these items mother made peanut butter fudge. She would make candy. She would put the candy in fruit jars and hide until Christmas time. The corn stalks were cut and looked like tepees. Mother hid a quart in one of the stalks. My brother found it and at that time, we had a large bin of shelled corn so he hid it. He forgot until spring and found the jar of candy when the corn was being used. The jar of candy was as good as when it was out in the cold corn. Years later, I made the fudge with raisins, which was from my grandmother's recipe. My aunt was in a nursing home; I visited her after and took her some fudge. She said, "That isn't what mommy made." When I asked why she said, "It didn't have any black walnuts in it." That was the first I knew there were nuts added.

In the one-room school, there were several instances that shows perhaps I was a rebellion child. I was disciplined to go to a corner and turn my back to the rest of students and teacher. Years later, the teacher was in a clinic in our town. Thanks to Miss Lewis, she said she couldn't remember me, but my sister (Selma Mabel four years older and the one four years younger and told her it was because she didn't see my face for I was sent to a corner to stand facing the wall. We got quite a laugh and for several years kept in contact with her and went to Fulton where she lived.

Living on a Farm Meant Work, Work, Work!
By Marsha Dale of Platte City, Missouri
Born 1951

I have lived in Platte County since 1960 and in Platte City School District since 1963. These years were spent on my parent's farm (Ralph and Waneta Kneuven.) I remember always asking my daddy for a horse and he said not until we lived in the country, so when we moved to the country I started bugging him and he said I would have to wait. My daddy was a sweetheart and one day we went to visit relatives and daddy, my uncle, and brother Donald left and were gone for quite a while. When they returned daddy said we had to go home. When we got there he said, "What is running around the house?" He began to walk that direction with me of course in his footsteps and there next to a tree was tied the most beautiful horse and his named was Danny. He was three years old and lived to be 21 and I cherished him all those years. He was trained for kids and would stop immediately if you fell off and they trained him to take his bridle and saddle off so you had to watch him closely if you tied him up for a minute. When I would go the field to get him, I would have to hide the bridle under my shirt or he wouldn't let me get close.

One time I remember going to get him and daddy had rented a bull for the cows that was mean and he saw me and I climbed the nearest tree as fast as I could. I sat in that tree for over an hour waiting for that silly bull to go away, but he stood at the foot of the tree stomping his feet. Sure glad he couldn't climb trees. Finally he went far enough that I thought I could get to Danny and get riding, however, just as I got to Danny the bull came running so I grabbed Danny's mane and pulled myself on and we took out on a run. The bull finally gave up. When I told my daddy what happened, that bull went bye-bye and a new nice bull came to replace him. I had two very close friends (Patty Moses and Penny Martin) within a mile of our house and we spent a lot of time together. One day we decided to ride the horses to Farley, Missouri so we could go buy some penny candy at the little grocery store. It was so much fun. One day my brother Donald thought he would go to the field and get Danny and ride him without a bridle like I did. I told him to hang on and he did because Danny began running towards the house, came in the yard, and instantly took him off under the clothesline. My brother wasn't very happy about that, but I think the horse smiled.

I loved being on the farm, even if it meant work, work, work! We had chickens, which I didn't like because they pecked me when I went to gather eggs. I found a solution to that and used the wire leg catcher my daddy had made up to catch the chickens, but it worked quite well getting them off the nests. We had milk cows, which was a lot of work. My momma always said the milk barn was cleaner than her house. When the milk cows had babies they only got to be with their momma for three days, then it was to the bucket with a feeding tube. You had to get a good stance, brace yourself, and wait for the butts of those baby calves and boy were they strong. You had to have old clothes on when you did this job. It was a fun job. Rusty, our dog, brought in the milk cows. All you had to do was tell him to go get the cows and within 10 minutes, they were at the gate coming from the backfield. If they didn't move, he bit at their legs and he was good at dodging those kicking legs. Daddy put two calves in our yard to eat the grass and Patty, Penny, and I worked on them until we could ride them just like the horses. We named them Sammy Davis Jr. and Penny. Soon they got too big to be in the yard, so Penny was off to field and Sammy was off to the market.

Raising pigs had to be the worst idea my daddy had about farm animals. They were messy and sometimes mean. Then when they

Marsha's parents, Ralph and Waneta Kneuven

were in labor and daddy was out in the field, momma would have to help the pigs. If they were having lots of problems, she would call Dr. McCrea and he would come out and deliver the pigs. One day he had to come out three times for different pigs and he told momma to get in there because he was going to teach her how to deliver them and she did. We had one runt pig that we brought to the house and kept him in the bathroom next to the heater to help him keep warm and fed him bottles. We named him Herman and just so you know, our family named every animal we had. That was a chore to remember. Anyway, Herman got bigger, so we put him on our back porch, then he got too big and we put him in the yard to get him ready to go live with the rest of the pigs. However, Herman decided he was not a pig, but a human and since our back door was easy to open, he would nudge it open and then next thing you knew, Herman would come running through the house. He did this one time when momma was talking to an insurance salesman. She was so embarrassed and not too long after that, he proceeded to go with the other pigs, but he still wanted to come to the house, so daddy had to take him off to the market, which was a sad day for me.

The farmers around our house always asked my daddy if he needed money to buy me some shoes since I never wore them. I could walk across gravel without any pain. Eldon Cannon, one of our neighbors, came one day and handed me two baby kitties and asked me to raise them. Their mother had got run over in front of his house. I proceeded to find a doll bottle and began feeding them. One of them didn't make it and went to heaven, but the other one lived and her name was Tiger. I would sneak her in the house when daddy wasn't looking and play with her on my bed. She got pregnant and then decided the perfect place to have them was in the middle of my pink chenille bedspread. Boy was I in trouble, but daddy got over it and loved that cat too.

Daddy had farm equipment to put in crops and two of my least favorite was the disk and plow. Why you ask, is this my least favorite; because I had to scrape all the dirt and mud off of them and grease them with a paintbrush put in this yucky black grease. He also put up hay bales so we would have food for the cattle. He always made me drive the tractor,

Marsha, Cindy Curry, and Donald on Danny the horse in 1960

which I hated to do since I thought I could do something more fun, so I decided I would wear my swimsuit and tan while I was doing it so it wasn't a total waste of my time. I found out years later that the boys who always helped daddy did it because his daughter drove the tractor in her swimsuit. Guess I was really naïve. Momma always took daddy lunch when he was in the fields. She would take her embroidery or crocheting with her and sit and wait until he came to eat. One day I was with her and daddy and my brother Donald were farming on the farm that had rattlesnakes on it. Momma and I walked down the lane very carefully with her watching one side and me the other. We finally got to them and my brother played a trick on my momma. He had killed a rattler before we got there, curled it up in the tractor toolbox, and then asked momma to go get a tool out of the box and surprise, what a scream!

In the mid-1960s, our milk barn caught on fire from lightning around 9:30 p.m. Momma, daddy, and I were all in bed asleep. My brother had just gotten home from work and he heard the loud clap, looked out the kitchen window, and saw the fire coming out of the barn. He woke daddy and of course, momma and I awoke too. My brother ran to the barn and tried to open the doors to get the tractor out, but flames had totally engulfed the barn. The fire department from Farley, Missouri got there with a tank of water. There was no putting out the fire, but they helped spray water on the other two barns and a gas tank

242

that had just been filled to keep them from catching on fire. We also hooked up hoses and sprayed the house roof. We did lose the tractor, 28 cats, 3 baby calves, and all of our milking equipment. A neighbor came over and helped my parents milk the cows until they could get some new equipment. Firemen said if my brother had not come home when he did that all the barns and house would have been up in flames.

We also had a large garden with quite a few strawberries. We canned and froze garden items, which kept us in lots of food. We had a party line and if someone was talking when you picked up the phone, you knew the neighbor beat you to the phone. Momma and I were so excited the day daddy brought home a real washer. We had electric washer, but you had to wring the clothes through the ringer on top and it was so much work.

When we first moved into the Platte City School District, the school was overcrowded so the 6th graders had to come via bus to school and get on another bus and be bused to Linkville Missouri School. Thank goodness, this was only for one year. My junior high school of 7th and 8th grade was in the old high school building. I remember that Mr. Neal nominated me to work in his office during my study hall, which I loved to do except when a classmate, mainly boys, would walk in and be taken into the principal's office and it was not sound proof and I could hear, "Whop! Whop! Whop!" Now I hated those days. I still to this day remember the first boy that I got to experience this sound from, but I won't tell; it's a secret.

Sweet 16! We would ask daddy if we could take the car to town and most of the time the answer was yes. I would go get Penny and Patty and we would cruise around Platte City for several hours. Of course, we didn't want daddy to see how much gas we wasted, so we pooled our money together and got a couple quarters worth of gas. My senior year in high school, my daddy got a new car, so he said he would trade me Babe, my cow for the old car, a 1963 Tan Chevrolet Impala four-door. At the time, I thought that was a cool deal, that is, until my cow started having babies and daddy collected the money for their sale. I had a smart daddy!

The Teacher's Nap
By James Mills of Big Spring, Texas
Born 1939

I was born and raised in the small, rural town of Chula, in north central Missouri— population 214, which is about the same today. My dad worked for the post office. His job was to pick up the outgoing mailbag each morning, afternoon, and at night, take it to the train station, and hang it on a hook on a pole. The train did not stop, just slowed down enough for them to grab the mailbag with a hook, and kick the bag of incoming mail off the train, which he would then pick up and deliver to the post office.

One of my earliest, but not good, memories is of our home burning down. At the age of five, I was sick in bed with pneumonia. Daddy got up that morning as usual, about 4:00, to go to work. When he opened the kitchen door to leave, it created a vacuum, sweeping fire through the house. My parents were preoccupied with fighting the fire, completely forgetting about me. Had it not been for my older Sister Bessie, I would not be here to write this story. She was my hero, as she remembered I was lying sick in bed, came to rescue me, and carried me to a friend's house. Our home burned to the ground and everything we had was lost. We then moved into a two-room house where we lived several years.

My Sister Dixie and I walked to the small school where everyone knew everyone else. My 1st grade teacher, Ms. Jennings, was very old. At the time, I thought she must have been 90 years old! I remember that she would take a nap every day after lunch while sitting at her desk. We all looked forward to that time, as no one stayed in his or her seats! My 2nd grade teacher, and my favorite, was Mrs. Johnson. She was very strict and demanded our attention. She had her way of keeping ours, by smacking our hands with a wooden ruler or pulling our rooster tail hair. I am surprised I had any hair left after that year. Mr. Moppins, my 4th grade teacher, was a World War II veteran who seemed to be still practicing war tactics with the students at recess time.

We were extremely poor. Our house had no running water, an outside toilet, and a coal stove for heat. I can remember waking up one winter morning and going in to wash my

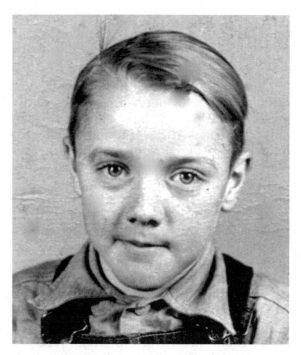

Jim Mills in 1945

face, found the water in the pan was frozen. I walked the mile or so to school, often with a sole on my shoe flapping all the way. Thank the good Lord at least I had shoes! We ate a lot of beans and cornbread and fried potatoes with fried chicken occasionally. Daddy had a small flock, which gave us eggs. A farmer let me raise a few pigs on halves and let me take care of a cow for a time, which gave us milk.

At an early age, I began working to help provide for our family. When I was eight years old I worked for a farmer, running a Poppin' Johnny (John Deere tractor), during the summer. At the age of 11, I helped to build a brick home, by mixing mortar and carrying bricks. During high school, I had a full time job at Kolbohn Bakery in Chillicothe, working from 11:00 p.m. to 7:00 a.m., as a pastry baker. I also had a part-time job, after school, helping to lay carpet for a furniture store.

I met my sweetheart Judy when I was 17 and she was 15 at Lamp's Grocery, a small store where she worked, owned by her sister and brother-in-law Clyde and Ruby Lamp. I joined the U.S. Air Force at the age of 18 and we were married six months later at the ages of 16 and 18. We will celebrate our 55th anniversary on April 28, 2013. We had four children (one recently deceased), seven grandchildren, and at the present time, have five great-grandchildren.

After my time in the Air Force, I worked at various occupations, the latest being Pastor of a small Baptist Church, from which I retired last year. I will continue preaching God's word, whenever I am called upon, as long as He allows. I would not trade or take away from what I call the "Good Ole Days." I treasure each memory and thank my God for all His blessings throughout my life.

Shopping at the Grocery Store
By Vaden Hopkins of Gladstone, Missouri
Born 1917

I was born at home on August 15, 1917 in Revere, Missouri. My family moved to the Kansas City area when I was about a year old to look for work. My father left when I was about three. Clark County was filled with my relatives, the Days and Christy's. I was able to visit our relatives in the Revere-Kahoka area when I was a youngster. I wasn't in school yet, or it was summer and I was visiting with my Aunt Neve and Uncle Oath on their farm.

The old farmhouse had 10-foot ceilings, had no closets, and used Chifforobes to put clothes in. The chifforobes were so large they had to be brought into the house through the upstairs windows because they would not go up the steep staircase to the upstairs. There was no heat except through the floor registers from the downstairs. There were four bedrooms and we use to sleep in feather beds. My Aunt Olive and Uncle Arthur (Aunt Neve and Uncle Oath's daughter and husband) had a bedroom downstairs off the living room. There was a

Harry, Vaden, and Myrtle Hopkins around 1919

244

Vaden Gilbert Hopkins seven weeks old

large kitchen with a big dining table. A large cook stove was on one side of the kitchen with a water tank on one end for hot dishwater, the oven in the middle and several burners on the other end. There were shelves lining the wall, which held the "mustache" cups for Uncle Oath to drink his coffee from. A big separating machine stood in the corner for separating the cream from the milk. There were swinging doors into the parlor and large dining room from the kitchen. There was a small glass windowed lean-to porch on the back of the kitchen where they had a little five-legged table with porcelain wheels to hold crocks of milk until it clabbered. They hung the soured milk to drain and made cottage cheese or fed it

Olive, Myrt, Grandpa Day, Aunt Neve, Lynn, and Vaden's mom

to the chickens. They would keep a bucket of corncobs on the porch to make a hot breakfast fire or a bucket of coal or wood for the day fire in the old cook stove. They had a 12-foot wide porch around the house from the kitchen door to the front door. Often time's traveling salesmen pulling small wagons behind their trucks came through the area selling kitchen utensils, spices, and seasonings. All of these purchases and dealings were usually held on the big front porch of the house.

One Saturday evening after chores were done, they hitched the team to the wagon and put a quilt in back for me and drove to Peaksville to the large one-room grocery store. There were shelves from the floor to the ceiling. They had a long handled pole with a clamp on the end to reach the high shelves. Aunt Olive would give her list to the grocery man and they would gather and visit while he filled their grocery order. They would trade a crate of eggs and a big cream can full of cream for the groceries. Aunt Olive would take two ½ gallon buckets with them, one to fill with peanut butter and the other for syrup from the two large barrels at the end of the counter.

The Brown family lived in a house behind the grocery store. They had three girls and we would play hide and seek by the full moon while the adults visited and the grocery order was filled. After Aunt Olive and Uncle Arthur sold the farm and moved into Kahoka, Missouri many years later, my wife and I, along with our family, still visited them. On one of our visits, Aunt Olive said she wanted to give me the little table from the back porch of the farm. I rented a trailer and we took it home. It was solid oak with five legs and little white porcelain wheels. I removed 10 layers of paint from the table and then refinished it with clear varnish. I still eat my meals on it and think about the good times we had through the years.

Under Quarantine
By Dorothy Roberts of Bethany, Missouri
Born 1921

On the afternoon of April 18, 1921, a baby girl named Dorothy Rhea was born to Elgin Merle and Lorana Vista Hickman, on a farm northwest of Ridgeway, Missouri, in the Buckley Chapel community. There had been

Dorothy's graduation from high school in 1939

a big snowstorm so the snow was over the fences, which blocked the roads. At that time, babies were born in homes and the doctors came to the homes. Dr. Lake Brewer of Ridgeway could not make it so Dr. Robertson of Eagleville came after neighbors helped find a route through fields.

When I was three years old the family moved 4 ½ miles northeast of Ridgeway in the Pleasant Valley community. I started 1st grade where they taught from the 1st grade through the 8th grade. I went all eight grades there. We walked ¾ of a mile to school. This was a one-room school with a small room for a library and a hall for wraps. There was a large stove with a jacket, which burned coal, carried by the teacher or larger students, in a coal hood from a coal shed. We had a well to supply water and had outdoor toilets, which were cold on winter days.

When I started 1st grade there were 21 students with only 20 desks. Hurbert Sutton was also in the 1st grade and brought his desk from home. We had several programs for the parents and neighbors. Each fall we would have box suppers where girls and women brought decorated boxes filled with food. They were auctioned off for the boys and men to buy. They would also give one cent per point for the man with the dirtiest feet, most lovesick couple, etc. We also had a Christmas program where we drew names and had a gift exchange. On my first Christmas program, Hurbert and I were to play marbles on the stage while the rest of the pupils sang "School Days" behind the curtains. As a girl, I did not want to do this and was so happy

when Hurbert forgot his marbles. This was during the depression days and we had a large family, so mother made me a dress from a pair of brown wool pants. It was not very bright so my teacher put a red crepe paper hanky in the pocket. Country schools years were only eight months.

The house we lived in was an old, small, four-room house. That was a little crowded for nine people. My four sisters and I slept in one bedroom in one full and one-half bed. In the wintertime, we slept on a thick feather bed under several heavy covers to keep warm. On very cold nights mother would heat bricks in the stove, wrap in newspapers, and put at the foot of the bed to keep our feet warm. We went to the outside john no matter how hot or cold it was. This was a good time to shop through the catalogs, especially when it was time to do dishes or other chores. As we had no bathrooms, we took baths each Saturday in a round washtub. In the winter, we could get close to the heating stove and put a blanket over the backs of two chairs for privacy.

We had cows to provide enough milk, cream, and butter for family use. We used a cream separator to separate milk and cream and sold cream. We churned butter with a daisy churn where you turned a crank or a stone churn with a wooden dasher we worked up and down. We raised several pigs and butchered some for our meat. As we did not have freezers, we cured and canned meat. We would grind our sausage, fry it down, and can in jars. We raised chickens each year. Mother

Wayne and Dorothy Roberts in 1955

would put eggs in an incubator in the cave. She would turn eggs every day and then let them cool a while. She would piece quilts while they were cooling. We would fry the roosters and keep hens to supply eggs. We would sell eggs and cream to do our trading or buy groceries. We always had a big garden and canned all the fruits and vegetables we could.

As farmers were busy in the fields during the summer, there was always a large crowd in town on Saturday nights. We would usually stay until midnight visiting with neighbors and friends. Our allowance was five cents, which we could buy a large sack of candy with. If there was a Shirley Temple, Jane Withers, or Will Rogers show in town, we would get 10 cents to go to the show. Shows were 10 cents for children and 25 cents for adults.

As we walked to school and it was so cold, we wore boy's long underwear and long cotton ribbed stockings. We could wear jeans to school, but we were not allowed to wear them during school hours. Mother did the washing for nine people on the washboard and then later on a hand powered washing machine. We did not have running water so we carried wash water in to heat on the stove and then carried it back out when the washing was done. Clothes were hung out on the line except in the cold wintertime. We would put quilting frames on chairs around the heating stove. We carried our drinking water in a bucket and drank from a dipper. Mother could always tell if we had been into the peanut butter, as we would get a drink afterwards.

My first money I earned was when I was about 10 years old helping an elderly neighbor by making a garden. She gave me $1.00 and I bought a new dress. Our clothes were homemade or hand-me-downs. We furnished our own entertainment. We had an old brooder house for a playhouse. Our dishes were old pans and tin cans. In the winter, we would cut out paper dolls of the family and furniture for each room from old catalogs. We made good use of the Sears Roebuck and Montgomery Ward catalogs. When we got all the paper dolls, we wanted they would be taken to the john to finish using.

Our meals were cooked on a wood cook stove, which also made the kitchen warm in the winter and summer. We bought flour in 25-pound sacks as we baked our own bread. It

Dorothy's children in 1945
Annette, Raymond, Noveta, and Janice

was a great treat to have a loaf of store bought bread. The white flour sacks were used for tea towels and flour and feed sacks were used for dresses, shirts, and other clothing. All of our clothes needed to be ironed, as there was no permanent press. We had three irons with one handle. We kept two irons on the cook stove to heat while we used the other iron.

A special treat in the summer was ice cream as we had a two-gallon freezer. We used our own milk, cream, and eggs. All we needed was ice, which we would buy at the icehouse in town. In the winter, we enjoyed popcorn and milk. We never went on a vacation. My vacation was to spend a week with Aunt Jennie who lived about five miles from us. I always enjoyed this. One day we were in the basement and I looked at the sun shining in the window. I said, "Look at that dust." Aunt Jennie said, "That isn't dust, it's the sunbeams." From then on, it was sunbeams to me.

Our farming was done much different then. There were no tractors so farming was done with horses. Plowing was done with a walking plow and two horses. You needed to walk behind the plow and hold the handles so you tied reins together around your waist to guide the horses. For a disk, you used four horses, harrow two horses, and corn planter two horses. Corn was cultivated with horses two or three times each year as there were no herbicides. Corn was picked by hand with horses on a wagon with a high buckboard to throw corn in the wagon. It was then scooped into the corncrib. Hay was mowed, raked, and stacked loose or put in the hayloft loose.

We had a Model T Ford. It was opened on both sides, but in the winter, we had waterproof canvas to enclose it. We had a long rock hill to go up when going to town. Sometimes the Model T did not have enough power to pull the hill so we would walk up the hill and sometimes push the car to get up. At that time, most of our roads were dirt, so ruts got pretty deep when it rained. Each farmer took care of his or her part of the road. Road drags were made from two boards about 2'x8'x2' and were fastened about 4 feet apart and pulled by a team of horses to smooth out ruts. In wintertime farmers worked together to scoop snow out of the roads by hand.

The year I was in the 5th grade Thelma and Deloris got sick during the bad winter. The county health nurse came to our house and said they had Scarlet Fever. She put a quarantine sign on the house, which meant no one in the family could go off the land as long as the sign was up. We could also have no company. As soon as they got over Scarlet Fever, Hazel and Garvin took it. They just got over it when I took it. We had to be in bed for at least two weeks. As soon as we all got over the Scarlet Fever, everything in the house had to be fumigated. We missed four months of school that year, but our teacher helped us and we studied a lot at home to catch up on our studies so we could pass. The next year Leroy took Diphtheria so we were quarantined again. The doctor gave the rest of us shots so no one else took it.

When I started to Ridgeway High School, I rode a small school bus when the roads were good. When the roads were muddy or drifted we went 2 ½ miles in a box school wagon drawn by horses. The last two miles were gravel roads so we rode the school bus on to school. It took quite a while to go by horses. If it stormed during the school day I would stay with my Uncle Ira and Aunt Gladys Chapman who lived in Ridgeway. In the spring of my freshman year we moved two miles north of Ridgeway on blacktop roads so we rode a large school bus. I went all eight years of grade school at Pleasant Valley School and four years at Ridgeway High School where I graduated in May 1939.

On July 22, 1939 I married my husband, Wayne Roberts. We moved northeast of Blythedale on a farm where we worked for a college professor in Iowa for 12.5 cents an hour. We had a lot of snow that winter. When the roads were too bad for a car Wayne would walk a mile then ride the train to Blythedale for groceries. We had a lot of gooseberries on the farm. Wayne would usually pick gooseberries, but sometimes I would take all four kids and help pick. One year I canned 80 quarts of gooseberries. I always had a big garden and canned a lot. Wayne would have a large woodpile to saw every year.

Pack Rat with False Teeth
By Stan Peery of Jamesport, Missouri
Born 1933

This story is true. Joe was a bachelor living alone. He lived in an old farmhouse with an attic with an opening to get there if necessary.

Joe had been missing things like scraps from his table. He had heard some noise in the attic like a mouse, which was common in his house. Then one night something happened. His false teeth, which he kept in a cup on the table, were missing. He decided to get the ladder and look up through the opening to the attic.

With his flashlight, he could see back in the corner. There were bread wrappers and, yes, there were his false teeth.

When he told me the story I said, "Joe, what did you do with your teeth?" He smiled and said, "I'm wearing them."

Joe said, "I guess it must be a pack rat. I've never seen one but always heard of them."

Scrappy in Shanghai
By Dorothy J. McLaughlin of Kansas City, Missouri
Born 1920

The love of my childhood was my cat and dogs. I remember one sad incident when the cat and dog were playing together. It had rained and water from the downspout had frozen. Kitty Cat was small and slid under the house. When Scrappy the dog came along, he was not so fortunate. He hit the brick corner of the house and broke his neck and died instantly. When I came upon the scene, I broke out in tears. My mother came out and saw what happened; she was sure the angels were singing "Amazing Grace." It was such a catastrophe that all the neighbors came around, even Mr. Cooper who owned the place.

Thelma, my friend from Kansas City, loved cats and dogs. She had her parents bring her down to see me to find out about Scrappy and Kitty. "Are you going to bury Scrappy in Norborne or in Shanghai?" Shanghai was on the farm with about a dozen houses scattered around, the original house right in the middle, along with the Court House where people came to vote. We buried Scrappy in the orchard under the apple tree. People ask if I got lonely. "Not on this farm, you don't!"

Extreme Weather Around 1937
By James D. Parman of Billings, Montana
Born 1928

I grew up in Northwest Missouri, born on a farm near Worth, Missouri, in Worth County.

In 1937, we had an ice storm when we had sleet 3 to 4 inches deep. Then it rained and froze, forming ice 3 to 4 inches deep all over everything.

My brother, my sister, and I skated to school. One morning my sister lost her footing and ended up on her backside sliding all the way down a long steep hill. We carried our lunch in tin buckets and she scattered her lunch all over the hillside. We laughed until we cried.

Later in the spring while walking to school along the same trail to school, I jumped over a log landing on a bull snake and sat down on the snake. I believe it frightened the snake as much as it did me.

In contrast to the ice storm, about the same time, we had a very hot dry summer, which destroyed our crops, and in order to find something to eat, our pigs and turkeys spent the summer in a dense timber adjacent to our farm. They ate acorns from on the ground and the pig's hair and the turkey's feathers became very shiny from having eaten the acorns.

We went to school in a one-room schoolhouse through the eighth grade. We had a good life growing up on a farm. Our mother attended college long enough to acquire a teaching degree. She was excellent on an old sewing machine. She was an excellent cook and cooked on an old wood-burning stove. She canned everything, fruit, meat, and vegetables, because we had no electricity or running water. She churned butter, made bread, butter, cottage cheese, and made her own soap.

I feel blessed to have grown up on a farm.

A Howl That Could Have Been Heard In China
By Susie L. Berry of Atchison, Kansas
Born 1928

There are many humorous incidents that come to my mind about our childhood. We lived on a small farm in Northeast Kansas.

Our oldest brother kept himself busy tormenting his younger siblings. We five girls played house in the backyard under a shade tree. Our mother had given us some damaged kitchen utensils: a colander with no legs, an eggbeater that "clicked" and went off balance, a leaky pot, some big spoons, a measuring cup, and several other things. We were soooo happy playing out there. We had a barbed wire fence to hang our dishtowels, rags, and doll clothes on. There was a small creek that ran at the edge of our play area. That is where we got our water for our "baking sessions" and "cooking."

All of our "baked goods" were naturally chocolate because our main ingredient was dirt. Not just any dirt, as we made superior products, so our ingredients had to be superior. We wanted dirt free from chunks, bugs dead or alive, dried weeds, etc. Our dirt had to be free of all these things. We would work and work and scrape to get a pile big enough for our next baking session. We would then go to our "kitchen" to get containers to transport it to our working area. We no sooner left the selected soil when our oldest brother would come running and kick through it and scatter it in all directions. We would cry and go screaming to our dad.

It was a few weeks later that we found a fresh cow-pile that was still steaming. We very quickly and quietly carried our dirt and covered it up. We talked about how this was the biggest and best pile of dirt we had ever accumulated and was just perfect for our next baking session. We heard him coming and bragging about what he was going to do. We got away from the "pile" and hid behind some weeds.

When he kicked through the dirt, he let out a howl that could have been heard in China. He was going to tell our dad and he was going to whoop us until we bled. And our dad would put us to bed without supper for a month (Our dad never did such a thing). At supper that night when we were all gathered at the table, our dad looked directly at our brother and said, "You got what you deserved." That is all that was ever said about the incident and it never happened again.

Did I mention that we were all barefoot?

Squirrel in the Bed
By Patricia A. Jones of St. Joseph, Missouri
Born 1942

At the age of seven, we lived in a house that had a toilet in our shed. It was a stool that had a chain you pulled when you were done. At night, it was scary. You only had a flashlight to see to go. For years, this is all we had. Winter was awful and, yes, we used a slop jar. What made it worse was a man hung himself using this chain. Then our landlord put a toilet in a small closet, and was I ever happy.

In this same house, we heated water on the cook stove and our galvanized bathtub was placed behind the heating stove. We bathed both my sister and I together because it did not take the water long to cool down. We washed each other's backs. It was fun back then.

My sister was a tomboy. We never had a lawn mower, there was no grass in our yard, and we used the broom to sweep it instead. Then we would play marbles or cut the pie with her knives. We played a lot of hide and seek.

I pulled a chair up to the old wringer washing machine and by accident; my sister got her hand caught in it. I got an awful whipping. My sister's hand was scarred for life. We never got to help on washday again.

My grandmother cut out all of our dress patterns from newspapers. None were ever bought.

We had a pet squirrel: unlike today, no laws kept us from having it. When bedtime came, we pulled our rollaway bed out and the squirrel went to sleep with my sister and I.

We took care of our cardboard ice cards. You had several for what weight you wanted for delivery day. We ate the ice shavings out of the truck while he took ice inside the house.

Road Trip in a '37 Ford Coupe
By Lester Estill of King City, Missouri
Born 1920

In the summer of 1941, my good friend Gordon Howitt and I decided to see some of this wonderful country we live in. We were farm lads with little money, but Gordon had a '37 Ford coupe to go in. His uncle sold Pheister seed corn, and got us a job detasseling seed corn at El Paso, Illinois. In the drive over there, we used 5 gallons of motor oil. We only had about sixty dollars each and it cost us a little under a hundred dollars to get the car overhauled while we were working.

We both had relatives living on the West coast, so we decided to go work for the wheat harvest in North Dakota. We toured Chicago in one day's drive and spent the night in a cabin on a fishing lake in Minnesota. We rented a motorboat the next day and enjoyed riding around the lake.

Then, on to Minot, North Dakota, and a job shocking wheat. It was hot and the bundles were large and heavy. The only place for us to sleep was in a slatted corncrib. It would have been OK except that we had no mosquito nets, so after two or three days we quit the job. That night the last lodging available only had one bunk, which was no problem as we had folding cots, and usually just pulled off to the side of the road to sleep. We needed showers after working a few days, so we tossed a coin to see who had to sleep on a folding cot. Gordon won the bunk, but the next morning, the laugh was on him, as he found the bed crawling with bed bugs and was pretty well chewed up.

Lester's friend, Gordon Howitt

250

Lester Estill and Gordon Howitt

Then, on to Seattle, Washington, for a visit with Gordon's aunt and uncle and cousins. Glacier National Park and the Grand Coulee dam were in fairly early stages then. Little did we know then, that we would be back there for our military training in providing communications and ground support for the Fifth Fighter Command, which controlled all the army fighter planes in the SW Pacific, starting operations in Port Moresby, New Guinea.

Our next stop was Los Angeles, where we both had uncles and aunts and cousins. We drove down Highway 101 all along the coastline. We crossed the new Golden Gate Bridge (and sailed out under it a year later). My uncle took us deep sea fishing one day as part of our experience there.

After several days, we headed for Missouri. We went through Las Vegas, which was just a small town then. We slept in our cots one night on the south rim of the Grand Canyon. When traveling we ate snack food and relied on our relatives for a lot of our needs. While in Los Angeles, the battery on his car developed a bad cell and would not retain a charge. Consequently, as we didn't have the money for a new one, we had to carefully park on a high ground so that we could push it off to get it started. We successfully did that all the way home. I don't recall having any tire trouble on the whole trip; which was very unusual at that time.

Our next stop was Kingman, Kansas, where I had a cousin. We arrived dirty, hungry, and broke. She didn't know we were coming, but happily put us up for a night and cashed a

five dollar check for me (about what I had in the bank), so that we could buy enough gas to get on home.

Then we went on to Emporia, Kansas. We spent a day or so there with my Uncle Wilford and Aunt Lura. He took us out to his farm and we had great fun shooting jackrabbits with my .22 rifle.

On the last leg of our journey, we got to drive on the newly completed 169 highway from St. Joseph up to King City, Missouri. Our native home was in the heart of GOD'S COUNTRY; better than any of the wonderful places we had seen.

Adventures in the Old Mill
By Vincent L. Scott of Freeport, Texas
Born 1919

It stood there in faded grandeur. Five stories high above a half basement in a residential neighborhood of one and two story homes. Hundreds of pigeons nested in the upper floors and half of the many windows were broken. Doors and windows in the first floor and half basement were locked or boarded up in a futile attempt to keep adventuresome boys from exploring the interior.

Every boy in town who wanted to raise pigeons got his start by trapping adults or risking life and limb by climbing to those inaccessible recesses to take squabs from their nest. There were so many that you could specialize in the rare all white, blue and white, brown and white, mottled, etc. There was a lot of trading going on.

Most of the equipment was intact. When the business failed, the creditors engaged a local lawyer to look after the premises until a buyer could be found. Nobody wanted a flourmill during the Depression. I never got to ride the freight elevator. Before we moved into the neighborhood several older boys, who were playing with it overloaded it. It came down through the first floor stop into the pit, the counter weights broke off, and it went back up, fast. All but one boy got off at the first floor and he managed to jump off as it passed the third floor. When it got to the top, the cables broke and it crashed into the basement. That incident brought a temporary halt to playing in the old mill.

Every mill had a pond. Since this one was

251

not used, it only contained rainwater, which had not evaporated. No fish, just crawdads. These were caught with a gunnysack seine for bait at other fishing spots. One group of boys built a raft so they could seine the middle of the pond where the water was about three feet deep. After the raft became waterlogged, it sank with one of the boys and he had to wade out dripping wet and muddy to his waist. His friends immediately nicknamed him "Half Wet." In a few minutes, this became "Half Wit" which stuck.

As you would imagine, this incident caused a lot of concern among parents and city officials. With visions of 'public nuisance' dancing in his head, the lawyer/caretaker had the levee breached so that the pond would drain into a roadside ditch.

One summer a city boy came to spend a month with his grandmother who lived in the neighborhood. We who were about his age were enlisted to help entertain him. In due time he was shown how to remove the boards from one of the half-basement windows and roll through onto the stairs, which were next to the wall. We usually toured the mill in small groups of three or four to minimize detection, but never alone. This city boy became enamored with shooing all the pigeons from their roosts on the top floor and wanted to go up every day. One day when I was the only one he could talk into going with him, he bolted up the stairs while I was replacing the boards in the window. I heard him cry out from two floors above and met him coming back down, beating the air with his hands and crying. He had decided to tear down some yellow jacket nests and shoo them out of the mill! We beat a hasty retreat to our house where Mother doctored the stings on the back of his neck and down his back with baking soda.

We were also ordered never to enter the Old Mill again.

N. 4th Street Neighborhood in the 1940s
By Neal E. Arnold of St. Joseph, Missouri

This is the story about a neighborhood and some of the folks in it. It was the early 1940s and people were frightened. We were at war, but life in St. Joseph, Missouri, had to go on.

These people are some I remember, even though I was very young. For some unknown reason I have thought about those times often. I am 76 now. So this is my first 7 years.

We lived at 702 N. 4th Street in St. Joseph, MO.

There was Ms. Limmel, who lived upstairs that thought Germany would win the war.

There was my grandpa, who I looked up to. He had a minnow pond in the backyard and sold bait to fishermen.

There were one-room apartments that were at about 706 N. 4th Street that is where my grandpa lived. The units were called the Chinese Flats. I never knew why, I still don't. They had one room for each tenant, a total of 24 rooms: six up and six down on both sides. There was a bathroom at the end, total 4 shared by all the tenants. Later he moved to the state of Oregon to work in the shipyards.

There was Violet and Emerson Hughes, our next-door neighbors who was like family. They had an older daughter and son. The son's name was Jesse; he had poor eyesight so volunteered for the Civil service. The day he left to go to the train station, my mom took me out to the model A to tell him good-bye and I got my hand shut in the car door. A few weeks later his parents received a letter telling them the ship, *The Lady Hawkins*, was torpedoed, and several St. Joseph men lost their lives. Jesse was one of them. A brief time after that, the family received a letter Jesse had written, and he asked how my hand was doing.

There was the neighbor, Wilber Taylor,

Neal with his neighbor, Emerson Hughes

Neal and Norman bumming a ride

who worked at Walnut Products that kept us in firewood. We were very grateful for that.

There was Mrs. Boyer, who ran a small store south of our home. She would stand on the sidewalk until I got home, after my candy purchase.

There was a friend of my mother's who came by our house to sell/play Policy. I have no idea what that was. A form of gambling I believe. My mom called her "Dago" Mary. When I asked why Mom said because she was from Italy.

There was a crippled man pushing the Tamale Cart down our street.

There was the blind man selling brooms door to door. Mom always said a good broom had five strands of cord, and his did so she would buy his brooms.

There was Mary Sherman, who lived up the hill on 5th Street. She was a friend of my mother's. Mary never liked to pull her blinds during an air raid drill, so the Civil Defense Warden would have to remind her of the rules. The blinds were dark green to keep the light in. Mary had two sons, George and Jimmie. Jimmie raised carrier pigeons and sold them to the military, I was told by my mom.

There was the Army Air Corps fuel that was stored in town on our street. It came by rail to that point, and then Rosecrans Field was 5 miles away. At night in the summer with the windows open, we could hear the fuel trucks

coming. Back then they drug a chain with a round steel ring that sparked when it drug on the pavement. They thought this made the truck grounded, that practice was stopped long ago.

There was the policeman, Arch Albertson, who would sometimes walk his beat in our neighborhood. He was very nice.

There was the chain driven fire trucks built about 1925 that would come up 4th Street, which was a busy street, but the trucks only ran about 15 miles an hour.

There was a boyhood friend, Harold Cole. He lived across the street from me. He later became president of the St. Joseph Water Company, and he was also one of the first people to have a successful heart transplant.

There was the neighborhood pub called Dominos. They sold buckets of beer, if you brought your own bucket. The pub was divided into 2 parts, one sold 5% beer 6 days a week; the other sold 3.2% beer on Sunday only. They would give me an Italian hamburger when I went in with my grandpa. It was a real treat.

There was the small smoking steam engine that came up a high-rise trestle behind our house going to businesses like the Hillyards, Batreall Shoe Company, and many others. When my mom would hear the engine, she would hurry to the clothesline to take them in before they were covered with black soot from the coal.

These are a few of my early memories.

Dubious Dub and the Brand New Stop Sign
By Jerry Kincannon of Zebulon, North Carolina

This story is about the goins-on in a small town on a particular warm summer Saturday night, long before the Interstate highway was completed just on the other side of the tall sugared soil bluffs that stood about half way to the Missouri River, and hastened the painful decline of a rural Midwestern community, which even then, had little to brag about, economically speaking.

Let me tell you a little about the community of Fairfax, Missouri, where the goins-on were going on. If you enter town from the north, you quickly come to a point where US Hwy 59 makes a hard 90 degree left turn and becomes Main Street, easing up a moderate slope in an easterly direction for about 7 blocks to the top of the hill, and then starting down a steep grade a whole fifty yards or so from the east city limits sign. And, you, armed with this information, might now ask yourself...

"What kinda story worth reading can come out of a town only 7 1/2 blocks long?"

Well, to answer that, you might need to know a little more about some of the 7 1/2 blocks. We will start from the Texaco Station and Cafe on the west edge of town, which would be "Intersection A" and is where the Highway makes the hard left turn. Going east one block, passing the hardware store, bank (with its polished black marble facade), one of the three local grocery stores on the left and another on the right, and a small appliance store. Not to mention Ms. Bullah's, which had all sorts of novelties to be had, and the local pharmacy which had one of those warm roasted peanut machines which normally got about half of my available money...

OH, and Polly's, which also had all the toys and 1 cent candy one could ever hope to imagine and is where I normally got rid of the other half of my available money. Then you would find Intersection 1. This is where both the telephone booth and the local cop sit. Even though the cop normally stays up a little later on Saturday night than usual, the telephone booth always out lasted him. Well, that is except the Saturday night the town drunk decided the phone booth would look much better horizontal then vertical and made an immediate start of this city beautification project by running over it with his pickup truck, but that is another story.

Then proceeding up Main Street another block, past the dry goods store and blacksmith shop, which had a whole assortment of penetrating sounds and strange smells to keep any inquisitive young man busy for hours, and just past that still another hardware store. These could all be found on the left. The produce and hatchery (locally known as the "Hatch and Scratch"), Café, and DX gas station, with its big red and white diamond shaped sign, could be found on the right. And at the end of this block, there is Intersection 2, which marks the west edge of the City Park, and directly across the street from there is the location of the local Dairy Dinner, which used to be a Dairy Queen until the owner decided the royalties were too high and the two organizations parted company. But, not before a fight ensued over who owned the sign out front. The court decided that the sign belonged to the owner, but that the little curly Q on the top of the sign was a trademark belonging to Dairy Queen. So, Dairy Queen brought in a big truck and proceeded to cut off the Curly Q. But that too is another story.

Oh ya, back to the geography lesson... after passing along the south edge of the city park with so many giant oak and maple trees that during the summer not a single beam of sunlight could penetrate their overlapping branches and reach the soft grass of the park floor, you come to Intersection 3, the east edge of the City Park, where all the bored kids hung out, especially on Saturday nights. This group pretty well included about all the kids in town who either didn't have a date, or weren't out tryin' to catch one of the local High School teachers out foggin' up the windows of a particular model of Ford product (which should probably go unmentioned at this point) with one of the Senior Cheerleaders!!, but that is definitely another story.

Well, on this one particular Saturday night, we were all sittin' there watching all the big rigs roll down the seven blocks to the bottom of Main Street and fade out of sight around the corner. One of the guys came into town with a Stop sign that he figured one of the backcountry roads really didn't need. Well, it just happens that at Intersection 2 there was a survey marker post across the street from the Dairy Diner, and one of those looks a lot like the mileage marker poles on the modern interstates today. We all decided that the Stop sign would look a whole lot groovier (a word of the period) hung on top of that survey marker than it did in the trunk of this un-named person's car, so that's what we proceeded to do. With just a little bit of the bailing wire that was holding "Saint's" '54 violet Chevy together we snuck down through the park and hung that Stop sign on the survey marker pole.

Then something happened that we had not really expected. These big rigs came rollin' down the hill, and the first thing they saw was this brand new Stop sign... about just one instant before they saw "Dubious Dub's" police car—you do remember about the local

254

cop sitting by the phone booth, right? Well, in about one more split second, all you could hear is the skidding of eighteen tires on the pavement trying to stop on the EAST side of that new Stop sign. This, of course, was followed very closely by extreme laughter of the now not-so-bored kids at Intersection 3.

I did mention that there were no interstate highways around yet, right? Well our town got lots of big rigs rollin' down that hill, and they had all been "Six Days on the Road" and in a hurry to get home. Unfortunately, in about 30 minutes, after the smell of burning rubber and brakes and the lingering cloud of smoke got really heavy, "Dubious Dub" finally decided to burn a little gas to see about the goins-on that had been goin on. And to this day, I am not certain which was louder, the skidding of the truck tires trying to stop at that new Stop sign, or the squalling of our tires (sneaker soles for many of us) getting' the hell out of there before "Dubious Dub" saw that beautiful new sign for himself and would also, in about one more instant, figure out precisely who the culprits were.

Epilogue: I was told not long after writing this story (about 45 years after it happened and part of the story I never knew) that just after Dubious Dub saw the new Stop sign, he pulled into the DX station where a few of the crowd were sitting by then, and not to mention any names, but my old friend tells me that "Uncle Dub", in that slow, well meaning way he had, told them "I don't know where that sign came from, but I am going to drive up to the Sinclair station and back, and when I get back that sign best be off of that pole and on its way back to the pole it belongs on, or there is going to be a whole lot of trouble around here!" He did, and it was!

Good Food Made All the Hard Work Worthwhile
By Linda Lintner of Platte City, Missouri
Born 1951

Looking back on my childhood, I can't imagine a better life than the one we had on the farm. We didn't always have what we wanted, but we always seemed to have what we needed.

In many ways, I think growing up on the

Linda's grandpa in the tobacco patch

farm helped prepare me for life in general. My parents worked hard to provide us with a stable life. My mother was always at home doing the normal domestic chores. I sometimes wonder how she kept going every day. We were a family of nine, with four girls and three boys, and the chores were never ending. There was always something cooking on the stove and several times a week you would hear the hum of the ringer washer out on the back porch as Mom did the wash. We must have had a half a mile of clothesline strung up around the yard. I remember watching the sheets whipping in the wind and thinking how good they would smell that night.

Spring cleaning was an annual event at our home, which included everything from removing the cobwebs to washing the woodwork. The summer would bring the canning and the gathering of vegetables out of the garden. I especially remember the green beans and tomatoes. It seemed we would never finish gathering and snapping the beans. Canning was a long tedious hot job. I can still see the tomatoes boiling and my mother removing the skins. There are jars to wash and lids to find. Also, the pressure cooker heating up the house and hoping it didn't blow its lid. The finished product was stored in the cellar and by winter, we were all glad to have those canned goods.

Along with those canned goods, we ate a lot of fried chicken. We raised our own chickens, which is not the most pleasant of jobs. My mother would also oversee the chicken coop.

Linda's dad, Dean Lintner on the tractor in 1948

Baby chicks are cute to look at but they require constant care to keep them alive. They need to be kept warm with heat lamps, have enough room to run without smothering each other, and water and feed at all times. Occasionally, I would help out with their care. I recall the water device was a glass jar with a small cut out along the rim to allow the water to run into the trough around the lid. You had to fill the jar with water, place the glass lid on top, and invert it without losing all the water on the ground. The feed troughs had to be filled daily. Imagine doing this with 200 baby chicks running across your feet. It was usually a good idea to take a deep breath and hold it before entering the chicken coop. The smell and heat was so overwhelming that you sometimes had to go in and out several times before the job was done. Also, you didn't want to be wearing your best shoes, if you know what I mean.

Once the chickens were grown, they would either be laying hens for eggs or eaten. Plucking the feathers and cutting up the chickens was my mom's job because she didn't trust anyone else to get them clean enough. Like the canned goods, that big plate of fried chicken on the table made all the hard work worthwhile.

My father was a farmer and always busy working in the field. Whether he was preparing the ground for a crop, planting the crop, harvesting the crop, tending to the farm animals, chopping wood, or making repairs to broken down equipment, my father's job seemed endless. When you're not physically working the farm, you're planning the next day, worrying if the equipment will last another year, or praying for good weather.

Just as we helped around the house, we also helped out in the fields after school and on weekends. My brother and I hauled many bales of hay to the barn and stacked them in the loft. I had the easy part of driving the tractor while he loaded the hay bales on the wagon. I remember one incident when I made a sharp turn and dumped the entire wagon. Needless to say, my brother did not think much of my driving skills. One crop where the entire family got involved was the tobacco patch. There was always something to be done and we didn't whine very often about having nothing to do because we knew our father would find something.

Living on the farm however was not all work. Our parents instilled in us that you have to work for what you have. Just as we knew the canned goods and fried chicken were well worth the work, we also understood the kind of Christmas we would have and whether we would get new clothes and shoes for the school year, depended on the success of the farm crops. There was always time to explore the creek, watch the frogs jumping in the pond, swinging in the shade of a large tree, or going wherever your imagination took you. There was the weekly trip into town on Saturday night and Sunday school and church on Sunday. The Easter Bunny, Tooth Fairy, and Santa Claus always seemed to find their way to our house and birthday celebrations made each of us feel special for the day.

I'm grateful to my parents for giving me many wonderful childhood memories that helped shape my character to become the person I am today.

Trimble School's Playground Equipment
By Betty Williams of Edgerton, Missouri
Born 1948

I was a little girl growing up in Trimble, MO, and got the privilege to start 1st grade in a one-room school with 1 teacher, 30 kids, and 8 grades. This would have been in 1952. I walked with my older sister three blocks up the gravel road where the schoolhouse sat. There were two tiny buildings in the back yard. This was the bathrooms, one for boys and one for girls (the old 2 seaters)...

The yard had a merry go round that you hung on to and someone that could run fast would run beside it and get it going and jump on and you hung on for dear life. It also had two tall rope swings. I remember one girl coming in as a new girl and she was shy so when we went out to recess to play she got in one swing and twirled around and around but when she went to get off her long hair had gotten caught in the rope and she cried and cried when the teacher had to cut some of her hair to get her out.

The yard also had a teeter-totter. A huge board balanced on a metal bar. One of my first tragedies was when I got on the teeter-totter and the girl on the other side decided to jump off leaving me to fall very quickly to the ground. Besides scaring me and jarring me, I had a dress on (common in 1952) and it had got caught underneath the board so when I tried to get up I couldn't and so being the brave 1st grader I was, I started crying. My sister came and picked up the board enough to get my dress out and helped me up (very traumatic).

The yard's other form of play equipment was a huge giant strike. It was a big metal pole and about 15 feet in the air. It had probably 20 chains hanging from the top and they had handles that you hung on to and started running and then it would go fast enough you could pick up your feet and twirl and fly around. That went well until one day I was tired and dropped loose of my handle, which proceeded to fling backward, and it hit a little boy's hand that was in my grade. He got a black fingernail from the deal. He followed me around for weeks showing me his finger that I had hit.

When you went into the school, girls went

Betty Taylor in 1950

to the little room on the right to hang up their coats; the boys went to the left. Then we went into the main room where there were eight rows of desks and two huge chalkboards up front and the main desk where the schoolteacher sat. Each grade had from three to eight kids. The teacher taught 1st, 2nd, 3rd, 4th, and then 5th and 6th together and 7th and 8th together. So if you start on the odd year you went 1st, 2nd, 3rd, 4th 6th, 5th, 8th, 7th, and then went to high school.

In the first grade, the schoolteacher had been there a long time and that was her last year of teaching. She would drive to school from Plattsburg and one day she forgot to stop and hit the school building. If you didn't feel good she would have you lay on a table that was used for projects, etc. She would have spelling bees and if you didn't know how to spell a word you watched her mouth and she would silently mouth the letter you needed. In about the 3rd grade the town built another room on the back of the building and it was a kitchen. All the mothers took turns coming to the school and cooking the lunch for the kids. We also had a man that raised popcorn and 1 or 2 times a year he would come to school with cooked popcorn for all of us and would sometimes bring a half dollar for all the kids. When I learned to ride my bike, me and my sister would ride the bikes to school. One day going home I skidded on the gravel road going home and slid down the hill on my face. It was never pretty but when we had group pictures taken the next day I really looked a mess.

Later the town had the school just for six grades. The older kids had the option of going to Plattsburg or Smithville. Buses came to Trimble. After the 6th grade, I went to Plattsburg grade 7th, 8th, 9th, and then finished 10th, 11th, and 12th at North Platte. The school was closed but remained on the hill for a lot of years. I took my kids there one day in the '70s and showed them my school for the first 6 years. Later the school burned down and the town built a community building which is used for community functions or for family gatherings or auctions or reunions. The Trimble school holds a lot of nice memories.

In the winter, a farmer next door to the school had a little pond and he would take an axe to check the depth of the ice and if it was thick enough we all got to go to it with sleds or just our boots and play on the pond. One day we looked out the window and saw black smoke and flames coming from the middle of town. The teacher sent an 8th grader down to see what it was and it was someone's house but no one was hurt and it was none of the school kid's houses. I had new red boots on that day with fur on the top and after school, we went to the burned house and walked among the ashes and got to see the burned appliances. I had nightmares for 2 weeks from that episode.

During the summer months, I would put my dolls in my red wagon and covered them with blankets and walked about five blocks to my grandparents' house. In those days, it was safe to walk all through town. My grandparents lived across from the Baptist church where I went to Sunday school and church and every 4th Sunday the preacher came home and Mama fixed him and his wife a good fried chicken dinner. That was the church I was baptized in.

In the winter we had a hill and sharp corner in front of our house and when the snow got real deep the people that got stuck on the corner would knock on our door and my dad would dump the ashes from our coal burning stove and dump that under their tires and push and get them on their way. When I got older (about 9), I loved horses and a friend of my mom's loaned us an old mare and we kept her in our little pasture and I rode her all over Trimble. Of course I couldn't get back on if I got off so I had to always came back home before I dismounted. One day when my mom was bringing her up to the house so I could ride her, the mare decided to take a big bite out of Mama's hind side so she had to go back to the farmer. Later we moved 4 miles to Mama's farm and I had a little pinto mare that

I rode every day after school in the woods and I was even in the Dearborn Saddle Club and we went to horse shows and I was in the drill team that the saddle club had. Those were fun, fun days also.

Horse Trading With Jesse James and Other Stories
By Rebecca Ann (Howe) Taylor of Trenton, Missouri
Born 1935

I was born on a farm 5 miles from Spickard, MO, and about 12 miles from Trenton, MO, in December 1935. My parents had seven girls. Three of them died in infancy before I was born.

My grandfather, Matt Howe who was in his '80s, lived with us until he died at 99 years of age. He looked like pictures of Santa Claus. He had a long white beard, a big white mustache, and big bushy eyebrows. Mom would shave him now and then. He taught us girls to count, our ABCs, memorized little poems, etc., before we went to school. He wore glasses when he was younger, but the doctor said he got "second eyesight" and he could see and read as good as anyone when I was born. He also didn't have any teeth left but could eat almost anything, except cornbread.

We had kerosene lamps, one wood stove to heat with and cook on, a wringer washer, old radio, old crank wall phone, a wooden icebox outside on a small step, and water in a well outside with a pump and handle that would go dry sometimes and Dad would haul

Rebecca's mom, Dessie, her dad, Earl, Pa Howe, Dixie, Becky, and Barbara in the '40s

258

water from town. And, once in a while, he would climb down in it to clean it out. That was scary.

We went to a one-room schoolhouse, Denslow School, about ¾ of a mile away. Half of the way was a dirt road and the rest gravel. The dirt road was bad in winter, so we girls went through Dad's pasture down to the gravel road a lot. I went to 1st grade when I was five and the teacher asked if any 1st graders could count to 100. She said she'd give a nickel to anyone that could. I was very bashful, but held up my hand and did it and got a shiny nickel to take home. No one else did it.

One year, in the '40s, they couldn't find a teacher for Denslow, and they told my oldest sister, Nellie Howe if she'd take a test and pass, she could teach. She was 11 years older than me and had a little college, so she did and taught all three of us for 2 years and was responsible for getting hot lunches started in country schools in MO. Boy, were they good. It was strange having her teach us, but we made good grades. She could help us at home, too.

One winter one of the lady schoolteachers boarded at our house. And for 1 or 2 years, we had a man teacher, Franklin Bosley a bachelor, that had a twin brother, Fredrick Bosley also a bachelor and teacher. They lived together until they died in 2012. They looked so much alike, I couldn't tell them apart sometimes. They were in their 90s when they died.

One winter day, we were walking home from school, and it was snowing so hard we could barely see the road, and all at once, a car appeared in front of us. It was an old couple that lived down the road, and we hurried to get out of the way, but I slipped and fell down and crawled to the edge of the road but felt a tire scrape the bottom of my foot, and they never saw us. Mom heard the woman talking on the phone to someone else that evening and she said they never saw a soul on the way home.

Another scary thing that happened was to my grandpa. Dad was gone to town, and we had about 20 hives of honey bees, and one hive swarmed and lit in a tree, and Grandpa got a pan and was pounding on it to get them to come out and go in their hive, and they landed on him instead. Mom called the old doctor in Trenton and he came out and gave him penicillin shots. He was down for a few

The house that Rebecca was born in 1938

days then up and ready to go. We picked out many stingers and were afraid he would die, but he didn't. The bees were between our house and the outhouse, and they liked to get in us girls' hair, so we'd run to the outhouse and back, but they usually got us anyway and stung us.

We girls usually had homemade clothes and were handed down as long as they lasted. Mom made quilts for every girl, and later after I married and had twin daughters, Lisa and Teresa Lynn she made "sunbonnet girls" quilts for their twin beds. Our twins are 50 years old now, and were a month premature, born in the hospital in Trenton and weighed 4 lbs., 1 oz., and 3 lbs., 7 oz., so they stayed in the hospital a month and in the only incubator the hospital had most of that time, sometimes naked and sometimes in tiny plastic diapers. I went to the dime store (Kress) and bought doll dresses to take them home in (I still have them), and they went to their feet. They were identical, so we left hospital bracelets on them as long as we could, and we didn't know we were having twins, so we weren't prepared. We had one bassinet and the other slept in a clothesbasket for a while. We stayed at Mom's for 8 or 9 months as they had colic and cried constantly. They are fine now, married, and have children of their own.

I spent some time in Phoenix, Arizona, where one sister, Barbara Miller lived after high school. I stayed with her in the winter and in Trenton, MO, with Mom, Dessie Howe in the summer, and worked part time in Phoenix. In the '50s, I got a job for a week or two as a movie extra at the fairgrounds in Phoenix for the movie "Bus Stop" with Marilyn Monroe and Don Murray. I got both of their autographs but have lost them during the years. I saw the movie at least 3 times but haven't seen myself, ha, and I was sitting a few bleachers behind

Ivan and Rebecca Taylor with their twin daughters, Lisa and Teresa in 1972

Marilyn. It was exciting.

I finally bought a car, a '57 Chevy convertible in Phoenix, aqua, with the pretty chrome, and a girlfriend, Beverly Davis and I drove to MO in it on vacation in the summer, and I met my husband, Ivan Taylor in Trenton, and he moved to Phoenix. We dated for 3 months, got married in 1961, moved back to MO in '62, and had identical twins. We have been married for 51 years and have three grandchildren.

My father-in-law, Thomas Taylor told us about a time when his father, John Price Taylor, knew Jesse James. John lived on a farm by Pattonsburg, MO, and Jesse and his gang would come by and trade for fresh horses, and Mrs. Taylor would feed them.

My grandfather, Matt Howe, told me about his great-great-grandfather, Noel Howe, being killed by Indians in a massacre in Iowa at Lake Okoboji, near Spirit Lake, in 1857, at his home. Seven children were killed and at least nine adults. My sister, Barbara Oswalt has a book about it called <u>The Spirit Lake Massacre</u>. She has been where it happened, but I haven't.

My husband, Ivan Taylor was in the army, but before I met him, in Japan in Korea, for 5 years in the '50s. There wasn't much fighting where he was. He was a Communications Specialist, so he climbed poles, strung wire, etc. Sometimes he'd spend the night out in the cold with only his Jeep for company, and wake up covered in snow. He had to watch for snipers all the time.

We girls worked in the fields with Dad, Earl Howe and one sister, Dixie Belle helped milk the cows. She was a tomboy.

A Pony Named Sparkle
By Donna Keever Pitts of Burlington
Junction, Missouri
Born 1947

I was born and raised in a little town in Nodaway County called Quitman, Missouri. The corner of northwest Missouri near the Iowa line.

My fondest memories were of Earl, Doris, and Sharon McDonald.

Their home was my home away from home.

Sharon was an only child and we were buddies. Best friends! We are still friends today.

Sharon had a pony named Sparkle, a dapple-gray Shetland. Just big enough for her and me. Now if a pony ran off when two girls came into the pasture, would you think it wanted to be rode? I don't think Sparkle wanted to be rode. Every time we would put the saddle on, he would make his belly swell! Therefore, we couldn't get the saddle cinched tight enough. Thinking everything was tight and ready to ride like cowgirls do, we got on.

Quitman had a back road that went around the town and back in like a "U."

I was in the saddle and Sharon in back. As we were trotting along the pony was startled by something in the road. Sparkle took off like a racehorse and, of course, the saddle started slipping off to the side. Over, over, and under.

Sharon fell off. I hung on. He finally came to a sudden stop. Sharon came running to us. Where was I? I was still in the saddle hanging on, upside down, looking at the underneath part of Sparkle's belly, wondering how in the world I was going to get off.

I finally managed to get out of that saddle. It was so funny.

Sharon McDonald and I had many of those funny and not so funny memories. Growing up in a little town called Quitman, Missouri, a dot in the road.

It was the Fourth of July about 1959. Sharon and I were about 12 years old.

We had been to town and got a few

260

fireworks, but we forgot our punk (a small twig-like stick) that you could light and then it would smolder so you could light your fireworks.

Not wanting to light a match every time, we sneaked one of her dad's, Earl's, cigarettes. It was a Camel cigarette, no filter. Straight stuff. Course you had to keep it going, so we took turns puffing on it. We really thought we were big time, smoking a cigarette. We even showed each other how we would hold the cigarette and smoke if we actually smoked.

Unfortunately, our fun turned to headaches and upset stomachs. Plus getting in trouble for getting Earl's cigarettes.

The Headless Chickens and Outdoor Movies
By Everett Dale Thompson of Savannah, Missouri
Born 1942

Can you imagine coming home from school and seeing 15 or 20 chickens running around in the front and side yards of your house without their heads?

Yes, that happened to me. I was eight years old when I came home that day. I couldn't believe what I was seeing.

I ran around the house and there was my dad with a chicken in each of his hands. He had them by the heads. Then he snapped his hands in a twist and the heads came off. The chickens started running around the back yard. Dad said it was their nerves that keep them running. Then they would just fall over.

Dad had a barrel that he cut in half and put on some concrete blocks with a tire under it so he could heat water. This is how he plucked chickens. ("Pluck," means taking the feathers off.)

He would put the chickens in the hot water, then take them out and start pulling the feathers out. The hot water made the feathers come out easier.

My dad raised chickens to sell eggs and chickens.

Years ago, there was a small community called Industrial City, which is now part of St. Joseph, Missouri.

This is where I lived. Everybody knew all their neighbors. The kids all played together after school and weekends.

There was not a lot to do except play games like Blind Man's Bluff, Kick the Can, and Hide and Seek.

Then we heard about the outside movies that they were going to show on Saturday nights.

They painted the side of the grocery store white for a screen. Then they would block off the road so people could sit in chairs or on blankets.

The movies would start as soon as it got dark. They would show three movies and a cartoon. Two of them would be funny and other a Frankenstein movie.

My dad sold popcorn and pop and they would take up a donation to pay for the movies.

As most people walked to the movies, they would talk about the movies on their way home.

We kids would try to scare each other by playing Frankenstein.

We had a great time at the movies.

A Long Friendship
By Ruby Lamp of Chillicothe, Missouri
Born 1931

I was born in 1931 in Chillicothe, Missouri. I had a sister two years older. We were as poor as church mice, but happy as meadowlarks. It was mostly the same food every day—rice and oatmeal for breakfast, fried potatoes, biscuits, and gravy for dinner. Our only milk was canned, diluted milk. My dad fished and trapped, so we had a lot of fish and rabbit. Momma made our dresses out of feed sacks. She was a wonderful seamstress. We lived in a two-room house. No water or electricity. We packed water from the nearest free hydrant. There were several in our town.

We moved to Idaho when I was nine. By then there was another sister. My aunt lived there and had wanted us to come out. Also had an uncle there. Daddy found work and we began having a better life. I met a girl and we became close friends. When daddy decide to move back to Missouri because the war had started, mom and us girls didn't want to leave, but he was afraid the West coast might be bombed. I watched my friend's house until I

Ruby, Bonnie, Judy, and Norma

could no longer see it. I cried all day.

We were 12 years old then and have kept in touch all these years. We send cards and letters on our birthdays, Christmas and exchange photos. I am now 81 and can remember her like I've been around her all this time. Another sister was born in Idaho, then two brothers and three more sisters in Missouri. Mom, one of the sisters and her husband went back to Idaho several years ago. They looked my friend up and visited with her and took pictures.

We've both lost our parents, husbands, and I've lost one sister. I've had a long, wonderful life and I thank God every day for my family and friends.

Born At Home
By Duane Taylor of Gladstone, Missouri
Born 1948

Christmas was in the air when I entered the world on December 23, 1948. My maternal grandparents' small farmhouse, devoid of indoor plumbing or electricity, was my place of entry. Attended by a doctor, non-hospitalized births were common in rural areas at that time. My grandparents were farmers, their small farm being located outside the small farming community of Lawson in northwest Missouri. At the time of my birth, they were still using horses for their farm work. Some

of my first memories were of the smell and sight of these animals, which I thought to be fearsome creatures. Great-grandfather farmed with mules. These animals were extremely tall and loud and I hated it when my father lifted me up to sit on them. My great-grandfather farmed all his life with mules and retired never owning motorized farming equipment.

Another custom of the time was for all family members to gather together one day in the fall for butchering day. A hog was slain and butchered, and the meat prepared and preserved for upcoming winter meals. Everyone had a job. The men's job was to butcher the animal and cut up the meat. The women's job was to prepare the meat for storage. My job was to stay out of the way. A hog was killed with a bullet fired from my grandfather's rifle. Next, he was placed into boiling water to soften the bristles for removal by a scraper device. Then it was skinned and disemboweled. I can still taste that home-cured, salty tasting ham and thick sliced bacon, served with farm fresh eggs and my grandmother's hot, homemade biscuits.

Jameson and Pattonsburg
By Deborah Dilks of Sibley, Missouri
Born 1951

From the day my parents brought me home from the hospital until I was almost six years old, I lived in Jameson, Missouri. While we lived in four different rental houses in and around Jameson in those six years, my most vivid memories were in only two of them. The first one was a red house with white vertical stripes that sat on the most northern road going out of town and straight to Highway 13. We didn't have running water in the house and the trek to the outhouse was a cold one on a brisk morning. We had a galvanized tub that we drug out from the back porch and placed in the middle of the kitchen floor. Cold water was poured into the tub and then we boiled water on the stove and poured into the tub until it was the right temperature. The kitchen could be closed off by shutting the two doors leading to other parts of the house and the gas oven was on with the door open to heat the kitchen. At three years old, I remember walking into the kitchen when my father was seated in the tub. I couldn't understand what all of the yelling to get out was about or what I did wrong, but I was promptly ushered out of the room by my mother.

By four, we had moved to the white house with green trim that was on the same road, but in town. The people who lived next door often babysat with me. They didn't own a car and had a wagon with two horses for their mode of transportation. They also didn't have electricity and used an icebox to refrigerate their food. Stepping into their house was a big step back in time with no modern contraptions such as a telephone. This was especially interesting since the local telephone operator lived right across the street from them and us. Frankie Trimble, the telephone operator, also babysat with me from time to time. In her house was a switchboard. I watched her sit at the switchboard, place the headphone on her head and the speaker hung around her neck. When it buzzed, she would plug a wire into the spot where the light was flashing and answer, "Number please?" She would then grab another wire and plug it into another slot and ring the call through. Sometimes, she would put me on her lap and allow me to plug the wires into the slots. We had a big, brown telephone box that hung on our wall in the kitchen. When it rang two shorts and a long, we knew the call was for us and my mother would pick up the earpiece and speak into the mouthpiece as she stood at the phone. If she needed to write something down, a pencil hung from a string and paper stayed on the tray for just such occasions. Probably out of boredom, some folks would pick up the receiver and listen to the conversation when they knew it wasn't their ring code. No one had any secrets in a small town and sometimes a private conversation was joined in by at least one busy body on the party line.

Main Street was two blocks away from this house and I loved to walk with my mom to Harry Wheeler's café, which was actually three blocks from us. Opening the screen door to his café, you were greeted with a big smile and a friendly greeting by the elder Wheeler (his son and grandson shared his name) who always wore a long, white apron and garters on his shirtsleeves, making him look like a gambler. Every time I entered his café he was always wiping down the bar, "What can I getcha?" I climbed up onto the high stool and looked at my mommy for permission to order

something. To the right, just inside the door, he had a soda pop cooler that was filled to the brim with icy cold water and bottled sodas. My reply was always a Nehi soda, either grape or orange. He would reach down into the icy water and pull the bottle out, wipe it off and use the church key attached to the end of the bar to pop the top off. When he placed it on the counter in front of me, a small piece of ice would slowly descend from the neck of the bottle. Sometimes I would put Spanish peanuts in the soda, a trick I learned from my brother and sister.

Best of all was the fact that this house was only one block from the revered Jameson Picnic. Tenderloins, homemade pies, baby shows, Ferris wheels, swings, carnival games, free drawings, and hometown people; all these things describe the "Annual Jameson Picnic." Jameson had a population of 120 people, but in early August, the population would swell to well over 500 returning to their roots, honoring a tradition that started in 1891. My beloved uncle would always give me and my cousins 25 cents to buy five rides.

You will notice that the first sentence of the previous paragraph doesn't mention the typical picnic things. The name is a misnomer, but the original Jameson Picnic was a picnic. Timed to occur right after harvest, the picnic has been in August every year but one and the weekend around August 9th is Jameson Picnic weekend. It was started to bring together the farmers and town folk in camaraderie after the busy summer farming season and celebrate the harvest.

Because of this celebration, August had always been a very special time of the year for the children in Jameson. It ranks with Christmas and birthdays for excitement and special times. Smells of popcorn and cotton candy mingle with hamburgers and tenderloins. Yellow lights outline the Lion's Club cook shack where most of the food is sold. Generation after generation of residents have worked in the cook shack and emceed the activities on stage. For three nights, activities are presented to the attendees. Thursday night is more for the locals, with a talent show followed by a local band. Friday and Saturday nights are the big nights where everyone takes part in making it a huge success,

Other Saturday nights in Jameson the whole town, carrying blankets and lawn chairs, would walk to a vacant lot at the corner of the two main business streets and pick out their spot for the evening. Bob Duly, who not only owned the local garage, but also served as school bus driver, would back up the school bus at the very extreme corner of that lot and open the back end of the bus revealing a movie projector. On the opposite corner sat a big, white billboard-type screen, where Bob would project some "free" movie to the townsfolk. I don't remember how he powered it up, maybe running extension cords from a power pole or from the garage. I just remember the movie.

In 1957 when I was six years old, we moved to Pattonsburg, Missouri where I started first grade. We didn't have kindergarten. My parents were excited to finally purchase their own home with the help of the GI Bill and with my brother and sister out of the house, (they graduated high school in 1956), and the two-bedroom bungalow had plenty of room for the three of us. Not only did it have electricity, but it also had running water! The water came from a well that, if you used too much water too fast, could run dry. So I learned to take a shower in about a quart of water. Jump in, wet down, turn the water off, and soap down. Then turn the water on and rinse off. Repeat for washing hair.

Pattonsburg was a whole new experience for me. I moved from having lots of friends within easy walking distance from my house to a house in the country and the nearest neighbor one mile away. I didn't know anyone, school hadn't started yet and with my sister and brother both joining the Marines, I went from little Miss center of attention to a very lonely little girl. Then my mother took me to meet the next-door neighbor, her cousin, who also had a little girl around my age. We became fast friends with a friendship that endures today. I loved it when my mom took me to visit Jan. She not only had cool toys, like a pedal tractor and a tricycle, but she also had a nice house with an almost vacant basement that we could ride those toys around and around in. When I got older, I learned to ride my sister's bicycle so I could ride to Jan's house whenever I wanted so we could play. I also learned that a mile in the opposite direction was another cousin with a little girl the same age as Jan. Her name was Evelyn. The three of us often walked the tree-lined country road beside my house that led to Evelyn's house. We gathered pretty rocks, talked, and shared several summer afternoons in the shady lane. Halfway between Evelyn's house and mine stood an old two-story house where the old man died on the front porch. When we came to "that" house, we always walked a little faster. Who am I kidding, we ran past it. As we got older, we became more adventurous and dared to walk around the house looking in the windows. Contributing to its ghostly appearance was the fact that it was fully furnished still—with no one living there!

Pattonsburg was at least twice the size of Jameson, if not more, and it had a lot of businesses lining its Main Street. It had a grocery store, not a general store, a dry goods store, a pharmacy, two cafés, three banks, a newspaper, a cap factory, a smattering of beauty shops, a barber shop, three or four bars, AND a movie theater! Saturday nights in Pattonsburg were a lot different than Saturday nights in Jameson. People came in from the country and parked wherever they could find a spot, and start walking up one sidewalk and down the other one on the other side of the street. Friends greeted each other and stopped to talk while other folks continued their journey. After dark and closer to nine o'clock, the crowd would start to thin out as one by one folks returned home. This, like the Jameson Picnic, was a long-standing tradition dating back to the turn of the Twentieth Century that is.

During the cooler months, everyone would crowd into the city hall where they would dance the Virginia Reel or a square dance or somewhere in the night the band would play the Shotsee (I'm not sure of the spelling of this dance), which was an old folk dance. Girls danced with girls, boys danced with boys, or boy girl, boy girl; no one thought anything of it. When the Shotsee started, we always linked arms and circled the dance floor—one, two, three, skip. One, two, three, skip.

In school, we practiced once a week, hiding under our open desks in case of a nuclear attack by the Russians. Nurses came to school to administer giving us TB tests and Polio shots. We lined up and one by one, we took our turn to offer them our arm or shoulder. From the Polio shot, everyone ended with a scab and when it dropped off it left a scar. Teachers were the ultimate authority and no girl wanted to have the stigma of getting into trouble with the teacher, heaven forbid she should get a spanking. Boys, it seemed were always in trouble, which meant they had to sit under the teacher's desk with a wad of gum stuck to their nose or they sat in a corner with a dunce cap on their head. Repeat offenders were told to lie across the teacher's lap or bend over as the teacher took the big wooden paddle that hung in view of everyone every day and gave several hard swats to the child's posterior. Girls were never allowed to wear jeans or slacks to school. We always had to wear dresses and on cold days, we wore slacks under the dresses.

Corky
By Iris Boyle of Jamesport, Missouri
Born 1930

From the time I was small I loved animals and had pets. One was a Plymouth Rock Rooster I named Dee Dee. I had one bunch of chickens and my mother another. When we sold them, I had my own money. Dee Dee weighed 14 pounds.

Another pet we had was a squirrel we named Bushy Tail. He slept in the sleeve of an old cowhide coat. When we turned him loose he came back to see us two years in the spring. He'd had his tail broke off so we recognized him, hence his name.

I had a dog given to me that was part Chow. It showed up in the big curl in his tail. He wouldn't stay home. Butch kept going to the same place so I asked if they would want him. Yes, they'd take him.

Next was a pup of mixed breeds. Showed Collie black and white fur and had short bench legs. I named him Corky. I spent lots of time with Corky. He wouldn't eat dog food, just table scraps. His favorite was biscuits. My mom made extra ones for him. When he thought it was time for breakfast he'd bark. My dad would go to the porch, feed him one, and he'd bark for another one until he was full or there was no more biscuits.

He enjoyed the 4th of July. We threw out firecrackers and he'd pick them up in his mouth and toss them in the air where they went off. We always worried they would go

Corky in 1953

off in his mouth, but never did.

We lived next to the railroad track and every day he went across the track. Corky got hard of hearing and nearly blind. Last time he went across the track a train ran over him and killed him. Corky was 17 years old. We wondered how long he would have lived. We had other dogs, which we thought a lot of, but Corky was special. He was my buddy.

The Good Life
By Duane Stuart of Stanberry, Missouri
Born 1939

I will start with a little history of how the Stuarts came to northwest Missouri. It started in Beanblossem, Indiana 1889. They came by horse and wagon. They sent machinery and large house goods by train to Gilford, Missouri. My great-grandfather and grandfather when they got to Gilford only one piece of land was left to homestead. Great-grandfather stayed. Grandfather, his wife, Eva, and his sister Emma went to Ravenwood to find land. Found a house in Ravenwood to stay in. The house had a solid walnut drop-leaf table and a walnut day bed.

I have these today. They got word there was land around Stanberry, Missouri. Grandfather and wife came to Stanberry and homestead. Emma stayed in Ravenwood. My father, Roy, was the youngest of 11 children to Edward and Eva Stuart. Dad was born 1913. They had a large garden. Dad always had a garden. Dad worked for a farmer his junior and senior year in high school in fall shucking corn. After school, he started farming.

My mother, Mildred Gunter, her father was from around Stanberry. He went to work for an uncle in western Kansas in a blacksmith shop in Studley, where he met Kate Morgan from Hoxie. Kate's father had come to western Kansas and homesteaded in the mid-1850s. She had six brothers and sisters. They lived in a dugout with sod roof. Where the dugout was, was a live spring. When the herd came through, they would have buffalo for meat. Also, Indians would come to get water. They pick up buffalo chips for heat in winter.

They met at a dance. My grandfather, Egbert Gunter, and Kate Morgan were married May 1, 1912 and move back to Stanberry. Kate had never seen a greener grass and good garden. They had two sons and one girl, Mildred. How dad and mom met was one of dad's older sisters taught at mom's school. They got married and started their life together. My sister, Beverly, was born February 1936. Roads was all full with snow. Dad went with wagon to get doc. Mom's mother was already there. I was born March 1939. In 1940, mom and dad moved to the farm where I now live 73 years later.

As a boy, I was outside doing something. We had a garden. Help with planting, weeding, and picking, get ready for mom to can for winter use. We had horses and mules to farm with, cows for beef, milk cows, sheep, hogs, chicken for meat and eggs. Four or five farm families in the fall would come to our farm to butcher. Dad had a big kettle to heat water. Would do five or six hogs and two beef that day. Would get a hog dressed so we would have liver for the dinner all the women would bring other dishes. The next day after meat had cold down would cut up sausage, make and cook the lard. Grandmother Gunter wanted the crackling to make soup.

My schooling, the first through seventh grade was at the Star school about one-and-a-quarter mile's walk each way, Eighth grade

I went to Stanberry. We rode in a panel truck with planks on each side. The summer '54 I got a job to work on a farm owned by the man who owned the five-and-dime store for $4.50 per day. If it rained, I could work in store, $4 per day. By the end of summer I had saved, I bought my first car, 1950 Chevy for $350. Dad paid my insurance first year. Worked other job in early '60s. Moved to Omaha Council Bluffs and work 'til 2001. Retired, came back to Stanberry to help mom with health problem. I feel I have had a good life.

Free Shows
By Jean E. Beery of Plattsburg, Missouri
Born 1932

Do you remember the "Free Shows?" I grew up in a small farming community where the main street of town was one block long. I am the oldest of three children. The one boy in our family did not come along until I was 11. Even though I am a girl, I also had the substitute role of being the only "boy" that daddy had for those 11 years. I worked along with daddy in the fields and also helped my mother with household chores. She loved to garden and to do the other work that required her to be outside. So I pretty much did the inside things such as ironing with a flat iron or helping prepare meals.

Neighbors would help each other with the crop harvest, and when it was thrashing day it was a busy day. When it was our turn for neighbors to come to help, it would take my mother and me all morning to prepare the noon meal. We would gather items from the garden and then prepare the food to have the noon meal ready for the ten or 12 people served. Each farmer's wife would gain a reputation for preparing the very best rolls or pies, etc. and the workers would look forward to that specialty being part of the dinner served at that farm.

After supper, in the evening, I would study my school lessons by a coal oil lamp, which did not give out much light unless you were right by the lamp. When the Aladdin lamp came along it was a big improvement. Well, Saturday night would eventually arrive and this meant that it was Free Show night in our little town. It also meant that I had to have the chores done when daddy came in from the field if daddy and mom were to take me to the Free Show in the park. The chores included the milking of the one milk cow we kept to furnish us with milk and cream, the gathering of eggs from the hen houses; where to my consternation the nest could also have a snake as well as eggs, and carrying wood for our wood stove. If the chores were not complete when daddy got in from the field, there would not be any trip into town that night. I did not want to miss a showing as before each main movie a serial would be shown that was ongoing from week to week and it kept you wondering what was going to happen next.

We would take folding chairs or blankets to spread on the grass to view the outdoor movie screen which was located near the bandstand in the park. If you got there early you could visit with the neighbors, and oftentimes the visiting would continue after the show, as people would stand around in the stores on Main Street or just linger on the sidewalks talking. This was the one night that you got some slack about bedtime. It is hard for me to believe when I go to see a movie now and the prices are so high that there was ever a time there was such a thing as free movies in the park.

Wash Day
By Irene Ellis of Missouri
Born 1926, Deceased 2008
Submitted by Peggy Smith, daughter

I was born and lived all my life on a farm. We had no conveniences, as we know them today. Work was hard. But being young and healthy, we accepted things as they were.

I was next to the oldest of a large family so I had to help with the housework and care for the younger children.

Washday was an almost all day affair. Water had to be carried in, heat on the wood range, clothes had to be soaked and then scrubbed on a washboard. White clothes were boiled after they were scrubbed, then rinsed and hung out to dry. It was an all day task.

I married at the age of 19. Of course, I married a farmer. I still had to carry in water and heat it on the wood range, soak and scrub clothes on the washboard.

I was allergic to harsh soaps so washdays were bad for me. My hands would become so dry and sore from all the soapy water, they would crack and bleed. Friend husband would help but this type of work was not his cup of tea.

One day he came home from town and announced he had looked at washing machines that day that was powered by a gasoline motor. Really, I couldn't believe what I was hearing. I didn't think we could afford one. A week later, he came home with a gas-powered washing machine, plus double tubs on rollers and a gas iron.

Needless to say, I was in seventh heaven. I still had to carry water and heat it on the kitchen range but that was minor. On washday, it set in the middle of the kitchen floor with the exhaust pipe run outside the kitchen door when in use. It was a little cool in the winter months but the convenience was so great we could put up with a little cool air. Just add a little more wood to the round oak heater.

I had a short paddle to stir the clothes and lift them out of the water to the wringer and swish them around in the rinse water and thru the wringer again.

What pleasure and how much better my hands felt and the washing was done in half the time. How I loved that washing machine and the gas iron. Ironing was made so easy. No more heating irons on the wood range. I could iron a bushel basket of clothes in an hour. Glory bee. Also, by this time we had seven children.

Rural electric companies began to develop and since we had purchased land, we began to anticipate getting electricity. Sure enough, by 1945 they were setting poles and stringing wire in our area.

We became very excited and got ready for it. We had our house wired for electricity and purchased a new refrigerator, electric washing machine, and an electric iron. These set in the house for three months waiting for the electric current to be turned on.

What a wonderful day it was when the electric current was turned on. The party lines were really busy.

As time went by, we enlarged our farming operations. We purchased another farm and remodeled the house on it. We installed a bathroom and had running water in the house with an electric hot water heater. No more heating water on the kitchen range. It sure sped up the family wash. How we loved it.

In 1965, I had to go to the hospital for some surgery. When I came home from the hospital, I found a new automatic washer and dryer in the basement. My good husband had them installed while I was in the hospital. I was so surprised, I cried. How much easier could was day get.

I love washday. Automatic washers and dryers and wrinkle-free clothes make washing so easy. I haven't discarded the iron. I still like to spray starch the shirt collars and lightly press a few things.

One of my daughters told me she loved washday as a child. She said when she came home from school everything smelled so good and clean. Of course, wash day was always a day for cooking a pot of beans on the back of the kitchen range. That called for some fresh baked bread with home-churned butter and molasses.

Of course, the rinse water was used to scrub all the floors (no wall-to-wall carpets then), the porches, and so on. We made good use of all that water.

Do I want to go back to those days? No, not really. They were happy days. A lot of hard work, but we were young and healthy. We didn't mind the work. We have a lot of good memories, a few sad ones mixed in.

We are retired now and I love my home in town, with all its conveniences. I now have time to putter around with flowers. I didn't have time on the farm. Life is still good and I love my automatic washing machine and dryer.

Best Time to Be Alive
By Randell McCloud of Spickard, Missouri
Born 1931

I was born July 30, 1931. I was born in the Depression years, times were hard. No one had anything, we was poor but didn't know it. We lived on a farm and growed our own food. Had a big garden. We had a milk cow and some hogs, chickens and mom would can stuff from the garden to eat all winter. Our home was heated by a wood stove and that kept us warm. There were seven of us kids and we all had chores to do and we did them. Back then, they paddled at school one time

Randell McCloud
A hard working man!

and when I got home.

The outhouse was out from the school and you would lift one finger or two if you had to go out there. You know, that is how the 100-yard dash got started. We went to a one-room school. All the grades in one room, first grade to eighth grade, and then you went to town to junior and senior high school. They called us "hicks." But the football coach loved to have us country boys on the team.

Our country home didn't have electric until about 1939. We had a kerosene lamp to see by, not very bright, battery radio. We kept the milk and butter down in the well. The well was our water supply and that would kept it cool and last longer. We would sat around the radio at night and listen to Jack Armstrong, Captain Midnight, Jack Benny, to name a few. We went barefoot all summer or 'til school started.

We had traps set to catch raccoons, skunks, opossum, mink. We would check them at mornings before school. We skinned them an sold the hides, all the way from 25 cents to $2.50. You had to be good if you could skin a skunk without hitting the scent glan.

We always went swimming on the first day of April in the creek we lived by, and it was skinny dippin'—no swimming suits. We play in that creek a lot. We would make believe farms and fences, cows and all we could think of. Then we would go upstream and dam up the waterway to hold the water back. When it got full we would break the dam and run back down the creek to watch the flood. We would find young trees, about 20 feet tall. Tried to pick Hickory or Elm, they won't break. Climb up in them and sway back and forth until we could touch the ground. No one ever got hurt.

I believe I have lived in the best time in history. I started farming out in a stump-filled field with a team of horses and a walking plow, planted it to corn and picked it by hand.

And now you see these nice John Deere tractors with GPS guidance systems and taking 30- to 40-foot wide tools, cell phones, microwaves, TV, jet airplanes, in-state highways, and nice cars that can driving through big cities without stopping. The early settlers wouldn't believe it.

Snake Killer
By Goldie E. Little of Chillicothe, Missouri
Born 1937

My sister was five years older than I was. We had snowdrifts high as the fences. She drug me to school as I was in the first grade. She got her feet frostbit. I came through fine. I love my sister very much. She is gone now. Sure do miss her. I was always getting into something.

Our schoolteacher was a man and he got one of the boys to dress up like Santa Claus. He would peak in the windows and scare some of the kids.

We had a well we drank from and only one tin cup. Sure was good water and a good excuse if we got tired of sitting.

We liked to kill snakes. There were plenty of black snakes around the farm because the chickens laid eggs in the barn. My oldest sister was going to get eggs from the manger. When she went to put her hand in to get them a huge black snake was having its dinner. She screamed and hollered for our dog. He was part Collie. That dog jumped in the manger and grabbed that snake. He started to shaking it and we all ran. Eggs were going everywhere.

My sister and cousin ran across a big black snake so they had an ax and hoe. One raised the ax and got its tail so it couldn't go anyplace. Then they tried to get the head but that old snake followed them around and around until they decided to one go one way and the other another until they finally killed it.

We loved to play in the creek. We built stuff in the sand. One day we found a water moccasin that someone, I suppose it was dad, had killed it and left. There were several babies crawling out of that snake. That's when we learned not all snakes lay eggs.

When I was about 14 mom and dad went to town and left us five kids at home.

I decided to help mom kill chicken. She had been cutting their heads off. Well, I decided to try one and make her proud. I lifted the ax, shut my eyes and put the ax over my shoulder, and let it down. When I opened my eyes I had cut its beak off. Knew I had to finish so kept chopping until the chicken's head was off. Needless to say, never tried that again.

Dad used to walk out in the pasture, so we tagged along. He asked me, the daredevil, to climb up in the tree then he said go out on the limb as far as you can. I did and the limb started to bow to the ground. We had more fun just climbing and riding the limbs to the ground.

My little sis and I loved to sit out in the shade and play our records on the old phonograph.

We used to take baths in a shed in summer and by the wood stove in the winter.

I had a favorite teacher. She always read from the Bible and say a prayer before school. We all loved her.

One time dad fill the haymow with hay. There was a place cut into the floor to put hay down to the cows, but the hay covered it, so dad told us to jump up and down in that spot. Of course there was a pile of hay below to fall through and land on. We jumped until we fell through. It was so much fun. Our little brother came out so we decided to take him with us. We sat down around the hole, took ahold of hands. When we fell through his eyes got as big as saucers. My sis and I laughed. She laughed so hard she took off for the outhouse, but never made it.

My sis and I were playing outside when we decided to sit on a log and rest. It was covered with red ants. They got up our clothes. Did we ever run for the house. Them things can really bite.

My two brothers decided to ride our horse so both got on but the one brother fell off right in a cow pile. Was he ever mad.

My oldest sister had a pet lamb and I wanted to feed it. She let me and it got too much air and died. We both felt sad.

My siblings and I liked to listen to The Lone Ranger and other programs on the radio, but we had to do our chores. Get in wood, get the cows up so they could milk. Gather eggs. Dad would take the battery off of the car and hook up the radio.

I liked to play with the neighbor girls. One

day, since they had no phone and we had no phone, they wanted to go to the neighbors since they weren't home. They had one. We called people we did not know and ask if their refrigerator was running. Then telling them to catch it.

I was raised on a farm. Dad was planting. He decided to take me and my older sister with him. It was a very hot day. He showed us how to plant pumpkin seeds then left us alone. We planted a while. Finally, we got tired so I decided to pour the seeds down a crawdad hole. We never told anyone until we got older.

Turkey Farming
By George Bowles of Bethany, Missouri
Born 1940

I was born April 29, 1940. The farmhouse was located in Harrison County, four miles north of Blythedale, Missouri. The house did not have heat, electricity, or running water. The roads were dirt. My dad went approximately five miles one-way to meet the doctor and bring him to the house with a team and buggy.

My first four-and-a-half years of school I walked one-and-a-half miles to a country school called "Cisco." The first eight grades were taught by one teacher in one room plus a coatroom. All children brought their lunch. In cold weather your lunch was partially frozen. The classroom had a coal stove for heat. Sometimes in the winter, my dad would come and pick us up at school with a team and sled when the snow was deep.

There were four children in my family and I was number three. I had one older brother, one older sister, myself, and one younger sister. My dad and mom worked hard to feed and clothe their family. We never went hungry. My mom had a wood cook stove for cooking and to heat the kitchen. On Saturday night, the old galvanized tub was put by the stove in the winter months for your bath. If you didn't do a good job cleaning yourself, mom did it and you didn't want that! We all had chores after school. Carry in wood, help milk by hand, and put livestock inside during winter when you were expecting offspring. You did your part! If you got a spanking at school, you went to the woodshed and got another when you got home. There was a good chance you had to cut

George Bowles

your own switch. Mom gave me a spanking once for going fishing. Bless her heart; I never got one I didn't deserve.

In those days, the neighbors all helped one another. In summer, harvest was the old threshing machine. There were more oats than anything else. There was lots of help with teams and wagons to haul in bundles into the threshing machine. I would estimate the crew to be around 20 people. When I was eight years old, I rode a 900-pound pony and was the water boy for the crew. I had two-gallon jugs that were wrapped with burlap. We used well water and no ice. You made your rounds, went and got fresh well water, and started around again. I got $1 a job, and was glad to get it. A job would last two to three days. The farmer you were working for always had dinner at their house. Once you started harvest, everyone on the crew helped out. No one quit until everyone on the crew was completely finished.

When I was nine years old, my dad and mom bought a 120-acre farm by Ridgeway, Missouri. It was located in Grant Township. The move was approximately 15 miles and was in January. I rode my 900-pound pony 15 miles that day. I finished the rest of my 12 years of school at Ridgeway. I graduated in 1958 with a total of 14 in my class. There were ten boys and four girls, and those girls were very well respected! I can remember shucking corn by hand to help my dad. On school days, I would get up early and shuck through the field then walk another half-mile to catch the bus for school.

I loved my family very much and I don't feel in any way I was mistreated or abused. I was taught respect. My first year out of high school I helped dad and worked for a farmer when he needed it. The farmer paid me $1 per hour. This was fair at that time. Gas was 16 to 20 cents.

At age 18, I went on the wheat harvest. We started in Oklahoma and ended in South Dakota. It lasted 60 days. I ran a combine with a 10-foot head. There were three machines in one crew.

I was no little angel. I sowed a few wild oats in my younger days. I got that out of my system and married the love of my life July 16, 1961. God found a way to put us together. I worked on a turkey farm for six years. Those people treated me as one of the family. The last year I was there, we raised 30,000 birds. When market time came (which wasn't all at once) we caught by hand and loaded semi's. My paycheck at the end of the six-day workweek was $42. This was appropriate for that time. I usually worked about ten-hour days. I was 21 when I married my wife. She was 18. We were in love, but after 44 years of marriage, we knew what love really was. I lost her with cancer July 4, 2005. Things will never be the same.

Self Service Hen
By Janice L. Miller of Trenton, Missouri
Born 1943

I was born at home on the 24th of February 1943. Mother, Gladys Taylor was assisted by two midwives, one of whom I got my middle name of Lucille.

Home on farm north of Trenton, Missouri, just off Route A. Farm owned by a Dr. C. H. Cullers and, later, his two sons, George and Robert. Not to get away from my story, these two boys were bankers.

This was a happy time for me. I was the youngest of a sister and seven brothers.

My dad, Tom Taylor and five of my brothers were always farm hands at this time in my life. Cattle, hay, crops, some hogs were raised. The crops were all put back into feed for the stock. On this farm was a foreman and 12 to 15 hands. Were five homes hands lived in.

The Doctor also had a big barn for show

horses, the high stepping kind, "gaited." Also, trotters that he showed and raced.

We raised large gardens, canned. All we needed from town was sugar, coffee, flour—we canned beef and salted pork down on closed-in back porch. The loin, liver, and heart had to be eaten right away because you could not salt it down.

I helped when I was old enough by cutting up fat for making lard. We would render it down in oven in large pans. A large bucket of homemade lard would last a long time. Hands were given one hog a year and one beef steer to share.

I remember getting in on dressing chickens for a meal, three at a time. Picking feathers off after mom put them in real hot water. Made the plucking of feathers easy. Then would hold them up over a fire and singe them. That would take care of what we did not get when pulling feathers.

Now when you removed the insides—"guts"—of the chicken, you had to be sure not to bust the goaul for it would spoil the chicken. This I was always told.

Cutting up a chick, I would have to show you. Ha!

Had a big, black kettle. Would build fire under it out back of house and we would cook beets in it, then we would peel off skin and

Bobby and Janice Taylor

271

can pickled beets—spices, sugar, vinegar.

After canning, we would listen for jars to seal, count them off. For you had to find the one that didn't seal and we would eat them next meal.

Back to the chickens, I was maybe 11 years old. We had a laying hen would pick on screen door, kitchen. She would come in, use wood box back of cook stove, lay her egg, go to the door to be let out, Road Island Reds.

As a child, I had the disappointment of "Little Orphan Annie" and the decoder ring, and what it spelled out.

Saturday afternoon at the movies, what a deal. Ten-cent box of the best popcorn in the world, 15-cent movie charge, and later even a pop machine. Five cents for about four ounces of root beer or Coke, etc. The cup would tip over most of the time.

My favorite movie stars, Roy Rogers and Trigger, Gene Autry and Champ, Ret Allen and Coco, Allen "Rocky" Lane and Black Jack, Lone Ranger and Silver, all the best, list could go on and on.

When I was 12, I had a pet steer, Hereford Whiteface. His name was Pete. I broke him to ride. Not long after that, the Doctor sent a pony out to the farm for me to ride.

As a child of maybe five or six, my mother bought a Maytag ringer washing machine, $5 down, $2 a week. Only thing was we had no electric lights. Burned oil lamps. Lights were put in later so it was worth it. Before we used the washboard.

In the fall we would go on a Sunday afternoon, mom, dad, and I, horse and wagon, pick up the large, very large, Hickory nuts and also Black Walnuts. Most of the trees still stand today on what we called "Billy Goat Hill" because goats were pastured there of course.

Growing up we lived in houses you could throw a cat through the cracks when the wind blew.

In the spring, April, my brothers would go out and find mushrooms, bring them home in baskets.

Also in spring, May, we girls would go out and cut wild greens, such as wild lettuce, pigweeds, wild onions, dandelions, sour dock, and deer tongue. There's more am sure, but I can't remember all.

Oh, I'll tell you about our milk cows. We had two because of large family. In the spring, they would have calves, so I had new playmates. Boy, they would eat those wild onions and that is just what the milk tasted like!

In the winter, dad and boys would hunt. Rabbits was my best but they also hunted ducks, geese, and we eat squirrels. Today I put corn and nuts out for them all winter, but we had to eat.

"Hunkie dory, kiddo, okie dokey" were used a lot when I was a kid. "Will shut my big mouth" was "will box my jaws."

We had large, truck-patch gardens. Long rows corn, green beans, butter beans, potatoes, rows of them. It was nothing to can 100 to 150 quart jars of each in summer. Tomatoes, also tomato juice, in large jars. We canned sweet and dill pickles. Not as many. Canned peaches, pears. We had to! My job was to pull weeds between the rows.

As a kid, I would climb trees. My daughter of 35 never did. My two grandkids never have.

Also would swing out over the creek with a rope, then drop in the water. They don't do that today. And I still can't swim.

Two country schools. First, one was two rooms divided. One through fourth grades was my room, heated with coal. My teacher was nice young lady, Hazel Herring (three years). We did not have Headstart or kindergarten so first grade was for learning to read, write, some math numbers, ABC's.

The next school was small, one-room basement heated by coal. Four through seven-and-a-half years at that one.

It was a blast. Our teacher was a tomboy. Man, we did play lots of softball, ice-skating. She would let class out and we would play ball all afternoon. Her name was Betty Hall. The bus driver was a nice man. His name was Arty Hall.

The outhouses were too far from the schoolhouses.

I remember school, West Fairview, northeast of Trenton because I and one of the boys were really slow about spelling. So once a week on Friday would have our words for the week, 12 words. This one week Betty told the two of us if we both made a 100% on Friday, we'll play ball rest of the afternoon. Of course, we both knew if we didn't come through, they would just kill both of us and be done with it. But we worked hard all week on those words and, sure enough, we made a 100.

I did not have time for radio programs. Wind-up record player we had. Also had album of Tex Ritter, records 78 inches, and Gene Autry.

I never was spanked at school, but I took home a few notes from the teacher to mom.

Saturday nights my tub was a washtub.

World War II, my brothers, Russell and George, served. My brother-in-law William "Bill" Taul also. My brother Ivan served in Korean Conflict. By the way, my name is Janice Lucille Taylor "Miller."

We had lots of pets, dogs, and cats. Loved them all.

Memorable person in my life, my parents of course and my uncle Harvey Taylor. World War I he lived with us a lot. Never married and he would play ball and other games with me. Very special to all of us. JFK was first President old enough to vote for. My late husband, Buddy Miller. He was my world. He also was in service, Navy.

My first love was Billy Harris from Kansas City. His grandparents lived here. My first kiss. The mischief I got into came in later years.

Playmates—Helen was her name. We rode horses every day. Lived close as a child, and cattle and horses were my playmates also.

Went to town every Saturday to do our trading, as they called it. Five-cent ice cream cone.

Had a wood icebox. Got ice for it once a week. Mr. Dinison stopped door-to-door selling ice, pop, candy bars, gum, tobacco for the men. With the ice, mom could make a Jello box. Now that was a treat.

Family time was every night after meal as a kid.

At school, we had the "March of Dimes'" cards passed out to fill. I think it held maybe $1 or $2 in dimes. This was in the early '50s.

Also, doctors came to the school and give polio shots,

Our little country school did have a yearbook.

Later years, my last three years of high school, was the best years of my life, 1961.

As a child, we played marbles, jacks, Old Maid, and checkers.

We had sand boxes and, most of all; we played in the dirt, made mud pies.

I have ration stamps still that my name is on. The war ended, so they were no longer used. People in town would trade stamps with us to get vegetables and fruits for they did not raise gardens.

Games: Kick the can; Blind Man's Bluff; Fox and the Geese (had to snow); tag; hide and go seek.

We said the Pledge of Allegiance to the Flag every day.

We had chores at school too. Sweeping out, the Flag, trash, blackboard, erasers—beat them on side of schoolhouse—and cleaning toilets.

One of the farms my dad and mom lived on taking care of it for owners living away. At night time they put the horses and cows in the barn, shut it up good.

The next morning the livestock would all be gone to pasture, the barn doors would be standing open, and this would happen again and again. Guess it was haunted.

School Was Worth the Hardship
By Doris J. Edwards of Cameron, Missouri
Born 1916

We lived in Bethany, Missouri when my dad bought one hundred and twenty acres seven miles northwest of Bethany. I was four years old when we moved to our new home. My mom and I rode in a cab with a large fern flower in the seat between us to our new home.

I had four older brothers, so I was a tomboy, peeking around the corners to see what they were doing so I could tell Mom and Dad if they were planning something bad. Once, they were smoking grapevines. They made me smoke some, too, so I wouldn't tell Mom.

When I was six years old, I walked a mile through the timber and meadow to the schoolhouse and then a mile back home. I did this for eight years. When I completed the eight grades of school there, I took the exams to graduate from the eighth grade. Then I was eligible to go to high school.

I went to Bethany High School my freshman year and I stayed with a couple in town. My sophomore year, I rode a horse five miles to Martinsville High School. I rented a room in my junior and senior years. I did my own cooking and you know, I didn't mind the hardship because I was happy and enjoyed school. I graduated from Martinsville High School in 1934.

Riding Sidesaddle
By Lorraine S. Walter of Waldport, Oregon
Born 1943

Can you imagine riding sidesaddle in a Foxhunt? In the fall of 1910, there was a foxhunt just for women entries on the Witt farm, just west of Ridgeway. It was conducted by John Leazenby. Witt Hill was a landmark in northern Missouri because of its elevation and steepness. It rose abruptly from the bottomland along E. Big Creek. Five women entered the hunt that day: Lola McGowan, May Young, Gertrude Polley, Leila Lair, and Eva Woods. McGowan and Lair were the only two in sidesaddles; the rest used regular saddles. People were perched all over Witt Hill to watch the hunt. They were all dressed up for the occasion and many of the women wore nice, white dresses. McGowan, one of the ladies who used a sidesaddle, ended up being the winner.

Fox hunt in 1910

Telephone Lines
By Neal Wharton Lawhon of Gladstone,
Missouri
Born 1931

On March 4, 1931, I was born in a farmhouse in Gentry County, Missouri. I had a great childhood there, and still own the farm. In 1945, we had heavy rains in May, which washed onto three bridges over the Grand River. The one near us took out the telephone line. In those days, farmers maintained the lines to keep the old crank phones working. We tried to tie line on rocks and throw it to the other side, to no avail. My dog, Mickey, followed me everywhere. So my dad, Ray, drove Mickey several miles around to the other side and tied the line to her collar. When I called her, she swam across with it and the line was spliced together again!

A Story Never Before Told
By Norma Appleman of Branson, Missouri
Born 1935

As a ten year old living next to Franklin Park, I spent many hours with neighborhood friends playing on equipment left from the old Franklin School. In fact, the old school was still standing. Usually, we did not venture into the old building, but one day we bravely went in.

In those days, the railroad was used daily by trains and also by people who "rode the rails." On this occasion, we entered the old school to look around and were surprised by a gruff voice asking, "What are you doing in here?"

We got out in a hurry and never felt the need to explore the old school again.

What a Coincidence
By Dorothy Essig of Excelsior Springs,
Missouri
Born 1938

I had several wonderful teachers but one really stood out. I attended a one-room schoolhouse called "The Red Brush School." In 1948 or so, I was ten years old and my teacher was Miss Susan Pigg from Orrick, Missouri. She was young and pretty, and she invited a few of the girls to spend the night with her in her apartment in Excelsior Springs. Living in the country, we didn't get to town much, so that was a real treat to be entertained by our teacher. I remember that her apartment was on the second floor.

Who would know that in about ten years, I would get married and move to Excelsior Springs, and our very first apartment was the very same one that Miss Pigg had lived in all those years earlier.

When we lived in the apartment, there was this real sweet elderly lady that lived across the hall from us. She was always telling me about being a relative to Jesse James!

Now, the apartment house has been torn down and that entire street has brand new homes built in their place, but I'll always remember that place.

Rainbow Park
By Mary M. Roach of Grant City, Missouri
Born 1927

As a very young child in the early 1930s, I will never forget going to the Rainbow Park in Grant City, Missouri and celebrating the Fourth of July there. My mother always made me a red and white dress to wear. We would pack a picnic lunch of fried chicken, and drive in our 1928 Chevrolet the five miles into Grant City. There was always a huge crowd and lots of entertainment on the stage. There was a movie screen where I once saw a silent movie. There was also a swimming pool and a dance hall. Once there was even a carnival there.

Later on in the '30s, they added a skating rink where I learned to roller skate. They also added a restaurant with a small dance floor. At one time, there was a radio station, KGIZ, which was later moved into town. We could walk from town to the park west of town on a good sidewalk. Ed Kelso was the owner of the park at the time. Of course, it has been gone many years, but it was the best place for entertainment that Grant City ever had.

Old-time Education
By Shirley (Edwards) Otis of Lees Summit, Missouri

I was born at home on a farm north of Bethany, Missouri. The doctor stayed overnight at our house until I was born. My parents paid him with fence posts and corn. That sounds unbelievable, doesn't it? I went to a one-room country school where I spent all eight years. I had to jump from the fifth to the seventh grade, then back to the sixth in order to have enough students in each particular grade. We had an outdoor bathroom and when

we needed to go, we held up our hand to ask for permission. We all brought our lunch to school and naturally, someone else's lunch always looked better than our own. We usually did some trading! Our teacher, Miss Nina, was responsible for teaching 18 students and did a very good job preparing us for high school.

I attended all four years of high school in Bethany. There were 62 students in my freshmen through senior classes. I have a lot of great memories from those school years. I took a lot of shorthand, typing and accounting classes. I thought that I would like to be a CPA, but after a couple of college classes and a very strange teacher, my mind was quickly changed. I still love accounting and keeping books. The years in the '50s were the best!

Service in the Army Air Force
By Jack Mehaffey of Tarkio, Missouri
Born 1922

I am sure most people can remember where they were when the Japanese bombed Pearl Harbor on December 7, 1941. I was a sophomore at Tarkio College and remember all of us being called to the Chapel in Rankin Hall by Dr. Earl Collins. We listened to President Franklin D. Roosevelt announcing that we were at war.

At the time, several of us were taking Civilian Pilot Training through the college and were grounded until we could prove our citizenship with a birth certificate. We were then allowed to finish the course and received a private pilot license along with college credit.

The next summer (1942), several college programs were set up by the Army, Navy, and Army Air Force. If we enlisted, we would be exempt from the draft and could continue our college education. I chose the Army Air Force and enlisted on September 2, 1942.

Even though we were promised we could graduate before being called up, in February 1943, the different services started calling us to active duty. My orders, along with two other classmates, Ralph Stava and Ed Chase, came for us to report to Jefferson Barracks in St. Louis on February 20, 1943. So began my tour of duty in the United States Army Air Force or US Army Air Corps, as it was called then. Eventually my assignment as a cryptographic security officer took me to Wakde Island off the coast of New Guinea in the South Pacific and then up to Loag Air Force Base in the Philippines.

After serving 41 months in the Army Air Force, I was granted terminal leave and returned to finish my last year of college at Tarkio, graduating in May of 1947.

Memories from the '30s
By Norma I. Bush of Liberty, Missouri
Born 1924

I was born July 24, 1924 at Maple Park, Missouri, which I think was a small suburb of North Kansas City. In May of 1929, my mother died, so my dad took my three year old sister and myself to my grandparents' home on the farm about seven miles east of Lawson, Missouri in Ray County. There we lived for fifty years or more. After my grandparents' death, my dad, my husband, and our three children moved to Lawson.

Life on the farm was never dull! In the '30s, during the Depression, the drought and dust storms, my sister and I took our toys, which were very few, and played on the old cellar steps where it was cooler. We hardly ever went all the way down the cellar for it was dark down there, damp and scary.

On Sunday, we all got into the old Model

Norma and her sister, Nadine in 1929

T and went to the little country church. The women in their hats and gloves sat in the center section. The men in their Sunday suits and ties, sat to the left of the pulpit. The young people sat to the right. If the children weren't old enough to sit with the young people, they had to sit with their parents. Many Sundays, my grandmother stayed home from church to cook a big dinner of chicken and dumplings, potatoes, vegetables, and a large fruit cobbler for dessert. Sometimes there were other family members or neighbors there for dinner. The men ate first, and then the women, and last of all, the kids.

There was always plenty to eat. During the dry years, the garden was scarce, but we managed to have plenty of meat, eggs, butter, cream, and milk, and some fruit from the orchard.

When it came time to go to school, we walked one mile down a country road to a one-room schoolhouse for all eight grades. The neighborhood kids all walked together. We sometimes waded in snowdrifts over knee deep. No shovels or plows cleared the roads. We had one boy who delighted in sneaking up behind the girls' backs and putting a handful of snow down our backs.

I have a lot of memories of those days back in the early '30s and on. The hard times didn't hurt us, and I think they helped us grow stronger!

Tornados and Baby Coyotes
By Philip R. Clark of Tarkio, Missouri
Born 1931

I was five years old when I started school in 1936. It was a two-mile journey down dirt roads to get to the one-room schoolhouse. Dad took me there the first day. After that, I always walked to and from school. We lived on Ranch number five of the David Rankin family holdings.

I remember hearing about Germany starting war in Europe on our battery radio. In the summertime, there was a man who would bring ice for our icebox. We kids would meet him at the front gate to get chips. That iceman was drafted into the army and later killed in Germany. Some of the older boys from my grade school were also drafted and several of them lost their lives as well.

In about the mid-forties, World War II was winding down. Around that time, an insurance company had taken possession of the Rankin holdings. A corporation in Kansas City bought most of it. Mom and Dad bought one section of Ranch number five and a quarter section of ranch number seven.

After I completed the eighth grade, I started high school in Tarkio. It was in September of 1945. We still had dirt roads and no school bus. My grandma lived in Tarkio, so it was decided that I would stay with her throughout the week and go home on the weekend. This worked out well until my junior year when my brother started high school. By then, dad had a herd of about 25 cows to hand-milk every morning and night. He needed help to milk them, so he purchased an old pickup truck for us to drive to school and back home.

I graduated from THS in 1949. Around that time, we acquired a baby coyote. We put him in with an old mama cat with babies. She nursed him until he was old enough to survive on his own. When he was big enough to catch Mom's old hens, Dad gave him to a neighbor. We had other pets, too. Mom had Sugar-foot, a black and white cat. Dad had a brindle boxer. There was also a pet raccoon, Cesar, and Murtle the pig.

One day in early June of 1949, and at about 8:00PM a tornado struck our place. The house was completely demolished and lots of people and livestock were injured. My 14 year old sister died from the injuries she received from the tornado. We gathered ourselves and began planning physical and financial recovery. We purchased materials for buildings and livestock. We stayed in town at Grandma's until a garage was built on our land that we lived in until we made the house livable again. The neighbors took the surviving livestock and pets until we could repair fences and build new buildings to keep them at home.

Everything I Needed to Know, I Learned In Missouri
By Marilyn N. Brown of Kansas City, Missouri
Born 1939

You have heard of the book <u>Everything I Needed to Know in Life, I Learned in Kindergarten</u>. Well, everything I needed to know, with a few exceptions, to survive in the barrios of the Philippines during my 1962-1964 Peace Corps years, I learned in northwest Missouri.

As a teen, I learned how to swim (the nipa hut I lived in was a few yards from Iligan Bay in the Philippines). I learned how to ride a bike (we had no other transportation except walking). As a young adult, I learned how to deal with rural life on the farms of Davies and Harrison Counties during the summer of 1959.

This was the summer I worked for the Southern Baptist Sunday School board as superintendent of Vacation Bible School in those counties. I had to live with farm families and teach in the small churches in their areas. Most of the time, I had to use the outside privies, deal with bugs and bug bites, farm animals, summer heat with no air conditioning, and use a pump for well water. I had to use home remedies for minor illnesses, deal with bad backcountry roads, and the culture of small town living. In order to get the news of the world we couldn't rely on computers or television, but we had to read magazines. We didn't have a lot of people around, so we had to learn to entertain ourselves by playing board games or cards. I learned country people had a way that was much better at surviving than the city of St. Joseph where I had grown up.

I did learn from my grandparents how to raise chickens, cut off their heads, dip them in hot water, and pull off the feathers. I got used to the smell and wasn't afraid to cut them open and pull out the innards. I learned to cook from scratch and to fish and garden from my mom and dad, who had grown up on farms. All in all, I was much better prepared for the primitive life in the barrios than my fellow volunteers from the east and west coasts who had grown up in the cities and suburbs. I still had a lot to learn to adjust to the life in the barrios, where no one had electricity, running water, or toilets. We had no telephone, so when President Kennedy died, we got a telegram, which was delivered three days late.

However, the people in the Philippines had a love of life and learning and could sing, dance, and enjoy nature as much as or more than anyone else I had met during my growing up years in northwest Missouri.

Skunks and Snow
By Ivala L. Taylor of Cameron, Missouri
Born 1920

I went to a county school for eight years. One teacher taught all eight grades. My favorite teacher was Miss Louise Dyer. She taught when I was in the first and second grades. I still can recite two poems that I learned back then. We had programs at Christmas time and at the end of the school year. Some of the games we played were Ante Over, Blind Man's Bluff, Mother May I, Hide and Seek, and Fox and Geese. One time after a big snowstorm, the snow was piled up high in places; the big boys dug a tunnel in the snow. They persuaded a little boy to crawl in it. The older boys jumped on the top of the tunnel and it caved in on him. They really had to dig to get him out. That really frightened me. Another time, we had skunks under the schoolhouse. One day, a dog got under there and disturbed them. The odor was so bad that we had to move out to the coalhouse to finish that day of school. Our water was carried from a well in a bucket. We all had our own drinking cups. There was an outhouse for the boys and one for the girls.

My mother was a very good seamstress. She made all of our clothes from material that was given to her. She washed good clothes, ripped them up, and made our dresses. We even had feed sacks that were made into clothes. I never had a store bought coat till I was 16 years old. Mother crocheted and tatted many beautiful things. I have a pair of shoes that she tatted for me when I was a baby. Our baths were taken in an old number two tub behind the cook stove.

Pleasant Valley School
Class of 1934-35

Big Snowfall in the '30s
By Robert Shaney of Hamilton, Missouri
Born 1925

I was in grade school in Nettleton, Missouri when it snowed about three feet one day. On the next day, it snowed another two to three feet. After that, the weather warmed some and it rained, and then turned cold; everything froze up. My Grandparents lived three miles south of town and I decided to try out my skates on the frozen snow. After asking my folks, I thought I would try to skate to Town. I took off in the morning and went "as the crow flies" across fields and over fences. I had ice skates that fit over my shoes. They had clamps on the toes, a strap in the back, and another strap in the middle of each foot to help steady the skates. I didn't have any problem with the skates staying on or the icy snow breaking under my weight. It didn't take long to go cross-country. It came as a surprise to my grandparents when I showed up. It was a good trip and I learned to skate uphill.

Taking Care of Turkeys
About a mile and a half from town was a family by the name of Yakley. We had about a 10-20 Farmall and I had fixed it up. I was very proud of it. I started it up for Mr. Yakley one day and asked him if I could plow some ground for him. I spent two to three evenings after school plowing. My plow had a trip rope to put plow in and out of ground. As I pulled the rope plow, it dropped back in the front end of the tractor up into the fence. I was stuck. A neighbor came by with a wagon and team of horses. He looked it over and said he'd be back in a few minutes to pull me out. He came back with his team of horses. He tied them on to the plow and within minutes, I was out. I was amazed, to say the least. Most farming was done with horses. I gave him a great "thank you" and finished my job. Those days you traded work not dollars. As I was visiting, I noticed that every turkey hens had saddle blankets covering it. Mrs. Yakley had made them. I asked what they were, and she explained to me that during the breeding season the hens need protection from the toms.

I had never seen that before or ever again.

The Ride
We had a good grocery store in town. Many farmers came on Saturdays to get supplies for the next week. They would bring

chickens, eggs, and cream to sell. They would also purchase all of their needs. I was raised in Nettleton (former name Gomer) in Caldwell County. Most had teams of horses and needed them to get over wet and snow-covered roads. The boys in town would meet at old 36 Highway, which was one block south of town. We had a 15-20 foot rope attached to each sled, and we asked the farmers if we could catch a ride. The answer was always, "Sure." We would slip our rope onto the wagon and hang on to it. Mud and water would fly. If we got into trouble, we would release the rope and hopefully it wouldn't catch in the process. Riding through those water holes was a blast.

Memories of the One-room School
By Darlene Holliday of Albuquerque, New Mexico
Born 1928

I was born July 5, 1928. This is my story as I remember it. We lived on a farm five miles southeast of Hardin, Missouri. Dr. Grimes came out from Hardin in a buggy driven by a man with the last name of Phillips. The doctor had celebrated a little too much on the Fourth and had quite a hangover. He could not get me to breathe, so he tossed me on the bed. Mrs. Mallory and Mrs. Fuller were there. One of them picked me up, took me to the kitchen, lit the oil stove, and worked on me until she got me to breathe. I did not know this story of my birth until I was 12 years old and overheard my mother tell a neighbor.

I am the oldest of five girls, and looking back, I realize what a wonderful childhood I had. Two years before I started the first grade, my parents took in a couple to live with them. They were Virgil and Charlene Moyer. Virgil was the teacher at Mallory School, which was located a mile and a quarter from our farm. When I was ready to start school, my dad thought it would not be right to have the teacher live with us any longer, so the Moyers moved to a house just west of the school. If I thought he would be partial to me, I was sadly mistaken. I shared a double desk with Pamelia Strider. One day we looked at each other and Mr. Moyer tapped each one of us on the head with a ruler.

Our one-room school did not have electricity or running water. We had to go to the pump, fill the water bucket, and bring it into the schoolroom. We had one dipper in the bucket, and I do not remember ever having individual cups to drink from. Generally, two of the older boys would raise the flag on the flagpole. At nine o'clock, we would recite the Pledge of Allegiance. Afterward, the teacher would put on a record and we would march around the school singing, "Marching, marching, all around the schoolroom; heads erect, eyes ahead, like the soldiers on parade. Marching, marching, by the open door; now we stand by our desks once more."

Our teachers taught all eight grades and had a course of study, which they followed very closely. Mr. Otis Chandler was our superintendent of the schools. We had reading, writing, arithmetic, spelling, history, geography, science, and music. Somehow, we even had time for spelling bees, geography matches, arithmetic contests, and school programs at Christmastime and on the last day of school. One year I participated in a declamation contest on the county level. Mr. Moyer taught there for my first and second grades, and then I had Helen Stoutimore for three years. She told us that if we didn't miss a day of school that she would take us to a movie. I got to go to a movie two of the three years. One year we went to Lexington, and one year we went to Richmond. At recess and noon hours, if the weather was nice, we played Town Ball, French and English War, Sheep-in-my-pen; Kick the Wicket, and Handy-Over. In the winter, we played jacks. When I was in the sixth and seventh grades, we had a teacher who taught us girls to crochet potholders out of store string from sugar and flour sacks. I also printed an annual listing of all of our grades and each student's story.

Choke It, It'll Start!
By Norman Provow of Holt, Missouri
Born 1935

To the uninformed and younger generation, autos and trucks of yesteryear did not have automatic chokes to start the engines. There was usually a hand choke on the dash, which you pulled out before cranking the engine. When the engine started, you simply pushed the choke throttle back in. Clarifying that, here is my story.

Several years ago, I needed a pair of work boots, which also served as hunting and everyday boots. I went to a western wear store, as I do like the odor of leather in these stores. A young, pretty little farm girl waited on me. I could tell she was a farm girl by her run-over cowgirl boots, jeans, etc. I picked out a pair of boots I liked and she got my apparent size. She sat down in front of me on the old-type seats that had the front part sloped, so I could place my foot and shoe there, and pull on my boot or shoe. These particular boots had inside pull-on straps, which could be grasped to really assist in pulling on the boots.

Well, I have on my right foot a kind of a high arch. I had my right leg kind of high and was straining a lot, pulling on those straps. As a rule, one can tell when he is going to pass some gas. I let the longest and loudest one I had ever let. The poor little farm girl took the velocity, etc. I was truly mortified, to say the least. You could hear it all over the store.

One old rancher, after hearing it, hollered out, "Choke it, it'll start!" With that, the farm girl and I started laughing and everyone else in the crowded store did, too. She was so nice. I apologized to her at least twenty times.

I guess to ease my guilt, she replied, "My dad, brothers, uncles, and grandpas all sit around playing poker, drinking beer, and eating hard boiled eggs, and they, too break a lot of wind. And sometimes they light the gas with matches!" I replied to her, "I'm not related to you, and I don't have any matches!" I bought the boots, and they lasted a long time.

Now when I am around somebody new, and they break wind, I'll just holler, "Choke it, it'll start!"

Norman Provow with his trusted boots

I did not mean for this to be a vulgar thing, but it did happen.

I am a retired Railroad Police Officer and really know some humorous things that happened in my thirty years as a Special Agent.

Good Old Day Memories
By Priscilla Faulkner of Holt, Missouri
Born 1938

I was born in the year of 1938 in Richmond, Missouri. The place where I was born was Bob Ford's parent's home. This is a story for another time and place.

My parents were very poor, and going through the great depression was a very hard task. I had two older sisters. Mom and dad were very hard workers and never gave up. Daddy would farm, work in a grocery store, and work in a coal mine, too. Sometimes he would do this all in a day's time. He never complained, and was always there for us whenever he was needed.

Mama was a stay-at-home mom and kept the household in order. It was so nice to come home from school every day with a delicious odor of homemade bread in the air or a nice, juicy cobbler waiting on the table. The house we lived in had no electricity, no running water, and no inside bathroom. We used kerosene lamps for doing our homework and lighting the rooms. In the winter, it was very cold, and the only heat we had was a black pot-bellied stove. The stove had to be filled with wood that Daddy chopped with an ax, or coal, if we could afford it.

Mama did the laundry by using a washboard until the wringer-type washer was made. The clothes were hung on a line that was stretched across a room inside the house. When weather permitted, clothes were hung outside on a line.

Every Monday it was time to do laundry. Tuesdays were ironing days. Everything that was washed had to be ironed. In those days, perma-press was not available. Old flat irons were heated on the stove till they were hot enough to press the clothes. Men's and Women's clothes were made from pretty cotton prints that came from feed sacks.

There were several wells on the land that were used for gathering water for drinking and washing. Bath time was usually on Saturdays. The water was heated on the stove and then poured into a large tub. The only soap we had was lye soap, made from the grease from a hog we had butchered for our meat.

We had no telephones, televisions, Playstations, DSIs, or computers. As kids, we made up our own games, and sometimes we had to make our own toys to play with. Outside games, such as hide and seek, leapfrog, baseball, and football were all greatly enjoyed by the whole family and neighbors. Family and friends were very important in those good old days. Memories will never be forgotten. We spent our evenings at home, eating popcorn together that we shelled ourselves from the corn that we grew in the garden. Back then, there was no Orville's or microwave popcorn.

Making homemade ice cream was always a good old get-together time. Fresh whole milk and good, rich, thick cream were the key ingredients. In the winter, when ice covered the pond, Daddy would chop the ice and put the pieces in buckets for our ice cream. Afterward, we would hitch our favorite horse to a sled and ride to the pond to get the ice. The crank type freezer was then made ready for some hardy churning. All of us would take turns turning the crank until the ice cream was frozen. What a delicious treat that was!

Saturday night was movie night at the in-town theatre. We watched mostly westerns, with the good old cowboys. These movies were appropriate for all ages. Admission, soft drinks, candy bars, and ice cream were all a nickel apiece. Popcorn was five cents for a sack and ten cents for a box. These are some of my memories that can never be taken away or replaced by the modern day world of electronics.

Warm Lunches and the School Band
By Charles G. Cotton of Agency, Missouri
Born 1924

Burr Oak was a one-room school in the Missouri River bottoms west of Forest City. It was north of White Cloud, Kansas. In the building, the blackboards were at the north end, a big coal stove (with metal jacket for safety) was in the southeast corner, and windows were on the west and south sides. That is where I got my first eight grades of education. Mrs. Wagoner was my teacher for the first two

years. Even then, in 1929 and 1930 we had a hot lunch program. Potato soup, vegetable soup, and ham and beans were some of the staples. Most families had milk cows, and raised beans and potatoes. Some would bring milk, others would bring the other ingredients, and others would be cooks that week. There was a kerosene cook stove with an oven on top, so sometimes we had baked potatoes or cornbread. The general idea was to have something hot to supplement whatever was in our lunch buckets. Also, as this was at the start of the depression years, it assured that everyone had something to eat. At that time, most of us were not aware of the financial disaster. We were in a farming community, and food and heat were available because we would raise our own food, and wood heat was the norm. There was very little money-changed hands, as it was in short supply, and people traded for most of their needs. Forest City had a grain elevator capable of milling flour. Dad would take very many sacks of wheat, and trade it all for flour. He raised cattle and hogs, and butchered his own meat.

I attended Forest City High School. In 1937, the depression had eased, and money had begun to appear more freely. I got a dollar per week for lunch money, and most of the time, I could stretch it to cover things like typing paper, clarinet reeds, etc. Lunch was usually a ten-cent hamburger or a fifteen-cent bowl of chili.

I have always felt that I got an exceptionally good twelve grades of education. We had available all the basics, as well as geometry, algebra, some trigonometry, chemistry, biology, two years of typing, bookkeeping, speech, band and a good many more. Our marching band marched in the Apple Blossom Parade in St. Joseph every year, and had a standing invitation to most of the ball tournaments in the surrounding area. My instrument was a twenty-dollar clarinet. We marched across the Rulo Bridge on a cold, windy day, when the bridge was dedicated. Our bass drummer was a small girl, and two of us had to grab her and her drum to keep her from being blown off the bridge.

Local crime was minimal, but we read of Dillinger, Bonnie and Clyde, and Pretty-boy Floyd. More locally, Ma Barker and her sons were caught throwing boxes of merchandise from the back of a truck going north on highway 71, north of St. Joseph. I became acquainted with several highway patrolmen who would come to hunt ducks and geese with my cousin and I. Over the years, I have known, worked with, and highly respected many highway patrolmen. They were fine men, worthy of respect.

Mom got a new Maytag washer with a Briggs and Stratton engine in the mid-thirties. It was fine when it decided to work good, but if stopped during washday, it often would refuse to start again. The rest of the washing was done on the washboard if we couldn't get it to work. Laundry soap was homemade lye soap, and wash water was heated in a forty gallon cast iron black kettle over an outdoor fire. Water was carried in a three-gallon bucket from a hand pump. With eight of us to wash for, that was quite an accomplishment! Usually one of us would carry water, and carry baskets of wet clothes to the clothesline. I have seen clothes frozen stiff on the clothesline many times.

Buggies and Strawtick Beds
By Mildred Irene Adkison of Kansas City,
Missouri
Born 1923

Mom was a schoolteacher up until she married Dad and gave birth to seven children. Dad was a farmer. Whenever each child was born, Dad would hook up the horse and buggy so that he could pick up the doctor who was five miles away in Lathop, Missouri. For the payment of delivering the baby, Dad would give the doctor a pig or some cured ham.

My folks had two wood-burning stoves in the house. One was in the living room with a pipe that went up through the ceiling. It was vented all the way to the roof, and it helped to keep the upstairs warm in the winter. The kitchen stove had a ten-gallon reservoir on the side filled with water. When the stove was burning, we had warm water to use. We kept an iron on the stove, the kind you snap the handle on. We slept on straw-tick beds made from several flour sacks sewn together. It was filled with straw that was thrashed from dad's bundled oats. We had no refrigeration, so we lowered five-gallon buckets down into the water in the well to keep the milk, butter, and homemade cheese cool. We used kerosene lamps and lanterns.

Mildred's dad, Clate Hubbard and his team of mules in 1934

There was no electricity, no bathroom, no telephone, and no fans. We only had outside toilets and a washtub and washboard with lye soap for the laundry. We four older sisters had to gather a sufficient amount of water for the day, milk the cows, and cut enough wood for the day. We cut the wood with a crosscut saw. Two of us would maneuver the saw while one sat on the log. One would be responsible for carrying the wood to the porch.

We walked a mile and a half to a one-room schoolhouse. It was called the Brooking School and had grades one through eight. We had outside toilets, one for boys, and one for girls. Coal furnaces heated up the school. My favorite teacher was Mrs. Dorsey. We took our lunch to school. Mom made homemade biscuits so we usually had sausage and biscuits. The kids always wanted to trade lunches with us to get the homemade biscuits.

One winter day, my sisters and I rode our horse to school. We had to cross a cement bridge that had frost on it. Our horse's hind feet slid down and all of us fell off. I was the fourth one on the back, so all of my sisters fell on top of me and knocked the wind out of me. We ended up leading the horse by foot to the school where we put him in the barn.

One summer day, a neighbor man walked to our house and said he needed to go to the store to buy groceries. My oldest sister and I took it upon ourselves to take this neighbor five miles to Lathrop for groceries with our horse and two -seated buggy. As we made a left turn, crossing a shallow ditch, the neighbor bounced out of the back seat and the back wheel ran him over! He got up and said he was okay and so we took him on to get his groceries and then back home.

I remember when the war was on and the sugar and gasoline was rationed. To buy tires or coffee you had to have a special stamp. The years of 1934-1936 were tough years. It was so dry and there was no wind. Kansas had a dust storm that blew over us, too. There was not enough wind to turn the windmill, so we four older sisters had to pump water up by the hand pump to keep the horse and cattle tanks full. The grasshoppers and potato bugs ate up our garden and crops.

Around Thanksgiving, Dad would butcher a big hog. He sugar cured the hams and Mom cold packed the sausage. We rendered off the lard and ate some of the cracklins. Around Christmastime, Mom's aunt would send her a box of her dresses. They were way too big for us, so I would take them apart and make myself a few clothes on Mom's foot-petal-operated Singer sewing machine. Dad bought our shoes at used shoe stores. He would always bring home the high-heeled lace up shoes. I'll never forget wearing those.

When I was about 14, I quit high school and went to work at Becket's Grocery Store south of Cameron, Missouri. I worked there for one summer. After that, I stayed at home and took in ironing from three homes a week, working one day for each one. After a few years of doing that, I got a job at the Standard station on Highway 69. I lived with another family about three or four years. That is where I met my boyfriend. We went together for several years. Later, we got married and moved to Polo, Missouri.

The Booking School class of 1963

We were married for 63 ½ years and have two children together. I lost Archie in 2004.

Spitting in the Sorghum
By William F. Yates of Burlington Junction, Missouri
Born 1931

I am eighty-one years old now, and when I was about six to eight years old, we lived on the north-west side of town. I was allowed to go about a block west of our house, down to the old brickyard, where some of the old men in town cooked sorghum. Sometimes they would tell me to bring a jar and they would fill it, and I would take it home to my mother. They had a big vat-type thing with a fire built under it, and these old men would all walk around the vat in a circle, stirring the cooking sorghum with long paddles. Farmers would bring in the cane to be cooked. It always fascinated me to watch them, walking and stirring the sorghum and as they all chewed tobacco, as they walked and stirred, they would spit in the sorghum!

We had ration stamps, red for meat and blue or green for sugar and coffee. I don't remember which color it was. There were also ration stamps for gas, but we didn't have a car so we didn't have gas stamps. My mother would trade her meat stamps for sugar and coffee stamps, and then she would can fruit that she could get during the summer for our winter supply. We also used pear juice to sweeten our coffee instead of sugar.

Farmers also had access to meat, and with cream from their cows, they would churn butter, but we lived in town and had neither meat nor milk nor cream. Margarine was then called oleo, and we would get it in the commodities given to us by the county. It would look like a solid pound of lard. We would put the pound of lard looking stuff in a bowl, and then there was a little orange capsule that we would break over the white margarine and mix it all in until it was a uniform yellow. It sounded like fun at first, but it was hard to do, as my mother wanted it all mixed in smoothly to a uniform color, and that was not fun.

As we lived about a block away from the old brickyard, the railroad tracks were right there, too, between the brickyard and

283

the house. As the train would be going slow through town, the fireman would often throw out a couple of scoops of coal when they crossed near our house. We would go get the coal for our heating.

My dad would go hunting for rabbits for the meat, and he used a .12 gage shotgun to hunt with. He got rabbits, but when my mother would cook them, we usually had to pick out the pellets from the meat, as he was never careful where he aimed when shooting them.

Scarlet Fever and Quarantine
By Thelma C. Harrold of Kansas City, Missouri
Born 1922

I was in the fourth grade, so it must have been 1932. I got up not feeling good so my mother, Lorana Hickman, let me stay at home. The next day, my younger sister, Deloris, got up not feeling good, so she stayed home. The two of us were sitting in the floor cutting out paper dolls. Around 10:00am, we saw a man out front talking to our dad, Elgin Hickman. Mom said, "That must be a salesman, and I hope he doesn't let him in." But just in a few minutes, here they come into the kitchen and on to the living room. My dad said, "This is Dr. Harnod, and he thinks we have scarlet fever." Well, sure enough, we did. The doctor said, "Get these girls in bed." There was no penicillin then, so we were quarantined. The doctor put a sign on our house. I don't remember what it said, but it meant that no one could come in and no one could go out. By the time Deloris and I got over it, Dorothy, Garvin, and Hazel got it. We were quarantined for four months. The two older kids, Leroy and Juanita, stayed with our grandparents, Will and Rosa Hickman. Both the oldest kids were in high school at Ridgeway, but the rest of us were going to Pleasant Valley School, a one-room country schoolhouse.

There was a family named Roache and they had a son, Jack. Jack was ill, and they called the doctor. The doctor said Jack had scarlet fever. Then the doctor stopped at the school to ask if there were other kids absent. The teacher, Dorothy Wiggins, told him about Deloris and me, so he came to our house. That is when he said we had scarlet fever and put the sign on our house.

After four months of quarantine, to be allowed out, my mom had to fumigate the house. We lived in a four-room house. She had two candles, so she had to shut the kitchen off, and we all stayed in the kitchen. It was a large kitchen. Then when that candle was burned, we had to wait so many hours, and then we moved in the living room and bedrooms. Then when that was done, we could go away from home and people could come to visit us. But after so long a time, my dad felt like he had to get out and attend to business. We had a neighbor man that lived alone, so my dad went through a procedure to be able to move out to live with this man. My mom would cook soup and bread for these men. Mom would take it hot from the stove and hand it to my dad. They felt hot food would not have any germs.

The very next year, Leroy got diphtheria and we were quarantined for a month that time. My parents had him stay in a bedroom with a door, and no one went in there but our mom. The doctor came out to give all of us shots, and none of the rest of us got it.

We lived five miles northeast of Ridgeway, Missouri in the Pleasant Valley School District.

Tidy Whities?
By Richard C. Edwards of Platte City, Missouri
Born 1949

Around 1958 or 1959, when I was eight or nine years old, we went to my grandparents' home in Dearborn, and we took my new bike. I decided to ride my bike the three blocks to Main Street. I had a stomachache, and I tried to pass a little gas. Big mistake. I soiled myself. There was an outhouse close to the road. I don't know whose outhouse it was, but I left those people a gift of my tidy whities, which were not as white as they were supposed to be.

My other grandpa was afraid of storms for good reason. When he was a young man, he and my uncle, who was a young boy, were caught outside during a tornado. My grandpa wrapped one arm around my uncle and the other around a small tree and lay flat on the ground. The tornado took all of the big trees close to them but didn't take them. So when a big storm came, we went to the cellar where they kept their potatoes and their canned vegetables they got out of their garden.

One Halloween when I was in high school, some friends and I went around town and set up roadblocks and the police chief, who was a cool guy, followed us around out of uniform and took them down after we left. We didn't find this out until later. Then we went to the sale barn at the end of Main Street and let all of the cows out. It was pretty funny watching all of the cows trotting down Main Street.

In 1953, Mom had her own beauty shop in Dearborn. She had to fix the ladies' hair and watch my sister and me at the same time. One day, she noticed my sister had been quiet for a while, and that was unusual. So she went to check on her. She found my sister with her diaper full of poop. My sister had reached into the diaper and gotten poop on her hand, and she had wiped it on the walls and everything else she could reach.

In 1963, when I was in the seventh grade, our principal had a paddle made in shop class that was about two feet long, and he had holes drilled in it. He had students bend over his desk, and he would swing the paddle like a baseball bat. The only swats I ever got at school were two swats from a ping-pong paddle from a different principal, but I had a friend who got ten swats from the big paddle. He was given the option of taking them all at once or two a day for five days. He chose all at once, but after two, he stood up and decided he would take them two a day.

When I was a senior in 1968, my family took a trip way up into Canada to a place called Lake Louise. Gas in Platte City was 25 cents a gallon and had recently been as low as 19 cents a gallon. On our way, we saw the Badlands, the Grand Canyon, and Yellowstone with Old Faithful and Mt. Rushmore. When we got to Canada, gas was 50 cents a gallon and it didn't take long before it was 50 cents a gallon in Platte City.

Everyone in my family, including both of my sons and my wife, are afraid of snakes. One day, when my youngest son was the only one home, he was leaving the house. As he opened the front door, a three-foot blacksnake crawled in the house. He didn't see where it went because he left as fast as he could. We called animal control, but they could not find the snake. They said the snake probably left because we had a dog in the house and two cats in the house. Three days later, I was in my bedroom when I heard a scream coming from the living room. I ran into the living room to find a three foot blacksnake coming down the wall.

Sally Aardvark
By Don Foster of Smithville, Missouri
Born 1933

There are all kinds of things in a person's life that leave strong memories of people, places, and things. I would like to share with you one of my memories of a character that is a little hard to classify in just one category.

Memories of Sally Aardvark began with her name. She wasn't really an aardvark, but rather, a horse. Why in the world, you might ask, would anybody name a horse Sally Aardvark? My son gave her the aardvark part of her name after the first time he saw her. He was playing in the hayloft of our old barn, looked down through an opening in one of the stalls, and saw this creature. He couldn't figure out why we were keeping an aardvark in our barn! Anyway, the name stuck.

Sally was a Missouri Foxtrotter, and was orphaned soon after her birth. She was raised on a bucket. Needless to say, she became very people-oriented. If she could see you, she wanted to join you. This became a problem for her owner, who was a friend of mine who lived in southern Missouri. He lived on a little acreage in the middle of a subdivision. If Sally got out of her pen, away she'd go to the house and try to get in through the patio doors. This made the house a little crowded, so we decided to pasture her at our place.

Once she was in the field with the older mares, Sally had a rough time. They were mean to her, so when I was around the house I would let her roam around our unfenced yard. In the beginning, this didn't seem like it would be of any harm since we were outside the city limits and had lots of space. In doing this, we experienced many adventures with Sally that summer. As I said before, she was a people horse.

One day, while trying to paint the picket fence around our patio, I noticed Sally waiting close to the pasture gate. Feeling sorry for her, I let her into the yard. She must have been watching me paint because she made a beeline to the bucket. Before I could stop her, she put her nose into the white paint! I guess she must have thought it was her milk bucket. She ran around for a couple of weeks with an extra snip of white on her nose!

There was another time, on a Sunday afternoon that we were having an outdoor lunch, as we often did in the summer. My father was sitting in the shade at the patio table. One of the kids had left the patio gate open. Sally had been in the yard most of the day with the kids and me. Well, my wife had just brought out a big bowl of mashed potatoes. Big mistake. Sally saw the bowl with the white potatoes in it and knew where she wanted to be. Before my father knew what was happening, Sally had her nose in our mashed potatoes! She seemed to like them better than the paint. We all got a big laugh out of that one, although, we obviously had no potatoes for dinner.

One of the more embarrassing situations in which Sally was involved happened later that summer. We lived across the street from a large cemetery. On this particular day, I was working on the yard and had Sally out with me. Well, I was deep into my yard work and didn't even notice the funeral procession that entered the cemetery. Sally did. Boy was I surprised when I rounded the corner of the house and saw one of our local undertakers leading Sally down our drive to the house. Yes, Sally had gone to the funeral. Thankfully, no one in our small farming community was too upset. There were lots of chuckles, and to this day, I am still reminded of the horse that joined the funeral.

Sally Aardvark gave us many entertaining memories that summer. If only my son had known that he had not seen an aardvark that day, but rather an addition to the family, we might have been a little bit more prepared. But, if so, things would definitely not have been as fun.

Our New House
By Alice Nathan of Chatham, Illinois
Born 1953

I was born in Culler's Hospital in Trenton in 1953 to George and Mildred (Chambers) Taylor. The delivery doctor was Dr. Fuson. We lived south of Trenton in the old Belshe School, a one-room schoolhouse about five miles south of Trenton. Dad had partitioned off a small kitchen, two bedrooms, and a

common area for dining and living rooms. My brother, Dwight, who was only 20 months older than I, slept in the only crib, so my first bed at home was a dresser drawer placed on a chair. My first real bed was an army cot that Mom set up every night by the kitchen table. The second bedroom had bunk beds for my two older brothers, George Roy and Dwight.

We did not have indoor plumbing, so there was an outhouse in the back corner of our one-acre place. Mom was so delighted that we had a three-hole outhouse—not the usual two-holer. Dad had cut a smaller hole for me with a little step stool. My oldest brother, George Roy, was tasked with shoveling the path to the outhouse when it snowed. Snakes also habitated our outhouse from time to time. This created a phobia for me that I still carry to this day. Water for the house was carried in from the outside hand pump by the water bucket that stood on a small red cabinet that was just large enough for the bucket and a small basin. It was there that my mother taught me how to wash my hair. Dwight and I would brush our teeth on the back porch and often had a contest to see who could spit the farthest.

Bathing was a special task that involved all of us. We would haul in enough water from the pump to fill four pots and pans that we would heat on the stove in the kitchen. The galvanized oval bathtub was carried in and placed in the tiny space between the stove and table. When the hot water was ready, it was added to some cold water in the tub. I was the lucky one in the family. Being the youngest, I got to take my bath first. That meant that my bathwater was clean. My brothers then each took a bath, with Mom adding more hot water as needed. Next came Dad, and then Mom. She always was the last, and her bathwater was the dirtiest. Because the bathtub was so big, we did not empty it between baths. We did not go through this every Saturday night like some people. We only did it once a month. Sponge baths were taken during the rest of the month.

When I was in the first grade at Pleasant View R-6 School (which was built right across the road from us,) my parents decided to build a bigger house for us. They decided to build it in thirds. The first third was built right up next to the old schoolhouse and had three bedrooms upstairs and a double garage on ground level. That summer we "moved" into that new section of our new house while the schoolhouse was torn down. Dad covered the dirt floor of the garage with plywood. He did not nail them together, just laid them side-by-side. It made for some interesting walking across the room! The television sat on top of the refrigerator, the water bucket was temporarily hung close to the screen door, and there was room for my parents' bed and dresser and the kitchen table. Frogs became our guests during heavy rain, so Dwight and I were responsible for catching the frogs and throwing them out the door. Next was the building of the middle section of the house. This was to be our living room and kitchen, with room for a bathroom someday. I remember helping shingle that section when I was seven. I would climb the ladder holding one shingle at a time. I even learned how to use the hammer to nail down the shingle.

Eventually, the house was completed, but the house was extremely drafty. The water bucket in the kitchen sat next to the north wall. On exceptionally cold nights, the bucket would freeze over. We had no indoor plumbing until 1970 when I was a senior in high school. I vividly remember the first shower I took in our new house. I thought it was the most glorious thing in the world!

Opening Up a Spring
By Earnest Johnson of Pasadena Maryland
Born 1939

Following the death of my father, Lowell Johnson, in 1956, my mother, Eula, and little sister, Kristie, decided to move back to Joplin. My aunt and uncle, Jean and Marvin Weaver, said I could live and work for them and they would put me through high school in Ravanna if I didn't want to go back to Joplin. This is when I started my education about day-to-day farm life.

One day, Marvin said that one of the spring-fed ponds wasn't providing enough water for the cattle so we would have to "open up the spring." I had no idea how to "open up the spring" but I was willing to learn. Marvin cranked up the bulldozer, I took the truck, and we went to the pond. He used the dozer to break the pond dam, drain the water, and then he proceeded to clean out the mud from the bottom. Boy what a mess that was! He couldn't get the spring to open with the dozer, so I was elected to get the shovel and see if I could open

up the area where the spring ran into the pond.

After considerable digging with the shovel, and being covered in mud from top to bottom, we still couldn't open the spring. Marvin said, "Let's go to Vanner, get some dynamite and blow the damned thing open!" Now, being 16 year old who loved fireworks (still do) it sounded like a *great* idea. We went to Ravanna, and made a stop at Barrett's Hardware. When we walked in, Barrett said, "Howdy boys, what can I do for you today?" Marvin explained to Barrett what we were doing and Barrett replied, "Okay, how much dynamite do you need?" The three of us kind of looked at each other with blank looks. (I was 16. What did I know about dynamite and opening springs?) Barrett said, "Why don't you take the whole case, use what you need, and then just bring back the rest?" Sounded like a plan! Then Barrett asked how much wire we needed to connect the plunger to the dynamite. After the blank stare again, he said, "Hell, just take a new roll and what you don't use you can bring back." Once again, it sounded like a plan.

Back at the pond, we cussed and discussed how much "powder" to use. After a lot of serious thought and meditation, Marvin said, "Hell, let's just use the whole damned case." Hot dog, now you're talking my language! We dug a fairly deep hole approximately where the spring entered the pond, hooked up the blasting caps, wired it up, and then covered it with mud. Afterward, we rolled out the wire as far as it would reach (500 feet) and brought the dozer over to hide behind for protection.

Marvin hooked up the plunger and asked me, "Are you ready?" He pushed the plunger down and nothing happened. Maybe God was trying to tell us, "Don't do this!" Regardless, we weren't listening. Marvin pushed the plunger down a second time and immediately I wished we had listened. The dozer came off the ground about three inches (seemed like a foot) because of the shock wave, and knocked us end over end. What had started out as a beautiful, sunshiny day was starting to turn dark! I looked up and there was a sky full of small, medium, and large chunks of mud. Had either of us been hit with one of those large chunks, I think it would have done serious damage to our bodies and souls! After getting up on my hands and knees, I looked over at Marvin and he looked as though he was laughing but no sound came out. I started to ask him if he was all right, but no sound came out. We started stumbling around, in shock, trying to see if the other was all right and in one piece. Apparently, there was no major damage to either of us, so we just started laughing. Very gradually, our hearing came back.

About that time one of our neighbors who lived around a quarter of a mile away came roaring across the pasture in his truck, wanting to know what in the world happened. Seems as though we rattled his house so bad that it knocked down some dishes. Good thing it didn't break them. Marvin assured him that we were okay, even though we were a little hard of hearing.

The spring did open up. We rebuilt the dam, and it was still providing plenty of water when I left the farm.

One-Room School and a Dreaded Disease
By Darline Kussmann of Brunswick, Missouri
Born 1932

I attended a one-room school in a small rural Missouri community. My younger sister, brother, and I walked two miles one-way from our farm home to the school. On cold winter mornings, our hands and feet were numb. There was one teacher to teach all eight grades, with an enrollment of about 25 to 30 students. There were two outhouses, one for boys, and one for girls. Sometimes in winter, they were used as shelter during fierce snowball fights. A hand-held pump to provide drinking water stood in the front of the school. I still remember the collapsible cups we each had to drink from. Playground equipment consisted of a seesaw, slide, and swings. This was magic to me, as we

One-room school students and the teacher in Missouri

had none of this at home. There was an old horse barn on the playground, but at the time I attended there was no one riding horses to school, so the barn was torn down.

When you entered the building you put your lunchbox, coats, caps, gloves, and boots in a small room called a cloakroom. Inside, the library was to the left in the corner area. I was fascinated with books and magazines, which were few or nonexistent in our home. I remember loving to read the teacher's copy of *The Instructor* magazine. I think it inspired me because later I indeed became a teacher. Inside the school, the desks were attached to runners. The floor was wooden and it was oiled to keep down the dust. The teacher's desk was at the front of the room. A big black-jacketed stove stood to the right, in the front corner. It was stoked with coal by the teacher or the older boys. In the winter, sometimes students would bring food to set on the stove so they could have a warm meal for lunch. Most students did not have this. There were no hot lunches provided and some students brought their lunches to school in tin buckets.

A piano stood on the left of the room; it was an old upright that I played to accompany our singing. The teacher usually had no musical training, so the children sort-of taught themselves, and amazingly, sang with gusto. We loved singing *America, America the Beautiful, The Star-spangled Banner,* and many others. During the war, we sang *Let's Remember Pearl Harbor, as We did the Alamo* and *Yes, We Have No Bananas.* There was rationing in those days. Every morning we sang America and said the Pledge of Allegiance. A picture of George Washington hung on the wall in front along with the flag.

Everyone went to recess at the same time, and it was a cherished time. It was not supervised, but older students looked out for the younger ones. Games such as Cops and Robbers, Red Rover, and Andy Over were played. One winter we built a magnificent snow fort out of blocks of snow. The teacher or a student who had been given the privilege would ring a big hand bell to call the children back to their studies. The students, when called by class, would come to the front and be seated before the teacher, where she would teach the lesson. The slate blackboards were used often, during class and also during indoor recess.

Christmas programs were a highlight of the year. A Christmas tree was cut, put up in front, and decorated. I remember my sister, who was a very good artist, painted a picture of the Wise Men on the window above the door. The program consisted of singing and a play or two performed by the children. Sheets were hung on wires in front to make a stage. Santa played a part, making his entrance at some point in the program. The school was usually packed with parents and grandparents. Sometimes the school was so full that some people had to stand outside and look in through the windows.

Discipline didn't seem to be a big problem, although I remember one boy who was in trouble was asked by the teacher to go out and get a stick to be disciplined with. He came back with a cornstalk, roots still attached. That happened at the end of the day and we were leaving, which made me happy. I don't know what happened after that.

One day in early fall we were all in school when the boy sitting in front of me started throwing up and became very sick. His parents took him to the doctor. He was diagnosed with infantile paralysis (polio), the dreaded disease of that time. The school was closed and I remember my parents being very upset since my sister, brother, and I were exposed. This was one time I saw my parents really dote over us. The student lived, but was badly crippled in his back. His siblings, who were also in school there, became ill, but had a milder form of the disease. They were not crippled. Amazingly, no one else came down with the disease. Since the Salk vaccine came to be, we don't hear about this dreaded disease today. When I was a child, it was something to be feared.

I am now 80 years old, a widowed farm wife, retired teacher, mother, and grandmother. The little school where I went to school is now painted red. It was white during the eight years I attended. It is a community center for the area and is kept up for that reason. It is one of the few still in existence. By the way, my sister's picture of the Wise Men is still above that door on the transom window!

When I talk to my grandchildren, I realize they can't imagine what it would be like to go to a one-room school. I plan to take them to the school one day. I do not wish for the "good old days," because I remember the good and the bad of those days. I look at the schools of today and wonder which is best. For sure, there never has been and never will be utopia on earth, whether in schools or anything else, but I do have good memories of going to that one-room school.

It Was a Privilege Growing up in Denver
By Avis Parman of Albany, Missouri
Born 1923

Growing up in the '30s in Denver, Missouri, Worth County, gave me the foundation for my future endeavors. I remember the hardships many families faced during that period. My family was lucky as my dad was appointed Postmaster for the Denver Post Office in 1932 at a salary of $90.00 a month.

I remember one evening our neighbor came to our house and with tears in his eye, asked my dad if he could borrow $5.00 to buy flour, sugar, and other staples to feed his family. Of course, my dad gave him the money. My dad was always helping people in many ways, which taught me to give back and to be thankful for what I have been given.

Another neighbor, Uncle Tom, as we called him, called up the spirits and people came from all areas to watch him. He put his hands on a table and folks could ask a question and the table leg would come up two times for "no" and three times for "yes." All that is still a mystery to me. Some people believed while others did not.

Denver was a very active place, with many stores, a service station, a restaurant, a theater, a produce buying store, a doctor, three churches, an undertaker, and especially Findley Graces Furniture Store. Also, in the winter, a person cut ice from the Grand River, which went through the edge of Denver. The ice was stored and then was used in an icebox in the spring to keep food cool.

Saturday night was a big night for the young people. They could go to the theater show for ten cents and have popcorn or candy for one cent. A few years later, a band was formed and concerts were held in the park, which had a bandstand that was made from locally made cement bricks. Of course, on Halloween an outhouse was always put on the bandstand or on top of another building.

Our school consisted of grades one through eight, plus two years of high school.

289

Years later, it was consolidated with the Grant City School District. One day, as Denver was hosting an area track meet, a dust storm with a strong wind came up. It was so dark we had to wait to finish after the dust storm had passed. It was red dirt from Oklahoma. Many times after a dust storm, when we dusted the dust rag was red.

Also, we had no school buses, so we had to walk everywhere, through mud, snow, and sleet. One winter, the ice stayed on for around two weeks, and we ice skated to school. People had the local blacksmith shop make cleats with straps that would fit over their shoes and over shoes, so that they could walk better on the ice and would not fall. It was a bad time for livestock on the farms as well as during the summer drought.

There was no grass so sometimes trees were trimmed and leaves fed to the livestock. Water was a problem also during that period. When possible, everyone planted a garden and canned the product for winter, keeping it in a cave. Also, each year the neighbors would get together and butcher hogs, calves, and then chickens and turkeys. As Grand River ran through our farm, my dad always fished the "rock," giving us fish to eat.

We had no TV, no iPads, etc. The only communication was the party telephone line where several neighbors were on the line and could listen to what we were talking about. Therefore, we were careful what was said.

We made our own fun and games, plus we had chores to do. We didn't sit inside on the couch. We played games like three deep, black man, hide and seek, and softball. Our chores were mowing the lawn, helping to stack the hay, and many other activities such as 4-H, where we learned to sew. We made skirts out of feed sacks, which today they would not believe. We were proud to have them.

One summer, my mother was ill, and the local doctor could not find out what was wrong. He suggested going to St. Joseph to a doctor. It was an infection from a tooth. During that time, I did all of the housework and learned to cook for the family, company, and hay hands. The only thing I didn't do was the washing. My dad did that using the gasoline-powered washing machine with a wringer to take the water out of the clothes.

After graduating from Grant City High School, I took the teachers examination and passed, which gave me the privilege to teach in a one-room school. I taught at Pine School located north of Denver for two years. I rode a horse most of the time each day, except in bad weather when I stayed with a family near the school. Building a fire, carrying in water, and teaching was a challenge during those years but a great experience.

Yes, it was a privilege to grow up in the Denver community, where everyone cared about each other and helped each other and were truly interested in making the town a better place to live, work, and play. How times have changed!

Sledding, Brewing, and Fishing
By Norman O. Steidel of St. Joseph, Missouri
Born 1934

Back when I was in grade school, there was a big snow. A friend of mine and I took my brother's bobsled up the hill about two and a half blocks from the house where I lived. We thought we would have some fun.

My brother had built this bobsled from the plans in a book that he had. It was for four people. There was just the two of us. Well, to make a long story short, we thought that we two could handle it. We got it up where we wanted it, got on, and away we went: down the first hill, turned the first corner, to the next, and then turned the next. We thought that we would stop at about two blocks down the street, but we went on down and up another and down another. When we did stop, we were more than eight blocks away from where we started. We had to pull that thing back up to the last hill, and we slid down to the next flat street and pulled it to my house.

That sled was about 100 pounds, and we were only about 60 pounds each. But that was sure some ride. That was the last time that I took that sled for a ride.

One other time, this friend of mine and I were having a good time on a Saturday morning at my house. My mother had made up about two boxes of root beer for all of us kids at home. I think she made up as many as 48 bottles of root beer at a time and put it in the basement to keep it cool. My dad made home brew and kept it in the basement also. My job was to bring up about four to six bottles of

Dad's brew and put them in the icebox each weekend.

The home brew and the root beer were on the same shelf. My friend and I thought that we had root beer, but we opened up two of Dad's brews and started to drink it. We both passed out and fell asleep on the floor.

Nobody knew where we were. I think that Mom and Dad on his jobs were all looking for us. My dad always looked in the icebox for a cold one and there were not any there. So he told Mom that he would go and get some of his brew, and then help look for me and my friend. When Dad went to the basement, there we were, sound asleep. He brought me up and then took my friend up to his house. He took about four or five of the brews, also. He told my friend's dad, "When he wakes up, give him a glass of the brew. Make him drink all of it." That is what he did to me also. I did not drink any more beer until about when I was in the Army. I was only about seven when this happened. My friend was like me and did not drink until later. I think that was about fifteen years.

I went fishing with my brother-in-law and his wife. We were sitting on a lake bank. To the north of us, there were a lot of white birds on the lake. Something caused them to fly up.

My sister-in-law said they were sure pretty. Then the birds flew right over her and me. We both looked up at them and she had said that they looked pretty and about that time a couple of them dropped a load right on her, one on her forehead and one on her chin. If her mouth was opened, it would have hit her mouth. Then she said, "Boy that was the nastiest bunch of birds I have ever seen."

Another time all three of us were fishing at another lake. I hooked a snapping turtle and brought it in. I picked it up and took it about a hundred feet up from the lake and threw it as far as I could. Then I went back to fish. About a half an hour or so later, we heard a noise in the grass and here comes the snapper. He was coming right at me. Everywhere I went he followed me. He chased me no matter where I went. We got a big stick and worked him over but didn't kill him. Finally, he went back in the lake and didn't trouble us. It was sure as funny as the birds with my sister-in-law. We still have a laugh about it each time that all three of us go fishing. Yes, we still go to each lake to fish.

The Forties: An Education for Life
By Marie Wheeler of Mound City, Missouri
Born 1935

Being five years old in 1940, I wasn't particularly concerned about the effects from the Depression years. I knew that we lived with my great-grandfather in a big house that he had built. It was on a farm a mile from town. We had electricity, telephone, a radio, a well for water, and an old truck for travel. Didn't everyone? We had plenty of food because we butchered two or three hogs and two calves each winter. My job was to cut up the fat into small chunks for rendering. In the summer, we dressed many young chickens. We always had eggs, milk, cream, and butter. Mom would can beef, sausage, and ribs. Dad would salt-cure the hams and bacon in the smoke house. I learned where our meat came from and how to preserve it so that it would last all year. In the spring, summer, and fall, we had plenty of vegetables: peas, carrots, potatoes, beans, beets, tomatoes, corn, and cabbage. These would be preserved by canning into jars in a hot water canner, as no pressure canner was available. This food was consumed throughout the year. Freezers were not available but later our town installed freezer lockers that you could rent. What a wonderful invention! When you went to town for groceries, you could take your locker key and get several frozen packages to prepare for meals later. I learned that food didn't just "jump" into jars; it took a lot of work to prepare food for preservation. We always had plenty of fruit: peaches strawberries, cherries, grapes, apricots, apples, and pears. These were canned or frozen for the locker, which tasted so fresh in the winter. All were so delicious except for the canned strawberries. They were canned without sugar during World War II. Sugar was in short supply and was rationed out. I learned the value of preserving food and to make do with what we had.

Saturday nights in town was a major event. Taking a bath was a big chore because we had to heat the water on the stove since we did not have indoor plumbing. I took an early bath on Saturdays, got dressed, and loaded into the pick-up truck to drive into town with my parents and little brother. Once we got there, we unloaded the eggs and cream to sell at the creamery and found a place to park since there was always a big crowd. We went to the movies for 10 to 25 cents while our parents shopped or visited with friends and relatives. After the movie, we looked for our grandmother as she would give us each a nickel for an ice cream cone. Then we would meet our friends and walk up and down the street to window shop or find more friends to visit with. When it was time to go home, Mom would buy four wieners or four bologna slices for sandwiches to eat when we got home. Yum! I learned that socializing builds character and friendships. I learned that socializing didn't require a lot of money to have fun, either.

There were no televisions in the '40s, just newspapers, magazines, comic books, and the newsreel at the movies. World War II was hard to imagine unless you talked to someone with more information. I was worried that my Daddy would get drafted and leave, but he was a farmer and was needed at home. Many relatives and friends did fight the battle. I remember collecting milkweed pods to be used as stuffing in uniforms. I took a dime to school each week to buy a stamp for a savings bond. I learned the need to help others and the need to save for the future.

Alma, Leota, Dora, and Marie in about 1938

There were always chores to do on the farm. We would milk cows twice a day, feed and gather eggs from the chickens, bring in firewood for the cook stove and heating stove, garden, and do the washing and ironing. We had no air conditioning or refrigerator. We would get a 50-pound block of ice from the icehouse in town for the icebox. We kept the milk, cream, and butter in the cellar to keep cool. There was no indoor toilet, just a path and an outhouse. The water bucket was filled from the pump and well outside the porch. We used a white water bucket and dipper to get a drink. The dipper was washed every day or so. We did have an electric wringer

washer. The water had to be heated in copper boilers on the stove on washday. This was a very hot job in the summer. The clothes were hung on the lines outside. We always cleaned the lines with a wet cloth first because the birds used the lines too! The final step was ironing the clothes, towels, handkerchiefs, etc. From this, I learned the value of taking pride in my work and helping my family.

After World War II, my folks began to sell cream, milk, butter, and eggs to customers in town. Delivery was every Wednesday and Saturday. In the summer, Mom dressed young chickens to sell. The money was used to buy groceries such as bread, flour, sugar, cereal, etc. We only got the necessities. I learned the value of money; if you couldn't' afford it, you didn't buy it.

Social life was very important in the '40s. We went to church each Sunday. Celebrations were eventful. My great-granddad always celebrated his May birthday with a public basket dinner. Dad would set up sawhorses with boards on top for tables under the shade trees. Relatives, friends, and neighbors, would come from miles around to wish him a happy birthday. They would bring a basket filled with delicious food. Great-granddad would get dressed in his best suit and sit on the south porch where he could see cars coming in from town. We lived on a high hill a mile from town. I learned what birthday celebrations meant to my elders and the importance of friends and neighbors.

Other celebrations included the annual summer dinner at the Bethel Country Church and family reunions. There were other church dinners, my mother's club dinners, and the 4-H Weiner Roast in the fall. Family traditions included Fourth of July ice cream suppers with fireworks, Thanksgiving dinners, Easter egg hunts, and New Year's Eve soup suppers. Of course, Christmas was a time to celebrate at each of the grandparents' with food and gifts. Gifts were simple and inexpensive. We received things like socks, handkerchiefs, a towel, perfume, or something handmade. My great-grandfather gave each person a fifty-cent coin. Oh, how rich I felt! I learned the importance of traditions and that the price of a gift is not important, it is the thought that counts.

Relatives and friends loved to visit my folks as they lived next to a major highway and had easy access to our home. There was always a dinner to celebrate our company's visit. Sometimes the visitors would stay three or four days. During a flood, friends would stay with my folks till the waters receded and they could go back home. When they stayed, I learned how our families were related. I wish I had listened more to their stories. Genealogy became important in my later years. How I wish I could talk to my relatives now and learn of their background!

Yes, the '40s was an interesting time. We didn't know that we were poor. We had food on the table and clothes to wear which were usually hand-me-downs or homemade. I had family and grandparents to guide me. We didn't miss what we didn't have, like running water, air conditioning, and indoor bathrooms. We learned to work and make do with what we had and still have fun. We learned to be creative and use our imagination. We learned love, compassion, and to live by the Ten Commandments from the Bible. Would I want to relive the '40s? No! I now realize that life was difficult without money and modern conveniences, but my parents never dwelled on that. They took one day at a time and kept smiling. I do wish our children and grandchildren could experience just for one week some of our "education" instead of reading it in story form. "Hands-on" experience can be a great teacher.

My Big Fear!
By Lucille Zimmerman of Maryville, Missouri
Born 1940

I can still remember as a very young child,
Running, and singing, and playing in the wild.
We picked lots of vegetables for our mom.
We even picked some for our uncle, Tom.

We had lots of chores to do.
But chores were all we knew.
We learned to play and have fun.
We laughed until our work was done.
Mom always had fixed a wonderful meal.
As we came in, we cheered and gave a squeal.
There was Mom's good old homemade bread.
We had no money, but were always well fed.
We climbed trees and sat high on the limbs.
We were never sad or had any big whims.
Travel consisted of trips to church on Sunday.
If you missed, it was hell to pay.
We didn't know what "town" even was about.
So we didn't waste our time and sit and pout.
We were up early as I helped milk the cows.
Brother Paul and I also had to feed the sows.
When it was time to put the loose hay up in the barn,
Paul would bribe me into his job. Oh, darn!
He had to lead the fork horse, to lift the hay.
He would talk me into it, and then never stay.
The big workhorse was always gentle and very calm.
I slipped and fell, running a big thorn into my palm.
Then the horse stepped on the back of my heel.
As I looked down, I saw that the skin began to peel.
Back then, you only wore shoes to church and school.
You went barefoot, saving shoes. That was the rule.
Paul got a big lecture from our dad.
And that made me feel really sad!
I never did want my brother Paul to get into trouble.
If he got yelled at, it would burst my happy bubble.
We were bosom buddies, only two years apart.
He was my buddy from the very start.
My January 4th birthday was only two years behind.
His was January 5th, and we were one of a kind.
We played a lot and did all the chores together.
The big five-gallon buckets required help from one another.

We pumped water every day by the hour.
It took muscles and lots of arm power.
As she got older, we got little sister Mary's help.
Brother Paul used to say she was just a "little whelp."
He didn't think that she could pump for very long,
But Mary was very thin and soon proved him wrong.
Big sister, Joan, always worked more in the house.
She wouldn't have like our job of killing a mouse.
Paul and I had to take clubs to clear the corncribs.
The huge rats and mice were hit hard in the ribs.
We aimed at the biggest part of their bodies it seems.
If we missed, they would bite us and foul up our dreams.
Luckily, I don't ever remember either of us hurt.
I do remember one running up under my skirt!
Believe me I got rid of him very quick!
Paul came to my rescue with a huge stick.
I still didn't have a fear of mice or rats.
We also had a few flying prey, called bats.
Dad told us to let them alone as they helped us.
They killed mosquitoes while making no noise or fuss.
But as a child, I developed a fear that has never gone away!
My encounters with snakes caused a fear that is here to stay.
I can remember digging postholes with our dad.
He dug into a bull snake, making him feel sad.
We were told that snakes do good for the farm.
He didn't intend to kill the snake causing alarm.
The snake was full of eggs that she was ready to lay.
But the babies would die and didn't have long to stay.
They weren't quite far enough along to live.
There was nothing we could do, no food to give.
I had no fear whatever at that time.

I even remember writing a little rhyme.
I had never had a fear or been afraid of a snake.
I would push them out of the garden with a rake.
I did a book report and got an "A." I was thrilled!
I didn't want any snake to get in our way or be killed.
Then one day as I rode our one bicycle down a steep hill,
Our neighbor lady was making a new dress for this little pill.
We used our old flour sacks for the new dress.
I hated to wear new clothes and made a mess.
I wanted to go climb trees and play ball.
So I was late and started to slow and stall.
I had to ride fast down that big long hill by then.
I hadn't ridden on the road since I don't know when.
About half way down, I saw this big snake.
I tried to avoid hitting him, for heaven's sake!
But it was too late, as I hit the brakes, skidding to a stop,
That flipped my bicycle and over I fell, landing right on his top,
He got tangled up in the spokes of the bike.
I was pinned underneath by that time. That I didn't like!
And then my dress got caught in the bicycle chain.
No matter what I tried, there was not an inch to gain.
The big snake's head came round and round.
I screamed, thinking, "For the grave I'm bound."
There was no one anywhere around to help me.
There was no one that I could even find or see.
To this day, I don't know how I got out of there.
He couldn't quite reach me, only my long hair.
I don't know how that wheel kept on spinning.
His big body got more tangled, he wasn't winning.
I tore my dress to get loose and limped back home
I was bloodied and hysterical, vowing never

to roam.
My dear brother, Paul, went to rescue the wrecked bike for me.
He wasn't afraid of snakes and was my good buddy, you see.
So my mom bandaged all of my wounds and cuts.
She said, "Oh, I think you must have hit some ruts."
Our roads back then were only dirt.
I also heard about ripping my skirt.
My mom didn't have time to sew, as we had a handicapped brother.
There were two babies, as little sister, Theresa, was the other.
She was younger, it's true, but Mom had a big job!
Of any spare time the six of us kids did rob.
So sewing was left to the neighbor, who was very good!
Mom in exchange gave her milk and eggs whenever we could.
So I had missed my appointment and added to more work.
How could I have been so careless, what a jerk!
That night, I began to have my lifetime of nightmares.
I have never been free of them, at my heart, it still tears.
My horrors grew, as months later we went for a ride.
Six kids and Mom and Dad piled into our old buggy, side by side.
We were so packed we could hardly move.
But we were having fun, in a party groove.
The wheels on the buggy were high above the side.
I was on the side next to the wheel for the ride.
We drove through our pasture to check on the crops.
Our buggy was loaded and full of fun, making no stops.
Something was hitting my hair and I brushed it away.
But as we went on, the pest was there to stay.
I turned to try and see what was hitting my head.
It was the one horrible thing I had come to dread!
A big snake's head kept coming around very fast.
It just can't be, I thought. My heart won't

last!
I began my loud and famous scream, trying to lean over.
We were packed so tight, I couldn't jump out into the clover.
My dad told us to stop fighting, right now!
Screaming, I had to get away, I didn't care how.
Finally, my brother, Paul, saw the snake, too.
He screamed also, not knowing what to do.
One by one, all the kids joined in, making lots of noise.
No one in that back seat felt anything close to our early joys.
Dad finally spotted the snake and helped us get free.
There was no way anyone could console me.
Dad tried and tried to pull that snake loose,
But he hung on tightly, there was no truce.
Dad finally said there was only one thing to do.
"I'm going to have to kill it before it bites you."
By then, I had climbed to top of our fifty-foot windmill.
It was close and not very far to that area on top of the hill.
I could go on forever, as that was just the very start.
It had gotten to the point "snake" words tasted tart.
I still am afraid of live pictures on TV
And the big one high up in my backyard tree.
So almost everyone who knows me knows my deep fear.
If you tease me with anything, it will produce a big tear!
I'm seventy-three, and it never, ever leaves my mind.
It keeps my heart and mind in an uncommon bind.
But the rest of our fifty-four years of marriage has been great!
With five children and twelve grandchildren, we really do rate!
In my lifetime, my encounters with snakes have never stopped.
Of all the things that have happened, snakes can't be topped.
I try to avoid any encounters with the slimy things.
Just seeing them on TV, horrible memories it brings.
But my life is still happy and filed with lots

of love!
I constantly lean on Him and ask for
guidance from above.
He guides me and shows me the right way.
In my life, I'm begging Him to always stay.
The good old country life has been really
neat!
It is really a life that is fun and can't be beat!
Thank you, God, even if you did have to
create snakes!
I guess everyone has to at one time make
some mistakes!
But the Blessed Mother Mary had her foot on
that snake's back.
Why didn't she kill him, his skull would
have taken one whack.
Maybe God didn't want her to do that to him.
She could have eliminated the snake so long
and slim.
So for now, I guess I will just have to watch
my step!
And so for heaven, my life I will have to now
prep.

Life and Worship in Clarksdale, Missouri
By Marilyn Moran of Savannah, Missouri
Born 1939

The First Baptist Church in Clarksdale, Missouri was located on the west side of the park. It was a white, steepled building with a big bell that was rung for church services by a person pulling a rope from inside the vestibule. We entered the sanctuary through swinging doors. As we entered, we met the morning with the sun shinning through the many stained-glass windows. The windows had been given to the church by families in memory of loved ones who had passed on. This scene set the mood for our worship.

Roberta Clinton was our church pianist for the worship service, and she played beautifully. The choir was led by Dwayne Fagan, and we almost always sang the same hymn special for worship service: *Let Others See Jesus in You*. I think it was the one that sounded best with our limited talents. God told us to make a joyful noise, so we did our best.

I played for Sunday school for three years, when I was twelve to fifteen years old, but my talent was limited. However, the early experience prepared me for playing in several churches throughout my life.

We had Sunday school classes in the basement with a wood stove for heat. Alice Anderson was one of my teachers. She was the mother of Iona, Ava, and Ralph Anderson, who were my friends. She was a wonderful Christian lady.

We had a GA (Girls in Action) group that met during the week to learn Bible verses and study about missionaries. Esther Ketchem was our leader. Esther was a great Christian lady who wanted all her girls to know Christ as their savior. Her husband was Guy.

Bible school was held in the summertime when school was out. It was a fun time for learning about God and the Bible and also for playing with our friends We had several ministers at different times, but I especially remember a young pastor named Tom Bray, because he invited us to come to Christ during Bible school one day. The Holy Spirit came into my heart, and I went forward and accepted the invitation. That summer, I was baptized in a pond in Whitesville, Missouri by Tom Bray. We had a cement baptismal tank in our church basement, but at the time, it leaked, so we didn't put water in it.

In November of 1957, I was married in this church to Jim Schottel. My parents celebrated their 50th Wedding Anniversary there also in 1982.

Many times during church, we would notice the side door opening and someone would head out. They were headed to the two-holer outhouse. We didn't have inside plumbing then.

Leaders in the Baptist Church are called deacons. Amos Fry was a deacon from the old school. He was a tall, lanky man and was intimidating to me. He always prayed long, long prayers and said, "Amen" a lot during services. He knew his Bible well and studied it a lot. His son, Armond Fry, went on to be a Baptist preacher. He and his wife, Madeline, had two daughters, Lavern and Phyllis. Phyllis was one of my friends and a cousin to my future husband.

Ed Veraguth was a deacon also. He sang in the choir and men's quartet with his deep and loud bass voice.

The Baptist Church was one of three churches in Clarksdale. There were the Methodist and the Christian Churches, also. They all played a part in our lives as citizens of the Clarksdale community.

Clarksdale was a great town to grow up in. We learned good values and morals. It was definitely a different lifestyle than today, and we can't go back in time. The simpler life we had back then looks inviting sometimes as we compare it with the hustle and bustle of our lives today. Maybe?

Saturday Night in Clarksdale, MO

We looked forward to Saturday night. For my family, Emerson and Lois Shirk, my brother, Ronald, and me, Marilyn, Saturday night was a big social event. It was a break from our daily work on the farm. After the chores were done on the farm, and we had eaten supper, we went to Clarksdale. We tried to get a place to park in front of Don Pearson's grocery store, because that was where the action was on Saturday night.

Main Street was packed with cars parked solid on the east side of the street. The Barber Shop, owned by Ray Clinton, was next to Pearson's, so the men went in there to get a haircut or just visit and catch up on the latest town gossip. The other grocery store in town was owned by Ted and Oma Arnold and later by Albert Anderson.

When the car was parked, we kids headed out down the sidewalk to find our friends. Mom and Dad sat in the car and watched people come and go into the businesses. People sometimes stopped and visited with friends in the cars along the street and sometimes got in the car and visited a while. Eventually Mom went to the grocery store and bought our groceries for the week. Then about 9:30pm, the grownups went to Clark's Drug Store and Soda Fountain and ordered malts all around and proceeded to the wooden booths to drink their malts and visit until time to go home.

My brother and I each got ten cents for the night to spend on the treats we wanted. We could buy one-cent candy and get a sack full for ten cents or we could buy a Cherry Coke for five cents and sit at the booths with our friends and make it last most of the evening. It was a time for teasing and flirting, as we grew older.

On some summer nights, some motion pictures were shown in the park on a big screen there. Everyone brought blankets for their families, and we all enjoyed the movies. This was before we had TVs and we didn't go to St Joe for movies very often in those days.

The feed store was on the north end of Main Street. They sold feed and bought cream and eggs from the farmers. Ladies bought flour in printed sacks and when the flour was used, they washed the sacks and took them to the feed store and traded their sacks for others to match. With several sacks, children's clothes were made, along with shirts, blouses, and skirts for adults. We didn't always have money to buy new material. I had many clothes from this source and was proud to have a new dress now and then.

When I think back on Saturday nights in Clarksdale, I have fond memories, and I think it was a learning time. We learned to communicate with all ages of people. Our parents were good examples of how to live life. Men worked hard, and women worked by their side to help, and the children had their chores to do. We worked together for the good of us all. We were happy and hopeful for the future. We were taught that if we worked hard and long, we would eventually reap our reward. My mother and dad were successful farmers and lived by Christian principles. My brother, Ron, and his wife, Joyce Shirk, are still living on the farm one and one-half miles north of Clarksdale. It was, and still is, a good life.

I'm Lucky My Parents Met Each Other
By Janice Lathrop of St. Joseph, Missouri
Born 1938

Rev. John Lowthropp was born December 20, 1584 in Etton, Yorkshire, England and died November 8, 1653 in Barnstable, Massachusetts. He immigrated to America on September 18, 1634 aboard the ship Griffin, and had married Hannah Howse, his first wife on October 16, 1610 in Eastwell, Kent. She was born about 1594 and died February 16, 1633/34 in London. He then married Anna Hammond on June 14, 1635 in Scituate, MA. They had four children.

Robert Foster was born in 1856 in Roanoke, Virginia. His mother is listed in a marriage bond on April 10, 1847 for the sum of one-hundred fifty dollars. She married a Charly Minnicks. From the 1860 census records for Buchanan County, there is a record of William Foster, whose wife was Minna or Minerva. Their bond date is August 8, 1841 in Botetourt, Virginia, with his date of birth around 1817. The Foster families traveled to Kentucky and onward to Missouri's Platte Purchase with seven children and Savannah Walker, who is listed as 85 years old in the census records. John Board Foster was born in February 1854 and died in 1931 in Severance, Kansas. He married Catherine "Molly" Walters (1860-1937), and they had six children. The third one was Rebecca Lee Foster, my grandmother. She was born June 3, 1889 and died February 9, 1975. Rebecca married Joseph Levandowski on January 3, 1913 in St. Joseph, Missouri. There were four children born Frances, Lillian Marie, Molly, and Leo. Marie married Dale Edmond Lathrop on January 20, 1937. To this union was born Janice in 1938, Marilyn in 1939, and Ronald E. in 1942.

The story that tells the tale of my parents, and how they got together begins in the Depression years of the 1930s. My mother's family had settled on a farm located between the southern city limits of St Joseph and the junction of old US 71 and Route A to Facuette, Missouri. She attended a single room schoolhouse consisting of eight grades and one teacher, where she and her sisters and brother walked or rode a mule approximately one mile each day. Economic times were tough, and crop prices were too scarce to keep the family's budget from collapsing, so they moved to a rented house on South 22nd Street in St Joseph.

About 1934, tragedy struck the Lathrops on a farm near Axtell, Nebraska. The head of this family, George Elver Lathrop, died of complications from a blood clot. Dale Lathrop became the head of the family, but he could not run the farm tasks without help. Although he had a football scholarship to the University of Nebraska at Lincoln, his sister, Leona Lucille, and her husband, Rufus Taylor, convinced the family to move to St Joseph, MO, where a job at a small diner near the West Tab factory awaited him. They moved in 1936 or 1937. Dad's older sister got a job at the telephone company, and they moved to a rental on South 18th.

Would you believe my parents met when Lillian Marie went to work at the diner as a waitress where my dad cooked? They knew each other for about two months before marrying at the Buchanan County Courthouse on January 20, 1937. I was born the next year in February 1938. Dad worked for a carpenter who could not afford to pay him much, and he soon got a job at Quaker Oats, where he loaded trucks with feed sacks for animals.

Somehow, they managed to buy from my mom's sister, Molly, the house next door to her on South 20th. Since my grandparents lived on 22nd Street, this extended family actually owned half a block of city property from 20th to 22nd facing Sacramento Street. A very large part of it was a garden, which my grandfather made available for the large victory garden. He enlarged it after the war to peach and apple trees, strawberry and gooseberry bushes, and grape vines. He also maintained a junk garage where he kept iron, chickens, and the meanest goose that ever walked the earth.

The earliest memories I have were those of starting elementary school at age six, when I began first grade and my sister was in kindergarten. The end of World War II was a year away, and I had three uncles who joined up. My uncle, David Averett, was wounded on Omaha Beach, on the second day of the invasion. My uncle, Leo Levandowski, was wounded in the Battle of the Bulge, and my uncle, Odell McIntosh, served in the Navy. My family fought the war on the home front with a huge victory garden and ration books for tires, sugar, and staples. The only candy I remember was homemade fudge and divinity that my mother made.

Hall School was five long city blocks from our house, and there was no such thing as a bus for pick-up and delivery of schoolchildren. We all walked with the older neighbor children, and they watched out for the younger school kids. We were instilled with responsibility very early and passed it on by assembling before and after school in a group walk. Along with personal responsibilities, we were taught civil patriotism in the form of collection of tin cans and newspapers for the war effort. We had no idea what these things were used for in winning the war, but it was my job to collect old and used newspapers in my little red wagon and bring them to school, where they were recycled periodically. I got a paper trooper badge to wear for turning in however many newspapers it took to get one.

My father worked for Quaker Oats, which was considered an industry vital to the war effort, and those who worked there were deferred, although he was told he might be called up for the invasion of Japan. My sister and I wore dresses and pinafores sown by Mother from feed sacks brought home by Dad, who I was told threw them around at his work. My grandmother used the leftover material to make quilts. Grandfather's garden included peach and apple trees, raspberry and gooseberry bushes and a lot of strawberries, from which he made wine, although none was used until the end of the war.

The war in Europe ended at the end of the school year in 1945. I remember the excitement of riding the bus downtown. The adults in my world were full of joy. There was a parade with a band playing and people marching. The biggest disappointment of the day was standing on the corner of Seventh and Edmond waiting for the bus to take us home and seeing all the newspapers I had collected for school blowing in the wind down the street.

The Great Depression was not ended until World War II geared up with massive armament build-ups for the coming conflict. The efforts of my parents, who lived through it, and the sacrifices made by them and others and the financial outlay of the Roosevelt Administration was the real end to the Depression.

With the end of the war, the returning servicemen looked toward employment efforts, and my uncles and their families settled down near each other. I had a number of cousins, most of whom were younger than me, which was a deciding factor in who was the boss and who got to plan the weekend and summer activities. It also made me the responsible one when trouble erupted. I can count on all my digits the times I didn't get punished for the four or five times I did get caught. My two older cousins, Bonnie and Dean Taylor, moved in the 1950s with my grandmother Lathrop and Aunt Doris, to northern California for employment and left me in charge of my maternal cousins. Since we didn't get a TV until I was in the seventh grade, it was my job to keep my cousins occupied by playing outdoor games, or riding bicycles to the park. Quite often, I was appointed babysitter for one or the other while the mother was busy with household task.

My grandparents kept chickens for years, starting early in the spring with one hundred chicks, which grew all summer. Then one day the kettle would come out of storage, a fire was lit under it, and Grandpa would chop off the chickens' heads, plop them in the kettle, and Grandma would pluck feathers all day. We would freeze all we could and eat a lot of chicken all winter. I had a pet hen named Betty one summer, whose short life made me a lifelong consumer of beef.

I can remember the flood of 1952, when the Missouri River filled the land between the bluffs for weeks. My parents had taken a trip to California and on their return could not cross the bridge because the river cut through Highway 36. Grandma Lathrop said they would just have to stay in Kansas until the water receded. Later, I found out that they had crossed the river at Atchison and returned to St Joseph on Highway 71. This was before Interstate 29 was built.

The family history and the stories of my two lines of ancestors' travels have been lost from the decades, but the fact that my parents met in the closing years of the Great Depression is one that I can recount here because I asked them how they met. I compiled a genealogical history in 1982 from census records. I guessed from the chronological dates and ancestor's births and burial places and from the journeys from Massachusetts and Virginia of these forbearers that I was extremely lucky that my parents ever got together.

To call these years the "good old days" discounts the medical advances of penicillin, modern sanitation practices, and technical inventions. The best thing about this time was that we survived it with a little help from our friends, families, and neighbors.

Quarantined
By Nita Waterman of Kansas City, Missouri
Born 1941

One day, as I approached our house carefully and stepped onto the front porch, I saw a large purple sign with white letters on our front door. It read one word: "Quarantined." What did it mean and who put it there? It wasn't there when I went out to play. I entered the house cautiously, looking for Mom who always had all the answers to my questions. "We have scarlet fever at our house; a man from the health department put the sign on the door," she said. She explained that because of this sickness, we could not leave our house and no one could come over to play for ten days. It felt like we were in prison. If I wasn't sick, then why did I have to stay home? It was not unusual for someone to be sick at our house because I was one of eight kids. I had seen the "sick" kids; why was this different?

Suddenly things were different. Dr. Harned was the family doctor and he came to our house when needed. Mom said that the quarantined sign meant that we would be seeing him shortly. When we saw him parking his car in front of our house, we knew that was our cue to run and hide. No doubt, someone was going to be given medicine, or worse, a shot in the butt! Dr Harned wore a brightly colored necktie with a skeleton sitting on two sawhorses printed on it. It had "old sawbones" written across it. Mom and Dad revered Dr. Harned. They always welcomed him in to our home and gave him their utmost attention. He was a soft-spoken man with a gentle nature and they trusted his expertise in treating us. If he said, "We need to paint their throats with purple medicine," that is exactly what happened. He looked in our ears and mouth and put a cold, round, silver disk on our chest that plugged into his ears. Dad asked us not to talk while the doctor listened to our chest.

Nita's family
In the middle row is Nita, Sandra, and Helen

We weren't used to having a stranger touch us and weren't sure what he would do next. He was a kind and gentle man that seemed to like kids, but we were still afraid of him. We were afraid of what he had in his mysterious black bag. That's where he kept the hypodermic needle and foul-tasting medicine. We watched carefully as he opened his bag, and if we saw that hypodermic needle, we felt our fear building. The needle looked big and scary and since he examined all of us kids, I wondered which one of us was going to get a shot. I hoped it wasn't me. To sterilize the needle, he placed it in the flame on the gas stove that Mom used for cooking. After holding it there for a minute, he said it was sterile, wiped it on a clean cloth, and held it carefully so that it did not touch anything. To us kids, it looked like he was heating it up like a hot poker to give us a shot in the butt. That alone was reason enough to hide. When Dad said, "come over here and raise your shirt," we feared that he would spot tiny red bumps. Those would almost guarantee a shot was coming. From then on, we checked ourselves often for any red bumps and if they appeared, we kept a close watch for cars pulling up in front of the house.

My sister Sandra, the mud-pie baker, had pneumonia more than once, and sometimes Dr. Harned would come to the house and give her a shot. She screamed so loud we thought he was killing her, so we all ran up the street where he couldn't' find us. We hid behind a big tree or ducked down behind fences. We watched the house to see if Dad was coming out to look for us. When we saw Dr. Harned's car leave the curb, we knew it was safe to come home.

Polio

Helen went on a church picnic one day and got sick shortly afterward. It was a cool, windy day, and she didn't take a sweater with her. We thought she had caught the flu or a bad cold. Helen was one year older than me and liked to go places and do things a lot more than I did. She felt at ease with people and was friendly and outgoing. She was always going somewhere to be with people. Helen slept in the same bedroom with my sister Sandra and me, and usually we didn't think anything of it when she was kept in another bed because of a fever. This time something was different. She had a high fever, and her legs and ankles became very stiff. She was very sick and couldn't walk normally. This was not the measles.

Sandra, Juanita, and Helen

The mood at our house seemed grim and I expected to see her getting better, but she didn't seem to improve. Even though I slept in the same room with her, I was kept away from her the rest of the time. The room was kept dark. She was getting a lot more attention than usual. Mom fixed her meals and took them to her. She helped her to the bathroom, sat by her bedside, and talked with her. There were whispered conversations at home phone calls. A person from the health department came and again, the purple sign with white letters was placed on our front door. We were quarantined again. Why was this happening to us again? I never saw any of the neighbors have a sign like that! Once again, it meant that we couldn't play with the neighbor kids. Again, Dr. Harned came to see Helen. After her examination, he stated that she had Polio. We had never heard of it. Mom explained to us that it was a disease much worse than the measles. We didn't know where Helen got it, or if the rest of us kids would get it but we knew, it meant Dr. Harned would no doubt be coming back.

After Helen was diagnosed with Polio, the rest of us kids were sent home from school and we didn't know when we could return. The neighbors didn't want anything to do with us. A couple of weeks went by and nothing improved. We lost our friends and playmates, but why? I slept in the same room with Helen and nothing happened to me. We tried several times to play with our friends but the answer was always the same: "not today, now you kids go home and don't come back." I was crushed. I just didn't understand diseases, and I didn't understand why no one liked us anymore. Polio was an epidemic spreading throughout the country and people were very afraid of it.

Things changed in my sister's life. She had surgery on her ankle to correct the paralysis that turned her left foot inward. She was admitted to the hospital and this was new to us. We knew how bad a shot in the butt hurt, but she was going to have an operation. None of us had ever been away from home overnight for something like surgery. Things didn't seem right with one of us gone. I missed her; I was scared for her, and wondered what they would do to her. When I visited her in the hospital, I wanted to take something to cheer her up. The only thing I could think of was my Mickey Mouse ears that a neighbor brought back from their trip to Disneyland. I walked in her hospital room wearing those mouse ears and Helen immediately showed off a big grin on her face. She lit up when she saw me and I put the ears on her head. I wanted to be selfish and tell her she could only wear them for a while, but when I saw how happy she was, I decided to give them to her to keep.

When she came home, she was in a wheelchair. In our very small house, it was not easy for her to move around. Eventually, she was fitted with a leg brace and a special shoe, so she didn't need the wheelchair any more. When she had to rest in bed, the rest of us kids asked if we could wear her brace and limp around. She got a lot of attention by doing it, so maybe it would bring us a lot of attention too. Helen didn't care; I guess she wanted us to know that it was not all that much fun to wear it. It was like a game to us, but we didn't have the pain that Helen dealt with. We liked to ride around in her wheelchair, but Mom put a stop to that.

Soon a special bus started stopping at our house to pick her up for school. She didn't want to go to a different school; unfortunately, she was told that things are different and that's just the way things are. The school for handicapped children did not have stairs, so it was much easier for children with walking difficulties to attend. Mom and Dad helped her to the bus and encouraged her to do her best. The rest of us were envious because we had to walk to school, whether it was raining or the sun shining. Helen got a lot of attention, and maybe that was a fair trade for her having the crippling disease of Polio. She would have preferred walking to school with the rest of us, but Polio made one leg smaller than the other. She walked with a limp, so she was destined to ride the special bus. We all looked out for her, but she didn't need that help from us. She attended the special school several years, and she walks with a limp even to this day.

Dad thought for years that Helen contracted Polio because she didn't wear a sweater to the church picnic. We never knew exactly how or where she got this terrible disease. People back then were uneducated regarding contagious diseases, but they could definitely see the damage that Polio did to a person's body. For that reason, they wanted nothing to do with any person who had it. There was no vaccine at that time and we always thought that it was strange that none of the rest of us contracted Polio.

Even afterwards, Helen was still very friendly and got to know all the neighbors. She knew all their kids and relatives and what was happening in their lives. She visited with them and stayed gone for long periods of time. Often I wondered where she might have gone to. She continued to be outgoing and made her own way. Since she was limited in playing with us, she found a new interest: people. She knew the pulse of the neighborhood and what was happening. We liked hearing her stories at the dinner table about our neighbors and the latest gossip. Some of it was funny and sometimes shocking! Helen told it all! I was not so brave as to go into our neighbors' houses and visit. I always just asked the parents for their kids to come out and play. It was a long time before our neighbors became friendly with us again, so we learned to love and rely on each other as a family.

A few years earlier, all of the schools tested for another disease; smallpox. We were all required to get vaccinated in our arm. I wished we could go back in time when there were no diseases or worry of them. I wish we never had to have a purple sign on our front door.

Crawl Spaces, Crazy Roosters, and Good Teachers
By Lavena Lowrey of Pattonsburg, Missouri
Born 1924

I really don't remember much about the first house I lived in as a child. I do, however,

remember that my dad and brother Chloral spent all of their spare time in the summers getting things ready to build the new house. They would cut trees to be made into lumber. They would also haul in rock and break it up with a hammer within the shade of a tree. It was hot during those summers in the 1930s and I remember that I spent a lot of time playing out by the hen house in the shade of that pear tree. I remember being out there under that tree when my dad and Chloral came home from the road, riding in a wagon with their team of horses. When my dad had to gather wood for the cook stove and heating stove, he would carry the long branches in that wagon. Usually the branches were so long that they would hang off of the back of it. When I would see him coming, I would run down the road to climb on the back and ride on the ends of the tree branches. I would bounce along all the way back to the yard.

Speaking of the hen house, there was a rooster that always wanted to fight us. He would run up to my legs and flop his wings. Our toilet was also out by the hen house, so I learned to carry a stick so I could fight him off. After a few times of poking him, the rooster learned not to flog me when I needed to use the toilet! There was a fence around that side of the yard so the chickens and roosters could not get in the yard and garden. The garden was on the South side of the house. We also had a building that we called the "smoke house" because that was where we smoked meat. Whenever we butchered a hog, we would hang the sides of meat on wires hanging from the ceiling, and then build a fire in the stove. The smoke from the fire would cure the meat so that it would not spoil. We cured our meats like that for several years because we did not have electricity to freeze the meat. At the corner of that building, I had a play house complete with play dishes, etc. I spent lots of time playing there.

Sometime in early 1930 the construction of the new house started. My dad, Clarence Gardner, built it with the help of a few relatives. One day when after they had most of the framework done, I was in the house playing around and spotted a little space under the stairway steps that was going to be used as an out-of-sight storage place in the future. I went in and shut the door. I found that it was a nice little place to sit and play. To my surprise, when I tried to push the door to get out, the door did not budge. One could only open the door from the outside! I just took advantage of the time and sat there and sang. One of the carpenters came back through, heard me inside, and let me out. That door was never fixed to open from the inside as long as we lived there.

We did not have electricity or a radio, so Chloral and I had to make do with the resources that we had on hand. We would let the sun shine through a magnifying glass so that we could burn letters in pieces of wood. Also, we made toy wagons, chairs, etc. out of the clay dirt located on the south side bank. We would set them in the sun to dry out and they would retain their shape. I remember that I would affix old buttons onto small cards that I received at Sunday school.

I went to Heath School House for my first eight years of school. I started in the month of August when I was five years old. The schoolhouse was just a short way from our house. Chloral and I walked together in my first year. After that first year, Chloral was out of school so I had to walk by myself. My teacher for the first six years was Stella Stratton from McFall. She rode a horse to the school. As far as my memory goes, she never did drive a car there. I remember that her older sister, Ada Stratton, was also a teacher, and taught at the school in Elam. For my seventh and eighth year of school, my teacher was Maxine Giles. Back then, you could graduate from high school, go to college during that summer, and be able to teach school the following fall. That is what she did. She actually drove a car to school, as long as the weather and roads were suitable. One day Maxine picked me up in her car when I was on my way to school. I was just riding on the running board of the car and when she made the curve to pull into the schoolyard, I fell off the side of the car! I guess I landed on my feet because I don't remember really landing on the ground. All was well. We took our lunch to school, and on some cold winter days, the teacher would fix potato soup early in the morning and set it on top of the tall round stove. By noon, it would be cooked and we would have a nice hot lunch.

In grade school, we were all in the same room from the first grade till the eighth. By listening in on other grade's class time, we learned extra things. We had spelling, math, and geography matches that we usually held on Fridays. They were like play time, a game. We always looked forward to them. At the beginning of the day, the teacher would read aloud for all of us from a book from the library. I mostly remember her reading the Bobbsey Twin books. She also gave them as gifts at the end of the year for perfect attendance. I still have five of those that I got from her. We had a small library at school; I read every book in the library. To this day, I still like to read.

We had recess outside during the noon hour whenever the weather was nice. If snow was on the ground, we still played. One game we played was "Fox and Goose." One kid would be the fox and the rest were geese. The fox would catch a goose; in turn, the caught goose would become the fox who had to catch another goose. Another game was "Andy Over." We would divide ourselves up into two teams then each team would stand on opposite sides of the coal shed. One team would throw a ball over the roof of the shed and the other team would run around to the other side. I don't remember the specifics of that game, but I know we got our exercise!

When it came to the end of the eighth grade, we had to take a county test at Pattonsburg School House to see if we were ready for high school. I remember one question on the test was to name a legume plant. A couple of Pattonsburg town girls who were also taking the test turned to me and asked me for the answer. Well this old hick country girl told them "soybean" was one. I made a hit with the town girls. When we started our freshman year together the next year, we became friends. My second year of high school I switched high schools because it was a long way to the bus route for my current school. The McFall High School started a bus route that went right by my house, so I attended there until I graduated in 1941.

Dad's Hawk
By Maurice C. Wheeler of Mound City, Missouri
Born 1933

Dad was in need of a new car, or at least one that was new to him. He was looking for something sporty, and his decision came down to either a 1957 Alfa Romeo or a 1957 Studebaker Golden Hawk. Both were the same price and had about the same mileage, but something about the Hawk just caught his eye. It was bright gold with pearl white inserts in the fins, and not a scratch on her. "Don't crank her up too far, too fast" the salesman warned as he took it out for a test drive. It seemed the previous owner had been racing her around the country, but was too eager on one occasion He had raced her cold and damaged the connecting rods. "I'll be careful," Dad said as he started it up. It drove out like a dream. The engine ran a little rough, but he could fix that. He looked it all over. "What's this?" he asked, motioning for the salesman to come over. "Oh, the last owner welded weights under the front to keep the front end on the ground during races," the salesman replied. Dad also found out from him that the previous owner had additionally increased the blower strength from 10 pounds to 15. The salesman gave Dad the whole story. "The Golden Hawk is a factory-made hot rod. With the super charge, this little 289 can produce over 310 horsepower and deliver that power to the locking differential." He was sold on it. After going over the budget, and with a little convincing, his wife allowed him to bring it home. Once he had rebuilt the engine and had it bored and stroked, he set out breaking-in his "new" car. He had never driven a locking differential before, and his first experience was almost his last. With this locking differential, when you accelerated, the car locked the rear wheels so that both would pull straight forward. Unfortunately, this action overrode the steering. When he went to pass a grain truck on the road, as he sped up, the car locked the driver wheels even with the steering hard over. It would only go straight, and he almost rear-ended the truck in front of him. The problem was, when he hit the brakes to overt a collision, this action unlocked the rear wheels, and with the steering hard over, it shot him across the road, and then in and out of a ditch. A couple of times doing that quickly taught him that in order to pass, he must first pull out, then hit the gas, and then when he had passed the other car, he could let off the gas and pull back in.

He would tell me that when the Hawk was properly tuned, he could pull out, pass a car, and be in front of it in the time it took to pass one telephone pole. If he could not accomplish this, he would go home and tune it up some more. All that power had a drawback, though. He couldn't' keep tires on it. Every time he would "step on it," the tires would roll out of their skins, leaving the treads lying on the highway. After about the third or fourth time he had taken the tires in for warranty replacement, the salesman gave him his money back and told him to find another dealer. Asking around about what to do, one dealer sold him new type of tires that were made by Firestone called radials. At that time, that type of tires was developed to be used on the racing circuit. While costing considerably more, they were worth it. He never peeled out of tread again.

So, he set back out on the road again at about 70 miles per hour. He would always tell us, "The Hawk would ride as smooth as a boat on calm water." He said that it would force the wind under the front of the car, and lift it up onto a cushion of air. Then you would hardly feel a bump in the road. From zero to 35 miles per hour the acceleration was sluggish, but when the blower kicked in, he could burn two lines of black on the road for as long as you had your foot on the gas. He said it was the fastest car that he had ever been in. "You had to keep an eye on your speed though. At about 135 miles per hour, the front end would start to lift off the ground, even with the extra weight in the front. Only two cars of the day could match the acceleration of my Hawk," he would tell, "the Corvette and the big block Thunderbird. If you could beat the T-bird off the line, you could stay ahead of him."

My parents enjoyed taking trips and traveling around the country in their Hawk. One day while coming home from college, they stopped to get gas. As the attendant was filling the car, he had made the comment, "Nice little car; must get good gas mileage." Dad liked showing off his car and thought it would be fun for him to see the engine in his "nice little car." "Why don't' you check the oil while you are at it?" Dad beamed as he walked up to the front of the car and unlatched the hood for him. As the attendant raised the hood, he was so surprised at the sight of the Hawk's engine that he fell into the engine compartment and the hood fell on top of him! Dad had to help him out." Oh my, Oh my!" the attendant kept repeating. "My brother is never going to believe this!" He pleaded with Dad to stay while he called his brother to come see the Hawk for himself. It was getting late, so Dad insisted that they needed to get on their way. They left him there still standing with his jaw hanging open with disbelief.

While traveling on vacation one summer, dad had stopped to fill up the hawk again when a fellow in a Hudson Hornet drove in and blocked him in. A good-sized, hot-tempered man got out and confronted him. "You been out to the salt flats with that?" he asked, pointing at the car. Startled, Dad explained that they were just passing through on vacation. He pointed at his wife, brother, and his parents sitting in the car. The man paced back and forth a couple of times, looking in the car to see Mom in the front seat and his brother and parents packed into the back, looking at a map. "Mind if I take a look under the hood?" Not sure, what to make of that, Dad lifted the hood for him. The man was stunned. "Well, no wonder!" he exclaimed as he looked it over. Dad couldn't take it anymore. "What is this all about?" The fellow went on to explain that he had overhauled his Hornet to race, and had thought it to be unbeatable. He brought it out to the salt flats to race and make some money. After several matches, he had won a good sum of money, and asked for challengers to try to build his money farther. He noticed two Hawks off to the side. They got out and tossed a coin to see who would take him. "I didn't see anything but dust and tail lights, and by the time I got back, both cars and the money were gone," he explained. He had never seen anything like it.

Mom liked to drive the Hawk as well. On one occasion while driving along at medium pace, a man in a truck started to pass them. Dad, who was sitting in the passenger seat, jokingly asked her if she was going to let him pass her. She mashed the gas pedal, and by the time she let up, they were on top of the next hill, ahead of him. Looking back, they noticed that he had stopped and was out looking in the field, searching the ditches. With all the squealing tires and smoke, he had thought that Mom and Dad had run off of the road. He couldn't find them anywhere!

They enjoyed their Hawk for several years, but it was not to last. While returning from doing chores on Granddad's farm, Dad, Mom, and Dad's brother were coming off of a one-lane bridge when a lady in an old Pontiac failed to yield the right-of-way. Taking the center of the road, she plowed over the driver's side of the Hawk. Dad dove in Mom's lap to protect her and avoid injury, but the car still managed to hit his back. Mom, who was pregnant with their first child at the time, crushed her wrist and received a cut on her chin. His brother was sitting on the outside passenger side. He was flung forward and broke the visor mirror with his head. The Hawk was completely totaled. Dad still has trouble with his back to this day, and it took him many years before he could wear a seat belt again, because he knew that if he had worn a seatbelt on the day of the collision, he would have been killed, and I would have never have been born to write this account on their behalf. He misses his Hawk and all the fun he had in it. After hearing these stories for years, I bought one myself to rebuild and take to shows. Dad's memories live on.

War Life
By Shirley Averett of Kansas City, Missouri
Born 1942

I was only three when the war was ending, I can only recount family stories from these years. We also had pictures to help me remember. One of the best memories was parading around the yard of my cousin's house that was next door to where I lived. We wore paper hats and had American flags to wave. My mother had a brother serving in the Army in Europe. She had a sister with a husband in the Navy in the Pacific. My own father was in the Army and had been wounded on Omaha Beach during the "D" Day invasion.

Another memory my cousins told was playing soldiers. They usually were fighting the Japanese. If the American soldier was hit, he would just lie down, but the enemy soldier would have to spin around and make a big deal out of falling down. I don't think we were allowed to have anyone pretend to die. At the time, we felt our side would be victorious.

We had a lot of feelings of patriotism, which last until today. Another way to show our patriotism was to have a victory garden with vegetables and fruit trees. My grandmother, who also lived in a house next door, raised chickens. Our fathers fished and hunted to supplement the meat supply. One thing my mother told me was about putting yellow dye in the margarine to make it look like butter.

We had ration books for various items that were in short supply or needed for the war effort. We walked to a local movie house instead of driving because of gas rationing and tire rationing. One of my young cousins wore a suit and hat that looked like a Navy uniform. We had pictures of the soldiers in the family, some of them with the entire until they were part of hanging on the walls. Every one of my close family came home from the war, but with wounds that never fully healed. Out of this experience, we gained a feeling of pride in our country and the people who put so much effort in helping to win the war at home and abroad.

One-Room Schoolhouse
By Mary Ann (Hughs) Allen of St. Charles, Missouri
Born 1934

My family lived on a farm about three miles from a little town called Brimson, Missouri. It is about eight to ten miles northwest of Trenton, Missouri.

Our little, one-room school was called Cole School.

Some of the children walked several miles to get to school. We had no buses.

School had no running water or electricity. We pumped water from a well outside. We used the water to wash our hands and to drink. We had tin cups to drink from. We brought our lunches from home.

Heat was a stove with a metal jacket around it. Coal was used as fuel. The stove was at the back of the room.

The toilets had two holes (seats). During class if you had to go, you raised your hand and one or two fingers, indicating which job it was for. The boys' and girls' toilets were several feet apart.

Each week a student was chosen to care for the flag, raising it before class, and to bring it in after school. We always said the Pledge of Allegiance.

The only trouble I can remember kids getting into during class was whispering to each other or throwing a paper spit wad at someone.

Winter was great fun for kids. One family had a large sled. Several could pile on and go

a great distance. It took two or three kids to pull it back up the hill.

When our lunch hour was over, the teacher came outside and rang a handheld bell, letting us know it was time to come in.

My maiden name was Mary Ann Hughs.

Class of 1945 at Cole School

A Barber, a Butcher, and a Paperhanger
By Dawn Blair of Rosendale, Missouri
Born 1939

Before Joy Mitchell was Circuit and Probate Judge in the 1950s, he spent some time barbering at Workman's Barbershop, 405 W. Main, Savannah, Missouri. The following story was told to Donnie Blair, present owner, who has been employed in the profession since 1958.

A stranger to town came in for a haircut and shave, and placed himself in Joy's chair. The haircut went well, but, when doing the shave, Joy nicked him with the razor. When Joy reached for the styptic powder to stop the bleeding, he discovered the vial empty. Joy proceeded to tear a small piece of paper from the headrest cover and placed it on the cut. With the procedure completed, the customer removed himself from the chair and handed Joy 35 cents for his services and also gave him a $1 tip. Joy, no doubt gratified but a little amazed, questioned his client as to the added bonus. The fellow replied, "I've been in many tonsorial establishments, but this is the first time I've been worked on by a barber, a butcher, and a paperhanger."

Sulfur Treatment
By Bonnie Hoecker of St. Joseph, Missouri
Born 1924

When I was in the second grade at Washington grade school in St. Joseph, my best friend and I both got a bad rash. How or from where I don't know,

We were sent home to stay until it was cleared up. To get rid of it mom sprinkled my bed sheet with this crumbly, yellowish stuff. I think it was sulfur. It was awful to sleep on and smelled bad too. After a couple of weeks, I went back to school. My friend did too. The teacher called us up to the front of the room by her desk. She pulled our skirts up to look at our stomachs to see if the rash was gone. How embarrassing that was in front of the whole class. I was six years old at the time, and I'm 85 now.

Super Price on a Deformed Hog
By Doyle H. Parman of Grant City, Missouri
Born 1938

Back in 1941, a neighbor turned a barrow (castrated pig) loose because it had a deformed head. They were afraid of it, like it had a disease or something and didn't want it mixed in with their other pigs. He was the only one in the neighborhood (3 miles northwest of Denver, MO) that had spotted hogs so everybody knew who it belonged to!

We asked him if it was his but he shook his head, "No." My brother Duane and I, who were 13 and 11 at the time, asked our dad if we could catch this pig. Dad didn't want it in with his hogs either, so we caught it and put it in a little shed with a pen around it, away from the other buildings. We were supposed to take turns feeding the pig, but Duane didn't like to do chores so I took care of him most of the time. We slopped the hog until he was big enough to sell, about 200 pounds.

Ed Holmes was hauling Dad's hogs to the St. Joseph Stockyards 75 miles away. They sold our deformed hog separately. Ed stayed in the city overnight and brought the checks back to us the next day. Ed said, "You won't believe what the boys' hog brought: $25!"

Super price for a deformed stray animal no one wanted. Of course, Duane and I had to split the money.

Not My New Ones
By Una Buck of Cameron, Missouri
Born 1943

I had polio when I was seven. I endured many surgeries and wore leg braces for 4 years. I eventually weaned myself from these braces and was able to walk without them with only a little difficulty walking. I also had to learn to talk again. The other children made fun of me, and because I was alone so much, I began writing in my private time. I have enjoyed writing since I was a young girl.

When I became a Christian, God began speaking many different things to me. Some were instructions, some were poems, and some were songs. As I learned to listen to Him, I would write them down quickly as He was speaking. I have written several poems and songs, which I sing in my church. Below is a sample of an occurrence in which God spoke to me.

Not My New Ones
Sometime back I had ordered
some Microwave dishes.
Finally they came.
Dee asked me if I had got them from the
kitchen.
I said, "No, I didn't know they were in
but I'll pick them up after the service.
We were in a revival
and before the service started
a voice said unto me,
"Dishes to Charity."
I nudged the one sitting by me.
"Did you say something?"
She said "No."
Again the voice said, "Dishes to Charity."
And then I knew.
"But Lord, not my new ones, I just got them."
"I know, but Charity needs them," He said.
"You'll be blessed by giving them to her."
I gave the dishes to Charity; she did need them for she had no dishes at all. God has blessed me by giving me many more writings.

The Lord has been with me down through the years. I had a kidney transplant. God has been so good to me. I still do writing because I believe I should write what He speaks to me.

The Best Christmas Ever with Babe and Doll
By Joyce Mendenhall of Fayetteville, Arkansas
Born 1947

Hopkins, MO, population 725, was an ideal place to grow up. Everyone knew everyone else and if a stranger came to town, most likely everyone knew that too. No one locked their doors or windows, night or day, and kids were allowed to play all over town. No one cared if you ran across their back yard or climbed their apple tree. One little neighbor boy would sometimes visit when we weren't home and help himself to the soda crackers my mother kept in one side of the stove. Once the town drunk got stuck in the ditch and "borrowed" our telephone to call someone to pull him out. We probably would never have known it except that he tracked muddy boot prints on my mom's new carpet.

Most of us "town" kids went home from school for lunch every day and as soon as the last school bell rang, we raced down "schoolhouse hill" to the Rexall Drug Store to buy a cherry Coke, lime river, or cherry phosphate at the soda fountain. Sometimes we would linger at the comic book rack, but most times, we went straight home to change clothes and play outside until the 6 o'clock whistle blew. That was our signal to come home for supper, where our entire family would gather around one table, eat, and talk about the events of the day.

I remember one night when the whistle blew and I did not come home for supper. My older sister and cousin had decided it would be fun to bury me up to my head in sand at the local lumberyard. When my sister finally confessed to knowing where I was, my dad had to come and rescue me!

Another "fun" thing we liked to do in Hopkins was to get a large piece of cardboard from the local hardware store such as a refrigerator would come in and use it to slide down the grassy slope in front of our house. The only problem with that was that there was

an open sewer ditch at the bottom and if you didn't jump off at the right time you would land in the sewage. There were many times when I would have to take an "extra" bath in the middle of the day because of not jumping in time.

Several of the neighborhood kids formed a club, which we named appropriately "The Fun Club." We met inside our "clubhouse" whenever the notion hit us. The clubhouse was actually a playhouse that my dad hauled into town when he purchased a farm it was located on. It had once been a model, which some homebuilder had given away so it was really very unique. The Fun Club decided to have a carnival to make some money. We put our youngest member in the "kissing booth" handing out candy kisses. We also had various dart and ball games of skill, a fortuneteller, and a lemonade stand. Our parents were our best customers of course.

We all looked forward to the annual Hopkins Picnic each summer. This was a three-day event with lots of local entertainment and hamburger and ice cream stands as well as

Joyce's great-grandpa, John Campbell

308

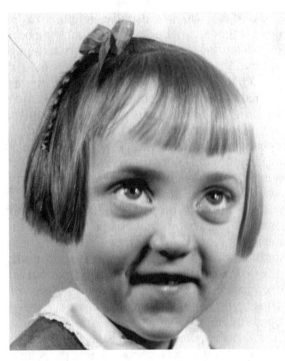

Joyce in 1947

a real carnival with lots of rides. When the carnies arrived in town us kids would gather along the sidewalk and watch for hours as they set up the rides and tents on Main Street. Sometimes we would even run errands or fetch drinks for the workers. Even then, our parents never seemed to worry about us.

One Sunday afternoon when I was five years old a tornado hit Hopkins and destroyed many buildings. We had just finished a family dinner with my grandparents, aunt, uncle, and cousins. My grandparents left to go home and do chores just before the storm hit which knocked out all the power and telephone lines. Our family stood in the front room and watched the roof blow off the house across the street. We had no warning systems at the time. As soon as the storm passed, my father and uncle went to check on my grandparents. They had to go around downed power lines and trees lying across the roads but they were able to get to my grandparent's farm. My grandparents had missed the storm and had no idea what had happened. We were without power for the next two weeks, but luckily, we had a gas cooking stove, which my parents allowed everyone in town to use.

I'm proud of the fact that my great-grandfather came directly from Ireland to Northwest Missouri where he worked to purchase land that he farmed all of his life and my grandfather farmed all of his life. The old farm is no longer in our family but about once a year I like to drive by and remember all the good times I spent there growing up. My cousins and I knew every square inch of the massive barn and other outbuildings. There was even an area behind the house, which Grandpa called the timber that we loved to explore. It was made up mostly of small trees and shrubs full of discarded rusty farm implements that we would climb on. I even enjoyed gathering eggs for my grandmother even though my cousins were scared to death that the chickens would peck them. We climbed up in the hay mow and threw corn cobs down at the pigs. Don't ask me why. The house of balls that kids climb in today reminds me of the corn crib we played in. We would try to climb to the top of the pile and then slide down. We made our own fun and never lacked for amusement.

Any mention of my grandfather's farm would not be complete without telling you about Babe and Doll. Babe and Doll were Grandpa's team of work horses that did everything there was to do on the farm, especially before he got a small Ford tractor, but even after that. Grandpa plowed and planted acres and acres of fields, picked bushels of corn, hauled dozens of bales of hay, pulled stuck vehicles out of the mud, and even rescued Christmas dinner using those faithful horses.

That Christmas there was a huge snow storm and our families from town could only drive our cars as far as the old country schoolhouse which was about 3 miles (although it seemed much farther to me at the time) from my grandparent's house. When we arrived, my grandpa along with Babe and Doll was waiting to transport us in a high wheel wagon to the farmhouse. We all piled in and sang Christmas carols all the way. It was one of the best Christmases ever!

The Feline Parachute
By Laurel Evans of Stanberry, Missouri
Born 1927

My husband, Russell, was the second of four brothers born two years apart on a farm southwest of Stanberry, Missouri to Homer and Angie Evans before, during, and after WW I. The oldest was Vernon, then Russell, followed by Harold, who died at birth, and Kenneth four years younger than Russell.

As they grew, according to information gleaned from much nostalgic reminiscing, the three Evans brothers resembled some of the adventurous boys of fiction. They and their friends who lived on neighboring farms did many of the things boys loved to do before TV and other modern devices distracted them.

The boys roamed the hills and dales of their home with carefree abandon, hunting small animals and hooking catfish as food for the table. They went swimming in the creeks and ponds, and spent many hours playing in the fragrant hay in the mow of the big barn on the farm.

This was during the time when mechanization was coming more and more into the picture of life in their part of the world. Automobiles were replacing the horse and buggy and Homer bought a tractor to take over some of the fieldwork necessary to every farm operation. However, the most intriguing of the new machines to the Evans boys were the ones that flew through the air.

Vernon and Russell often hatched boyish schemes, and the one most persistent was their dream of flying an airplane. They carried it to the point of building a crude craft of boards, nails, and wheels from one of their wagons. Russell didn't remember what they used for a propeller, but I'm sure they found something for this essential component because this was long before the age of jet propulsion.

Vernon was so convinced their contraption would fly that he felt it necessary to equip it with a parachute in case the pilot had to bail out in flight. The nearest replica to a real parachute was one of his mother's umbrellas." He believed that if he clutched the shaft of the umbrella tightly and jumped off a high place it would waft him gently to a soft landing on the ground. To test his plan he scrambled onto the roof of the house by scaling the hump of earth, which covered the cave, and boosting himself onto a low section of the roof on the house. From there he climbed to the highest level of the roof with the umbrella in tow, and set sail. The umbrella turned inside out in flight and a cut lip as a result of the sudden stop at the bottom of the jump revealed a glaring fault in the premise of an umbrella as a parachute.

Kenneth was not usually included in his big brothers escapades, which might have been the best thing for his health and wellbeing, especially when Vernon enlisted his help in another one of his parachute experiments. He tied ropes to a corner of one of his dad's tarpaulins where he had positioned it on the ground. He instructed his brothers to hold the ropes while he lifted the corner of the tarp so the strong wind blowing that day could fill it, thus, hopefully to lift it and boys into the sky. When Vernon raised his corner of the tarp, it ballooned into a monster. It took flight, not upward, but along the ground yanking the three helpless boys off their feet where they tumbled over each other while still clinging to the ropes on the tarp. Kenneth came out the loser in that fiasco with several contusions bruises and bumps to show his tenacity as a rope holder.

Even then Vernon and Russell could not give up trying to perfect a workable parachute. Despite the failure of their first two attempts to figure out the combination of factors to accomplish their purpose they hung onto their dream. Their next effort to make a parachute involved one of their cats. They found a piece of discarded fabric and cut it into a large circle and tied cords at even spaces around its outer edge. The ends of the cords were gathered together and tied to a makeshift harness the boys concocted for the cat to wear. With preparations complete they climbed to the roof and launched the frightened cat into space. Again the carefully planned plot to prove their ability as parachute makers fell short of success. The parachute failed to open, and when the cat hit the ground, the four feet he landed on took him rapidly to parts unknown by two very young would be aeronautical engineers. He shed the harness and I am sure made himself scarce anywhere near those two boys. As far as I know that was the last effort to make a parachute, but their yen to fly continued to when Russell and Kenneth were in the Air Force during WW II.

It's All Relative!
By Jeanie (Garner) Moore of Pleasant Hill, Missouri
Born 1941

When I was a child, growing up in DeKalb County, I soon discovered that most of my friends had "cousins by the dozens" living in close proximity. My mother's five siblings had scattered to the four corners of the U.S., and my father's sister rarely lived within 100 miles. It seemed to me that most of my "close" relatives were in the Cameron and Kidder cemeteries!

So, naturally, I was extremely envious of my friend Alice Ann Dyer, who went to a family reunion almost every Sunday during the summer. I would try to wheedle an invitation and talk my parents into letting me go with her to these grand occasions. I usually could talk them into it once or twice each summer, and I always had an amazing time.

When I was in high school, Alice Ann invited me to go to dinner when her parents were invited to the Moore household in Amity. There I met my future in-laws, Herbert and Irene Moore, although I didn't start dating Philip until about 4 years later. I've always told Phil I fell in love with my father-in law before him because Phil's dad was fun to be around!

Anyway, when I married Phil Moore, I figured I was probably related to half the county. But... we have never lived in De Kalb County during our now 52 years of married life. Instead, we moved to the Pleasant Hill community in Cass County, Missouri, where (you guessed it!), everyone was related.

However, since we retired, we've been able to attend the White family reunion (Phil's mother's family), descendants of John Arthur and Melissa White every other year.

In addition, we were fortunate to have a family reunion of descendants of my mother's grandparents, John and Mary Whitelaw, a few years ago in Kidder, Missouri.

So, I'm proud to say, I now get to go to family reunions of my own!

Our Cave Shelter
By Betty J. Clement of Augusta, Georgia
Born 1935

I was born in 1935, on a farm northwest of Maryville, Missouri. I have many, happy memories of my childhood, especially living on the farm with my dad, mother, and brother. I am so blessed to have had a loving, Christian family.

I started first grade when I was four years

Betty with her brother, Eldon Jenson in 1938

old. Mt. Vernon was a one-room school, with a foyer in front for coats and boots, and a potbelly stove, which the teacher kept burning. Windows were on one side of the room, desks with ink wells scattered about. Blackboards covered the front wall, with erasers, which were cleaned every Friday afternoon, hitting them together outside. There was a large bell on top of the school, which the teacher rang each morning. There were two outhouses, boys' and girls', quite far from the schoolhouse, very cold in the winter.

My brother, who was in the sixth grade, and I walked to school, bringing our lunch each day. During the winter it was so cold and a lot of snow, I could hardly pick my feet up over the snowdrifts. We did a lot of coasting, bringing our sleds to school. It was a lot of fun going down the long hill, but no fun walking back up, pulling the sled. We threw a lot of snowballs and made snow forts. My dad always said I was the only little girl he knew that didn't like winter, especially playing in the snow.

I attended Mt. Vernon for three years, until my brother and two others graduated from the eighth grade. My friend and I were the only students left, transferring to Ireland School, two-and-a-half miles from our house, also a one-room school.

After going to elementary school for eight years, I attended Horace Mann High

School in Maryville, meeting the school bus at Highway 71, three-and-a-half miles from home. I enjoyed my years in high school, active in many groups. After graduation, I attended Northwest Missouri College.

Two of my best girlfriends and I attended a 4-H gathering at Missouri University in Columbia, singing "Three Little Maids in a Row." We attended a banquet and were introduced to Mr. J. C. Penney, shaking his hand.

Every home had a crank telephone. When you wanted to call someone, you gave the crank different turns. Ours was one long and one short. Everyone on the line heard the rings and could pick up their phone and listen to all conversations.

Drinking water was pumped from a well outside the house. We all used the same dipper, didn't think about germs, everyone was family.

My mother made all of my clothes until I went to high school. Livestock feed came in pretty feed sacks. Dad always bought the ones we liked best.

There was an outside, underground cave not far from our house. Whenever a bad storm came up, we would get crackers and spoons before entering the cave, opening a jar of fruit, which my mother had canned. Dad would take the lantern for light and an ax, in case something blew on the cave door. It was always pouring down rain when we came back inside the house.

Wash day was always on Monday. My job was pumping water from the well outside, carrying the buckets to the basement, making many trips, spilling a lot. The water was heated early in the morning on a wood stove. After washing and rinsing, the clothes were hung on outside lines to dry.

My family usually went to Maryville on a Saturday afternoon, doing their shopping, and I took my piano lesson. In the summertime, everyone went to town on Saturday nights, visiting, and course going to double feature movies at the Tivoli or the Missouri Theaters. Dad and mom would wait until the movie ended, late. A great time to be with your friends.

Marrying my U. S. Army husband, also growing up in northwest Missouri, in 1955, we have lived in Texas, Alaska, Virginia, and Georgia. My husband retired from the Army, after serving 22 years, retiring in Augusta, Georgia. We have three children, three grandchildren, and two great-grandsons. I have had a very wonderful and fulfilling life, continuing to share these memories with family and friends.

Lincoln Township Odd Jobs in the '50s
By Barbara A. Butler of Burlington Junction, Missouri
Born 1939

I grew up in the country and went to a one-room country school for 1 1/2 years, then moved to a small town in Lincoln Township.

I attended school 1st-12th and graduated from there.

Snowdrifts were so high that my brother and I could walk on top of it to get to school. Town children had school on snow days, but the country children only went if they could. There were no Make Up Days.

We went sledding all winter down a steep hill, around four blocks. State Hwy was blocked so that we could cross it on the way down the hill. We went really fast down the hill.

We played croquet, hide and seek, swinging on bag swings, handy over, may I, rode bicycles all over, roller skated, and spent a lot of time in our tree house.

Saturday in the small country town was special: Movies, drug store with a fountain, all kinds of drinks, malts shakes, and sodas. The streets were full of cars and people. We all had a good time. A nickel could buy kits, cinnamon squares, bubble gum, and lots more.

I had friends sleep over during the summer. We slept outside so we could watch the boys go by. It was fun.

We lived behind the business buildings on Main Street, across the alley. We could watch the people on Saturday nights coming and going from the bar, to the outhouse, what a sight! We had an outside toilet, a two-holer, with catalogues for paper. It was cold in the winter.

My dad had the farm and we raised chickens for eating. I dressed chickens and sold them in town for $2.50 apiece. I worked at the Telephone Co. as a switchboard operator, where everything was done by hand, for $0.35 an hour. This job helped me pay for my senior ring and pictures. I also worked at the Printing Co., which printed the small town paper. I was paid $0.35 an hour for this job. I ironed for several families, too, which helped with expenses.

We caught rainwater in a stock tank by the house, and we washed our hair in the water. There was a cellar for vegetables, fruits, and canned goods including meats. We made dolls out of hollyhocks, smoked grape vines, and wore dresses, skirts, and blouses to school; No jeans or pants (Girls). We made hand cranked, homemade ice cream all winter using pond ice. We hung clothes outside in the winter to freeze dry.

Quotes From the Rural Communities:

Harder than a brickbat (like hard candy/ frozen ice cream).

Don't start anything on Friday (you can't finish).

You lay with the hogs; you'll smell like the hogs.

Study your lesson (think deeply about what you plan to do).

Birds of a feather flock together. (like same ideas, attitudes).

Don't throw stones at glass houses (clean up your own mess first).

He/She made their bed, let them lay in it (your choice).

Watch pot never boils (be patient).

Drought and Grasshoppers
By Lois Pauline (Clark) Peterson of
Aberdeen, Washington
Born 1926

When I was six years old, we moved from the Jefferson place, the "old house", to the little white square house where both Betty Jo and Colleen were born.

In 1934 and likewise 1935, we had severe droughts. Very few crops were raised and livestock had to be sold or eaten. Mom even canned rabbit, wild ones, which were actually very good. And then in 1936 grasshoppers moved in and proceeded to eat everything edible and also some things non-edible such as pitchfork handles, clothes on the line, and straw hats still on our heads. I remember Mom hanging clothes on the line but removing them long before they were dry as grasshoppers would be devouring them!

This meant gathering up corncobs, building a hot fire and getting the irons hot for ironing. Everything was ironed even dishtowels.

Gardens were devoured; they even ate little potatoes into the ground.

The chickens thrived from eating the pests and I'm sure we had lots of eggs that year.

Many young men of the Half Rock area became disillusioned and decided to go west to search for work. In the fall or winter of 1936, Ernie and Jake bought a worn out car from Ted Regger and with help from a man in Half Rock who was more mechanically inclined than they were, they finally got it to run. They sold it and with the money from it and some other funds probably from shucking corn in Iowa, they bought a 1934 or 1935 Ford truck in Iowa.

They brought it home, bought lumber and other materials, and set to work building a camper type cabin on it. It was equipped with a small coal stove, beds, and a table. Even curtains on the windows! All the comforts of home. A family from Osgood rode in this camper.

Loyd was desperate to find 'work too, so they had a sale and joined the others in their car. They travelled together to Idaho but first came to Utah.

They all left Missouri in Feb. of 1937. I never heard of any trouble getting over the mountains but that time of the year, I can't imagine how they did it. It had to have been the northern route, Highway 30, and that was rugged even in the summer.

Ernie saved enough money to have Nada come out in May of 1937 when they were married. She was only 16. She and another woman came by car. They were in a minor accident and not seriously hurt.

Then in June of 1938, the copper mine started laying men off so they all came home. Somehow, Mom knew they were coming and had been planning for months. She ordered extra baby chicks and planted more garden. We put new wallpaper on most of the rooms. Every room was scrubbed and woodwork painted. Loyd, Gussie, Betty Jo, Norma, and Donnie stayed with us all summer, which pleased me a lot. One of the girls had the mumps when they came and Gussie and I soon came down with them. Jim refused to get them and boy! How he rubbed it in.

313

Sheep Dip and a Permanent Wave
By Sylvia M. Eads of Green Castle, Missouri
Born 1917

One pretty day in the fall of 1934, my next-door neighbor, Elsie Brown, called me and asked me if I would drive her into town to get a permanent wave put in her hair. I asked her whose car I would be driving and she said it belonged to John Carter who left it at their house every day and rode to work with her husband Vic. She assured me that John would not mind and I knew him well enough to agree.

I was 17 years of age and Elsie was 19 and she was newly married. She had never driven a car at all and me only a few times. I had two older brothers so that explains why. Most old cars that we farmers could afford to buy had something wrong with them. This one was no exception as you are about to learn.

I agreed to drive for her and when I arrived, I looked the car over. It was a Model "T" Ford, open-air four door. Elsie had been to her chicken yard and caught two old hens. She tied their legs together so they couldn't flop around and pitched them onto the back floorboard. She would sell them at the poultry house for $1.00 each and that would more than pay for her perm. She was too excited to notice there was something else sitting on the floorboard with her hens.

We were finally ready for take-off and the Model "T" started immediately and we were on our way. I discovered immediately why John didn't want to drive it any farther than he had to. The steering wheel had to make two complete turns before it would hold! Believe it or not, I fought the thing 4 miles into the edge of Gallatin before putting it into a rather deep ditch.

Both old hens were thrown out into the road. The other item we had not been aware of, a container of vile smelling sheep dip, broke open and some of it splashed on Elsie's clothes. We got out of the car and put the hens back in the car. I told Elsie I didn't think I could drive it out, but she was sure I could, so I did. Those old Fords could do wonders and take lots of abuse.

Our new problem after we sold the hens was getting Elsie cleaned up. Our "good luck" kicked in. She had a relative who lived in town and they wore the same size clothes. We found her at home and soon Elsie was presentable. We were finally ready for the beauty shop, our last stop. It went well and we headed for home. We arrived safely and I parked the car in exactly the same spot, but somehow it did not smell the same.

To my knowledge, this incident has never been told by anyone. Not a complaint not a question. My parents never learned about it and the law was never notified. If they had been, what would have happened? I was not of age; I had no driver's license and took a car without asking the owner.

Toothpick for a Show
By Judy Wallace of Los Lunas, New Mexico
Born 1923

My name is Julia Mae Wallace and I was born April 15, 1923 in a small town, Richmond Missouri, just east of Kansas City, Missouri. The population was 1,000 people. Everyone knew every bodies business, including my mom and dad's.

First of all, we didn't have much in the good old days, as they were called, but we were happy with what we did have because I guess we didn't know any better.

My dad worked in a store called "Fletcher & Simms Groceries." He was known as the groceries deliveryman who delivered groceries to their houses when they would call in for their groceries, if they were lucky enough to even have a phone. Sometimes the people would give him tips for his quick, speed work, plus what they owed for the groceries. In those days, my dad was paid 50 cents a day, which made him very tight with his money. Once in a while, he would take my older sister and myself with him in the little pickup truck that he used to make the deliveries so my mom could have a little time to relax. She stayed home to clean the house, cook three meals a day, and then managed to entertain us in the evening for hours until we had to go to bed. Oh yes, those were the good old days!

As my sister and I got a little older, my mom and dad taught us to play a card game called Casino. We also learned how to play Ball and Jacks and Dominos. My mom would get on the linoleum floor we had and play Ball and Jacks with us and my dad would take his

Judy's mom, Ethel Snyder

turn playing games like Dominos. It was a lot of fun, oh yes, we would also play checkers, which my dad would win most of the time.

I remember the outside toilet as well. That was quite the thing when it wasn't too cold. I would go and sit on this hole in outhouse, look through these catalogues from Montgomery Wards, J. C. Penny, and Sears that we used for toilet paper and I would pretend that I was rich and would buy a lot of things to put in an imaginary home.

I remember my mom's kitchen, she had a big, old, round table that we ate on, big, cast iron cook stove, with four grates to cook on, and a reservoir built on the side of this stove to heat water in, as we never had electricity. My mom had several old coal oil lamps that she would light up, which made enough light to see whatever you were doing. We also did not have indoor plumbing, but there was a deep well outside, which we would have to pump to bring water up so we could use it to cook with, drink, to pour into the reservoir on the side of the stove to heat water for our bath and whatever else she needed hot water for, yes, these were the good old days to remember!

We had a big, round, potbelly stove that was in the living room that my dad, mom, my sister, and myself would sit around this old potbelly stove and my dad would tell us stories of his childhood and his life. We all

would get so tickled. These are very good memories of mine. We had an old radio ran by batteries, but half the time you could not hear it. We would listen to the "Grand Old Opry" every Saturday night if my mom, sister, and me didn't go to the picture show while my daddy was still working at the grocery store. If we went to the picture show, by the time it was over, my dad would be getting off work so then we would all go home.

I remember my grandma and grandpa lived close by and my grandma use to sew for the rich people. When my dad had little chickens he would bring the chicken feed home in bags that were made out of a printed cotton material and my grandmother would make my sister and I little gathered skirts with a band of elastic running through it to hold them up. These skirts were called durndell or peasant skirts, why we thought we were really dressed up and very proud of these skirts. Whenever we wore out our shoes or didn't out grow them, we would take them to the shoe repairman and have him to re-sole the shoes, making them almost new again, but the next time the shoes wore out my dad would buy us a new pair.

I also remember, my grandma would have all of us over to her house on Saturday or Sunday for dinner or my mom would have them over to our house and a little later on in the evening they would pop popcorn, then when it was finished they would pour the popped corn into the middle of the table, which was always clean, for all of us to enjoy. While all of us sat around the table and enjoyed the popcorn, we would tell stories, jokes, and sing. Now these were the good old days!

My grandmother was a Sioux Indian, whenever we would start telling stories, she would tell all about the way she was raised. So then my sister and I would say to her, "Guess we are the lucky ones to have what we have." Oh, there is one more thing, like I said we didn't have much, for example, we never had a telephone. So one time my dad found a telephone, that someone would give away, all they had to do was come in and pick it up, so that's what he did. It was the kind you would hang on the wall and you had to ring it with a handle on the side of it to get the operator, then you would give her the number or the person's name you were wanting to call. In those days, you would be hooked up to a party line that everyone else could hear what you were talking about, so right there, people really knew your business. So one day my dad had to make an important call, so when he got the person on the line to talk to, he said you could tell people were listening in, just by the way it sounded. So he decided to fix them, when the man answered, daddy told him he had a joke to tell him (which wasn't going to be a clean one), he said you could hear or tell these people who was listening on his conversation start hanging up their receivers. So after that, daddy said he never had any trouble with people listening to his calls.

I use to love to go to my grandma's whenever she would do her washing. She had an old stand sitting by where she washed clothes and there was something that looked like a machine with a handle on the side of it and she called this her wringer machine to run the clothes threw before she put them into another wash tub filled with water so the clothes would get rinsed off and she would let me crank the handle on the side of the wringer to wring out the clothes. It was a lot of fun to do that. As I look back on the wringing, I have to say that in today's standards, other people would probably think it was pretty silly to think that something that simple could be so much fun for me. Whenever I was at my grandma's house and she would be sewing on the sewing machine she had, which was an old Singer sewing machine, I remember it had a foot pedal attached to it that was on the floor and in order to make it work you would have to petal it and that was my job if she happened to be sewing when I was there.

I remember the first television that we had. It was a Majestic with a black and white screen. We got the television once my dad had the electricity put in the house. Then a little later on, someone invented a sorta clear plastic shield you could see threw which was tinted with a blue and green color and you could place that over your TV screen aloud you to then have colored television. We thought we were rich then.

I also remember my mom would let us have some of our girlfriends over and we would make up a dance and sing and pretend we were movie stars and if any other kids would come over to see our show, they had to pay to watch our show, which was one toothpick to get in. Then my mom joined the show and she would tie a sheet onto a long rope and hook it over nails out on the front porch and when the time came for us to put on the show, she would slide that sheet back and our show would begin. Very fun memories. I always wanted to be some kind of an entertainer, but my dad did not allow it because he was afraid it would cost too much.

Well, now I am getting older and going to junior high school. My dad still saving money had an old Chevy four-door car, but in order to keep two of the doors closed he had to use bailing wire that he used to bail hay with and he would pull up right in front of the school and drop us off. My sister and I were so embarrassed; however, our friends at school didn't care.

My First Box Supper
By Christine K. Punzo of Maryville,
Missouri
Born 1924

In front of the mirror, I shook my short brown hair, trying to make it bounce like the ladies I'd seen in the movies. It didn't seem to bounce at all, but I comforted myself by thinking about the Box Supper I'd be going to later that day. After all, being almost thirteen and in the eighth grade, and being able to fix my own box of food for the occasion was pretty special. I wondered who would buy my box. Who would sit beside me in the double seat and enjoy the supper I'd prepare? Maybe it would be Ray Rowlette, a very handsome young neighbor, probably in his twenties. My heart skipped a beat just thinking of the possibility!

I decorated my box with scraps of paper pasted to it like a crazy quilt. I thought it looked really attractive and searched for an artificial flower to glue on the top. (It would be so easy nowadays; and there'd be scotch tape to attach it.)

What would I fix for the supper? I could imagine the fancier boxes that the older young ladies would cram with fried chicken, potato salad, maybe even fresh hot rolls, though of course they wouldn't be still hot when they were eaten, hours later. My thirteen year old idea of what would be an appropriate offering at the time, leaned toward pimento cheese sandwiches, something a bit different, but easy to fix. I mashed the cheese with a fork, tilted the bottle of pimentos so that a good supply fell into the concoction. I went to the cellar to get some pretty red apples to put into the box, polishing them on my apron as I hurried back to my task. What else? I reached for the cookie jar. Mom had baked some peanut butter cookies just yesterday, so I added a few of them to my treasures.

(Friends, to my thirteen year old mind, this menu seemed quite suitable at the time!)

That evening the school house was alight with several coal oil lamps.

Everything looked so splendid! People were arriving in their Model A Fords, and one or two buggies were also still in vogue. A few people who lived nearby walked to the entertainment.

A Box Supper was a bit of a fundraiser. If the school was needing funds for books or other special needs, the young bachelors would bid on the decorated boxes the young women had prepared full of food. Sometimes the girl whispered to her beau when her box came up for sale, and sometimes the young man would bid way more than he could afford just to get her special box!

I looked around and noticed that the handsome Ray Rowlette was there, sitting quietly on one of the side benches. I wondered if he had a special girl whose box would be offered and if he would dig deep to pay a high price for her creation?

As the evening progressed, it seemed to me that he was hardly bidding on any of them.

The auctioneer was hamming it up, teasing the fellows. "Boys, this one really smells good!" he'd say, and pretend that he wanted that one for himself. Of course, his small bids were quickly surpassed by the wealthier young bachelors. There was a lot of laughter and back-slapping among the prospective buyers. Some of them blushed furiously as they led their unexpected partner to one of the double seats.

The auctioneer was getting down to the plainer boxes now. My own box looked not nearly so fetching beside the fancier, be-ribboned boxes that had already been sold.

Finally, third from the last, my box came up for bidding. Suddenly, seized by the terrible realization that it might not get any bid at all, I wanted to bury my face in my lap and cry. But I had prepared the box with such high hopes! Surely, someone would want it!

Suddenly a hand shot up. I couldn't believe it. It was the good-looking Ray Rowlette! And he pronounced his bid, "I'll give a quarter for it.," he said quietly. Of course, the auctioneer didn't let that small bid go unnoticed; he talked it up quite a bit.

So that's the story of my first Box Supper. I ate my lumpy sandwiches with the handsomest man in the room. We hardly said a word to each other the entire evening. Oh well, there would be other Box Suppers. And I'd learned a couple of things about the boxes that were considered most desirable.

Orrsburg Store and its Memorable Owners
By Ron Wray of Bonner Springs, Kansas
Born 1934

Some of the most memorable days of my young life were spent around a small place northeast of Maryville, MO. It was called Orrsburg. To get there one travelled east on Highway 46 to Route E going north. This road is also called the Gaynor Ridge Road. Up Route E, about 7.2 miles (according to my aunt), you would be at the Orrsburg Corner.

According to my dad, who was a local history buff, a store in Orrsburg was started in 1881. Later, about 1900, a phone service and switchboard was added. The store had many owners through the years. At one time, there was a blacksmith; eggs and cream were bought at the store; and a "pick up route" was run from the store.

One of the owners, whom I will always remember, was Buddy Bloomfield. He ran the store through the World War II years: rumpled straw hat, glasses kind of down on his nose, and a great, friendly disposition, especially with us kids. The store's inventory, as I remember, carried a little bit of a lot of things one might need to exist in a rural farm community. The meat cooler was stocked mostly with lunchmeat and cheese, there was a cooler for pop, and a freezer for ice cream like Eskimo Pies or a cone could be dipped up. The store was one big room with shelves along the sides. A candy counter was up by the front door just to your left as you came in. There was a big heating stove in the center of the store for the long winter months, which was only taken down with the advent of spring.

In those days, a gravel road ran up from Highway 46 to the Harmony Church and Harmony High School, a distance of about two miles. The rest of the way on the Gaynor Ridge Road to Orrsburg was dirt with heavy overgrowth along both roadsides. Most all the rural roads were dirt. Folks couldn't run to town like they do today. This made Orrsburg store the social center for lots of folks who lived on those farms in the surrounding area. I have seen the store full of men on Saturday night just sitting around and "shooting the breeze."

A later owner of the store, Clyde Dorrel, even had outdoor movies for ten cents on Saturday nights. One of the things I vividly remember was on a hot summer day going into the store, over to the pop cooler and getting out a Pepsi and dumping half a bag of Planters Peanuts in it then sitting back and enjoying it. I forgot to mention that fuel was sold from a hand pump located just east of the main door. My dad related in some of his writings that early on there was a small shed across the road from the store that contained a can and funnel for early purchasers of gasoline. When Clyde Dorrel bought the store, he added another pump that ran on electricity.

With the advent of WWII, things changed around Orrsburg. My grandparents Wray, whose house sat just north of the store, saw three of their boys go off to war. One by one, each was drafted. After a family dinner, each said his "good bye" to his tearful mother, my grandmother, and was whisked off to Maryville to catch the bus to Kansas City and the induction center. One became a tail gunner on a B-17 and flew 33 missions over Germany, one participated in the Alaska Campaign, and one went to India. My grandmother wrote each one of them every day. I also had another uncle, Jim, who went into the Marine Corps. He was my aunt's husband and he served in the South Pacific. They all came back.

Things were rationed then and things were collected for the war effort. Common Sense School was a mile east of Orrsburg. My sister and I attended Common Sense along with seven other kids. We collected scrap iron, bacon grease, milkweed pods, and bought war bonds and stamps.

In the long winter evenings my grandfather,

my uncles (who weren't draft eligible), and I would go down to Orrsbug store and Buddy Bloomfield would read us the latest Life Magazine accounts of the war. No TV in those days, so that (and the radio) was how we learned how the war was going. We were told that the scrap iron we collected would be melted down to make tanks and guns, the grease would be used for nitroglycerine for ammo, and the milkweed pods would be dried for the lining of life vests.

Sugar and canned goods were also rationed (I think my grandmother hoarded lots of canned goods). Another rationed item I should mention was tires and, last but not least, gasoline. You had stamps for that. If you had a truck and you were somehow helping the war effort, you got a "T" stamp, which was worth more than other stamps (but I can't recall what they were).

Today, Orrsburg store is gone. One of my uncles tore it down when he bought the town of Orrsburg. And also gone is the switchboard. One of my other uncles now owns the house. Little remains but memories from old guys like me. It was a great experience!

I will close with one of us kid's favorite patriotic songs:
"Oh, the Fuehrer says we gotta go to bed,
"So we'll Heil! Poop! Heil poop!
"Right in the Fuhrer's face!"

The Herbert Ridge Barn
By Joyce Ridge of Agency, Missouri
Born 1943

The barn on the Herbert Ridge Farm southeast of Agency, MO, has gone the way of most old farm barns that used to be scattered across the landscape. The barn was no longer functional for today's farming operation. It became cost prohibitive to maintain unless it could be turned into a practical or profitable use. The Ridge barn had been neglected and in a state of disrepair for many years. The barn gave a final death groan and collapsed after a heavy rain in 2010.

My first verified memory has to do with the barn. As an adult, one day I was recalling out loud to my mother about some black pups born in the barn on her birthday. She was amazed I could remember this because I was barely three years old. Mom remembered the

The Herbert Ridge Barn in 1975

event because it was a sweltering hot July 26th. She was quite uncomfortable being eight months pregnant with my sister, Janice. She remembered climbing with me in tow into a corn crib where there was no moving air to see the newborn puppies.

The barn conjures up many other memories such as the time my brother, Carl, was clowning around in the loft, and stabbed a pitchfork through his big toe. My sister and I used to stalk cats whose appearance revealed they had recently given birth. We were relentless trying to locate where the kittens were hidden. Often we watched the mother cat crawl down a crevice between hay bales in the loft. We had to really do a lot of work sliding bales aside to get to the kittens. It was always fun to watch Daddy milk our one cow at the barn. He gave most of the milk to his barn cats. You see, Daddy had his cats at the barn and Mom had her cats at the house. You need to wonder no more, why I grew up to consider our cats members of the family. A fun time with Daddy was being in the barn with him when he was operating the grinder. I have no idea now why it was so fascinating to watch what we called "corn chop," otherwise known as cracked corn, flow out of the grinder.

The barn was the site of pig inoculation day. Janice and I were given the task of catching and holding the pigs while Daddy vaccinated them. My dad became frustrated with our efforts and finally decided we were old enough to do the vaccinations so we switched jobs. It was a very happy day for me when Daddy concluded Janice was an expert and she was awarded the job of full time vaccination specialist. The pigs were probably happy as well to be rid of my painful stabs.

Sheep shearing was an all-day springtime event at the barn. Everything else was put aside for that day. Sheep shearing was a unique skill. The sheep shearer was booked in advance as he travelled from farm to farm doing his work. We watched each ewe being sheared one at a time with wool taken off in almost one piece. The wool was then packed into a long, approximately 4 foot wide burlap sack and taken to market for sale. I always felt sorry for the ewes because they looked naked and often shivered in spite of it being a warm day.

My always ornery brother, Carl, took advantage of the barn as a good place to scare or taunt his sisters. Such was the case when he tried to convince me that jumping out of the hay loft would give me the same sensation as parachute jumpers when they hit the ground. I can't remember why that was something I was curious about, but fortunately, I was not so gullible to his suggestion. The barn was also where Carl and I had heart to heart talks of a more serious nature. I remember one of his life learning lessons he gave me just before the U. S. Army sent him for an 18 month tour of duty in Korea. He told me to learn how to take care of myself. He tried to impress on me that we never know what the future holds so having knowledge and skills for self-reliance would be valuable if needed.

After my dad died in 1965, our neighbor Charlie Kline and joined later by his twin sons, Dale and Gale, did our farm work and still do so today. One day when they were taking hay bales out of the barn loft the twins, then teenagers, were fighting about something. Charlie was below watching the bales pitched out and wondering what the outcome would be of the loud yelling. Then, out came a bale with Dale partially attached as it fell to the ground. On that occasion Gale ended the fight by throwing out his brother. I suspect the score was evened up shortly thereafter.

The barn is gone but not the memories.

Gone Fishin'
By Buford Weddle of Ravenwood, Missouri
Born 1929

The following event took place in the early 1940s. I was in my teens. My folks were farmers. They always went to town on Saturday to bring the cream and eggs to the poultry house. Then buying the next week's supply of staples. I usually stayed at home watching over things. This was my time to practice the mischief I had dreamed up all week. Of course, we all went to town on Saturday evening. This was girl-chasing time.

A logging company moved in down on the creek bottom. They purchased some large timber they were cutting for lumber. Part of their deal was to remove the large stumps, which they blasted out. They did not work on Saturday.

There was always a deep hole of water in a bend in the river. This was our usual fishing hole.

This outfit kept their blasting products locked in a small building. My buddy and I got this idea of going fishing with blasting products, potash, sugar, and gunpowder.

So we called in the troops, neighborhood boys that wouldn't tell. We go down to the little hut armed with hammers and crowbars. We were soon in the little building. We came out with plenty of blasting paraphernalia. Lots of fuse.

We had four glass gallon jugs with lids, which we cut a hole in for the fuse. One jug would have been enough. We went over to an old yellow clay bank and got us the packing material. Packed and set up. Pack in some clay, blasting products, fuse, and then more clay. All set, ready for the fun. We scattered around the old fishing hole, lit the fuse, and threw them in.

We stepped back what we thought was far enough but miscalculated badly. Those things blew at the same time, blowing mud all over us. We had fish, frogs, turtles, snakes, and muskrats scattered over one-half acre of ground. Boy! Did that stuff blow. We laughed. The old fishing hole was almost dry.

We dug some mud off of each other and started picking up fish. Heard someone coming through the cornfield and weeds. Was an old man who owned the land. Surprised at the amount of fish we got, he started a big belly laugh that lasted a while. Gave him all the fish he wanted, not to tell, but he did both. We took all the fish we could carry. My buddy and I cleaned ours.

My dad was not a mean man. Quite the opposite. He had his standards to live by and expected his household to do the same. It was evident there was too many fish obtained not to be some illegal action, so dad ask me what had happened. I knew better than not tell him. He did not bring out the razor strap, but he tore my heart out with words for stealing what we did. His bit of stealing education.

Summers and Saturday Nights in King City
By Janet M. Preston of Perry, Kansas
Born 1940

I was born in King City, Missouri in 1940. I left soon after, but always come back in the summer to visit grandparents, aunts, uncles, and cousins. In the '50s when I would visit, usually two weeks in the summer, we always had a good time. We would go uptown on Saturday nights. The town was full of kids and people.

Grandpa would take the car uptown early in the afternoon and park on Main Street. About 5:30 or 6:00, someone would come and get grandma and I and we would go get into the parked car. Other people, aunts or cousins, would come by and get into the car. Grandma would send us to the "Men's Club" to get money from grandpa to go to the movies. I didn't like to go in the "Men's Club" because it was full of old men smoking cigars and the smoke was so thick you couldn't breathe. Grandpa would always act like he didn't know us, then he would say, "Oh these are my grandchildren." He would give us $1.00 apiece, and then we would get a hot dog before the movie. We had two movie theatres in town, the Royal on the south side and the Danbury on the north side. We would watch and see where our friends went, and then we would all go there. It cost 12 cents to see the movie. Sometimes we would get a jar of dill pickles before we went in. We would pass them around and then we would roll the jar down the aisle and they would stop the movies and tell us to calm down. My husband who was born and raised in King City said he only got ten cents a week allowance, so he could only go ever-other week to the movies. They would wait outside and when the other kids come out, they would tell them about the movie. After we got out of the movies, we would go to a soda shop and get a Coke or root beer float. About 10:00, we would check in with grandma and it was time to go home.

She had been in the grocery store and bought her groceries and they would put them in the cooler till she was ready to go home. My husband said they would get a half-gallon of ice cream and go home and divide it five ways and then pour Karo Syrup on top (yuk). The town was so crowded you could hardly walk down Main Street.

There were three grocery stores, two movie theaters, three drug stores, two clothing store, a dime store. To me it was so big when I was eight or ten years old. Now when we visit there is no one up town on Saturday night. I have to stop and think that was 60 years ago.

Other things we did in the summer was, stealing watermelon (only once); getting dumped in the country with my friends because they were freshmen; going to the old chicken coop for teen town. We made a playhouse in Grandpa's barn. Got into trouble because we took mattress from my cousins house. Played baseball almost every day in a field where every-one in town came to play.

When I was 17, I moved back to King City and finished high school there. After graduation (1957), I went to work at the First State Bank. I met my husband and got married and lived there for five years. We then moved to Kansas. We have been here for 45 years. We were married in the First Baptist Church there June 6, 1959. We still get back to King City every month or so. My childhood memories are something I will never forget in the small town of King City, Missouri.

Parties and Square Dances
By Anna Lou Webster of Oregon, Missouri
Born 1928

I was born approximately six to seven miles northeast of Oregon. At about two years of age, my family moved to another home on the same farm. It was about one-quarter-mile from where I was born, making us closer to Oregon. I went to the New Point School all 12 years, graduating high school in 1946. My primary teacher taught for many years. She taught several generations and was loved by all. Each morning she led us in the pledge to the flag. She always found time to read to us out of the Bible. We sang religious songs, also Patriot songs. No one complained the one before and after did the same.

My first cousin was two months younger than I. He was in the same class until during our fourth grade when he and his family moved. I was lost without him. We never got spanked at school. Miss Lydia could humble us without spanking. I remember three little boys in our room (she taught three classes) who she tied in their sears because they would not stay put. She used twine string. Of course, they could have gotten out, but they didn't. Their parents did not complain, if kids misbehaved, she handled it—no spanking.

High school was fun. We learned bur we had parties (for any reason). This involved party games and refreshments. I remember one Halloween party held in a vacant house. We put bales of straw for seating. My mom made 24 dozen raised donuts. Don't remember what we had to drink, probably cider. We played party games a had great fun. This was typical of all our parties. Our party games were "Skip to My Lou," "Miller Boy," "Three Deep," and others. We also had square dances at various homes. One family in particular had square dance parties in their home. She played the piano, he called the dance, the son, and the rest of us rolled the carpet back and danced.

I was married in 1946, we moved a house to the farm, and lived there until the 1960's when we moved to Oregon.

I had worked as deputy circuit clerk/recorder for three years. The lady who was the circuit clerk/recorder decided to retire and she wanted me to run for the office. I had never held a political office but she said she would help me, so I ran for the office, was elected, and held the office for 16 years (four-year terms for four years). Since we heard they were going to computers that let me out. So my deputy won.

My husband and I joined a square dance club and we danced until the wee hours of the morning. Then we all went out to eat breakfast.

We had two children, Steve and Sandra. We had four and five generations in our family at various times.

At one time when we lived on the farm, but both of us were working in Oregon, we got stranded in a snowstorm about a mile from home. Both of us stayed at a farmhouse, since two other cars were stranded also. We enjoyed chicken and noodles with our neighbor and her husband. We walked home the next day—

321

left the car in the ditch covered with snow, only the radio antenna showed where it was.

I have never lived more than approximately seven miles from Oregon. Lots of living in a small area!

Clover Hill, a One-Room Country School
By Deloris (Tyler) Reeves of Tarkio, Missouri
Born 1932

Of the 8 years that I attended elementary school, all but one and a half of them were spent in a one-room country school known as Clover Hill. The school was given a certificate as a first class school in 1923 and was located 3 miles north and a quarter mile west of the Tarkio, MO, city limits.

The year was 1938, the month was September, and the day Monday. I was both excited and scared on my first really big venture into the world outside my home. There were no buses in those days to pick us up at our door and deliver us to the steps of the school. Nope, it was "shank's pony" (our own two feet) all the way. Sunny, rain or snow, hot or cold, it was all the same.

On this warm fall morning with my little tin dinner bucket in hand, my shorter legs

Deloris Tyler in 1937

tried their best to keep up with the longer ones of my brothers as I headed out up that dirt road walking a mile and a quarter to my first day of school.

What a journey in life this would prove to be. Clover Hill was equipped with at least 200 books in its cupboard library: Books for study and learning purposes and books filled with stories and exciting adventure known as outside reading books. But the ones that caught my eye and held my interest those first few days of school were the Dick and Jane books, which had covers in different colors for each different story contained inside. I loved those books and they hold an interest for me even to this day. I have a treasured two or three in my own library. The technique of pictures and words were used in clever ways, not only to teach me how to read, but woven into the stories were learning tools of respect for others, sharing, cleanliness, and so much more that melted in and extended what we were taught at home.

What a glorious sight my eyes beheld as I stepped through the doors that first day. Seats and desk were set one behind the other on runners. Each runner of seats and desk were placed in rows across the width of the room. As the rows made their progress across the room, so did the ages of the pupils starting with the 1st grade up to the 8th. Each desk held a compartment to hold books, paste jar, Big Chief tablet, penny pencils, crayons, etc. The top of the desk had a small hole up in the right hand corner to recess an inkbottle in, and a narrow slot across the top to hold a pencil.

Such wonders did my blue eyes behold. At the front of the room a long blackboard stretched with a chalk rail below and over it hung a container holding a series of maps on rollers that pulled down to share their secret of the world. A globe of the world rested on the teacher's desk as well as her Course of Study book, which contained daily lessons. A piano stood in one corner of the room, and there was a picture of a man I later learned was the first president, George Washington.

The floors of the schoolroom were clean and well oiled. In the winter a furnace in the basement belched black smoke from the chimney as the banked coals from the day before were encouraged back to life as new coal was added.

I soon found school a place of both fun and learning, with new friends to make, and for some even a crush on some unsuspecting boy or girl. Recess times were always looked forward to with much pleasure, a 15 minute break both morning and afternoon with an hour at noon. At noon, you'd swallow your food half eaten so you could find more time to play. Playtime could be both fun and painful, especially on the teeter-totter. If your partner on the opposite end happened to be a little on the ornery side and jumped off while you were up in the air, it was a spine jolting butt bustin' experience when you landed hard on the ground.

Clover Hill had a playground of grass, which during the summer months was allowed to go wild without any form of tending. When it was finally mowed just before school began in the fall, it left stubs to stab the ankle and stubble to scuff up new shoes. The yard was large with ample ground to play Cowboys and Indians, replaying a Saturday night western. Softball, Blackman, Ante-Over, and many other games were enjoyed. Fox and Geese was a lot of fun when the ground was covered in snow.

Over to the side were two swings, two of those gosh awful teeter-totters, and the most fun of all, a merry-go-round. It lent a lot in the way of both exercise and working off excess energy.

If the weather was bad and we couldn't go outside to play there were plenty of things to keep us entertained inside. There were spelling and ciphering matches, a piano to play, and a record player to march to band tunes to. We had crafts to make and monthly we traced and colored pictures that matched the theme of the month and were placed in the windows.

In Clover Hill, and I imagine, other one room country schools, age didn't seem a factor. We had respect for our teachers, even a crush on them from some of the older kids. Some of the upperclassmen were looked up to as heroes.

Drugs were not in our vocabulary. Grass was something one played on and adults mowed, certainly not referred to something to smoke. Gay was being happy and enjoying life and Pot was a utensil your mother cooked beans in.

Long handles (underwear with arms and legs) were the 'must' on cold winter days for both boys and girls, as well as long brown cotton stockings for the girls. Many of our dresses were made from the colorful sacks that our parents bought chicken feed in. We were especially appreciative of warm Mackinaw coats and wool scarves and mittens when we walked to school on cold, cold days, oft times on snowdrifts that had been cleared from the middle of the road. Some days the snow and mud would melt during the day and by the time we headed for home, the mud was thick and deep and would ball up around our overshoes making our feet twice their size and hard to walk.

It was a joy to see the American flag with its 48 stars and 13 red and white stripes waving freely, greeting us each morning as we arrived at school. The old pump stood bravely by with a tin cup hung from a wire hook to be shared by anyone with a thirst for a cold drink.

Sometime during the year, the County Health Nurse came around and ran tests for such things as hearing, sight, teeth, etc. Children worked hard to achieve the steps that it took to earn Nine Point Buttons. These were pins about the size of a silver dollar and came in a different color every year. They were health awards and represented nutrition, posture, throat, teeth, birth certificate, hearing, vision, diphtheria immunization, and smallpox immunization, the nine achievements needed for the pin.

Certificates were also awarded by the teacher for perfect spelling and perfect attendance. Many of the children learned from watching the upper class doing spelling or arithmetic at the blackboard or listening to them recite or read standing by the teacher's desk.

School programs were put on at Christmas time by the children. Most were held at night after the farmers were out of the field or free from other daily work. Heavy floral curtains were hung from a strong wire across the front of the classroom and small rooms were formed at either side for the changing of costumes. In the middle was the stage where the program was acted out.

No electricity had yet come to our school in the '30s. Lighting came from kerosene lamps with reflectors positioned between each window. Later Aladdin lanterns on wires hung from the ceiling gave more light.

When we older folks talk about the Good Old Days, it is very likely the old one room country school will enter somewhere into the conversation. There is much more to be said about those humble learning centers, for they were indeed special and wonderful days for me. If only we had some of that good old-fashioned down to earth learning these days, when we worked our brains to learn, not by a computer that has all the answers for one.

A big year for all the old one-room country schools and the many teachers who taught in them! Yea for Clover Hill!

After the Thunderstorm; the Rainbow
By Anna Egli-Maynard of Lee's Summit, Missouri
Born 1930

God said, "When the rainbow appears in the clouds, I will see it and remember the everlasting covenant between me and all living beings on earth." Genesis 9:16 (TEV)

It was a hot August day and the farmers were in the midst of harvest. Ma, my younger brother and sister, and I had spent the day with the neighbor: the farmer's wife who had been recruited to finish the term in our one room school after our teacher was drafted for military service. The farm where she lived was less than a mile from the south forty acres where our family threshing crew was working. Seldom did Ma leave work at home to visit during the week, so this day away from home had been exciting for us.

Now we waited. To the southeast, moving over the crest of the hill, we could see the approaching horses and wagon, our ride home. The driver was hardly discernible in the distance but we knew it was John, my older brother, coming across the stubble field with a load of newly threshed wheat. The threshing operation—the threshing machine, the John Deere tractor, the hay racks, the teams of working horses, the crew of men—and the stack of new straw were out of view over the hill.

The late afternoon sun was beginning its westward descent toward the horizon where there was a hint of gathering gray clouds. For us the day had started early. Now as we stood watching our transportation coming, we were ready to go home. The wind was blowing. It always blew. We were used to pushing from our eyes the strings of hair that whipped across our faces.

As the horse-drawn wagon arrived, we could smell the newly harvested grain.

John signaled for us to get on and we wasted no time climbing up the wood spokes of the iron-rimmed wheels to clamber onto the grain. Ma came up last, after exchanging parting words with our hostess. Our feet sank into the wheat as we moved to seat ourselves, with legs dangling over the side of the wagon box.

John looked over his shoulder to check on passengers and called, "Everybody on?" We heard the slap of leather on leather as he gave a sharp flick of the reins. "Giddap!" and we were moving.

The horses were eager. They always are when homeward bound. We scarcely had time to wave "Good bye" before the jolts of the moving wagon forced us to hang on to secure our perch.

We knew we had a long ride ahead of us. It would take an hour or more before we reached the homestead: an hour of jarring, jiggling, and bouncing. Frequently, we repositioned ourselves as the jolting settled our seats deeper into shifting wheat.

The shortest route took us across the flat, tilled fields of neighboring farms where farm machinery had smoothed a trail. It took us over un-graded county roads between pasture and corn fields, where ruts had dried after spring rains. There were gates to open and close. As we came over the crest of one hill and continued down the slope of the next, the distance between us and home shortened. We bumped steadily along not talking much, our tired bodies absorbing the shock.

By now, the sun had receded behind the gathering clouds. Overhead the vast expanse of sky was darker. We saw the sheet lightning in the west and heard the thunder rumbling in the distance. The new chill in the air brought the smell of rain. The horses quickened their pace as John allowed more slack in the reins. The rhythm of hooves beating on earth blended with the creaking sounds of the moving wagon. We knew the race was on to reach shelter before the brewing storm hit.

Now we could see our house on the hill a mile or so ahead of us. My five year old brother spoke, "I wish we was home." "We will be soon," Ma replied calmly, but there was a note of anxiety in her voice. I knew Ma was praying.

The team needed no coaxing and John let them break into a slow gallop. We huddled together as the dome of threatening clouds above seemed closer—closing in. The wind ceased. An ominous presence filled the air. Big raindrops began pelting. It was cold.

Suddenly we sensed the sizzle of electricity as lightning crackled, followed by thunder clapping so close we ducked instinctively. A new surge of wind rushed the torrents of rain that burst from the sky. Within seconds, we were drenched.

The frightened horses bolted into a full gallop.

"WHOA! WHOA! WHOA NOW!" Above the eruption of storm, John shouted to control the team as he braced himself to tug tightly on the long lines until he slowed the horses and wagon to a halt. While John struggled to unhitch the prancing horses, we all scrambled to the ground and leaned closely to the side of the wagon to seek protection from the buffeting wind and rain. Then the vibration of hooves pounding against the earth faded into the weather as the harnessed team disappeared toward home. Hurriedly, John joined us as we bent to huddle closer. Lightning split the sky and the thunder reverberated louder and nearer in the violence of the storm.

Clinging together against the grain wagon, we waited out the repeated cycles of lightning and thunder that blasted through the steady downpour. In time, the storm began to subside. Wind and rain slowed.

Dripping and chilled we took off our shoes and socks and turned homeward.

Wet clothes pasted to skin, hair clinging to cheeks, we trudged barefoot through mud and splashed through puddles. Occasionally one would stop to wait for another.

As we ran and walked, the rain receded to a sprinkle. Thunder rumbled, echoed, and then faded away. By the time we crossed the main highway that slices through our farmland a fourth of a mile from home, the dark clouds had moved over us and on to the northeast.

Now on home territory, we could see the harnessed horses standing at the barn with heads reaching over the corral gate. As the sun low in the west peeked from behind a cloud, a rainbow arched over the eastern horizon. Calmness had returned to our freshly washed world and we were home.

The Old Outhouse
By Dixie L. Swafford of Rayville, Missouri
Born 1948

I remember the old outhouse way out back when I was a little girl. It was so small, the best way to enter it was, as mom would say, "Just turn around and back in." It was just a little one-holer.

Mom finally talked dad into building a new one. So the process began. It was a stately outhouse; it had two holes with toilet seats over each hole. Windows with lace curtains, toilet paper holders on each side, a small chest to hold books, a small lamp, and radio set on the chest, linoleum on the floor, with a shag throw rug. When you hit the switch on the back porch, the lights and radio came on in the outhouse. People said, "Lucy's outhouse was much cleaner than most people's indoor toilets," and it was. In the summer, she also kept an electric fan that came on with the switch too. All the comforts of home.

I always wanted a playhouse like the outhouse that daddy built. Well, years down the road the outhouse was moved, cleaned, and became the playhouse for my children, and they loved it. But the old saying stands true. Hottest place in the summer time, coldest place in the winter.

Castor Oil

I remember as a very young girl, maybe five or six years old, my mother decided I needed some castor oil for some reason that I don't remember. I do remember, however, that she had to call in the neighbors to hold me down in order to get it down me. One held my arms, one my legs, and one to hold my nose. A lady named Francis Sanderson, mother's good friend who lived across the street, was the one who held my nose. They laid me out on the kitchen table for the procedure. And the memory has lasted my lifetime.

I was invited years later to Francis' 90th birthday celebration. As I gave her a hug, I whispered in her ear that I still haven't forgiven her for holding my nose for the dose of castor oil, but loved her to death any way. She told me she remembered it as though it was yesterday, and had thought of it many times with a laugh.

It makes for a good story and a good memory, but it wasn't funny at the time. I still shudder at the thought.

Party Line

These were days of easy information, just pick up the receiver and listen, much to everyone's dismay. The switchboard operator, Tavie, was a lady with all the information. You needed to know anything, call Tavie. After all, she sat all day with the headphones on. Just a little switchboard set up in her home. I remember always wanting to be like Tavie. I would take a piece of cardboard, poke holes in it, and use my grandma's silver, metal hair curlers as my connectors on the board. What an imagination, and what fun I had. I would play for hours. I still remember our ring was two longs and two shorts on the old crank phone.

Spankings at School

I never got a spanking, but I sure remember one on someone else that made a lasting impression on me.

I was in the first grade and one of the eighth grader bus riders have got into trouble on the bus that morning. The eighth-grade teacher just happened to be the principal too. So she brought the girl that had gotten into trouble on the bus into our room, laid her across my desk,

Dixie's parents Lucy and Strother McGinnis with Dixie

and proceeded to break a yardstick over her bottom side. She had gotten my full attention, for eight years!

Those were the days when discipline was used and kids learned from it. It is a shame those days are gone and kids now days don't know what the meaning of respect is, at school, on the job, or in the home. I'm very thankful that my parents loved me enough to discipline me.

Saturday Night Baths

We were uptown because we had one of those oblong bathtubs, not just a little, round one. Every Saturday night the tub was set up in the kitchen right in front of the oven door in the winter and on the back porch in the summer. A big, metal bucket of water was heated on the stove. It helped to heat the house in the wintertime. And in the summer, mom and dad used an electric heater that went into the bucket.

I always got the first bath. Water was hot! I always told mom she tried to scale me, but her comment was, "It had to be hot so it would stay warm for daddy." You see, after I got done, she would take hers, and then dad after that. Same water and it never killed any of us. We just didn't know any difference. There were only three of us though. A friend told me one time, there were eight of them in the family and the water got a little thick before the last one was done. I told my daughter-in-law this story not too long ago and her comment was, "O, YUCK!"

Wringer Washer

I awoke on Monday mornings to the smell of Clorox water, and beans cooking on the stove. You see it was washday. The sound of the old Maytag's swooshing and humming on the back porch was a sign mom was busy. Two rinse waters, one with bluing to whiten the whites. I was always asking to put the clothes through the ringer, but was always told no because mom was afraid I'd get my fingers caught in the ringer.

She used a little, wooden stick to dip the clothes out of the washer because the water was so hot.

The clothes were then hung on the line. If it was raining, then the clothes were hung on the line that dad would string through the house. O, the smell of clothes drying in the house, and brother, let me tell you, you'd better not run through them either.

Dixie and Suzanne (best-friends)

To this day, the smell of Clorox or beans cooking brings back some beautiful memories.

Homemade Clothes

Mom loved to sew and was very good at it. She had an old Singer petal sewing machine. A pull of the wheel and perfect timing on the petal, and she had it humming.

I had a schoolmate, Suzanne that was my best friend and she was at my house more than her own. Mom just kind of adopted her as hers, so if she made me something, she made her the same thing. Most of the time we looked like twins. To this day, we are still best friends. We just don't dress alike. When we get together, we have so many good laughs about the "Good Old Days," and our many clothes of many colors.

Blizzards

I remember one year when I was in the third grade at Rayville it began to snow and blow really bad. No fancy weather forecast in those days. They called the bus drivers back in and closed school. Mom new it was gonna be bad so she walked to school and brought my boots. We lived across town so I always walked or rode my bike. This day I had walked with little, red boots, and my headscarf tied tight, we set out for home. By the time we got there, it was blowing and snowing so hard we could hardly see where to walk because it was stinging our faces so bad. It was the blizzard of the year. Dad didn't get home so it kept me and mom busy keeping coal in the stove. I'd fill the bucket with coal and she attended the stove. I don't think mom slept all night for worrying about daddy. He finally got home around three o'clock the next day. He had gotten stuck and had walked to a house and stayed the night there.

Tales and People Remembered

I loved to set and listen to mom and dad tell stories of the days when they were young. Reminiscing always brings so much joy.

Mom would always talk of the days when she and her friend, Grace, would take out for Kansas City in the old truck, with four bad tires. Those were the days when tires were hard to come by, so they carried a bag of rags and newspapers with them and, when a tire would go flat, they would stuff it with rags and papers.

Another story I always loved was when one of Grace's chickens died and they decided to give it a funeral. Grace preached the funeral and mom sang. She said they closed the service with a little saying: Ashes to ashes and dust to dust, if we don't get you buried, you're gonna bust.

Stories like dancing the soles off her shoes on the streets of Camden, spring house cleaning, turning the mattress on the beds, putting clean newspapers under the linoleum, and etc.

I still love to set till this day and listen to my memories, in my thoughts. How beautiful they are to me.

Hit and Miss of My Life

I have so many special memories of my childhood. What a childhood I had. I would gladly go back and take it all over again.

I remember the ice man came through the neighborhood. The bread man came to the door; you could buy a loaf of bread for 17 cents. Ball games played on every corner lot after school. I lived to play ball. I was a tomboy from the word go. Mom tried to teach me girly things, but I never had time because there was always a ballgame being played somewhere. We would go to the old, concrete slab to wash our cars and swim, then drive back home on the gravel roads; cars would be as dirty as ever.

We played hid and seek all over town, not a worry in the world. Stores closed at 5:00 p.m. Families had one vehicle and meals were taken together. Life was beautiful for me. The Lord has truly blessed my life. I grew up

327

poor, but didn't know it. I was so rich in good family and friends. Time spent at home was so special to me. Mom always made it special. Bottle of cold Pepsi and popcorn while watching the Andy Griffith show. Now that made for a good night. Dad worked nights, so it was usually just me and mom

I never had a room of my own. Slept on a roll-away bed in the front room. My clothes hung on a broom handle across the corner in another room. No indoor plumbing of any kind till I was married. Then I moved one-and-a-half miles north of town. We built a new home at that time, $14,000. We paid $73 a month house payment, and that was tough. We still live in the same house till this day.

We were grade school, high school sweet hearts. Neither ever dated anyone else. We now have been married 46 years. We have three children and nine grandchildren, all of whom attend the same church, and all come home on Sundays for dinner. I wouldn't trade my life for the best of the best or the richest of the rich that this world has to offer. Because I have the best and I am rich with things that money can't buy.

Stories My Grandmother Told
By Marguerite Smith of Savannah, Missouri

The Rooster: Life is interesting. I like cute pets like cats, dogs, pigs, calves, sheep, and goats. I had them all. But you have to meet the rooster, there is nothing like The Rooster.

I guess the first rooster I remember was the Bandie. He didn't like me at all. I was a little girl and Grandmother tried to show me how to get the eggs. That rooster came all the way from the back of the hen house to get at me. Grandmother kept the rooster away from me.

Then came the time when I was a little older. I had been walking in my garden, going to the bathroom. That's when you had the outdoor one. There was a big white rooster and he would bite me. I had a rake in my hand and I hit him about 100 times. I thought I was going to kill him, but he still would not let me out, my father had to come and get me. I think HE killed the rooster.

Then there was a time, a long time later, the rooster took out after my husband and

my husband hit the rooster with his truck and knocked the rooster out. I killed the rooster but I never got him cooked.

Then there was the time when a friend and I got some chickens together. I had one rooster and one little hen. I had them at my home, outdoors. I thought it was too cold in the winter, so I let a friend take them. So, one day I went to see them. I wore a red coat and the rooster came from the back of the hen house to get me. So, I took the rooster back to the lady I got him from. She had a little grandson and the rooster took off and the rooster was nowhere to be found.

One day when we went to church in Savannah, a preacher was preaching about the Rooster in the Bible that Jesus told the Rooster to crow three times to Peter and that made me think of my Roosters.

The Day the Pastor Came to Supper: It had been a nice day. The Pastor and his wife and little girl were coming to dinner.

I went to the store and got chicken and potato salad. I came home, made a cake, and set the table. I just set the table for five people, but it turned out that there were just four of us. I thought I knew who was coming to supper and that I'd set the right number of places. The Pastor didn't mind and I guess I didn't count, but The Pastor just said it was room for Jesus.

When We Found a Home: We were little girls. I was six and my sister was four and we had lost our mother. So our father took us girls back to his mother, father, and brother. There were now six of us in our home and that's the time our family was renting our home.
Then, our family thought we needed a home of our own. So, my grandfather said we were going to buy a farm so we could have a home. So we all went together and got a home, our home. We had all kinds of pets. Grandmother raised hens and chickens and Grandfather and Daddy and Uncle had cows and pigs. Later, I got sheep and goats and a lot of pets. We got our home in 1949.

Grandmother read and told us stories. One of the stories she told us was about Grandfather and his first car. It was a model T car. A little after he got it, he was putting it in the garage. He started to put it in, but he forgot how to stop, so he shouted "WHOA," but it didn't stop, it just kept on going.

Grandmother and Grandfather showed us

a lot of things. They showed us how to make a garden, but most of all they showed us how to do right. Daddy and Uncle and Grandmother and Grandfather showed us how to have a home and how to take care of each other and took us to church when they could.

Do You Remember the 1940s and 1950s? I remember the first school bus I ever rode on. It had brand new seats and one time it left me and another girl at school. We had had to go to the bathroom and my father had to come to school to get us. The bus driver didn't do that again. That was back in 1943.

Then in 1944, when we moved in with my grandmother and family, she had a wood stove to cook on. I saw my grandmother was making a cake so I thought I would make a chocolate cake. So, I stirred one up and just got it in the oven and Grandmother came in and asked if I had put any baking powder and I had not. My grandmother had me take it out of the oven and put the baking powder in and it turned out good.

The Wood Stove that Took a Ride: We had a wood stove for over twenty years that we had to cook on. There were times it got so hot I thought it would bum the house down. I thought I would get the stove out of the house, but it would take about six people to move it. So, a friend of ours said we could put a chain on it and pull it out with our Model A. They did move it and it turned out that my husband's brother wanted it, so he took it to his house, and he used it for about 3 years. When he passed away, his wife sold the old stove for $10.00 and she gave me the $10.00.

The Stories My Grandmother Told Us: Grandmother told us stories while we helped with the housework. Grandmother told us that when she and Grandfather were married Grandmother was 17 and Grandfather was 19. They had four boys.

She told us about her oldest son. When he was one year old, she went to take something outdoors. When she came back in he had a chair on top of the sofa and was trying to get down and Grandmother had to grab him before he fell. Then she told us about taking the 3 year old and the one year old to the well to get water. This is back in the late 1800s. I don't know what year. She gave the 3 year old a small 1/2 gallon bucket and she carried the one year old and bucket. They were getting the water and the three year old started yelling the

"cotton" was after him. When Grandmother looked around there was the sheep coming after him. She had a cap on her head. She took her cap off her head and put it on the sheep's head so that he couldn't see. So Grandmother and the boys went home.

A few years later, when the boys had grown some, one day Grandmother was home alone. Grandfather had gone to town. So, Grandmother went to feed and water the chickens. There she found a possum in the water pond taking a drink of water. Possums will kill chickens, so she had to kill the possum. So, when Grandfather came back, Grandmother told him she had killed the possum. Grandfather didn't think she did. She took an axe and cut off its head.

We also had an outhouse. Ours had a light in it and also had a black snake in it. I also saw my grandmother kill a rattlesnake with a hoe.

One year my grandmother had a big garden. One day my sister and grandmother went to get beans and in their way was a big black snake. You should have seen her run. That year my grandmother canned 200 cans of green beans for the winter.

Maysville Memories
By V. Cooper of Berryville, Arkansas
Born 1927

The time I put my male and female rabbits together, Max, and Betty Pearl were there. We lived northwest of Maysville and they lived in Fairport. Well, it was really a funny ordeal. Rabbits were up and down running, about to tear the pen up. For 15 minutes we laughed and laughed—then guess what happen—we found out we had put the SAME SEX together—to this day we still enjoy a hearty laugh—yes, we had no babies.

This was probably the 1938-39, early '40s. Where I always lived Maysville, DeKalb County—had an annual horse show. It was a big one. Riders with their fancy horses and the clothes they wore was first class. As the fairgrounds and school football field was out our back door, my mother rented our downstairs bedroom to a woman in Kansas City each year and she would come and stay. One of her luggage pieces was her ribbons and awards she had won. They were beautiful

John E. Davies

to me.

The county fair with everything was held at the county farm—rides, cotton candy, machine to set in for your picture. Sometime only one person, sometime two, or three made more fun. At night, there would be a special show of comedy, singing, etc.

World War II was classes trying to get more paper than others. Also, selling tickets to March of Dimes, dances and parties. Classes would buy ten-cent tickets and try to fill a book to get it full, ten-cents a walk. What has happened to one-cent candy and ten-cent cigarette package?

I've been in Arkansas 50 years, July 2012 and Maysville is still my home town, the problem is of the over 100+ people I knew and visited are now gone. The days of visiting, going to dance "Frog Hop," St. Joe picnics, dinner and parties, and Saturday night card games, I've been blessed to remember so much.

Remember the cars were few in the '20s and '30s, so we had just about everything we needed right in town—McAdams Drug, Mi Drug, Quiley Cafe, Jim & Yvonne Brock Cafe, Donald Young family, the Hatchery, Weidermier feed & seed, Goble Feed & Baby Chicks, OE Rose Dry Goods, Davidson Mercantile. Really early The Blue Bird Café with large bar and stools lined up, now corner of Casey's Record Journal paper. Mrs. Pollard had what they called her girls—high school students lived in country, she let them come live with her and they helped her with her home and paper. School buses probably

hadn't come to be yet.

Drs. R. R. Reynolds, Johnson, Dr. Dosch Eye Harold Fowler, Dunham Café, Saturday night Jiggerbug dance and large tenderloin sandwiches.

The Herald paper was Ficklin and their daughter was our Girl Scout leader. She had a sleepover one night and we were on the floor and everywhere. She came to check us and not a stitch of clothes on. Can you see six or eight little girls eyes pop out? In that day, I wonder if any of us went home and told mother.

I'm sure the first hotel was probably the brick two-story house on Main next to City Hall that was a service station.

I lived next to school. After school, students would gather, joke, talk, and enjoy, waiting for second bus to take them home. Other nights, you hurry home to the radio for Little Orphan Annie, Tom Mix, Lone Ranger, Captain Midnight. My first TV must have been 1951. The first color was Jim and Yvonne Brock. They have been many improvements in them. Or they wouldn't have made it.

When I would go to the farm to spend the night with my friend, Eileen Hunt Lam, she milked the cow and her cat would stand for her to milk and hit the cat's mouth with the milk. We still write and visit after 80 years.

Owen Harris and I were neighbors. We were always riding bicycles, playing games, and we both messed around with baby owls and snakes. One day he came down and had baby snakes he had found. They were in his pockets and hands. He passed away several years ago, but I'm sure he would have remembered.

Another time Owen Harris and Jean Rainey (they moved) were riding in car and Jr. Cooper and myself saw a snake on the road. Jr. stopped for Owen to get it. Jr. hated snakes and he drove off, left Owen, he didn't want it in the car. Yes, we went back. No snake.

I was born and spent many days on the square of Maysville. All of the businesses knew me and I knew them. I first made the news at four-and-a-half months old.

My dad was very proud of his firstborn. So when the editor of the Herald brought a pair of pants in, "Rosy" decided he would deliver them and his little daughter to the Herald. I believe the editor would have been Mr. Ficklin. The story goes like this. Of course, we don't want to embarrass Carl by quoting his fatherly utterances, as he beamed on his daughter. He cut loose something like this, "Here's dist four month, 15-days old today and here's got a tooth. We noticed her were just a slobbering and spittin' a dood deal and we didn't know what vas do matter with her and den we dust noticed she had a tooth. Er, we did." Carl is a regular dad. But he could have said, "toof furr," instead of tooth.

My memories start from the time I guess I was born. The reason my parents, Carl "Rosy" and Alta Cogdill had the Wardrobe Cleaners, they work side-by-side for 25 years. I', V. Deloris Cogdill and I had one sister, Donnis Jane Cogdill. I married Glen Jr. Cooper and Donnis, Stanley McCrea.

The Cooper family came from St. Joseph, Missouri. Had a 900 acres in northwest DeKalb County in 1940s.

The McCrea family had always been in DeKalb County, some farmers and others business and school employees.

The Cogdill family was from Woods Community. In 2007 I wrote saying Cogdill started the church and home. But my Grandmother Cogdill was a Stewart and it was her dad who built the first buildings. So I was wrong, hopefully not to often.

The family winter sport was skating and sliding The King Hill, northeast of Maysville was a big one. We used anything that would move, shovel, spade, board, tire, regular sled, and a large bobsled that held four to six people. It was a place Sunday afternoon was always a crowd.

V.'s parents, Carl and Alta Cogdill

Donnis, my sister, Stanley McC have passed on in the '70s. My husband died March 2011. We each lost a daughter, Melody and Candace.

Saturday was the day for everyone to shop. No WalMart every day, no extra trips to town for groceries. Saturday started early A.M. It was the day to shop, visit with friends you hadn't seen all week.

Kids went to movie, played together in courthouse yard. The Maysville Band would play a couple hours. I know the women did all these things, no hurry to go home. The men were having a beer. Sometimes to many. They went for the groceries and pick up cleaning and business people waited on them. I know it was always around midnight to 2 a.m. Sunday morning before we got home. I know Donnie and I would go to sleep in the cleaners or in the car. After all, we had been there all week.

Donnis and I would set in the car because we had a new one and it had a radio. Parked in front of the cleaning shop. That was lots of fun. Dad stopped us when he was afraid we run down the battery.

men jobs. The camp was a government project.

On highway going to Fairport, south of town was good for raising watermelon and Mr. Bledsabo would always bring a load to town on a flat bed.

Also a Fairport famer there had a bicycle, no car, and he would ride the bicycle everywhere he went.

River was also in that area and when it rained it would flood the highway. In Maysville they would put out a sign to let you know about it, normally saying "Bridge Out North." One time it read, "Bride Out North." I'm sure the men all went to see her.

Northeast of Mayville, several miles, there was a Phelps Pond. It was a large farm pond. In summer it was a family place to go swim. There was always a crowd.

Inside Owen Roller Skate Rink, north side square, great floor. Everyone skated. Our daughter started at three years old.

When I graduated 1945 the country schools were to close the next year. The County office hired three girls just out of school to teach. We went to Maryville Teachers College for a three-month course and then we taught. It was Marie and Noami Beckwick and myself. We were paid $100 month. I'm sure that couldn't be done today. My seven in five grades, all

The Cogdill family

became wonderful young people and family members. Thank God.

My favorite dog was black and white, medium size "Judy." Another dog because we had two dogs and mother said only one. Dad gave "Rosco" to a friend and she lived to be 22 years old. The one we kept was a toy name Rags. She finally got run over. We lived on Main Street.

We made our kits out of small wood, newspaper, and a cloth tail. They flew.

Mr. Allen spanked a senior with a whack from a wood paddle on last day school. I babyset his kids one day.

Donald Newcom had a Chevrolet coupe with a rumble seat. He taught Eileen Hunt, myself, and his future wife, Martha Ward, to drive.

As I said, I not only knew the businesses, but I remember their families. I could take you there and if the homes are still there I can tell you who lived in them. Not only around the square people, but those that worked in the courthouse—Miss Stutton Battinger, Perry, Morman, Assel Whiteaker, Mr. Lee, Mr. Allen, Coach Calvert. B. W. Sheperd, Miss Hite, and George Mackley, these were teachers. Rile Henry, night watchman, with his German shepherd dog that went with him. When I was very small, the night watchman was Mr. Law. They lived next door and I called her grandma. I remember Mrs. Wingate across the street with a big, beautiful yard. She was mother-in-law of Mr. Brown at lumber yard. Then three ladies (sister) never married. The Mathis girls lived on West Main in town. One worked at paper, one in courthouse, and I kept house for them. Then the Pollard girls. The

Record Journal editor, Mrs. Edna Pollard, use to have students living in the country come and live with her, do house work, and help at the paper so they could get to school. No buses. Her pay I'm sure was their room and board. Evelyn Beckwith Bray at Weatherby was one of these girls. Evelyn was a sister to Noami and Marie Beckwith Boyd (twins).

The Herald (the Early Pilot), the Record Journal went together, then called Record Herald, And Byron Lord was a early employ there.

World War II I remember the day with my parents and many others from Maysville. We went to Kansas City to see places of interest. Swope Park, museum, train depot. The day was a time of fun and families together. I remember the paper boys on the streets and corners yelling the news that Japan hit Hawaii with everything they had. Many killed, ships and planes were being bombed.

I Was My Daddy's "Boy"
By Joyce A. Bell of Belleville, Illinois
Born 1932

I was born in August 1932 to A. Wayne and Julia Nauman Staley on the hottest day of the summer or at least so my mother always said. It was a time when all the hogs up in the barn lot would not pay for my grandfather's funeral a couple of months earlier. It had been hot and dry for a long time and these were hard times for all farmers in the area.

I was born on Aunt Ella's place some six miles south and east of Mound City in Benton Township, Holt Count, MO. Today you use 1-29 and exit at #79, the Squaw Creek truck stop. You turn left, go over the highway, then again turn left on County BB, a gravel road, and you are on your way. When my grandmother moved off the farm to town, we moved into the bigger house with a big wrap-around porch on two sides. We had electricity but no running water or indoor plumbing. We had the usual wood/coal burning potbelly stove for heat but I do not remember having a radio or an icebox. The cellar was the ice box/refrigerator—a cool place to keep milk. Mother was scared to go down there because she had seen a snake and my baby sister almost starved. We had a party line and if we wanted to call Uncle Newell in Phoenix, Arizona, that was long distance. To do that, we went to the telephone office in town, where an operator placed our call through her switchboard. I was fascinated with all the holes and cords that went together and thought, "What a great job."

Mother had an electric iron. It had no temperature control so she would plug it in until it was hot enough and then unplug it to use it. What an improvement this was to heating an iron on the cook stove and ironing until it got cold. I decided to imitate this action and put a hairpin into the electric socket and burned an imprint on my forefinger and thumb which really hurt a lot. I guess I'm lucky to be alive. Today these antique irons are used to hold the door open.

I always wanted to help and get into everything. We had a wringer washer and my dad would put me in front of him so I could help put the clothes through the wringer. Pretty soon my little hand was coming through the wringer with the bedding. I sat down in a bucket of milk, I dropped the eggs, and I loved to go visit Aunt Nelly who lived a quarter mile down the road. Mom decided to tie me to the clothesline to keep track of me and cut down on my travels as a two year old.

There were no Pound a Peg toys back then but I found a sack of penny nails and had the best time pounding every one of them into a board I had found. Why I wasn't caught before I accomplished this feat I do not know. Penny nails were not cheap and Dad was not happy.

I wanted to write one Sunday morning. Mother had gotten a gross (13 writing tablets). She had them stored on the shelf up high in the closet. Before they were out of bed, I used a chair to get the tablets down and proceeded to scribble/write on every page. We also took a Saturday night bath in a metal round tub. Kids first, Mother next, and Dad last. The next morning I tripped over Dad's work shoes and hit my chin on the edge of the tub. The cut bled profusely and I have a nice scar even today, 80 years later. My sister and I always weighed within five pounds of one another and were the same height with dark brown hair. We would fight over the same dress and Mom resolved our fighting by just dressing us alike and many thought we were twins. Of course, my sister has beautiful big, blue eyes and mine are not so big and hazel.

I started first grade at six at Benton School, a one-room school house (grades one through eight) about one mile west of our house. I attended 1st, 2nd, and most of 3rd grade there before moving. All roads were dirt (now they are gravel) and the bridge crossing a fairly large "crick" (creek) was wood. Today it is concrete. To get to school, you went up the steepest hill in the county. My family considers it to be a VERY steep hill today. I walked by myself but suppose I joined the Andlers kids when I got to their drive at the top of this hill. I cannot imagine what it would be like to bundle up your six year old and send her out the door in every kind of weather to walk one mile every day to school. Eventually, Dad got Chester, a Shetland pony, for me to ride. Chester came from a farm to the east and always wanted to go home or back east. Because I was older, my sister and I would ride Chester east to visit Aunt Nelly but when it came time to go home, my sister would ride while I walked and lead Chester home. Dad provided quite a rodeo getting Chester to let me ride him the one mile farther west to school. During the day, he would get the saddle down around his belly and of course, I was not tall or strong enough to get it back upright. One of the older boys always had to get the saddle cinched up tight enough for me to ride home every day.

I'm not sure if Chester was the result of an accident I had or not. But one afternoon, we were walking home from school along with others on horseback. I elected to be on the inside of the curve in the road and here comes a Model T. The driver sees all the kids on the opposite side and takes the curve short, shearing the bank, and I end up under the car unconscious. When I came to my senses under the car, my hand was about six inches from the tire. One of the boys let me ride home with him on the back of his horse. Definitely the highlight of my day.

The boys hid cigarettes or I should say hid tobacco and papers in a bank along the road. You rolled your own and they would smoke on the way home; then eat onions to cover the smoke smell on their breath. I'm sure they weren't fooling anyone.

At school we played Andy Over, had swings, and played baseball. I got to be pitcher probably because I was too small to do much else (everyone had to play) and one of the eighth grade boys hit a ball directly into my stomach. I don't remember what happened after that. Then one day I jumped out of a swing going a little too high and hurt my elbow. I couldn't straighten my arm all the way for many years. No trips to the doctor back then either. Andy Over was a game of throwing a baseball over the roof of the school building (Andy Over) then running as fast as you could around the building. I don't remember exactly what that was all about but I thought it fun. The older girls told me there was no Santa Claus one day, which was really hard to take. This school building no longer exists, closing its doors in the 1950s.

One summer my sister and I took water out to the field where Dad was plowing with horses. We were almost home when a ram sheep came toward us and knocked one of us to the ground. Then the ram turned around and knocked down the other and before you could get up, he would knock you down again. Mother was on the porch waving a board and screaming. All the noise brought Dad running from the field to our rescue. He ran the sole off his shoe trying to catch this sheep. I'm sure he would have killed it if he could have caught it. I guess the sheep were mowing our grass. While my sister and I were scared to death, we really were not hurt.

My mother nicknamed us after a couple of popular songs of the day. My sister was "Chatter Box" and I was "Scatter Brain." My sister came down with Scarlet Fever but none of the family got it then; some seven years later (I was 13), I brought home Scarlet Fever from school. We were quarantined for THREE WEEKS with a big sign on the door to warn of no entry. About two weeks later Mother became sick with Scarlet Fever, which added another three weeks (now a total of five weeks). On the last day of this quarantine my father became sick. He was the sickest of us all and all the calluses peeled from his hands and feet making them soft as a baby's. By this time I had missed a lot of school, so my clothes were fumigated and I moved to town with my sister who had been living with Aunt Ida.

In the third grade, my folks moved to a different farm. March 1 is moving date so the farmers can get the land ready for that year's crop. I then transferred to the Mound City Public School and had a hard time with spelling. All the farmhouses I lived in growing up have been bulldozed and one would not know anyone ever lived there today except for the house where I was born (Aunt Ella's place) and my grandparents' home. They were still occupied at least five years ago.

My dad had a harelip and a hole in the roof of his mouth. He was difficult to understand particularly in a phone conversation. There was no corrective surgery back then. When he was older, he needed to have some teeth pulled and got a partial plate; this covered that hole and he could speak plainer. According to others, he was babied and given whatever he wanted. He did not finish high school, was teased/bullied about his speech impediment, and became what I would call "wild" today. And he had a car. His brothers became mechanics, the leading edge technology of the day. Automatic transmissions had not been developed yet and Mother provided excitement for us whenever she drove. She was not so good with the clutch. Dad attended the last lynching in Maryville.

He met Mother on a blind date, a friend of a friend. And he had the wheels. They were married in December 1930 by the mailman who was also a minister in Forest City. Her birthday was 20 Dec and with Christmas on the 25th, I asked her why so many anniversaries to remember in one week? She replied, "I had to be 18" although the license shows Grandma signed for her. Mother wore her older sister's wedding dress, a dark brown number. And another sister was her Maid of Honor.

I was pretty much my daddy's boy and learned to milk the cows, do all the farm chores, and eventually drive the tractor. My grandfather and great-grandfather were active in the small Benton Evangelical Church with a cemetery not far from that one room school and when I die, I will be buried in the same plot beside my grandfather and not that far from Aunt Nelly. Church services are still held in this church one Sunday each month.

No Work No Money
By Bonnie (Sherwood) Allwood of
Norborne, Missouri
Born 1938

My first recognition of life was when I was about a year old. Dad had gone to the Missouri State fair and gotten or won a big candy cane. I had my picture taken with my

Bonnie in 1939

sister and brother where we used to live. It wasn't long after that that LuDean (my sister) took sick with scarlet fever and died. She was four. I do remember looking for her, not knowing or understanding where she went. Another brother died before I was born, then I had another one 5 years older than me. I was always giving him trouble.

We moved to the home place 7 miles west of Carrollton when I was almost two. I was 5 years old when I went to Russellville, Arkansas, to see my grandpa Ward (Mom's Dad). He had broken his leg and we went to see him. I also remember fighting with my two aunts over who was going to sit on a big lard can to eat.

I just had only one grandparent living and a step-grandmother. The others had passed on before I was born.

As I said, anything that my brother could do I thought I could too. We had a tree that fell across the pond (a deep pond) and he used it to walk across. I had watched him several times, thinking, "I can do that." When I started to go across, my foot slipped and off the log, I fell into the pond. Here is where I am not normal. I went straight to the bottom first. I felt the mud on my feet, I was about to panic when he pulled me out to the bank. To this day, I don't like water over my head.

By the time I was six my uncle Bill gave me my first dog. I named him Tippy. Now that I had my own dog, I had lots of fun. There were a few blanks, but our lives were happy

and busy. My dad was a farmer, carpenter, moved houses, and did a lot of odd jobs to make ends meet. My mother took care of the house, garden, yard, and anything she thought needed to be done.

We had chores to do, cows to milk (13 of them), chickens to feed, hogs to feed, grass to cut, and hay to put up. We raised a lot of cane, that is, we had a molasses (sorghum) mill that we made molasses and sold. They put the cane through a press to get the juice then cooked it.

We raise our own meat—hogs, beef, chicken—vegetables, and fruit of all kinds. And we had cows for the milk.

Winters seemed to be cold, snowy, and windy. We had wood stoves, which meant on nice winter days we went to saw wood. Mom cooked on a wood stove too. She did a lot of hard work but I never heard her complain about anything.

Mondays, both summer and winter, were washdays. I had to carry water to an old iron kettle outside to heat the water up then carry it to the tub on the porch to wash. The washboard was first; sometimes you skinned your fingers rubbing the clothes. They were hung outside on the line to dry, summer or winter. I always thought that is why my mother's hands were so crippled from the cold and hanging out the clothes. This was the time I remember Mom setting the leg of the bed on my dress tail to keep me away from the stove. Oh, and she had a window so she could look in on me too. In

Bonnie, Barbara, and Dorothy in 1944

Bonnie Sherwood with Snowball and Corky in 1951

this day and time, I guess people would think this was abusive. I knew to stay there till she came back. And at this time, we got a gas Maytag washer that was a big help. We still had to carry water. But you could hear them start up all over the country on Mondays.

School started for me in 1944; I was five but turned six in Dec. This was in a one-room schoolhouse. The name was Star; it had no kindergarten class. Now my first teacher was also my preacher—Brother Baker—that is what we called him too. And he meant business, so when he spoke you took notice. I just had three teachers in grade school. We walked 3 1/2 miles to school and back. It sort of takes the spunk out of you. My brother Charles always walked with me. I never got a spanking, not because I didn't need one. I do remember standing up at the blackboard with my nose in a circle through.

Then of course, there were the outhouses that seemed to be a mile away when you had to go. The worst was getting up in the middle of the night to go, especially in the winter.

There were some older boys in school that trapped to sell the fur. Sometimes they would trap a skunk. When they came in, we would have to dismiss school for the day. We had box suppers at school. For those who don't know what that is, the ladies fixed a fancy box with food in it that was sold to the highest bidder. No one was supposed to know who fixed the box. The money was turned in to the school (at that time) for picnics or whatever.

During the school night, we had to get our lessons with a coal oil lamp, and for the life of me now I don't know how we ever saw anything. I still have the one that I study with. But then wouldn't it be nice to go back just

one of those times. We listened to the radio in the evenings, to Gang Buster, Fibber McGee & Molly, and Amos & Andy. But Mom and Dad always had time for us, whether it was playing games or studying the Bible. We always entertained ourselves. Heck, I rode the range with Roy Rogers, Gene Autry, and some others, all on the stick horse I had. I always liked to try and sing, so I would go out in the backyard and sing all day. Little did I know till many years later that the neighbors would hear me, stop their horses, and listen.

We went to church on Sunday mornings and all the revivals. There was a church picnic every year, where people gather that hadn't been back for years.

I remember castor oil too. That was something you took for everything from an upset stomach to constipation, diarrhea, and even if you felt good, it cleaned you out. (I can still taste it.)

In 1948 or 1949, we got electricity; now talk about being uptown. I finally found out what my room looked like after dark. I loved the lights, at last, I could see like never before. We didn't have a phone yet.

I remember Dad saying when he was a kid they had a phone with about 20 or 25 people on the line. He would ring his own number and listen to see how many others picked up the phone to listen. Dad did fix the washing machine into electricity. That helped Mom a lot.

Most of the toys we had Daddy had made them. I did have a little red wagon painted green; I usually hooked the dog to it.

The Christmas I was 12 we didn't have much at that time. I remember that was when the big Hershey candy bars came out. It was a cool winter. Daddy had gotten us two big bars and buried them in the snow to keep. That and two oranges are what we got. But we got something so that didn't matter. I guess we were poor, but we didn't care. Everyone was.

My brother Charles had worked and had gotten him a bicycle for $15. Naturally, I wanted one too. I was told to work for the money. I did that year for neighbors to get money to save. I did a lot of ironing and cleaning for them. I finally saved enough to get one. Mine was $20. It was a blue, which I rode to school. Wasn't long after that I wanted a horse, but knew that would be out of the question. And I would have to work a long

336

time for that money. But I could dream. My parents provided for us, we didn't starve, we were happy.

We had a rooster that I was a little afraid of. Daddy told me to take the broom handle out with me and tap him a little and he would leave me alone. I did and when he came up after me, I tapped him, right in the neck, a little too hard. I broke his neck. The worst part was I had to dress and cook him, and we had tough rooster and noodles. I loved all my pets. We always had a dog and lots of cats. On rainy spring days, we played games like fox & goose, checkers, or some card game. Then we had times of sharing the Bible and stories from it. I had a lot of memorable aunts, uncles, and cousins, some on the serious side, but most on the funny.

Going to town consisted of going once a week on Saturday evening. We sold 12 dozen eggs and 5 gallons of cream to the grocery store on the square in Carrollton (McGee's). You could buy 3 or 4 sacks and still get money back. Coming home, we went by the ice plant to get ice to bring home to put in the icebox to keep food cool for a few days.

I can barely remember hearing the words that Pearl Harbor had been bombed. There was a young man that lived across the road from us who went into the service. I remember hearing his mother scream when she got the letter he was killed in action. His name was Johnny Hardwick, maybe 22 or 23 years old.

As I said before, we didn't have to buy much food. But did have to use ration stamps for sugar, flour, coffee, and gas. The stamps were brown, red, blue, and green.

When you are young and go out to gather the eggs out of the nest and feel something slick and slimy in there besides eggs, a snake that makes you step back a little.

Now baths were something else. In this old washtub, the cleanest went first. Now you know that wasn't me. I was last for dirt stuck to me like glue. Wonder how many can remember your mother taking her handkerchief and wiping your face?

After age 12, I got a quarter a week. I had to work for that, no work no money. I could go to the Saturday evening shows. I never went to the Saturday afternoon or Sunday movies. I had no way to go unless I walked, so I stayed at home.

I had never been to too many places in Kansas City, but the last of November 1952 my brother had been drafted, because of the Korean War. He wanted in the Air Force so he enlisted into that. Dec. 12th we took him to the Union Station to leave. A sad day for us all. I often wonder how my folks made it with him being gone. I knew we had to get along without him and I tried to keep up with all I could at home.

We enjoyed life; my dad could always look at the bright side of things and make a joke of it. Mom did well too. Sometimes I could see a faraway look in their eyes. And I knew what they were thinking. But thanks to the good Lord, time goes on.

"Tradin'" By Horse and Wagon in the '40s
By George Lee, Sr. of Portland, Oregon
Born 1929

I would like to write about growing up during the Depression years. I was born in December in the year of 1929. And as the records show, that was the beginning of some very hard times for many of the farm folks in Daviess County, Missouri. After my parents separated and then were divorced, I lived with my grandparents on their farm along with my father and younger brother.

My grandparents were the third owners of the land. In the early to the middle 1800s, a family by the name of McGaugh was the first owners of record. They had slaves and the original house was a square two story with a dining room and a parlor on the first floor and there was a building in the back of the house that had a finished room with a chimney for a cook stove. The slaves, I would think, cooked in the cook room and then served meals in the main house in the dining room. I would assume that the slaves lived in the unfinished portion of the same building. Around the time of the Civil War, a family by the name of Hartman bought the land and lived there till 1907. They also added a room on the east side of the house and this then became the dining room. This addition also had a front door and porch and a back door and a porch and a basement. Then what was the original dining room was now the kitchen.

George Lee, my grandfather, arrived in western Kansas around McDonald in the late 1800s. He met and courted Lucy Louella

Knapp and they were married. Sometime in 1906 or 1907, the Lees moved from western Kansas to Daviess County, Missouri.

He owned a big team of Percheron mares, Kit and Bird they were named. He acquired them at the time he lived in southern Iowa and he lived for a time at New Hampton, Missouri. How he got the team to western Kansas I never heard it told. They produced two colts, fillies that were named Minnie and Mae. Minnie and Mae had some colts but the only ones retained on the farm were a mare named Lady and another mare named Fanny. These third generation mares are the ones I learned to drive and work as a team of horses. I do think that eight years of age is a bit young to have a kid handle a team. The mares were very gentle and well trained; still I question my father's judgment. The next generation of horses was Fannie's colts. This is the team that I actually grew up with. Jocko and Roxy were sired by a stallion that was on the old J.C. Penny horse farm that was located a few miles east of Hamilton.

During the Depression years, we didn't always have an automobile. Therefore, we would take a team and a wagon to transport our eggs and cream to town to sell at the MFA produce station. It wasn't called going to town to do the shopping, it was called going to town to do the "trading." It was pronounced in those days as "tradin'." I think this terminology was a carryover from as far back as possibly the pioneer days.

Almost all of the farmers in Daviess County farmed what was called diversified type farming. They would have a flock of 200 to 350 laying hens. They would milk five or six cows and would have two to four brood sows. And some folks would have a little flock of sheep as well. The way this worked out was the laying hen's eggs were gathered each evening at chore time and put into the thirty dozen-egg case. The cows were milked twice a day and the milk was run through the old Delaval cream separator. The skim milk was put in the swill barrel for the hogs. The cream was run into the 10-gallon cream can and then taken to the basement to keep cool until it could be transported along with the egg cases to the produce house. The sheep were sheared in the spring and the wool taken to the MFA store and sold. The lamb crop was marketed in the fall and this gave the farmer

a little bit more money to apply to the taxes and the fire insurance on the farm buildings. The brood sows would produce a piglet crop and these would be fattened up to about 200 pounds and then sent to the stockyards in St. Joseph. This provided some more money to be used where needed and also the calves would be taken to the stockyards and sold. Also there would be a cornfield as well as wheat or oats to harvest and put in the granary for hog feed as well as chicken feed. Altogether a farm would function, although I never knew of any rich farmers. They had a place to sleep in the dry, plenty of food to eat, and work clothes to wear.

As a teenager I did notice a few farmers that always dressed up to go to town. The fellows that I remember wore a nice hat, a good suit coat, tie and dress shirt. This was all over a nearly new pair of overalls and clean and shined pair of "plow" shoes. These men all drove a Model A Ford. I remember one drove a 1929 two door sedan, another had a 1930 four door sedan, and another a 1931 two door sedan. During the 1930s and 1940s most people went to town to do the "tradin" on a Saturday. And the stores and the restaurants stayed open till midnight or till no one came in. Many neighbors would stand on the sidewalks and visit. Some would go by the drugstore and have a dish of ice cream at the soda fountain. Others would drop in to Woodruff's ice cream shop. It was a great social event as well as shopping. This custom didn't change till sometime in the late 1940s. I was surprised when I went to town on a Saturday evening and found that all the merchants went home at six o'clock. I was shocked and going to town on Saturday evening was never the same.

Another happening was coming to its end. That was going to town with a team and wagon. One of my memories was driving the team that I pretty much grew up with, 'Ole' Jocko and Roxy, to town on the Peter Shutler high wheel wagon that my father owned. I had the usual can of cream and two 30 dozen cases of eggs. Also on this day I had five or six sacks of grain to take to the MFA mill to be ground. I drove up in front of the store and everything was unloaded. Then I drove around the corner to the left and then at the next corner I made another left turn to tie up my team to the hitch racks. But to my surprise they had been removed. So I made a left turn at the alley and drove into a lot where two more teams were tied to the fence and tied my team there also. Then I proceeded to tend to the business that I was sent to town to do. About two hours later I went to retrieve the team and wagon and the lot entrances were blocked. As I started to do whatever was necessary to retrieve my team and wagon a young man about ten years older than I approached me and explained to me that he and his brother had renovated the building on the corner and had opened a soda shop and had spread some gravel on this lot for customer parking and we couldn't tie up here anymore. It seemed the health department didn't like the horse manure or the flies that followed. The Gatenby Brothers were starting their business and definitely we could not tie our teams there anymore. I must say he was very pleasant about all this but I could tell he meant business.

That was incident number one that day, the next thing I drove the team and wagon around to in front of the MFA feed and produce store and loaded up the feed sacks, egg cases and cream can as well as the purchases we had made. Incident number two happened while loading up the wagon. There was a truck scale in front of the store and Jocko raised his head just a bit with his ears pointed forward, He then stepped his hind legs back about a half step. Then he raised his tail and began urinating. He ran the water over both sides of the truck scales. As a 16 year old kid, I was mortified. As soon as I could get in the wagon and get under way, we did so.

The next incident happened at about two miles west of town on Highway 6. We were just about a hundred yards from the Cope school house. I heard a truck engine moaning right along and as it passed us, the tarp over the box came loose and was whip-whopping. That team of horses bolted right together and our spring seat flipped over backwards and dumped us on top of the ground grain sacks. Oh boy I thought a runaway team. I scrambled over the out of place seat and then stepped over the front end gate and was reaching for the lines to try to control my team. As I retrieved the first line the horses resumed their usual walking gate as if nothing had happened. I was more relieved than anyone could ever know.

The town of Gallatin didn't ban anyone driving their team and wagon to town but still all the hitch racks were removed and that was in the summer of 1946. After that I tied my waiting team in an alley to a utility pole. My last time to drive a team and wagon was in August of 1947. I drove my dad's team of black Percheron geldings. They were full brothers and sired by a stallion at the JC Penny horse farm. They were at this time in the prime of their lives. I had driven them to town several times before this time. On this last trip to town I retrieved my team and wagon from the alley and pulled them up in front of the MFA Store. I then loaded up the empty egg cases and also the cream can. It seemed to me that this team was displaying a bit more energy than when we were coming to town. They seemed to know we were going home. I drove them ahead to the stop sign. Then I turned them to the left and just sort of let them have their heads. They were trotting down the hill going west and a gas transport was coming up the hill pulling a full load of gasoline. The gas transport cleared the street as I arrived at the end of the block. I turned the team right in behind the transport going to the left or south. The black geldings were trotting with a lot of energy and actually slung the old Peter Shutler high wheeled wagon out straight behind them. The commotion of their hooves pounding the cement and the old wagon rattling, it might have sounded like a runaway team as three fellows came running from the old Tolbert gas station. I took off my straw hat and bowed to them and then replaced my hat and let the horses go at a full trot for another block and a half where I pulled them into a walk. After all we had five more miles to go.

Wild, Rough Life
By Marj Locker of Ludlow, Missouri
Told to by Clifford Webb
Born 1921

Carved into the beams that span the combined living and dining area of the country home of Clifford Webb, west of Ludlow, is the phrase, "Bless This House O' Lord We Pray And All Who Etnter In. Amen." When you turn around and face north, you can see another phrase that says, "As For Me And My House, We Will Serve The Lord."

The phrases were the favorites of Clifford and his late wife, Lola, who had the idea to

Lora Smith Webb, Arlie Webb, and Will Warner in 1905

have the words carved into the wood to serve as permanent reminders of the importance of family and church in their lives. "When our family is in this home we have a good time and we don't fight," commented Clifford about the large family gatherings he has been a part of in his home, with the latest being a celebration of his 89th birthday.

One of Clifford's birthday presents was a commemorative century farm sign that had his name on it. But the farm is much older than a hundred years. It all started at a location northeast of Ludlow across from the present home of Clifford's grandson, Ramey. It was there that in 1848 the land was homesteaded by Clifford's great-grandparents, Silas and Salena (McCoskrie) Smith.

Silas Smith was a Scottish sailor who ventured to the Dawn area at around the age of 50 and purchased Dawn's original business, Whitney's Mill. While he worked the mill, a young Salena traveled to the mill with her family where she met and then married Silas. Silas was 50 at the time and Salina only 16. They then homesteaded the original farm near Ludlow and had seven children and had their mail delivered through the Austinville post office in what was known as District 51. One of those children was Clifford's grandmother, Lora, who was born along with her twin, Flora, in 1863.

The 1860s was the decade of the Civil War, which created tragedy for the Smith family. With raiders such as the Quantrill and Anderson gangs roaming the countryside of Howard County (at this time Livingston County was part of the much larger Howard Couty), daily life could be very dangerous. The closest law to the Dawn and Ludlow area was located in Hannibal, so people traveled armed and leery of strangers.

One rainy day in 1866 Silas rode his horse to the mill to conduct a business transaction to sell the mill. Afterwards he rode home to lay down for a nap while his wife and 14-year-old son, Sanford, went to the barn to do chores. While in the barn, they heard gunshots. In the house, at least three marauders had ransacked the home looking for the sale money from the mill not knowing that there wouldn't be any to be found, and shot Silas to death with black powder guns as he lay sleeping. The couch was caught on fire from the gunshot and Salena was left with seven young children to care for and no home went it burnt. Sanford said she recognized one of the killers, but no one ever was convicted of the crime.

Sad as this story is, it could have been worse. With no husband, seven children, and no home, the Smith family could very easily of fallen apart. But through the grace of caring friends, the family were kept together when neighbors stepped in and built a new home for Salena in the late 1870s. The home was two stories high with three bedrooms up and one down. It also had a kitchen. Their new post office was the Bluff City post office.

Clifford's grandma Lora (Silas and Salena's daughter) had a sister, Molly, who married Robert Jones and moved to Colorado Springs, Colorado around 1880 to establish a general store. At that time, Colorado Springs had about 120 people and today it counts over 380,000. Lora then followed them to Colorado to work in the store and that is where she met Joseph Webb from Dunklin County, Missouri, near Clarkton (according to the census), who traveled to Colorado with supplies in his wagon pulled by a team. They married in 1885 and homesteaded near Colorado Springs. Joseph was 27 and Lora 21. They had three boys, Arlie in 1886 and later Seth and Buford.

Tragedy brought them back home to Missouri.

In 1898 a devastating blizzard termed, "The worst blizzard in U.S. history," swept across the country and killed all of Lora and Joseph Webb's livestock and they decided to travel back home to Missouri. "The streets, with their immense banks of snow, look more like those of a Klondike Village," said the author of an article in the Emmitsburg Chronicle. Joseph packed up his wife and three boys and deposited them on a passenger train headed for Ludlow and he hopped on a freight train. Joseph arrived on time to

Ludlow, but his family was nowhere to be found. Three days later, they finally arrived after being stuck in the banks of snow from the blizzard.

In the early 1900s, the Webb family moved near the McCoskrie Cemetery located northwest of Ludlow and built a house south of there, near the home place where Lora was raised. The farm contained a large orchard of nearly 1,000 trees on 80 acres and there were many trips to local towns with fruit for sale. Neighbor kids worked the orchard and the family had settled in for more comfortable conditions than that they had experienced in Colorado. The family situation changed drastically again in 1906 when Joseph Webb's horse came home without its rider.

The day was wet from large amounts of rainfall when Joseph headed out to a farm sale near County Line Road. Water was out in the area and by the time, Joseph left the sale he was heading home in the dark. It was in the darkness that he failed to see that the bridge he was riding across was missing some boards, removed by the rushing water, and he fell through. The next day his lifeless body was found lodged in a tree with a gash on his head. Lora had suffered the same fate as her mother, losing her husband with small children to feed. Unfortunately, her misfortunes had just begun.

In the early 1900s cattle drives still took place from Texas along trails such as the Chisolm, the Goodnight-Loving, and the Shawnee Trail. Seth Webb, Lora's then 17-year-old son, was a good roper who took off for Kansas to work the cattle drive along with a friend named Hammond around 1915. Life was a struggle on the trail with menus

Bettie Well, Molly Jones, Salina Smith, "Shang" William Sandford Smith, Francis Austin, "Das" Daniel Andrew Smith, Flora, and Lora Smith

limited to items, which would keep, such as biscuits, beans, and coffee or the occasional "slow elk," a cow belonging to another outfit. Oftentimes cattle from other outfits were simply pushed into other herds to enlarge numbers and wars broke out between outfitters. Stampedes, rushing rivers, drought, loneliness, snakebites, and broken bones were hazards of the trail and perhaps one of those was responsible for the disappearance of Seth and his friend. For whatever reason, neither was heard from again and Lora lost her youngest son.

Buford, Lora's middle son, served in World War I and when discharged, homesteaded in Montana on 320 acres that was blessed with running water. There he raised livestock and became involved in a dispute with his employer in October of 1919, near Rosebud, a village along the Yellowstone River, and was shot to death at the age of 26 by a posse of nearly 200 men. The posse was after Buford for shooting his employer in the back over wages and then killing two sheriff's deputies who had travelled to his home to arrest him. Buford had held off the posse for a number of hours before being shot. Lora travelled to Montana to claim her son's body and buried him with her family in McCoskrie Cemetery. "Men had a hard survival," Clifford said about the early Webbs.

Arlie Webb, Lora's eldest and lone surviving son, remained in the Ludlow area where he prospered on the family farm. Arlie never had a middle name so he is listed on records as Arlie X. He died in 1980 at the age of 93. He had married Amie and in 1921, Amie gave birth to 11-and-a-half- pound Clifford in the two-story farmhouse after an all-day labor. Finally, the cycle had been broken and Lora was there to witness the birth of her grandson. Today, Brad Webb's (Clifford's grandson) in-ground home stands at the location of Clifford's birth.

At the time of Clifford's birth Lora still was living on the old place and Clifford remembers riding his tricycle on a path to her house for cookies. "She spoiled me rotten," Clifford said. He also remembers sitting on the step with her eating those cookies when he was 11 and Grandma Lora giving his only sex talk. The content of the entire talk was, "Don't get too familiar with girls."

Clifford grew up strong; despite having

341

Clifford Webb age 89

to wear dreaded knickers and until boys were potty-trained dresses. Life was hard for the Webb family and other area farmers, but they endured. Next time we will visit what life was like for Clifford as he grew up and met the love of his life, Lola. He grew up on the family farm, pampered by his grandmother, Lora, and experiencing the hardships of farm living without today's luxuries of electricity, speedy cars, and, quite often, indoor plumbing.

As the economy of the late 1920s headed towards the Depression, Clifford attended school and graduated from Ludlow High School at the age of 16 in 1937. He worked on the farm and did the normal ornery boy activities getting into trouble now and again. "Young boys would use table legs to hold down the tales of the girls' dresses," Clifford related, and then do something to the girls to get them to chase the boys. "I spent time doing chores. We had to raise turkeys and chickens and a garden to feed the family. You can't picture what it took, there were no pleasures, just one day at a time," added Clifford.

One job Clifford did was to work in the Sid Kingdom traveling show when it came to town. The show had three acts and included Vaudeville entertainment between them. Adults were asked to pay 25 cents, while children coughed up a dime. Clifford's job was raising the curtain free tickets to the show. "One time I got the ropes tangled," Clifford exclaimed. By 1939, the show had

one admittance fee of a dime for all.

The children wore hand-me-down clothing and Clifford was quick to point out how much he disliked wearing knickers that were popular for the boys of the time. More often than not, the boys of the area were found wearing overalls. Clifford remembers riding horses to school and at the old Warner School (located two miles west of Ludlow); children would show up riding bareback and keep the horses at the school all day before returning home in the afternoon.

Also growing up during the rough times of the 1930s was Lola Eichler of Braymer. One of 15 children (two sets of twins) Lola endured the hardships of the Depression with her family lead by her father Lawrence who was a native farmer of Braymer, and her mother Natty McBee Eichler. In 1933-1934 Lola attended five schools as her family moved first to Lamar County then to Ray County to horse ranch. They were back in 1935 were Lawrence landed a job with the WPA (Works Progress Administration). The WPA did projects such as housing, road building, and dam building. Locally, a quarry was begun at Blue Mound to supply stone for local roads that provided jobs for many men that was begun with WPA funds.

Golf Courses Aren't Just for Golf
By Rick Folsom of Atchison, Kansas
Born 1948

Today I'm an avid golfer, but when I was a kid, the golf course was my winter wonderland. My two brothers and I would walk up there in the morning and not come home until it was getting dark. By the time we got home, our pants would be frozen from the knee down. They would actually stand by themselves after we'd taken them off. Our feet and hands were so cold and red that we couldn't wait to put hot water on them. That turned out to be a big mistake. It really made it sting. Then my dad said to use cold water, which didn't make a whole lot of sense, but it worked. Go figure.

We all had sleds. Mine was higher which allowed it to go through deeper snow and consequently be faster. The extra weight could also have had something to do with it too. I have always been a lot larger then my friends.

I wasn't fat. I was just a big kid. I grew to be 6'8" and 260 pounds as an adult. The best ride was the one that started at the top #9 fairway where there was an access road in the shape of an "S." This road ended at the base of #9 where we then had to cut through an opening wide enough for two sleds and onto a narrow path through the woods that ended up on #7 fairway. It was at least a 700-yard ride. Today I'd say it would be an extremely long par five. We would start out with five sleds abreast. As we flew down the road, we'd shove and push each other trying to be the first one to that small opening into the woods. That's where the speed of my sled really came in handy. Once in the woods, there were three trees we had to watch out for before we reached the safety of the seventh fairway. It was a thrilling ride. The only problem was the long hike back to the top.

We also had a toboggan. It was a six-foot-long wooden sled with no runners and a big curved front on it. It kind of looked like a candy cane laid on its side. You could fit four to five kids on it. You would wrap your legs around the person in front of you. (As I got older, it was nice to have some girls sledding with you.) The front person was in charge of steering. He had to lift up the front and tell everyone to lean left or right. Being bigger, I usually got that job. When we got all that weight going down #9 fairway (the longest and steepest hill) the snow would come flying up over the front, blinding us. That's probably where my size worked against me. Every once in a while we slid into a sand trap and deeper snow which caused us to come to an abrupt halt throwing us all over. We liked to hit moguls though, because they acted like a jump. Sometimes we'd get two or three feet off the ground. One time we hit one and Johnny Gambel's leg came unwrapped from around the person in front of him and ended up under the toboggan breaking his leg. We didn't have cell phones back then, so we pulled him home on the toboggan. I doubt an ambulance could have gotten to him anyway. I guess if we could've called, they could've met us at the nearest road.

The best time we had with the toboggan was when we played BOMBER. The toboggan was a B-29 and all the kids with sleds were fighter pilots. We'd send the toboggan first and we'd attack it. We'd jump for our sleds trying to knock those on the toboggan off and vice versa. Most of the time we'd be lying all over the hill and our sleds had to be retrieved wherever they ended up.

We also had our first exposure to skiing on the golf course. My dad had brought home two wooden skies. They didn't have bindings, so we drove a nail into both sides of each ski. Then we cut an old car inter tube into two-inch strips. We then put the cut pieces over our toes and pulled them under the nails and up over our heels. This kind of held our feet on the ski like a pair of primitive bindings. Next, we got a couple of old broom handles as poles. None of us knew what we were doing. We didn't even know how to snowplow. We could all skate, but balancing on these things was a chore. We'd go ten feet, fall, and have to chase our skis 20 feet. We got tired of that really quickly. I was 30 before I went skiing again. My wife and I went out to Winter Park in Colorado and were smart enough to take lessons. Today, I enjoy it. The acceleration of downhill is only surpassed by white water rafting.

I'd say the craziest thing we did on the golf course was with my dad's old World War II cargo parachute. He was a medic with the Fifth Armored Division and drove a halftrack with a big red cross on it. (He'd always patch us up if we hurt ourselves. If it was something big, we'd go to the doctor.) Anyway, he got a hold of this huge camouflaged parachute, the type they used to drop heavy equipment. It was much larger than an individual chute. Well, we took it and attached it to an old car trunk. We took it to the par five #4 fairway that was straight and long. We had to start on the end from which then wind was blowing. Once the chute started to become full of wind, we'd all jump on the trunk. It would hold about six of us. It didn't take long before we were going lickety split down the fairway. We couldn't see anything in front of us except the chute. We decided it was dangerous when we saw a crease in the chute as it engulfed something. It was a small tree that we promptly snapped off at the ground. We were all thankful it wasn't a mature tree. We could've all been injured or even killed, so we decided to retire the chute.

Today I go sledding with my five grandkids, but they get cold in an hour. They just don't make them like they used to. Of course, at my age, an hour is good.

Trips to Town
By Martha (Rinehart) Groom of Grant City,
Missouri
Born 1933

The year was 1937 in which I would turn four years of age and I had begun to have bits and pieces of memories if things that happened on the road to town.

The windshield on my dad's 1928 Chevrolet would open out at the bottom like an awning to let more air into the car. On this particular trip, I guess too much air was coming in so my dad started to close the windshield not noticing my hands was on the dash with my fingers in the way. I remember the howl I let out and dad was quick to open the windshield back up. No damage was done.

My parents and I lived in northwest Missouri on a farm in Worth County near the small community of Irena and five miles to the south, on 169 Highway, was the county seat of Grant City where most of the shopping was done. The country road past our farm was dirt as were all the country roads then— no graveled or blacktopped at that time. Fortunately, our farm was only half-mile from the hard-topped highway. Many farms were several miles away. After a rain and the roads had dried, dad would hitch a team of workhorses to a "road drag" and smooth out the ruts that had been made by the passing horses and wagons. A disk or harrow could be used if the roads were not rutted too bad.

The day of the anticipated trip to town would have to dawn bright and clear with no threat of rain anywhere. Occasionally at the start of a trip, I remember my mother saying, "I hope we don't meet one of those old fruit trucks."

The cab of the truck was somewhat larger than the front seat of the cars of the day and there was a wooden box somewhat taller than the cab built over the bed of the truck and it did look rather spooky coming down the road toward you. Its purpose was to take fresh fruit to the grocery stores. Sure enough, on one of our trips, we did meet a fruit truck, but it was lying on its side at the edge of the highway with fruit scattered around. Several men and horses were around, probably discussing how to get it back on its wheels.

After reaching town, the first stop would be at the "poultry house" to sell the eggs, which was in an "egg crate." My memory is not good on the size of the crate—it was a square wooden box maybe one foot by one foot and as tall. But I do remember the cardboard-like sheets that went between each layer with indentions the size of the end of an egg. These were separated by a flat cardboard that unfolded into separate sections to fit each indention into which each egg was placed to keep them breaking during the trip to town. The "egg money" was used at the grocery store.

My mother always went to the grocery store on the southwest corner of the square to do her "trading" because she had a niece who clerked there. Her grocery list was handed to the clerk who went around the store gathering up the items and bringing them back to the counter where my mother waited. The clerk them wrote the name and price of each item on a special pad and added up the total herself (no adding machines). With groceries sacked and loaded, we were ready to start the trip home.

If gasoline was needed for the car on the way home there was a "filling station" about two miles north of town and one at Irena. The round bottom of the gas pump was four or five feet tall (painted red) with a round, clear glass tube on up a ways with the number of the gallons of gas in the tube printed on it. The operator would pull a lever back and forth, which would pump gas up into the tube to the amount you wanted. The rubber hose, which was attached to the gas tank, was then placed into the car's tank and gravity let the gas empty (no electricity in the country then).

If a "blow out" (flat tire) was encountered on the road, my dad fixed it on the spot with tire patches and a tire pump. A patch was placed over the hole (possibly glued on). The tire pump was a small, round, metal cylinder with a rubber hose inside with a handle on top. When the handle was pulled, the cylinder would slide up and down, causing air to flow through the hose that had been attached to the stem on the inner tube, thus filling it. I do not remember our car having a spare tire.

My maternal grandparents lived in the same area as we did, on a farm about two miles from the main highway. During one of the years in the 1920s, my grandmother was taken very ill with pneumonia and needed to be moved to a hospital. It was in the dead of winter and the road was drifted shut from bank to bank with heavy snow. The men of the neighborhood gathered together and with shovels scooped the road out so that a team and wagon could bring grandma out to the highway where the hearse was waiting to take her to a hospital some 70 miles away. In those days, the funeral home's hearse was also used as an ambulance. Grandma lived to be an old, old lady. I bring this up at this point because if it had not been for the determination of the neighbors she would not have lived. Today, decades later, one thing has not changed and that is the willingness of people to still so whatever is necessary to come to the aid of anyone or anything that is in need.

City Girl at a Country School
By Melville Booher Davis of Washington Center, Missouri
Submitted by her daughter Helen Nichols
Born 1922

We moved from Des Moines in the Depression days about 1932-33 to a farm two miles west of Washington Center, Missouri. We had no electricity like we did in Des Moines. Mom had an electric washing machine. Grandma Hook had a hand one with a wooden tub. You had to hand-operate the handle on top to make the dasher work. Anyway, we traded machines with grandma. I remember the washdays as Galilia, Dad, and I took turns making the machine work. We had a hand-crank wringer. Mom sorted, loaded, rinsed, and hung the clothes on the outside line. Mom had a cow that Uncle John Smith raised from a calf and kept on his farm for her. We moved the cow to our house and also got a few hens somewhere. We ate what we could get. It was a hard winter and the cow was dry and the hens did not lay eggs. I remember taking a jar of grape juice to school for my lunch. We had grape vines in Des Moines and mom had caned the juice. It seems like we had gravy and bread mostly. My sister, Galilia Booher Hill, and I had to go to the Zimmerman County School. We walked to get there. It was different to have only few kids and go to the front of the room for class. In Des Moines, we changed rooms when the bell rang. Pauline Zimmerman was the teacher. I was the only one in my class. We talked city streets, instead

Melville Booher Davis

of roads, etc. and the kids made fun of us. We both hated every minute of it.

School was out in early April, so we did not have to go long. They had a picnic the last day of school and Galilia and I refused to go, and mom did not make us. I remember some mules in the pasture by the schoolhouse. They lay down and rolled over with their feet in the air. Galilia and I thought that was funny. We had never seen anything like that. The kids made fun of us again. One day in March, it started snowing right after we got to school. Parents kept coming and taking their kids home. Dad finally came after us. It was snowing so hard he could have gotten lost. He covered our faces with scarfs and led us home. I balked at the gate and said I wasn't there. Dad had to uncover my face before I would go through the gate. It didn't take long for me to know dad was being good to me when he covered my face. I remember mom and dad going to Grandma Hook's one day while we were in school. I don't know how they got gas for the Model T. We saved it, I suppose, as we always walked to Washington Center. Mom came home from Grandma Hook's with potatoes cooked in meat broth. I will never forget what a treat that was and wondered since how Grandma Hook had it to give. In the spring, we planted a garden. I don't know how we got the seeds. With good care, the garden grew and I'll never forget how good the food was and we could eat all we wanted to. In July, we dug potatoes and took all we could out of the garden and moved to New Hampton, Missouri. I remember the back enclosed porch had potatoes spread out so they could dry. We moved our cow and put her on pasture. Our next-door neighbors were Scott and Dolly Christi and daughter Anna May. We became good friends and remain

Melville Booher Davis, Ina Hook Booher, and Galilia Booher Hill in 1929

good friends. I remember going to their house and eating fried biscuits and, years later, waffles. John and Leota Mock was an older couple next door on the other side. John had a stroke and walked with a crutch and cane. Leota had a garden and I remember spending a lot of time in their yard. I helped shell peas, break beans, or whatever needed to be done. I always brought them their mail. When I went to the post office for ours. Galilia and I drew a picture of John with his crutch and put it in an envelope and addressed to him. We put a used stamp on it and drew the postmark. When I went to the post office, I delivered it to him. He was so pleased that we had done it for him. Franklin D. Roosevelt was elected President that year. He started the WPA and the CCC and put people back to work. The economy improved and we gradually came out of the Depression. Dad got a truck and went into business for himself. He hauled livestock hay or whatever for farmers. I was his right hand companion and helper. We loaded a load of baled hay one summer and put it in a building in New Hampton. I also remember going to the threshing machine when I spent time at Uncle John and Aunt Alta Smith's farm in the summer. Grant Galloway's were their neighbors. I remember going there. They had three daughters and a son. The girls and Aunt Alta and her daughters, Mildred and Deween, helped cook for the thrashers. I remember going to the field and playing in the oats and

wheat. It was mostly oats and they were sticky. At noon, the table was groaning with the most delicious-looking food I had ever seen.

Galilia and I went to New Hampton School and walked to get there. It was better than country school. We had three grades in one room. I was in the fourth grade.

We went to the Christian Church and Sunday school in New Hampton. I remember a new dress on Easter and getting up early to go to sunrise services.

I remember the bread starter that Mom, Leota, and Dolly shared to bake bread. The more it was used the better it got. We were the only ones that had a cellar and the starter was kept there. We did not have iceboxes or refrigerators then.

I remember Tweedle's Grocery Store in New Hampton. It had ceiling fans to help cool it. It had a soda fountain and we could get a double-dip ice cream cone for five cents. I also remember Noble's store. It was run by Will Noble and his son, Carol. They had groceries and dry goods and were also funeral directors and took care of the bodies in the back part really next door. The railroad was a big part of New Hampton at that time. Livestock were trucked or driven to the pens along the tracks and held until loaded on the train for shipment. Dad's business was better after they quit shipping the livestock by train. The train brought the mail. The postmaster met the train and took it to the post office where it was sorted. Lots of town people would be waiting in the post office until the job was finished. I always went when the train whistle blew and delivered mail to all of our older neighbors. I also went to the store and ran other errands for them. During this time, our old landlord in Des Moines had moved to Mt. Ayr, Iowa. Galilia and I got our first train ride going to visit them. I graduated in 1940 and went to Northwest Missouri State College in Maryville that summer. Galilia was going to Maryville also and had taught one term at the Solomon, a one-room school east of Washington Center. I borrowed $65 from the First National Bank in Bethany to go to school on. Dad signed the note. I had a teaching job in the fall at the Bush County School north of Brooklyn, Missouri. My students were Cheryl Montgomery, Roland, and Estel Rucker, Patty and Billy Lacy, Lyle Edwards, and Bobby Chandler. The Bush

School was familiar to dad as he attended there when he was a boy. Later, my kids, Donald, Shirley, Helen, and Nancy, attended there also. It was consolidated with Eagleville in the middle of the year when Nancy was in the first grade 1953-54.

Therefore, my other kids, Johnnie and Jimmie, started to school in Eagleville. I made $35 a month for teaching. I had to do the janitor work and build a wood fire to heat the school. It never got warm until time to go home. Even though I put big chucks of wood in at 4 p.m., it was always out and cold the next day. I also had to carry the water up a hill from where Lacy's lived. I walked to school from Marco Davis' home, where I had a sleeping room and cooking privileges. I paid $3 a month for this. I got my $65 note paid off and money to buy a new, white, enamel cook stove when in the spring of 1941 I married Marco's brother, Louis, nickname "Binger," Davis and moved to his farm on Big Creek a short distance away. We had no electricity and I carried the water from a spring at the foot of the hill. Brooklyn, Missouri was a booming little town at that time. It had two general stores that bought cream and eggs and supplied our needs. Joe and Effie Stanton ran the store on the south side. It finally burned. The north-side store was run by Ed Derr, Vernon Fitzgerald, and Clyle and Mary Allen at one time. Bud Fitzgerald also had a gas pump at his store. It was the old kind. It had a glass tank on the top with measuring marks. They had to pull the handle back and forth before you could put gas in your car. Saturday nights were big as Bud was a musician and many musician friends. They had live music every Saturday night and the whole country went. Garland Edwards was one of the

Bush Country School, class of 1951-52

musicians and his son, Lyle, followed.

When I was young, my grandparents, Marchie and Sylvanus "Vanus" Hook ran the switchboard called the Central Office in Martinsville for many years out of their home. Grandma could not leave it until 9 a.m. on Sundays. Then people were not to call anyone until 4 p.m. unless it was an emergency. When someone called in, the square button on the back panel dropped down. Then she pulled up one of the wires and plugged it in to find out who they wanted to talk to then she pulled up the black wire and plugged it into another outlet. There were different lines. Then she used the front buttons, pulled them over and held however long needed to compete that person's ring. There were shorts and longs. She held the button over longer to get a long rang. When the person's phone rang their ring, maybe two longs and one short or one long one short and one long etc. they answered the phone. That ring went to everyone's house that had a phone on the same party line. Everyone went to the phone too, to eves drop. Most would say they did that in case something was wrong or someone needed help. Grandma listened in too unless everyone decided to call at one and the other lines were busy. They had what they called a side phone in the bedroom. It was mounted on the wall and was the regular, old, crank type. Sometimes people who needed to make a call had no phone would come and grandma put the call though for them and they talked on the side phones. Grandpa Hook helped with the switchboard, but not often.

Old Sum Bitchee
By Marie E. Bird of Dearborn, Missouri
Born 1941

As children, my mother survived immigration from Poland, my father homesteading in Colorado. Married, they weathered the Depression and days before Pearl Harbor, they were handed me on November 3rd, 1941. My dad moved my sister, brother, and me into the mercantile store with a lodge hall overhead, to the town of Faucett. My baby sister was a month old before mom joined us, so Lelah, the postmistress, a tiny, little woman whose shoulders shook when she laughed and daughters, Anna Lou and Twyla took me under wing. Raised not only in the center of town, but the hub of communication, activity, and love doted out by elderly, lonely folks whose children, for the most part, had moved away to find jobs or serve in the military. I was blessed to play among the ruins of the old town, grow up through several innocent, progressive eras, surrounded and taught by a farming community of hardworking, fun-loving, dedicated folks with solid, Christian morals.

My new home was in the back of a grocery store with a toilet stool at the end of a long, dark hallway with only a single, pull-string light bulb that we shared on lodge nights. An icehouse attached to an open front porch with oak vinegar barrel, empty chicken crates, gunnysacks of potatoes, chairs, and benches, where old men sat to pass the time of day. At first, it was little privacy, dusty wood floors, tall ceilings, and a coal furnace, but my dad remodeled the old Confectionary Building next door and that house held a lot of my memories. My toys were there when we returned from Midnight Mass in St. Joe, making Santa real.

I was given my first and only two bare bottom spankings: one for not minding, the other for lying. Dad caught me climbing in the window, when I was supposed to be taking a nap. Mom got word I'd been lying about having a horse like Black Beauty, then denied it to her, and got caught. They sat the first television in town, with a large, concave, magnifying glass, on top of the meat counter to share and many came in. Each purchase was recorded with the amount. When folks paid, they got the original, if they charged, they got the copy. Many families had their own book and charged from January through December, paying along when grain or livestock sold, usually clearing their debt when their tobacco sold at the end of the year. My folks bartered or paid for cans of milk, cream, chickens, and eggs. Some folks worked out their bill during lean times and mom never charged interest. Next, they bought the old barbershop and converted it into a home for their handyman. He planted and tended a large rose garden for mother, emptied and burned her trash, and helped dad. He taught me to pull nails out of boards and straighten them on a hard surface so they could be reused.

Born allergic to a wide variety of things,

I would scratch till I bled. They tried tying my hands and feet to the baby bed, but one night I slipped out of the bindings and the next morning blood was running down the floor. Bananas were all I could eat, so when the war broke out, our pharmacist got mom dried bananas. Mom contacted a doctor, who was passing through Kansas City that might have a curing salve. Mom never knew what it was, remembering only that he stood on the steps of the train, handed it to her where she stood on the platform, and it worked, but turned her hands purple. I quit whining about pimples when my dad explained how my face once looked like bloody hamburger.

In the kitchen area of the store, we had a two-burner, gas, camp stove. My first boyfriend, Phillip, lit the stove with a match so he could help me wash dishes, and then stuck the match in his pocket. Pretty soon, his pocket started smoking and I instinctively doused him with the water.

My first girlfriend, Fayetta, stayed with her grandmother across the road. Starting in the first grade and graduating together, we learned to pledge the flag, recite the Lord's Prayer; everyone took turns praying before lunch.

My childhood was a safe adventure with freedom to roam, but my "do it if I want to" attitude plus my curiosity always got me disciplined. Complaints like ringing the Church bell during the week, playing with the robes in the Lodge Hall, and accidentally catching the Christian Church yard on fire with a firecracker. One morning Lelah scolded me for picking her tulips. Throwing them down, I started home, stopping in the middle of the road, called her an old sum bitchee, and when she laughed, I stomped my foot, cussed her again. I returned the next morning for the junk mail so I could play "business." She loved me dearly, telling mom how tickled she got, but mother told me in no uncertain terms never to use that kind of language or pick her flowers again. There were plenty of barns with high rafters where I'd climb, lying quietly, catching birds then turning them loose. I learned my lesson when leaning over the rail I jumped off the storage loft upon a very large wood crate with a nail that went through my foot. I couldn't scream or cry out as I pulled my foot off and slipped out of the barn. I couldn't limp for fear someone might see me and tell mom, so I slowly walked to the house. Soaking my foot in hot creosol water, so it wouldn't fester. I told God I'd never go back if He wouldn't let anyone know I'd been where I wasn't supposed to be.

I'd walk cross-country to my older sister's home, in time for milking. Rose Marie's husband showed me how he could hit the mouths of the cats sitting around, and squirted me a time or two before I ran off to gather eggs. I spent a lot of time with her, learning how to cook and work in the fields. My reward was going to the "free show," a movie screen outside, sponsored by the businesses in Dearborn and Faucett. We'd watch "Francis, the Talking Mule," "Ma & Pa Kettle," and cartoons. Bebe, sister's nickname, took adversity in stride and set a lasting, endurance trend for me.

I'd help unload the trucks who delivered in the wee morning hours. These were good times mom and I shared over hot, buttered rolls, milk, and coffee. Mother ran the store and daddy worked an eight-hour job, plus helped her do the butchering and picked up extra supplies that weren't delivered. I remember one time we took the truck, with racks but no gate, and an angry dad, as we picked up the broken, scattered boxes of straws strewn all over the highway. Mother always had a delicious treat for me after school, baked sweet potato, hot rice, or T-bone. I swept, candled eggs, stocked shelves, washed out the meat case, waited on people, learned to make change. Dad taught me to drive when the automatic shift came in, so I could deliver groceries to widow ladies, pick up produce and other supplies from town.

The Christian Church gave me a white Bible, engraved in gold, Marie Elaina Bird, on the cover signed inside July 13, 1947, for perfect attendance for six months, Mrs. Brown. I went to Bible School for two weeks at both churches. Mother, a Catholic, allowed me at 16 to be baptized in the Faucett Baptist Church and at 17 I married a farmer there. We experienced the rise and fall of farming methods, farm divisions, two farm crises, and raised four children. Gary's deceased, but I still live on 90 acres of the original 350-acre farm.

Never afraid of snakes, walking home at night over Bee Creek, I'd pray the boogieman wouldn't get me. I dealt with all the childhood traumas like ants in my pants from playing in an old car, chiggers, fleas, lice, and ticks. Ran away once, but not for long, maybe half-hour, as my big suitcase, full of everything I called mine, was too heavy. Being a tomboy, my dad bought me a boy's, chrome, Schwinn bicycle with hand brakes. I was showing my rider how fast I could go, coming down the paved hill, when I hit gravel, applied the hand brakes, flipping Fayetta and I off in a heap. Disoriented and shocked, we got back on and rode some more. I never hunted but became a good shot from target practicing with my dad's 22-rifle, along the railroad track and in the timber. I traveled barefoot, visiting some in town, others in the country, taking my meals, listening to their stories, and staying several days with some. I was forbidden to call adults by their first name, it was Uncle, Aunt, Mr. or Mrs. Aunt Marie and Uncle Larson taught me to milk and run the cream separator. Uncle Bill would leave Aunt Docie's grocery list with mom, then go to the beer joint; on his way back he'd load his groceries and hand me the reins. She taught me to pray before meals and at bedtime, he would tell me stories as we sat on the glider swinging. As a child, one of my proudest accomplishments was driving the horse, not realizing the horse knew its way home. Mrs. Humphrey showed me how to card wool and gave me a small "treasures" trunk.

My dad raised hogs in the foundation of the old mill and we had been warned not to play there because of the deep, uncovered well. Secretly, it was one of my many playhouses. Arms outstretched I'd balance my walk over the old hardware store foundation and sit on its steps, watching and wondering. The bank became a barbershop, then the Post Office. Folks could park on the road and climb the steep stairway to the Baptist Church, as did pall bearers to the cemetery. After Interstate 29, our main street became a speedway to Highway 371, making it unsafe. I snooped out the train depot and peeked in the windows of Faucett's one-room school before they were torn down. I only heard about the other two churches and interurban trolley, which shuttled between St. Joseph and Kansas City.

My past allergies left me thin and anemic, so Mrs. Habluetzel brought me fresh eggnog daily. I must have been curious in mouth, as well as in mind, because I was always given challenges to get me out from underfoot. I'd spend hours lying on the ground trying to catch gophers, with a slip knot at the end of a long string, on a fishing pole, stalk turkey hens to find their hidden nests out in the timbered pasture, or watch the clock to see how long I could sit quietly, besides swimming, tap dancing, 4-H meetings, cooking and sewing projects. Hugh Coker brought in fresh, bottled milk ever evening, and then played tic-tac-toe with me. I won until he was ready to go home, then he'd put his glasses on, he called cheaters, win several games, and say it was time to go. The '50s, as a teen, were fun with rock 'n roll music, dancing, sleigh ride parties, playing basketball, and dating. It was safe to hitch a ride with someone and leave your doors unlocked. I would lock the store door when I came in from a date, but one time mom was surprised when the Sheriff entered instead. I watched homes moved, our Beacon light disappear, and Interstate 29, a four-lane highway being built.

Marilyn, Mary, Betty, and Nancy in 1950

what had happened. Now you need to know what a fantastic sense of humor my sweet and crazy best pal Mary has. Without skipping a beat, although she was sprawled on the floor, she calmly picked up the sugar bowl and the spoon and started spooning up the sugar that had ended in her lap. I'm ashamed to say I was laughing so hard I didn't even help her up! Every last soul in the shop gave her a glorious and rousing applause.

We departed soon after and I can testify, we continued to have some other fun adventures. What were they? I can't tell you now, because I haven't started my novel on all that fun just yet.

The High-Heel Meets a Chair
By Nancy Browne of St. Joseph, Missouri
Born 1932

About a zillion years ago, 1952 to be exact, my best friend Mary and I had been planning a weekend at the prestigious Hotel President in the huge metropolis of Kansas City. That's the way we pictured any large city because we were just babes in the woods. We had just crossed over to the sophisticated age of 20. Headed down the highway in my sporty little Henry J we were all freshly permed, nails polished sparkly red, new dresses, and high heels as pretty as any Betty Grable wore in her movies.

Before checking in the hotel, we stopped at a popular coffee shop. Strutting in, we sat down at those cute little ice cream tables and ordered coffee. We were so excited as we had never stayed at a hotel. As we got up to leave, somehow, Mary got her three-inch high heel caught on one of those darling little chairs. Everything broke loose about that time. Down went Mary, the table and chairs, the coffee cups, the spoons, and the sugar bowl. The coffee shop was packed with customers and with all the clatter, everyone turned to see

Testing Out Chewing Tobacco
By Ron Searcy of Albany, Missouri
Born 1936

When we were about 15 or 16 it was decided to do a Boy Scout project by moving large rocks to form the entrance gate to Camp Anove (that's Evona spelled backwards) south of Albany. It was a scorching hot July day so my mom furnished a half-gallon glass jar of ice water for the most enthusiastic guys to quench our thirst. Well, Harry and I had to wait for Norman or Benny to pick us up. We did not have transportation, but the other two did. Norman could borrow something from the dealership or Benny could use the panel truck from the plant. We had to always be on our best behavior so we wouldn't ruin the reputation of the business printed on the side.

Norman showed up in a jeep, which had an open top and sides (no one ever knew about seatbelts at that time). Norman drove, Benny riding shotgun and Harry and Ronnie Paul sitting in the back.

Wind whistling around our flat top crew cuts, the sun overhead, and my jar of water in hand and all was well with the world. This was until Benny proudly displayed his treasure of the day, a sack of beechnut chewing tobacco. We all had our share of lucky strikes, but had never tried Benny's chew. We had a saying around AHS that no one messed with The Lone Ranger or spit in the wind. We got the part about the Lone Ranger, but must have missed the part when it came to spitting in the wind. We all took a big drink of mom's cold water and then a healthy mouth of chew. We didn't know if it was to fit in the side of the cheek, under the tongue, or under the upper or lower lip. We tried them all, alternating with another slug of cold water. All of a sudden, Harry and I started seeing these strange brown things flying towards our freshly laundered white t-shirts and blue jeans. Benny and Norman would spit out the side of the jeep and you guessed it, it flew in the back on the unsuspecting Boy Scouts. When we got to Camp Anove, we all had tried to remember not to swallow the juice but somehow, some got to our tummies and the rockwork got us very sick.

We had to fess up when we got home, because of the speckled clothes Harry and Ronnie Paul had on. My dad Tom and my uncle Clarence got a big kick out of the rite of passage to manhood–all in the name of Boy Scouts.

The Getaway Man
By Richard Barrett of Mound City, Missouri
Born 1924

How we long for the good old days. Do you remember as far back as the days of the depression era? The days of the drought in the mid-1930s? The days of Maud and Bess, nice tempered, black in color, mares compared to "ol" Sam and Dan, the gray colored mules, Sam the ornery character that the Barrett Twins, were not given the chance to harness. If Sam didn't get the chance to kick you, then he would bite.

That's the introduction leading up to the school days, when Richard and Robert walked ¾ a mile to school, attending Goodwill Country School, four miles west and one mile south, then back ½ mile east from Skidmore, Missouri.

Now picture this in the days of the 1930s, farmers would break stalks in the early spring using their homemade "stalk breaker", maybe a two section harrow, follow that up with a dump rake, which would provide a meandering windrow allowing us to burn the corn stalks on a still cool night giving the farmer, in our case Floyd Barrett, our dad, a decent seed bed provided by plowing and disking. Little did we realize nutrients being removed robbing each succeeding crop of plant food. Now J.R. Keever and Lee Metcalf would meet the Barrett Boys up at the corner ¼ mile north of Floyd and Jodie's to walk on east to Goodwill School. On this particular day, Lee Metcalf's dad had burned his stalks the night before. Lee found a hedge post in the fencerow that had caught fire so what a weapon we had to destroy clumps of foxtail grass to torch and clean the country roads providing beauty to rural America. I guess we could call the last member of the four as being the getaway man, his responsibility to put out the fires. The burning hedge post made it all the way to the school ground and found an old dead stump of a tree, about five feet in height. Here provided the boys to continue the beautification project. The fires were "put out" following the bell for recess. Let's continue at noon. We did. Between 1:00 p.m. and about 1:30 p.m. J.R. in his seat behind me, leaned forward and said, "Richard, there's an awful lot of smoke blowing across the school ground." J.R. held up one finger and Mrs. Beverlin gave him permission to leave the room, going out to the outhouse. J.R. came barreling back in and said to me, a muted whisper, the school ground is on fire and heading toward Mrs. Beverlin's 1934 Chevy. I held up one finger, yes, "Richard, you may leave the room." I went out the door and in less than 10 seconds came running back in and shouted, "The school ground is on fire and almost to Mrs. Beverlin's car." The building emptied, probably 10 to 12 boys and girls were firefighters supreme. The fire was contained, blackish smoke and dirt was washed from the heroes. The car was saved! They returned to their proper desks and this was follow by the owner of the 34 Chevy making this announcement. Action will be taken tomorrow at noon.

At noon, this appointed hour, the disciplinarian's voice rang out loud and clear. Lee, J.R., Robert, and Richard go to the willow tree and each one of you will bring back a strong willow switch, 24-30 inches long, capable of standing strong usage up to fight swats each. The four death row criminals held their breath. With their heads hanging down to their shoe tops, the accused waited for the dreaded voice to announce! Here it comes. "Frieda Barrett and Fay Randall, tell me that Robert, J.R., and Lee kept setting the stump on fire and Richard kept trying to put the fire out. Richard, you did the right thing. You don't have to go to the basement." I smiled. Robert, J.R., and Lee came back up from the basement with scowls on their faces. That scowl said, "yah, yah, yah, teacher's pet, little goodie, goodie two shoes, didn't get a whipping, teacher's pet, teacher's pet, yah, yah. I'm still smiling, no willow switch for me!

Living Through Rations
By Bonnie Carroll of Lawson, Missouri
Born 1933

Some of you may remember the war ration books issued by the government during World War II. That meant you couldn't buy certain items without coupons from the book. I don't remember everything that was rationed. I was just eight years old. I remember that sugar was the one that we struggled with. My folks lived on a small farm and we produced and processed our own food. Beside a large garden and strawberry bed. We had an orchard of apples, apricots, cherries, and pears. We also picked and canned wild berries such as gooseberries and blackberries. That year we couldn't get enough sugar so there were no jellies and jams. Mom tried canning some fruit without sugar but when we opened them, it seems like we couldn't ever get them to taste sweet. My mom baked our desserts so there weren't many cookies, cakes, and pies. We also butchered our own hogs, which we usually sugar cured. The R.E.A. hadn't

reached us with electricity so we couldn't freeze anything. Everything had to be canned. We were glad to do without if it helped our boys overseas but sometimes we wondered. The other things rationed were tires, cars, and bicycles. Gas, fuel, and kerosene, solid fuel, stoves, rubber footwear, shoes, sugar, coffee, processed food, meat, canned fish, cheese, canned milk, fat, and typewriters.

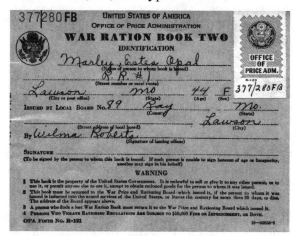

A War Ration Book Two

I Got My Spanking and I Deserved It
By Ruthanna Ezzell of Savannah, Missouri
Born 1929

I was born in a three-room farmhouse in Dearhorn, Missouri. The doctor delivered me at home and charged my dad $5.00 and dad fixed dinner for him. A few years later, we moved to a five-room farmhouse in Edgerton, Missouri where my dad worked on shares. He got $5.00 a week pay. I always got a nickel for candy. I got a big sack of different candy. On Saturday nights, we would go to town in the wagon pulled by two horses. Mom put a pillow and blanket in the wagon because I would go to sleep on the way home.

School started for me I walked and sometimes I rode my horse. There were eight or nine kids in the school. We took turns carrying in the wood for the stove in the wintertime. At Christmas, the teacher would put up a set of sheets across the front of the one room schoolhouse and we would come out and sing Christmas songs. I had to carry in wood in the wintertime and summer time because mom cooked on a wood stove.

On Saturday nights, she would bring in the big round tub that she washed our clothes in on a washboard with the good old lye soap. She would heat buckets of water on the heating stove then pour it in the tub for us to bathe in. I remember standing on a chair and listening in on the phone and people talking. There were a lot of people on one line. My clothes were made out of flour sacks that my mom bought flour in, also our underpants. We wore high top wool stockings.

Dad was in the field one day and it was getting stormy. Mom sent me to the field to tell dad to come home. He said you go to the house I'm going around the field one more time. I got half way there and then the storm hit. I jumped in a ditch in a creek and a big tree went flying over my head. A few branches hit me but I wasn't hurt.

One-day mom got after me for something I'd done. I ran and climbed up a tree. She said you are going to get a spanking when you come down, about that time, I spit, and it hit her in the face. She went back in the house, but was waiting for me. When I came in, I got my spanking, which I deserved. We had kerosene lamps for light. Mom had a big metal iron that she would sit on the wood stove to iron our clothes. She put a blanket on the kitchen table to iron our clothes. I got two pairs of shoes a year, one pair in the fall and one pair in the spring. I went bare footed all summer.

The farmers could take turns on Saturday nights having dances. Mom would clean out the front room and they would dance in there and when they went home there was lots of dishes to wash and I would stand in a chair and dry them. We had the chamber pot by our bed every night. Being a clumsy kid, I spilt it a couple of times. Mom said, "from now on you will wash and empty it every morning," which was fine with me. I went out to the outhouse or privy as we called it and a lot of times there was a big snake up in the rafters and I came out screaming. Then there was the old Sears and Montgomery Ward catalogs in there that we would tear out a page and wad it up and rub the paper together to make it softer to clean ourselves with.

Dad killed our meat in the winter and hung it in the smoke house all winter so we would have something to eat. Dad would go out and cut off what mom needed to cook for the day. Dad would wring the chicken's neck off. Mom would not do it. She forgot to tell dad one morning we would have chicken for supper. He was in the field. Being brave, I said I could do it. I grabbed the chicken and twisted him round and round then dropped him on the ground. The chicken then got up, shaking his head, and ran away. All of our food was home canned.

One-day mom said I'm going out to weed the garden. I went with her and was playing in the grass; all at once, I thought I could pull those weeds. I went down the row behind her. She got to the end of the row and I said, "I helped you." She turned around and saw that I had pulled up a whole row of tomato plants. We got an icebox. We liked that we thought we were rich. It was my job to empty the pan you put under it to catch the water as the ice melted. We moved to St. Joseph when I was nine years old. I was really made fun of in my homemade clothes. I remember a kid grabbing my coat and ripping the pocket because it was homemade. In the summertime, we slept in our bed outside under a tree. It was too hot in the house from the cook stove. I also enjoyed our first car as I rode in the rumble sent.

The Blizzard of 1961
By Sandra Kay Ashler of St. Joseph, Missouri
Born 1940

On Friday, December 22, 1961 after our morning office Christmas party at the St. Joseph Stockyards company, my parents picked me up at 1:00 p.m. to take me home with them for Christmas. Home being the farm five miles east of Pickering. It was snowing when we left St. Joseph and headed north towards Maryville on Highway 71. Bear in mind that Highway 71 at that time was only two lanes wide – not four as of today. The further north we went we got into a blizzard with howling and fierce winds and frigid temperatures.

Driving was hazardous and visibility was very poor. Dad was having trouble getting up the hills in the car, so mom and I would get out and push. The wind lashed at our faces and clothing and we would be encrusted with snow and ice when we would finally get up the hill and jump back in the car. This happened repeatedly! At one point, we even slid clear across the highway into a snow bank in the ditch. Dad had bought a scoop shovel while in St. Joe and we were frantically trying to scoop ourselves out worrying about getting hit by southbound traffic. We had no way of knowing southbound traffic had already been halted.

When we reached the Fillmore Road, which intersects with Highway 71, we pulled into the service station and called it quits. People kept coming into the station all night long and we were literally packed in there like "peas in a pod" before morning. There was no place to move anywhere; however, as people kept coming we did some sort of a shuffle to accommodate them. We made it work. Now this was togetherness! At least we were inside out of the elements and never lost power. These people would tell us of the huge, deep snowdrifts they had to wade through to get to the station and of the people; they came by stranded in their vehicles.

One man came in carrying a ham his employer had given him for Christmas and told the couple who owned the station to slice and serve it to everyone. There was a very small room on north side of the station where the owner's wife and my mother went to slice the ham and make sandwiches. There was bread, chips, pickles, candy bars, pop, milk, etc. at this station like a convenience store of today but on a very, very small scale. As people kept "drifting" in and I use that word loosely, all night long they shared food they brought with them. One man came in with a big sack of bananas and proceeded to get them out and they were frozen solid. Gives you an idea of how far he had walked in the frigid temperatures, howling winds and blinding snow to get to the station from his stranded vehicle.

In the meantime, I'm frantically trying to call my two younger brothers at home. This was way before the advent of cell phones. It took quite a while to secure use of the station phone and then the line would be busy as this was a party line wherein several farm homes were on the same line. I finally reached them and said we were stranded and that dad said not to worry about farm chores. Their concern, after knowing we were okay, was the livestock. I told them to stay inside and see what the conditions were like the next morning before venturing out to milk the cows, feed the hogs, horses, sheep, goats, chickens, cats, and dogs.

By Saturday morning, there wasn't a morsel of food left in that station. The shelves were totally bare. A hat was passed to take up a collection for the station owners in appreciation for spending the night inside. As daylight came, we could see the snowstorm was over. The sun came out and the howling winds had stopped, but it was extremely cold.

Late Saturday morning we decided to try our luck in getting to Maryville as the snowplow had opened up the highway, but only one lane wide. The drifts were so tall that when we came to a curve, I would jump out and run ahead to make sure there was no traffic coming, then motion for dad to come ahead. That made for a very long process in getting to Maryville. We finally arrived there in the evening. Dad did some checking and learned our country road had not been opened up so we spent that night in a hotel in Maryville. Wow! We actually had a bed to sleep in! And we were exhausted.

Neighbors to the west of us had sick children so they called the county to make arrangements to get the road opened up to their house so dad could bring medicine to them. On Saturday afternoon, we got to their place with this much-needed medicine and then the snowplow continued on to our farm. They plowed out our driveway, as there was no way we could have gotten through those drifts.

This was the most unusual Christmas in my life and one I'll never forget. Here we had left St. Joseph on Friday at 1:00 p.m. and did not arrive home until 4:00 p.m. on Sunday– Christmas Eve. A distance of 65 miles. Needless to say, we were so glad to be home and my two brothers were just fine. They had done all the chores and scooped snow. This was a very special Christmas day and we were so thankful to be home together.

Thankful For My Horse
By Gene Prindle of Jameson, Missouri
Born 1936

One morning, on my way to my country school, I was riding on my horse named Babe. Before I got my horse, I had to walk to school. I was really fortunate to be riding my horse

Gene Prindle

that morning. About half a ¼ mile ahead as I topped the hill, I saw a neighbor lady and her son running out of their yard and up the road. Then I saw her husband running across the barn. I could see he didn't have any shoes on. I never thought anything unusual about it at the time because I had seen him go barefoot in the summer time. Being eight years old, I never realized it was 4°F. As I came on up the road and got even with the place, he was out in the garden next to the road. He commenced taking off his clothes, like a dummy I thought he was going to the bathroom. When he looked up and saw me, he started cursing me and saying, "I'm going to kill you." The garden had a real tall woven wire fence to keep the chickens out. He ran and jumped with one big leap and landed on the top of the fence with both feet like a bird. That's when my horse and I left town. When I got to the schoolhouse and slid off ole Babe, I just fell down to the ground because I was so weak and scared I didn't even remember tying up my horse but I did because she would have went back home if I didn't tie her up.

I got into the schoolhouse and told the teacher this fellow has gone crazy and is heading this way. At first, she didn't believe me, but she locked the door anyway and had the 8th grade boys get the ball bats. All the windows at the schoolhouse faced the road and we all stood by the windows. We could see him coming, stark naked with a brick in each hand. As he got on down the road, a ways he got so cold he got down and couldn't go any further. One of the parents that brought kids to school in their car had to pull around him. After dropping the kids off he went back and got a neighbor to help pick the man up. He was headed up north to a ladies house to kill her and take her to Heaven with him. That was his destination. He was at St. Joseph No. 2 for some time. I never went that way to school for the rest of the years I went to school there.

Chasing Airplanes
By Col. Robert Smith (Ret. USAF) of
Mound City, Missouri
Born 1921

One of the first things I can remember about growing up occurred one very cold night in December. I was three years old, it was early morning, and there was quite a commotion in our house. My dad was frantically ringing the wall telephone and shouting at the telephone central in town in an attempt to reach our country doctor, Doctor Hogan. It was 2:00 a.m. and my baby sister was about to be born. Doctor Hogan, being a faithful country doctor, soon arrived via horse and buggy over frozen muddy roads. There was no gravel, asphalt, or pavement in those days. He travelled 4 ½ miles that cold night and delivered my baby sister. His fee, I have been told, was "whatever you can afford." My parents told me that all the change they could find in the house amounted to less than $2.00.

Life progressed pleasantly for me as I remember, traveling 2 ½ miles to Sunday school in my dad's 1918 Buick Touring car with only side curtains to keep out the cold air. My mother would heat bricks and we rode under a heavy lap robe to church and learned with the other country kids to sing *Jesus Loves Me*. My great friend and companion was my collie dog, Fritz, who went everywhere with me. Along came a terrier named Fido and the three of us would go ground hog hunting. Fido would go down in the hole and arouse the ground hog that would chase Fido out only to be nabbed and killed by Fritz. One day Fido failed to come out of the ground hog hole. I waited for him until dark when I had to go into the house, certain that the ground hog had eaten Fido. He came home the next afternoon all chewed up and bloody and never again went back down a ground hog hole. That was the end of that hunting expedition!

About 1925 or 1926, the airline was established between Kansas City and Omaha. Open cockpit bi-planes began traveling daily right over our farm. They were probably at about 500 feet altitude, but looked to me to be about three feet off the ground. I decided to try to catch one by chasing the plane across the field, thinking that if I could just catch one, I would have my own airplane and little pilot to fly. My collie could hear the coming plan before I could and would alert me by jumping and barking. I often wonder what those pilots talked about, "Did you see that crazy little kid and his dog chase us?" Life went on and as the airplanes flying over each day progressed to small cabin models carrying passengers, I decided to build models of them out of orange crates and paint them with small cans of different colored paint purchased at the variety store for $0.10 a can. I had my own landing field scraped out of a patch in the backyard right by the family outhouse.

About this time, I was approaching 10 years old and traveled two miles to country school with my sister riding along behind my pony Ginger. My dad being a farmer and my mother raising about everything we ate, we needed very little money to survive. One day a neighbor called on our party telephone line– our ring was a long and a short. He wanted my pony Ginger and I to carry water to the threshing crew out in the field. My dad covered two glass gallon jugs with burlap and used a short piece of corncob as a stopper. My job was to soak the covered jugs in water, which was usually the horse tank, then ride around to where the workers were pitching bundles onto the hayrack wagons and give them a drink of cool water. Everyone drank out of the same jug and nobody complained. At the end of the day, the neighbor gave me $0.35! Oh boy–I had a business going! I carried water all summer to haying and threshing crews and along with my ground hog scalps, (the county paid $0.10 per scalp for the little pests); I was able to buy my first leather jacket for about $3.75.

Many days as my dad was farming in the field, I was instructed to carry him a cold drink of water twice a day on old Ginger. One day he asked me to bring along a twist of honey dip chewing tobacco, which he could get away with before my mother would find it and throw it away. I decided while in route to the field to try a bite as I had seen my dad do. Needless to say, I became quite green, as I had not learned that to chew tobacco you had better spit or get sick! One look at my dad and me knew I had sampled the chewing tobacco. He kept quiet about it until several years later when he confirmed that I was very green around the gills.

A couple of years later I learned to drive my dad's 1928 Chevy. During a Friday night supper, get together at the neighbor's house, three, or four of us 12-14 year old kids decided to go out in the garage and start up the neighbor's 1920 Dodge touring car. I was the sole smart aleck because I had driven my dad's Chevy. I put the Dodge in reverse to back out of the garage to take all of us on a ride, without permission of course. The only trouble was the Dodge transmission was backwards from the 1928 Chevy and as I revved up the engine we lurched forward right through the back of Buck Zachary's garage. We all took off running like deer and hid in the creek about ¼ mile away. You guessed it– we all got a licking and the car owner thought it was hilarious.

As a farmer, my dad needed my help as his workload involved farming a whole 180 acres of land with horses and mules. I learned how to make very straight cornrows driving six mules abreast on a two-row lister/planter. The mules were all tied together with leather lines so it only required you drive the two leaders in the center on the tongue of the lister.

When I was a sophomore in high school, we had a severe ice storm. It snowed over a foot of ice pellets, then two inches of clear ice on top of that. Everything came to a standstill. Two or three of us kids decided to ice skate over the fields about six miles to high school. That lasted about two days and those of us in the country got to play legal hooky. The school kept going for those who slipped and slid on the ice, but the teachers enjoyed small attendance for about a week.

Saturday night baths were quite different back then. We had no hot or cold water in the house and no electricity until I was a junior in high school. We all took a bath in turns in

356

a galvanized tub in the kitchen in front of the cook stove using the teakettle for warm water. My dad was always the last one to bathe in the same water as the first person. Our only water source in the house was a well on the open back porch. We didn't know what luxury was and probably couldn't spell the word anyway!

The depression years were here but we didn't know we were poor–everybody was! We always had plenty of healthy food to eat, chickens and eggs and home canned vegetables. We butchered four hogs every fall then salted the meat in a large box packed with Morton curing salt. Later we hung the meat in the smokehouse and smoked it with green apple wood for two weeks. It was cured to perfection and very tasty. My dad kept a whiskey bottle hidden, but not hidden well enough that I couldn't find it. It was called Crab Orchard. It tasted great when I would sneak a swallow! I haven't tasted whiskey for a long time now–nothing like the old stuff!

I soon learned the value of a 10-cent piece, as my granddad would give me a dime to go to the picture show on our Saturday night shopping trips to town. I also learned to drive my dad's Model T truck, but only around the farm and through the fence gates. He eventually traded the Buick in on a 1928 Chevrolet 2-door with roll up and down windows. I drove this vehicle to high school two years before I was 16 years old. This was before everyone in the state had to have a driver's license.

By the end of my high school years Germany had begun occupying countries in Europe and it looked threatening that the United States would be involved. Upon graduation from high school in 1939, I along with several from my hometown decided to travel to California and get deferred from the draft by working at a defense plant. Five of us rented a double apartment in Hollywood, California one block off Hollywood Boulevard and began living as bachelors, even doing our own cooking–taking turns of course. I was bringing home $32.00 a week and sending home $20.00. We were really living it up right in the middle of Hollywood near Linda Darnell, Ava Gardener, Mickey Rooney, James Gleason, Marjorie Main, and the Dead End Boys, two of which lived in our apartment complex, the Gorey Brothers.

All was going well. I was employed by Lockheed Aircraft Corporation and was actually taxiing the finished aircraft for engine slow time before they were delivered to the USAF Corps. The Japanese attacked Pearl Harbor December 7, 1941 and the whole world changed overnight. We all threw our deferment cards away and enlisted in the Navy, Army, Marines, or in my case, the US Army Air Corps, as I wanted to be a pilot. Since I did not have the required two year college education, I had to pass the equivalent examination of Algebra, Trigonometry, Logarithms, etc., which I strenuously studied while working in the defense plant. To this day, I have only used the mathematics and air navigation. I was accepted into the Aviation Cadet Program with flight training in primary, basic, and advanced flying. I graduated June 27, 1943 as a 2nd Lieutenant with assignment as a flight instructor. Soon I was allowed to transfer to fighter training in the "P-38 Lightning" which I had worked on at the Lockheed Factory.

Now after surviving combat in three wars– WWII, Korea, and Vietnam, 320 combat missions mostly in fighter aircraft, over 10,000 military flying hours, several hundred more in my own antique 1937 Waco biplane, I have retired after 34 years in the Air Force, settled down just outside my hometown in a log home with my lovely wife, Joan and am living happily ever after. I have traveled the full circle in my 91 years. I have been in 14 countries and all of the 50 states finally arriving back in my hometown, just four miles from where I was born.

Maintaining Perfect Attendance Through Blizzards
By Florence Flanary of Burlington Junction, Missouri
Born 1926

Until February, the winter of 1935-1936 was a normal, northwest Missouri winter. There was some snow, but the days were warm enough to turn that snow into days of muddy roads and feed lots. The freezing nights firmed up the ruts to make early morning walks toward school easier. Mid February changed everything. Snow fell endlessly, blocking the roads completely. The thermometer mercury tried to escape at the bottom as it fell to -30°F night after night.

My sister who was seven, myself at nine, and two next-door neighbor boys the same ages, were accustomed to walking the two miles each day and evening to attend our rural school. Now we faced roads so deep in snow that the fence posts on either side were hidden under the four and five feet of snow, even more in some of the worst drifted areas. Because of the intense cold, the snow was heavily crusted and could be walked on without breaking through.

Perhaps there might have been a day or so of intense blizzards when school was called off, but no more than that. Each morning my sister and I were bundled into overalls pulled over our dresses – there were no jeans then – sweaters, coats, caps, scarves, mittens, and boots and then we were handed our dinner buckets and started off to school. Mostly the four of us walked together, sometimes joined by other kids who lived much closer than we did.

Without today's snowplows and heavy equipment, there was no way to open up the roads, so families were isolated, unable to go for mail or supplies. Most of the men of our neighborhood, and many others in the area, cared for their livestock as best they could then spent the remainder of their days scooping snow to try to open the roads. I remember one Friday evening going home from school to find the road cleared so we walked between the fence posts instead of on top of them. All the families planned to take their Model A's and Whippets out to go into town, Maryville, on Saturday for groceries and other supplies. However when daylight came, it revealed some more snow and the result of a lot of wind during the night, the roads were full again. Gradually the storms

Bloomfield School in a mock wedding

eased, but it was the middle of March, almost a full month, before the weather moderated and the snow melted. We went to school over the drifts and sometimes across fields instead of remaining on the road.

Now I think about what might have happened if one of us had fallen through a softened crust and been swallowed up in snow far deeper than we were tall! But that didn't happen and we never missed a day of school. Farm kids were tough kids in those days. One thing spoiled our perfect attendance. When the snow finally melted, the river couldn't carry all of the snow water and the consequent flooding kept us out of school for one day. For we lived on the other side of the river and we couldn't talk our school board member dad into calling off school that one day. We were sure a pair of unhappy little girls for a little while, that perfect attendance certificate was a special prize in those days.

Santa Claus Commotion
By Betty Smith of Trenton, Missouri
Born 1929

The day I was born they had spent the day at Grandma Clark's. Daddy had bought some new shoestrings and after they got home he took the old ones out of his shoes, but he decided not to put the new ones in until morning. Mama told him he had better put them in because he might need to wear his shoes before morning, but he didn't think so. Shortly after they went to bed she started labor so he got up and put in his new shoestrings and went to get Grandma Clark. Grandma left orders for Aunt Helen to call the doctor but she couldn't get the one grandma had told her to call so my uncle went down to tell them – the folks lived just down the road from grandma's. Just as he stuck his head in the door, mama let out a scream so he rushed back home and told Aunt Helen that they just had to get a doctor. They sent my uncle to town to meet the doctor with the horses and sleigh because there was a lot of snow with big drifts. Mama's labor was short and I was born long before the doctor got there. When the doctor finally got there he was drunk. She can't remember what time I was born, but daddy always told me on my birthdays that I wouldn't be a year older, which I was always anxious to be, until 10 o'clock that night and that always aggravated me because we always had to go to bed at 8 o'clock at night.

When I was a baby Old Dad, my great grandfather, taught me to bawl like a calf. One night at church he came in and sat down right on front of us. Mama said she knew what he was going to do and sure enough, he whispered to me to bawl like a calf and I did – right up in front of the church. It seems that when I was around two years old while mama and daddy were out choring, mama had gathered the eggs and just set them in the kitchen in a bucket. When they came in I was breaking eggs, putting part of them up on the cabinet and part of them in the slop bucket. She said the way I looked at her she just couldn't spank me, but they ate eggs for quite a while using up the ones I had put up on the cabinet. One time when Grandpa Curtis stopped on his way home from town and Norma and I went home with him in the buggy, I can remember Norma telling some big story and she said, "I'm just like daddy; I always get the little end of the horn." Grandpa got a big laugh out of that. At the time I didn't think it was that funny.

On Saturdays when we knew Old Dad would be going to town Norma and I would wait for him out by the road and tell him what kind of candy we wanted. I'm sure he probably brought us a big stick of peppermint candy. I don't remember ever going to their house when he didn't give us each a penny. He taught me to tie my shoes.

On Christmas Eve that year it seemed that there was a commotion outside that I didn't understand, it was Santa Claus. He came in and brought us a little table. I don't know if I knew at the time that it was or if I just remember them telling me. It was a neighbor. But I do know that his brother mysteriously showed up right after that. Just before Christmas daddy came home from town one day with what seemed to me at the time, two big sacks and set them on top of the cabinet and we weren't to bother them until Christmas and we didn't. I don't think we even considered bothering it. When Christmas finally came one sack had hard Christmas candy and the other had shell peanuts – what a treat that was. We would always have a coconut under the Christmas tree every year and on Christmas Eve daddy would crack it and we would get to drink the milk from it and then eat the coconut in chunks. I think that became a Christmas tradition. The second Christmas I can remember we had company. We kids were in the kitchen with grandma and when we went into the dining room we saw Santa Claus run across the living room and out the front door. It scared Norma so bad she went back in the kitchen and got behind grandma and wouldn't come out. Santa had brought us little baby dolls with some doll clothes. I remember mama sewing on something every night for a while before Christmas. She sat next to the table, which held the kerosene lamp. When I asked her what she was making she said she was making some handkerchiefs for my aunt. I didn't doubt her, but she wouldn't let us get very close to her for some reason. It was probably this same Christmas that when we were at church and Santa came in and ran up front. Norma was so scared she crawled in behind daddy and wouldn't come out.

There was always the boogeyman that stayed up in the attic. If we were naughty he would come down and get us. We were afraid to go through that room at night by ourselves. I had no doubt that he was there. It made good little girls out of us even if it did scare us to death. One evening mama went over to the neighbors and left us kids home with daddy. It was something I didn't understand but I knew it was something serious. I think as it turned out, one of the kids had eaten green apples and had a bad stomachache.

One time Norma and I were sitting out behind the hen house. That was the place we went to talk things over. We were discussing whether to go over to town and let our uncles take off our freckles with the coal chisel like they had told us they could. We hated those freckles so bad we would have done almost anything, but we were so bashful we couldn't get up the nerve to go through with it. We had no idea what a coal chisel was. That was the only time I remember ever considering running off. Up to this time most of the things I remember were things Norma and I did together. Donna was still too young to be out playing with us, but from now on she was included more. We took her up in the hayloft one time. Norma went ahead of her and I went behind her to make sure she didn't fall. We got her up there but we couldn't get her down so she sat in the big open door in the hayloft and cried until mama saw her. I'm sure we about gave mama a heart attack when she saw her because she came running to get her down. I don't remember but I imagine we got a good spanking.

About this time is my first remembrance of going to Sunday school and church. We would walk over to grandmas and go to Sunday school with them in the Model T Ford. I don't remember us having a car until I was seven or eight years old. The folks would take us to church on Sunday nights sometimes in the summer and to revivals. I never liked going to the Baptist church as well as I did to the Christian church for two reasons; I didn't like to hear those Baptist preachers holler and I liked the seats in the Christian church. I thought they were pretty neat. One night coming home from the Baptist church, Donna asked what the preacher was so mad about because he hollered so much. We always walked everywhere we went unless we went with grandma and grandpa in the Model T Ford.

I started to school at the country school about a mile from where we lived when I was five years old. Sometimes I would walk across the field and down the main road to school. The first day of school I got off to a bad start. When school took up everyone went to their seats, which they had decided on before. I knew nothing about choosing a seat and seatmate before school took up so I just stood there and cried. My Aunt Jenny took me to her seat, which she shared with another girl. The desks were two seaters so you always shared with somebody else. I sat with Aunt Jenny and her friend for a while then I sat with my cousin. All eight grades were together in one room with one teacher. My only classmate was a boy that I was afraid of for some reason. When our class time came we went up front and sat on a bench, I would sit as far away from him as possible. We also had to say apiece together at the Christmas program where we stood as far apart as we could. The whole school drew names for Christmas and he drew mine, I got a set of little toy pans. The thing we usually did for our mothers was we made a gift for them at school during recess time. That year we embroidered a dishtowel made out of a flower sack. Everyone bought their flour in 50-pound sacks. Sometimes mama would make whip cream with coloring

in it in my little pans and put in my lunch bucket.

We lived close to my grandparents. Mama and grandma used the same bread starter so mama would send me over to grandma's to get the starter when she made bread. I would go across the pasture. There was a cow path I followed. I always went barefoot for every day in the summer. That cow path was so hot on my bare feet that I sure didn't tarry any.

It was on one of our Sunday visits to Grandma Clark's that all of us Clark cousins almost got into trouble and I don't think any of our parents ever knew about it. It was in the early spring when the ponds were beginning to thaw out. We had all the little cousins with us and we were skating on the pond when the ice began to crack and weave. We would all take hands forming a chain clear across the pond and we would go from one end of the pond to the other. The ice would go down then up and finally the water was coming up over the ice and we decided it was too dangerous for the little kids, so all of us "big" kids would go across and make the little ones stay on the bank. Oh, it was great fun and very daring. It makes me shudder to think what might have happened. We might have wiped out one whole generation of Clarks.

Puppy Wisdom
By Margie Buescher of St. Joseph, Missouri
Born 1924

I wrote this story for the sole purpose of keeping my brother-in-law Richard Buescher informed of the progress we were making in the training of his puppy, Rebel. We had kept best of litter for a gift to him. My husband and I owned the only stud dogs for the Vizsla breed in this area. We belonged to the St. Joseph Kennel Club for over 10 years, which is one of the oldest clubs registered with the AKC. We trained, showed, and hunted with this breed.

Hey there! I ended up with four big boys. When I arrived, I was housed in a garage most of the time attached to the house of course. Except for play time and necessary walks (a few of which come a wee bit late) well, I hit the pee paper most of the time; except when I just got so excited and let it fly any ole' place to get rid of the pressure.

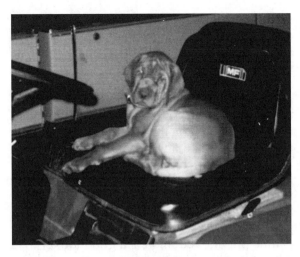

Rebel

Lots of people came to see me; boy did I feel important. The big boys were all related to me and they sort of fussed that I was getting most of the attention, so I'd run down to the kennel to touch noses every so often. This was hard work for a little fella like me, there were stepping stone and the slope to the kennel made me take a few tumbles end over end, maybe I was trying to move too fast but there were seven people up by the garage telling me what a good looking pup I was now that's hard to ignore while still trying to get acquainted with the big boys. I was bound to be good looking with a mom like Hannah and a dad like King, both champions in their own rights.

Last evening some guy mentioned how much I had grown in a week's time. Gee whiz, I thought that was what I was supposed to do, I eat everything put in front of me and a little more if given half a chance. I learned to be exceptionally good in that garage, figured it could be a real haven for a little guy like me. I only whimpered that first night when the lady put me back in the dark after 2:00 a.m. potty call. I was wet on my tummy from the grass, she wouldn't let me go on the sidewalk, and you can bet I tried. Now I was cold and needed someone to snuggle with, I whimpered a few times, but that didn't work so I decided I had to entertain myself. I tore up the pee paper, but didn't upset the water bucket. We went through this same procedure for four nights before a new routine was started.

I'd been introduced to my dad and brother one day while the owner painted two boxes on the other side of the fence of the kennel where my Grandpa Hans and his running mate Duke

lived. Guess they figured it was smart to keep an eye on me being my first time with the big boys. I overheard the lady telling them to be nice to me and take it easy; I was just a little fella. Made me feel good that she was giving them the what's for. I felt like hot stuff going down to that kennel for the first time but when we got there and the lead came off my neck and the gate opened up to go in I pulled back, but the lady pushed me in. I thought this might not be such a good idea after all. She reminded them again to be nice to me, I thought yeah - I'm related you know. I just wondered around carefully as they sniffed me out, okay that went pretty good, they didn't reject me. After a little time passed, I thought I might encourage a little play. I sort of jumped at my Brother Ace, he just moved back and away. My dad King wasn't going to have any part of this game, he jumped up on top of his box and lay down. Now that wasn't any way to get acquainted with your son, but maybe I was lucky at that, one at a time could be the way to go. That didn't last long soon feeding time was at hand and I got to go back up the hill to my safe haven.

The following day I was introduced to my granddaddy and the one they called Duke, now he was the biggest of all. Wow! Could I ever get that big, he had legs that never stopped or so it seemed too little me. Granddaddy more or less ignored me after a couple sniffs and Duke was like Ace and jumped back and away from me, they really took that lady seriously. This wasn't going to be near as much fun as I thought.

Finally, on the fifth day I was told I had to give up my haven and learn to sleep with my dad or brother. Now dad was all stretched out in his box and didn't act like he was ready for this, so I eased over to the next box to take up residency with my Brother Ace. He was curled up in a ball so plenty of room for little me, I carefully crawled in beside him being careful not to disturb him I wanted him to like me. I just couldn't sleep but Ace soon let me know the middle of the night wasn't the time for games or we'd both be in trouble, especially him he had some sort of strange box hanging around his neck, I haven't figured out what that thing is. Anyway, I settled down real fast and played the silent act. I catch on real fast, for a little fella; must be in my breeding.

There are times during the day when

I get too noisy and I hear that word "quiet" Rebel coming from up by my haven. I run to the gate and look up there but seldom see anyone, maybe I'm too short, but that voice always comes from the same direction. If I see someone I give a couple quick barks as much as to say come get me and let's play; these guys aren't any fun. That usually doesn't work; they seem to think when I'm the quietest is the time to take me out. I also learned when they poke me in that wire cage in my safe haven yowling doesn't work either. The quieter you are around this place the more fun times we have in romping in the grass and running after a ball we do. Life sure is confusing for a little fella like me. If I can just stay cute I might have it made.

This ball is changing too, now I'm supposed to bring it back when they say fetch Rebel. If I don't bring it back they take it away from me put a lead on my neck and prance me up and down the sidewalk. Then we stop, my front paws have to be just so, stretch my neck so my head is up in the air and whoopee pick my hind end up and stretch the hind legs out so far I nearly loose my balance. Don't they know those little legs are still like Jell-O? It helps if the kids across the street are playing so I have something to take my mind off what they are doing to me. This must be important because when I don't move they tell me what a good boy I am.

I think the big boys are getting used to me, they play a little bit now. I learned to be careful where you stand, I don't know if it was intentional or I just got caught in the line of fire but I yowled and the lady came running to help me. I was shaking off the wet stuff and she said, "Shame on you" to my granddaddy then took me up to my safe haven, dried me off, and sprayed some good smelling stuff on me.

Another time when it was so hot the big boys put their front feet in the water bucket and made water fly, now that looked like fun, but it was deeper than I thought. They say I'm growing by leaps and bounds bet I'll be able to swim before you know it. I'll get to be one of the big boys yet. If I let out a yelp those guys all look up yonder as if to say we didn't hurt him, like the day I tried to squeeze between the tree and the fence well it worked the first time.

Today even before breakfast King and Ace sit down half way in the run and looked up in a tree that's on the other side. So I followed suit and sat down behind dad and looked up in that tree, I didn't see a thing and wondered what kind of game this was. Now granddaddy and Duke had whatever was in that tree in their sight cause their paws was as high as they could reach on the trunk. Oh! Something moved and Duke shifted his position as Mr. Squirrel scampered from one limb to the next with such sure footness he was quickly in the tree outside the run. Duke is waiting for him to make one false move someday. I got to visit across the street after a new little canine pup moved in, he's a good looker to, a couple weeks older then me but all together a different color. We played well together, he's more my size. I show off for neighbors and friends all this attention is great, hope it keeps up after I grow some more.

Oh! Labor Day they taped my antics and me I performed well, took a couple tumbles off the patio step and trimmed the lady's flowers. My to be owners had come up to see me, I made a hit with them too, even his wife who I heard doesn't like pets gave me a pat on the head and said just don't bite at me and I'll like you. She even joined in when they decided to give me my full name. They all agreed I should be named after my dad, my new owner, and my call name, so I ended up as King Richard's Rebel, impressive for those AKC papers.

The Escape of the Bull
By Ethel Bledsoe of St. Joseph, Missouri
Born 1920

My husband and I owned and operated the Rough Acres Angus Farm, which meant we raised registered Black Angus cattle. The heifers he kept the bulls he sold. One morning before leaving for work, he told me he had put a bull in the barn and a man would be coming to look at it to decide if he wanted to buy it. I looked out the kitchen window about mid-morning; I saw a bull on the lot south of the barn, so I went out slowly and opened the door to the barn and there was no bull inside the barn. I called my husband to tell him the bull was out of the barn and in the lot. He thought I was going over the hill! He thought it was funny; he did come home to check and sure enough; there was no bull in the barn. The one that was out in the lot was the bull he shut in the barn. He decided to put the bull in the cattle chute to check for injuries. On one of the hind legs, there was a small 3-inch patch of hair and skin missing. It was red, but not bleeding. Then he decided to check the room in the barn. The door was locked and secured. The window was open. It was a sliding window so he believed the bull pushed it open. Sure enough on the windowsill area the skin and hair was proof. That was the only way the bull could have gotten out of the barn. He relocated the bull in another place of the barn. The man came and decided to buy the bull. After filling out the registration papers and paying for it, the bull was loaded in a truck and hauled off the farm. That was 54 years ago. I still live on the farm; have the same barn and window where the bull escaped. My family and I often think about it. I have lived here 66 years ago.

The bull

Shame on Me
By Frankie Haggard of Princeton, Missouri
Born 1919

I am a 93-year-old lady. I am in pretty good shape for my age, I think. I live in Princeton, Missouri. Many years ago, when I was in the 6th grade, in Lineville, Iowa, my mom gave me permission to go home with my girlfriends after school. What did I do but do just that. Well, I slid off the back end to the gravel to get a big bump on my lip. What was I going to tell mom. Well, I told her I was on the swing and fell out. I don't think she believed me. Shame on me.

Discipline and Teaching
By C. Max Randal of Grand Rapids, Michigan
Born 1928

One of my favorite memories as a student of Maysville High School in Maysville, Missouri was the type, degree, and effectiveness of one teacher's, B. W. Sheperd discipline, and teaching. Our superintendent frequently would stroll through study hall, quiet as a mouse, with the stealth of a cat and apply a bit of his discipline if needed. For anyone caught napping or not, at least pretending to be, engrossed in study could be abruptly brought to attention by a sharp rap of his thumb and forefinger to the back of your head or an ear. He taught math as well. Throughout my career, I have remembered and used some of the simple shortcuts he taught us in multiplication and division problems. I have used as examples quiet and effective lessons of discipline and simple mathematical shortcuts, many times throughout my career. Today's teachers often don't have this freedom and flexibility.

Too Young to Understand
By Mary Lou Leslie of Richmond, Missouri
Born 1938

I was between three and four years old when Pearl Harbor was bombed. We were at my Grandpa and Grandma Skiles house for Sunday dinner. They lived one mile east of Rayville, Missouri. Everyone was screaming, crying, and wailing. I was too young to know that my Uncle Gene and Charlie were on the battleship Arizona and that my mother had just lost two of her brothers. Gerold, her cousin, was on the battleship Oklahoma. He was gone too. Gerold and Gene waited for Charlie to turn 18 so they could all join the Navy together. Gene and Charlie were self-taught fiddle players. I remember my aunts dancing on the porch while guitars and fiddles played happy music. Both boys played in the Navy band and had performed the night before the bombs hit. We still have Gene's old fiddle. I have a photo of Gene in front of their house playing his fiddle with the curtain blowing out the open window. Their loss did not stop the music forever. Their legacy still lives on; many members of our family still enjoy playing music and dancing.

Since grandpa knew President Truman, they wrote a letter telling of their desire to greet the remaining ships and sailors. You see, her sons remains are still at rest aboard the Arizona. The President forwarded their letter to the Department of navy and they granted their wish. They were flown by the Department of Navy to San Diego, California, where hundreds of sailors greeted them with open arms.

Today my uncles' pictures hang in the Ray County Courthouse and the Veterans building in Richmond, Missouri. As a family, we are very proud of them, but we should never forget all who served our country. History has record what happened there. This is the story of three farm boys who have done their duty and served our country and is a reminder of how precious our God given right of freedom really is!

Freeze Drying Clothes
By Pat Hall of King City, Missouri

Starting in the year of 1978, we moved to north Missouri from south Missouri. My five children and a dog went to live on a farm owned by Kenneth Arm Field. It was an old two-story farmhouse, which needed a lot of work before winter set in. We cleaned and cut grass. We were very happy there. It was ideal for five children to play in with lots of room. It was cold those years, we burned wood, had an old wood stove to keep the house warm, also cooked on it too. The water froze usually every year. My husband did all he could to unfreeze the pipes. I would use a wringer washer to wash clothes and hang them out to freeze dry. My hands would be chapped all winter long. Then I would bring them in to dry behind the wood stove.

Winters were hard and cold. One Christmas we took the kids to town, it was warm enough they could ride in the back of the truck. By the time we got on the road to come home, it was so cold we all rode up front in the truck. We have so many good memories. The years the kids would go to school and graduate. The year the tornado hit us also was in 1993. It was a hot night in June, the animals were all upset

as I remember and the sky was dark. I was fixing supper for my husband and I looked out the window. The cloud was so dark and brown and ugly. Before I knew it, it hit us. I prayed to God to save us. That was the first tornado I was ever in; it was so scary too. Lost all out trees, roof, back doors, and so much damage. But we were lucky; one neighbor lost her life, so sad.

All three years we had done so much to build a life on that farm. Children married, babies being born. In 2004, we lost all our life dreams, our place burned to the ground. We were so shocked; we had nothing at all left. We moved to the King City, Missouri. We were blessed. So many people gave us a lot of furniture, clothes, and money. Today I still live here, but my husband passed away in 2010 of cancer. We had a lot of good times.

Learning a Dis-stink-tive Lesson
By Darrell Bashford of Liberty, Missouri
Born 1931

It was a very hot day back in the '40s in Altamont, Missouri. A bunch of boys decided after riding their bikes around town they would go out to the Altamont Lake for a swim to cool off. Arriving at the lake, clothes were hastily pulled off in anticipation of swimming and hung on the fence. Then a mad dash toward the lake and the cool water. We didn't see a car slowly pull up and stop. The next thing we knew, girls hollered and we looked up to see the car driving off with our clothes hanging out the windows and the girls howling with laughter. We screamed and hollered begging them to bring our clothes back to no avail. Ever so often, they would drive back by and taunt us to come and get our clothes. This went on for about an hour and I was getting very nervous. My problem was I delivered the K.C. Star and I had to get home to start my route. I headed for town stark naked, hiding behind trees, and ducking down in tall grass whenever a car went by. The other boys stayed in the lake until dark before they headed home. My mother let out a shriek when I entered the house without a stitch of clothes on and after a quick explanation, I was dressed and out the door on my way to deliver the K.C. Star, a day I will never forget.

It was Halloween in the late 40's in Altamont. I was a young man with his first car, a used 1939 Plymouth coupe. I was driving ever so slowly around town to see what the younger boys were up to when my younger brother stepped out from behind some bushes and motioned for me to stop. He was laughing so hard I couldn't understand what he was saying, but I could smell something as a breeze blew in my window. "What is that smell?" I asked my brother, which only made him laugh harder. Finally, I got the story out of him. There was an old man that lived in town that most of the kids disliked, so every year they would tip his outhouse over. This year was the year the old man was going to get even, so he had his outhouse moved forward a few feet. That night as the boys moved toward the back of the outhouse to give that big shove, there was a splashing sound and a scream. What on earth was going on the young man thought as he slowly sank in the mire. The rest of the gang pulled him out and that's when my brother found me and wanted me to drive his friend home so he could clean up. Not in my 1939 Plymouth, the most precious thing I ever owned. I told him to sit on the fender and we slowly drove him home, stopping at a small creek where he got in and tried to clean up the best he could. That was probably the last Halloween the old man's toilet was tipped over; at least by one Altamont boy who learned a dis-stink-tive lesson that night.

We Learned How to Be Self-Sufficient
By Judith Bailey Hoyt of Independence, Missouri
Born 1935

In 1944, during World War II, we moved to Darlington, Missouri in Gentry County. The town had about 344 people in the little farming community where everyone knew everybody and were related to most. We quickly learned not to gossip. The town had been built around the spot where two railroads met, which helped farmers in shipping. A few horses and wagons as well as pre-war vehicles were driven as long as possible until new cars came on the market again. The town consisted of a grocery store, post office, drugstore, produce and filling station combined, and a general merchandise store where one could hitch a team, buy groceries, kerosene, fabric and notions, candy bars, penny candy, and even get a document notarized. Groceries could be put "on tab." To get other services, one had to know who was handy at barbering, fixing machinery, giving Toni perms, sewing, cobbling shoes, and firewood.

Darlington had no running water, but we had a sink with a bucket underneath. We got water from the neighbor's pump. We had outdoor plumbing attached to the house by way of a 60-foot path. That room also served as our library, but we only had two books, one from Sears Roebuck, and the other from Montgomery Ward. This little room is also, where we did a lot of our shopping. In extreme weather, Mama allowed us to use the slop bucket. Many had no phones. The phone company was Margaret's living room where she had a switchboard and knew every number. Usually only one name was sufficient in our town. Keys were for cars, not homes.

Our food was of the "tater and bean" variety, plus foods we had grown and canned. We usually had a little meat or cheese on Sunday. We walked home to lunches in grade school. We bought one slice of meat at a time for high school lunches with our homemade bread. In summer, the children went barefoot a lot. At I5, I realized I was a young lady. Gentlemen touched their hats and called me that. I decided it was time to start wearing shoes to town. In winter, we sometimes wore cardboard in our shoes until we could order from the catalog.

The Bailey family in 1954

Our home was modern; we had an electric light on a cord in every room of the house and even double and triple sockets for other inventions. Try doing homework as your sister is ironing with a light bulb swinging over her head. Only one room was heated in winter and us eight children stayed close to the pot-bellied stove. Bricks were heated and even the stove skirts were wrapped in rags and carried to bed to warm feet.

At the age of nine, I stayed nights with a 93-year-old lady for six weeks. My job was to get up on the stool and ring Central to have her alert the lady's daughters. I got $0.50 a week. I became known for such help and worked in 25 homes before graduating. I became a hired girl in an age when girls my age did not do such work.

In 1945, our schoolhouse burned. We were without school from December 15 until February 1, 1946. The two Protestant Churches provided temporary classrooms for the displaced pupils. We were very cramped in the small rooms until a new school was readied for us the next November. Games at grade school were softball games on a Friday afternoon sometimes or hopscotch and jacks. In high school, we were bussed to the big town of Albany, which had a population of 1,800.

One, hot, August day, I walked barefoot 1-½ miles out in the country to get buttermilk for my brother's runt pig. The lady told me the radio was broadcasting the news that the war was over. I ran home on that hot asphalt to tell Mama. That night church bells rang. The children were the ones pulling that long rope over and over again and no one tried to stop us. Our bubble gum was soon available again, new cars were ordered by some. One day my bicycle frightened horses pulling a wagon and they pawed wildly in the air a block away. I was ordered to hide my bike in the weeds until they passed. They had never seen a "wheel" before.

Our area was accustomed to flooding being near three forks of the Grand River. When the Grennell Ford Bridge washed out, George took his daughter and the two of us girls to see the damage. We entered a house nearby. I recall seeing a ham hanging from a ceiling. We started to enter a bedroom when George told us not to. A huge snake was wrapped around the head of the bed. It raised its head and George shot. We watched it unwind, drop to the soaked mattress. That image frightened me. I was afraid to sleep after that unless my head was at the foot.

We learned many lessons at Darlington, which helped us to mature in life and be self-sufficient. We learned how to do for ourselves. Today our town is nearly a ghost town, but when there is a school reunion, former students come from far and near. Many now live in cities, but remember our roots. More people often attend the reunion than the present population. The town we could hardly wait to get out of, we can hardly wait to get back to.

Mini Vacations
By Betty Boettcher of Liberty, Missouri
Born 1930

I was a young mother when my husband and I moved our two children to rural Liberty, Missouri. At least our new home had a bathroom and that was better than the outhouses most of our family had in Iowa. I did babysitting at home because we did not have a second car for traveling into Liberty or Kansas City to work. My husband did not have a job and he controlled out car. I made the best of our situation staying home six days a week.

Sunday was my day off and they were special to explore our new surroundings. So we packed up the kids and away we would go. Every Sunday we went in a different direction and increasingly further away. Sometimes we made a picnic lunch to stop at a local park and eat. Barbecue was a new passion for my husband, but he really never mastered it. We ate his creations with potato salad, pork 'n beans, and a desert and had a feast all on our dishes and silverware from home. We packed up the leftovers and did not worry about refrigeration too badly. Dirty dishes were put in a roast pan to wash later at home. Some Sundays we would go to the Kansas City Memorial Hall for country shows from Nashville, Tennessee. It was a large variety of talent of comedy, singing, and playing of instruments. Our local radio station, KCKN, in Kansas City was our biggest source of music and advertisement for each show. For a small price of $4.00 to $5.00 for adults and

$1.50 to $2.00 for children, we saw all the big stars of the Grand Ole Opry. That was a big thing in this area! After the shows, the kids got to collect autographs and visit the stars. The shows provided an escape of reality, but sometimes the reality came out unexpectedly. Women openly breastfed in the bathrooms. Once Johnny Cash was drunk and fell into the folding chairs right beside us after wavering repeatedly before he fell. The kids would interact with the stars because we usually sat front and center in the first four rows. They learned about loss when Patsy Cline died in a plane crash with other members of the show after we had seen them. My daughter with her new camera was taking a photo of Patsy and her steel guitarist. She could not quite get the photo she wanted, so she kept moving up. It tickled those on stage! Finally, when she got the photo she wanted, Patsy curtsied and the steel guitarist, who was sitting, bowed his head as to say, "Thank you" to the young, but new photographer. But our delight from the experience was short lied when the news came of the plan crash on our favorite radio station, KCKN.

Finally, my husband got a job after almost a year. He worked as a crew worker for the Missouri Department of Transportation. He then drove a truck for Oldham's Gravel and Concrete Company and then Denny Concrete Company. The jobs were all within a city block of our house. On the later job, his boss was Gilbert "Gib" Denny, who owned many three and five gaited horses. My husband really enjoyed the exposure of the high-spirited horses that they were much different then the farm working horses he was used to. Gib showed the horses in all the local horseshoes in several counties, but the prize show was the American Royal, next to the old stockyards in the west bottoms of Kansas City was the top show. He showed his horses in the pleasure and buggy classes. It took lots of money to compete from training, equipment, tack, horses, transportation, confinement, pasture, hay, and feed. Definitely out of our league! The kids spent a lot of time with their dad and time at the concrete company, so they got allocated to the horse environment in a very short time. They wanted their own horses, but we started small and progressed to bigger ones. We never showed at the American Royal, but they did at local shows after they rode them back down the roads to get there and back home. My oldest three children eventually were animal groomers and rode in the American Royal from the rodeo to the regular horse and livestock show. Today, one of them is involved heavy in the barbecue part of the American Royal.

Our family mini vacations were once a month that were drives to Iowa to visit our family. They were spur of the moment of throw the clothes in a suitcase and barrel out the door for the car. One of those trips was about 1964; we did not listen to the weather forecast and drove into a blizzard in Savannah, Missouri. We got to town finally and ended up in a mom and pop unheated roadside motel. They did not plan for winter patrons. We slept in all our clothes and all the blankets they had on top. All four of us in one bed. We were never so glad to hear the road was open going north that next morning and we left immediately in a nice, warm car. Another one of those mini vacations we were going back to Iowa at night and the lightening flashed and there was a big tornado in front of us on the road and coming at us. Good thing the road had a bend in it or I probably would not have been here to write about our ordeal. It was very scary to think that your family, in an instant, could be gone. Then be so happy that in the next instant know that they are still here.

Speaking of tornadoes, Liberty's tornado alley was from our house north of Highway 152, on Church road, north to the concrete company where my husband worked. Every year we had several of them. Part of them hit the other side, 69 Highway (now I-35) and slam into the Hillcrest Trailer Park on the southwest side of the hill next to Highway 71 (now Highway 291). That happened every year until Liberty's landscape started to change with more roads than housing and last businesses. We would watch them pop up behind our house and be aloft as they swirled around. Very few times were we ever scared to run to the basement because we had lived through a direct hit, a few years earlier from a water spout on the south side Big Spirit in Orleans, Dickinson County, Iowa that wiped out my husband's brothers business and part of his home.

On the average, I had 10 children to babysit every day in my home. We usually started in the kitchen or living room, then taking turns to go to the bathroom, then off to the basement, or in the yard depending on the weather. At the end of the day, we were back in the house for cartoons and for me to fix dinner. They all played together without much fighting. If they did, they all knew what they would get. Most only got one swat on their butt with dipper or clothes, but hard enough that it would be just enough to smart real good. That usually took care of the problem. After that, if they needed a reminder, I got down on their level and told them to get busy and go play. You know I never had to give them another swat or even another warning after the first one as they then got busy playing real quick. For breakfast was a choice of toast, butter, and jelly or cereal with milk. Lunch was a variety of peanut butter and/or jelly, cold meat, or hot cheese sandwiches with potato chips, a hot vegetable, and ice cream. Snacks were cookies and milk. They had a nap in the afternoon. By the time they went home they had played hard and were ready to go.

My kids babysat outside of the home and started about 13 until high school. My daughter was so popular with some of the line workers at the Ford Company that she babysat from Friday night to Sunday night at one of their local apartments. She usually had up to 20 children all weekend under the age of three. The workers wives were always impressed by all being fed, clean diapers and clothes, and all happy and not crying. My daughter always said she raised other people's children so she never had time to have any of her own. I figure that was true as she missed out on a lot of things on the weekends for school. After babysitting with my kids around me, I know I was a good role model for my children to do this job.

The oddest experience I had at this job was a lady came and brought her son with a suitcase for the day. But the day went to night to the next day and then the next for a week. Emergency numbers were not heard of back then, but I sure should have had one. Her and her husband finally showed up to pick up their son and told me that they had been on vacation to California. She left her little boy with a complete stranger from a newspaper ad and not much more information. It was the oddest thing I ever saw that a mother would do. Nope, I never saw them again either.

When my fourth child came along, I was ready to get a job outside of the house. We were closer to downtown Liberty then. I went to work in the kitchen at Franklin School. My young son and I would walk to a babysitter close to our house. After he started to school he suggested that I pay him instead of the babysitter to get himself ready, lock the house, and get on the bus. It ended up giving him responsibility, but also a little spending money. I never regretted doing this because he did a great job and never missed the bus. Currently, I am still working for the school district, after retiring at 25 years as a kitchen manager and subbing in the kitchen since, for a total of almost 40 years.

I never had any real hobbies, but I had lots of work to do at home. I washed and ironed clothes, prepared our food for lunch and dinner, cleaned house, sewed light type clothes, and embroidered niceties for our home. I was constantly on the run to get things done. My husband enjoyed doing the breakfasts as he got up early every morning. He fixed sausage and eggs every morning, especially when the two oldest kids were young. He was raised on lots of grease in his meals. He did not drain it off and the kids eventually could not eat it. He changed to hot oatmeal till they got tired of it too. Now none of my children will eat breakfast, let alone something greasy first thing in the morning. Two will drink coffee, but no food for any of them. They all brought their appetites for me to feed them at lunch and dinner instead. We did not eat out at all except on special occasions and they were far and few between. Our meals otherwise consisted of meat, potatoes, a vegetable, and a small desert with a wholesome beverage. Everyone ate good helpings of what was put on the table, but did not graze at a meal like today. I could make better meals at home to everybody's liking compared to eating out. Even today, we do not eat out much because of the variety of fresh food from the garden and hunting.

The Bed Was Too High
By Julie Gilland of Mound City, Missouri
Born 1917

I am writing about my hometown of Bigelow, Missouri located about 40 miles north of St. Joseph, Missouri, about four miles

Old motel

west of Mound City, Missouri. Our school was a 12 grade school, in later years was cut down to the 10th grade, 8th grade, then finally to Mound City. My favorite teacher was Miss Irene Keith, who taught 1st grade through 3rd grade. We walked to school lots of time on frozen snow, over the fencerows. We enjoyed playing fox and geese, making snow angels, snowball fights during recess, but we really like ice cream made with the snow. When I graduated from the 10th grade, we had four boys and four girls, our dresses cost us $3.00.

We had a small train called the "bug" come up from Napier and bring kids up at 8:00 a.m. to schools and returned at 4:00 p.m. to pick them up. A bunch of us would go to the elevators and play in the piles of corn shucks until the train came by. We listened to *Fibber McGee and Molly, Guiding Light*, and *The Squeaking Door* on the radio every evening. We had a wind up tube shaped Edison Record Player with a big horn, dad's favorite songs were "Bird on Nellies Hat" and "Slow Boat through China." It is still in my family. We also had a wooden ringer type telephone; our ring was two long and one short. Everybody knew everyone's business and we could hear receivers clicking. We had coal oil lights as well.

We did our washing on a washboard and used homemade lye soap. We had plenty of blisters from rubbing so hard to get clothes clean. We hung clothes out on a line, during summer and winter. They would be frozen so

hard they would stand up when we brought them in the house. Our Saturday night baths were in an oval shaped galvanized tub in our kitchen, water was heated on the kitchen stove. During the depression years, men worked for $4.50 a week, groceries were cheap. A loaf of bread was $0.10 a loaf and rent was $10.00 a month. I remember going to one movie when I was young, it was Ben Hur at Craig, Missouri. Our homemade clothes were made from feed sacks at the seed store for $0.25 each. Dress material ran $0.17 a yard. Most of the girls wore dresses made from feed sacks. They were very pretty.

We had a wooden icebox, which held 50-pounds of ice. My dad went to the lake or river and cut blocks of ice. We stored it in a shed with sawdust between each blocks. We had ice all summer. There was a pan set under the icebox to catch the water as the ice melted. Later on we cut a round hole in the floor under the icebox, running a hose down through the floor; water went under the house. A train called the Zelpher came through town twice a day and picked mail up from an iron arm; it was fast and never stopped. Our town had a store, restaurant, post office, elevator, depot, hotel, skating rink, three churches, school, grocery store, filling station, doctor, garage, stockyard, basketball court, Bank of Bigelow, weight station, big hay barn, and a mail carrier. We had PTA meetings once a month with a supper and program. In the evening during summer, the kids all met at the schoolyard and played ball and games. We received a magazine every month with the story Cimarron in it. Mom read that to all of us as soon as we got it. It was real good. We had a toilet, which we papered the inside; used Sears catalog for toilet tissue, and washed out the toilet every washday with our wash water.

Flood of 1993

The toilet seat inside a lot where we had a horse would make a mad dash to the toilet and wait until the horse got over in the lot to go in or out.

My granddad used to tell about the flood of '81, water from Nebraska Bluffs to Mound City. We saw men drive, from our front porch, drive herds of horses and cattle down to the stockyards. They would stay overnight and shipped out by stock cars the next day. Also, trains took loads of army boys being transferred and some prisoners. Our streets were muddy and full of ruts, sometimes almost impassible. Our schoolhouse was converted into a Sportsman Lodge and still is. It has a restaurant and pull in trailers all over town. I loved to stay all night with my grandmother; she was a tiny little woman. She would take me upstairs to bed at night and I could hardly get up into bed it was so high, made with corn shucks, but it sure was warm. We rode horses to school and all rode to the Crossroad Corner after school. I had several close classmates who lived in the country and we still are together after marriages and I kept in touch with to the best of my knowledge I think I am the only one living.

I was born on July 14, 1917 in Bigelow. The doctor sent my birth certificate on July 13 and my middle name was Elizabeth, which should have been Ellen and my birth date should have been July 14, 1917. I could celebrate two birthdays, but I am 95 and one birthday is enough. I lived in Bigelow until 2011 when I sold out and moved to Evans Circle in Mound City and went from a seven-room house to a small apartment here. We bought our home and raised two boys and two girls there. I lost both my boys, one daughter lives in Arizona, and the other is my right hand man here with me. This is a real good place, real good neighbors who look after me all the time. After over 60 years there, it's kind of hard to get use to. But it is my home now. I sit and watch my little finches and hummingbirds around the feeders. My brother greased the pole where the feeders sat on; the squirrels would run and grab the pole and start up and would slide back down. It was fun to watch them. My schoolmate of years ago at Bigelow school moved in here where I live now; we visited and talk about old times in school, I really enjoy it.

A Horse with Determination!
By Karen Farrell of Effingham, Kansas
Born 1957

Where does one begin to tell their childhood story one might ask? I suppose it should start as early as one remembers and what stands out in their memory. Back in the good old days and being reared in the 1960s and 1970s, I can say my family was not wealthy, one might even say we were poor and did without the finer things in life. Money wasn't everything and it certainly didn't change the love we all had for each other, in fact, I believe it made us stronger and our time together more memorable.

I grew up in a small rural area outside of Hiawatha, Kansas, in an old two-story house with my parents and siblings. I remember waking one morning, as did my brother who is younger than me. I can't recall whose idea it was or who woke up whom, but I do remember the both of us looking out the bedroom window. It had rained that night and there was this huge area that resembled a mud pit. We scrambled back to our bedrooms, threw our clothes on, and outside we flew. It was like skating in the mud! We were having a grand ole time, until mother spotted what we were doing! We were caked with mud from head to toe! Mother was very upset and told us we had to bathe outside! Now mind you, this old house didn't have running water, or a hot water tank. All we had were buckets of water pumped from the well. Mother was so mad at us she made us take a bath in that freezing cold well water! We found out later that she had just planted seeds to create a flower garden and we had just completely destroyed it.

Now I already have mentioned there wasn't piped running water in the old house. That meant bathing, dishwashing, and the washing of clothes were done the old way. I always felt different than my classmates because there wasn't a shower stall, bathtub, or instant heated water in the house. We did have a toilet in the house, but it wasn't flushable, well not by hand, instead you had to pour a bucket of water down the bowl. We hauled water in the house, took a bath in a metal tub, washed our hair in a bucket of water, and heated water in a teakettle on top of the stove. Dishes were done in tubs instead of the sink so the water could be easily taken out to dump. It was like camping in your own home.

We had quite the imagination as we built our very own circus out of barrels, boards, and other material for make-believe rides and games. We would invite the neighbors to come and join us. One playmate's mother would make little baggies of toasted Cheerio's and mother would make sweet tea. All the playmates said she made the best sweet tea ever. We would also all get together and play softball at the sale barn. Dad junked out old cars and warned us kids to stay away from them, as he didn't want us to get hurt or possibly run into a snake. He showed us a really big one he had killed, just to show us, but that didn't stop us from flipping a car shell on its hood. Now this was a lot of fun because it now became our ship and we would play pirates. We would get our ship rocking back and forth, as if it were rocking against tidal waves from the ocean. Using our imagination and pretending was the best fun anyone could ask for. Ahoy there mate!

Sometimes dad would let us kids drive around one of his junk cars (that still had a motor and was drivable) in the fields beside the house. It was fun learning to drive that way at a young age. The only problem was there were not any seats in the car; instead, we sat on top of an upside down bucket. My older sisters decided they would let our little brother give it a try, even though he wasn't tall enough to see over the steering wheel and almost drove us off into a creek! We all laughed and still had fun regardless and knowing we really were not in immediate danger.

Saturday morning's mother would be busy cleaning and washing clothes using the old wringer washer. The water was brought in the night before and the rinse tubs filled so it would be ready to do laundry. She would also hang the clothes outside on the clothesline, as we didn't have a clothes dryer. It was funny when the clothes were brought in to fold because they were always as stiff as a board. You could easily pretend someone was walking beside you using a pair of jeans. As kids, we would be sitting in front of the television watching cartoons or our morning shows like *My Friend Flicka, Sky King,* and other oldies. Saturday evenings were considered family night. Sometimes we would all load up and head for the drive-in theater with a cooler of soda pop. Or we would stay at home and mother would make popcorn and by dad's request, cocoa fudge. Saturday nights were the only time we were allowed to have soda pop.

As kids we truly wanted to buy a horse, it was discussed as a family and mom and dad made the decision that we would have to save up our allowance if we truly wanted one. After we pooled our money together, we set out to look for and purchase one. It took us a couple of weeks, but we found a chestnut gelding. The owner at the time had his son ride him over to our house, they removed their saddle and left. My sister hopped up on him and took him around the barn as the before owners feared if he saw them leave he would want to follow and head back to his old pasture. A few minutes after they left, we looked up and here came my sister and our new horse in a full run, ran right past us and onto the road! Dad jumped in his old Chevy Impala and chased after them. Man could that horse run! Dad caught up and got around them, pulled out in front of the horse sideways, thinking maybe he would stop, but no, he took to the ditch and my sister was hanging on tight and couldn't get him to stop. He was a horse with determination! After about a mile, he finally got winded and my sister was able to get him to stop running. She jumped off him and was shaking. Another quarter of a mile and they would have ran out onto the highway! That gave everyone a scare! Later as years had passed she confessed to me that she kicked him into the run, but didn't think she would had such a tough time to get him to stop. Needless to say, she didn't do that again. Dad went out and bought a new saddle and bridle soon after that incident. Brownie was the name of that horse and every time you rode, you had to hold on for dear life when you headed the direction back home. I took a piece of rope and tied it to the bridle around his nose to help slow him down. He should have been a racehorse because he ran so fast!

I cannot forget to tell about our mushroom hunting days. This was always a favorite for us kids. Have you ever been mushroom hunting? It was an adventurous trip as not only would we find mushrooms, but we could wade through creeks, listen to a few waterfalls, and even play Tarzan using the vines that grew along the trees and swing with them. Dad was usually the one that took us and once in a while mother would go with us. The only problem with mother joining us was she always found snakes! Dad knew she was terrified of them and had no problem teasing her with them. I swear dad wasn't afraid of anything! He would grab up a snake by their tail and give them a snap like a whip, killing them so we could continue to mushroom hunt or scare mother with one.

I would not want to grow up in this crazy old world now days. It was a safer world back in the day; the laws of life were so different than compared to what it is like now. Reminds me of the song I hear every now and then by Bucky Covington, "A Different World."

Virginia and her teacher, Miss Jessie Baldwin

People Knew Hard Times
By Virginia Cruth of Clearmont, Missouri
Born 1932

I was born in 1932 in a country home near Conception Junction, Missouri in northwest Missouri. My father was George Downing, and mother, Frances Downing. My father farmed and my mother was a housewife and later a schoolteacher. My father farmed there only one year. I was one year old. They moved to the Hopkins, Missouri area to my mother's father's home site (my grandfather, Frank Miller). It was located southeast of Hopkins. There were five children and times were very hard as that was called the Depression years. People knew hard times. Mother washed on a washboard, soap was handmade, we cooked on an old-fashioned cook stove, and ironed by heating heavy irons on top of the stove. She made our clothes from flour sacks, which at that time were purposely printed to make our dresses to wear to school.

My sister and I had a 2-½ mile walk to get to school. At that time roads were not graveled so there were many times I had to pull my sister from the mud. Sometimes her shoes would come out of the overshoes and "ook the mud." The schoolhouse was Prairie Flower. We had to wear long brown stockings, which we both hated when the weather was cold. We walked in all kinds of weather, rain, snow, sleet, and sun. Miss Baldwin was our teacher and a very good one. She taught all eight grades, having to build a fire in cold

weather, it was just one large room. She also had to clean after school for the next day. That is not done now. We drank water from a large crock fountain. Many things are far different than today. She taught us several games to play at recess time. Some I remember were Hide and Seek, Anti-Over, Run Sheep Run, and Baseball. The larger boys would hit the ball and they would grab my hand and would I run. Older kids would look out after the small kids of which is not done these days. I recall one ornery boy that thought it would be funny to sneak in and hit the blackboard with a roll of mud when everyone was not looking, including Miss Baldwin. She was a little angry, when she asked who did that, no one would admit to it. She decided if no one would admit it she would keep us all after school and that she did until someone would admit it or tattled on the other who did. It was well after 4:00 p.m. when someone finally told. She let us out and before we got home here came my very angry father with a flashlight to find us. There were no telephones at that time. Well that meant that when we got home, it was razor strap spankings for us. Our father thought we were lying to him. It's one spanking I never forgot!

Miss Baldwin was a wonderful teacher, she later married and is now Mrs. Jesse Fine and is living at the Parkdale Manor nursing home in Maryville, Missouri. I visit her regularly. I am 80 plus years of age now and

I believe she is 95. I have a picture of her and she still remembers those days and has a very good mind.

Another thing I remember is taking cold sandwiches to school for lunch. Almost always peanut butter or sandwich spread. Glad that was all in the yesterdays. In the 3rd grade, I was attending another one-room school northeast of Pickering, Missouri, a school called Zenia. Two and a half months into that school year, my dad decided to move west to the state of Oregon and we all left in an old 1928 Chevrolet. That is quite another story, but in the end, I lived in five states and ended up graduating from Pickering High School. My mother taught in most of those states and we've seen and done a lot in all. I am now married and have three children and a very good husband and still living in northwest Missouri.

Neighbors Shaped Me into What I Am Today
By Dorothy Taul of Trenton, Missouri
Born 1949

Born in 1949, life on the farm was simple and very north-central Missouri rural. I was raised on a farm near Coon Creek and Wilson Hollow. As a matter of fact, one year at Halloween I dressed up as Miss Wilson Hollow. My family consisted of parents, Bill and Betty Taul and two brother, Ike and Billy, as well as four sisters, Doris, Linda, Nancy, and Peggy. We had many animals most necessary for the farm, but others were simply there to love and please us farm kids.

Each year when our old sows had pigs and one being of "runt" size my dad would bring him to the yard for me to love and care for. Of course, I seemed to always name him after the cutest boy at Edinburg School, "Jimmy." Each spring it was always the same when it came to naming the pet pig, "Jimmy" seemed to always win year after year. Jimmy would eat in the yard out of a pan with the chickens or cats. He would grow and thrive. He would follow us kids around squealing each step as he ran close behind us.

One of the hardest times in my life with a pet was when our pony Kennedy got sleeping sickness and was sick for weeks in the horse barn. Each day we got off the bus at the end of our lane and walked down our private road, we would quickly change our school clothes and head for the barn hoping Kennedy was feeling better. This was not to be each week; it was not good. To us kids we never gave up hope we always thought just one day he would be standing, eating, drinking water, and running in the green pasture. Finally, he died and was buried on the slop just past he lot fence. Oh did we cry. Our ponies were our loves of our lives. We road each day and especially in the summer I would ride back north and pick when in season, gooseberries and blackberries. I trained our horses to eat the leaves while I set on their back picking and eating. What a wonderful memory.

We had many dogs as children. My dad and Brother Ike had coon, squirrel, and coyote dogs. Our yard dog always seemed to be a collie. Our collie dog let us put dresses and hats on him. We ran and played in the front yard; he thought he was a kid just like us. Some days he would be a kid other days a baby, depending on what we found to dress him up in. He was very protective of us and when anyone pretended like they were yelling, made, or would raise a hand, he would stand ready to protect us and barking his head off.

I live on that same farm where I grew up with one of my daughters and her family. We have three horses – Fancy, Ginger, and Cookie; one cat named Jelly Bean; and one dog, Peaches. My grandchildren play outside and enjoy farm life. Kids in today's world have video games, computers, iPods, and cell phones. They do not have the time or life to have pets as I did. This is why I have tried to expose my grandchildren to as many farm animals as possible. I have a deep love in my heart for animals and enjoy attending country fairs and parades just to see the animals.

I grew up in the 1950s and 1960s along Wilson Hollow and Coon creek. I was a girl living in a big farm family, with not a care in the world. I loved being outside, playing cowboys and Indians in the back timber with my brothers and sisters. We killed Indians and outlaws and threw them across our pony for a ride to the house. We made corrals out of old limbs and had a wonderful time.

Our neighbors were few in number, but influenced me in many different ways. Fay was the first "working woman"; I mean working outside of the home woman. She worked at

Trenton Foods, a factory that employed most workers in our community. She took us to the movie to see *Swiss Family Robinson*, my first movie experience. Fay also paid our way into our first circus, she had to work but she bought us tickets and her children tickets and my mother took us to the "Big Top." Wow! Country kids go to town with the neighbor woman who worked and had extra money to spend on her children and us children. One thing I will never forget was when she brought a little jar to our house and showed all of us her gallstones; they were marble sized rocks of multicolor.

Dolly was my favorite. She would invite me to go to town with her on Saturday morning once in a while. I would put on my skirt and blouse, yes, there were no jeans or slacks for girls back then, and off to town we would go. First, we sold her cream, then her eggs, now she had money for the "dime" store and then groceries before we left for home. She loved to look and touch almost everything in the store. I even was allowed to go upstairs to the toy section. Dolly was entertaining; she had all kinds of animals - guineas, ducks, chicks, cows, pigs, geese, pet calves, etc. She talked funny, the television "antannie" was one of my favorite words she had her own way of saying it. Her yard and farm lot was fenced in a very different way, posts, wire, bedsprings, metal, and anything else to block up a hole so all of her many animals could be fenced in. Now I also loved Vernie, she and I were gooseberry pickers together. I would get my two lard buckets and off over the hill, I would go and meet her half way between her farm and ours. I loved to talk and pick berries, we talked about all kinds of things while we picked. I also rode my pony back north to bushes and stop and eat and pick. My pony learned to stop at each gooseberry bush. According to Vernie, "if you don't look for a rattle snake, they will not let you see them while picking berries." If you have never eaten a green gooseberry, you must try one or a handful as I prefer and as you chew, squeeze the sour juice out of them. Oh, what a wonderful refreshing taste!

Eula was one neighbor who had a John Deere spray painted evergreen tree at Christmas and a beautiful fern plant that I adored. She made macaroni and cheese in a small counter top oven and homemade bread too. Her kitchen always smelled so good.

Her son, Herbie, went to college and that really impressed me. Lottie was the neighbor where I got kissed playing "spin the bottle" at a community block party. A boy who I swear looked dark complexion just like Elvis Presley. Each month neighbors would rotate the block party from house to house. We had good friends, adults played cards, and talk, us kids played outside. Her sons, Edmund and Billy, were teachers and that impressed this little country girl.

Neighbors were important to my growing years and making me who I am today. Each one had a big influence on me, from the stories I heard and events I witness. They all helped me from my personality and actions I use every day. All are long gone now and most of these home sites are bulldozed under and are now farm ground. This has not stopped my wonderful memories. As I sit in my backyard swing on my parent's farm and look across the farm lot and pastures where I grew up, my mom and I can reminisce when I walked this same land as a young child with my neighbors. Yes our farm and home still exist, now my grandchildren run and play at the creek and pond, just like me and my brothers, Ike and Billy, and sisters, Doris, Linda, Nancy, and Peggy once did.

When we went Square Dancing
By John E. Wolfe of Faucett, Missouri
Born 1937

At the old one-room schoolhouse, everybody was welcome to come. There was music by the Grable family or anybody that could play. Joe and Lee Grable played the fiddle. There were many others who played the guitar. Dortha Grable Wolfe played the piano. It was just one room, but they could do two sets at a time in there. The women fixed sandwiches to eat before we went home at about 11:30 to midnight. We had a great time there. Then, we went to Platte Falls Inn at Raster Falls in the summer. The first time we went we didn't have a room to stay in. we danced outside in the dirt. The owner said if we could come back the next week that they would have a dance floor to dance on; he did. The next week he had a roof on it. By the winter, he had a heater in it. At about 11:30, they served fried fish or chicken. There

Joe Grable

Dad's Hunting Trip
By Sharon Aring of Smithville, Missouri
Born 1941

I grew up on a farm near La Cygne, Kansas and moved in the third grade. However, my dad told me about how he and my grandpa would catch the streetcar on Independence Avenue and Cliff Drive. They would ride it to where they could buy tickets on the inter-urban railway (I do not know where this was.) Dad, Fred Monteil, and his father, Joe Monteil, went north to go hunting. They each had a shotgun and gunnysacks. Just imagine that happening now! They went through Ferrahview and before they crossed the Little Platte River, they got off and started hunting. My dad was a good shot, and they always filled both gunnysacks. (Gunnysacks are now known as burlap bags.) I can't imagine anyone being able to go hunting on a streetcar with guns in this day.

Homemade Clothes and Early Cars
By Nadine Gatterman Baugher of Liberty, Missouri
Born 1917

I was born on a farm in Chariton County, Cockrell Township, Missouri on July 6, 1917. There was no running water or electricity in the house. We managed just fine. I attended a country school. My father was a member of the school board. I walked a mile and a half to school with my sister and brother. My father would come for us after school if it was raining. My mother was very bright, and taught us each night at the kitchen table after supper. I could read and write before attending school at age six. My grandmother made my clothes to wear to school. She was a gifted sewer. I recall our first car—a model-T Ford. It had to be cranked and had a gas, a spark, and a brake. I later dated a boy who had a Ford V8 that had a rumble seat for two. It was a beauty!

I taught at a country school at age 18 after being qualified to teach. The way I qualified was by taking a test at the county seat in Keytesville, Missouri. I later attended Kirksville State Teacher's College in Kirksville, Missouri. It is now Truman University. I met my husband in the Sunken Garden on that campus. I now live on a farm in Clay County, Missouri.

was plenty to eat. That went on for about two years, and then I met my wife, Candy, and we got married. We went to Savannah, Missouri one Saturday night and a member of the Legion had died, so there was no dance. There was a bad snowstorm that day and we got six or eight inches of snow. Lavern said, "Let's go somewhere else to dance." It was ten degrees below zero when we came home. We went to many other places before we finally found a place. We went to Wallace, Missouri to Lodge Hall and went upstairs. We had a good time there. We met a lot of good people.

Clifford, Winifred, and Ruby

375

Daily Chores and Drive-in Movies
By Emma F. Patterson of St. Joseph,
Missouri
Born 1926

It was a cold and snowy day in the small town of Amazonia, Missouri on March 28, 1926. I was born to Thomas and Sarah Harman on that day, and they named me Emma Frances. I was the youngest of seven children. When I was three, my mother died in childbirth. I had to go lived with my father's sister, Ollie Smith on a farm in Gilford, Missouri. I learned to do chores like gathering eggs and bringing in wood for the heat stove. There was always chores do before and after school. There was no inside plumbing or electricity. I had to walk to school till I was 12, then I got my first horse. I rode that horse until the eighth grade to the Whiteford School. It was a one-room schoolhouse. When I was young, I loved to play baseball. I was a catcher. One time while playing, I got hit in the nose. On Saturday, the family, Ollie and Allie Manship, would hook up the mule to a wagon and ride to town. We had free drive in movies. Ollie would buy me a bag full of candy for a nickel.

In 1941, I married Richard Johnson. I had my first child, James William, on July 31, 1947. When James was two, I divorced Richard and married Roy Patterson on June 12, 1949. Roy and I had six children. I am an amazing woman, wife, mother, grandma, and great-grandma. Roy died on April 22, 1988.

Thank Goodness for Kind Strangers
By Lora Ellen Crowley of Savannah,
Missouri

This 1880s story is about a young northern German girl who immigrated to the United States—my grandmother, Elisabeth (Sander) Uhl. Barely 20 years of age, she traveled first from her homeland to Liverpool, England. She was employed there as a house servant for about a year. She then embarked for America, sailing for 49 days. At that time, immigrants coming through New York City were processed at Castle Garden, now a historical site. I wish I had asked my grandma many more questions about leaving home and coming to a new country and about the upscale hotel restaurant that her family operated in Germany.

What happened (or didn't happen) at Castle Garden has impacted our family to this day. As Grandma was getting her bearings, she was not aware that a "bad man" had spotted her and determined that she would be a likely candidate for his evil purposes. Meanwhile, he was unaware that he, too, had been spotted. An astute observer realized that he was certainly after Grandma, and stepped in, literally saving Grandma. The interceptor was an African American woman who took Grandma under her wing. She saw to it that Grandma boarded the correct train to come to Saint Joseph, Missouri. Grandma, until then, had never seen a person of a different race other than white. What if this compassionate woman had not intercepted? What if Grandma had not accepted her kindness?

Although no pictures exist to validate this story, my imagination and emotions can see this incident very clearly. Yet today, more than a century later, my family is grateful for the positive conclusion.

Life with No Cell Phones or K.F.C.
By Nancy Styhl of Liberty, Missouri
Born 1942

I was born in 1942. We lived on a farm on the outskirts of Kansas City, Missouri. Often I think how my grandchildren could manage back then. They walk around texting on their cell phones, have a television bigger than our icebox was, hot showers, and electric clothes dryers. I wish I could take them back to the good old days!

Our phone was a rotary party line phone. Of course, there was only one in the house. The radio was our entertainment. We listened to country music, Arthur Godfrey, and the Lone Ranger. For some reason, the kids today like their jeans with holes in them. Ours were patched. My dresses were made out of the cotton chicken feed sacks. They were cute, too. I can still remember the chickens having their necks twisted. I would help pull the feathers off. The smell when you dipped the chicken in a bucket of hot water is what I remember the most. We had to do it because there was no K.F.C. around! When TV showed up, there were very few channels. Howdy Doody with Big Bob, Clarabelle the Clown, and Princess Summer

Fall Winter Spring were the stars back then.

Behind the house was a low spot. When rainwater filled it up, it became a pool of tadpoles. The water would start to dry up, so my brother and I would catch the tadpoles in buckets and tubs to "save the frogs." We would watch them grow and hop away. We were one of the first animal activists, and we didn't even know it!

Some would look back at these times as hard, but I think they really were the "good ole days!"

Lloyd's Experiences
By Mildred Koontz of Norborne, Missouri

I married Lloyd in 1946. We have been together for 67 years in good times and bad. We both are in good health, except old age has caught up with us. My knee gives me lots of trouble, but still I can work six to ten hours a day, or as long as I can.

Lloyd was a small boy doing a man's job. One summer, we were working in the hay, and I left the pitchfork in the haystack, went home for dinner, went back to finish the hay, and the grasshopper crewed on our pitchfork handle. We had to use broken glass to smooth up the handle. From that day on, we buried our handle in the stack.

Every Saturday, we always had a job to clean the old hen house. All of a sudden, we couldn't find Lloyd. He was hiding under the hay. He had everyone hunting for him. We were scared to death. We had to find him before dad got home or they would skin him alive.

In the middle of 1900, we had an awful ice storm. We went to school on ice skates over the fences. We didn't have to walk the mile and a half around the road. We thought that was fun. Our teacher taught first grade to eighth grade in a one-room schoolhouse. She just had a high school diploma. The ice was so bad that we made a patch out of straw for the horses to walk on to the tank to drink.

In the year of 1934 or 1936, they cut trees down for cattle to eat the leaves for food. Two older people passing by in a bugger, the boys thought it would be a good idea who could hit that back glass out of that old bugger. Guess what? Lloyd picked up a clod of dirt and broke that glass out.

Wall Phones and Homemade Games
By Eunice Rader of Fairfax, Missouri
Born 1923

I went to a one-room country school from the first grade through the eighth. We walked three quarters of a mile all through the grades. The only time Dad came and picked us up was when it rained or snowed. It wasn't in a car either—it was in a wagon with horses. I remember getting punished for telling the teacher a lie. She spanked my hand good with a ruler. I was about eight or nine years old. We always had two outhouses at school—one for the boys and one for the girls. During the drought in the early thirties, we kids had to herd Dad's cattle to keep them out of the cornfields. Dad farmed with horses. We had to do the chores. We were responsible for milking the cows and feeding the hogs. We knew we better get them done before he got in.

We went to town every Saturday night. Dad would give us all a dime. We could either go to the show or buy a sack of candy. You could get a pretty large sack of candy for a dime. On Sunday, we often hitched up the horses to the wagon and went to church and Sunday school. Afterwards, we went to Grandma's for dinner. Mother always made us girls clothes for school. She would order fabric bundles from Sears and Roebuck or Montgomery Wards. She always made us three dresses apiece. There was three of us. We would pick out a dress in the catalog that we liked and she made it like that.

We had a wall phone. Everyone on the line had a certain ring. We would listen on the phone so that we knew what was going on in the neighborhood. Mom would put a boiler on the stove and we had to fill it with water on washday. We carried in wood for the stove. Dad had a huge stack of wood that he sawed up every fall to use in the winter for the heater and cook stove. He and neighbors cut wood and Dad had a tractor with a saw that he made on the front end. He went around to the neighbor's houses and sawed up the wood.

When Christmastime came, there was not much money for presents. Mom was good at making us all gifts. She would make us some games. One year she made a croquet game to play on the dinner table. She used spools, sucker sticks, and wire. We played a lot of games with it. She also made us checker boards.

Mud Roads and Chicken Feed Sack Dresses
By Verba Massey of St. Joseph, Missouri
Born 1926

My school days story happened in the thirties in Doniphan County, Kansas, just across the river from St. Joseph, Missouri. I had one older sister and one younger brother. We lived on a farm two and a half miles from Leona. We had mostly mud roads. During my early school days, we went to a one-room school. Sometimes, we rode a white pony. My sister sat in the saddle and I rode on the back. Often times we didn't get our ponies tied securely at school, so they went home to the barn early. We still had to walk. Also, this same pony would go where she pleased. Sometimes she would go under low hanging tree limbs and rake the rider off. She'd stop and eat along the road or fields. She'd also shy at trucks with floppy tarps. I really don't have any fond horse stories.

For some reason, we transferred to Leona school. It was the same distance, and mostly mud roads. When it rained, our overshoes got so big, heavy, and tiring. An older girl had a car, and when we'd see her coming, it was great because she always stopped for us.

I remember having unforgettable lunches. There was no refrigeration, so my mom bought canned sardines and instant ready sandwich meat. She baked bread, which seemed to be a bit more porous. By noon, it was so soaked through that we needed a spoon to eat it. We did not have finger foods. Often, mom sent a dime with us to bring home a fresh loaf of bread. As we walked, we ate the fresh bread. Very little of the bread actually made it home.

We weren't exactly overdressed. When buying chicken feed, it was important to choose three of four bags of the same design for making a dress. My mom used to order bloomers from the Sears catalog. They came with two pink pairs and one black pair per package. My sister had more class, so guess who wore the black ones? We always had chores to do when we got home from school. We gathered eggs, split fire wood, and carried a good supply to the kitchen for cold evenings. On really cold nights, we'd take a warm flat iron to bed and push it out when we warmed up. Thanksgiving vacation usually meant that we'd have to spend three days in the cornfield with our team of horses and a box wagon. My sister was the horse handler. By Christmas, we fared better. We had "running" water—the kind where we ran outside to get it from the windmill.

The Hog Mishap
By Carol Kay Wolf of Amity, Missouri
Born 1942

Speaking for most farm wives in DeKalb County, women were partners in the farming operation. We drove a truck and stock trailer; tractors with various equipment attached, and got parts in the surrounding area. We also worked the farrowing houses, mowed the yard, cooked meals for hired help, and did various other jobs and projects as needed. The list is limitless.

On one occasion, I drove to St. Joseph, Missouri delivering hogs. At the docks, I became an excellent backer—one that most of the men at the docks couldn't believe. However, my backing of a fifth wheel stock trailer was not practiced at the docks. Prior to this, Larry, my husband had said, "Learn to back this gravity flow wagon." He didn't give much advice or information as to how to accomplish this feat, so I just learned to back it through a gate. Learning on the farm was less nerve racking when no one was looking or waiting for me to get out of the way. I was talking to my neighbor, George Pulley one day about this when he said, "As you back, just turn your wheels in the direction that the wagon is going." Simple enough, I thought. As I practiced, this bit of information was very helpful; thus, that was the beginning of my trucking career.

One day, I was to go to the Oak feeding floor. We were fortunate to rent this floor from Jim Rosier. Larry and Charles Rogers, our hired man, were loading hogs when one or two escaped. The hogs were not far from Highway 6, so it was important to catch them quickly. After catching them, Larry shut the rear sliding door on the stock trailer. Immediately, I drove to St. Joseph Stockyards with 20 butchers. I traveled Highway 6 to St. Joseph, turned south on Riverside Road, and as I began to merge onto Highway 36, a car pulled around me with their window down.

378

The man yelled, "Do you know your back end gate to the stock trailer is open?" "Oh, no," I said. While thanking them, I jumped out of the truck and went to the back. Most generally, hogs always wedge themselves against the back end gate. However, this time they were as far forward as they could get. They were probably scared of the moving highway at the end of the trailer. No wonder they were frightened. I counted the hogs. I called Larry asking him how many hogs I was supposed to have. I told him that six were missing. He called Hubert Schneider, the commission man, to inform him of my plight. He said that if anyone found the hogs, they belonged to us.

After unloading the hogs I had, I decided to return on the same highway, thinking that perhaps I could find them somewhere. Approaching an area on Highway 6, about halfway home, cars, a highway patrolman, McShoggey's Animal Shelter vehicle, and others were stopped on the highway. I thought I was in real trouble with the patrolman and an animal shelter person there; however, they were just helping Larry and Charles to load three hogs into another truck and stock trailer. There was still some missing.

About a week later, via Highway 36, Larry had gone to St. Joseph with the stock trailer, when out in the median near the weigh scales were some men trying to corral a hog. He stopped to see if he could help since he had some hog panels with him. They were successful in loading the hog into the stock trailer. Larry then took him to the stockyards and told them that he had found the hog if someone had one missing. No one ever inquired about this hog; thus we regained one hog of our lost ones.

Carol Kay Wolf

Grandpa Burns
By Beverly Stevens of Bethany, Missouri
Born 1934

Way back in the early 1900s, a little over 100 years ago, there was a man named Benjamin Franklin Burns. He was a mailman. He delivered mail out of Cainsville, Missouri—a little thriving town that had about everything that anyone would need. This town was on the Grand River in Madison Township in the northeast corner of Harrison County. Cainsville also had a coalmine and a train. Cainsville and a big area around it had earlier been a settlement for many families from Bohemia. They came over on boats. They landed at the east coast of the United States and then came across Ohio and Indiana. There were also families from Ireland and Germany here, as well as Native Americans. Mr. Burns had relatives here, as he was the step-great-grandfather of some children in Cainsville. The children and many others knew him as Grandpa Burns.

He had a horse that pulled a high wheeled, homemade mail wagon. It didn't look like other covered wagons. It had a seat across the front but it was just a rectangle shape that was covered with cowhides. When it was very cold in the winter and early spring, he had a metal stove that burned wood and coal in the back of his wagon. He would go back and warm up every now and again on his route.

After a long winter and spring, with many days of freezing and thawing he went out on a route. While he was out delivering mail that day, his two wagon wheels on one side slipped off into a deep wagon track. His wagon tipped over on the side, and before he could get his hot stove moved, it had burnt a big hole in the cowhides that covered the side of the wagon. Just like all mail carriers, he was very aggressive about knowing that the mail route had to be run every day except Sunday.

Mr. Burns enjoyed being a mail carrier, and told many stories about it. He told the children and people that his horse knew his route so well that many days he'd stop and go right when he needed to. He never had to tell him, "Giddy up," or "Whoa!" Some days he'd take one of the great-grandchildren with him on his route. Sometimes he'd tell the kids that someone at a certain home must have had a birthday because one person had gotten five cards or letters in the last two days.

The family was always happy to meet Grandpa Burns and his horse each evening when they got home from the mail route. Sometimes when the weather was hot in the summer, his horse was wet with sweat so that he looked black instead of brown. Other times they returned home in the winter when the horse had large puffs of snowflakes frozen on his mane and eyelashes.

Hand-milking and Outhouses
By Nancy Thompson of St. Joseph, Missouri
Born 1958

Many memories and history flash through my mind as I think of when I was a little girl. I lived down by Lake Contrary in a house with a small path to the outhouse. Chickens pecked me on the butt all the way there! My mother told us that we were not allowed to go to the lake house by ourselves. She didn't want us by the rock and roll band that played there at the roadhouse by the beach. We didn't have running water in the house, so Mom and Dad would drive to town to get drinking water and cooking water. Otherwise, we used water from a well. Drawing up the water took a lot of elbow grease. We raised our own cows for milking. We sat the bucket down and squeezed each teat to get the milk out.

My mother wrote a book about history and memories of her childhood. In this book, she told of her grandfather whom she grew up with. Her grandparents raised her because her mother died from giving birth to her. She was born at home with a midwife. One memory in her book told of her walking up a hill with her grandmother at age three or four years old to take her grandfather a drink and lunch. He had been plowing a field with his team of horses. He would be walking behind his horses holding the wooden handles of the plow, turning the black dirt over in rows. She wrote that she could still see his blue, long sleeved shirt soaked with sweat and his striped overalls and cap. Grandma would always have a cold jar of tea, sandwiches, fried chicken, and salad for him for lunch. All of their food was homegrown and raised. Grandma would can the harvest and store it up for winter in the storm cellars. The cellar was their icebox, too.

There was no electricity. They used coal oil lamps for visibility at night. They cooked on a wood stove and had a path to a two-hole motel. The Sears and Roebuck catalog was used for toilet tissue, and there were many uninvited spectators watching—about seven or eight feet long with beady eyes and slithering tongues.

Hospitality and Young "Love"
By Donna L. Thomas of St. Joseph, Missouri
Born 1941

As a young girl in St. Joseph, Missouri, my father was a used furniture dealer. Times were rough for everyone. My parents, my brother, and I stood in long lines around Townsend and Wall department store to get rations of coffee, tea, and sugar. There was also a city market down by the Missouri River where we could pick up groceries cheaper. I remember although we didn't have much; my dad would cook extra on the weekends. When the hobos got word of it, they would come two or three at time for free food on our back porch. My father knew how grateful they were because he had to do the same in his younger years.

When I was about seven years old, we did not have a TV. Our cabinet radio was the only activity for us. I would put a blanket and pillows down, gather up cheese and crackers, fruit, and soda pop. Then, my brother, sister, and I would listen to *Roy Rogers, The Shadow,* and *The Three*

Donna's parents Mary and Fountain Parker with their children in 1952

Karen Root, Donna Parker, and Carol Poe

stooges. We were happy just being a family.

When I and my cousins Karen and Sharon stayed overnight with Aunt Marie and Uncle George, Aunt Marie would round us up, make us take our baths, then here she came with the bottle of castor oil or milk of magnesia. We all grabbed our noses before the tablespoon hit our mouths. She said it was good for "what ailed us," but it sure was nasty tasting!

I had a very close friend named Carol Poe whose father owned his own candy factory. It was called Poe's Candy Company. The family lived on the second floor of the factory and Carol and I played in the very large packing boxes. We also played hide and seek when more friends came. Then, we all went downstairs in the candy factory and ate all of the peco flakes, bon-bons, coconut stacks, and fudge that we could get down. Sometimes her mother let her invite some boys over and we all sat in the living room and played spin-the-bottle. It was all silly, embarrassing, and fun back then. We also were all good roller skaters and we all met at Skateland and Pony Express Rink.

Whenever I could, I loved to go to "Teen Town," as we called it. I think I "fell in love" with a different guy at every dance. At a Halloween dance, I dressed up as a little girl with braids, big ribbon in the back, polka dot puffed sleeves, and a big gathered skirt just above my knees. I thought it was a neat idea to put a thin piece of wire through the bottom of my dress all around to make it stand out like a hoop skirt. Later, I realized why I had a group of guys waiting to dance with me. My skirt went straight up in the back, and my white, ruffled bloomers were showing. I was trying to hold onto my very large striped sucker while dancing, and I couldn't do too much about the skirt situation. Anyway, the boys liked it!

I did have a lot of boyfriends during grade and high school. I had a special, very popular dancer who I really liked. He asked me to go to the Ringling Brothers Circus at the old St. Joseph Auditorium. He chose to sit in the third balcony, so everyone else did so as well. We watched the high wire family group, and as the lights went down after the performances, I felt Jerry get really close. All of a sudden, he gave me the tenderest kiss. I realized the house lights were still off, but a very large round spotlight was suddenly on us for all to see. I did enjoy that, of course, and he bought me a chameleon that changed colors to go on my blouse. Play that scene back again!

Learning to Drive
By V.M. Wood of Plattsburg, Missouri
Born 1927

In 1947, I was 20 years old and soon to be married. I went to apply for my driver's license. Our plan was to drive to North Carolina, have a reception, and then spend our honeymoon at a cabin named Burnstead. I believe license cost one dollar back then. Since our wedding was only a week off, I signed my license with what my new name would be. I don't remember them asking me any questions and there was no training.

We also had a plan B. My husband was in Sea Bees and was out on the ship when his mother, Zula Iris Wood died at age 38. The Red Cross was to get in touch with him, but that didn't happen. He did not find out till March when he went home. She died December 18th, and they held her body until Christmas day. They could not wait any longer. There were three siblings younger than he was, so I agreed that if he got a job in Arkansas in a week then we would stay in Arkansas. We ended back up in Kansas after six months. I renewed my driver's license each year by taking the bus downtown. The only driving I did was doing was backing out the cars we had that we were selling to the end of the drive. Basically, I could start the car and put the car in drive.

When my third son was about three, he got sick. He was burning up with a fever and was very sick. The bus ran by the hour, so I decided I would drive him to the doctor. It was starting to snow, and my dad went along. He had already had a couple of strokes but he could move. The doctor was about six miles away and I was terrified. My son had an ear infection and got a shot. We all made it home safely. I did not intend to drive ever again! A week later, another son was sick. Back we went to the doctor! Very shortly after that, my mom was in the hospital. I drove my youngest son to my sister-in-laws and to the hospital to check on Mom. After that, I had taught myself how to drive. I was driving!

When we moved from Kansas to Missouri, I took my first driving test. My husband had told me the year the boys got ill that we were not paying for the fee to renew the license anymore. We did make it to North Carolina when our youngest son went to Knoxville, Tennessee for a playoff ballgame. I had an aunt in Chimney Rock, and I wanted her to meet my prince. We drove down to meet another aunt and to the church were some relatives are buried in Mill Springs. We spent one night in Chimney Rock. The cabin named Burnstead burned down, so he did not get to see it.

My husband died at age 56. The lord blessed me, and believe it or not, I am still driving around in town at almost 86 years old—if my car runs!

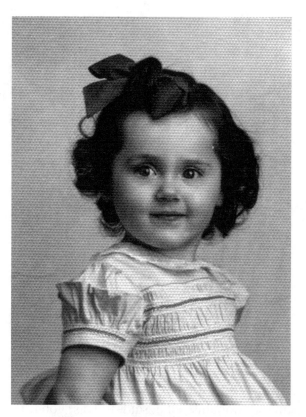
Virginia (Letzig) Miller at age 2

Home Life in the 1940s and 1950s
By Virginia Miller of Richmond, Missouri
Born 1941

I was born at home in 1941 on a farm five and a half miles north of Hardin, Missouri. As a small child, we had kerosene lamps, then carbide lights, and finally electricity. Our home was heated with wood and coal, and then finally propane gas. We did not have running water until the 1950s. We carried buckets of water for cooking, drinking, laundry, and bathing. I can remember an old icebox we put milk, eggs, butter, and meat in. It was cooled by a large block of ice that we purchased in town at the icehouse. Oh yes; we had a cellar (everyone did) which was in the ground. We stored our canned good, eggs, potatoes, carrots, turnips, and fresh fruit. It was "creepy" and also had snakes and lizards in it, which I dearly hated. We used the cellar to take shelter in during the bad storms and cyclones (now called tornados). My Mother canned our fresh garden vegetables and some meat products (sausage, ribs, fish, etc.). We, like everyone else, had an outhouse. Our toilet paper was usually an old catalog or newspaper and was they ever harsh!

At Christmastime, my parents and I would load up in our Chevrolet two-ton pickup and go to Kansas City to the Montgomery Ward store on Chouteau Street. It was always a real treat to go, as the store was decorated up so pretty and Santa was there, too. I would sit on his lap and tell him what I most wanted for Christmas. On the way out of the store, we stopped and got either cotton candy or a red candied apple. Oh, what a treat! My parents bought their only deep freeze there, a chest type. It lasted over 60 years. You won't find any appliances today that will last that long. Once in a while, we would catch a commuter train to Kansas City called the Doodle Bug. It ran from Moberly, Missouri to Kansas City, Missouri and stopped at every train station between. It had an engine, a freight car, and two passenger cars. It was usually full. Seven days a week, it would go to Kansas City in the morning and back to Moberly in the evening. It was always a real treat to get to ride to Kansas City to shop for the day and then ride back home.

Hardin was a very busy small town when I was young. There were three churches, Methodist, Baptist, and Christian. In the late 1940s, the Assembly of God Church was established. They had church in a tent first and then built a church building. There were two railroad tracks that ran through town. The Wabash tracks ran on the south side of town and the Santa Fe tracks were the north tracks and had a train station. There were four grocery stores—Dan and Claude Myers Store, Underwood Grocery, Clyde Stratton, J.K. Summer Grocery, and Georgie Mae Wilson Grocery and Soda Fountain. There were two banks—Hardin Building and Loan, ran by Allen Rhodes and the Hardin State Bank, which was run by the Bond Family after the Great Depression.

The Tinsley Hotel was located on First Street, which is on the south side of the north railroad tracks. Mrs. Tabler rented out rooms in her home located on Main Street. There were two barbershops in town. One was beside the Tabler Boarding Home and was run by Dick and Red Smith and later by Sneak Halterman. The barbershop had a pool hall in it also. The other barbershop was on East Elm Street and was run by Boyd Myers and Mr. Godsey. In the 1950s, it was turned into a clock and jewelry shop that was run by H.H. Walker. There was a lumberyard run by Ed Chase and Dan Stratton. Harrison Lumber burned out in the big fire in 1938. There were a couple of drug stores—Brown's Drugs and Lucy William's Drug Store. It was at Lucy's that I first received mills in the change I got back when I got an ice cream cone. We had three doctors in town—Dr. Grimes, Dr. Reed, and Dr. Bittiker. The Howell Shoe and Repair Store was later run by Jake Grove. We had Tablers Café on the east side of the square. Walls Produce with fresh eggs, chicken feed, and other supplies was run by Bill Wall. Reds Dry Goods with a walk through into Underwood Grocery. On the south side of the square was Ray-Carroll Elevator run by Bob Carter, the icehouse was run by Clint and Lewis Harlin and Bartlett Elevator (formally Seward Elevator) which went broke during the Great Depression. On the west side of the square was a Case-Oliver Dealership run by Herbert Wilson and Art Socheck with Jerry

Kist as the head mechanic. On the north side of the same building was a car repair shop run by Fred Summers and Glenn Lynn. The Odeon Theatre showed the silent movies and then the talkies. There was a blacksmith shop that was later run by Walt Hesterburg. A funeral home was located in the home of John W. Knipschild on Parkway. In the 1950's a home was bought on West Elm Street and made into the funeral home. It was later run by Gus Borcherding. There was a Chevrolet Dealership on Elm Street owned by Bill Ferguson. Bill's son-in-law Virgil Shirkey was the head salesman and always drove the nicest car in town. In the early 1950s, Virgil built a soft serve ice cream shop. There were a couple of beauty shops in town. One was run by the Palmer sisters, Gladys and Dorothy, and the other by Lilly Brown. She later sold to Jessie May Lydia Mason. The (party-line) telephone office was run by Mrs. Patton and later by Sadie Oster Clemens and her teenage daughter, Elizabeth Oster McGraw. If you wanted to know what was going on in town you could just stop by the telephone office and they could clue you in on the latest happenings. Wilmer Sadler opened a TV shop in the late 1940s or early 1950s. It was then sold to Beverly Myers, and his main helper was Dorsey Lentz.

Virgil Boggess had a full service gas station in town and Jake Stratton only sold

Don and Virginia (Letzig) Miller in 1912

383

gas. There were three stations on the outskirts of town on Highway 10. There was the Standard Oil Station with gas and oil only. It was later sold to Mattie Blankenship who tore the old station down and built a new station. It is still in operation today and run by Mattie's sons Danny, Gary, and Stanley Blankenship. The Paul Stewart station was at the corner of Highway 10 and Highway A and a mile west of town was the Lentz Brothers Station. It was also a full service station. We had a cleaning shop run by Louise Grimes who later sold it to Jimmy George. It closed in the 1950s. The dentist in town was Dr. Wallace. Mr. Z.A. Berry had a confectionary shop, and there was also a bowling alley beside the Odeon Theatre. On the north side of the Santa Fe railroad tracks was Hales Farmers Exchange. He sold eggs, feed, and other items. The livestock and chicken feed came in pretty printed cotton feed sacks, and I loved to go with my Dad to get feed and pick out enough of the same pattern on the sacks to make a new blouse or dress. There was a furniture store run by Mr. and Mrs. Knipschild, and you could even go there to pick out your casket.

Our school was at the east end of Elm Street and was a three-story brick building with the gym on the top floor. In 1954, a new school was built on the corner of Northeast First Street and Highway 10. It is still in operation today and has approximately 250 students. The Hardin Journal was the newspaper for the town. It was run by Howard Rhodes and later by Lee Meador until it ceased publication. On the south edge of town Robert Letzig ran a dairy and sold and delivered milk, cream, butter, fruit juices, and other items. Ed Summers also sold dairy products and delivered in town. He lived a couple of miles east of Hardin on Highway 10. I am sure I have missed some businesses that were in operation in the 1940s and 1950s.

Hardin sets in the Missouri River Bottoms and has seen its fair share of floods. There were two major floods. During the 1951 flood, water flooded from the bluff at Lexington to the bluff north of Hardin. In 1993 the levees started breaking up closer to Kansas City, letting walls of water out headed east. By the time it got to Hardin, the pressure was very great and it washed out half or more of the Hardin Cemetery. Caskets were floating for miles east of Hardin and also skeletons

that were in the old wooden boxes. It was a very sad thing because we expect our loved ones to stay put once they are buried. It took many hours and lots of manpower trying to find and relocate each and every casket or corpse. Some were never found.

Today Hardin is struggling to stay alive just like every small town. There are several businesses still in operation, Farmers and Merchants Bank, the Post Office, SeAirLan World Tours run by Jim and Sharon Strain, Ray Carroll County Grain Growers, the biggest business In town, Herring Carpet and Floor Covering, Missouri River Flood Plain Antique Store, Thurman Funeral Home, Hardin City Hall, and Hardin Fire Department, and a car wash, a laundry mat, and RV campground that are run by Jason Raasch are all located in town. On Highway 10 is Blankenship Service Station, MFA Propane, Hardin Mini Mart run by Debbie Rodgers, and Luff's Welding Shop, run by Bill Luff.

Roller Skating and a Hardworking Grandpa
By Terry Barnett of Plattsburg, Missouri
Born 1953

My birthday was a month before school was out. I received a pair of roller skates that clamped onto my shoes and a key to hang around my neck. When I first started skating, Mom would walk me down the side walk and then back up the side walk, time after time. On one trip, she took me down, and then left me. I was on my own to learn how to skate. After I was good on the skates, my most daring feat was Power House Hill. We had spotters watching at the bottom of the hill, and down I went. What a ride! Halfway down, a bearing went out of one of the wheels. The ride was then like a car with a flat tire, and my foot was shaking violently. Sometime later, Mom and I were at an old neighbor's house and he was repacking the wheel on the skate and telling her he had never seen this happen before, I was probably in my forties before I confessed.

Family called him, Pap, I called him Grandpa. I was number 28 of 33 first cousins. My grandfather died at 92 when I was only eleven years old. I remember what he looked like. He was short and wore boots that came up to his knees. We would be in the car, and he would come from his garden with a handful of cherry tomatoes for us. My parents would take my grandparents to the city to get groceries, and we would sit in the car with Dad while Mom went inside with Grandma and Grandpa. Grandpa always came out first with a box of crackers and a box of chocolate covered cherries. We would get one of each. I was learning to knit, and I made a pair of slippers for my grandfather for his birthday. My dad said it was okay to give them to him, but that I should not mention that it was for his birthday because he did not take it very well.

Years later, an uncle shared with me that his love for foxhunting came from my grandpa. He went on to share that when my grandpa went out of town to go foxhunting, he would walk his dogs out with his fox horn over his shoulder. As he walked down the middle of the road and not a sign of a dog anywhere, he would pick up the cow horn and do a blast on it. Then, all the dogs would come from every direction and go walking beside him. One at a time, they would start wandering off again. The process continued until they made it out into the countryside.

Another person who shared about my grandfather was a man in his nineties. I met him in a nursing home, and he shared that he worked on the same farm as my grandfather, as hired hands. He and other young bucks (as he called himself) were to work a field with my grandfather. At that time, my grandfather was an old man, so the young bucks decided they were going to prove just how old this man was. They started working across the field, and he described that and he and the other young bucks worked hard all day trying to keep up with this old man. They could not come close to catching him all day! They were a bunch of tired young bucks at the end of that day. He said that he never lost respect for that old man, my grandfather.

Hang On
By Neva Lyons of St. Joseph, Missouri
Born 1931

In October 1919, my mother and dad drove to Santa Ana, California from St. Joseph, Missouri to be married. There were only dirt roads to drive on and sometimes you

Neva's parents, Eldora Evelyn and Alvin Franklin Howard in 1919

had to make your own.

Dad bought a new model T Ford and they were well on their way until as they approached a bridge two robbers were hiding under the bridge. Dad stopped at the top of the hill and told mom to hang on, he raced across the bridge and left the robbers in the dust, and they made the rest of the trip fine.

When they were to come back dad took the car to be washed, as he was standing in front of the hotel a man came up and asked dad if he would sell the car. He sold the car and they came back on the train.

Mother passed away in 1957 and dad in 1961, but he talked about this trip so many times!

Neva's parents, Eldora Evelyn and Alvin Franklin Howard in 1919

Coast Down the Hill
By Sylvia Sweeney of Bethany, Missouri
Born 1912

My memories go quite a ways back as I was born on December 1, 1912. I think this memory was about 1918 or 1919.

I don't know if other people had antifreeze for their cars or not but we didn't. My dad would heat a kettle of water and fill the radiator we would be ready and we would climb into the model T and go to Lone Rock Church, he would park just over the turn of the hill and drain the radiator so it wouldn't freeze while we were in church. When church was over we would all get back in the car dad would release the brake and we would coast down the hill and part way up the next one then he would turn the key the motor would start and up over the next one, that way we would make it home without the motor getting too hot.

The church is still standing next to the Payne Cemetery about 5 or 6 miles north and East of Hatfield in Harrison County Missouri.

Stand Up or Get Shot
By Maxine Pew of St. Joseph, Missouri
Born 1923

My early years were during the depression, but we lived on a farm, where my dad worked by the month and mother could raise all the garden she wanted, and believe it or not many homeowners wouldn't let you have a garden spot.

Our meat was also furnished, so we would have a butchering day and all neighbors would come to help. Women and kids came too and every woman brought a dish and we all had a lovely meal, and fun!

Mother canned the meat and dad knew how to cure the hams and they were delicious. This cellar also had folding cots, a lamp, jars for mother, Minnie Hilchcock, matches to light lamp, and an axe.

Mother was so afraid of storms, so she would say, "Grab a blanket" and we all went running to the cellar, until the storm was over. Several times, we would share it with a neighbor who would get caught in a storm before getting home.

I remember one time mother woke dad,

Frank Messner up and said there was someone all hunkered down out by the clothes line pole and he got his gun and went to the door and said "Stand up or get shot" and when no one moved he shot and it turned out to be our little red wagon.

I was always afraid of my shadow, so just at bedtime mother would go to the outhouse with us and I would run as fast as I could to get back to the house, and the chamber pot was always there if needed at night.

I lost my baby brother Bobby Messner when he was 2 years old, I was 5. Then in later years, I lost another brother, Charles "Bud" Messner due to a tractor accident. That was so hard for all of us.

Three Real Dolls
By Betty Reavis of Kansas City, Missouri
Born 1934

I came into this world on May 2, 1934 in rural Buchanan County, Missouri to join my parents, two brothers, and two sisters. We were a very poor family by today's standards. My father was a tenant farmer, and did not own his own land, which meant that we usually moved each spring to a different farm.

My earliest memory of the first time we moved to another farm was basically over the top of the ridge in a steel-wheeled wagon pulled by our two workhorses containing all of our furniture to a new home, which consisted of four rooms.

I didn't know we were poor because everyone else was in the same boat. Most little girls had a doll to play with- I had a baby lamb, which I fed on a bottle and adored. My family lived in this house until 1941- we raised our own meat, veggies, eggs, milk etc. canned on a wood cook stove and were very happy. There was no electricity, running water or indoor plumbing. This all changed June 18, 1941 when my father told me and my younger brother Joe that we were to go to the Johnson house (neighbor) and stay until he came to get us. It was Mulberry time so we spent the day in the trees with the neighbor boys eating mulberries. My father came after us late in the evening to take us home to see our new triplet baby sisters. We got a small peek and to see our mom for a minute before we were put in the wagon and taken to my granny's house to stay for one month. My mother almost died with this birthing without any prenatal care but came through in flying colors.

Upon returning home, I was introduced to diaper duty on a washboard and tub. I got the great opportunity to play with three real dolls instead of my lamb which was long gone by now!

Who Ruined All Those Melons
By Marolynn Shafer of Waukee, Iowa
Born 1926

I was born on a farm east of Mill Grove, Missouri in 1926 the youngest of fourteen children; all were married except three of us.

We had to walk wherever we wanted to go. We did have a pony named Beauty and had a buggy that she pulled and that's how we went to church but mother drove.

If we rode her and she saw a car she would throw us and then run home. If she showed up without us the folks knew to come looking for us. One time a car popped over a hill and my sister and I were thrown off her shoulder blade hurt her real bad. There were two well dressed men in suits and they wanted to take us home but we refused. We had been taught never to get into a car with anyone, especially strangers.

One day my sister, who was four years older than me, and I decided to walk to our older sisters farm which was several miles away. When we were half way to her house my sister invariably had to go to the toilet. There was a culvert close by so she decided to go in it. Lo and behold it was crammed full of watermelons. She couldn't figure why they were in there. We proceeded to burst every one of them and ate our fill of the middle parts.

Many years later when we were both married I was visiting her house and we were reminiscing about our younger days. One of us mentioned about the watermelon episode, her husband was listening and the funniest look came on his face and he said we've wondered all these years who had ruined all those melons.

He and three of his buddies had raided a farmer's patch and hid them in the culvert with the intention of getting them the next night. All these years we've wondered who on earth found them and done such a trick.

All Day to do the Wash
By Lorena Stevens of Fairfax, Missouri
Born 1928

I'll start my story in the 1934 time frame. My folks moved from Agency, Missouri to a farm in Atchison, County. I had to walk or ride my horse to school one and a half miles from home. We had no running water and as most places a privy out back. When it snowed, the path was usually crooked, so a few accidents happened along the way. Of course, I watched for snakes, used old catalogs for paper, and of course, the softest sheets were used first. A chamber pot was used often.

I had several teachers in a one-room schoolhouse. Some I liked better than others. Of course, there were older boys in school, and were usually doing things to cause trouble. One teacher made the whole school stay in when the boys caused trouble.

In the summer, the washtub would be put out in the sun to warm for baths.

Mom washed clothes using a washboard, and it took about all day to do the wash. She helped my dad do field work. When I was too young to stay by myself, they wound a tarp over a wagon and parked it at the end of the field. When I was old enough to stay by myself, I'd do some of the cooking for lunch and dinner. We always had a big garden, and homemade bread.

I wore flour sack clothes mom made. Store bought bread was a luxury. High school was not too eventful. We either walked or rode a horse the two and half miles to the highway to get on the bus.

I had a room in town where I stayed if the roads and weather was good.

Church was in the country about a half mile from home. Saturday night was usually a trip to town. If I was lucky, I'd get a nickel or dime to spend. There was a movie house but rarely had the money to go. Time passed and I married a wonderful man we had four children that have turned out to be great adults.

I'm a widow now as I end this chapter in my life.

Spelling Bee
By Athel McIntosh of Lebanon, Missouri
Born 1930

I attended a country school for the first eight grades; we would look forward to Friday afternoon when the last period we "ciphered," had a geography contest or spelling bee. It was a small school, at one time we had three boys and two girls, the memory I want to share is a spelling bee we had one Friday when some of our graduated pupils came back to visit. We were having a spelling bee, so they joined in. We were rather nervous having to compete with high school students. We did it "railroad" fashion most of the time but this time words were pronounced by the teacher. If the first person could not spell the word, they were out and the word passed to the next in line. I was in 4th grade. The teacher gave the word "quail" when there were two of the high school students and I left to spell. I couldn't believe it when the other two were down and it was my turn. I spelled the word correctly and won the spelling bee!

When I finished 8th grade at my country school I joined the other 8th graders at Princeton to take our 8th grade exams. If we passed, we would go on to high school. I was very nervous about going on the school bus for 20 miles to such a big school compared to our country school. I met some girls that day that are still my friends some 70 years later. A few weeks later we were all back at Princeton for our 8th grade graduation, May 5, 1944. It

was a special occasion; mother made me a new dress to wear. As we were going into the church where the ceremony was held we had snow flurries! When we got inside, I was told to sit on the front row. Then they announced that Paul Minshall had the highest test score in the county so he was valedictorian. Frena Golden and I scored the same so she was second and I was third since her name came before mine alphabetically. They went on to announce the remaining of who made up the 10 highest scores. I was so surprised and stumbled when I went up to receive my diploma. I felt embarrassed to be so clumsy. It was one of those unforgettable events in my life.

A Snake in Each Hand
By Martha Smith of Rock Port, Missouri
Born 1933

My family lived on what was referred to as Ranch 14. There were a lot of outbuildings so we had lots of places to play. We had chickens and my sisters and I had to gather the eggs. The rooster was mean and always chased us and flogged us so we really didn't like to do it. One day my sister Lucille went to gather the eggs and the rooster started after her, she picked up a piece of wood and hit him on the side of the head and he went staggering off. He was still mean so one day mom fixed him for dinner.

I was the youngest of 5 children with 2 older brothers and 2 older sisters.

We went to school at South York in Atchison County Missouri. I started to school when I was 5 years old and we had to walk a mile and a half to school in the mud and snow. I don't remember the mud so much but the snow would drift and was hard for a 5 year old to wade through. Sometimes my oldest brother would carry me home on his back and my mother would tell him not to do that to make me walk.

We usually played and had fun on the way to and from school. It was a one room school on the side of a hill with all eight grades in the one room. There were two outhouses, boys and girls, some swings and things and a grove of trees toward the bottom of the hill where we sometimes played.

One day after our brothers had gone on

Athel's friends in front of Princeton High School

to high school my sisters and I were about a quarter of a mile from school and an older neighbor boy came out from a ditch, he had a snake in each hand and chased us almost to school. The snakes were probably dead and maybe two feet long, but to me they were at least 5 feet long and I was scared to death.

When I was in 3rd grade, we moved up by Westboro, Missouri still in Atchison County and attended Moulton School. It was another one room school with all 8 grades. There were close to 30 kids going there. We had to walk 2 miles to school and sometimes we would ride a horse but he didn't like bridges and we had to cross the Tarkio River twice to get to school and we would have to get off and push and pull him across the bridges. His name was Chuck and he was red colored, chubby and stubborn. It was almost as easy to just walk.

Running From a Game Warden
By Bill Prindle of Buckner, Missouri

My brother and I tagged along with my older brother and his friend driving through the country road hunting rabbits. Ever so often, we would stop and shoot rabbits. We ran on to a place we called Rabbit Town where someone had dozed up a bunch of brush piles. We saw rabbits everywhere. We decided not to stop because the road was slick and we had a steep hill to climb, so we decided to turn around and head back where we come from.

Just as we started to turn around, we saw the game warden coming. We took off because we knew he had heard us shooting. He kept following us. We could only go so fast because of the slick roads. He couldn't gain on us either.

The reasons, and there were many, why we were running was:
1. We had no hunting license
2. We had the trunk full of rabbits, squirrels and quails
3. The squirrels and quail were out of season
4. We were over the quota of rabbits
5. We couldn't have paid the fine and we would have to go to jail

My brother knew if we got on the highway, we wouldn't be able to out run the game warden. He had a new '55 Ford and my brother had a

'53 Plymouth. We didn't stand a chance of out running him.

So we stayed on the country road and came upon an old side road that had been closed. The weeds were higher than our heads.

The game warden was still hot on our heels as we topped over the hill, we could see that at the bottom of the road the bridge was out. There was nothing to do but try to jump. Luckily, the ditch wasn't that deep. As the car dived off where the bridge was supposed to be, I saw the dirt on the floor boards come up as high as the dash. Luckily, the car came up on the other side and we were in the clear.

We ran on home, got rid of all our game, and waited for the game warden. We knew he had passed our house many times and knew my brother's car. He never came.

My brother's friend was in town the next day and saw the game warden's car at the Ford dealer's being work on. His car didn't make it across.

It was a good thing the Plymouth had a real short body and the warden's vehicle had a long body that is why he wrecked his car.

A few weeks later my brother was sitting at a little country store having a Pepsi. When he looked out the window, he saw the game warden drive up.

When he came in the store, my brother thought he had had it, but the game warden just looked at him and grinned. Whew!

A Barrel of Mischief
By Esther Dauma of Kansas City, Missouri
Born 1944

Growing up on a farm long before cell phones, tweets, and video games was a very different world. After several hours of daily farm chores, it was up to my younger brother, Ernie, and me to provide our own entertainment. The best entertainment involved some degree of mischief.

The farmhouse sat atop a very high hill and was surrounded by other steep hills. The hills were great for sledding, or just lying down and rolling all the way to the bottom.

One memory that does stand out from the rest involves a 55-gallon metal barrel that became a source of fun for Ernie and me. We had used the barrel in various ways. We sat astraddle the barrel when it was on its side and pretended it was a horse. We jumped over it. We rolled it around with the dog inside. We bounced balls off the barrel.

But one exciting day, I had another idea. I thought it would be fun to roll the barrel down one of the steepest hills with me inside it. So, we pushed and rolled the barrel to the hilltop, I got into the barrel and had Ernie give the barrel a big push. The ride down would be a thrill. What I didn't consider was that a small creek ran at the bottom of the hill with some mid-sized willows growing along the creek.

My 11 year old body was literally stuffed into the barrel. Ernie said I'd get stuck. Though it was a tight fit, on the LONG ride to the bottom of the hill, my head was slamming into the side of the barrel. The top edge of the barrel had a sharp metal rim, which inflicted cuts as the barrel careened down the hill.

After what seemed an hour of being slammed and cut, the barrel crashed into a willow tree and into the creek. Ernie ran down the hill as fast as his 7 year old legs would carry him screaming, "Are you alright?"

With creek water flowing into the barrel I managed to extricate myself by pulling on the willow before Ernie reached me. I was wet, cut, bloody, bruised, but an imp on my shoulder immediately decided that I should not be the only one to partake in this adventure. With much effort, due to the pain level, I convinced Ernie that all that red stuff covering me was rust from the barrel, not blood, and that the ride down the hill was great fun. Ernie remained skeptical even while we rolled and pushed the barrel back to the hilltop. He made it clear he did not want to ride the barrel down the hill as I had.

I convinced him to get inside the barrel to see how well he fit. As soon as he got inside, I shoved the barrel and it began its rapid descent down the hill with Ernie screaming and crying all the way down.

As soon as I shoved though, panic set in. What if he were to get hurt?

Then it was my turn to run down the hill screaming, "Are you alright?"

I helped him out of the barrel, and moved it out of the creek so it didn't look so bad and with my crying little brother, went up the hill to the house and mom's wrath.

He told mom the whole sordid story and she sent me out to find the appropriate switch for my punishment. As much trouble as I was

in, a bit more didn't matter. I went on a lengthy journey out of sight into the timber to find an "easy" switch. It took over an hour and I was hoping with every breath that mom would forget. But, of course, she didn't. However, my choice of a switch was excellent. It was a long, dead woody stick, which broke into many pieces with the first swat, but I acted as if I were mortally wounded.

The day of the barrel ended with an attempt at a well-deserved switching, and dad got rid of the barrel so the little imp on my shoulder could not tempt me again.

To this day, I love roller coasters, Ernie however does not.

Ill Fated Odds
By Lois Prindle of Jameson, Missouri

My father-in-laws dad, Alva, was born in 1887. He only had one sister Goldia born in 1896.

At the age of 9, his father died with appendicitis. His mother took his sister leaving him to live with his uncle to be raised.

Goldia got married in 1921 to a fine young man. Paul was a thrifty energetic farmer and a dealer of real estate.

They had one little daughter, Gwendon.

Gwendon Shaffer

390

Paul and Goldie Shaffer
They were killed in a train accident

One time Alva was riding in the country with Paul, when they came to a railroad crossing, Paul just ran across the tracks not looking one way or the other as if they weren't even there.

Alva got on to him about not stopping; Paul just quoted the odds of a train being there. The next day Paul, his wife and 5 year old daughter was going with his friend, wife, and young son on a trip to Colorado on some business venture.

They were tragically killed at a railroad crossing at Kearney, Missouri.

The two children were the only survivors. Goldia was killed on the cow catcher with her daughter in her arms. Her daughter didn't have a scratch on her.

Walking Through Gumbo
By Ruby Allen of Weston, Missouri
Born 1925

My first memory, when I was five years old, was my grandmother's death. Friends and family would come and sit up all night with my dead grandma, I couldn't understand why. She was dead. Some of the family brought her body in a casket to the house. There weren't any flowers on her casket. It was spring and the lilacs were in full bloom. My father went outside and picked a big bouquet. He put them in a fruit jar with water and placed on her casket. The whole house smelled of the lilacs. To this day, I can't stand their smell.

We moved to another small town about five miles north when I was eight. Our school was out in the country and my sisters and brother and I had to walk through gumbo (which is mud). My brother was in the eighth grade and he loved to hunt. The day before school, he went hunting and got mixed up with a skunk. He went to school the next day smelling very bad. The teacher sent him home to change clothes. He also went hunting for some birds. He killed some blackbirds. Mom told him if he cleaned them, she would cook them. He took one bite of one and that was the end of blackbird hunting.

While we lived in this town, my parents bought us a wagon. I was standing up in the wagon and I fell out and broke my arm. My mother scolded me but she took me to a doctor and I had to have a cast.

My father was a railroad worker and he was the lowest in seniority so we had to move often. I went to three different schools in one year. I hated the last school I went to. We were very poor and I had to wear black socks with the holes in the heel. Some boys made fun of me.

While we lived in this last town, my father would make grape wine. My sisters and I would sneak down in the cellar and drink some. It was lucky we never got caught.

When I was in the third grade, we moved south of St. Joseph to a small town. I made friends there and was happy. One of my sisters and I were playing outside with some kittens we had acquired. My sister was holding a kitten and took it over to a well that you had to pull water up with a rope. The kitten scratched her and she dropped it in the well. Some neighbors helped get the kitten out, and he was still alive. They also took all the water out of the well. She really got in trouble.

We always had plenty to eat. It consisted mostly of chicken, which my mother raised. We also had navy beans, fried potatoes, and homemade bread. My mother made bread every day.

In the spring, my dad would take us younger children down to the railroad tracks and we would pick a bushel of nettles. My mother would cook them with some bacon. We would have them along with boiled eggs. My sister and I would go to the woods and pick wild strawberries. My mother would make a cobbler out of them, which everyone enjoyed.

Because my father was a railroad man, we burned railroad ties. I can remember the stove getting red hot. I have often remarked that God was looking down on us because the stove got so hot, and the house didn't burn down.

My parents were very good to us at Christmas. Dad would take me to the woods and we would cut down a cedar tree. We decorated it with strings of popcorn and round rings made out of art paper. Our treats were orange slices and chocolate covered cherries. I was very disappointed when I found out who was Santa.

We took a bath once a week. My mother would heat a big pail of water on the old wood stove. We had a big oval tub. My older sisters would bathe first and then us younger ones.

I believe my childhood made me a stronger person as I grew older. I dedicate this to my dear mother, Anna Mae.

Which Paddle Would Be Used
By Diana Arn of Savannah, Missouri
Born 1947

Back in the '50s and early '60s the phrase, "spare the rod, spoil the child" was followed not only at home, but at school as well. According to my husband, Duane, at Lafayette High School the vice-principal administered the discipline to the boys. He had three different size wooden paddles. The student got to choose which paddle would be used. The smaller paddle meant more swats. But if the larger paddle was chosen, knowing it was less swats, it seemed "Old man Hoehn," as he was referred to, although he was only in his 30's at the time, really laid into it!

The boys had to bend over the vice principal's desk and the swats were delivered to the boy's bottom. The larger paddle would raise you off the floor, and bring tears to your eyes, according to Duane. The boy's got to put their names on the paddle that was used on them, and Duane said he had his name on all

three.

I guess Duane thought he deserved the swats, or at least he held no grudge, as he asked to have his picture taken with the vice principal at the Class of 61's 50th reunion. And I guess the vice principal liked Duane too as he came to see him at the funeral home when Duane passed away last year.

A Very Real Castle
By Lu Durham of Dearborn, Missouri
Born 1920

Her name was Cousin Hattie and she and her older sister, Cousin Sally, lived in the last house down our side street, which was a dead end. A gate there opened into a pasture. A smaller gate on the other side of the side street opened into a magic world for me. Cousin Hattie was the cook and housekeeper and my savior.

My mother has told me how I would escape her care, run down our side of the dead end street calling "Hattie! Hattie! Come and get me!"

Cousin Hattie would open her gate and call "Run, Lula Margaret! Run!"

Inside her gate, I was safe. A narrow sidewalk led from the front gate to the front door of their spotless home. The door opened into the parlor and in the parlor was a player piano! How I did perform! I was a concert pianist, entertaining a huge audience, which was very appreciative of my efforts.

I realize now that the rooms were quite small, but at the age of about five, I felt those rooms formed a castle for me, a castle still visible in my mind some ninety years later.

At the south wall of the parlor were two doors. The door on the left opened into their guest bedroom, which was just big enough to hold an iron bed and a washstand. A white counterpane covered the feather mattress, making the bed so high that I couldn't see how anyone could climb into it.

The other door in the south wall of the parlor opened onto a stairway that led to cousin Sally's bedroom, the only upstairs room. It was a long room, between dormer windows on the north and south. I was up there only once when Cousin Sally sent me to get something for her.

A third opening from the parlor led to the

dining room, the biggest room in the house. It was where they spent their evenings, and it was the only room that was heated. Rocking chairs were gathered around the wood burning heating stove. In one corner was a round dining table and rather uncomfortable straight back chairs. There was a large opening on the north side of the room. A heavy curtain could be pulled across the opening to close off the bed and dresser, which made up Cousin Hattie's room.

The dining room was a special spot because it was where we played games. My favorite game consisted of using the Sears/Roebuck or Montgomery Ward Catalog. Cousin Hattie and I would sit on the floor with the catalog between us and take turns closing our eyes and pointing to something on a page. Whoever got the most expensive item won! After I learned to add, I would keep score. Such simple things entertained us.

An opening by the heating stove led to another stove, the cooking stove in the kitchen. It was a big black thing with all sorts of doors and lids: a place for the fire, a well for hot water, a big oven, a warming oven, and burners. Cooking on that stove was like being captain on a ship and oh the smell! Can there be anything more enticing than bread baking? It was here that cousin Hattie was in charge, cooking, baking, and preserving.

The kitchen cabinet was another object of interest. There was a tall door where the flour bin could dispense sifted flour if you turned a small crank. A hard surface shelf about the middle of the cabinet was the spot where Cousin Hattie made up the dough for her bread. Shelves above that held ingredients needed in cooking- spices, etc. But my favorite ingredient and one I'm afraid I let it be known that I really liked bars of chocolate.

A kitchen table with an oilcloth cover was where I sat to share a meal with them. It also was the place where coal-oil lamps were cleaned. Having no electricity, the house at night depended on these lamps to dispel the darkness.

On the south side of the house there was a screened in porch. Doors from the dining room and the kitchen gave access to the porch where there were washtubs, a row of chairs, and all kinds of potted plants, the water bucket, and dipper.

Not only did I know the inside of that house, but I also was allowed to explore outside. There was a boardwalk from the porch to the garden, and along one side of the walk were the rain barrel, cave, outhouse, shed, chicken yard, and barn.

The cave (we called ours the cellar) was opened by what looked like a door in the ground. Steps led down to a long room with a brick floor, shelves along both sides, and an arched ceiling of bricks. No matter how hot it was outside it was cool down there, and that's where they stored apples, fresh vegetables, and all sorts of canned products: preserves, canned vegetables, and meat and their milk and butter. There was a lamp down there so that even when the door was closed we were not in the dark, although eerie shadows filled the cave.

Cousin Sally was the local postmaster. She always dressed in black, black shirt, long black skirt, black shoes, and stockings, and she always carried a black umbrella. They never owned a car and Cousin Sally walked to and from the post office, and came home for lunch. At the end of the day when she came home she liked to have toast and milk. I was allowed to go to the cave, ladle milk from a big crock into a tin can whose edges had been hammered smooth and bring it and a crock of butter to the kitchen. The cave was their refrigerator and the milk in that can was always cold. Cousin Hattie would take a thick slice of bread from the warming oven spread it with butter and place it on the table for cousin Sally who would then change her clothes and head outside to milk the cow and do whatever needed to be done.

The outhouse was also of great interest to me because we had indoor plumbing. I was always afraid of outside toilets as that seemed to be the favorite place for wasps to build nests, but no wasp would dare to build a nest where Cousin Sally was in charge.

Next along the boardwalk was a shed where meat was hung to cure. Their father lived on a farm just south of town where pigs and cows were butchered and the meat preserved by rubbing a mixture of salt and sugar and pepper into the flesh of the hams and shoulders. Then they were wrapped in heavy paper and put in canvas sacks and suspended from the rafters to cure.

The last building was a small barn where Cousin Sally milked and fed their cow, which had spent the day in the pasture back of our house. Behind the barn was the fenced in chicken yard where Cousin Hattie fed and watered the chickens and gathered the eggs. Water had to be carried from a well in the corner of their yard.

From the barn to a creek was the garden where Cousin Sally raised the vegetables that Cousin Hattie preserved and stored in the cellar.

Don't you agree that all this made up a very real castle?

Much to my regret I outgrew my need for Cousin Hattie, and I'm afraid she never knew how precious the time was that I spent with her.

The Outhouse Diary
By Kay Jean Pierpoint of Platte City,
Missouri
Born 1938

My sister and I often stayed with our grandparents, Perry and Anna Boswell, during the forties. The school bus driver or hack driver as they were sometimes called would let us off at their farmhouse. The house they lived in between New Point and Oregon, Missouri in Holt County was built by my grandpa with his brother's help. He was a hunter and trapper and often went coon hunting at night with his hounds. He had a red fox stole made for my grandma. The stole was lifelike with a head, tail, and four claw feet. In winter, he would chase me and my sister around the house with that red fox stole. Grandma would finally say, "Perry put that thing away!" I don't remember grandma ever wearing the stole.

Without TV, we made our own entertainment. Grandma and we girls would make cookies, candy, or doughnuts in the evenings. Grandpa would smoke his pipe and listen to the radio. Later my sister and I would sleep on a feathered mattress in an unheated bedroom. A chamber pot was placed in the room for our convenience. Otherwise, we would have had to make a trip to the outhouse in the cold.

The outhouse was an important structure on the farm. My grandparents had to build a new one in later years, which became known as "The Outhouse Diary." Grandma would

The old outhouse

write on the outhouse walls about daily happenings and family celebrations, which can still be read today. The Sears Roebuck Catalog could often be found in the outhouse for reading and for another functional purpose if needed.

Grandma would get up early and fire up the cook stove using corncobs and wood. That stove heated water, cooked meals, and heated the house. Before they had running water in the house, they had a pump outside in the back yard, which provided water. In the early morning hours while grandma was preparing breakfast, they would plan their day's work activities together.

Grandpa and grandma lived off the farm from food they produced. Grandma raised chickens for eggs and meat and grandpa raised hogs and cattle. They always had a big garden and an orchard. Before she had a deep freeze, grandma would can meat in jars. They would collect walnuts from the trees in the fall. To get the outer shell off the walnuts, grandpa would run over them in the barn with his truck. Later, he would pick the meat out of the shells on winter evenings so grandma could make her wonderful divinity and fudge candy.

Before grandma had a refrigerator, she had an icebox. In Oregon, they bought a large block of ice and put it in the icebox. How long the ice lasted would depend on the temperature and how often the icebox was opened. Even when they purchased a refrigerator, grandma still referred to it as an icebox.

Before air conditioning, I can remember my grandparents sitting outside on those warm summer evenings under the large maple tree in the back yard. Grandma had a long bench-like worktable against that tree. Grandpa's rocking chair and other mismatched chairs were also placed under the tree. They used the table for eating and preparing vegetables and fruit for canning, and the chairs were for visitors who often stopped to pass the time.

Family reunions were sometimes held under grandma's whitewashed locust trees between the driveway and the east side of the house in the summertime. The Boswells were wonderful cooks and they enjoyed the fellowship of family at these gatherings. My family lived a little over a mile from my grandparents. By 1960 or 1961, my sister and I were both married. It was Christmas and the roads were impassable due to a large snowstorm. Grandma was so disappointed that no one could get to their house because of the snow packed roads. She had been preparing food for days. My dad hitched up a team of horses to a beautiful red bobsled he had recently purchased and away all nine of us went through the fields to my grandparent's house.

Above all, the indelible memories of my grandparents are precious because they genuinely enjoyed each other, their family, and the simple pleasures in life.

Snow on the Bed
By Donald Daugherty of Rock Port, Missouri
Born 1943

My name is Donald Daugherty, I was born December 5, 1943, and I grew up in the small town of Phelps City, Missouri. The population in 1950 was 139, and in 2010 the population was 24. The flood of 2011 was the end of my hometown. The population in 2012 is 0.

My first memories are just playing with other kids in town. The schoolhouse was a two story built out of wood but only the first floor was used for the classroom. Grades one through eight, I remember my dad taking me to school for the first time. I was five and had never been left anywhere by dad or mom. It was a shock when dad left me there, and I didn't like it, so I took off and beat him home. When he got home he just took me back to school. He told me it was the law and I couldn't go with him during the day anymore.

At school the teacher, Mrs. Thompson, would lead us in the pledge of allegiance to the flag, then she would check each one of us to see if we had brushed our teeth, washed our face, our hands and behind our ears. If you were clean you got a good mark on your line if not you got a bad mark. I didn't know at the time she was teaching us about hygiene.

Then she would have each grade, one at a time, come to the front of the room and she would teach reading, writing and arithmetic and history. Each was a separate trip up front for each grade. When you weren't up front you were to be working on your last assignment.

There were two outhouses on the back line of the schoolyard one for the boys and one for the girls. We all had outhouses at home so that was no big deal. The whole town was poor but as kids we didn't know that. Nobody had indoor plumbing, but some did have a pitcher pump in the kitchen for water. Most were outside, and in the wintertime you had to make sure it was drained after each use or it would freeze and break. You also had to leave enough water to prime the pump the next time.

The winters were the worst time of year, the houses didn't have insulation and were not built that tight, when the first wind driven snow fell I would wake up with snow on the bed, and we would have to stuff rags in the cracks.

The heat was a wood burning stove, and it would go out at night, and it would be freezing in the house, and in the morning the water bucket would freeze solid. Once the heating stove got going it warmed up pretty fast. Mom's cook stove was wood also, and when it got going it was real warm in there. The house was only two rooms, and on the flip side of winter summer left much to be desired.

The wood cook stove made it almost unbearable in the house and we didn't even have a fan, so we spent most of the summer outside. After the supper meal was cooked, the coals and ashes would be taken out so the house could cool to the outside temperature, and we still stayed outside as long as possible.

The town had a small grocery store, that also sold gasoline from a hand pump that filled a glass tank on the top of it, and then into the car. Minnie Wells owned the store and would make sandwiches for men that worked on the farms around town. I remember the pop was always cold from the water cooler and cost five cents. The store also had one of the two telephones in town.

The railroad split the town and my mom would hate it when the train came through and its black smoke on washday and the clothes on the line. The town had a depot on the main line and a cattle pen and elevator on the sidetrack, and a post office across the road from the depot. The farmers would drive their cattle through town to the rail pens and load them on the trains. I always liked to watch that.

We had a lady postmaster she lived just across the street from us. She would put the outgoing mail in a canvas bag with a lock on it, and take it over to the railroad and climb up and hang it on the pole. When the train came by it would hook that bag, and throw out the bag of mail for us. The boys in town, me included, would race to get the mailbag and take it to her, because the one that got it she would give a candy bar. I remember one day one boy said, "I'm getting it today for sure" he had it for a while, but he tried to catch it in the air. By the time he could get up and go I was eating my candy bar. The guys on the trains knew how poor we were, they would throw coal off in the winter and ice in the summer. We picked up the coal for the heating stove and the ice for the ice box.

It was a great day when a guy showed up with a gas cook stove and an electric refrigerator. I remember mom telling him he has the wrong house. He said, "Is this Bill Daugherty's house?" She said yes, "Well, he bought these, and told me to deliver them and hook them up." I think that is about the time we got a radio because dad liked to listen to boxing and have some beer. Dad would make home brew, and would fill the bottles and would let me cap them. I loved being with my dad, but I never did like home brew. One time dad bottled a batch too green, and the bottles started to blow up. We were having supper and heard pop, pop, dad jumped up and grabbed the bottle opener and said "son, go get the neighbors" it was a good time in the old town that night.

Another thing that happened about this time, we were going to one of mom's brothers or sisters I don't remember which one, she was one of fifteen. I always had a rope and was roping things just as we were going to leave I roped mom's pet goose, it didn't like it and I pulled a little hard and broke its neck. The trip was called off, and I was in trouble, and mom was picking her pet goose.

Dad worked as the saw man at Stiver's saw mill in Brownville, Nebraska. This was in 1952 and dad had the mumps and they went down on him, he was in bad shape and the county said they was told to get everybody off the bottom it was going to flood. Dad's friends at work come and moved us to Brownville they even had to carry dad he was too bad to walk. We moved back home after about six weeks, being a kid I didn't know how bad things were, but they were bad. Having been through them as a man I now know how bad.

Dad was back at work and things were getting better. By the end of 1952 dad bought a TV and we were the place to be in town our house was like a movie house dad put the TV up high so no matter where you sit you could see it. The teacher got all us kids together at our house to watch Eisenhower sworn in as president.

My favorite thing to do was fish. I had a piece of string, a hook, and an old tap for a weight. I would dig some worms for bait and I'm off. I fished at a place called the willow patch; it was a place on a drainage ditch my uncle dug extra deep and wide when he dredged the ditch. I would just cut a good willow for a pole and start fishing. It was always fun and it seemed like the fish were always biting.

When I was thirteen I went to work on the saw mill for my dad and uncle, Dale, my dad's brother. I would sight the log and catch the slab and carry it to the slab pile, and be back to catch the next one. When all the slabs were off, and the log was square, then the boards would come off. They had to be carried to the right pile and stacked tight. If there was no lumber to saw I would go to work for my uncle Ralph, my mom's brother. He had a corn sheller and trucks and did custom shelling and hulling for farmers. I would scoop ear corn for him.

Back to the saw mill, I remember every time uncle Dale would pay me he would say you make sure you get your dad to pay his half, and you buy land don't chase girls. Two things I never did get the half from dad, and I don't own any land. Uncle Dale gave me good advice, but at fifteen I didn't listen, land was $50 to $125 per acre on that old bottom, who wants that? Now it's selling for $6,000 to $12,000 per acre dumb kid anyway.

My uncle Dale died when I was fifteen, he was only forty six years old, and colon cancer took him fast. The mill had to be sold to cover all the bills. Dad bought two trucks and him and I cut and hulled logs to a mill in Brownville. We would hull two loads of logs each and every day. We did this till I turned sixteen, I wasn't paid, but I had a place to live and food to eat so that was all right. But when I turned sixteen I wanted a car and some money to run on. I found a job at a nursery in Hamburg, Iowa. I bought and paid for a car. I was still living at home, so I was paying mom and dad to live there. I got a job helping build grain storage, it paid better so I went to work there.

When I was seventeen my best friend and I were out on a Saturday night in his '57 Chevy, it was foggy, and we crashed. We were lucky we lived. He was not hurt bad but I was laid up for six months. The next spring I met my one and only love, I was eighteen, and we were married two months after I turned nineteen. February 13, 2013 makes fifty years with my love and the only woman that would put up with some of the things I have done. I love her more every day.

Large Dust Storm Coming
By Iona D. Coult of Chillicothe, Missouri
Born 1927

It was a hot, dry, summer day, July 30, 1927, when I was born at Ames, Nebraska. My parents were John Cummings from Ireland (illegally we later were told), and Lena Isabelle

Oliver, John, Lena, and Iona in 1940

Stone Larkins Cummings. We lived on a farm (rented), no electricity, telephone, bathroom, or modern conveniences. Our neighbor had either homesteaded or been brought as children to America from Europe. They spoke broken English, but had many characteristics of European culture- children were loved but made to mind adults with respect- seen but not heard. I learned early to mind. They were all good, happy, people, and very helpful. The women were good cooks and household managers, and the men worked hard and made home brew. They all seemed to enjoy life.

I was raised with a half-brother, Johnny, 16 years older, half-sister Clara 13 years older, and Raymond 4 ½ years older. My parents were married in 1919 after mother's first husband died.

I started school in rural District 30 at age 5 on July 30th that year. We had eight grades taught by one teacher, and she also did all the janitor work, making fires in a large belly stove with wood etc. In winter, I wore long underwear and long stockings to keep warm. We rode a pony in the spring and fall and had shaded areas to tie up with water troughs and hay. It was about four miles and in winter either my dad or a neighbor hitched to a wagon, took my brother and I, and picked up children along the way. He would take a cream can of drinking water to the school, and it would freeze on top in cold weather. We had straw to sit on and an old buffalo skin to cover up. My half-sister, and half-brother finished at a different school and Clara went to high school in a town, but had to pay tuition. She stayed about ten miles from our farm and did housework for room and board.

We had a metal cyclone shelter halfway in ground at our school and were taught to lay flat in a ditch if a cyclone overtook us going home.

One summer day, after we had a rural telephone, probably ten or twelve on line, we received an emergency call. This was long continuous rings and all got on the line. There was a large dust storm coming from the north. My mother and sister hurried stuffing dishtowels and old cloth in cracks of the windows, and we ran to a deep cellar. I remember tumbleweeds came first and then the sky turned dark and we closed the cellar doors. The noise was great and after it passed, we tried to open the doors but dirt had blown against them and it took all our strength to push out. Dirt was piled two feet high around the kitchen door, and it had sifted in all the cracks in spite of the towels.

We had a picnic at the end of school in May. Mothers brought food and young children, dads were working in the fields, and I always remember older eighth grade girls taking us on a teeter-totter and we played other games. I uncovered pennies in a sand pile and would take them home and play same way. Money was so scarce so to have four pennies was so great.

We moved to Missouri in 1937 after the drought and grasshoppers hit us in 1935 and 1936. It was different as roads were muddy and had to leave car a half mile from farm and walk in. Missouri had been settled earlier and it seemed like every ten miles was a little town, and people in our community were related through marriage etc. Everyone seemed to have large families. Customs were different but people were nice. Farming was

Iona and Raymond in 1934

behind.

We finally had a gas engine wringer washer and only eight people on rural telephone line. My mother made my clothes out of old things given to her. Now I marvel how well she sewed, cooked and cleaned, as she had lived in an old covered wagon and travelled never having any land or home. She attended to third grade in school but taught herself to write and read.

Missouri had mills for tax and we used them to purchase anything- we had green, red, even cardboard tokens. They finally did away with this and had a state income tax.

I graduated at fifteen in May 1943. World War II had started when I was a junior in high school. I took the civil services test and finally assigned to Quartermaster Depot in Kansas City. Women had taken men's jobs when the war was going on. It was so devastating and everything seemed to be rationed. We had coupons for sugar, shoes, gas etc. We were so poor it was hard to get to town, our car was old, and there was hardly any gas. During the war, everyone seemed to prosper more. I still wore feed sack clothes even to Business College later.

We got to see "Gone with the Wind" at a movie theatre, previously we would watch outdoors at the schoolhouse in summer, and we sat on the grass. We later called this our outdoor theatre. They hung sheets from the second story and showed the picture.

They later got electricity on the farm, and it was difficult to pay the minimum, we only had a light bulb in the center of the living room, and very few wall plugs.

I was married in 1947 and my husband helped wire my parents' home and we were able to buy them a refrigerator the first year they had electricity. They cost about $150. We were married in March and my husband had returned to meat cutter at the A&P. Then he and another friend bought a restaurant and we run it until my second son was born.

We had four children and saved and sent all of them through high school and the boys all went to college. Our daughter was the youngest and did not want to go. My second son had attended one year at the University and then his draft number was close; since my oldest son was drafted, he enlisted. It was so terrifying having one son near the Russian border and the other son in Vietnam. Our second was killed in Vietnam, and after forty years, it is still so hard to recall.

We had bought a house with a G.I. Loan at 4% and as children were born, added on and remodeled. We played lots of cards and many games. Both sons now have masters and special degrees. They taught math and since computers came in my eldest son retired as computer programmer at a bank. He then was asked to teach because of the shortage of math teachers. He had taught math both in high school and university so he had degrees. Now he subs some and volunteers in the sports department. He prefers not working too much.

My father never received his U.S. Citizenship. It was not important in 1900 when he came and only during World War II, they checked on him and in 1960 final visit to farm the Feds casually stated his records would probably get lost in files.

My mother and father were such true Americans and taught their children to love and appreciate this country.

I am now almost 86 years old, live alone in the same house my husband and I bought in 1950 and still using rotary dial phone.

I have seen land homesteaded and people earn their citizenship, the dust storm through Nebraska and Kansas, World War II and men going to the moon. Having lived and worked 53 years and raised four children, so happy to be in the USA.

Joe Town
By Shirley Peterson of Shelbyville, Texas
Born 1946

I was born and spent the major part of my growing up years in the worst neighborhood my town had to offer, Florence Addition. A town that thrived and grew due to the large number of packing plants located there. I remember Swift, Seitz, Armour, and Dugdale without even thinking. My hometown was a trading post in the early days when the pioneers were heading west in hopes of brighter horizons. The town that hails as "Where the Pony Express started and Jesse James ended" is my hometown. Yes, my hometown, St. Joseph, Missouri or "Joe Town" as locals sometimes call it is where most of my memories have been made.

I recall the large railroad yards and have often missed the fact that we always had to wait for the long trains to pass before we could get to our destinations. The numerous and colorful cars of various types cannot be forgotten and always the thrill of the caboose and knowing the reward for waiting would be the waves from the crewmen on board- quite a thrill for an impatient youngster. The whistle and racket of the trains passing over the tracks is a sound my mind can still hear. The clang and clatter as the cars of the train were disconnected and switched to another rail and the cars reconnected. We knew the trains carried nearly everything that was needed into our town and everything manufactured there to other destinations.

Should I tell you about the time a bear escaped from the circus at the Fair Grounds on 6th and Atchison Streets? The radio announced that the bear was loose and could be in the proximity of our neighborhood so to be on the watch. My girlfriend from next door was sitting on my porch with me and we weren't supposed to leave the porch. We saw her two older brothers going to the outhouse, yes, we still used them, and they acted very afraid so we both got a stick and went quietly behind the outhouse and started scratching and growling! Those boys may have been her bigger brothers but they didn't act like it then, they went running out of the outhouse with their pants down screaming! We were both laughing, but not for long. Our mothers didn't find our prank as funny as we did.

One of the memories that bothers me still is the one related to the segregation of the schools. The school bus picked me and my fellow students from our neighborhood up down on the corner from my house. There were some "colored" children in our neighborhood who rode the same bus but they went to another school, which was for "colored" kids only.

They were not allowed to sit on the bus-they had to stand in the aisles. The "white" children got onto the bus first and sat in the seats but the other children had to stand. Even as a child I thought this was unfair and unjust as there were plenty of empty seats. I devised a plan to correct the situation. I got on the bus and went straight to the backbench seat. I sat on one side of it and then told some of the "colored" girls to sit beside me. They said they couldn't because they would get in trouble. I told them the bus driver couldn't see back there if they sat in the middle because all the kids standing in the aisle would block his view! I finally convinced them to sit beside me! So actually, we made our own statement before Rosa Parks was heard of. The bus would stop and let them off by what used to be Ozenberger Ice Cream on King Hill and Lake Avenues and they walked up the hill to their school. I often wonder if those girls remember that and the girl who convinced them to sit instead of stand.

One of my fondest memories was of Lake Contrary Amusement Park. I didn't get to go many places or do many things but once a year my dad's employer, Dugdale Packing Plant, hosted an Employee picnic there. It was a huge thing in my eyes. There was a picnic area at the amusement park where they had covered shelters and Dugdales had Robidoux Hotel cater the event. They had a vast array of foods, things this little girl had never seen or tasted before. They also had big tanks full of iced down soda pop of all flavors and beer for the adults. It was an all you can eat and drink affair and we got the privilege of riding all the rides at the park for free and that was unlimited times. I can still see many of them in my mind, the "shoot the shoot," where it was like a boat ride that shot down into water and everyone got splashed, the "Giant Dipper," a huge wicked wooden roller coaster, and my all time favorite, The Carousel, or what is better known as the Merry Go Round. I loved

it and it was always hard to make a selection of which steed you would ride this time. You may get on one and the spot a better one up ahead. It was so colorful and the horses had real horsehair tails. I always had to have one that went up and down on the pole and not a stationary one. It was sad to see the demise of the amusement park due to numerous times it was flooded and the age and failing health of the owners.

One of the strangest things to those that knew me then was the religious upbringing I had. I was raised, but no longer follow the beliefs of a Jehovah Witness and that caused troubles at school because I could not salute the flag by placing my hand on my heart when we stood each morning for the Pledge of Allegiance. I could not take part in Valentines exchanges or in any Christmas celebrations. Every year when we returned to school after Christmas vacation the teachers would have us take turns standing and tell what we got for Christmas. I would say I didn't get anything and the other kids made fun of me and said I was a liar so I devised my own plans. The next time I got something new prior to Christmas I did not wear it, new shoes, a dress or whatever and then I wore it the first day back to school and when it was my turn I said I got that for Christmas and I didn't feel I was lying because I did, I gave it to myself for Christmas.

When I was in first grade, the teacher was telling the class about Santa Claus and I raised my hand and when she called on me I said, "You are not telling the truth because there is no Santa Claus." She came to me, slapped me in the face, and took me into the hall and made me stand in the coat closet. I was only doing what I had been told. When I told my mother about it, she said the Bible says you should "turn the other cheek." She did not contact the teacher about it or the school.

St. Joseph, Missouri had many factories as well as the packing plants. There were sewing factories such as Nelly Don Garment Co., Big Smith, and H.D. Lee. Driving along Frederick Ave. around 23rd St. or on 11th St. south of Mitchell one could inhale the wonderful aroma of fresh baked bread when you passed by the Rainbow bakery or the Wonder Bread Company. Travelers in the north portion of the city got the aroma of fresh brew when they were in the area of Pearl Brewery.

Salesmen used to go door to door bringing

variety to the lives of the stay at home moms. There were the Watkins, Rawleigh, L.B. Price companies as well as the local milkman and the huckster who sold his homegrown produce from the back of his truck. As a youngster, I was always inspired by an older gentleman named "Joe" who was an L.B. Price representative. He always brought me Tootsie Rolls, I hated them but he never knew, and he called me The Tootsie Roll Kid. He always talked about Russia and how the United States wasn't very smart. He said everything we do is supposed to be top secret but we print it in the paper and put it on the news. "Don't they know those Russians can read?" he would say.

When I was a teenager, I always went to the local mom and pop grocery near our home. An older couple ran it and lived upstairs. I spent a lot of time visiting them. The gentleman told me that one of these days there would be no more stores like theirs. He said some big company will come and give everyone better prices than the smaller operations could afford to do. They would gradually force all the smaller operations to close and then they could raise their prices and charge the people whatever they wanted because there would be no places to shop other than there. I didn't fully understand what he was talking about but now I see what he meant with the influx of big corporations such as Wal-Mart.

My memories of the "good old days" are a menagerie to me. I need someone to weave me a memory keeper like they do to for the Indian Dream Catchers; only mine will have to be much bigger and stronger as to hold a heavy load. I am always just one-step away from memory lane- maybe I should write a book and have you join me on my memory trip by reading it.

Party Line Cure
By Georgia Corbin of Bethany, Missouri
Born 1944

My grandparents, Elmer and Georgie Tipton, lived on a farm northwest of Lucerne, Missouri. My mother, Hildred, told me that when she was quite young, she jumped out of the hayloft and ran a rusty nail that was on a board into her foot. She said she suffered, so she couldn't sleep at night. In those days, they didn't go to the doctor often. Grandma

was on a telephone party line with a total of eight people. She was talking with a friend about the problem, and someone interrupted and told Grandma to follow a cow around and get some fresh manure. They told her to make a poultice out of that hot manure, put it in a white cloth, and tie it around Mom's foot. Mom said that is what Grandma did. She slept for the first time in a while. The next morning, it was all puckered up and white. The manure had drawn out the infection and it was on its way to healing.

Grandpa's First Car
By Julie Coffman of Gallatin, Missouri
Born 1969

My paternal grandfather, or Grandpa as I called him, was born in Lorado, Missouri in 1913. His name was Hayden Coffman. He was born into a prosperous farming family along with his brothers Herb and Floyd and his sister Ethel. Like many folks of Grandpa's generation, his family lost everything in the Great Depression. However, they survived! The story of Grandpa's first car speaks as a testament to the resourcefulness, fortitude, and the ability of the human spirit to soar in times of adversity.

When Grandpa was in his late teens, he couldn't afford a car. As chance would have it, while walking down a dirt road one day, he spotted an abandoned car in a ditch. What a car it must have been! It was a Ford Model-T from the 1920s. As was typical of the times, cars were often abandoned when a tire was blown. To make matters more interesting, the serial number had been filed off, indicating that the car probably had been stolen. Luckily, for my grandpa, he was able to walk home and bring back a team of horses to pull the car out of the ditch. For this trying feat, Grandpa enlisted the help of his two buddies, "Timer" and "Straight-Edge." Grandpa and his pals successfully pulled the Model-T from the ditch and towed it home.

The three of them set about making minor repairs, and soon the car was in working order. They just didn't know what to do with the blown out tire! Grandpa had little to no money to buy a tire. Well, Grandpa's dad (my great-grandfather) had an idea. He gave Grandpa some molasses that he had made to take to town and sell so that he could buy a tire. It must have been pretty darn good molasses because Grandpa came home with four tires! Grandpa eventually parted with his treasure and lived until the age of 84. Although he's been gone for almost 20 years, he continues to live in the hearts and memories of those who loved him.

The War Days
By Donna J. Perry of Helena, Missouri
Born 1933

The memories I have elected to write are about the World War II years. I remember the day of the attack on Pearl Harbor on December 7, 1941. We had moved from Helena, Missouri in November of 1941 to Oakland, California. I was eight years old. On the day of the attack, my uncle wanted to go to San Francisco and the Pacific Ocean. It took a little coaxing from Mother to have me stand in front of the waves for a picture. I still have the pictures. They are dated December 7, 1941.

Upon our return to Oakland, paperboys were everywhere selling papers. They would yell, "Extra! Extra! Read all about it!" My uncle decided to stop and buy a paper. It was hard to believe that such a horrible thing had happened. When we moved to Oakland, I remember beautiful Christmas decorations and cartoon characters in stove windows. Then, a cloud of darkness covered the city. Air raid wardens were assigned to specific

Donna and a sailor boy in 1941

blocks. Sometimes at night, we heard the drone of a plane. During the war years, my daddy worked as a stevedore, walking and unloading troop ships. Mother worked at a Caterpillar plant making parts for the war.

I have the autograph of a Japanese schoolmate. One day, she was no longer at school. In later years, I learned that Japanese people were located elsewhere at that time. I also remember the war rationing stamps on meat, sugar, and shoes. Mother gave blood as much as she could give. I have her pin that she received for doing that for the soldiers. Her brother was drafted at 18 years old. He served for four years and I still have his discharge papers.

We came back to Missouri shortly before the war was over. Mother and Daddy are gone now, as are my uncle and aunt. I'm the only one left to share some of my childhood experiences with my children, grandchildren, and great-grandchildren.

My Family's Start in Missouri
By Virginia Luikart of St. Joseph, Missouri
Born 1921

My story is about my family coming from Germany to settle on a farm in the Marian Township, just two and a half miles from the town of Cosby in Andrew County,

Donna Jean Perry in 1941

Missouri. My grandfather was William Christian Frederick Garbe. He came from Salghemenandant, Germany near Hannover in 1853 with his widowed mother, Charlotte Licki Garbe. He was given 20 acres from his stepfather as his mother remarried and then he bought 220 acres of hill and bottomland. He built fences, a well, planted fence hedgerows, and built a barn, granary, and many outbuildings. There were no power tools, so he did everything by hand. He was a part of the starting of the German Evangelical Church. His family and all of my sisters and brothers were baptized in the church. Our family is buried in the church cemetery. My grandfather helped to start the first school at the edge of the property. I attended the eight month, one-room school. Our teachers were close friends of the church or community. They had finished high school and had some summer instruction to become teachers. In the Depression years, a crude oil pipeline was laid the full length of the farm. It is still there today, and is maintained by an inspector.

In 1921, the farmers agreed to have the Platte River dredged. My parents said it was done that very summer that I was born. The river rarely spills out anymore. The first house the family lived in was a log cabin. In 1979, the house was built, and my father was the first child born in it. I was born at home in the same house, as was my daughter in 1943. My family had an interest in the telephone company, and that was installed in later years. A dozen families were on one line. There were series of long and short rings to identify who the phone call was for. We could listen in on other calls on the party line, though.

My sister Leatha learned to drive on a Model-T Ford. She bought her license at the barbershop in Cosby for 25 cents and drove until she was too old to drive. She wanted to drive to high school, as it was two and a half miles from our home. All the roads were muddy, but the wheels would go in most type of weather.

Making Soap and Picking Corn
By Beverley (Barton) Slemp of Fairfax,
Missouri
Born 1928

I grew up when we didn't have any electricity. I was born on July 25, 1928. My mother would make her own soap out of grease cracklings and several other items in a large, black kettle. We took a bath every Saturday night, all year long. Mother always had a large garden and canned a lot of vegetables in the summer. It was so hot, and she used her cook stove in the kitchen to can the vegetables. We had an outhouse and chamber pots. We used a Sears and Roebuck catalog in the outdoor toilet. There were always a lot of hollyhocks around the outhouse.

We had a party line phone on the wall, and our phone number was 2712—a long and two shorts. Mother always had a lot of chickens for eggs, and a lot of fried chicken in the summertime. It sure was good! Our radio had batteries, and I remember Mother listening to Stella Dallas every afternoon at 1:30 P.M. we listened to the Grand Ole Opry on Saturday evenings, too, from the station in Nashville, Tennessee. I and my two brothers went to a country school, which was a mile and a half from where we lived. There was one teacher for all eight grades. It was fun, too, especially at recess time. We all took our lunches in brown paper bags.

I fully remember when World War II started on Sunday, December 7, 1941. We got home from church, turned on the radio, and heard the news. The Depression years were bad, but we always had enough to eat. In 1935/1936, we had strong wind and sandstorms. The sand came in all around the windowsills and doors. I know my mother would get so tired of cleaning it up. I used to help my dad pick corn on Saturdays with a team of horses and a wagon. He milked two cows each evening and morning. He raised sheep, hogs, and cattle. Mother always made all my clothes until I got in high school and later. Most of them were made out of the real pretty feed sacks and flour sacks.

One-room Schools and Box Suppers
By Lucille Fletcher of Trenton, Missouri
Born 1925

I will write a couple things that I remember about my early rural school days. I lived in the country, and we moved quite often. I had many good friends and memories. The rural schools I attended were Union, Dunlap, Center Union, Grundy Center, and Mt. Pleasant. Later, I did attend one year at Central School in Trenton for the ninth grade and attended three years at Trenton High School, which is now the Adams Park Apartments. The teachers I had at the different schools were Evelyn Grubb, Elizabeth Shields, Willa Perry (Fulkerson), Irene McHargue, Rosella Dumbler, Marjorie Whan, Lorene Utterback, Louise Brassfield, and Linus Dowell. I will not attempt to name all of the children who attended school with us, but I will name my sisters and brothers who attended school. They were Mildred Chambers, Letha Mae Chambers, Eugene Chambers, and I, Lucille Chambers.

As rural children, we walked about one mile usually to school and carried our lunches to school in tin buckets, usually old syrup buckets. Before we ate lunch, we washed our hands with an older child pouring water over our hands. Some of the games we played were tag, marbles, races, hide and seek, Fox and Geese, Handy-over, teeter-totter, and swings. The schools sometimes had box suppers. The older girls brought decorated boxes and the boys and men bought them. When the program was over, the couples enjoyed their meal together. The schools received the money, and school supplies were purchased for the school. We always had Christmas programs and last day of school programs. The children would memorize plays, songs, and poems for the programs.

I remember sometimes when we had three or four children on our family, sometimes we had soup beans, which our mother cooked and they were kept warm in a wood stove that had a metal jacket around it. One thing we really enjoyed was in the winter, Mother would mix a little sugar with some milk, and then we would add snow. We really enjoyed the ice cream! As we became older, we helped with farm chores before and after school. The jobs we did were milking cows and feeding pigs and sheep. I remember one year, we had geese to feed, and sometimes we had guineas and ducks.

Neighbors Helping Neighbors to Harvest Oats
By Marjorie J. Roush of Pickering, Missouri
Born 1936

When the oats were ripe and ready to be harvested, the farmers used a binder to cut the grain. They then bundled it up and tied it with

Marjorie's grandpa, Luther Amos Pistole working the fields

heavy twine. After several bundles had been collected, a lever was tripped, and the bundles dropped in one place. Then, the farmer and his family worked together to prop the bundles together to form a small teepee. This helped to dry the oats and make it easier for the men with pitchforks to throw the bundles of oats on a hayrack. When the threshing machine arrived, the neighbors brought their grain wagons, scoops, hayracks, and pitchforks.

It was quite a chore arranging the tables and chairs the day before in the living room. That is where the men would eat. Some of the neighbor women helped with the meals. All the pies had to be made the day before so the oven could be used to cook other food the next day. Since there wasn't enough room for the men to wash up in the kitchen sink, a stool was carried outside with a wash pan and soap on it for the men to wash their hands. There was a tank of rainwater next to the house, so all they needed to do was to wash up in that and use a towel to dry off. The men had to take turns eating since there wasn't enough room for all the men to sit down and eat at the same time. Usually the men that helped with the threshing machine ate first so they would have time to check and oil the machine and make sure it was in good working order. They just needed to make sure that it was ready to go by the time the other men returned from eating their meals.

Every detail back then was important. A farmer couldn't get in a hurry, or he might miss seeing a problem that might cause a serious accident. As the men sat down in their chairs, they could smell the aroma of the delicious meal awaiting their tired, hungry bodies. All of their aches and pains were forgotten as the food was passed from one to the other. For a while, all you could hear

404

is their forks hitting their plates as the food is devoured. Sitting back in their chairs, they joked and waited patiently for the pie to be served. After eating their pie, they longed to stay longer at the table, but they knew other men were out in the hot sun. They rose from their chairs to join their comrades in the field.

After the last man left for the hayfield, the ladies headed for a chair to rest their tired, aching feet. They had been on their feet all morning as well, and it felt so good just to relax a bit before they went back into the hot kitchen to fill their own plates. There would be time enough later on to clean up the kitchen and wash the dishes, but right then, they were going to eat!

Grandma's Washday
By Patsy Pendergraph of Lee's Summit, Missouri
Born 1941

My paternal Grandma was born in 1888 and died in 1963.

Grandma had hollyhocks, marigolds and zinnias in her vegetable garden, one pink rosebush on the fence by the road and peonies at the front of her house. Her clothesline ran beside the garden.

On Washday, Grandma pulled, tugged and rolled the wringer wash machine from the back room to the middle of the kitchen floor. She heated wash water outside to almost boiling in a big aluminum tub sitting on cinder blocks over an open fire. Two people carried the steamy tub of hot water in, pouring half in the wringer washer. Cold water added to the other half left in the tub for rinse water was placed next to the wringer part of the washing machine.

She plugged the electric cord in the overhead light socket, added some Oxydol washing powder and Clorox until she was satisfied with the amount of suds. Sheets and pillowcases were washed first followed by the rest of the white clothes. Light colored next, and then Grandpa's blue overalls. The washing machine agitator mixed the clothes back and forth, until Grandma pulled the lever stopping the movement.

After shaking several drops of Mrs. Stewart's Liquid Bluing in the rinse water, she swished the water with her hand to mix it. Turning the small knob on the wringer set the two rollers in motion as she pulled the clothes out of the machine with her smooth wooden stick. The water was too hot, even for her work-toughened hands, as she held the steamy clothes to the wringer; Grandma pushed another lever swinging the wringer around to the edge of the rinse tub and doused the clothes up and down in the bluing rinse water to remove the soapsuds. Then she fed the clothes through the ringer again, letting them drop into the oilcloth lined bushel clothesbasket.

After throwing in another load of clothes, she tied the clothes pin bag filled with clothes pins around her waist, hefted the basket of heavy wet clothes to her hip and carried it out to the clothesline, the wonderful clean, fresh smell competing with the garden flowers.

Back inside, she poured Faultless Starch powder from the blue box into a pan of hot water boiling on the bottle gas stove, adjusting the flame and stirring until smooth and thick. Shirts, dresses, aprons, doilies, dresser scarves, pillowcases and tablecloths were starched.

Later in the day she brought in the stiff and dry clothes from the clothesline-some were folded and put away, others were sprinkled with the aluminum topped, sprinkler water bottle, rolled up, placed in the clothes basket, covered with a towel to be ironed the next day.

When the water was drained out of the rinse water tub, a bucketful was saved to mop the floor with the rag mop (a long wooden stick handle with a spring-wire head holding an old rag from a worn our garment). As I grew older, Grandma let me mop the linoleum floor of the kitchen and front room. I liked to help her and I loved to make things clean and shiny.

Fun with my Siblings
By Dorothy Mattox of Cameron, Missouri
Born 1929

I read this at my brother's 90th birthday party on September 16 2012. These stores are about part of my childhood. When this started, I was about eight years old. Jewell was about 14. The other two boys, Loren and Darrell were 13 and 12. There were seven of us—

five boys and two girls. The oldest was my sister. I am the youngest. I don't remember my two older brothers or my sister living at home. We lived on a 400-acre farm. The day my dad brought the tractor home, at least ten neighbors, men and women, came to look at it. They voiced their opinion at how foolish he was to spend all that money on a tractor. We have always been a close family. There are only three of us left—Dean, Jewell, and myself. That is why I started this story the way I did.

When we were growing up, we were not allowed to say the word "ain't." My dad was very conscious that we use proper English. Every meal that we had at home was on a white linen tablecloth. The boys and girls wore proper attire. No hats were allowed to be worn in the house. We did not know there was a Depression going on. We thought we were living a normal life, and we were.

Jewell liked to keep busy and tried to keep us three younger ones busy as well. He told us to clean the workshop, then the yard, then make this, and build that! We had a pony, Sparky. That pony would either go like the wind or wouldn't move one-step. This one day, we were going to build a pony cart. The wheels were old buggy wheels. He built a box, put a box on top with a lid, and sat on the lid. We put our picnic lunch in the box and drove off into the woods. When we got to our destination, we ate our lunch. It was butter, sugar, and cinnamon sandwiches.

On a cold winter day, we gathered at the shop to build a toboggan sled. It was streamlined! It had long steel strips on the runners to make it go fast. Five of us got on that sled from the barn to the creek. It was about six blocks downhill with lots of snow and lots of fun!

Our parents took Brother Dean back to Virginia for his next assignment in the Navy. Jewell was in charge of doing chores, cooking, getting us off to school, etc. What a deal this was! We had no groceries. Dad took our only car, but Jewell had a plan. He got grain out of the grain shed, washed the wheat, dried it in the oven; ground it up in the antique coffee grinder that was sitting on the top shelf on display. He cooked the wheat and lo and behold, we had cream of wheat! We ate that three times in one day.

Walking home from the country school that we attended, we were always so hungry, just starved! We put our books on the dining room table and looked over at the secretary with a glass door. Sitting on the shelf on my mother's best pink glass cake plate was a big plate of fudge, cut perfectly into square pieces. They were oozing with black walnuts, just waiting for us. However, the door was locked! Darrell scooted the secretary away from the wall and tried to pry the back off. That didn't work. If we were to break the glass door, our mother would not have believed that it would have been an accident, so we decided against it. We just gave up and ate a peanut butter and jelly sandwich…again.

A few years later, Jewel got a job in Kansas City working for the railroad. I went to visit him right before school started. He took me school shopping, and we bought a coat, shoes, and slacks. Slacks were in style right then, and I would be the only person to have some. Absolutely no one had them back where I lived. He also bought me a sterling silver bracelet. I knew that no one would have that either. What a way to start the new school year! Oh, happy day!

Remembering Grandpa and Grandma Swofford
By Frances J. Heman of Green Castle, Missouri
Born 1937

There were things that were very nice about overnights at my grandparents, like Grandma's cooking; the big featherbed you could sink out of sight in, sitting on Grandpa's lap, and listening to the pocket watch in his overall pockets. I remember listening to Grandpa singing "The Preacher and the Bear" and enjoyed the tales he would tell.

There were also things that were not so nice, like the big pictures on the walls of stern-looking ancestors that seemed to watch every move you made, the mount of a large deer with huge antlers that you had to pass by on the way to bed, and the fear of the bee stings from Grandpa's bees. If we got stung, Grandpa chewed up some tobacco and put a wad of it over the stung area. Then, Grandma would tie a rag over it. Yuck!

I liked to be at Grandma's on washday. Her washing machine didn't have a gasoline engine like Mom's. It just had a lever to push back and forth to stir the clothes. We kids liked to help with that. When there was a supply of cream, Grandma would put it in a daisy churn, hand it to Grandpa, and say, "Dad, I'm going to 'let' you churn." He always had a reply about how nice of her to "let" him do it. We kids would turn the handle for a while. It was sure more fun than shaking a quart jar to bring butter. We didn't have a regular churn, and Mom would give us a couple of jars to shake. Grandma's bread was so good. It had a special yeasty taste that I just loved. She mixed it in a big old wooden bowl. When I was about 16, I went over to watch how she made the bread and get the recipe. It turned out that there was no recipe. I just wrote "about a cup" and before I could even write it down, she'd grab a handful or so of something else and toss it in so quickly that I couldn't see how much went in. what I wrote was good reading, but sure didn't make good bread—absolutely nothing like hers!

A shopping trip to Gallatin (five miles away) with them in their old car was a hoot. You always went to the feed store to sell the eggs and cream. Then, you bought feed and groceries. The feed was always put on the front fenders of the car. The last stop was at the icehouse. The ice was put in a burlap bag and put on the front bumper.

When I was about 11, rural electricity became available in our area and our standard of living rose dramatically. After that, if the chickens wanted to roost in the outhouse, so be it! Speaking of that, Grandpa's outhouse had three varied-sized holes—for a custom fit, I guess. It didn't matter to me, as I was too afraid of mice, snakes, and spiders to sit flat on the board anyway.

One of Grandpa's stories was about a "dumb bull" that he and his friends when they were young would use to frighten the preachers. Back then, the preachers walked from homes to the church. After the evening service, it would be dark, and the boys would lie and wait till the pastor came by. Then, they would make the "bellow" sound.

When I was about 12, my brother and two of his friends were planning an overnight campout. I remembered Grandpa's story, so I went and asked him to tell me how to make a "dumb bull." The most important item was a fresh hide. My dad had just lost a ewe, so I skinned a piece of hide about 18 inches round and pulled the wool off the hide. Then, I nailed it on one open end of a nail keg and put it under a heat lamp to dry and draw up tight. When it was dry, a small hole was made in the center of the hide and a rosin cord that was about four feet long was pulled halfway into the hole. By pulling the cord back and forth, the sound is identical to that of a mad bull. We carried that "bull" about a quarter mile that night, sneaking up to their tent and pulling the cord! Believe me, the evening commotion and clamor was worth every effort we had put into creating the "bull." My brother had the scare coming, as he had disrupted a couple of my campouts that my friends and I had.

Proud to be Raised on a Farm
By Charlene Cashatt of Mesa, Arizona
Born 1933

I was born in 1933 on a 40-acre farm a couple miles outside of Norborne, Missouri. I was the second of eight children. My life was probably like most kids born in that era—the Saturday night baths, going barefoot all summer, which meant daily foot washing before bedtime. Our shoes, more than likely, had cardboard innersoles. We all had chores to do, even at an early age. The older children always looked after the younger ones.

I was so excited about going to school. The third day of school was my birthday. For the first time ever, my mom curled my hair, using rags. We always wore our hair straight with bangs. Our dad cut our hair until we were teenagers. Anyway, I felt so special with my curly hair. I noticed some of the kids pointing at me and smiling. I smiled back, of course, because I thought they were admiring my hair. What a letdown when my sister whispered to me that my dress was wrong side outward! Would I ever live that down?

We didn't go to movies; there was no money for that. What excitement when our neighbors asked us to go to the Missouri State Fair! Mr. Burton put racks on their 1937 Plymouth pickup, and then covered the racks with a tarp. My mom, dad, and we six kids crawled in the back where we sat on blanket-covered straw bales. When we went through the gate, all the kids were given a ticket. There was to be a drawing for a bicycle for the boys and a watch for the girls. We kids gave the tickets to dad for safekeeping. At the appointed time, we all gathered at this big arena. Dad handed us the tickets. My sister looked at her ticket and said, "Mine had a five," so we traded tickets. Well, you guessed it, my ticket was drawn. I was so frightened to walk down to that platform in front of those thousands of people. The announcer asked my name and where I came from. I replied, "The farm." He said, "No; where do you live?" I said, "On a farm." I had him flustered good. Then, he asked if my mom was there. Mom was always an "in the background" type of person. I'm sure she was totally embarrassed. This was in august of 1941, just a couple of weeks before I turned seven years old. The watch was a Waltham, and it had "Missouri State Fair, 1941" inscribed on the back. I still have the watch, which is a miracle. You see, I begged my mom to let me take the watch to school so I could show it to my teacher. She finally relented. She said that I if kept it in my lunch bucket, that I could take it. As we walked home through the hayfields, I lost the watch! I had taken it out of the lunch bucket to admire it, I'm sure. Then I had put it in my pocket. I had disobeyed! I don't remember whether the tears were because of losing the watch or for what would happen to me when I got home. Praise God, my sister found it a couple hundred yards back.

Besides the farming, my folks and my aunt made sorghum. People from miles around brought their cane to us. This was during the war, so sugar, as well as lots of other things, was rationed. Sorghum was a regular at our table. On special occasions, Mom baked sorghum cake. During the early 1940s, grade schools (not sure about high schools) would dismiss school for an hour or so in order for the kids to collect milkweed pods for the fluff inside. It was used to make parachutes for the war effort.

We always looked forward to Saturday nights when we went to town. The first stop was at the creamery where we sold our cream and eggs. Then, we went to the grocery store. If the weather permitted, we'd get in our neighbor's car, or they in ours, to visit and wait for the Saturday night drawing. If I remember correctly, the sum started out at ten dollars. After the drawing, most people headed home, as there was church the next day.

Yes, Mom made all of our clothing,

including unmentionables. Our shoes were ordered from the Sears and Roebuck catalogs. We stood on a piece of paper so that Mom could draw around our feet. She sent that along with the orders so that the shoes would fit us. Everyone had a garden, chickens, and hogs. It was a big event come butchering day. Most everything on the farm involved hard work and dedication. How proud I am that I was a part of it!

Bailing out of School and a Memorable Canoe Ride
By Dorothea Scott Payne of Weston, Missouri
Born 1932

Ten years and ten days after my parents were married, their first child was born. That was me. I guess you could say I was born in the suburbs of the little village of Madeline in Daviess County, Missouri. Sharing began when I was two. I had the measles, and gave them to my daddy and maternal grandmother. By the time I was three, I began saying what was on my mind. A neighbor came to visit and brought her daughter who was my age. Upon seeing her, I immediately put my hands on my hips and said, "Well, hello Dirty Socks." I guess I already knew that people should be clean.

We attended Old Scotland Church of Christ. When there was a baptism, it was always at a pond on my grandparents' farm. They would sing, *Shall We Gather at the River?* At the age of four, it was hard for me to understand why they would sing about a river when it was a pond. Many years later,

Dorothea's parents, Jim and Lela Scott

408

Bill Payne and Dorothea Scott in the 8th grade

I was baptized in March in the cold water of a creek north of Gilman City, Missouri.

My grandmother was not a loving person. She did teach me to read, and I read three books before starting to school. She also taught me to embroider. I still enjoy doing both.

I started school at Gilman City and loved it—probably because of all the children, as I was an only child. The first day, I met a girl named Lois Cutshall. We became good friends. While in the second grade, they were working on our restrooms, and we had to go to the outside toilets. They weren't too close to the schoolhouse. If I was out there too long, the teacher would send Lois after me—and vice versa. We would swing on the rafters and take our time going back to school. This continued, but our teacher either didn't catch on or didn't care. The friendship with Lois lasted throughout high school and has continued for almost 63 years since graduation. She lives in California now, and we still keep in close contact. She is my dearest friend.

Back then, tax was paid by mills. They were about the size of a nickel. The five mill had a hole in the middle. They were made of aluminum. During World War II, they were made of plastic and were red or white.

There was a lot of rationing then. Gasoline and tires were two things that were rationed, but that didn't bother us, as we didn't have a car. Candy and chewing gum was scarce. I had an aunt who worked a naval base and would send boxes of each to me. Carole Lowe was a grade ahead of me and her sister Peggy was a year behind. Their mother made the best candy from the sap of maple trees. It was boiled to make syrup. It was such a treat when they brought some to school. Rallies were held in town to sell war bonds or stamps. You could get a book, and when it was filled with stamps, you could trade it for a bond.

During the 1940s, chicken mash (feed) was put in floral sacks. It would take four sacks to make a dress. I had a very good 4-H sewing leader, and from the time I was in the fifth grade until I graduated from high school, I made all of my dresses but one were made by me. Mother made one for a Valentine party when I was in the eighth grade. I only remember having a suit and three dresses that were bought during that time. I made dresses, skirts, and suits. Later on, I did the same for our five daughters.

At the end of the school year when I was in the eighth grade, we had a class picnic at a lake. A boy named Bill took me for a canoe ride. That summer, the two of us were in the back seat of a car that his mother was driving. It was nighttime and raining and his mother had her window down. The rain was hitting us in the face, and he pulled a blanket over faces. That is when and where I received my first kiss.

There were six of us girls who ran around together during my sophomore, junior, and senior years. We all stayed the night at one girl's house. Her mother didn't awaken us in the morning, so by the time we were awake; we knew that we were already late for school. My grandparents lived on one street and one of the girl's parents lived on another, so we had to go out of the way to school. It was a beautiful morning, and as we were walking to school, and we decided not to go. We threw our jackets and books over a fence and walked the other direction. We went to a farm where trees had fallen, and sat on them. We were just laughing and having a good time. About noon, it started getting cold, so we retrieved our belongings and went to school just as it was resuming after lunch. When the superintendent finished his usual update, he said he wanted to see Dorothea Scott (it figures that he said my name first), followed by all the names of the other five girls. When we went to see him, all he told us was to never do that again, and we didn't. In fact, we didn't intend to that day.

So, back to that canoe ride and kiss. That has led to 61 years of marriage. We have six children, 20 grandchildren, and 26 great-grandchildren. There are 73 of us now, and it is a wonderful dream come true!

Hospitality Toward the Traveling Folk
By Kathleen Eckard of Stanberry, Missouri
Born 1931

There used to be a common belief that gypsies, hobos, peddlers, and other travelers had secret signs showing homes "friendly" to their kind. If so, my grandparents' farm home must have been marked. My grandpa always told of when the little band of gypsies camped near his house in the late 1890s. You have to know, my grandparents lived at a T-junction on roads that came from nowhere and went nowhere. For travelers to be so far off the beaten track was the first mystery, the second, why they would choose this particular place.

This little band of Gypsies appeared over the hill into the sheltered vale where my grandparents lived. Their chief asked if they could make camp under the big cottonwood tree down where the road from the north intersected the east and west road. My grandpa said, "Sure, and you can water your horses at the well across the road, but get your drinking water from the house well; it is the best in the country." I don't know if they did or not; you see, there were the two pine trees flanking the path to the front door, which was to deter gypsies. They would not pass between the "dead man's trees" or "cemetery trees." Yet, as Grandpa would say, "They made their camp and caused no trouble, though many neighbors later reported a shortage of chickens after the little band had passed through." He didn't lose any of his flock, and felt his good deed was thus appreciated.

Then, there was the tale of the two brother peddlers from Syria. This would have been a little later than the gypsies' encampment. According to my dad, the first time they appeared at his parents' farmhouse, he was nine or ten years old. He was born in 1897. Their names were Joe and Ed Stie. They came by about sundown, carrying packs on their backs filled with merchandise to sell to farm wives— buttons, thread, needles, lace, beads, and what have you. Things these women might need or want, women who seldom went into town.

They were invited to the supper table, and then invited to sleep in the same room as my ten year old father. He said they would talk in their native language, and he was scared to death. Were they plotting to kill them all? He didn't know. Inviting someone in like that would be an unthinkable circumstance today. Turns out, they were just hardworking men who had come to the United States of America. To earn enough money to return to their homeland and families, they had set themselves up a little business. Imagine leaving wives and children as twenty-somethings to do such a thing.

Every spring and every fall, they would make the trip through, going from walking with a backpack to having a one horse covered cart. It was probably about 1930 when Joe, the older brother, said he was going home. His son was now a grown man, and he said he had saved enough money so that he could set him up in a business in Syria. However, Ed, the younger brother, was staying on for a few more years, and continued to come through twice a year. Each time he stayed overnight and enjoyed two meals with my grandparents.

Then, one fall day in 1936 when I was five years old, my parents and I were at my grandparents' house. Down the hill from the north came the little black peddler cart with Joe Stie with his notions and goods. It was his farewell trip, so he couldn't take the time to stay overnight. He had to make time, for he was catching a train out of the Midwest and on to the coast to sail home. He was 18 or 19 when he came over here, and now he was a middle aged 45 or 46 year old man. He had saved his money and was going home to start his life anew. We still have the Kodak picture that Mom took of him coming down the hill on that final day. It gives me goose bumps.

We also had merchants who had a general type store in our county seat. They were twin brothers from Russia. They were Jews who had escaped the Tsars pogroms. Every summer, the twin who was more outgoing of personality would load up a selection of styles and sizes of what we called silk Sunday dresses. He had a fairly late model sedan. This was in the late 1920s, and the 1930s. He called on farm women, bringing the latest selections right into their homes. Guess where he planned to be at noon? You are right, at my grandparent's house. They just had to have her good fried chicken and a fully loaded table of fresh garden vegetables. The meal ended with pie, of course. It always amused me that Grandpa would say that his favorite piece of the chicken was the back. My dad said he had looked all his life for some sign that would inform those various migrant people, tramps, or hobos, if you will, who traveled the highways and byways, depending on the hospitality of folk for food and shelter. He never found one, yet he never disbelieved there wasn't one there, if you only knew how to read it.

The Time of my Life
By Emma Jane Summers of Liberty,
Missouri
Born 1936

I had the time of my life on a 120-acre farm my dad bought in 1942. Before he bought the farm, we lived in a small home with nine children. I don't know where mom put our clothes or where we slept. When we moved to the farm, it had two bedrooms, so mom and dad got bunk beds and four of us slept in the two bedrooms and mom and dad had a bed in the front room. My dad rented a store and frozen locker plant in town.

I remember playing with kittens. I just loved them! We would feed the kittens popcorn. It was a lot of fun to see them try to reach the bottom of a can of cat food. They would walk around with the can on their heads! It was so funny to see!

Mom always had baby chickens in the spring. She would put them in a big box and put a light in to keep them warm. They were so cute, but we could not hold them. When they got bigger and were put outside, we'd have to run outside and catch them when it would rain so they would not drown. We had a steam at the bottom of the hill that we would all play in. we would dam it up sometimes. I stepped on a piece of glass once and could not get it out, so Mom and Dad took me to the doctor. He cut the glass out without numbing it. I guess I kicked him with my other foot and got blood all over him. He was sure mad, but my mom said he deserved it.

We had a wood-shingled roof on our house and had a wood stove to cook with. The house was always catching on fire. Mom did not get too excited; she would send the boys to the well for water and send the rest of us outside. One time, she called the fire department. I was really afraid of the fire, and they caught me walking up the road carrying my doll. I remember the pretty dresses my sister made for me.

I started to school at five years old. There was no kindergarten. We had fun until a little girl did not want me to play with my brothers and sisters. She kept bothering me, so I punched her in the nose. She went to the teacher crying. I had to sit at my desk the rest of the day, but I learned to take up for myself.

One evening, we were listening to the radio when it announced that Pearl Harbor had been attacked by Japan. President Roosevelt said we were going to war. We were very scared because we had to turn out the lights at night and pull the window shades if we heard an airplane. We went to the show every Saturday night and they would always show pictures of the war. *Nyoki the Jungle Girl* and *the Lone Ranger* helped a lot to ease our fears. We made a victory garden and recycled tin cans and any iron that we had.   We also picked milkweed pods for parachutes. It was fun because we did it together.

While the war was going on, there was rationing of sugar and gas. There was also not much meat to be found, so my dad bought some black Angus cattle and some pigs and built a slaughterhouse. He also had the boys to build a trailer to haul the meat into town. They worked every night until one or two o'clock. They had customers a half a block down the street to buy meat. My mom saved some of the money to build on to our house. They eventually made it into a two-story house with two bedrooms upstairs and a large front room with a fireplace. We also had a new school to go to. It had a cloakroom, a schoolroom, and a small library.

In the fall when school started, the grass was very tall and had been mowed with a sickle. The girls made an outline of a home, and we played with it until it fell apart. We had Christmas plays, thanksgiving plays, and pie suppers. I loved the library. There was fiction books and non-fiction. I read every one of them. We played games like the Flying Dutchman, tag, and played on the swings and slide. We belonged to the 4-H Club in the summer, so we got to see our playmates at meetings. We had spelling bees and art when it rained. I had a favorite teacher, Martha Miller. She liked me, and had a niece my size. She gave me a beautiful apricot dress with long puffy sleeves and a full skirt. I felt very beautiful in it. At home, we played jump rope, croquet, and baseball. We had five-gallon cans, and rolled on them standing up. It was very good to practice balancing. When it was very hot, we could sometimes fill up the metal bathtub with water from the well and put it in the sun until it got warm. Then, we took tin cans and threw water at each other. Sometimes, we just went fishing in the pond.

These are the memories I hold dear of my childhood. We had a very happy family, working together and playing together.

Jenny Beutler in 1944

Didn't Have a Lot, but in Ways, Had it All
By Jenny Beutler of Watson, Missouri
Born 1944

I was born and raised in Atchison County. My dad was Leo (Little) Holmes. He had a twin brother by the name of Leland (Big) Holmes. My Grandma Annie Holmes told me that when the boys were born, my dad only weighed a little over one pound. The doctor said he would never live. She said she made him a bed out of a shoebox and set him by the wood stove. She fed him a little at a time. She saved him. She called the two brothers Big Sweet and Little Sweet. They went by Big and Little for the rest of their lives. They both were coon hunters and watermelon raisers. Dad also had cows and pigs, chickens. We milked cows, and sold the cream and eggs. We traded the eggs in for other things we needed.

When my brother, Gilbert, and I got home from school, we had chores to do. We would gather eggs and milk cows. My brother had to milk the cows because I could never get that milk out! We broke corn for the steers. We all picked up corn left on the ground after the harvest. We chopped sunflowers and

shatter cane out of corn. We used to butcher a hog for meat. We had a big black pot that we made a fire under. We rendered lard by cooking the fat until we had lard. Then, we had what was called "cracklings" left. That was used for dog food. We kept the lard in the cellar. We canned everything. My mom even canned meat. We would all sit around and pod peas. We would break beans after supper that night. We had about an acre of garden that we hoed at night. I was always glad when Mom would tell me to get supper out. I helped my dad hoe watermelons every year. We would meet at 6:00 A.M. and hoe until it started to get hot, around 10:00 A.M. He would then say, "Same time, same place, tomorrow." Of course, I said, "Yes, I will, Dad."

We never had a TV until I was in the sixth grade. We listened to westerns on the radio.

Dad would go coon hunting. Sometimes we would go to someone's house while he was gone. We had to ride in the back of a Model-T car with the coon dogs. That was the life! One night we were skinning coons in the timber so that they wouldn't be so heavy for me to carry. I said, "Dad, I smell something burning." He always wore a carbide light hat with a flame. While Dad was bent over skinning the coon, he had scorched my hair! We raised several baby coons and two squirrels. When they were old enough, we let the squirrels go. The coons ran in and out of the house; they were never pinned up.

My Grandma Holmes told us about Jesse James and his brother Frank coming to her house. She said they would bet on how many flies would sit on the sugar bowl. They were related to us, but I don't remember how.

Dad used to walk to school very early and get the fire going so that it would be warm for others when they got there. In front of my house used to be called the head of the lake. Dad said that's where the kids (him included) would ice skate. He said he could jump logs and limbs in the lake. He could do the figure eight. When he was older, they picked corn by hand by the wagonloads and caught rainwater for washing clothes. Grandma always had a tub at the corner of the house to catch it.

My mother, Ruby Johnson Holmes, came to Atchison County from Syracuse, Nebraska. My grandpa Johnson had a lot of Indian in him. My mom worked in the field like a man. She was a hard worker. While she worked in the field, I was the cook and housekeeper at the young age of nine years old. She picked up corn to get us a little Christmas gift. I can remember living in a house just up the road from where I live now with no electricity and no restroom. We took baths in tubs and had an outside toilet. We had a good life. Nowadays, kids just play games and watch TV. Dad and I used to go mushroom hunting. He would say, "This is Hairpen Hollar," or "This is Horseshoe Hollar." Now I don't know which one is which.

I used to get a dip of ice cream and a pop for ten cents at the little drug store in Watson, Missouri. Bread was only a nickel. Another thing that was much cheaper was pop. It was only five cents a bottle. We wore longer dresses and skirts with bobby socks. We bobby pinned our hair to curl it. I remember only going to a show twice when I was younger.

We carried a lot of water, and washed clothes in a wringer washer and rinse tubs. We also carried a lot of water to drink. We lived by the hills, so we climbed the hills a lot. They were just behind the house. Dad used to go to the hills to pick paw-paws. He called them "Missouri bananas." They were the worst bananas that I ever tasted, but he ate them. He liked them. My mom and my aunt used to go to the hills and pick the biggest blackberries that I have ever seen. I looked for the patch when I was older, but I never did find it.

Life was much better back then. We didn't have to lock doors or take keys out of the cars. I wish my kids and grandkids could live the life I lived. We had loving families and neighbors. My grandkids are not as lucky. I knew nothing about drugs when I was in school. We never did hear of them. We went to drive-in movies and had roller-skating parties. We had a good life; we didn't have a lot, but in many ways, we had it all. We had a good family life and worked hard as kids, and didn't expect to be paid for any of it.

Home Remedies, Hunting, and the War
By Twilla Hughes Yandell of Mound City,
Missouri
Born 1935

I was born at home on June 27, 1935. My sister Phyllis was 22 months younger than I. I was the oldest of three sisters. My first memories are of beginning the first grade in a one-room schoolhouse called Lonesome. My teacher's name was Burdabell Fullwider. All the kids walked to school in those days. Even after I started high school, I walked about two miles to meet the bus. In the first grade, I walked across the country with the neighbor kids to save time. Sometimes the snow covered the fence posts and we walked over the fences on snowdrifts. There were no gravel roads, so when we had more than a half inch of rain, we could not drive a car anywhere. I remember riding a wagon to town to buy groceries many times.

When I started school, we lived on a farm owned by two brothers who raised sheep. I

Leo (Little) Holmes and Leland (Big) Holmes

413

loved the little lambs. Mom raised one on a bottle because it was born small. I was always out in the barn with those sheep. One day I stepped on a board with a nail in it. It punctured the bottom of my foot and became infected. It swelled so badly that I couldn't wear my new black patent leather shoes that Mother had bought for Easter. Mother soaked my foot in something she called crelen water. It took a long time to heal and was very painful.

When I started first grade, my parents bought me a black tin lunch bucket. I couldn't wait to take it to school. I carried that bucket all eight grades and in high school. There were a couple times I used it to defend myself and my sister. It was dented on both ends. My first year of school was the years of 1941 and 1942. We were given ration books to fill with ration stamps. Everything was rationed then, like sugar, flour, tires, gasoline. That was to provide more for the war effort. If anyone was known to be hoarding, everyone thought they were "un-American," as we called it. This was 1941 and everything was rationed through the next four or five years till the end of the war. I believe it was before I started second grade when we moved to a farm south a Mound City, Missouri. This was near Blair Hill (named after one of the original settlers.) it was owned by Mrs. "Mam" Gould. She lived by herself in one half of the house. We lived in one large room where we all slept, cooked our meals, and basically did everything. There was no electricity. There was a pitcher pump in the kitchen area, but no bathroom. We had one Aladdin lamp for light at night. Mother had a large garden spot and grew most of our vegetables. We also had chickens. Sometimes I had to gather the eggs and one day I found a large blacksnake in the nest box they like chicken eggs obviously, because there were always snakes in the chicken house. I've hated snakes ever since then. When Mother found one, she threw it over the fence for the pigs to eat. They crunched them right down. It made me feel sick.

My youngest sister Karen was born there in the spring. Our Aunt Katherine was the midwife. Because of the mud roads, our local doctor, Dr. Hogan, could not make it for the delivery. In the fall and winter, my daddy would hunt and trap animals and sold the hides for Christmas money. He would skin and stretch the hides on boards to dry. He hung them overhead in a shed. The odor was overwhelming! He made good money because there was a market for pelts back then. He sold mainly raccoon and sometimes skunk.

I and my sister Phyllis went to Blair School. I started the second grade and she started the first. Our teacher's name was Mrs. Kenny. We liked her very much. I believe she retired because the following year we had a new man teacher. We didn't like him because he would not help us with our studies and let the older boys pick on us.

My sister and I loved to play in the hayloft in the big barn in the summer. All the years we were growing up on the farm, several of the neighbors got together and helped Daddy put up hay. We always had good neighbors and Daddy always helped them in return. After approximately the year of 1942, one of the neighbors bought a new hay baler and offered to bale Daddy's hay. I think that really astonished him, but he agreed. Up to that time, hay was stored loose inside the barn. We moved again to Uncle Lee's farm. I was approximately nine years old at that time. It was only a few miles east and south of the Blair Hill area. It must have been late fall or early spring because I remember it started raining then turned to sleet, then snow. The furniture and household goods were moved in wagons, and of course, it all got wet. That upset my mother. The wet blistered the varnish on her dresser. She still had that dresser long after I was married. There wasn't' money to buy new furniture. We made do with what we had. My sister and I had one wagon, sled, and one doll apiece. I never felt deprived. I remember my mother saving printed flour sacks to make us girls dresses. In the years that we lived there, the house was wired for electricity and the first rotary type wall phones were installed. We and the neighbors were on the same line or "party line." You could listen in on everyone's conversations. Several of the neighbor ladies would get on the line and visit. It was an easy way of keeping up with the local news. It took the place of the daily paper. I listened to the "Grand Ole Opry" on the radio on Saturday night. It was powered by the car battery.

Mother always had laying hens. We also had milk cows and butchered our own hog in the late fall. Neighbors pitched in to help with the butchering, also. There was a large garden spot and strawberry bed, an orchard with apples, peaches, plums, cherries, and grapevines. Mother canned everything because no one had a freezer. My folks bought their first refrigerator after I graduated from high school. Up until then, we had an icebox. Daddy bought a block of ice once a week from the icehouse in Mound City.

We had four cousins who served in the army during World War II. One was killed in action in Germany. One fought in the Japanese invasion of Okinawa. He later married a girl from that island. She was very shy and soft spoken. We all liked her immediately. She died of cancer years later, still married to my cousin. Her name was Sadaki. During the war, any family who had sons or a daughter was honored to display a blue banner in their window with a gold star. This represented their service.

Sometime after the war, our cousin Sammy gave us a puppy. He had named it McArthur after General McArthur. But, he said that we could call him Macky for short. That was a tough little dog. Whatever we did, wherever we went, he was right there. I believe he would have fought to the death for us. He lived to be fourteen years old.

When I was about 15, we moved again to a farm about six miles northwest of our Uncle Lee's farm. This was a much larger home with four bedrooms and a big kitchen with running water. There was a wood burning furnace in the basement, and a bathroom with running water and a bathtub, but no toilet stool. All those things were new conveniences for us. My first memory of coon hunting with my dad was while we lived in the Dooley farm. My sister and I went with our dad mainly to help carry back the dead coons. Sometimes they could weigh as much as 20 pounds. Daddy had two purebred coonhounds that were his pride and joy. When they "treed" a coon, you could hear them a long distance at night. Daddy would aim his gun above his head with only a flashlight for illumination and shoot the coon out the tree, dead every time. It had to be a head shot because a hole in the pelt meant less pay for the pelt.

I graduated from high school in 1953. I got my first real job filling catalog orders for Nellie Don, a women's clothing catalog in St. Joseph, Missouri. My sister Phyllis also worked there. We rode to work with the neighbors who also worked in St. Joseph. We gave them $5.00 each week for gas. That job only lasted a few months. My sister started dating a fellow who drove our school bus. They were later married and I was her maid of honor.

The owner of the Dooley farm wanted Daddy to buy his farm so that he could retire, but Daddy was afraid he couldn't make the payments, so he had to turn him down. I think Mother was disappointed, but she never said a word. I started dating a friend of my girlfriend's husband. He was in the air force and stationed at Ellsworth Air Force Base in Rapid City, South Dakota. He was on leave at the time.

My mom, dad, my sister Karen, and I moved from that farm to another smaller farm. The house was only three rooms and had no running water. It was quite a letdown from that nice big house on the Dooley farm. I was married while they lived there. We moved to Rapid City, South Dakota where my husband, Clyde Noland, was stationed as a jet mechanic. My parents didn't live on that farm long because Daddy disagreed with the owner's refusal to make improvements to the farm.

I will end my story here. My parents, Daniel and Bonnie were honest, hardworking people. We three sisters had a wonderful childhood. We lost our parents in 1971 and 1980. They say that "the good die young." In this case, that proved to be prophetic.

Days in Pawnee
By Nina L. Adkinson of Eagleville, Missouri
Born 1931

Growing up in Pawnee during the 1930s was quite different than children growing up during the 2000s. Pawnee had been much bigger in earlier years. It had many stores, such as millinery shop, a post office, a hotel, a barbershop, and a blacksmith. When I was born in 1931, it was just a crossroad with one store. The store was a large building with a cement floor and cement steps on one end. On the side next to the road was a wooden platform high enough for the horse drawn wagons to pull up next to. This made it possible to unload the cream and eggs that the farmers brought in to trade for the groceries and other supplies that they needed. The cream had been skimmed off the fresh milk with a separator, which was turned by hand. It was tested with a little machine by spinning it around. Then, the can was weighed to see how much money

Richard, Janet, Nina, and Janice

or credit the farmer would get. The eggs were put into 12 dozen or 24 dozen crates that had dividers in them to keep them from getting broken. The storekeeper had a way to hold each egg up to a light that was placed behind a board that had an egg-sized hole in it. By doing this, he would be able to see if the egg was fresh or not. This was called "candling" them. Most of the time, they were good, but once in a while the farmer would find a nest in the barn somewhere with a lot of eggs that didn't get gathered every day like they were in the hen house. Some of those eggs would be rotten. The good ones were counted, and the farmer was paid or given credit for them. We grew most of the food we had, but needed to buy things like coffee, sugar, flour, oatmeal, and raisins. Most of our small farms produced the fruits and vegetables that we raised and canned in Mason of Kerr canning jars. Most of us in this area butchered a hog or calf when we needed meat. We cured our own hams and bacon. We also canned beef and sausage.

There was a drought in 1937 and 1938, so many in the area didn't raise enough food for themselves or the livestock. The government furnished commodities for those who needed food. The storekeeper, Ben Jerome had a pickup, so he delivered those boxes of food to the families that didn't have transportation other than teams of horses or mules and wagons. It was a rare thing to see a car back then. The roads were all dirt, so when it rained, the mud was so deep that it was often difficult to travel with the horses and wagons. The men had poles in the wagons to punch mud out of the wagon spokes when it got so

thick that the horses couldn't pull the wagon.

The store had shelves on both sides with counters in front of them. Some of the counters were made with glass so you could see inside where the candy, thread, handkerchiefs, and may other things were without the items getting dusty. They also sold shoes, overalls, shirts, and oil for the few cars. There was standard gas from a pump outside that had a glass top with markings on it by gallons. They would pump up to the number of gallons the customer wanted, and then put it in their car or gas can. They also had a barrel of kerosene. People brought in their own gallon jugs with corks in them. Most people had kerosene lamps, but a few had Aladdin gas lamps for light. There was no rural electricity back then, and only a few people had telephones—even then, they were party lines. There were no radios or televisions then, so each family had to make their own fun or music. The neighbors got together and built a stage out in the open behind the store. All would come to town on Saturday night to listen to music. Some even got up and played. My Aunt Faye played piano and my Uncle Everett Sturdevant played the fiddle. Several others from the area played guitars and other instruments. Our neighbor boy, Darryl Sturdenvant around 18 years old, ordered parts to build a radio. It could be listened to by earphones. That was quite a treat when it was our turn to listen. Later on, he got a loud speaker for the whole family to listen at the same time. He could only get one or two stations to come in.

I had a sister, Cleora a year older than me and a brother, Richard two years younger. In 1936, when my sister started school, she had to walk a mile by herself. We moved into an old house in Pawnee so that there would be other children to walk together with her across the creek to the Ramey School. When the creek was flooded over the bridge, my dad hooked up the mules to the wagon and took all the kids to school. Dad said that horses would not cross water that way, but mules would.

Our one-room schoolhouse had first through the eighth grades. The Ramey schoolteacher, Miss Hope Prather roomed with us, but she always left about an hour before we did so that she could get a fire started in the stove at the schoolhouse. She just wanted the building to be heated for the schoolchildren's arrival. The bigger boys would have coal hoods filled and taken inside from the coalhouse the afternoon before. Most of the time, about ten to twelve of us walked together from Pawnee. The other children came from the other side of the school. In mid-morning, we had a 15-minute recess. We had another one in the midafternoon. We also had a one hour lunch period to eat our sack or dinner bucket lunches. The first thing we did in the morning was to raise the flag and say the Pledge of Allegiance to it. The last thing we did before leaving to go home at 4:00 was to take the flag inside again. In about 1940, the government sent commodities like canned fruit, etc., and we got a little gas stove to heat or cook things on. Sometimes, our teacher had us bring certain things from home so that we could make hot vegetable soup. That sure was good on a cold day.

Entertainment at school included programs at Christmas and at least one box supper every year. We would decorate some kind of shoebox (or whatever we could find) with crepe paper or ribbons. We would then fill them with good eats, like fried chicken, bread and butter, sandwiches, homemade cookies, or cake. These were always in the evenings after the family chores were done so that everyone could come. Someone would be the auctioneer and try to run the prices up to make as much money for the school as they possibly could. The person paying the most for a box was supposed to eat with the child that brought in the box. The proceeds went toward something

Nina's family in 1940-41

for the school, like balls and bats, etc.

In 1938, we moved to another location and were in a different school zone, so I attended Smith School. Our teacher there had organized a band with rhythm sticks for first graders, wrist bells for the next class, and tambourines, drums, trumpets, and other horns for older boys and girls.

Most families, like ours, had no money to spend, so homemade toys were the most usual kind. Dad made us stilts to walk with. He made whistles from tree roots and a scooter with two wheels from an old broken wagon. We played "house" with empty bottles and other discarded containers, using crates for cabinets out in a shed. Empty wooden thread spools came in handy for drawer pulls. I remember another use for them in the two-hole outhouse. When they cut the circle out in the seat, we saved the circle and fastened the spool to the center of it to make the lid. Dad fashioned what we called a toy "tractor" by using a rubber band, a tack, an empty wood thread spool, a matchstick, and a round sliver of hand soap about the size of the spool. He put the rubber band through the hole in the spool, tacked it in place on one end, made a small hole in the middle of the piece of soap, pushed the other end of the rubber band through the soap, and then put one end of the match a little ways through that end of the rubber band. We would wind it up and it would go!

The boys liked to play a made-up game in the middle of the crossroads on Saturday evenings or after school. They got an old rubber inner tube from a tire and they would see who could stay in the center of it. It was a rough and tumble way to play, and usually didn't end until they were all exhausted. We got a sled for Christmas one year, and it was long enough for all three of us to sit on and slide down the big hills in the road. There was no danger from playing in the road back then, as very seldom was any cars ever seen.

The big tin store had outlived its time, so in 1939, Ben Jerome, the storeowner, built a new wood, two-story building with living quarters in the upstairs. Unfortunately, he had a fatal heart attack about 1943, so our family took over the store and moved into the upstairs. Sometime in the early '40s, many people around northern Missouri started raising turkeys on their farms as we began coming out of the Depression years. We raised thousands of turkeys for two or more years. After a lot of hard work, we finally got to see what money was. My brother, sister, and I pumped several barrels of water each day to be hauled to the turkey pens. Dad had built a large wooden sled to hook the mules to so that they could pull the barrels of water wherever we needed them. It took many sacks of feed each day to feed the turkeys.

The empty sacks made many things for us since they all had pretty prints of flowers or plaid on them. At age 11, my mother, Vergie Ward had taught me to use our Singer sewing machine, so I made shirts for myself and my sister. Dad usually picked out pretty sacks, but one day we told him to get at least four alike so that I could make a bedspread for our beds. However, when he got home, he had four that were printed with the exact little flowery design, but two had blue flowers and two had pink flowers. We told him they weren't alike, but he couldn't see why not. Dad was colorblind and couldn't tell the difference! We just had a good laugh over that!

After I turned 12, we moved to Eagleville to a better school with separate grades. I've had a great life with very loving parents, grandparents, and a wonderful brother and sister. I also have many precious grandchildren and many great-grandchildren to help care for when needed. I still think that Pawnee during the Depression was a wonderful time out of my 82 years.

Merry-go-rounds and Buggy Mishaps
By Mary M. Bontrager of Jamesport,
Missouri
Born 1950

In 1959, my parents, Henry J. and Mary Mast, and their seven children moved from northern Indiana to Jamesport, Missouri. I was in the second grade, and we went to Gee School (pronounced Jē). It was a one-room country school with a small cloakroom with a sink and water bucket. We all drank from the same cup. That little room was always overflowing with coats, boot, and lunch boxes. The schoolroom was heated with a kerosene oil-burning stove. There were about two dozen scholars. Barbara Jean Jones was our beloved teacher. We called her Miss Barbara. She taught all eight grades and stressed reading, writing, and arithmetic.

There were some "English" students and some Amish students, but we were good friends. One thing that we all had in common was that none of the families had much money, so no one looked down their noses at anyone else. We "made do" with what we had.

My sister Elizabeth, two brothers, Eli and Joe, and I walked to school when the weather was nice. It was about two miles if we walked through a neighbor's pasture for a shortcut. We trudged through mud and snow, up the hills and down. Sometimes, we got a ride from John Peery, who worked on the railroad. We always cheered when he came along with his pickup truck. He would stick his head out the window and ask, "Ya wanna ride?" We hollered, "Sure!" We all piled in the back of the truck and went merrily on our way home. Sometimes we would take the horse and one-seater open buggy to school. However, we had to go around the road, so we couldn't take the short cut. It was quite a bit farther that way.

There was a swing set and an old merry-go-round at school. We spent many happy recesses on that merry-go-round. We would stand on the ground on the inside of the seats and push with all our might until it was going around pretty fast. Then, we'd hop on the seat and have a joyously dizzy ride, going 'round and 'round. One time when I was pushing, I hopped on the seat, missed my aim, and was drug 'round and 'round on the ground. I had hold of the bars, so all that was hurt was my pride. My boots and the back of my dress were muddy. Miss Barbara cleaned me up the best she could. That didn't' keep me from going on the merry-go-round the next day, or the days after that. I thought it was so much fun to get dizzy from going around so fast!

Every Friday afternoon, we had a special snack time. Usually we had bottles of pop and candy or some other snack. We were allowed to have a whole bottle of pop, which was a big treat for us poor folks. One time when I opened my bottle of pop, I accidentally dropped it and spilled some on the floor. I suppose I spilled some tears, too. Miss Barbara kindly took the partly spilled bottle and gave me a full one, bless her heart. There were two outhouses at school—one for the boys and one for the girls. The teacher would scatter powdered, white lime down the holes to keep odors down. It looked clean for a while. We didn't think it was gross because that was what we were used to at home as well.

One day on the way home from school, we were merrily riding along in the open buggy and singing silly songs. We went down a steep hill, and one side of the shafts came loose from the front of the buggy. We were weaving wildly from one side of the road to the other. We hung to the seat for dear life! About that time, the other side of the shaft broke loose and set the horse free, galloping away with the shafts and driving lines trailing behind. The seat was busted loose from the buggy, and we ended up in the ditch. None of us were hurt, so we gathered up our lunch boxes and walked the last ¾ mile to home. Our mom was frantic when we got home. After seeing the horse come charging home, she just knew that we were hurt.

I always thought that the seventh and eighth grade boys were so huge! I guess they were compared to this skinny little second grader. That was the last year that Gee School had classes. The next year, we were transferred to the Jamesport School in town. We rode the school bus. There, we had one grade in each classroom. After Gee School closed, the Welch family bought it, added partitions, and remodeled it quite a bit. They lived in it for several years, and then it burned down.

At home on the farm, we milked cows by hand and sold the milk in ten-gallon milk cans. John Treadway hoisted those heavy cans of milk into his truck and exchanged the full ones for empty ones. The cans had our number on them, so he knew which ones to leave. I learned that the milk cans made different tones when I tapped on them with a stick. I spent many happy Sunday afternoons tapping on the lids and sides of the milk cans, adjusting the lid for a wanted tone. It was amazing how close you could get to the "do re mi fa so la ti do" notes that we learned in school. I'm sure my family got tired of my tapping out tunes, but I loved it. They knew I wasn't' in any mischief as long as I was tapping. Then, the milk cans had to be filled with milk again, so my "music" was dismantled. That didn't keep me from using other cans later on, rearranging them in the right order to get the wanted sounds. This innocent way of making music would simply be unheard of and laughed at nowadays. I suppose this is what we consider the good old days—the precious memories, how they linger!

We did our farming with horses. We plowed, disked, harrowed, planted, and then cultivated the corn and soybeans one row at a time with a horse-drawn cultivator. Then, we had to take hoes and chop cockle-burrs, and button weeds in each field, plus thistles in all the pastures. We didn't use spray, but we used our muscles!

We took time for some fun, too. We went fishing, played croquet, Andy-over, and all kinds of outdoor games. We ice skated in the winter, read books, and put jigsaw puzzles together. What a simple life we lived! Everyone had time to help his neighbor, putting up hay, shocking oats, and threshing it, filling the silo and husking corn by hand. It was hard work. The parents worked side by side with their children. We all did our share of work, and we all needed our neighbors.

Phonographs and Spool Tractors
By Lettie Siddens of Marceline, Missouri
Born 1926

The 200 acre Mutton Ridge Ranch was my birthplace in 1926. I had a sister four years older and a brother who came along three years later. When about four years old I was allowed to go spend time with Grandma Maud and Grandpa Will Rodgers at Oakenstan about three miles from our home. It was a pleasant afternoon, but in the evening, there was a fire to the east of their home, the direction of my home but much closer. By bedtime, I became restless and could not go to sleep. Finally, I asked Grandma to call my parents to come for me. By lamp light, she went to the large wooden box fastened to the wall. A lever on the right side would turn to call central, on the left was a hook that held the receiver, in the middle of the front was the tube for receiving the message, and above it, two shiny knobs formed the bell that rang. Inside were two tube shaped batteries. Grandma took down the receiver but held her hand on the hook while turning the ringing lever. Hearing her asking for Dad to come, I fell asleep. Upon awakening the next morning and finding myself still at Grandma's, I was both angry (I had been deceived) and pleased (I would have another day to play.)

Years later, when we had moved to town we could not afford a telephone. One day I

Lettie's parents, Ruth and Edgar Lippincott in 1926

was asked to take a nickel to pay for a phone call at a neighbor's house. We needed to send a message to my dad. He was across town hanging wallpaper. Although embarrassed to have to use someone's phone, I was encouraged when she loaned me a book to read. That made the trip a joy. We did not a have a phone again in our home until I was in high school in Stanberry. That was about 1940 when my dad started speaking for the Bible Truth Radio program on KFNF at Shenandoah, Iowa. Now I prefer Skype because you can see the face of the person to whom you are talking and see facial expressions. That sometimes reveals as much information as words.

One summer morning after Dad had gone to the fields to work, we three children were ready for a delightful breakfast. Mother had prepared oatmeal with cream, toast, and jelly, with milk to drink. The table faced the south window, and to the left was an outside door going out to a nice porch. Mother glanced at the window in the upper half of the door, then turned to us and said, "Be still, and do not get out of your chairs." We then noticed a large black snake crawling up the screen outside the door, watching us eat. We were too enthralled to say a word but watched, speechless. Mother slipped out the north door, got a hoe, walked around to the porch, and removed the snake. She later cautioned us not to go to the strawberry

patch in the south edge of the yard. No doubt, she thought its mate might be lurking there.

A mile or so beyond Grandma's lived Great-grandmother Hannah and her daughter, who was a high school principal in a nearby town. She eventually resigned to stay with Great-grandma Hannah after Great-grandpa James Rodgers died. This homestead was a Rock of Gibraltar to me, having lived in Oklahoma, Florida, three farms in Missouri, and three towns before entering high school. What a glorious place to spend summer vacations! The house contained an organ in the parlor, lemon cookies in the pantry, many books, and a phonograph in the library. Hannah frowned at my playing the phonograph. They were classical records, I could not understand why. Probably she thought I should be listening to hymns. There was a lovely stand with two large books. One was the 1892 edition of the large self-pronouncing bible in parallel columns King James and Revised versions. It also had a complete Concordance, along with the Smith Bible Dictionary and 200 illustrations from steel and wood plates, some in color. The other book was "Webster's International Dictionary of the English Language" published in 1864. There was a Studebaker in the garage and a carriage in the barn. No one seemed to be interested in the car, but that carriage had two wide leather seats, isinglass side curtains, and two tiny kerosene lanterns up front. (I have one of those lanterns hanging in my workroom, it still works.) I would sit in the back seat and instruct my cousin in the front to take me to the Taj Mahal in India, or the Tower Bridge in London. It was great!

The Lippincott Family in 1937-39

Kites were easy to make if we could hunt up materials, but the most fascinating toy that we could make was a spool tractor. Materials needed were: a large wooden spool that once held thread, two matchsticks, a rubber band, a sharp knife, and a tiny sliver of soap. Notches were cut around the two edges of the spool for wheels. The rubber band was then threaded through the center hole. On one end of the spool, a piece of the matchstick was placed to hold the rubber band in place. Make a hole in the center of the soap and thread the rubber band through it. The end of the whole matchstick then would be placed between the soap and the end of the rubber. Then, you would hold the end of the spool carefully while you turn the long matchstick around until it was tight. All that was left to do was place the spool on the ground and watch it roll! If all goes well it will even pull up hills.

My school career started at Jackson Corners, a one-room building with a well on one side, a couple of toilets at the far end, a few trees for shade, and a flag pole. Mother made me a new yellow dress with a circular skirt, a sash at the waist and a small round pocket with blue cord around the edge. My initials were embroidered in the center of the pocket. My sister Faye walked with me that mile and quarter each day. The first year was a delight. There were five first graders, and at reading time, we walked to the front of the room and sat on a bench below the blackboard that reached clear across the front of the room. It was interesting to watch the third grade class at the board practice writing their multiplication tables.

At Christmastime, I was part of a small group of girls who pantomimed "Silent Night" with white crepe paper dresses and silver rope decorated headpieces. Older students sang the song. The next year, same school, same teacher, but I was in the second grade. It was time for reading class. This time we just stood by our seat when it was our turn to read. It was my turn. I stood and read until I came to a word I did not remember. The teacher became impatient and shook me because she decided that I knew the word but just refused to say it. My sister, across the room, put her head down on her desk and started to cry. This made the teacher angry, and she dismissed our class and reprimanded my sister for crying. I think the teacher was having a bad day.

Lettie Lippincott age 9

Thirteen years later, I was the teacher at a rural school at Island City. It was wartime. Teachers had joined the military or went to the city where high wages were available. The County superintendent suggested that I apply to teach. I was offered the job for $110.00 a month and I was to do my own janitorial work. I was not prepared to operate a coal/wood burning stove and had requested help. Instead of help, they just upped the wages $10 a month. I was to attend six weeks summer studies at Northwest Missouri State College. I was delighted to do that. The furnishings of the school were much the same as the one I attended at age five. However, the entry room was large enough for a tiny lunchroom. I didn't volunteer to prepare lunches, so we each brought our lunches from home. Five of the eleven students were first graders. That cut down on the number of classes I taught.

In October, the students prepared a short program and invited parents to come one evening. That gave me an opportunity to meet all the families. The students served hot chocolate and doughnuts while we visited. They were a well-behaved group of children and we had a good year together until the last good snow. They had a good time sleigh riding on the hill outside the schoolyard at their lunch period. I, with some of the smaller children, had stayed inside the building and supervised by watching out the window. When the recess was over, I rang the bell to resume classes.

Four of the students decided to continue riding on the next hill over. I could see them but did not feel able to go after them. The rest of us resumed our lessons and the recalcitrant students returned an hour and half later. When it was time for dismissal, we agreed that they would make up their time by staying 30 minutes after school each afternoon until they had made up their time. One mother sent a note each day to have her daughter excused to go to doctor, etc. Everyone else had made up their time, so she was required to make up her time during lunch period and afternoon recess. The mother appeared in person one evening after school. She gave her speech and after listening, I reminded her that the girl still had 15 minutes to work. All the children were happy with me at the last day of school and the board offered me a contract for the next school year. I had saved enough money to attend college a year, so I recommended they hire my older sister to teach instead.

There isn't room to record the many interesting happenings in high school. I will close my story with this one. During my senior year, I was employed to help in the office at the Big 4 Hardware. I worked a couple evenings each week after school and often a few hours on weekends. Our family had one car. Dad normally drove the car wherever he needed to go because of a crippled leg. My sister learned to drive because our Mother did not drive and it was helpful to have another driver in the family. My brother, being a boy, thought he should learn to drive also. I had no need to drive and no one had time to teach me anyway. A young man who worked full time at the hardware store offered to teach me to drive his green Ford coupe. A couple evenings a week, he would take time to give me a lesson. We usually drove on the paved roads going to King City or Albany. One evening, we were sailing along at 25 miles an hour and he said something unique and I returned with a "smart" remark. He said, "Don't you dare to say that again." Not realizing he was serious, I repeated my rejoinder. He reached across the seat and planted a kiss on my right cheek. Shocked and surprised, I turned to look at him and also turned the car to the right and almost drove over the curb before he grabbed the steering wheel and put us back in our side of the road. You know, as long as I knew him he never offered to kiss me again. Wonder Why?

The Unexpected Vacation
By Joanne Kline of Traverse City, Michigan
Born 1929

The year was 1953. I had graduated from college in 1951 with a bachelor's degree and a secondary teaching certificate and had married a man who was determined to become a physician. He had depleted his V.A. benefits in undergraduate school, having previously served two years in the Air Force. This meant that upon acceptance to medical school, Kirksville College of Osteopathic Medicine, we were totally dependent on my income in a small community with an abundance of married students with wives seeking employment, several of whom were qualified teachers.

We settled into a college–owned two-room apartment, under pressure as (my husband's classes began and I learned that my chance of obtaining a teaching position was slim to none. With great trepidation, I applied for a job as a nurse's aide in a nearby hospital. I did not have experience; I had no desire, nor real knowledge of what my duties would be. Besides, I would need to buy uniforms and shoes. Furthermore, my husband had made it clear that he would never marry a nurse. In the midst of my great anxiety, thankfully, a knock came on our door and it was the superintendent of an outlying small school district with an offer of a position in a one room rural school, where the previously hired teacher failed to show up. School had already begun and in the meantime, mothers, though unqualified, were attempting to hold some kind of order.

Although this offer of employment was even more frightening in many respects than the position in the hospital, the pay was better, the hours on the surface were shorter, and it seemed at the time to be my destiny, and even perhaps, God's intervention! And so the adventure began. Getting to this school, Ringo Point School meant driving 14 miles to the small town of Novinger where the consolidated high school was, then taking a school bus that went into the county to pick up high school students. That was a route of about 11 miles or so, but it didn't go as far as Ringo Point. That meant that I got off the bus and hiked a half mile or so, over a couple of barbed wire fences, through a snake infested cow pasture, to the school yard, which included a rickety outhouse that appeared to be barely clinging onto a small hill, and an outdoor hand pump for water.

Needless to say, I had some serious reservations about my decision to accept this "opportunity," but really, I had no choice at this point. The schoolhouse door was unlocked and as it opened, I could see 15 or 20 mice scurry from the tops of the desks to wherever they hid out when the room was occupied. I made a mental note to bring some poison the next day. Before long, I heard the sound of a bus unloading my students, 18 of them ranging from 1st to 8th grade. I don't know who of us were more frightened. There they stood, barely inside the only door, huddled together and looking at me as though I were from outer space. I might as well have been, I shared with them that I was from Michigan, I might as well have said, "Mars." Most of them were barefoot. Needless to say, I found preparing lesson plans for eight grades, plus a kindergartner five days a week, overwhelming. But it soon became clear that I would have no discipline problems. These children knew that if they caused any trouble in school, and if their parents learned of it, they would be in big trouble at home.

One ongoing problem involved a little 2nd grade girl who either couldn't hold it or chose not to leave her desk to go out to the outhouse. I can't say that I blamed her. So frequently, the noise of liquid splashing onto the wood floor was heard, along with some quiet giggles. This was not her only problem, but she was clearly loved by the other students. Her name was Judy. Then one spring day as I was teaching the older students and using the blackboard, I heard what sounded like a light knocking in the area of the chimney behind me. It persisted so I sent one of the older boys outside to see if anything was amiss. He quickly returned and said he couldn't see anything unusual, but then a rather rhythmic sound persisted even as I continued with the lesson. So I reluctantly decided to take a break and go outside myself to check the source of the noise. To my chagrin, the chimney was on fire! Did I mention that a coal furnace in the basement heated the building, which was also under my supervision and part of my janitorial duties? Needless to say, my mind and my body went into overdrive and I knew that first and foremost, I must get the children

out of the building, not at all difficult. Perhaps it was the most exciting thing they had ever witnessed.

Well, in the midst of my disaster, the neighbor nearest the school, where one of the older boys ran for help, came roaring out of his driveway, in his truck and leaning on his horn without a break. He sped past the school and up and down every local two-track. Miraculously, within minutes, the schoolyard was filled with trucks, tractors, and other odd farming implements, loaded with ladders and buckets. The ladders were quickly placed against the wall nearest the chimney. I frantically pumped water from the well, the children carried the water to the men on the ladders, all like a well-organized machine and time having been suspended, before long the flames and the smoke were defeated! And as a bonus, I got to meet some of the parents of my students as well as others who obviously cared about them, as well as the schoolhouse.

So school was suspended for a few days while repairs were made and I along with the children had an unexpected vacation. I spent many hours trying to get the black stains out of my clothing, rather unsuccessfully. That Christmas I decided to knit mittens for every student. I had observed that some of them came to school mittenless. Somewhere I have a picture of myself with the 18 pairs of mittens spread out on my bed. I don't know how they felt about it, but I felt content. That was the last year that Ringo Point School was open. The following years those students would be bussed to Novinger, the location of the newly consolidated school district. Every once in a while I think of those days and those students. I never had a single discipline problem. The 8th graders would be 60 now. I wonder where they are, what they're doing, and if they remember the day the schoolhouse caught fire.

The Life of Roy
By Roy D. Stuart of Stanberry, Missouri
Born 1913

This is the story of Roy, as I was told. Roy was the youngest of eleven children born to Ed and Eva Stuart. Roy went to Floyd school for the first eight grades and then went to high school in Stanberry. At home, they had a large garden that he liked to work in. He had a garden all of his life. During his senior year of high school, after school and on Saturdays, he would shuck corn in the fall for Clyde Ditter. After high school, he started farming one mile south of his father. It was hard times. In 1933 and 1934, Roy and the Murphy boys went to North Dakota to do the wheat harvest. When the C.C.C. came along, they were building the 136 Highway. He went to Stanberry and worked either shoveling sand or cement from railcars into buggies. In 1934 and 1935, Roy and the Murphy boys went to Treynor, Iowa to shuck corn for two cent per bushel. Roy worked both years for the Storkenbeckers.

On Easter Sunday of 1935, he married Mildred Gunter. In 1936, a girl was born to them, Beverly. That was the year of heavy snow. To go get the doctor, Roy drove a team and wagon over a fence and one mile south. In March of 1937, they moved one mile southwest to another farm. In March of 1939, a son was born, Duane. In 1940, they moved four and a half miles southwest of Stanberry. They had 160 acres of land. They had chickens, milk cows, sheep, hogs, and horses. Eggs and cream from the milk were saved to sell on Saturday nights. With the money made from selling that, they bought the groceries that they needed. The farm was owned by O.C. Bullock, an engineer on the Wabash Railroad. In 1954, O.C. said he wanted to sell the farm for $75 per acre. Dad and Mom got a loan. In years later, they stopped milking and raised more hogs and stock cows. In 1945, they got their first tractor, a John Deere. In the early 1980s, they bought another 60 acres. In the mid-'80s, he had some health problems and rented the farmland out. In Early 1986, the doctor said he had a brain tumor. Roy said life will throw you some curves and you just made the best of it. We lost Roy in 1986.

Flour Sack Dresses and Snakes
By Bonnie Swalley of Maryville, Missouri
Born 1940

Back when I was a kid, Saturday night was bath night. Mom would fill a galvanized tub with hot water that was heated on the old wood stove. She would put the tub in the middle of the kitchen floor and each of us kids would take turns with our baths. By the

Bonnie, Tanis, and Connie

time the last kid was done, the water would be getting pretty bad! As long as I can remember (as a kid), my mother made us our clothes. I remember she would take us to town to the grocery store and take us to the flour aisle. Mom would tell us to pick out a printed flour sack so that she could make us a dress out of it. We could hardly wait until the flour sack was empty so that she could make us a beautiful dress to wear! Back in the '40s, we used to have iceboxes instead of refrigerators. The iceboxes had two sides—one for food and the other for ice to keep the food cold. Sometimes when it was winter and we couldn't get to town, Dad would cut ice out of the old cow tank for the icebox.

I know the Depression years were rough because I can remember my parents talking about them. I can remember going to town in our Chevy Coupe and buying sugar with war stamps. Also, we used to buy tires with those war stamps. My sisters and I went to a one-room school with eight grades. We used to have community meetings where the whole neighborhood would get together once a month for some type of entertainment. One I can remember was the "box supper" night. We ladies would make boxes with crepe paper and try to make them as pretty as they could. Then we would fill them with food for two people. The men would bid on the boxes and whoever got your box would eat with you. That was lots of fun!

I have always hated snakes. I think the reason is because of an incident, which happened one sunny morning, years ago. My sister and I were sitting on the ledge of our picket fence in the corner of our yard. We were playing with our dolls, when a big old blue racer snake came out from under the fence. We dropped our dolls and the snake crawled over them. We jumped down off the fence and headed for the house. That big snake chased us with his head held high off the ground. He chased us around a tree three times, until finally we got brave enough to head for the house. That snake chased us halfway up the steps and fell back down. Mom came out and finished off the snake. To this day, I am scared to death of snakes! Our grandmother lived in Southern Missouri. When we would go visit her, we always wanted to go to our ole swimming hole that we often visited there. It was a spring fed water hole back in the deep woods. Probably not very safe because of all the copperhead snakes around, but it was still lots of fun!

Tarkio College Days
By Doug Kingery of St. Joseph, Missouri
Born 1949

During my senior year of high school in Glenwood, Iowa, I was either athletic enough or fortunate enough (or both) to have received an athletic scholarship to play for the Tarkio College Owls in Tarkio, Missouri. Tarkio College was located in Atchison County and had a college for over 100 years. I was to participate in football and baseball at the school.

I graduated in May of 1967 and when I left home in August to attend the college, it would be the farthest away from home that I had ever been by myself/on my own. Although it was only about 65 miles away, it might as well have been 650 miles. My parents took me to Tarkio about two weeks before school started, as football practice began way before the school term. I stayed in the football dormitory and began to make friends with my new teammates. We ate all of our meals together, had team meetings, and went on several team outings during this time. As early arrival football players, we were able to register for our classes before the other students and got practically all of the classes we wanted. My biggest and most dreaded class was a science/chemistry class that met four times a week. It also had a two-hour Saturday morning lab. Of course, this meant that I couldn't go home on the weekends. I really couldn't anyway because the football games were all on Saturday afternoons. Either way, I still disliked the morning lab!

Once school started, we freshmen football players found the things changed somewhat for us. Although we had an advantage over the other incoming freshmen, we found ourselves being treated equally. We had to wear these crazy little beanies that were alternating the school colors, purple and gray. We had to wear those beanies for about the first two weeks of class. If we were caught without our beanies on, we had to do some sort of silly dance, sing the school song, or some such thing. We also had convocation every Wednesday morning in the school gymnasium. The convocation lasted approximately one hour. We had to pick up a piece of paper prior to going into the gym, sign our name on the paper, and drop it in a plate or box upon leaving convocation. This was to prove that we had indeed attended. Tarkio College was a Presbyterian affiliated school, so we were told that the convocations were mandatory and that if you missed three in a trimester that you would be kicked out of school. I don't know the validity of that, but we all attended the convocations.

The college served the student meals in the school cafeteria, so there was always a line. For us football players, it made suppertime especially hectic. At Tarkio College, you had to dress up for supper. This means that the men wore shirts, ties, and most of the time dress coats. The women had to wear dresses. Football practices usually ran from around 3:00 or 3:30 P.M. until around 5:30 P.M. Supper was served at the cafeteria from around 4:30 to 6:00 P.M. Well, you can imagine the scurrying around the football players would have to do after practice to get ready for supper! With practice getting over at 5:30 P.M, that only gave us football players 30 minutes to get showered, put on our dinner clothing, and run the two to three blocks from the locker room to the cafeteria. Many times, most of the players skipped the shower and just got dressed over their sweaty bodies. It was either that or no supper in many instances.

I got to play a little football that fall and one memorable moment was up at Crete, Nebraska when we played Doane College. We had a pretty good team, but they were a really good team that I think was ranked very high in the national NAIA poll that year. Anyway, I was on the kickoff team. We kicked off to the Doane College Tigers. They had an All-American tackle and an All-American running back. Wouldn't you know it that the All-American tackle was in my lane of responsibility and the ball went to the All-American running back. I ran as hard as I could toward that tackle, staying in my lane of responsibility. Just as I got to him, I did the most spectacular "submarine" dive you have ever seen! I went right between his legs and came up just as that running back got there. I don't know that you could say I made the tackle, but he went down and I was congratulated by all of my teammates! I felt like I was at the top of the world! Well, unknown to us, there had been a penalty flag thrown. We, the kicking team, had been offsides and had to re-kick. We did, and that tackle was still in my lane. The ball once again went to that outstanding running back. Things did not turn out the same that second time around, as that All-American tackle ran over me like a locomotive! The running back gained considerable yardage. I think we only lost one or two games that year and that was one of them.

I left Tarkio College at the end of the term, joined the Marines for four years, and went to another college on the G.I. Bill. However, 22 years after attending Tarkio College, I came full-circle in 1989. I began a fourteen year teaching and coaching career at Tarkio High School that allowed me the opportunity to walk the grounds of the campus I had attended many years before!

Farm Life
By Ruth (Massey) Cave of Kearny, Missouri
Born 1921

I was born at Gower, Missouri, on a farm on March 26, 1921. One of my sisters was 15 years older that I am. I remember her boyfriends giving me gum to get out of the parlor when they came to see her. She went to Wyoming in 1927 to marry a man that had been to Missouri working on making a highway. My mother made her dresses. The waistline was below the hips. My sister got out of high school and went to college that summer. She was a country schoolteacher that fall.

At Christmastime, my mother could take cedar tree limbs and make a pretty Christmas tree in the corner of the room. My dolls were celluloid, like plastic. The arms and legs were on with rubber bands. My toys outside was two little wheels and a dog. My dad drove a buggy and horse to town. We didn't have a car. We had a garden and fruit trees. The groceries that were bought were put on a ticket at the store. When you sold a load of hogs or calves, you paid the grocery bill.

I say I was raised on a dirt farm, as we did all the farming with mules. We had wood stoves to cook on and for heating the house. We had to carry the water in and out. We had coal oil lamps to see with at night. We had to go down the path to the two holer in the daytime and had a pot (also called a slop jar) with a lid that we used at night. I rode a horse all 12 years to school. I remember being at school in 1929 when we heard that the banks were closing. I graduated in 1939. There were 21 students in my class. In the 1930s, they had a hog program that you could only have so many hogs. If you had just one hog too many it had to be done away with.

My husband was born June 28, 1917. After he got out of high school in 1936, he worked at a gas station for 30 dollars a month. He worked every day, every other night, and

Darrell and Ruth Cave in about 1938

426

every other Sunday. He did this for three years. I rode my horse to school by this gas station. One Sunday, he came out to my home and asked me if I wanted to go to a show with him. I had to ask him his name. I went. We went together for three years and have been married for 72 years. Our first home in 1940 had five rooms. There was no water. The rent was seven dollars a month. This was the first time I had had electric lights. We have lived on a 30-acre farm for 50 years. I am still on the farm. We have had a good life together. We have one daughter and son-in-law, one grandson and his wife, and three great grandchildren. My husband had to stop driving about two years ago. He has been in a nursing home for the last six months, and is unable to do anything. He is also in a wheelchair. He can still feed himself, though. I still drive and go five miles to see him every day.

My Horse Tony
By William D. Huffman of Palmyra,
Missouri
Born 1927

I was born on October 7, 1927, on a farm six miles northeast of Gilman city, Missouri. My parents were Oleath and Jennie (Shepherd) Huffman. A dirt road ran east to west and crossed the Sugar Creek and passed several houses and farms. One of those farms belonged to my grandfather, William F. Shepherd. A road running north and south intersected with this road and paralleled Sugar Creek for a mile or so. My home place was located at the base of a large hill that was spread out across the bottom of that land. Sugar Creek was notorious for flooding. It drained many acres up through the bottomland, and the day I was born was one of the times that it came out. Dr. Wilbur Warren from Gilman City was on the scene to deliver me. He was there overnight until the flood receded. I supposed my dad probably brought him in and out with a wagon and team of horses.

My parents moved to the hill farm that Grandfather owned by the time I started school. We farmed with horses, and I had a black colt named Tony who was two years old. He was broken to ride when I started to Rock Island, a one-room country school that I attended for eight years. I attended Milbourne

High School for the first two years. One teacher taught all the subjects to six or eight students in one room of the schoolhouse. Tony continued to carry me three miles to school. I put him in the school barn, and fed him at noon. By the time school was out, he was ready to run all the way home. The small black horse was my transportation all through school. Prior to going to high school, I would ride him to my grandparents' house, which was three quarters of a mile away. If my sister Bonnie tagged along, I had to ride slow and bareback because Mom was afraid that I would get a foot caught in the stirrups.

My father was a substitute mail carrier out of Brimson, Missouri. Part of the route was dirt roads. When the road was really muddy, about 20 miles of it was delivered on horseback. Later on, he turned the 20-mile jaunt over to me and Tony. Tony was well acquainted with the route, so I had no problems. Sometimes, I rode a mare that belonged to my grandfather so that Tony could have a rest. Of the years in the thirties, 1934 through 1936 were the dry years. There was nothing to feed the livestock. Dad and my grandfather hand pumped water for 40 head of cattle. To feed them, trees were cut and my dad would get on a horse and drive them down to sugar creek where horseweeds and other foliage grew abundantly. The hill farm had lots of water, which was provided by a well that was one half mile south of the house and a spring that was close by. In dry weather, the spring would dry up, and then it would become necessary to haul water for use at the house. That was put in 50-gallon drums. We moved back to the bottom farms, and water was plentiful. We would go to Gilman City on Saturday nights, weather permitting, and take eggs and cream to sell. We would use the money to buy needed items. We always had a garden, and Mom canned everything that she could. We always had plenty of meat, eggs, and milk. The merchants would hire someone to show movies. The theater was just a screen on the side of a building, with improvised seating on a vacant lot. If a cloud was visible in the west, I would keep one eye on the cloud. If it became threatening, Dad would come after me. It was imperative that we got home before the storm hit because we lived on a dirt road.

After high school, I worked for the Standard Service Station run by Fred Green. I worked there up until Uncle Sam called.

The service rejected me, and I was sent back home because of an old injury that I had suffered from getting knocked off a horse in my younger years. I then went to work for George Shepherd, my great uncle. I was responsible for hauling coal, delivering ice, and other things to local patrons. It was fun to hold 20 pounds of ice in my hands while the lady of the house made room for it in the icebox. After that, Noble Hardware needed someone, so I worked for Ed and Bernice for a few years. I sold appliances, propane gas, hardware, etc. we sold stoves and refrigerators to customers in Bethany. We delivered bottled gas all over the town. Freight came in on the train and we picked it up at the station for the store in Gilman City. I dated girls up there and attended movies. At that time, a small hangout was on the Wye. After a show, it was time for ice cream or a snack. I believe it was called the Tripp Inn.

After Nobles, in 1951 I married and moved to Trenton, Missouri. I spent 15 years with the Municipal Utilities, and then I moved to Palmyra, Missouri in 1966. I was in charge of the city utilities, power, water, and sewer. I retired at the end of 1992. I served as mayor for the next six years. I seldom come back to the Gilman City area. I have many fond memories growing up. When I think of memories of my family and friends who are no longer with us, I remember in sadness. I am astounded at the growth and changes in Bethany in the last 25 years. The square was the main drag during my younger years.

Living with my Aunt and Uncle
By Sharon Curren of St. Joseph, Missouri
Born 1945

I was born in 1945 and lived with my aunt and uncle, Ray and Opal Donahue in the small town of Grayson, Missouri. My life there was filled with memories. We had a tiny post office and a gas station where you could also get bread, milk, or pop. Since we lived close, many times my uncle would pull me and my doll, Susie, in my Steger Coaster to get mail and stop for a soda. We had one cow, Pocahontas, and a big bunch of chickens. My uncle got up very early to milk the cow. Sometimes I went to the barn. One morning, my uncle said that if I would sing to her, that

Aunt Opal, Uncle Ray Donahue, and Sharon

she would give more milk. I started to sing and she bellowed out so loud that I ran back to the house to hide. Chickens were my aunt's pride and joy. I was told to go get the eggs one morning, and I did try. Seems there was this hen sitting on the nest, so I got me a stick and tried to poke her. She would not budge, so I decided to whap her on the head. Just as I went to swing, my aunt grabbed the stick. Her words were enough. I knew I was wrong.   O n e day, I was told to get a bucket of chicken feed out of the building. I went back screaming, "I can't! There's a monster in the building!" My uncle took the ax and came back laughing. Yes, it was quite a monster: a dead mouse. Afternoons were fun. I played in our cellar or had tea parties for my doll underneath the lilac bush. Afterward, I would have a cool drink from the good old pump. On hot days, I took naps in the house on our linoleum floor with a pillow while my aunt churned butter. Sometimes my uncle would rock me in his rocking chair while I listened to the sound of his ticking pocket watch. We never had much company, but it was really special when we did. We had one church in town and whoever came around to preach was welcome. A preacher came to invite us to church while my uncle and I were in the pasture with a new Billy goat that he had gotten me. That goat went around back of that preacher and took those cigarettes right out of his back pocket! He was so embarrassed that he left!

Once a month, we went to the next town, Plattsburg, to get groceries. I got cinnamon balls. I loved to help shop and was real good at wanting all the things that we did not need. My aunt did lots of canning and her pickles were the best. The whole house smelled like vinegar when pickles were made.

There was an ornery side of me. I got made one night, as I did not want to go inside and go to bed. I took my shoes off on the porch and told my aunt, "I wish you'd see a snake!" Bad language was never tolerated. The next morning I got up and went out to get my shoes and a big black snake was curled up around them. It just don't pay to talk back. Today I truly miss my aunt and uncle, as they are with the Lord. Now, I sit in the rocking chair, and as I rock and think back, I would not trade those memoires of that great life for anything.

One-room School and WWII
By Carolyn S. Kiner of St. Joseph, Missouri
Born 1935

In the fall of 1941, I entered the first grade at Bowen District # 61, a one-room school in DeKalb County, Missouri. We lived about a mile and a half from the school on a mud road. When the weather was really bad, Daddy would hitch up Ole Buck and Sparkplug, our team of horses, to a farm wagon. Then he would take my sister and me to school. The school had one teacher for all grades. I only had two different teachers in my eight years there. The school had electricity, as it was on Highway 6, but farther out, no one had power. There was no plumbing, just two little houses by the back property line. We had no phone, but the nice lady across the road let us use hers in an emergency. The building was heated by a coal stove that the teacher kept going in the winter months. We students had chores to do. We would put up the United States flag each morning and bring it in at the close of the day. It was then folded properly and put away. It hung from a metal pole that was located in the front yard. Also, there was a well where we pumped fresh water to fill our earthen fountain. We would clean the blackboards and pound the erasers against the side of the building. We emptied the sharpener for our number two lead pencils, which was always overflowing. Our wooden desks stood in neat rows in front of the teacher's desk. We played Andy-over, tag and such during our

recesses. On the really cold days, we played games that we had brought from home. The card game, pitch, was always a favorite. We lived in a community where everybody played pitch. Our playground equipment consisted of two teeter-totters and two swings.

We were more like a family than a school, and our teachers stressed that fact. We had programs for Halloween, Christmas, and closing day. We always played to a full house, as the whole community would come. The school was built in what we called "shotgun configuration" with a stage at the far end where we performed our short plays, speeches, and boisterously sang our songs while the teacher played the old upright piano. There were rose colored denim curtains that were strung on a wire so they could be opened and closed. The ladies occupied the desks, and the gentlemen stood along the three open sides. Attached to the main structure were two small rooms. One was used to store coal for the stove. It had a door leading directly to the stove, which saved the teacher many steps. The second room was called the cloak room. That is where we hung our coats and put our lunches. When the temperature dropped, our lunches would be frozen by noontime. I feel truly blessed to have had the privilege of attending a one-room school. Bowen closed in 1952 and reverted back to the McDonald estate, the family who had donated the land years beforehand.

On December 7, 1941, our school days were suddenly changed. Japan attacked Pearl Harbor and threw the United States into World War II. I remember it was Sunday and some of Daddy's relatives were at our house for dinner. It must have been a fairly warm day, because my cousins and I were playing outdoors. One of Daddy's brother-in-laws had stopped in to relay the news. We knew by his demeanor that something was wrong. We trooped inside to see what was going on. A hush had fallen over the gathering, and everyone seemed to be talking in whispers. Our school was deeply involved in the war effort. We collected all kinds of things: tin foil, string, newspapers, to name a few. The whole nation rose up to help. We had special days to buy war stamps. When we filled our stamp books, we could turn them in for war bonds. We had ration books of stamps for certain items. Many common products were in short supply such as sugar, butter, coffee, and meat. I remember that ladies silk hose were almost impossible to find, so most women were using leg makeup. Extreme measures were needed to get tires for a car, as the government was using our rubber for the war vehicles. Doctors were granted tires, as they traveled a lot of miles, and they were still making house calls most of the time. People didn't call a doctor unless it was serious. My parents were farmers, so we had no trouble getting food on the table. My mother always had a huge garden, and we raised our own meat. Daddy planted molasses cane so that we could have our own sweetener. He had it processed at a nearby mill. It turned out to be a beautiful honey color. Mother made lots of gingerbread and gingersnaps.

I had one Uncle that served in the Navy. He never left the States. He was an athlete in college, but had health problems. He spent his service time teaching navy recruits to swim. Another uncle was in the Army. He was in the infantry and served in the Europe sector. An older cousin was in the Marines and fought in some of the bloodiest battles in the South Pacific. He was lucky to make it back. Another cousin was in the Air Force. He was part of a crew on a bomber stationed in England. He was killed on the return flight after a bombing mission over Berlin. He was a 19 year old college student. When the war ended in 1945, there was such joy in our land. Jobs were plentiful and the real estate market was booming due to the returning service men. You could quit a job one morning and have another by the next morning. A lot of servicemen were going back to college on the GI bill. We celebrated our freedom.

Frozen Fish and New Bicycle
By Ramona Cowger of DeKalb, Missouri
Born 1932

I was born February 4, 1932 during a terrible blizzard. My parents lived in a little house with no phone, no electricity, no indoor plumbing, and a wood heating and cooking stove. My dad had to walk a mile during the blizzard to reach a phone to call the doctor. Thankfully, the doctor arrived before my birth. Seventeen months later, my parents had a baby boy. When I was three years old and my brother, Dean was one and a half, my parents

Uncle Raymond Ford, Ramona, and Dean Long in 1942

moved to a four-room house that was three miles away. It was a very cold, blustery day when we moved. They put the heating stove, still hot, in the farm wagon, and then loaded the feather bed, quilts, and pillows in the wagon. Mother and we two toddlers were loaded among the bedding, and the horse-drawn wagon took us to our destination. Mother said that when she tried to scrub the kitchen floor the water would freeze on the floor.

When I was old enough to go to school, I walked across the fields a mile and a half to the one-room school. It had one teacher for all eight grades. School was never cancelled. For school, I had three dresses that were made from printed chicken feed sacks. We lived in that house until I was 11 years old. There was still no electricity, no indoor plumbing, no phone, and a wood stove for heating and cooking. The wood would burn out during the night. My two little fish would freeze solid many nights. When my dad got the fire going, the fish bowl would thaw and the little fish would start swimming again. We had a rooster that would flog me when I went out to the outhouse. He only bothered me. My brother and I had very few toys. One Christmas, my dad secretly bough and fixed up a bicycle for us to share. We were so excited. We took turns riding it to the first house next to ours and back. It felt wonderful traveling along with the wind blowing in our hair.

In 1943, when I was 11 years old, we moved to a home that my parents bought. We had electricity, indoor plumbing, an oil furnace, and an electric range for cooking. Still no phone, but how proud we were! Since my father was a farmer, he was exempt from the draft of World War II. Many things were rationed: sugar, tires, and cigarettes, to name a few. One evening when my parents were working at my grandparents tobacco barn, I decided to make fudge. I mixed the sugar, cocoa, and butter together. I found that we had no sweet milk. I knew I would be in trouble if I wasted the sugar. I found some clabbered milk and mixed in the curds. I cooked it, and it tasted just fine. We ate every bite. We never received an allowance. We would pick up corn and tobacco leaves after the harvest. My dad would sell them and give us the proceeds. We also raised runt pigs. It was really difficult to take them to market. However, this was our money for letter jackets, yearbooks, or a Coke with friends.

Accidents, Disappearances, and Snowstorms
By L. E. "Drifter" Place of Phoenix, Arizona Born 1945

I was in my graduation year at Gallatin R-5 in Gallatin, Missouri. I asked my mom if I could go to a dance at Chillicothe, Missouri with a friend. She asked me if I had my homework done. I replied, "Yes; I have it done," so she let me go to the dance with my buddy. I lied about having my homework done, and when I got home from school, she was waiting at the back door saying, "Your teacher called and told me that you got an F on your test because you didn't have any homework to turn in." She was boilin' mad to say the least! She then told me to go get a switch and go into my bedroom to wait. She came in and told me to bend over the bed, which I did. She gave me my few swats, and

when I faked a cry, she stopped. That's the last time I ever lied to my mom, or anyone.

One day, I was putting up hay at my folks' farm, and we were on the last load and last bale of the season. We were putting them in an old hay barn with a huge hayloft that was about 25 feet above the main barn. I had just thrown a bale on the "elevator" which was just an old steel conveyor of sorts. There were two farmhands in the loft, and they were always yelling at me to keep the hay coming. I was, to say the least, getting frustrated at their constant yelling at me, and threw the last bale on the elevator. However, the bale landed across the conveyor instead of the inline way it should have. I foolishly stepped across the elevator to straighten the bale, but my foot and leg went past the PTO shaft instead, and the rapidly turning shaft grabbed my Levi's leg. Of course, it began twisting it tightly and trying to pull my body with it. I jumped back and grabbed the sides of the elevator. Thank God, the elevator was heavy and was easy to hold onto. At the same time, I yelled at the two farmhands to get to the tractor and shut the power off. They both just gave me dumb looks. I was finally able to tear the remaining denim strip off the jeans and ride to the loft. I angrily yelled at the two stupid (I thought) farmhands, "I'm going to dinner!"

I drove to town and walked in the back door of my folks' house. Mom saw that I had one leg of my Levi's cut off. She asked me why I had ruined my jeans. I told her, "You'd better sit down." I told her what happened, and she told me that I'd better tell my dad what I had told her. Dad came in the door, and Mom said, "J, look at your son's jeans!" I told him the story and he did not say a word. He just ran to the truck, backed out of the driveway, and laid rubber for about a block. He came back in about a half an hour and said, "Boy, you are doing the farming now. I just fired two men that almost cost my son his life." He then put the square baler up for sale and bought a hayfork that mounted on the back of one of our John Deere diesel tractors. The next hay season I raked hay in from the local contractor who baled 2-ton round bales. I was so happy to not have to handle 150 to 200 pound hay bales anymore!

I rode the running boards of a 1951 Chevy pickup for quite some time early mornings around Gallatin. I delivered milk, cream, and butter to customers for Places Dairy in the early '50s. I was the milkman! We did this until good old USDA told us we were, like many farmers, "unhealthy."

When I was in my teens, I worked part time as what people nowadays call a bag-boy. I did this job at my parent's small town grocery store. It was chance that I met a very special and wonderful elderly lady, known locally as Miss Daisy. I believe she lived by herself in a somewhat rundown older home. She was on "relief," and was an aunt of a very wealthy farmer and his family. She rarely saw them except for her two nephews who came over every couple of weeks to mow her lawn. I was appalled what I found out through my mom about her relationship with her well-to-do nephew and family, until Mom told me she wanted nothing to do with her wealthy family, except for the nephews. She apparently was too proud to accept their help. God bless Miss Daisy! Vadis and Bertha Mae were a black couple who were common-law married for years and were two of the hardest working people I have ever met in my life. Vadis mowed lawns all over town sand rode his riding lawn mower all over town on side streets with Bertha Mae or "Bert," as she was nicknamed. They lived in the north end of town, a somewhat less desirable part of town for most Gallatin people. However, Vadis and Bertha Mae kept their home immaculate, unlike their neighbors. Unfortunately, their neighbors did not care about their homes. I delivered their groceries three times weekly. I commented to Vadis one day when I delivered, "Your home looks like a rose in the middle of a hog pen." Vadis looked at me and explained, "Well, I never gave it that much thought, but, by dang, you're right!" One day, Bertha Mae was doing yard work for my Mom. She was out in the hot sun raking the yard while Mom was doing the dishes. Mom looked out and saw Bert raking leaves. She yelled out the kitchen window, "Bertha Mae! Get out of the sun or you'll sunburn!" Then she realized she was black and yelled, "Bertha, I didn't mean..." then Bertha Mae sat down at a picnic table and started belly laughing to almost hysterics. Mom ran out to her, thinking she had gotten sick. She found her laughing so hard that she could hardly talk. Bertha Mae composed herself long enough to say, "Bonnie, we do sunburn, but thanks for your concern!"

In 1961, two years before I graduated Gallatin R-5, we had a blizzard in mid-December for several days. The closest radio station (long before good FM radio) broadcasted the school closings for several counties. The local reporter happened to be a good friend of our family and lived probably a block and a half from us. She always gave news reports from her bedroom. She had to be awake by 5:30 daily, except for Saturday and Sunday. I'll call her Janice in this story because I just cannot remember her name. She read the news of Daviess County from her bedroom desk. Well, the snow came for probably four days straight or more. I went out and put chains on the folk's new Chevy pickup, then went to the back door of their grocery store to retrieve two 150 pound, six foot long elevator weights for added traction. Boy, those things were heavy! The truck was obviously a 4x4. I went back to the house and picked up my dad and headed for the farm, or so we thought! We arrived at the beginning of our farm road, only to find a 20-foot wide and 20-foot high snowdrift. The road was completely impassable. We then drove a quarter mile east to the next road going south. We drove about two thirds of a mile south to a road going east. We then parked the pickup and started walking across the snow-covered, three to four foot deep pasture and stepped over the neighbor's fence. This I believe put a severe strain on my dad's heart, as he would stop to rest several times. That was the last time he walked to the farm over the snow. Fortunately, the diesel tractors had been equipped with block heaters, as the temp was around zero degrees. That was the winter average temperature that time of winter. The new township grader operator was fired, so the township had to hire a contract operator to bring in a crawler with a scoop. He worked the next three or four days to clear that road.

My grandparents owned a livestock market sale barn and my mom worked in the same city, St. Joseph, Missouri. She let me stay with Grandmother and my grandfather, Brownie, during the day. Mom came home from the shoe store where she worked and couldn't find me. I was only four or five years of age, so she panicked. She asked her foster sisters if they had seen me; they told her no. She had forgotten that every Saturday she let me follow Brownie around the sale

432

barn to talk to all the cattle buyers there, as they all knew me. She screamed, "Brownie! I can't find my son!" At that moment, Brownie grabbed the microphone from the auctioneer and announced to the entire crowd (which was probably a couple hundred cattle buyers) "This sale is on hold until I find my grandson!" He had cattle buyers from the lower 48 states walking around their 100-acre farm looking for me. Mom finally found me playing in a place that she had never imagined. The sale continued.

During the same time period, my mom came home from work one day and received a letter from a Boston attorney that stated that my natural father's parents from that area were sending an attorney to St. Joseph to retrieve me. They wanted to take me back to the East coast to be raised in a proper Catholic home. She tearfully showed Brownie the letter and asked for help. Brownie promptly called a Buchannan County circuit judge and advised him of the situation. The judge told Brownie to bring his daughter to the courthouse at 9:00 A.M. that Monday morning. We walked out of the judge's chambers in about an hour, with Mom having full, unconditional custody! Brownie commented, "It will be a cold day in hell when someone takes my grandson away!"

Gypsies and Strange Men
By Betty Taul of Trenton, Missouri
Born 1924

On April 14, 1928, I turned four years old. My sister was five years old. Things happened in my childhood that I have never forgotten. My mother and dad went to town (Gallatin), and left my two older brothers to watch my sister and me. As soon as our parents got out of sight, our brothers grabbed their poles and went fishing north of the house. We could see them from our home, so my sister and I played "house." That was our favorite thing to play. A huge, bearded, longhaired man knocked at our door. We were both afraid, but we opened the door anyway. He was the biggest old man that we had ever seen. He told us to tell our parents that the hogs were out. We were so afraid that we ran and got in Mom and Dad's bed. We stayed there until they got back home from town.

Another time the same summer, the other memorable even took place. Our grandparents were at our home visiting. We were busy in the garden, picking green beans, cutting heads of cabbage, digging new potatoes, and pulling some onions for our dinner. That is when we noticed that a group of gypsies had driven their wagons by our house and camped at the creek down the road. There was a big commotion because they were singing and their pans were rattling as they drove along. My granddad told my mother to run to the house and protect the baby. I got hold of my grandma around her leg and put my face under her apron. Later that day, three women came to our house. One was very old, one younger, and one middle aged. They asked for something to eat. We gave them some potatoes, green beans, and cabbage. My granddad took them in the hen house and gathered her some eggs and caught her cooking hen. After this, they went on their way to their creek campsite. We could hear music, singing, and saw them dancing that night. When we kids got up the next morning, they were gone.

September brought school days. We had to walk to school between two-cow pasture over wire fences that my dad and Mr. Miner

Vawnitha and Betty in 1928

433

made steps over. My sister and I were very afraid of the cows in the pastures. Our school, Spring Hill in Daviess County, sat right in the middle of the timber. One day, Mr. Miner was going to the schoolhouse, so he stopped by our house and invited us to ride with him in his two-wheel cart. The horse got spooked, and then everything went up in the air. We fell backwards into a muddy water puddle on the dirt road. We wanted to go back home, but he would not let us. We had to go to school muddy and dirty. Our teacher cleaned us up the best she could.

We did not live at that house very long. We moved to the Crab Hill School in DeKalb County. We had three women and one man teacher in our eight years of schooling. We lived in a nice white house on the corner. There was an orchard to pass as we walked to school. Oh, what fun it was growing up. Going to school each morning we said the Pledge of Allegiance to the flag, weather permitting. One of my teachers would not let me go to the bathroom when I asked, so I wet my pants. It ran all the way down to the blackboard. Guess what? My teacher had to clean that up! She sent me home to get cleaned up and then I had to return to school. I remember I was just four years old then. Each morning, for our health, we were checked for clean fingernails, ears, mouth, and hair. My sister, at age six, took sick and died. My teacher was very understanding; I could go home and be with my sister if she asked for me as she laid there sick. One time, my dad saw a picture of my teacher and said, "She's a cat's meow!" I did not know that that meant back then and often wondered what he meant. As of today, I know it meant she was beautiful, a princess, and precious.

The Kindness of Others
By Gladys Anderson of Holt, Missouri
Born 1911

If I make it to May 24, 2013, I will be 102 years old. I think that what helped me the most out of life is love, kindness, and work. I learned love from my parents, N.L. and Sarah Bogart. The beginning stages of my lessons of kindness I learned when I was five years old from our rural mail carrier, Pate Moberly, and a neighbor, Grace, Albright.

In 1916, we had no car, just a buggy, and

Gladys Anderson at age 100

a spring wagon, which only had two seats. We didn't go out much. One of the highlights of my days was to meet the carrier and get our mail. Mr. Moberly was so kind to me. He always fixed it so that I wouldn't lose any of it. My dad raised garden produce and fruit. I took the carrier apples, peaches, and grapes. One Christmas he brought me a package. Just imagine that! Me, a little girl, with a package of my own! I rushed to the house to open the package. Upon opening it, I found the most beautiful doll. She had curls and eyes that opened and shut. She was one of the most treasured gifts I ever received. Another kindness that was shown to me was from my neighbor, Grace. She lived about two miles from us and halfway to Pleasant Grove School where I started attending at six years old. I walked with my brother. I made it to school fine but on the road home, those little short legs got so tired! Grace knew that and always had me something ready to eat every day. I still remember those two people fondly.

In the fall of 1916, we moved to a farm near Holt, Missouri, and I started to school there. Holt was a different town then. It had 28 businesses, including two banks, a depot, and trains. One came from Kansas City at 6:00 A.M, and then came back again at 8:00 A.M. Once nice thing about Holt was that there was a livery stable nearby. You could leave your horse there in the warm place and pick it up ready to go home when you returned. There were three grocery stores, two restaurants, a drug store, two doctors, a dentist, a newspaper (The Holt Rustler), and two hotels. Traveling salesmen came on the

434

train and stayed at the hotels. They brought samples for merchants to select and order from.

I went eight years to grade school and four years to high school. I graduated in 1929 and married my school sweetheart, James Anderson. Later we ran the Phillips 66 Station for over 40 years. I hand pumped many gallons of gasoline, fixed some flat tires, and even greased a few cars. Those cars still run, by the way! We raised one daughter, Beverly. As time passed, an opening for a postal clerk came to pass. I took exams, passed, and went to work as a clerk with Lawrence Bartec as our postmaster. I also served with postmasters Lawrence Odor and Benton Kelp. I retired from that in 1976.

I drove for my Dad, taking produce and fruit to sell at Excelsior Springs, Missouri. I started driving when I was 13 years old. We didn't have to take a test back then. I drove until I was 97 years old. I enjoyed every minute of it. I went down one of those hills in Excelsior Springs and into a garage with the door closed. I had a few scrapes and there was lots of noise, but no one got hurt.

Through the years I have seen lots of changes. One change was from using kerosene lamps to using electric lights. That was good, as I didn't have to clean those sooty flues. Another change was that we used to use wood stoves and now we use gas and electric heat. No more carrying in wood and carrying ashes out. Before, it used to be sweltering hot inside. Now we have air conditioning. Cars have changed a lot, too, from Model-Ts to Cadillacs. Used to, we only had radios; now we have nice televisions. Wall phones were prevalent back then; now, we have cell phones. This I will just never understand. Back then, you had to ring a central operator. She would answer and would ring your number for you. But now, all you have to do is rub your fingers on a little box that you carry around with you, and up comes a message and even a picture! It just boggles my mind!

On my 100th birthday, I was privileged to play offertory at my church. In 30 minutes, pictures of me at the piano. I was at a friends' in California. That was amazing. I had a wonderful 100th celebration. 185 people came to wish me a happy birthday. It was so good to see all of them. Oh, something else about birthdays: I've been to Hayes Hamburger at Antioch the last four years.

They make the best cheeseburgers you could ever eat. I remember going to the Hayes Parent restaurant on the west side of square in Liberty, Missouri before as well.

This has been fun. It took me back in my memory. I thank my Lord Jesus every day for blessings that He has given me: a good family, good health, kindness, and a life with golden (old), to silver (new) friends. To reach 100 years was a blessing. It was also a blessing that I was able to see so many changes take place. The added one year (plus) is a double blessing. I'm sometimes achy but it is mostly wonderful.

My School and the Depression Years
By Norma Louise Barnes of St. Joseph,
Missouri
Born 1921

I remember attending a one-room country school with grades one through eight. I lived approximately one mile from the school and my cousins lived near my home. We would walk through the pastures and cornfields in all kinds of weather. When we had snow, sometimes we would fall down while crossing the ditches. We would be wet by the time we arrived at school. We would hang our wet coats, gloves, and socks behind the wood stove to dry. When we needed a drink of water, we would take a cup that was stored within our desks, go outside, and get the water from the well that had a pump handle. The outhouses were at the corners of the yard. Girls was on one corner and the boys was on the other. When we went to the outhouse, we would hurry, as it was so cold in the winter, and sometimes a snake would be inside. At recess, we would play a game called blackman. This was a game to choose up sides from one side of the yard to the other side without being tagged. We also played baseball.

At home, we would listen to the radio program, "Amos and Andy." We had a party line phone that hung on the wall; anyone could listen in. When we had a storm (called a cyclone at that time), we would disconnect the outside line from the house. If the storm was severe, we would go to the cave and take an ax and a lantern. The ax was taken in the cave in case a tree branch fell on the cave door. Butter, milk, and other foods were kept in the cave, as we did not have electricity. We bought ice blocks from the town icehouse. When it was harvest time for wheat, my father had a threshing machine and an old tractor. All the help (mostly neighbors and friends), would gather at noon for a big dinner. Sometimes my mother would have friends in and would quilt a cover. I remember playing under the quilt frame as she was making it. My mother washed clothes on a washboard and hung the clothes on a line outside to dry. When they were dry, two of us would help bring them inside. Then we would help fold and iron them with an iron heated on the woodstove. I helped

Baby Norma in 1922

with the garden and carried in wood for the stoves. Mostly, on Saturday nights, we would take a bath in a washtub. When it was cold, we took that bath by the heating stove. One of my farm chores was for me to bottle feed a three-legged calf. When I was older, I got to drive the car from the shed to the well, wash and dry the car, and then drive it back to the shed.

A memorable person in my life was my grandmother, Letitia Moseley who lived in town. I liked to go and stay with her. She and I would walk to the park, take some food, and have a sunrise breakfast. We would also go to the movies. I never had a pet of my own. My younger sister, Fontelle had a dog, Lucky and I liked to play with her. One day, her dog fell in a cistern well near the house. My father, Paul Dowell put a rope on a bucket and lowered it into the well. Thankfully, the dog climbed in and was brought back to safety. One time, I ran off with two of my cousins who lived nearby to ride their pony. My father came after us and all the way home (about a half mile); he used a little switch and gently hit us on our legs. The road was muddy and we were

barefooted. Needless to say, we didn't run away again.

The most embarrassing thing happened to me when I was very young. I was afraid of chicken feathers, so one day after a rain, I went into the muddy chicken yard. I picked up a feather to show that I was no longer afraid of feathers. On the way back to the house, I slipped and fell in the mud and got dirty. I cried because I never liked to get dirty. I still don't. I remember my uncle, Bert Moseley had a Model-A Ford with a rumble seat. I liked to sit in it and ride with him. He also drove that car to the Chicago World Fair.

During the Depression years, we lived on a farm and my mother, Virginia Dowell would sell eggs and butter. I would sit on the floor by the kitchen woodstove and churn the butter on a little Daisy churn. Also in the Depression years, one of our relatives, Dr. H. S. Dowell (who was a doctor in town), and his family drove to our house in a Packard car. I thought that they had to be rich to own that car. They would bring ice from town and mother would fix a big dinner of fried chicken. We had a lantern for light that had a mantel on it. To be mischievous, I would poke holes with my fingers on them. Of course, I was punished. My punishment was to do dishes or other chores. My dresses were made from any material available. During the depression years, our farm crops were destroyed by grasshoppers. At that time, there were no insecticides. We had to sell our cattle, horses, and chickens; we had to move to town. Franklin D. Roosevelt was elected president that year in 1933. Now, while I write this, I appreciate the time of remembering.

My Spirited Aunt Helen
By Mary Jane Fields of St. Joseph, Missouri
Born 1928

Every family that is honest enough to admit it has an Aunt Helen; or maybe it is an Uncle Joe. My Aunt Helen is one of my mother's younger sisters. My grandmother had ten children: five boys and five girls. The oldest and youngest boys died as very young children, but Grandma raised a couple of "strays," so it was a very full house. I never called my aunts and uncles "Aunt" or "Uncle," only by their first name or nickname. I meant no disrespect; that's just the way it was. Aunt Beck and Aunt Minnie were my great aunts and they had earned their titles somehow, unbeknownst to me. That's just the way it was. Sometimes Helen's brothers and sisters called her Hellie, a name well deserved. All her siblings had nicknames: Mary Naomi, my mother, was Sister; William Jackson was Bill; Winifred Clarissa was Joan, Beulah Carma was Beulie; Emery Leland was Jim; Faith Jane was Toots; Edward Rushworth was Bud.

Helen was the fun character of the family. She was always ready and willing to do anything mischievous. She was very limber and could do all sorts of what we called acrobatics. She might also have been heard calling down from the

Aunt Helen

roof, the top of the windmill, or a limb on a tree. She was generous, almost to a fault. She never had much in earthly goods, but she would gladly share it all with anyone. She was a hard worker, willing to undertake anything that didn't eat her first, with no though of the consequence. Helen had a great sense of humor and was my favorite fun aunt. I loved her and I felt that she loved me.

She did have one weakness, which became one big fault: booze. When she drank, she no longer was my favorite fun aunt. You never were quite sure what she might be, as different quantities, qualities, or wind directions might determine what attitude she developed. I knew one thing for sure: none were ones I wanted to be around. On one occasion during a Saturday night party at Grandma's, Helen got on a mad drunk and focused on Barney. Demonstrating great wisdom, she went across the road and threw her wedding ring into the raspberry patch. This made for an interesting Sunday morning group activity. The ring was found! Next to booze came cigarettes. This started with her smoking grape leaves behind the barn, and then escalated from there. She was not blessed with children, but married Barney, who had a four year old daughter, Audrey. Helen never called her "my daughter" ever! She was referred to as "Barney's girl" or "the girl I raised." The latter was a poor choice of words because Audrey pretty much raised herself while doing all the work and babysitting Helen.

In the early forties during World War II, there were few male members of the family around to manage and work on Grandma's truck farm or to sell cars on my uncle's used car lot. Helen helped with both. She was an excellent driver and went along with Uncle Bud and the men he hired to drive used cars back from Chicago. I suspect that they were black marketed, as cars were not being manufactured and used ones were at a premium. I do know that sometimes they smuggled black market sugar back in those cars. This was much like hard drugs are being

437

smuggled today. However, we welcomed the sugar, just as drugs are welcomed today. Once, after they picked up the cars, they stopped at the edge of Chicago for supper before starting the long nonstop trip back to St. Joe. About 50 miles out along the dark highway, Helen heard something in the back seat. Startled, she screamed, as she was driving solo, of course. When she screamed, the "something" sat up. People didn't lock their doors in those days. A drunk had crawled into the back seat to sleep it off in comfort while Helen was eating. She stopped the car and set him out along the highway to hitch his own way back to Chicago.

I spent my summers working out in the fields for ten cents an hour. My least favorite task was liming cucumbers. To do this, first I filled a gunny sack with as much lime as you can handle because I did not want to walk back to the shed for refills. Then I had to carry the lime-filled sack down to the cucumber patch and shake the lime onto the plants. I was hot: not perspiration hot, but very sweaty hot. There was no shade at all. I was in the middle of 35 acres of various vegetables, and that, I repeat, is hot. I could not stop breathing, so I had to breathe in the lime dust. That is not a pleasant experience. Then, my sweat would run. If I would reach to divert it, presto, more lime dust. Like I said, this was my least favorite job.

A cooler and perhaps more interesting summer job took place at night. The field hands would load the rusting pickup for its trip to the market. The various products would be put in bushel baskets, half bushel baskets, or pecks, as needed. About 10:00 at night, it was time for the trip to the Kansas City market. Remember, there's a shortage of men, and they can't work all day and go to the market at night. Helen was a good driver and at 14 years old, I am allowed (or drafted) to help her. All set, our trip's first stop is at the south end of the Belt, which in those days was way out of town. There she had a beer or two and I'd have a Coke and be given some nickels for the jukebox. There was no Interstate 29 back then. Eisenhower hadn't been elected yet. If we went down Highway 169, the next stop was Gower's bar. Here she had more beer, and I might have an ice cream cone. The next stops were in Grayson and then Smithville. By this time, I cannot possibly think of another Coke, but to her, the beer only tastes better. From there, it was a pretty straight nonstop trip to

the market, and we needed to hurry because the market opened at 2:00 A.M. Helen might have needed a couple potty stops, which were made behind a dark roadside bush or tree. If the potty break was an emergency, the bush, tree, and dark suddenly became non-essentials.

At the Kansas City market, we would find an open stall, probably not a good one, as we were late and the good ones were taken. If she was able, she would back the truck into a stall, lay down across the seat of the pickup, and go to sleep. If backing was a skill that she had temporarily lost, usually some other trucker would handle it. I was only 14, too young to drive. She would sleep until morning. I sold off the load, hired the shaggers to deliver what was not taken (cash and carry), and repacked what had not been sold in preparation for a much quicker trip back to St. Joe. When our tomatoes ripened, everyone's tomatoes ripened. As a result of this, we often hauled unsold tomatoes back home. A couple of trips and they were ready to be sold, with tomato juice dripping through the stained basket. In some cases, a little mold was peeking out. These went to Otoe Canning Company in Nebraska City. I never bought any Otoe brand, ever.

To her dying day, Helen believed that jackolopes existed and that she had seen a pig climb a tree in Arkansas. With all her smokin', drinkin', and cussin', she outlived all of her nine brothers and sisters. At her funeral, during our last look at an aunt we dearly loved, Trudi, my daughter, and I slipped a cigarette in her casket. We weren't sure if she'd need matches, so we didn't include those.

Snowstorms and Learning to Sew
By Elaine Grame of Weston, Missouri
Born 1944

My grandmother was one of 17 children, and my grandfather was one of seven. My mother was the youngest of seven, and I am the oldest of seven siblings. Having such large extended family, I spent much of my childhood learning how I was related to each person of the family. I enjoyed hearing many family stories that were passed down from one generation to the next. Through the years, due to our brother's extensive genealogy research, we discovered that our great, great, great, great, grandfather on our father's side

438

came to America from Germany in the 1760s and settled in the Mohawk Valley of New York and fought in the Revolutionary War. My brother and his wife, my sister, and I traveled to this area and found the original homestead and the cemetery in which many early family members are buried. During this visit, we learned stories of our ancestral family escaping from an Indian raid. We also learned how the homestead was the location of the local swimming hole for the surrounding neighborhood. Yearly family reunions were started long before I was born and still continue today. I have attended most of them, as it is a time to catch up on family happenings, get acquainted with the new family members, and enjoy the great food.

I was born in August of 1944 at Missouri Methodist Hospital in St. Joseph, Missouri, during World War II. My father was a medic in the army at the time and was given leave to come home a few days after my birth. When he was discharged a year later in 1945, he came home to Platte County and began a career of farming as his father had before him. Six siblings came along over the next 20 years. I enjoyed being the oldest, and was probably a little bossy and domineering at times. We had no close neighbors with children that we could socialize and play with, so we were each other's friends and playmates. We had exemplary parents who loved us, and each other, and with their guidance and direction, we became a very close-knit family. My siblings and I still enjoy that closeness today. We all worked together to help out with farm and household chores. We were raised in the Baptist church and we four older siblings loved to sing old gospel hymns. We were often asked to perform special music during church services. Our two story, eight-room farmhouse was cold and drafty in the winter and hot and stuffy in the summer. We used a couple of fans that moved the hot summer air around. In the winter, we only had one heating stove that warmed three rooms downstairs. We all slept in cold bedrooms with lots of blankets piled high over us. Many winter mornings our inside windows were covered with a thick frost.

My oldest sister and I attended a rural one-room schoolhouse. Thankfully, we only had to walk one mile to and from to attend. The school was heated by a large wood/coal stove. We often had to keep our coats on in the winter until the room warmed up. I attended four years until all rural schools were consolidated and students were bussed into Weston to the newly built elementary school in 1954. Most of the time during those four years, I was the only one in my class. I learned a lot from the classes higher than mine, as you could hear their lessons as well as your own. I remember an incident that occurred at recess when most of the students were playing follow-the-leader. Our teacher had just entered the outhouse, when the leader decided to lead us all behind the outhouse. Each one of us knocked on the back wall. Needless to say, the teacher was not amused and we all lost several recesses. My six siblings and I, my future husband and his six siblings, our three children, and our nine grandchildren all attended and graduated from West Platte R-II in Weston, Missouri. I do feel very fortunate to have had the opportunity to attend the one-room school, which still stands today. It is known as Swamp School.

We looked forward to Saturday nights, when the whole family went into our small town of Weston to buy the weekly supply of groceries and to visit on Main Street with neighbors and relatives, who were all in town for the same purpose. Our grandpa occasionally paid a quarter for the older grandchildren to see a movie, or maybe to get a small eight ounce Coke for ten cents at the pharmacy soda fountain. We were sometimes lucky and allowed to go home with our grandparents to spend the night. Grandma would make a fried chicken dinner for the whole family on Sunday when our parents came to take us home.

I remember that we got our first wall-mounted party line phone when I was about six years old. We knew who was being called by the long and short ring combinations.

Larry, Elaine, Diane, and Linda Lintner in 1961

Our ring was one long ring and two short rings. You could always count on a couple of neighboring parties to talk for an hour or so before the line would become free for anyone else. We got our first television when I was 11. We only had three network channels to watch, but those were the "good ole days" of decent family sitcoms, funny cartoons, and the cowboy and Indian western shows. We had no bathroom until I was approximately 15, but until then we all had our weekly baths in a round galvanized washtub in the kitchen. One after the other, we all bathed in the same water. I am not sure if the last person that took a bath in the water was any cleaner after the bath than before the bath. Our first bathroom was installed in a kitchen closet under the stairwell. It consisted of a stool, a small basin, and a shower. We were so happy to finally be rid of the outhouse, but soon we were told that we couldn't afford the water for the shower very often. When we were allowed, we were told to get wet, lather up, and rinse off as quickly as possible to conserve water. Luckily, we still had the old washtub. Our mother made our school clothes, bought us our one pair of shoes for the year, and made sure my sister and I had a curly perm for the school year. I would rather have had straight, stringy hair, but Mom insisted otherwise. Along with a pencil and our Big Chief tablet, we were ready for school. Mom also taught me how to sew. My grandpa bought me a used treadle sewing machine, and I began to make my own clothes. I later made most of my children's clothing. Sewing and reading were my favorite hobbies.

In 1958, our family, along with our Uncle's family, took our one and only vacation. It was a camping trip to the Black Hills of South Dakota. We had such a good time, made lots of memories, then came home to discover an 11 year old cousin had drowned in a farm pond while we were gone. The highway patrol had tried to locate us, but was unable to. The funeral had been held the day before we returned from vacation. We had the best and worst experience all within one week.

I remember several big snowstorms in our part of Missouri, one being when we were quite young. A big snowstorm prevented us from being able to drive to Grandma's on Christmas Day. As she only lived a mile away, Daddy hitched a wagon to a team of horses and we bundled up, and were able to celebrate Christmas with Grandma after all! One of the worst snow storms was the last few days of February 1960. We had at least a foot of blowing, drifting snow on the ground when our baby brother decided to come into this world. We four older siblings were taken to Grandma's and had to walk down a long drifted-in lane to her house from the main road. She did not have a phone, so she was not aware that we were coming. If they known, Grandpa would have bladed out the lane. The snow was up to our knees, but we finally made it to the house. The snow quit falling and Dad made it back after two long days to let us know of our brother's birth. He was born on February 29th, so he was a leap year baby. We think it is ironic that this brother has always loved big snow storms and still does today, 53 years later.

I would not trade growing up in the fabulous 1950s and early '60s in Northwest Missouri for anything in the world. It was a time of simplicity, contentment, hopes, and dreams of great things to come.

Horses, Tornadoes, and New Houses
By Sherry J. Brown of Kansas City, Missouri
Born 1936

Growing up in the '50s in small town USA was so different than today. We did not know of drugs. Alcohol was not served in either of our homes, and therefore presented no temptation until we were older teenagers. Even then, there was only beer, and it was not easily available. None of the girls I knew drank the stuff and the boys, when they could, might find someone to buy a six-pack for them.

I met a boy named John when I was in high school. I had seen him around the school, but had really never met him until I went roller-skating with my friend, Pat. We ventured across the Taneycomo Bridge, and skated on the blacktop road all the way to Hollister, Missouri. It was about a mile to get back to Branson, and John and his friend offered to give us a ride back on their horses. We thought this was a great idea, so we went. As it turned out, I got on John's horse, and Pat got on his friend's horse. After we girls had been deposited back in Branson, Pat was mad at me because I got to ride with the cutest boy. We started dating when I was 16 and he was 18. While we were dating, I had a small horse whose name was Cricket. John and I would sometimes ride together. One day, we wanted to race, but because my horse was smaller and I was a great deal less experienced than John, he gave me a head start. I raced off at full speed, and my saddle started to slip to the side. I went right over with it and the pony continued at full gallop. John galloped his horse to the rescue, just like John Wayne! He picked me right up off of Cricket! What a man!

We married in 1955, and the first place we lived was a little cabin in the woods on a property owned by John's dad. This little cabin had two rooms, and no running water. We scrubbed, painted, and I made curtains for the windows. We thought it was just as cute and snug as it could be! We had a cow that John's dad had loaned to us to milk. We called her Banana Tit. We lived there just a few months when John's friend told him about a good job that he had landed in Kansas City with a vending service. Since John was then working for my Dad, making $1.00 per hour clearing land, we decided that a job in the big city with a guarantee of $87.50 per week sounded like an opportunity that we needed to take. John went to the city and worked for three weeks until he could save enough money to pay a month's rent and bring me to Kansas

John and Sherry Brown on their wedding day

City with him. We found an apartment that had three rooms and had a private bath. This was a big step up from the cabin. It was also so close to John's work that he could walk there.

Our daughter, Sherry, was born on September 18, 1955 back in Branson because it was much cheaper to have a baby there. Three weeks later, we came home with our baby to our little apartment on Pennsylvania Avenue. On February 21, 1957, we brought home a baby boy named John Stephen. With two babies in the little apartment, we were starting to feel a little cramped. Since John had been a country boy, he had had enough of big city life, so we found a half-duplex to rent out by Stillwell Kansas. This duplex was an old schoolhouse that was so old it had been constructed with pegs instead of nails. It had been recently refurbished into two living units.

We were not to live in this peaceful setting very long, as on May 20, 1957, in the early evening we were watching television, and saw that there was a weather warning about a tornado that had been seen coming from the southwest. We ran to the door to see a huge tornado in the western sky. We watched, and as it came nearer it grew bigger and bigger, but did not veer left or right. It was coming straight at us. We ran to tell our neighbor that there was a tornado, seemingly coming straight in our direction. Since we had no basement or cellar, our only chance was to escape in the car. John, Jody, Steve, and I were in the front seat of our 1952 Mercury, and the neighbor and her baby were in the back seat. We drove as fast as the old Mercury would travel. By this time, the winds were screaming; the monster was all around us. I looked behind us and saw the roof our duplex go up in the air. I told John, "We are going to die!" Behind our Mercury, a giant oak tree went down across the road just seconds behind us. Finally, we could see the monster ahead of us on our left and it was safe to stop. John turned the car around to retrace our steps. We couldn't get back that way because of the giant oak tree had fallen across the road. When we finally got back to the duplex, we discovered that the house on one side of the duplex was only inches high, and the barn on the other side was also only inches high. The old peg-made schoolhouse was there, albeit with the roof removed and the structure yanked up off of the foundation. That night the other man and John stood guard over our few precious possessions while the other girl and I took our babies to relatives for the night and called our parents.

Our next home was compliments of the Salvation Army and some generous soul who had offered a one-room basement apartment to tornado victims. My mom and dad came to Kansas City to see about us, and suggested that we should look into buying a house. With a $500 down payment that we borrowed from my Dad, we soon moved into our very first real house, complete with a basement, two bedrooms, living room, dining room, kitchen, and one bath. Our babies were growing and everything seemed great. John soon won a bid on a job in a plant at the new overhaul base, out north by the airport. He was driving 30 miles each way to work every day, so we decided that we would be better off living north of the river to accommodate his employment. Soon we were looking for a new home.

We had saved $3000 (at that time that was a lot of money) but was told that to buy house with land, they required 25 to 30 percent down. John told one of his co-workers about our search for land, and he offered to sell 15 or 30 acres of his land southwest of Weatherby Lake Dam to us. We went out see the land and immediately fell in love with the rolling hills and the view of Adkison Lake below. The property had, at one time, been a home site for one of the first homesteads in the area. There were mature trees, perennial flowers, and an old cistern, and cellar from the old home place that had burned down many years before. Best of all, Bob Rich would sell us this wonderful piece of ground for $75 monthly payments and no money down on a contract for the deed. This would also leave our $3000 free to start construction on the house. We really were excited. John was 25 by then and I was 23. We were so ready to start on our big adventure.

After the paperwork was completed and we sold our little home on 39th Street, we moved into a small one-bedroom 4plex so we could work on the property and the house. The first thing we did was to plaster and clean the old cistern, as no county water was available. We staked out our new home, having decided on a true ranch. The $3000 was enough to pour the basement, put a top on it, and move in. we were so anxious to move and save the $50 per month that we were spending in rent that we moved in with only an extension cord into a window from the electric pole. No running water, no bathroom, except for a can. We could now put that $50 per month into lumber and things for our new home. Our first night in our new home was interesting indeed. We had just moved in boxes, and what little furniture we had. John had not had the time to put on the door, as he had worked till midnight the night before finishing the roof so that we could move the next day. We put a quilt around the door, stuck it in the hole, made our beds, and exhaustedly went to sleep. John found a used pump that was broken at the neighbors' house on the next hill north of us. It was of no use to these people as they had replaced it with a new one. The man gave it to John. John repaired the pipes and found someone to rewind the motor, as it was also kaput!

My parents came up to see our grand adventure and we were so proud. John had never hung a door, but he had hung gates on the farm, so he figured it couldn't be that hard. When Dad saw the door (which was hung with hinges on the outside, like a gate), he exclaimed, "And he is going to build this house?" Now that we had water in the house, we were certainly doing fine. It was Friday and John's sister, Louise, and family were scheduled to pay us a visit that weekend. This was the first time that they were to see our project. We had worked so hard so that everything would be just right, or at least as good as possible, in our still very primitive state. I had cleaned and cooked for hours so that we could entertain our guests. We were building the septic system, and as in everything else we were doing, we did most of it ourselves. However, we did hire someone to dig the septic hole and laterals. That rainy day, John was at work. The septic holes were dug, but we had to wait till it dried up to complete the task. In the meantime, a friend had a beagle dog in heat and needed a place to put her until her time had passed. John volunteered an old corncrib, which was on the property for the confinement of the dog. I was at home that day, getting ready for Louise's visit, when I looked out the window and saw the beagle dog running loose. I made Jody and Steve stay inside and went out in the rain to catch the dog. The county that we live in is not called Clay County, but the whole area could have been named this, as that is sure what is here! Clay, when wet, is extremely slick. I ran after the dog, fell, and came within inches of falling in the septic tank hole! When I staggered into the house, wet and muddy as could be, I looked up and saw a waterfall coming into the basement between the top of the concrete wall and the wooden board on top of it. This was the day when I was truly ready to move back to the city!

With a couple more loans, we finally got our house finished, and had two more babies, Tammy (born in 1962), and Kevin who was born in 1964.

Battling Scarlet Fever in 1941
By Carolyn S. Hughes of Carrollton,
Missouri
Born 1933

The summer of 1933, I was born the third daughter of four children to RA. (Bill) and Eva E. (Cochenour) Cox, in Hill Township, Carroll County, Missouri.

My daddy was a farmer of a rental property, raising corn, oats, and hay. We had milk cows, pigs, sheep, horses, chickens, and geese. Mother planted large gardens and canned everything she grew.

Daddy worked the farm using horses to pull the machinery. We milked four to six cows by hand twice a day.

My brother Billy Joe was born in early May of 1941 and it was that winter we became exposed to the disease Scarlet Fever. Our oldest sister Doris Lee became very ill, and our doctor took Daddy and Doris to Kansas City and entered Doris in Children's Mercy Hospital. She was a patient in the hospital for over a month. She was in the hospital at Christmas.

Because the disease was so contagious, we were not permitted visitors nor was Daddy allowed to go to the store (Braymer or Quote) for groceries.

Our good neighbors, the Stewarts and Sperry's, brought groceries, flour, sugar, coffee, etc. and left them at the end of our lane about a quarter mile from our house. They also picked up our mail at the mailbox a couple miles from our house and left it at the

Carolyn's parents, Bill and Eva Cox with Carolyn Sue and Billy Joe Cox

end of the lane with our groceries. Someone (I suppose the county health department) put a yellow flag on the yard gate so people would know we were quarantined. I will never forget that ugly yellow flag.

I remember Mother had a severe sore throat, but the doctor said since she had Scarlet Fever as a child she would not have it again.

My sister came home from the hospital with gifts she had received at Christmas: a beautiful doll and other gifts from clubs and organizations who donate gifts to the hospital.

I am very grateful to people who care about children who are in the hospital at Christmas.

My middle sister Evah Jean was covered with a rash that is the sign of the fever. I did not have the rash and as far as I know, I did not have Scarlet Fever. The doctor put us on a liquid diet. I thought I would starve, liquid food isn't very filling.

Our house had to be fumigated with formaldehyde to disinfect it from the germs. Mother strung twine from nails over the windows and hung books so they would be disinfected. She was about ready to fumigate when my baby brother broke out with the rash. He had a high temperature and very cross as an eight month old sick child can be.

I don't remember the length of time until we were all well and we three girls went to stay with Aunt Ruth and her family. Mother, Daddy, and Billy stayed at a neighbor's house overnight as the formaldehyde canisters had to be lit and left in the house overnight. Thank you for reading my story.

Riding the C B & Q in the '60s
By Lila Weatherford of Liberty, Missouri
Born 1925

Remember the old C B & Q railroad? That's Chicago, Burlington, and Quincy. It was fantastic in the sixties. We lived in the small town of Clarence, MO. It's still there, a few houses and some churches. It's mostly a farming community now. Highway MO 36 has now circumvented it also.

Our second son was born with a cleft lip at Smithville hospital. We were living in Nashua at the time. Dr. Spellman quickly sent him to Children's Mercy Hospital for surgery. He couldn't nurse so this was a life saving measure.

My husband was transferred back to Clarence for his work. I did not want to leave the city. But the Children's Mercy Hospital people assured me that we could do it.

So in Clarence MO on highway 36 my son and I would board the C B & Q railroad at 5am in the morning and ride the rails for three hours to Union Station in Kansas City. We would run outside and catch the street bus to 600 Woodland, where Children's Mercy Hospital was at that time. The school of Osteopathy is there now. Now that was fast: It is still a two hour and forty-five minute drive on the new four-lane highway.

Blessed to be able to keep our appointment, we bypassed some people waiting, and returned to Union Station by noon or one o'clock to catch the two p.m. train back home. I always felt guilty for doing that but it was the only way to get it all done in one day. By this time most of the work was all dental so didn't take quite so long. And we boarded the street bus back to Union Station as soon as we could.

We sat in one of the many rows of seats in Union Station and ate our lunch. Of course there was the Harvey Girls restaurant but we couldn't afford that. Then if we had the time we would walk around and view the beautiful station. I still like to do that.

Our train left at 2 p.m. to head back to northeast MO, arriving at 5 p.m. just in time to fix supper for the family.

My son just recently told me that he spent time every day watching the train come in town and slow down (this is not the one we rode) to pick up the mail. First the trainman would throw our incoming mailbag on the ground then grab the bag of outgoing mail from the long pole the station manager was holding out for the trainman to reach. This happened every day and he was fascinated. That is probably why he begged to ride the train to Kansas City.

The Worst Snowstorm I Ever Saw
By Adeline Flint of Savannah, Missouri
Born 1947

One very cold winter morning in the later '50s, just a few days before Christmas, my mother woke all of us up. She tells us we are going to St. Joseph to shop so we needed to get up and hurry getting dressed. There were six of us kids and my parents had a station wagon so we all piled into the car and off we went.

The day was lots of fun. We ate at McDonald's, eating the good old 10 cent or maybe 15-cent burgers, I'm not sure. Since I was the oldest and no longer believed in Santa, it was my job to steer my younger siblings away from an area when Mom found something she wanted to purchase for Santa. We were all having such a good day when Dad announced we must head for home and now. Well, when my father puts something that way we knew to get going. Back then, children didn't argue when parents told them to do something. Out of the store, we went and ran into a hard snowstorm, one that made it hard to see much ahead of yourself.

We lived about 1 hour away from St. Joseph and I watched my father drive 10 to 15 miles an hour when normally we could drive 50 to 55 mph. We were about 2 miles from home when the car got stuck on a very steep hill and there was no going further with it.

Well, Dad left Mom and all of us kids in the car and he walked home to get the tractor and a wagon. We all huddled on the wagon under blankets and got home. The very next day Dad and I took the tractor and wagon over to the car and got the Christmas gifts. Our car stayed stuck on that hill for several days until a snowplow came along and plowed it out. I believe that was the worst snowstorm I ever saw.

Hoover Baseball Players
By Betty Lutes Hoskins of Platte City, Missouri
Born 1932

The saying "It takes a village to raise a child" by Hillary Clinton, was never more true than in the Hoover community, where not only parents were watchful over their children, but friends and neighbors were diligent in efforts to raise good law-abiding Christian adults. If someone's child was misbehaving, it was not uncommon to be brought up short by someone other than your mother or dad. Although the Hoover Christian Church was the heart and soul of the area, the school came a close second, and Hoover Store was the social place to be each night. In the '30s and '40s television was unheard of, electricity was still a dream, and if you had a telephone, it was a "party line" with 4, 6, or even eight households on it and everyone had a separate ring. So you knew the neighbor that was being called, and when they answered (it stopped ringing), you felt perfectly comfortable "listening in" as everyone else was doing it too!

It was not a prosperous time due to the Depression and then WWII, but it was a time of closeness as we mourned the young men leaving our community to fight for us in far off places that we only knew by studying history. We only realized a little inconvenience due to rationing of certain items such as gasoline, sugar, and butter. As my parents had a Jersey cow, we always had cream for Mother to make butter. So she would give her ration stamps for butter to a neighbor in exchange for sugar, as she loved to bake. Gas stamps were shared with people that had a car and needed to get to work. Rides were shared, and people walked or rode their horses as much as possible. Very few people had bicycles as all the roads were either mud or gravel.

Our property had been cut in two pieces when Highway #92 was built between Platte City and Smithville, MO, leaving a triangle between us, church, store, and school.

Some of the men in the neighborhood decided they would build a baseball field to have some games and of course, it also became a magnet for the kids too. Since Hoover Store was close, soda pop was high on the list of treats for everyone. Some of the players were "Buzz" Allmon, "Judge" Badtke, Bob Conn, Russell Clifton, Orville 'The Mayor" Flowers, Graham Lutes, Eldon Mosby, and Audon Witt. A lot of teasing, joking, and just plain fun was the highlight of the games. In the winter, when snow came, 92 had a big hill that was terrific to go sleigh riding, and a pasture on our farm had a gentle slope that wasn't as dangerous as the highway so parents were more comfortable for the kids to use that hill.

Many times folk would gather and bring any item that was slick on the bottom: shovels, pieces of tin, and Judge even fashioned a toboggan so several people could ride down at the same time. I clearly remember a big snow that drifted badly. The school was closed and for three nights in a row, a bonfire was built in our pasture. Neighbors came bearing cookies and treats and Mother made gallons of hot chocolate for everyone. Even to this day, when snow is on the ground and it is a clear crisp night I can recall how bright the stars were and how happy and safe our little corner of the world seemed to be.

A Day with Spike and Uncle Bill
By Charles M. Turner of Kearney, Missouri
Born 1947

A mournful howl pierced the cold January morning interrupting the silence of a new day breaking. The fresh mounds of snow glistened like diamonds as the rising sun gave everything a rosy red hue. Spike had disappeared into the thick brush. He was in charge this morning, a conductor orchestrating a Missouri rabbit hunt. This was his performance. He knew the game and he knew the rules. The baying grew

louder; the air was tense, then—

In Kansas City, a father rises at 4:00 AM and wakes his two soundly sleeping boys.

"Let's go," said Dad. The day had started. We quickly gathered our hunting clothes and rubber boots. The two single shot Mossberg shotguns were carefully laid with Dad's in the trunk of the '57 Plymouth alongside the boxes of shells. A small plastic bag of Mom's homemade "Cowboy cookies" were also included. We were off to St. Joseph to meet up with Uncle Bill. Bill was a gunners mate and spotter aboard the USS Indiana during World War II. We boys loved to listen to the stories from his colorful life. It was a treat joining up with Uncle Bill and my cousins at the truck stop on "the Belt" in St. Joe for breakfast. Pancakes were quickly devoured amidst the noise of the diesels and constant moving of the waitresses bringing mugs of hot coffee to the truckers and hunters. "Time to go;" said Uncle Bill, "rabbits are waitin'".

Spike had a place in a small kennel tucked into the back of Bill's truck: plenty of straw, just right for a Beagle. Spike was a handsome tri-colored dog with a white tipped tail that stood out in the brush. If you looked close, you could almost see a grin on his face. A bundle of energy packed into a 28-pound frame.

Uncle Bill had a habit of rolling down the windows about 2 miles from the hunting spot.

Charles, Nancy, Jack, Uncle Bill, and John Turner, (Charles's father) with Spike the dog

"Just to get ya used to the cold," he would say. Spike was barking when we pulled up. We hurriedly loaded our guns. Bill unlatched the kennel door and said the four magical words, "Hunt 'em up Spike!" The beagle bounded off the tailgate with a yelp and quickly vanished into the thick brush. No need to tell him which way to go. His nose gave the direction.

The baying grew louder and louder. Uncle Bill yelled out, "Get ready!" The first two rabbits launched themselves from the brush into the open field. Guns started going off. Three more rushed from the thicket. Bang! Bang! Four more! Then the last two bolted out with Spike right behind baying loudly. When the smoke lifted, there were rabbits down all around us. Spike paused for a quick survey, and then promptly jumped back in the brush to hunt another bunch. We quickly gathered the rabbits and reloaded for the next encounter. Spike skillfully worked them to us during the morning hours. We stopped for lunch: peanut butter and (Aunt Verna's) jelly sandwiches with hot coffee and a thermos of milk. Bill gave Spike a little bite to eat with as much water as he desired.

We hunted at a slower pace that afternoon. Our boots seemed to gain weight during the day in the heavy snow. The sun made its trek westward, painting the horizon with spectacular reds and purples giving us a "hunter's delight" to end the day. The hunt was over, the rabbits field dressed, and loaded in large coolers.

Even Spike seemed to yearn for the soft straw in the kennel. He had done a good job.

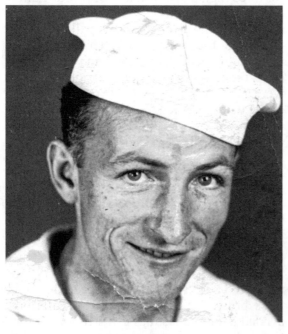

Uncle Bill Andrew

446

"He's the best rabbit dog I've ever had," said Bill. He was proud of old Spike. We said good-bye to Uncle Bill and my cousins. We got into our car and drove out of the field. My brother and I didn't remember much of the ride home as Dad turned the car south on old 71 highway. We were already fast asleep dreaming of rabbits and the hunt with Spike that would be forever etched in our minds.

Karo Syrup Bucket "Guitars"
By Anna L. Clark of Belton, Missouri
Born 1934

I was born in May 1934, on a farm southeast of Rock Port, MO, in Atchison County near Langdon. I was a middle child of nine children: eight girls and one boy. This was during the last part of the Great Depression. The after-effects of that Depression and the Dust Bowl still lingered. My dad's father died in 1924 and the family farm was lost. After that and many years after, my dad worked wherever work was available: on farms, the railroad, the original Brownville Bridge over the Missouri River, the Workman's Projects Administration (WPA) and many others. He was a quick learner and had a lot of common sense. These qualities usually kept him employed.

My dad's people were Welsh, English, and probably Irish. They migrated from New England, through Michigan, Minnesota, Montana, and then Missouri. My dad's father was the first sheriff of Rosebud County, Montana.

My mother's immediate and extended family lived and farmed a large portion of that general area. Many of those still living there are either direct descendants or related to descendants of the Coopers. My mother's parent's last names were Cooper ("oo" pronounced as in "look") and Smith. The names were originally spelled Kuper and Schmidt. Immigrants were once eager to Americanize their names.

One day, before starting school, I was with my dad at a neighbor's home where he was working. This gave my mother a break as it was just before one of my younger sisters was born. As we were eating lunch, I discovered the meat we were eating was cows tongue. I wouldn't eat another bite. The adults had a big laugh at my expense.

When I started first grade—no kindergarten at that time—we were still suffering from the drought. Part of our play at home was in the dust (no sand box). By adding water from the well, it made great mud pies. Maybe that's where we learned to be such good cooks! My oldest sisters attended school at Nishna Botna High School, which was later consolidated with Rock Port Schools. I and my two older sisters attended the one room school named Lincoln. Our home and the school were very near the Missouri River. That year, the river crested or was out of its banks, it seemed very deep at our house, as were the snowdrifts in winter. Actually, the water didn't come up to my knees and considering my age of 5 or 6, may have been seep water from the river. Perhaps, the snowdrifts were not too deep either!

When I was in second grade, we moved to a different school district. My brother, I, and my two older sisters attended another one-room school named Cooper. That year, we walked to school (probably a mile) crossing farm fields to reduce the distance of our walk. Part of our playtime during the summer months was spent climbing onto the roofs of the hog houses and singing. We thought we were every bit as good as the local radio singers. We serenaded the countryside, using one-gallon buckets that had held Karo syrup. We strummed across the circular ridges on the bottoms to accompany our great singing! We also harmonized while washing and drying dishes. There were a lot of dishes so we got a lot of practice.

I and these same two sisters had one set of new clothes consisting of blue sleeveless blouses buttoned in the front with celluloid buttons (celluloid because of WWII). We had matching blue striped dirndl skirts (we erroneously called them broomstick skirts). Handing down clothes from the eldest to the youngest was the norm. We also had clothes made from printed flour and printed feed sacks.

Later, when I was in third grade, we moved into Rock Port to live with my grandmother, who was in poor health. When she died a short time later, my parents bought the property and lived there until they passed away. At her death, it was the custom after the embalming for the body to be held in the home, where relatives took turns sitting up until the funeral. I attended the funeral at the Lutheran Church in Langdon. At the cemetery, it was my first experience of seeing the casket lowered and dirt thrown on the top. That picture stayed with me for a long time.

Moving into town was a time of great change for me. We had many kids in class and more to play with after school. I always walked home with a girlfriend. That same friend had a large boy's bicycle. One day we had walked to the top of a steep hill in town not far from the courthouse. We rode down the hill with one girl on the handlebars, one on the seat, one on the crossbars, one on the back fender, and she was standing up, doing the driving. We had no helmets, of course! The courthouse hill was where we rode sleds in the winter. The side streets were roped off for that purpose.

One day on the way home from school, reaching my friend's home before reaching mine, my friend's mother greeted us at the door crying, telling us that President Roosevelt had died.

This was also during WWII and the days of the big bands. With all the boys gone, my eldest sisters and their friends would gather in our living room and dance to the music on the radio. With no boys, we younger girls were used as partners. We learned to dance at an early age. Later days, my parents belonged to an organization they called Club Dancing. We learned to square dance that way.

The boys were always thrilled with the Friday and Saturday western movies. The greatest hit for me was Nyoka, Queen of the Jungle. They didn't have many girl heroines.

During the summer, one of my older sisters and I walked to the library which was then located in the courthouse. It was the greatest place in the world. One of my first books was Heidi. I haven't stopped reading since.

School Stories from the Class of '58, Albany High
By Carolyn Sue (Hathaway) Jones of Kansas City, Missouri
Born 1940

I was born in September, 1940, in a small house east of Darlington, MO, to Emery and

Annette Hathaway and Carolyn Sue Hathaway

Daisy Hathaway. I had two brothers, Eldon Lee and Stanley Keith, both now deceased, and a sister Annette Hathaway Rathbun, who lives in Independence; MO. I remember very little about my first 5 years, but I do remember starting first grade in a new brick Darlington School, a two-room schoolhouse. My first day is still very vivid, as I was very shy, and we had been told to raise our hand if we needed anything. I desperately needed to go to the bathroom, but was afraid to raise my hand, so I just sat there and cried. When the teacher noticed, she came and asked what was wrong, and led me to the bathroom. My teachers during my grade school years were Mildred Maris, Goldie Phillips, Raymond Whitmore and Iris Dean Hise.

We had moved to a farm south of Darlington, and it was a real treat to get to ride that yellow bus to school. Our bus driver was Mabel Hise. Mother usually had a surprise for us when we got home: home baked cookies, fresh fried bread, and when we got our first refrigerator, homemade vanilla ice cream.

We had an old wall party line telephone (our ring was 2 longs and a short), and no television, just a radio. It was a special treat when our neighbors, Fred and Lorena Minkner (their daughter Nellie Faye and husband Jerry McGinley now live at our old home) got a black and white TV and invited us over on Friday nights to watch 'The Pendulum Swings", and "Sergeant Preston of the Yukon".

When I reached 8th grade we were sent to Albany High School. Our bus driver was Clark Marsh. My teacher was Etta Meryl Stoner, and I was terrified of her and being with students,

I had never met. My friends were there also, who had been with me since first grade: my cousin Jerry Dodge, who lives in Raymore, MO, Carolyn (Hartman) Curtis, who lives in Lee's Summit, MO and Mary Ann (McNeese) Fetterley, who lives in Westminster, CA. I am still in contact with them. Our other class member was Bertha (McGinley) Sowards, who lives in Springfield, MO, and I also see her at the Darlington All-School reunion held once every three years at the Darlington Opry building.

My friend Carolyn (she was Carolyn Mae, I was Carolyn Sue) decided one day that we should get Social Security cards before we got a job. We went to the Darlington post office and filled out the information, but before signing decided, it would be cool to use different names. She used Carolyn Maella, I Carolyn Suzanne, but when we tried to get a job, these were incorrect so we had to re-apply using our correct names. We had a good laugh about this the last time we met.

Carolyn, in fact, had a huge impact in my life. When we were both working in Kansas City, MO, she set me up on a blind date with a cute guy, Phillip L. Jones, who would become my future husband. We have been together 43 years. Thank you, Carolyn Mae!

I have many fond memories of growing up in a small town in northwest Missouri, and return every Memorial Day weekend for our annual Hathaway family reunion, held at the Albany Community Center. My daughter, Tammy Sue Gamblin has recently moved to Albany, so I will be making more trips back there. It is fun to drive around the square and tell her "that used to be Hardin's Drug Store, run by the Barretts, who had the best spiced

The last students at Darlington Grade School

ham sandwiches and coke for 25 cents, or if you were lucky enough to have an extra nickel, you could add chips" and "at one time that was a Places store" then around the corner to the Rigney Theatre "where we went on Saturday night to see Ma and Pa Kettle in one of their hilarious shows" or "that was where I went to school and excelled in Shorthand at 120 words per minute."

It's great to reminisce about the "good old days," and there were many.

The Miraculous Surgery of Dr. Byland
By Peggy L. James of Ravenwood, Missouri
Born 1951

Let me start by clarifying something for you. My husband's name is Byland James, not James Byland. How does one obtain the first name of Byland you say? Well, here's how it all began.

On April 27, 1947, the lives of the 223 people living in the town of Worth were forever changed. The day started innocently enough, with people going about their various occupations. Then, at 2:35 p.m., tragedy struck in the form of a tornado cutting a path from west to east, starting at the schoolhouse and moving along Main Street, destroying homes and businesses in its path.

My father-in-law had gone into C. B. Adam's feed store to warn of the impending storm and, according to the article in the Maryville Daily Forum dated April 30, 1947, "Alton James received the most unusual injury when a plank as big as a man's fist was forced through his right leg about halfway between the ankle and the knee, and pinned him to a wall. Besides having the right leg splintered from this blow, his left leg was broken at the ankle." He was taken to St. Francis Hospital in Maryville.

Here's where the plot thickens. Seventeen doctors examined Alton's injuries and recommended that his right leg be amputated. Obviously, this was not an option he wanted to consider. The one doctor who thought it could be saved was, you guessed it, Dr. Benjamin Franklin Byland. Using stainless steel plates and screws, Dr. Byland connected the bones in Alton's right leg and set both legs in a cast. He was in the hospital for 18 months and walked with a limp, but Alton survived the Worth tornado with all of his limbs intact.

Dr. Byland would take no money for his services, so even though he was unmarried at the time, Alton told him he would name his first son Byland. Alton James and Ellen Robertson were married in June 1949. Byland Alton James was born in April 1950, and the rest, as they say, is history.

Please remember, my husband's first name is Byland, and he wears it proudly. We even named our son Donald Byland James.

It was the summer of 1970. I was 19 years old and had been staying with Mom and Dad while my husband was in National Guard basic training at Fort Bragg, North Carolina. His ART was in Fort Belvoir, Virginia. I was getting ready to ride a Greyhound bus from St. Joseph, MO, to Washington, D.C. to be with him. The ticket cost $33. Ma and Pa took me to the bus station and we waited for departure time to arrive. While I was boarding the bus, a middle-aged black man told Dad he would take care of me. This did nothing to boost Dad's confidence in the fact that I was going far from home for the first time in my life. I'll never forget looking out the window and watching my mama cry as we left the station. I found a seat by a nice looking lady about Mom's age and settled in for the ride. In Effingham, KS, I was supposed to layover an hour, but when I asked for the bus going to Washington, D.C., they told me there was one leaving right away, so I got on it.

We drove all night, making various stops along the way. Passengers dwindled down to a very few. At one stop, several people got on and sat in front of me. One man sat in the seat beside me and started acting like he was going to sleep and leaning on me. I got up and went to sit behind the bus driver. My mama didn't raise a fool. She had warned me about strangers taking advantage of me, and I'm sure there were angels watching over me, answering the prayers of my mom and dad to take care of me.

We finally arrived at the Washington, D.C. terminal. My husband was nowhere in sight. I tried calling his sergeant, but didn't know the information needed to get in touch with him. There were no cell phones then, just Ma Bell. In fact, when Byland called me, he had to wait in line to use the pay phone. He said some guys would talk for hours. Multiply, and that's

a long time. I walked outside and decided I had better stay where Byland could find me. I went inside and sat down to wait until 4:00 p.m. I was never so glad to see a familiar face as I was at that moment when he walked in with another G.I. and went to the information booth to find out if my bus had arrived yet. I walked up behind him and tapped him on the shoulder. At last, we were reunited! He left for basic before our first anniversary in June 1970, and this was July or August. We found out my bags had not arrived yet, so we took the bus going back to the base.

We stayed at the guesthouse for two weeks, but had to leave when our time was up. We only got to stay there because Byland's sergeant was romantically involved with the lady who ran it. We found an apartment not far from the base and soon discovered that when we took a shower, the water smelled like sewer. We made a lot of trips to the Seven Eleven across the street for drinks. We had no car, so we walked or took the bus everywhere we went. One day a plane flew over dropping leaflets protesting the water situation. It was unseasonably warm that September in Virginia, and we were more than ready to go home when October arrived. We decided to fly back home. Byland's duffel bag was stuffed so full he could barely drag it behind him. Dad and Eldon came to pick us up at KCI. We stayed up late talking and catching up with the family. I can't believe that was 43 years ago.

Our son, Donald Byland James, was born in January 1972. He is our firstborn and a new experience for Byland and me, his mom and dad. We moved from Worth, Missouri in December 1971 to the Ravenwood trailer court. Fuel oil for our furnace cost 17 and 9 tenths cents per gallon then, and we were saving all we could for the birth of our son. We often spent weekends with my folks, Marvin and Juna Graham at their home south of Stanberry.

The next morning, Byland went downstairs and Mom asked where I was. He said, "I think we're gonna have a baby today." We all piled in Dad's 1962 Chevy, and took off for the Albany hospital. Byland was driving and I was riding shotgun. He took every corner as fast as possible. Dad was worried about a tire going flat. He said they were smooth, like the back of your hand.

We made it to the hospital, and the nurse greeted us at the emergency room door. She asked what we needed, and I told her, "I'm going to have a baby." We were ushered inside, filled out some paperwork, and Dr. Parsons was called. It was about 11:00. I was lucky I had not eaten anything. That made labor and childbirth easier for me. At 3:29 p.m., Dr. Parsons looked at the clock. I made one final push, and Don was born.

Byland worked second shift at Lloyd Chain Co. and visiting hours were very strict then. He arrived the next morning to see us and was told he couldn't. He said he was the one paying the bill and wanted to see the head nurse. She finally relented and let him in. Our furnace had run out of fuel and Byland brought a list of the things that had frozen because of the cold weather: my goldfish, some colored water in a bottle, and our water pipes. Letters Byland and I had written to each other when he was in basic training were stored under the sink and ruined by the broken water pipes.

The hospital bill was $188. We went home to Ravenwood three days later. Dad said, "Beej grabbed that baby up and away we went." We stopped at the gas station on the edge of town to show Beany Owens our new baby. Don is grown now, and has blessed us with two grandchildren, Nicholas and Alicia, and a great grandchild, Conner. Where does the time go?

Our daughter, Angela Lea, was born in April 1975, at 4:28 p.m. Byland and I and our son, Donald Byland, lived in a trailer house on High School Avenue. We bought the trailer in the fall of 1973 and had to scrimp and save in order to pay the payment on it. I shopped for groceries with the kids and had to put stuff back at the cash register because we didn't have enough money to pay for it. We had no credit card. We operated on a cash only basis.

Angie was supposed to be born on March 28, but hadn't made an appearance yet. I had a doctor's appointment, so Don and I rode along with Byland in the Ravenwood city truck. He had business in Maryville, and my appointment was at 11:00 a.m.

When it came time for my appointment, we drove to St. Francis Hospital and Byland waited with Don while I went to see Dr. Stamos for my appointment. The doctor examined me and said he thought he felt a foot. He had an x-ray taken to confirm his suspicions.

He showed me the x-ray and I could see our beautiful baby, sweet and complete, but in the wrong position to be born. He admitted me to the hospital, and said our baby would be born Caesarean later that day. We didn't know if we were having a boy or a girl. There were no sonograms then to determine the sex of the baby ahead of time.

Byland called my mom and dad, and they came up to help care for Don and to await the birth of their grandchild. Dad brought Donnie to the window, and I waved to them from my second story window. That is a memory I will cherish always. I was a little apprehensive about the Caesarean, but very happy that my baby would soon be born.

St. Francis was founded by the nuns, and a nun prepared me for surgery. She shaved my stomach, and I thought, "I don't have any hair on my stomach!' She was very thorough, though, and did a good job. Kathleen Shunk, a neighbor from Ravenwood, gave me the anesthetic, and Dr. Stamos performed the surgery that brought our daughter into this world. Mom got to see the nurse, Brenda Wharton, a former classmate of mine at Stanberry High, clean Angie up. Mom said Angie was red and crying, and Brenda was talking so sweet and kind to her while she got her ready to meet us.

I was struggling to wake up from the ether they had given me when they brought Angie to me. I had to be sure and stay awake so that I didn't drop her. I found out later that the rest of the family went to KFC while I was in surgery. I always tease Byland and tell him he was eating chicken while Angie was being born. We had to pay off the hospital bill in payments. I tell Angie we thought about skipping a payment to see if they would take her back. She made our family complete. We have a boy and a girl, and they have made us all happy. She is grown now with a family of her own. She has my middle name and she is a blessing to all who know her.

Figuring Out Driving On My Own
By Lyllis Vette of Westboro, Missouri
Born 1931

I was one of eight children in our family. I had one brother two years older than I was and the rest of my siblings were all younger.

Lyllis and the Buick

In 1947, you could get your driver's license when you were sixteen. I was sixteen, and all of my friends either had their license or were in the process of learning to drive. I decided it was time I learned to drive and asked my dad and older brother to teach me to drive. Well, NO LUCK! (They didn't offer Driver's Education in high school at that time.)

I finally coaxed my six year old brother to ask my dad how to use the "stick" shift on an old pickup that sat in our driveway. Dad gave him the information that I needed. My younger brother showed me what I needed to do. I spent weeks in the old pickup. Driving forward a little ways, backing up, driving forward again, I soon got the feel of driving. Our neighbor was in a nearby field and saw the old pickup going back and forth and asked Dad what in the world was going on. Dad answered "Oh that is just Lyllis learning to drive.

My brother had an appendix operation and spent several days in the hospital. Mother and Dad went to the hospital to pick him up when he was released. While they were gone, I decided I would take a joy ride in the pickup. I asked my twelve year old sister to go with me but she refused, but my ten year sister consented to go. As we pulled out the driveway headed east, my Mother and Dad came over the hill from the West. My mother told my

dad to go after me, as I would probably kill myself. Dad told my mother that I would be all right. I decided to drive around the section and all was going well until I had to turn a corner and go up a hill. I didn't realize you had to shift down and I couldn't make the hill. I got it in reverse and backed up right into a ditch. Luckily, I was able to get out and drive on up the hill. We finally made it home the rest of the way safely. When I got home, I got a good lecture from Mom and Dad. Even though I was in trouble, I was pretty proud of myself for a successful "first drive"!

In 1945 when I was fourteen years of age, I was so excited anticipating the 4th of July. Dad had purchased fireworks for us and I could hardly wait to help set them off. When the big day finally arrived, I was so disappointed because I was upstairs in bed with the "Red Measles." I could hear all of my siblings outside popping firecrackers fast and furious. They felt sorry for me and brought me up some fireworks that I could set off later, when I was well. I decided I didn't want to wait so I lit one in my window. Luckily, it did not break the window, but gave it quite a jar. My siblings heard it and thought the neighbors were popping fireworks. Mother and Dad took the rest of the fireworks away from me until I got well. Well that finished my fun for the day.

Several months went by and I still didn't have a driver's license. I decided that I could drive Dad's car, even though I did not have a license. He had a Buick with a gear shift on the steering wheel. It was a lot easier to drive.

My younger siblings were going to Bible School at St. John's Lutheran Church, which was a mile east of our home. I decided that

The Bible School class in 1944

I should take them to Bible School in Dad's Buick. I didn't tell my mother because I knew she would not let me. I was proud as a peacock as I let them out and then made the trip there and back safely. When I got home my mother and older brother was standing at the yard gate. My mother said, "You are going to KILL those kids." Needless to say, I got another long lecture.

True Friends in a Simple (But Wonderful) Life
By Linda Kay Guy of Troy, Kansas
Born 1965

I am not over 60 and I honestly don't remember the days of rumble seats and iceboxes. My dad sometimes called our refrigerator an icebox, but that was just left over terminology from his youth. But, I do recall a life that was different than life today for most people: a time before computers and cell phones, iPods, video games, and Facebook.

I grew up in a small community in northwest Missouri called Frazier. When I was born in 1965, there were about 7 homes in Frazier but the Frazier community, as many rural people know, consists of anyone living within at least a 5-mile radius.

I admit that for young adults of the '60s and '70s my parents, Curtis Fisher originally from Maryville, MO, and Phyllis Shipps from Agency, MO, were pretty old-fashioned compared to some. We lived very simply. My parents did not rush out to buy the latest

Linda's parents Curtis and Phyllis Fisher with their children in 1973

gadgets and technologies. Mom cooked from scratch and we very rarely went out to eat. We grew most of our food and my mom made a lot of our clothes. We got new clothes before school started and at Christmas. There were no entire Saturdays spent at the mall. Well, except for 4-H Achievement Day. I can list on one hand the movies I saw in a theatre as a child. We lived in a small, older farmhouse and we burned wood for heat. We wore hand-me-downs and my dad drove used vehicles. My mother did not drive. I suppose some folks thought we were poor. But we were not poor. We had everything we needed and then some, as you are about to see.

Frazier had a general store where you could buy milk, eggs, butter, bread, flour, other staples, pop, and candy. You could also fill up your car with gasoline. When I was very young, the people who owned the store also lived there. As far as I know, it was simply called The Frazier Store.

I remember Dad occasionally buying bologna and longhorn cheese there. The clerk sliced circular chunks off and wrapped them up in white paper. You paid for it by the pound, very similar to going to the deli today, except you knew the person behind the counter and the selection was limited to three or four kinds of meat and cheese.

On rare occasions, Dad would let my two older brothers, Carroll and James, and I get a pop while he visited with the neighbors or the storeowner. The soda pop was kept cold in a metal cooler about waist high to an adult and about 2 1/2 x 3 ft. wide, with sliding doors on the top. The 16-ounce glass bottles stood upright in icy water inside the cooler. There was a bottle opener built into the side. If you took the bottle with you, you did not throw them away, as you could take them back to the store and get 10 cents for every bottle you returned. My favorite flavors were Ne-Hi grape and strawberry.

Every kid in the community went to Vacation Bible School at Frazier Baptist Church. Even though my family belonged to the Ebenezer United Methodist Church which was located another 8 miles away and closer to St. Joseph, my brothers and I always attended Bible School at Frazier and at Ebenezer. During the 1970s sometimes over 100 children attended Bible School there. Learning the Bible stories, singing songs, making crafts, and having fun with my friends while learning about Jesus was for me one small step toward the life-long love affair with Jesus and the church. There was always a certain scripture that we could memorize and recite to the VBS director to earn a small picture of Jesus or a bookmark. I still have some of those things tucked away in my first Bible. Bible School was held for two full weeks.

At junior high and high school age, my closest friends from the neighborhood were Yvonne Routh, Shannon Corkins, and Deann Walker. We all lived close. Yvonne and Deann are cousins. Shannon and Deann were in the same class in school. I was a year older and Yvonne was four years younger than I. The four of us spent a lot of time together. Yvonne and I lived the closest and spent the most time together.

Yvonne and I got acquainted shortly after her family built a house in the neighborhood. My middle brother James and I saw Yvonne outside one afternoon with some other kids and decided we would go say hello. It wasn't long after that when Yvonne's mother asked if I would stay with Yvonne in the summer during the day while she was at work. Yvonne was too old for a babysitter, yet too young to stay home alone all day. I was about 13 and she 9 at the time.

We ended up as best of friends spending every moment we could together after school and on weekends. In the summer our mothers would each leave lists of chores for us to do while they were at work during the day. I would go to her house and help her with her list and then she would help me with my list. We did not pout and whine about doing our chores or put it off until almost time for our parents to get home. We pitched in and got them done first thing. After they were done, we had the rest of the day to ourselves. We took turns eating lunch at each other's house.

It became a summer tradition to have a camp-out up the old dirt road in July for my birthday. The neighbor who lived behind the church was the only one who used it as a short cut once in a while for tractors and farm equipment, and sometimes for moving cows from one pasture to another. Deann and Yvonne's grandma, Bessie Amos, had a large canvas tent that we set up. We took blankets and sleeping bags to sleep on. We cooked eggs and bacon in my mom's cast iron skillet over

Linda Guy and her 3 friends in 1979

an open fire for breakfast the next morning. It also became a tradition for James to try to scare us at some point in the night. I don't think we were ever very scared. We told ghost stories and played truth or dare and talked and laughed until we all fell asleep.

My brothers and I belonged to the No. 5 4-H club. The club meetings were held at the old No. 5 one-room schoolhouse. The No. 5 Extension club kept the old school house in good repair. It had not been used as a school for many years. The only heat was a large, round wood stove. It was the largest wood stove I'd ever seen. Most people didn't realize that you needed to build the fire in it several hours before the 4-H meeting and keep it stoked in order for the building to be warm for the meeting. I remember sitting through some pretty chilly 4-H meetings. Mom volunteered our family to be hosts during a month in the winter, since we already had firewood for our own wood stove and lived close. My dad worked for himself as a carpenter and could go early and build the fire.

Almost everyone in the club took cooking, even the boys. I also learned to sew, knit, ceramics, and other crafts. My brothers also took woodworking and showed cattle. My brothers and I have several purple ribbons from judging vegetables and other projects. My brothers showed Holstein calves in 4-H. I never did. By the time I was old enough to not be scared of the livestock, my mother had taken a full-time job outside the home, and we couldn't make it to the shows in the summer. James and I were very active in the Junior Leader organization and the Buchanan

County 4-H Council, holding almost every office in both organizations until we were too old to be in 4-H. He also did very well in the public speaking contests. He and I earned several 4-H awards.

One Fourth of July, we were supposed to go to my aunt and uncle's for our family holiday gathering. That afternoon my mom saw my brothers and my cousin Terry Shipps running as fast as they could with buckets of water from the pond to the holler. They had been shooting fireworks near where my dad dumped all of our trash, brush, etc. and caught the trash pile on fire. We ended up having the family to our house because Mom and Dad were afraid to leave with the fire burning. It burned for 10 days.

I remember digging dandelion greens and picking green tomatoes to take to my Grandpa Roy Shipps to eat. My mother never fixed them for us. But, I learned to love fried green tomatoes when I lived in Alabama 2000-2005.

My extended family of cousins and aunts and uncles on my mom's side (Shipps) always gathered for the holidays. I remember times of my mom, or my aunt Marjory Shipps who played the piano by ear, playing hymns and country gospel songs at the piano and several family members—myself included—standing around singing. Eventually, I could play while they sang.

We fought and we did things that we weren't supposed to do. But we also loved each other and trusted each other, and took care of each other. We took care of our clothes and things because my parents couldn't afford to just go buy us new ones if we ruined them or lost them doing something foolish. We were taught the value of honesty and integrity. One of the many important things my mother taught me as a young lady was that it is more important to be pretty on the inside than on the outside.

My family did most everything together. We worked together to feed and take care of the livestock and animals. Everyone had responsibility. The animals ate before we ate. We all worked in the garden and did what we could to help with preparing and preserving. We all helped haul firewood. We played games together, watched wholesome family TV shows together, and we went to church together. We sat at the supper table together and said a blessing before we ate. We

basically learned by doing most everything that our parents did. We learned the value of hard work and money. Nothing was wasted or taken for granted.

There are probably few kids nowadays, maybe even then, who could be trusted to do the things that we did. We didn't steal or damage anything. We were taught to respect other people's property and other people. We were taught to leave things as we found them or better than we found them. We were taught to respect life and the world around us. We stayed away from danger if at all possible. We had a lot of fun together but took very few risks. We went home at the time our parents requested. We weren't angels by any means, but for the most part we respected our parents and didn't want to be in trouble with them or make them worry about us.

As for me and my three friends, there were very few, if any, arguments or disagreements between us. We did not talk behind each other's backs or treat each other unkindly or unfairly. We took turns and took votes and then went along happily. There was no jealousy or manipulation to get our way. There was no drama, as kids today would call it, between us. We were country kids, raised in Christian homes. We worked and played well together. We were true friends to each other while living a simple yet wonderful life.

Always Fresh Bread on Grandma's Table
By Mildred M. Hurst of Tarkio, Missouri
Born 1935

My grandpa and grandma Howard lived a mile east of us. My first memories of them began before the roads were hard surfaced and when it rained, we walked the mile to church, which was just a fourth of a mile past my grandparents'. We would go to Sunday school and then walk down to my grandparents when it was over. We loved stopping at Grandpa and Grandma's. She always had a loaf of fresh bread and a jar of mustard on her table. If she was not home, we would fix ourselves mustard and bread sandwiches. Then we would go up the creaky stairs to their bedrooms. There were two rooms, which had feather beds. Oh how we loved to jump into those feather beds. The rooms upstairs were not heated but you didn't have to lay in the feather bed very long

Grandpa and Grandma Howard with 2 of Mildred's Uncles in 1941

before you became warm and cozy. Then we decided it was time to head up the muddy road to our house in time for dinner. I am sure my grandma was shocked to find an entire loaf of bread had been devoured and she wasn't even home.

We would always stop at Grandpa and Grandma's whenever we passed by. She had goats. We liked the nanny goat but the Billy goat would chase us and butt us. We would wait until the Billy goat was as the far end of the yard before we would head to the outhouse. When it was time to go home, we would hurry to the car so Billy would not notice that we were outside. When I got older I always wondered if they got the goats to keep us from going in the house when they were not home and eating their food.

My uncles trapped and that is how they got their meat. When we stopped by, there was always rabbit, squirrel, and various other wild game cooked and on the table. They would encourage us to eat some. I did, but I am still not fond of wild game. There were always many pelts hanging on stretchers to dry. These were sold and helped purchase food other than their meat. Because of my uncle's trapping they were always bringing a wild pet home for Grandma to tame. I was usually afraid of them as well as the goats but it would not be long before she had made a pet of them and they would crawl all over her shoulders.

Grandma and Grandpa did not have a refrigerator. We were always impressed when she got ready to get a meal. She would go to the open well, lower a rope on a pulley, and bring up butter, milk, and cream. (Nanny supplied them with milk, cream, and butter.) That was their refrigerator. The chickens

scratching around in the front yard provided fried chicken and eggs for their breakfast. My grandpa and grandma did not have a lot of material things, and did not need much. They eked out a living with him working as a farm hand and Grandma cooking and sewing. Grandma was always jolly and happy and never complained. Grandpa was quiet and worked hard. I am glad that I was able to know and enjoy them.

I lived with my mom, dad, four sisters, and three brothers on a farm. Our farm was located on one corner of the square, St. John's Lutheran church was located a mile East on the corner, Farmers City Store a mile East and a mile North of our home, and North Polk School was located one fourth mile West and a mile North of our home. It was a four square mile area and an important part of our life was located on each corner of the square.

We raised cattle, hogs, chickens, geese, guineas, horses, and corn. We raised a big garden, had a big orchard, butchered hogs, and belonged to the beef club in our area so during the winter months we were supplied with fresh beef each week. We killed a couple of chickens a week for Sunday dinner and when hay men and threshers were there for a meal. We canned lots of fruits and vegetables. So most of our food was "home raised". With Mom and Dad many meals consisted of ten of us, and when Mom baked a cake in a nine by twelve pan, it was gone in one meal.

My mother was the disciplinarian and if we didn't behave after her tongue lashing, Dad would back her up and we knew when he spoke we'd best listen up.

One night at supper Mom had baked her usual 9 x 12 cake and I was just too full to eat my piece right then but planned to go back later and have mine after the dishes and homework were both done. Well, I was too late. My oldest sister had the nerve to eat her piece and mine too. I went in behind the bedroom door, lay down on the floor, and threw a screaming bawling fit! Dad, usually so quiet, had enough of that and came in, made me stand up, and gave me a good spanking. But then being the softy that he was he took us all over to Farmers City Store and bought us a big package of cookies. That satisfied me for a moment until I found out my sister got a cookie AND two pieces (which included my piece) of cake. So I threw another fit. Dad gave me another spanking. The only spanking I ever got from him and I got two in one night.

East White School in Mercer County
By Marian Moore of Princeton, Missouri
Born 1929

My first recollection of my early school days was when I attended a one-room country school west of Mercer, MO, in Mercer County. It was called the East White School. This was in 1935 and I was in the primary grades. I loved school and I vividly remember the learning experiences I had there. Some of the older students rode horseback to school but my sister Laura and I walked ½ a mile to school and back every day. We left home about 8:30 a.m. On rainy and muddy days, my neighbor who was a student at the school would sometimes carry me on her back.

After we arrived at school, the bell would ring and at least 15 students would assemble together in the one room schoolhouse. First of all, we recited the Pledge of Allegiance to the flag. For seating arrangements, two people sat at one long desk. The seats were fastened to the floor to keep the students from moving around. An ink well and quill pen was in the middle of the desk. Students who could afford them had Big Chief Tablets. The primary grades used slates and chalk. Our teacher Mr. Stoklasa was very strict but at the same time made the students feel that they were very special. I don't recall any harsh disciplinary action. He involved all of us in school activities. He presented the curriculum

in such an interesting and clear manner. The curriculum consisted of materials for different levels 1st through 8th grade. For the primary grades memorization, repetition, and recognition of sight words and math facts were stressed. Students were expected to print and recognize the alphabet and to write numbers to at least 100. They were expected to master good penmanship.

The students read from the Dick and Jane books and the McGuffey reader and spelling books. I have a copy of a McGuffey reader, which I treasure. We didn't have computers, calculators, TV, cell phones, iPads, or other electronic devices, but we mastered the 3 R's. The upper grades dwelt more on book assignments, which included history, English, math, geography, and science. The activities included group discussion and written assignments. Mr. Stoklasa wrote a lot on the blackboard. He had a pointer to point out certain information on charts and maps of the world. In history, the upper grade students were required to memorize and recite the Lincoln Gettysburg Address. Sometimes the older students would tutor the younger ones. Mr. Stoklasa had creative abilities and stressed it in his teaching. I remember two of the poems he read to us. They were "Little Orphan Annie," by James Whitcome Riley and "Wynken, Blynken, and Nod" by Eugene Field. The primary children dwelt on Nursery Rhymes and poems such as "The Purple Cow," by Gilett Burgess, "The Little Turtle," by Rachel Lindsey, and "My Shadow," by Robert Louis Stevenson. These poems have remained with me throughout the years. During the fall on nice days, Mr. Stoklasa took us outdoors to find leaves from different trees. The older students later pasted the leaves in a scrapbook and labeled the name of the tree they came from.

Christmas time at school was a very special time. We went to the woods together and the older boys chopped down a Christmas tree. When we returned to the schoolhouse, we set up the tree in front of the room in a bucket of sand. We made chain decorations for the tree from popcorn and construction paper. We also had store-bought tinsel and icicles for decorations. An angel made from white cloth was placed on top of the tree. We had a Christmas program and parents and family members were invited. My sister

East White School class of 1937

457

Evelyn came. My sister Laura and I sang "Up on the Housetop Reindeer Paws". The older children read the poem "A visit from St. Nicholas" by Clement Moore. My sister remembered this program as well as I and we discussed it in later years. After the program, we exchanged modest gifts that were made in class. Mr. Stoklasa treated us with peppermint candy canes and oranges. The parents who came also brought treats.

At recess time we younger children played games such as "Ring Around the Rosie," and "London Bridge". We swung in swings that were made from rope and lumber. The swings were attached to a strong limb on a tree. We played Tag and Hide and Go Seek. The older children participated in relays, hop scotch, and played marbles. In the fall of the year, I remember how I loved to eat the grapes from the grapevines near the schoolhouse. I vividly remember the sweet aroma. In the wintertime, we slid downhill on sleds. We stayed inside if the weather was bad. The students enjoyed participating in spelling bees, cyphering, Chinese checkers, and putting puzzles together.

The old schoolhouse had many inconveniences. It was very cold in the winter and some of us sat around the pot-bellied stove to keep warm. The teacher had the fire started when we arrived at school. In the wintertime, we drank water from an old oaken bucket inside the classroom. We used the same dipper to drink water from. Some children used a tin cup of their own. As I recall this little cup folded up in a unique way that resembled a small accordion. In the summertime, we drank water from the schoolyard pump. We of course had outside toilets that were very uncomfortable in the wintertime. In the summertime, it was full of wasp nests. Sears and Roebuck and Montgomery Ward catalogs came in handy and were used as toilet paper. This typical way of life was far from the modern conveniences we enjoy today. At a class reunion in later years, I was reminded by an old classmate that there was a peephole in the toilet that the boys looked through when the girls were in the toilet. The girls also remembered that the boys were caught urinating behind the grapevines.

My sister and I took our lunches to school, which usually consisted of a dry biscuit and an egg. My mother saved old lard buckets for us to use for our lunches. This led to an amusing incident. One day my sister Laura sat under a tree to eat her lunch and eagerly opened her bucket. To her surprise, she found a bucket of lard. She had grabbed the wrong bucket as she was walking out the house that morning. The children thought this was amusing but they came to her rescue and shared their lunch with her. We weren't as fortunate as some of the students who had decorative tin lunch boxes. This was during the Depression years and we were very poor. We couldn't afford nice lunch boxes.

As to dress, most of the girls dressed in a very modest fashion. They wore cotton and gingham dresses. The dresses were usually homemade. The girls usually had one good dress to wear for special occasions. Red silk was popular then. This was during the Depression days and the same clothes might be worn every day. The girls usually wore long cotton stockings and oxford shoes. Buster Brown shoes were beginning to be popular during this time as well as the Gibson Girl dresses. The boys wore overalls, boots, and rubber overshoes with buckles. Their shirts were usually made of denim or flannel.

After a long day at school sometimes my teacher, who dated my sister Evelyn, would drive us home in his one seated car. My sister and I rode in the rumble seat. We laughed with glee as we enjoyed seeing the lovers together. They later went their separate ways. In the 1980s, I went to the country to see the old schoolhouse once more. This brought back many pleasant memories. I looked through the windows. Some of the seats were still there as well as the blackboard and teacher's desk. I visualized the students sitting there and remembered the fun times we had together. The grapevines were still there but the outhouse was gone. These memories of the one room schoolhouse and the impact it had on my life no doubt helped to influence my decision to become a teacher.

When my family moved to town, I attended the town elementary school. The elementary classes were in the basement. Grades one through three were in a room together. The room was very cold and heated with steam. One of my favorite teachers was my second grade teacher, Mrs. Esther Shroyer. She encouraged children and brought out the best in them. She was patient and kind. Mrs. Shroyer was ahead of her time. Although they didn't have special programs during those years she had a talent for special needs children. She was a big help to my sister Laura who needed extra attention. Mrs. Shroyer sat us in little red chairs that were in a circle. We read round robin from the Dick and Jane books.

Another teacher that comes to mind was my third grade teacher. Her name was Miss Shaw. She was a short lady. Her hair was in a bun and she wore long silk dresses that came to the top of her black shoes. She wore no jewelry. She was single and devoted her life to teaching and her students. She had our class dramatize the Whippoorwill Song. One student would go behind a screen to portray the whippoorwill. The other students would sing The Whippoorwill Song. They would sing, "There is a cry beyond the hill." Then the student behind the screen would whistle the cry of the whippoorwill.

I also had an exceptional 8th grade teacher. Her name was Mrs. Stella Wickersham. She read a chapter from a book every morning of the school day. She read from the book *Girl of the Limberlost* by Jean Stratton Porter. In addition she read the *Shepherd of the Hills* by Harold Bell Wright and the famous books by Mark Twain, which included *The Adventures of Huckleberry Finn and Tom Sawyer*. She also had us present patriotic plays and sing the song *God Bless America* by Irving Berlin.

Every Friday there was a school assembly at school. Students were required to participate in the program. They sang, recited, and acted in plays. I have memories of participating in these assemblies. When I was in 8th grade, on Valentine's Day, I sang the song "Lollipop Lou." My aunt made me a white dress and gave me a heart necklace to wear on the day I sang. Later that year I sang "The Woodpecker Song" and recited the Lincoln Gettysburg Address at other assemblies. Our 8th grade class presented the play *Tom Sawyer and Huckleberry Finn* and I had the part of Becky Thatcher.

My elementary school years were most influenced by these three teachers: Mrs. Shroyer, Miss Shaw, and Mrs. Wickersham. They stand out in my mind and I will always have a place in my heart for them.

Rebirth of an Old Country Church
By Pastor James F. "Jim" Broker of
Skidmore, Missouri
Born 1939

It was a cold day in March 2005 when I once again entered the old country church that sets in Benton Cemetery, six miles south of Mound City, in Holt County, Missouri. This was the first church that I had ever pastored, way back when I was just beginning my ministry in 1969, so it had some pretty special memories for me. My years there had been good ones with some really nice country folks and good times worshipping together.

The land that contains the tombstones, pine trees, and the old church itself was deeded to the Evangelical Association of North America in 1882 by Benton community settler Washington Hutton and his wife Caroline for a church and cemetery and the church was built soon after.

That meant the old building was around 124 years old and it looked it, that cold March day. Although the ancient structure appeared fairly solid, paint was peeling off the outside, wet spots on the floor declared that the roof was leaking, and two or three major holes in the ceiling, which were leaking musty debris down onto the pulpit, pews, and floor, told me that we must have gained a family of raccoons in the thirty or so years that the old building

Benton Church

459

had set idle.

But it was like an old friend to me. I just couldn't stand to see it go, along with all those happy memories of days gone by when glowing testimonies, shouts of praise to God, and old-fashioned songs of faith resounded within those walls.

So I walked up to the front, brushed away some rubbish, and knelt to pray. I very earnestly asked our Heavenly Father to restore this building that His praise might resound once more from this hilltop and I believe He heard that prayer. But I never realized the extent He would go to fulfill it.

I knew the cemetery board had entertained thoughts about restoring it to its former glory, for this had been relayed to me three or four years earlier, while I was pastoring a large country church in Mississippi. Someone had called and asked if I had any interest in preaching in the old Missouri church again. I was nearing retirement age and told them yes, I was interested, but had heard no more about it. But that had planted a seed of thought, which remained after I moved back to NW Missouri and retired.

So I contacted one of the board members

Pastor Jim Broker in about 1970

and mentioned my interest to him. Maybe two or three weeks later I received a telephone call. The board was having a meeting in the old country church next Sunday and I was to be there, without fail. I replied in the affirmative and waited and prayed.

When Sunday afternoon came, the board seemed enthusiastic about restoring the old building. This had been their desire for the past few years and they immediately voted 100% for me to begin services there again, beginning the first Sunday in June 2005. Then I discovered they had a "working board." They rolled up their sleeves and set to work. Word got out on the street and even people with no former connection to the old church called me and offered their services to clean and/or help repair the old building. Two or three construction companies called and offered free labor to assist in the restoration, which was thankfully accepted and then a few checks began coming in the mail to help restore Benton.

The old building had settled some so was lifted up, leveled, and had a new basement built under it. Cracked plaster was repaired and a new roof installed. Then volunteers painted the inside and we hired a painter, with donated funds, to paint the outside.

I was happy to discover that one of our board members was a retired electrician, and still certified, who was willing to donate his time to completely rewire the whole building. Now the building was filled with a beautiful soft glow from the old fixtures once more.

After that, he and the Vice President went to town and bought a truckload of lumber, nails, and instant concrete, and came back and built a nice handicap ramp beside our concrete steps at the front door.

While they were doing that I painted the front entry gates and gate posts a nice golden color, which caused a passer-by to ask me if that "was the golden gate to heaven?" I replied, "We sure hope so."

In just a few weeks, we had the old building presentable again and a notice was placed in both local papers that "Benton Church Lives Again" and Sunday worship would begin at 10:30 AM on Sunday June 5th, 2005.

"Don't wear your best clothes as pews are rough. This is an 1880's church in the 21st Century; overalls or jeans and boots are welcome here.

"No collections and no membership book as we believe all the truly born-again are already members of the church and our Heavenly Father will finance His own work."

However, we put an empty coffee can, just inside the door, for those that wanted to help with finances.

The board president wasn't sure that not passing the plate was a good idea, but after a few services changed his mind and stated that he thought we were probably getting more this way. Can donations ran from a few dollars to $1,100 one Sunday. Plus we received nice checks, in the mail, from various locations and one lady even remembered us in her will for a nice sum. So all expenses were paid with some left over for future needs.

The Lord provided a semi-professional guitar player/singer to lead the music and a fine pianist to play the new piano, then a violin player joined us. All free-will service, and the people came! We soon had a lovely congregation numbering in the twenties or thirties coming from several area towns and all seemed to enjoy this old-fashioned church even though the sermons can sometimes get pretty warm, reminiscent of the 1800s. Hopefully we'll continue to grow.

Christmas in Missouri During the Depression
By Marilyn Maun of Odessa, Missouri
Born 1932

Many years ago on a little farm in Missouri, there lived a poor farmer, his wife, and four children. They didn't know they were poor as everyone was in the same situation. It was in the midst of the Great Depression and times were hard. They always had food to eat, clothes to wear, a warm house in which to live, and they had each other. What more could they want?

This was my family! Christmas was a special time of year, one the children looked forward to for months. It was a time of magic, secrets, and great expectations.

Children at that time did not expect great or magnificent gifts. They were used to playing with things that were on hand and making up their own games. They would be thrilled with anything they might receive.

At school, they spent the weeks before Christmas rehearsing the program that would be presented to their families shortly before the school break. It was an exciting time. All children had a part: reciting a poem, singing in the choir, or being in the special play. One really felt important if they were chosen to play a lead role.

Recess and the noon hour were spent stringing popcorn and cranberries to wrap around the tree. Paper cutouts were also made. Names were drawn for the gift exchange. The slips of paper were diligently guarded to keep anyone from finding out whose name they had. Sometimes names were exchanged in secret.

Finally, the night arrived. Parents streamed into the small schoolhouse, sitting at the student's desks. The children were all behind the makeshift curtains in anticipation of the big event, barely able to contain their energy.

The program opened with everyone joining in singing some of the favorite Christmas carols. The evening proceeded with several small glitches, which everyone overlooked. Afterward there were refreshments, and oranges were handed out to all the children present. Everyone went home with the joy of Christmas in their hearts to await their own Christmas with their families.

Mother was busy baking Christmas goodies. Every year she would make fruitcakes to give as gifts to relatives. These were filled with candied fruits and after baking, were wrapped in cloths soaked in brandy or whiskey. They were stored for several weeks in tins to let the flavors mingle. We children were glad they were to be given away, as we did not care much for them.

A weekly trip to Lexington, the local shopping center, was a special occasion. We could glory at the decorations strung across the streets and marvel at the beautiful store displays. It was truly a magic wonderland. The toys placed in the windows were magnificent and we would be in awe of the many wonderful things they had to offer. We knew they were not for us, but we could dream, as all children do.

A week or so before Christmas, our father would go out into the woods and select a tree that would be right for us. Sometimes, we children would get to go along, each having a different idea of the perfect tree. It was brought home, where a wooden stand was nailed to the bottom, or it was put in a large container filled with soil and rocks to hold it upright. Then came the fun part. We got out our assortment of decorations that had been used over and over. Like the tree at school, we had ropes of popcorn and cranberries, but we also had ropes of paper and fragile glass ornaments. After everything was lovingly placed, we added the finishing touch, the tinsel. Then we stood back and admired our handiwork. We thought it was the most beautiful tree we had ever seen.

I remember one Christmas time when a neighbor came to see my father about something and brought some of his children with him. Our tree stood in the corner where the light from the oil lamps reflected on the ornaments and the tinsel. We were so proud of our tree and so happy to share it with someone who had none.

Our parents somehow managed to get our gifts without our knowledge but my older brother was quite the detective and seemed to always know where they were. I was naive and waited for Santa to come.

Christmas Eve finally arrived and we could barely contain our excitement. We were told to go to bed so Santa could come. Of course, sleep was impossible. We would be up every half hour or so, asking, "Has he come yet, has he come?" I don't know how Mother and Dad managed to get the gifts under the tree, but somehow they did. I'm sure they were exhausted by the time morning arrived. At the first light of dawn, we were up and racing to the tree to see what magic Santa had brought. The gifts that were from Santa were never wrapped. Occasionally there would be other gifts that were wrapped from my aunt or uncle and sometimes we children would make something for the rest of the family and wrap them. There would be large bowls of hard candy and nuts for each of us, with a few chocolate peanut clusters mixed in. There would be oranges and apples and once in a while bananas.

We spent the rest of the day relishing our gifts, quite satisfied with the way things had gone.

Mother baked a scrumptious dinner complete with turkey or goose, dressing, mashed potatoes, gravy, vegetables of all kinds, and pie. We were living like royalty, if only one day in the year. Father tried to take a much deserved nap after dinner, but I'm sure with all the noise it wasn't easy.

The rest of the holiday was spent in contentment, playing with our gifts and each other. Sometimes there was snow and we would go out and build snowmen and snow houses, throw snowballs, and go out on the hills and ride our sled. What fun we had!

Through the years, our Christmas became more affluent, but the magic of Christmas and those early years are the ones we cherish and will live on in our memory forever.

Lucky 8s in My Life
By Judith Dunwoodie of Richmond, Missouri
Born 1941

My birth was on a Monday morning in December 1941. It was very close to December 7, 1941, when Pearl Harbor was bombed by the Japanese and so many of our countrymen were killed! I'm sure, without it being said, I was the last thing in the whole world my folks needed. Both my parents were in their middle 40's. I happened to be the eighth child of eight children. My three oldest siblings, all brothers, were in the war (Army) but were not in Hawaii. The oldest, age 23, was in Germany, the second in the U.S., age 21, and the third was in France, age 19. All three were spared and returned home safe. There were 4 boys and 4 girls. I became an Aunt at 4 months of age and being neighbors, was hardly ever separated from my nephew. So, Donny and I thought we were brother and sister until one of my sisters felt the need to tell us exactly how we were related. This was quite a shock, being all of 6 or 7 years old. The way our birthdays fell put me a year ahead of him in school.

The grade school we attended was a three-room school with grades 1 through 6, 2 grades to each room. I was such a baby I sat on my teacher's lap every day crying until lunch. Now she was teaching 1st and 2nd grades with me on her lap. I wouldn't eat lunch. My sister closest to me in age was 8 years older and in high school. She and another girl would walk to the grade school to make sure I would eat! But, then they had to go back to school. I would cry and hang onto her dress/

462

skirt begging her to not leave. That went on every day until Christmas I was told! My hair had never been cut and was braided in a French braid with a wide satin ribbon tied at the end of each braid and brought to the opposite side with the ribbon bow tied at the base of my neck creating "basket handles." Have you noticed throughout this writing how many times the number 8 played a role in my life?

I married my high school sweetheart. He died in our 42nd year of marriage. He was 3 years older than I was. He went to the Navy when he graduated high school and I finished school. He was back home after his discharge in 1959. We married that same year and I had a very good life with 3 children and now am blessed with 6 (two each) grandchildren.

I suffered a stroke at the age of 55 and was hospitalized 8 weeks and now walk with a leg brace and cane with left sided paralysis but can think on my own, live alone, and care for myself for the most part. My left side is stroke-affected but I'm alive and have a good family to draw on when I need them. I oil paint, still. I attend meetings of the local "Red Hats" and I'm a Beta Sigma Phi Sorority member since 1985. I miss driving and getting out when I want to and I miss the love of my life! It has now been 16 years since having my stroke and 11 years since my husband's death. It's a good life but I'd like it to be better, "easier."

My four brothers are all deceased. I lost a sister just a year ago, in March 2012. Of eight siblings, only three including myself are still living. My oldest sister now in her late eighties lives in Texas, my sister closest to me

Judy's sister Irene with Judy in 1945

in her late seventies lives in South Missouri, and myself now 71 years old lives in North Central Missouri. We are close only through mail and telephone. Nephews and nieces are plentiful and we stay in touch for the most part. Facebook is mostly a necessity in this day and age.

This area is just recovering from 2 heavy, back-to-back snowstorms both in the same week! But the only measurable snow in the past 3 winters. This locale (50 miles east of Kansas City, Missouri) is very short for moisture but hopefully will get much needed moisture support this coming spring and summer. I love to live here in Missouri and I'm glad to be able to experience the change of seasons. I've always loved snow: playing in it, shoveling it, and walking in it during a snowfall.

When my children were small (each of them being 6 years apart), the age differences kept them from being very compatible, but they helped one another and me and their dad in any capacity when asked. They were then and still are great human beings. Both my husband and I have been very fortunate to be given our marvelous family. I came along so far down the line my siblings were nearly all away from home, married and with their own families. I was raised pretty much like an only child. My folks died at young ages, each one 59 years old: Mother in 1956 and Daddy in 1958. It could be implied that they worked themselves to death. Both busy with family, working, and just plain everyday living.

I remember the days before "flash bulb" picture taking, how as a child the "Christmas presents" were taken outside to get photos taken, even in the snow! My head was always tied with a headscarf. Otherwise, I was likely to develop a cold, earache, or both!

At Christmas every year, we always had a live tree. It was never put inside or decorated until the week of Christmas. Our whole community, even families from neighboring towns, came to our Methodist Church on Christmas Eve for our program and live Santa Claus visit. Sacked treats with candy and an orange were given to everyone in attendance. It was also tradition to have a new outfit of clothes including new shoes and new coat because at that point it was a necessity due to growth. The former was given to a younger child, either family or neighbor. Shoes were generally totally worn out! There were certain things that were rationed during the 1940s: shoes, tires, and sugar. This was because of WWII. My father owned and operated a coalmine in those days with the help of sons not away at war. My youngest brother, 12 years my senior, had to quit school to help in the mine. My oldest sister, 16 years older than I, worked at the mine too in the office. I rode in the coal delivery truck with my brother from the time I could go with him delivering coal (shoveled on and off the truck by scoop shovel). I always had to sit in a cardboard box (original car seat, do you think?)

My mother and father each had only 8 years of schooling. Both were very learned and smart in all aspects of their educations.

Mother was the oldest of eight children born to Scottish immigrants. Her mother and father came to America on the same ship and came to Missouri and settled in the same area, married, and raised their family. I only knew one grandparent, my mother's mother. She suffered a stroke and was left an invalid. She lived with us and was left childlike after her stroke. She would snatch my doll away from me and stuff it behind her back. She was without teeth and mother would scrape a halved apple with a spoon to feed her. She also loved her hot tea and fried scones that she had for breakfast each morning. I was about 4+ years old when she died. I've been told I became an avid tea drinker too. I forever wanted what she had and she always wanted what was mine. Sounds like two kids, huh? Her name was Charlotte Diana Izett.

My folks led a hard, busy life. When my folks had their first 4 children, my father's parents, Grandma and Grandpa Woods, lived with them. My dad's brother's wife died. They had 3 small boys and came and lived at our house too. It was like raising 3 sets of twins plus one, as both Grandma and Grandpa were not very well at this time. I understand Mother did a lot of gardening, canning, sewing, etc. She was a very busy woman and hard worker.

She sewed all of the kid's school clothes including sewing for nieces too. When I went to school, I would pick out the school clothes from the catalog I liked and she would make them nearly exact from the catalog pictures. Different collars, sleeves, skirts, and trims. I always had nice clothes for school, and whatever my outfit, always hair ribbons to match. They were kept in a cigar box and pressed on ironing day. I didn't take our living to heart then but now realize how lucky I was.

There was never a drop of liquor in our home, nor foul language spoken. We were raised to be Christian, both at home or wherever we were.

Mother played the piano and sang soprano, and Daddy sang with a deep bass voice. There was hardly a gathering at our home without music. I later took piano lessons for several years from my cousin Marilyn (daughter of my mother's sister, Agnes). My family was very musical and not only sang but played instruments mostly by "ear."

No indoor plumbing. There were still a lot of outhouses during the '30s, '40s, and '50s. I never knew our kitchen without running water.

My dad worked 6 days a week. Mother didn't drive, so trips to town (Richmond, Missouri) occurred only once a week on Saturday nights after the Saturday workday ended. We always went to the grocery, 5&10, Penney's, and hardware store and stopped for an ice cream cone when leaving town at the Lillard Creamery—delicious!

My folk's first deep freeze was a used ice cream freezer from the Lillard Creamery. We used it for many years. We raised our own chickens, beef, pork, fruits, and vegetables. The freezer never failed, not once! This was such a very, very handy luxury for Mother.

I could go on for pages but better stop. Yes, this was easier than I thought it would be.

"Don't You Know There's a War On?"
By Barbara Boehner Cook of Chillicothe,
Missouri
Born 1935

My daughter Cyndy brought a book from the Field School library called "Don't You Know There's a War On?" by Avi, a nominee for the Mark Twain award for 2003-04. It was a story of a boy growing up who was in upper elementary school and though I was definitely lower elementary level at the time it brought back some childhood memories that perhaps some of our future family generations might be interested in hearing. I remember when the announcement was made over the radio that the War had been declared and I still see the faces of my parents and their reaction of shock. We were eating supper at the table and the radio was on. There was no TV then. Listening to certain radio programs was part of our entertainment. I never wanted to miss Fibber Magee and Molly and The Shadow.

The book mentioned tying packages with string and that was a common practice to bring home something from the store wrapped in paper and tied with string. Mother saved the string to use again. The book also mentioned having only one pair of shoes which I don't remember about that but I know I didn't have to think much about what I was going to wear, so I don't think I had a lot of clothes but I always had enough and was comfortable. Rationing coupons were common and my mother would figure out what she could buy at the grocery store with them because some items simply were not available unless a coupon was presented. Another grocery store item was white margarine with a yellow capsule in it. The yellow capsule had to be mixed through the margarine before using and then, of course, it looked like butter.

Windows of homes had blue stars in them if a member of the family was in the Service, and if one had been killed, it was gold. Saturday afternoon movies were the highlight of the week and I faithfully went each Saturday to see the current cowboy show, which was always shown in installments so you'd keep coming back. I liked Roy Rogers better than Gene Autry. I was tall for my age and when I was 11, they wouldn't let me in unless I paid adult fare. Of course, I didn't have the extra money, so I ran back home which was a block

away and told my mother. She walked right over and informed them my birthday hadn't come yet and I could still pay kid price. I was never asked again, but when my birthday actually came, Mother sent the full price with me. She was mad that I was questioned!

Furnaces were fueled with coal and certainly not automatic and my dad kept the furnace going at the building where we formerly lived along with other people in apartments. I remember him getting up early to do the same at our house and then go to the building to check it. Another thing we did to help the war effort was to collect newspapers to be recycled. It was our Girl Scout project and I jumped into it with energy and enthusiasm and ended up with enough pounds collected to be a princess to the Paper Queen, which was the Girl Scout who collected the most. That made me either the second or third highest! The *Kansas City Star* published paper dolls with clothes each Sunday and I loved to cut them out and dress them. My friend, Doris Ferguson Schworer, and I played many Sunday afternoon's together cutting out those dolls and then making clothes for them!

School had memories, too. When my mother and my dad got married, it was a secret until the school year was over. They always said someone in the family couldn't keep their mouth shut and it was known before the end of the school year, so she couldn't teach any more. The school days started with the pledge to the flag, a tradition that should have never been stopped. At recess we played a lot of hopscotch, jacks, jumped rope, chased each other, and when school was out, I lived for baseball. We also played after school a lot of games like Kick the Can. We had to make our own fun.

There were erasers at the blackboard and sometimes we would get to take them outside and pound the chalk out of them so they could be used again. We had head lice checks and had to line up in the room while the nurse looked at each of us. We also were weighed and measured for height in front of the class and I was mortified that the nurse would say the weight and height aloud and I was the tallest one in the class at 5'4" and weighed a little over 100 pounds. One other girl also got that dubious distinction. There was a drive through the schools to buy war stamps at either a dime or quarter each to paste in a book until it totaled $18.75. If we kept it for 10 yrs., it could be cashed in for $25.00. That was to raise money to help with war expenses. Crayons were not always available and I was mad at my brother for coming home with colored pencils for me when I specifically wanted crayons; of course they were not available at the time.

Rationing coupons were also used for things other than food. My aunt worked at Penney's and she would call Mother when some desired item came in and told her to get to the store quickly. She did and didn't waste any time about it. I think it was sheets that she bought. I think towels were included, too. I know she bought some one time and put them out to use. I grabbed one and wiped the back of my leg hard and looked down to see blood running. The stapled sticker was still on it and I cut a good long scar and still have it today! I remember Mother's face with that one, too! .

Blackouts were mentioned in the book but I don't think we ever had any; it was probably the cities where there would be many lights and easy for planes to find to bomb them. One more interesting one, is that Beverly's dad, Clayton, my brother-in-law brought back a parachute, and my mother sewed a wedding dress out of it for my sister. It was quite a special thing at the time.

The book brought back memories that I had not thought about for quite some time, and I hope that whoever is reading this will enjoy them too.

Chores on the Farm
By Duane Clement of Tarkio, Missouri
Born 1939

I was born in Northwest Missouri in December 1939. There wasn't much money so you raised your own food and butchered your own meat. There were lots of responsibilities even as a child back then.

Gardening was a full time job. You started in early spring and finished after a freeze in the fall. During the season, you had peas, green beans, hominy, sweet corn (field corn if the sweet corn failed), carrots, kraut, pickles, beets, tomatoes, tomato juice, and all kinds of relishes to can and place in the cellar. You also had to dig a huge amount of potatoes, turnips, parsnips, and sweet potatoes to store.

We also canned fruit. It could be apples, peaches, pears, apricots, cherries, blackberries, raspberries, plums, boysenberries, gooseberries, grapes, and even pumpkin. We could can the fruit or often we made jellies and preserves. We would melt paraffin and cover the tops of the jelly or preserves to seal it.

In the fall, we would gather walnuts and it would often be my lot to hull them so we could have a batch of fudge. We also added them to cakes, brownies, and cookies.

We had a major workday in the fall after it was cool. We would gather with the neighbors to butcher a bunch of hogs. The women were very proficient in the processing and even cleaned and processed the heart, liver, brains, jowls, and even the entrails (which was used for casing for sausage). The old saying was "they processed everything but the squeal." Everyone had a smokehouse to keep their meat. Hams and bacon were cured. Sausage was made, encased in the entrails, and buried in salt to keep it from spoiling. The lard was rendered and used for cooking and baking. Leftover from the rendering was called cracklins. This was used to flavor cornbread and was it ever good. We also canned a lot of meat to be used later. The meat was always so tender and tasty. If a jar would spoil, it was almost like losing a member of the family.

Everyone milked cows so they could sell the milk and cream. We milked between 15-20 head all the time. It was a job 2 times a day, 7 days a week, and 365 days a year. After milking all the cows by hand, we had to carry it to the house and down to the basement to run through the separator. The separated milk was then carried back upstairs and out to feed 15 or 20 calves. These were our bucket-fed calves and it could be a challenge to feed them without spilling the milk. When I was about 4 years old, I decided I was old enough to milk. I could milk a bucket full of milk but there was no way I could lift it. While waiting for Dad to come and move the bucket of milk one of our friendly cats decided to sharpen its claws on the back of the cow's hind leg. Needless to say the bucket of milk and I took a ride. Dad rushed over and asked if I was all right. I replied "Hell no! Give me another bucket and I'll finish milking that cow, but if I see that damned cat I will kill that S.O.B."

We always had a lot of farm cats; some

Duane Clement

were very gentle, some very wild. Our dog was very tolerant of the local cats but he hated any stray tomcat. One evening while I was milking the dog spotted a stray cat. The chase was on and the cat finally raced into the barn, up the back leg of the cow and across her back. Once again the bucket and I went flying.

We also had a lot of hogs ranging in size from baby pigs to fat hogs and even some sows and boars. Once the calves got big enough that they didn't need the separated milk we mixed it with oats and corn and let it soak. We used two 55-gallon barrels and would rotate from one barrel to the other. The hogs went wild over that feed. In the summertime, it smelled like a brewery. Sometimes we would sort off the smaller pigs and feed this mixture to them. They didn't stay small very long.

We took cream and eggs to town to sell 2 times a week. On Wednesdays, we might get a small dish of ice cream. I always got butter brickel—a real treat. On Saturday night, we took more cream and eggs to town. We purchased groceries and visited with friends. The town would be packed with people at 9:30 pm on Saturday night. We might even take in a movie. Everybody had to stop by the local restaurant "The Candy Kitchen." There

was always a huge crowd.

In the spring, we would always get 450 baby chicks. Before we could bring them home, we had to clean the brooder house real well. We scrubbed and disinfected it with "lye water." This was repeated at least 2 times. After the floor was completely dry, the bedding was scattered on it. Then the brooder stove was carried in and started to make sure it was going to work all right. This was done a week before the chicks were supposed to arrive. We had to be sure everything was going to work properly. It always smelled so good, and was so warm (about 90 degrees) that it was a pleasure to go in and sit. We had to pick up the baby chicks in Tarkio at the feed store or the post office. When we got them home, we filled the chick waters with warm water and medication. Then every chick's beak was dipped in the water to teach them how to drink. Feeders were placed near the edge of the brooder. Newspapers had to be put down under the brooder and a little feed was sprinkled on the papers. This was done to encourage the chicks to eat and drink and stay near the heat. This was a lot of work but it must have paid off because we seldom lost a chick. The chickens grew rapidly and the 150 Cornish rocks were ready to be dressed in about 7 weeks. We worked steadily at this because they would soon be too big to fry. We would leave a few and by Thanksgiving, they would be as large as a turkey. The remaining 300 were laying chickens to produce eggs for sale and eating. In early fall we began preparing the pullets for the laying house. A man would come and debeak and worm them. Worming consisted of poking a pill down each chicken and debeaking was done by burning off part of the top beak. This was done to prevent pecking one another and it helped prevent breaking eggs. Later in the fall, the older hens would begin to "molt" and lose their feathers as well as cut down on egg production. Mother Nature was telling them to take a rest. At this time we would get rid of the old hens and prepare the laying house for the new hens. After much cleaning, spraying, and disinfecting we were ready to move the pullets. We would enter the brooder house at night after the chickens had gotten on the roost and catch them asleep. We would carry them by hand to the laying house. It took many trips before we got it done.

We hand-pumped lots of water when I was a child. We had to pump and carry water for everything from drinking, cooking, canning, poultry, bathing, dishes, laundry, and cleaning to watering plants. We had a windmill for the livestock if the wind blew.

My father purchased a new tractor that had steel wheels. We were so excited but since Dad had bleeding ulcers the Doctor told him he would have to get rid of the tractor and go back to horses and mules if he wanted to farm. He bought horses and mules, which became another chore since they had to be watered and fed. Mom and Dad had to pick corn by hand. Two horses were hitched to a wagon and driven down 2 rows of stalks that had already been shucked. On weekends, I would help shuck and throw the corn into a wagon. It had boards on one side that raised it higher than the other side. This was called a bang board. The purpose of the higher side was to keep the corn from going over the wagon as we threw it inside. I would occasionally throw one over the other side. I knew I needed to get around there and pick it up because you didn't dare waste an ear of corn.

Another major project was putting up hay for our animals. The hay had to be mowed and left for 3 or 4 days to dry and cure. When it was cured, it had to be raked with a dump rake. When we stacked it outside a j-hawk stacker was used. If it was going to be put in the barn, it would be picked up with a buck rake and loaded on a hay rake to be hauled to the barn. The hayrack was pulled along one end of the barn and a long rope with a large hayfork was lowered to the rack. After the fork was filled with hay, it was pulled through the hayloft by the rope that was threaded through pulleys to the other side of the barn and hooked to a gentle horse. My job was to lead the horse when the men at the hayrack hollered. I would slowly lead the horse until someone thought the hay was in the right place in the barn and hollered for me to stop. After I stopped the horse, the hayfork was dumped. We would repeat this process until the hayrack was empty. Usually another hayrack was waiting to be emptied as soon as we finished the first one.

There were always many chores to be done and you could never feel like you had it all done. Every day there were animals to care for and gardening during spring until

fall. When you finished one job, it seemed like there were 2 or 3 more waiting on you. We never took time for a vacation because of the many responsibilities. You wouldn't ask a neighbor to help except in a crisis because they had their own chores to do. However, you always knew you could count on them if there was an emergency.

Class Reunion
By Paula Wilson of Chillicothe, Missouri
Born 1945

The month of May is the beginning of spring in our area, when class reunions are on the minds of many graduates. My dear friend Sandy called: "Hey girlfriend, let's go the Humphreys School Reunion. All classes are combined. Let's go!" Finally, I said "ok."

I had not graduated from Humphreys, but went to this school from first grade through my freshman year. Boundaries changed in the small counties, which had myself going to a different school. Leaving where I had been all my years as a child was sad, but now a chance to go back seeing school friends, teachers, was exciting.

Finally, the day came, Sandy arrived, and the visiting began. We were catching up on old times when we were neighbors. We would ride our ponies even though she had the best horse, mine being a Shetland pony who would try to bite me when I was getting on her and never wanted to run except when the barn was in her view. The conversation led to what dish each of us would be taking so the recipe box began being shifted though like powdered sugar on a cake. Finally, our choice was made.

Getting ready for the event didn't take long, at least not like our younger days. I remember when I was given permission to shave my legs, which my father soon learned to dread for his shaving cream disappeared all most as fast as he could purchase it. A dab was not enough; a handful worked great. Picking out what to wear wasn't a chore for we were not trying to impress anyone, just making sure, we would be comfortable, and in something we could recognize each other in a crowd.

Time to leave for the event. I guess in my head I had this idea that we were on our way to the best Hip Hop ever, seeing friends, rock 'n roll music, and good food, like traveling back in time. Before long we were pulling in the parking lot. The school building that used to seem so large now felt so small. Some of the single room buildings were gone along with the two big slides with the four favorite swings. All had been replaced with modern playground equipment plus a cafeteria. The school once for all grades was now an elementary school; the high school had combined with Galt.

As we entered with our prize dishes, me with my 9 x 13 blue carrier, perfectly baked pecan crust, first layer Philly cream cheese with powdered sugar, instant vanilla pudding, and the instant chocolate pudding with milk for the second layer, and a Cool Whip third layer, with nuts sprinkled on top. We signed in putting our maiden and married names on the tag and applying this to our clothing. While walking up the incline to the event all the time I am praying my hip doesn't pop out while carrying my 9 x 13 blue carrier. Finally we entered the auditorium, again, smaller than I remember. I looked up at the bleachers and could almost hear the cheers during a basketball game, the laughter during a pie box supper, or the cake walks to raise money for the school. The gym was the center of the community coming together. In grade school you were never to walk on the gym floor with shoes. Now the floor was showing all the layers of wax which had begun to turn a deep brown. As I sat my dish down looking around the room, there were no girls in poodle skirts with white blouses perfectly ironed, colored neck scarves around their necks, hair shining from being washed in rainwater, curled the night before with curlers and hairpins. Boys were not in dark blue jeans with each cuff turned up one fold, plaid shirts, hair combed to perfection

Paula's Grandpa Pete with Paula and her cousin Nadene

as the smell of Vitalis or Butch Wax that you could smell as they passed you in the halls. All I could see was white hair, some with hair dye to cover the white; Age seems to make us all look different. But after reading nametags it all came together. Yes we were all older, but the same people.

Our friend Joyce soon joined us. Now the three musketeers were together in school visiting like it was only yesterday. Joyce is one of these special persons who knows everyone, where they grew up, parents, grandparents, who they married, how many children, etc. If you need a friend to go to a boring party take Joyce, in no time at all everyone will be visiting and enjoying themselves. I do believe when her mother gave birth to her, she communicated all she had heard during the nine-month stay in the womb, a precious person. Suddenly Joyce says to Sandy and I "Hey look over there in the corner. Don't you girls remember him?" Remember how all the girls in school thought he was the best looking guy!

Now, we were raised not to stare, so slowly we turned our heads, looked for a second, and then slowly turned back toward each other with the reply of "YUCK," giggling as school girls do. I sat there thinking to myself that the gentleman probably had also been looking around the room, had noticed we three senior citizens, and expressed his "YUCK" too. Walking the halls of this school, we came to the trophy case and all the awards the school received with the many talents of students, or band trips our director managed to take our small school to, so we too could march in a parade. I carried my E flat alto saxophone to and from school each day from 4th grade through high school. I recall one day the school bully came up to me and asked if the suitcase was my lunchbox. Being hurt but determined not to cry, I turned around to him.

I said "It's full of candy bars" and he couldn't have one. He never bothered me again.

The reunion was a good experience. I realized all things change like our outward appearance. We still feel the same inside. I guess it is just the Lord's aging process, and I am thankful for all the memories. As we were walking away I felt blessed by the small school that had been a big part of my life. As we left I felt a tear run down my cheek. Good-bye Humphreys High School.

The Screen Door

Born in a small town and about to become a 4 year old, my life was about to change. This came about from an agreement between my mother and grandfather.

My mother had returned home expecting me, while my father was in WWII. After the birth she remained there until my father came home. This is when tempers began to flare for they were going to move to Ply Month, Indiana to run a sandwich coffee shop. My grandparent's hearts were broken. They had helped walk the floor at nights and you might say became parents all over again, therefore the agreement went into effect. I was to come back to the grandparents for summers when old enough.

I remember my first trip back to Reger, Missouri, and even though the Grandparents had come to Indiana several times I was more excited than I would be getting a new toy.

The trip began. I said goodbye to my cat Puff and the dog Skuff and we were off. Riding in the backseat in those days you had lots of room to play and pass the time. After what seemed like forever, Granny was telling me to "get up, we were home." I put my face against the car window and there it was the barn, house, orchard, and all of Granny's flowers all around the house. I jumped out of the car and ran to the old screen door.

This door at one time had been painted a bright forest green and was the prettiest door on the farm. Now the paint was peeling, and some of the spokes were missing. The handle had been moved several times for the nails would strip out of the wood but it was in my reach when I stood up on my tiptoes. I could open the door easily.

Once inside the wood floors were shining with a throw rug here and there. Granny took me to the room where I would be sleeping— oh my the feather bed. I needed a stool to get in this but once you got in the bed you would sink down and you felt surrounded by all the love in this house.

Next morning I heard my grandpa Pete calling and with Granny's help I was up and putting on my play dress, but I didn't have to wear any shoes for all was different on the farm. I could smell hot biscuits and the kitchen air was full of the smells of jams and jellies Granny had worked on this summer. Grandpa Pete had a big smile on his face and introduced me to the wire egg basket. Yes, this would be my job: gathering the eggs.

So after breakfast off we went to meet the hens. They were white and red ones. I had a box to step up on to reach the top nests. He failed to tell me about Mr. Black snake and sure enough on the first day reaching into the last nest I touched something that wasn't an egg. I dropped the basket and began running towards the screen door, stepping on stones, which hurt, but I kept on going, finally coming into the grass. I could see the screen door, which I flung open and at last safe inside Granny's kitchen. But the eggs never made it that morning.

The summer was busy that year, I made mud pies, and learned that when Granny's old wall phone rang not to pick up the receiver unless I heard one long ring and two short rings. Even Grandpa Pete's red Irish setter learned that if he could catch the screen door on the second slam he could open it with his nose and come into the house.

I remember the screen door most of all for it was always open in the summer months and was locked with a hook that could pull apart if opened hard. What a great time to remember. I'll never forget the screen door. It was inviting fresh air that would roll in on a windy day, and my first feel of independence going in and out. Time was so simple but the lasting effect it has on a person makes a memory that can never be forgotten.

Dad Raised All eight of Us on His Own
By Russell L. Gienapp of Cameron, Missouri
Born 1947

I was born in Iowa City, Iowa, in August 1947. I was the eighth to be born, two more came after me. We were a family of four boys and six girls. We were dairy farmers in NE

Russell's parents Ernest and Welma Stark Gienapp in 1937

Iowa.

In January 1951, we had a house fire. We lost our mother, oldest sister, and youngest sister in that fire.

Our dad was left to raise eight kids from 11 years old to a 2 year old. Our family was pictured on the front page of newspapers all across the country.

Public response to the 8 kids sitting on that couch in that picture was hundreds of letters, people asking to take and raise one or two—the county came in and tried to split us up—but our dad fought to keep us all together. Twenty years later, my wife's mother says she remembers it on the front page in their Kentucky newspaper. We continued to farm and Dad also worked out at a packinghouse.

The oldest child left was Ray, 11 years old. He watched after us and kept us in line when Dad was at work. Walt, second oldest, helped him.

We milked cows, raised pigs, chickens, and a huge garden every summer, and I am sure we raised lots of trouble for each other and for Dad. We were poor and we worked hard and eight kids could come up with thousands of ideas for fun things to so.

I really don't remember my mother, but I do remember the day of the fire. It was very cold and the snow was deep.

Sometime later Dad bought a farm. He had to put a lien on everything we had to get the farm. Then came a bad crop year and we lost the farm. I remember going to three different schools in 1 year. We were picked on and laughed at because we were so poor.

I swear I don't know how our dad did it, but he kept us all together and alive. All eight of us are still alive today.

Number 1 of a million: I was the second to the youngest left. I remember me and my brother David closest to me in age and our youngest sister Anna were sent to gather eggs. With baskets in hand, we headed out to the chicken house. Our ages were 4-5-6. We were gone a long time, but came back with no eggs.

Dad asked, "Where are the eggs?" We said, "There weren't any." He took us back out to the chicken house and there were eggs all busted on the end of the chicken house. We'd had a contest who could throw them the highest. We got a good working over!

Number 2 of a million things we did: One summer day David and I were riding calves in the barn. We were having a lot of fun when the calves broke out of the pen we were riding them in. I took off running to shut the barn door, so nobody would know what we were doing. We took off after the calves. I tripped on a string and fell on a hayfork. Two points went through my thigh and one into my stomach. My brother pulled it out. Calf riding was over.

Dad wasn't home. My sister Kate ran to the neighbor's for help. They carried me to their house. I nearly bled to death. Dad came and took me to the doctor. I spent the rest of the summer on crutches, when the other kids weren't taking them from me.

There was always something going on. Then at age 14, I left home.

I don't know how my dad "Ernest John Gienapp" did it all, but I've thanked God

Ernest John Gienapp with his family in 1975

471

many times for giving Dad the strength to do it all. I and my family have lived in Missouri for 35 years now.

Friday Nights in Carrollton
By Bettie Lee Sawatzky of Carrollton, Missouri

I lived through the Depression. On Friday evenings in Carrollton, my mom (Mary Walker), sister (Anna Walker), and myself would walk a mile to the band concerts on the square at the courthouse. All the stores and restaurants were open till 9 and 10 pm. We had a much larger population in those days.

You could get almost a pound of candy at the dime store for 25 cents.

If colder weather, people sat in their cars and visited. People loved to visit in those days.

Then we would walk another mile home, up and down those steep hills. My legs were short, so I often would run to keep up.

Elliott's Store in Laredo
By Louise M. Harris of Jameson, Missouri
Born 1915

My husband, Elmore Harris, liked to tell about going to Laredo, Missouri, on the train with his mother to visit his grandparents, Charlie and Lydia Elliott. They owned the village grocery store.

It was a long ride from McCook, in southwest Nebraska, so his mother packed a lunch to eat on the way. Five year old Elmore could hardly wait to see Grandpa and eat all the black gum drops, cookies, and peanuts that he could hold from Grandpa's store. By supper time, he had an upset stomach and he vomited. Grandpa was in trouble and he received a scolding from his wife and daughter!

It was 60 years later when I came to Missouri with my husband that I had a chance to see for myself that Canadian geese mated for life. We heard from a cousin living in Chillicothe, Missouri that goose hunting was very good at Swan Lake Refuge, south of Sumner. (Sumner, Missouri was considered the Canada Goose Capital as well as the birthplace of Senator Fullbright.)

We drove there in our travel trailer. A widow named Viola Roup owned the choice 20 acres joining the Refuge. Her three blinds were rented to hunters by the year. She let us park in her yard and hunt when the blinds were empty, providing we would dip out water after a rain. (Four-inch rains were common there.) I could sit at my window and watch the geese fly out to feed in the cornfields and come back to shallow water later. On flights out and back, the gun shots could be heard. One day a goose was hit and came down along the fence row. The mate swooped down to it, and then quickly joined the flight. I had to shed a few tears.

I am not a native of Northwest Missouri, but I've lived in Jameson, Daviess County, since 2004.

"Across the Wide Missouri"
By Dolores J. Huiatt of Mound City, Missouri
Born 1928

When I was eight years old, we had an extremely cold winter in Northwest Missouri. We lived in Mound City, which is about twenty miles from the Missouri River. The river had frozen so hard that cars were being driven across the river to Rulo, Nebraska.

We very often went to a restaurant across the river at Rulo. One night we drove to the place where people were crossing the river. My father decided that since the weather had been much warmer that afternoon, we would walk across and not drive the car.

I thought that was quite an adventure and the next day at school I told my classmates that I had walked across the river on the ice. None of them believed me and the boys teased me and said I was "telling a story."

However, I did walk "across the wide Missouri."

Memories of the 1947 Worth, Missouri Tornado
By Lila Kidney of Bethany, Missouri

A tragic day for Worth, Missouri, occurred on April 29, 1947, a Tuesday at about 2:30 P. M. The town was a small friendly, farm community of around 300 residents located in the southeast part of Worth County, Mo.

My parents had lived in town for several years, but when I started to school, the three of us moved to Grant City, MO, to the county seat of Worth, MO, where my dad was employed.

When I was a junior in Grant City High School, on this Tuesday, April 29, 1947, there was a track meet in Albany, MO, about 25 miles south.

The school bus was to take the students to the track meet that day. In the afternoon, rumor spread through the crowd that a bad storm had struck the town of Grant City, leveling it to the ground. We were all upset about our families, friends, and community. The school bus could not leave until the meet was over, but one boy, a student, had missed the bus that morning, so his parents had told him he could take the family car to the Albany Track Meet. He told us that he would take the car and the students that were with him, back to the school.

When we were traveling north on 169 Hwy., the traffic was stopped several miles south of Worth, MO, where we were told that the storm was at. Worth and the traffic was closed through the highway, only emergency vehicles were being allowed to travel. Everyone was running and walking, very worried, to find what had happened.

Arriving in the town of Worth, disaster was everywhere. The buildings were leveled, cars were damaged, and people were in disarray as what to do for their friends and relatives. Mrs. Meyers, the telephone operator, had time to warn many of the upcoming storm, so residents had time to get to storm cellars. The school had received the warning and the children were taken to fruit caves.

There were 15 killed and many injured.

The traffic was coming through town, and a semi-truck was along the highway, with many people riding on the back to see about their families. When I looked at the truck, there was my dad. We were so happy to find each other. He had told my mother that he would come to find me and what had happened.

Dad told me to go on home and tell everyone what I knew had happened, and to be with my mother, as she was very worried. He would stay and help his friends.

Now when I hear of the disaster of a tornado, I always remember the destruction that is caused and the feelings of everyone, families, and friends.

Give a Penny to the Poor
By Oleda Cooper of El Dorado, Kansas
Born 1933

From the Missouri River to the Iowa line, I lived almost 80 years in Northwest Missouri, in the towns of Wakenda, Carrollton, Braymer, Pilot Grove, Grant City, and Platte City. My first eight years I lived in a tarpaper shack my dad built on an island in the Missouri River south of Wakenda, a tiny town that existed until the Great Flood of '93 washed it away forever.

In those days, we went to Carrollton once a month in a horse-drawn wagon for groceries and livestock feed. In the thirties in small town America, before the warning: "Don't talk to strangers! A barefoot boy in patched bib overalls and a girl in a homemade feed sack dress usually moved one or two of the old men loitering on the street corner to slip them a penny or two. A penny would buy enough candy for a day. A harmless thing: giving a penny to the poor.

During World War II, our family was split. My dad worked in a defense plant in Kansas City, my brother lived with our grandfather, and I was sent to an aunt in Carrollton. Since my aunt worked all day in the chicken processing plant and school lunch was yet to be invented, I walked three blocks to a small, hole-in-the-wall diner. For 15 cents, I had a hot dog and milk. Occasionally the middle-aged man behind the counter would slip me a pack of gum: giving pennies to the poor.

After the war our family was together again, this time in the hills above Wakenda and away from the Missouri River, that had flooded our home almost every year. Going to school in Wakenda, we usually took a sack lunch, but once in a while, we could afford a lunchmeat sandwich at the little grocery store in town. As we walked back to school, every day a shy (but obviously rich) boy who had a crush on me threw a five-cent Hershey bar at me: throwing pennies at the poor.

During high school, I worked weekends at Pinky's Coffee Shop in Carrollton. Two or three teachers gave me a ride to town on Friday afternoon and often a ride back to

473

school on Monday morning. I usually stayed with the aunt who had kept me when I was ten, or if she was out of town, I stayed with my boss and his family: more pennies for the poor.

Andy Rupe, described by my boss as "the richest man in town," ate toast and tea alone every Sunday morning at Pinky's. The year Christmas fell on Sunday and we were closed, he came in on Saturday night for his usual tea and toast. This time he left a silver dollar under the saucer.

Today I like to tip generously, especially if the server is young (or bumbling) and if there's any semblance of poverty. But I know the automated giving of the credit card can never equate the surprise and the joy of finding a silver dollar under a saucer when the richest man in town gave a penny to the poor!

Mom's Wringer Washer
By Barbara J. Farris of Dearborn, Missouri
Born 1948

I don't remember my mother doing her family's wash on a washboard (although she did), and she never had an automatic washing machine, but she sure got a lot of mileage from the Maytag wringers.

Monday was usually washday, and that meant filling the washing machine with hot soapy water. There were two rinse tubs; one contained bleach. In addition, there was a bucket of starch water as well as a bucket of bluing which made the whites whiter. Mom started with the whites, followed by the colors, and last were Dad's overalls, and sometimes a throw rug or two to finish it off. There were several loads of whites and colors, and more hot water was added to each load. Washing for a family of six meant an entire morning would be spent doing the wash.

Clothes swish-swashed around the old wringer until my mother's inspection of cleanliness allowed them to move to the next step. The clothes were punched with her pointed wash stick into the wringer where they were squeezed into the rinse water. While some were washing, some were rinsing, and by the third load, the "hanging out clothes" on the outdoor clothesline had begun. Dad had

constructed the lines from two locust posts set deeply in the ground. To these posts, a 2 x 4 was securely nailed to the top of each. Then three strands of Number 9 wire were strung and wrapped from each 2 x 4. As the wet clothes hung to dry, they were propped by forked branches my dad cut from small saplings in the woods behind our farmhouse.

Just as there was a regimented system for washing, there was also a code of conduct for the drying on washday. Whites were placed on the front line; colors were hung from the seams on the middle line; and jeans, overalls, and throw rugs completely filled the three lines for the farm family of six. With the help of sunshine and wind, we had clean clothes for another week.

There were interruptions, however, and one we still laugh about.

Farming was a family endeavor, so one summer day when the milk cow jumped the fence and sought greener pastures, all of us immediately joined the chase. The wash had started, and when we were summoned to help get the cow in, the first load of clothes had just begun to wash. This cow chase went on for close to an hour over our farm, the neighbor's farm, and finally into another neighbor's barn lot. The cow was pursued through tall weeds, deep gullies, and green pastures. When we finally had her corralled, we headed down the road toward home. Mom said, "Gee, that load of clothes will be clean for sure." As we topped the hill toward home, we could see white sheets flying in the breeze. My aunt had dropped by, and finding no one home, but seeing signs of life, had continued doing laundry. It was just one ordinary day on the farm, but one we still remember.

Tuesday and Wednesday were days my mother labored over an ironing board putting creases in our jeans and shorts plus ironing wrinkles from our print dresses and blouses. We were kept very clean, thanks to the good old Maytag washer. Electric dryers have replaced the clotheslines in most people's homes, but I still have three lines of clothesline rope in my backyard, and when weather permits, I dry my sheets on an outdoor clothesline. As I rest my head at night, there is no better touch than crawling into a bed with line-dried sheets.

Yes, Mom's wringer washer saw a lot of heavy-duty work, and her efforts to keep us clean are to her credit. She also kept us

Barbara's mother, Helen Farris in the 1960s

safe. We could help pull the clothes from the wringer but cautioned to keep our fingers at a safe distance. We remember the starched jeans that were also wrung through and then drip-dried on the line. We walked around stiff-legged until finally they began to bend. We owed our clean appearance to the good old wringer washing machine and its knowledgeable operator, our dear mother.

Jack Benny Broadcast in St. Joseph
By Maurice Fothergill of Mound City, Missouri
Born 1933

I was born and raised on a farm, which provided many memories and experiences that lots of kids never have.

Summers on the farm were full of activities, most of which involved playing when I was younger. Since I had cousins and other kids living close we spent many hours together building dams across the creek to make a pond for boats made from small boards. At times, we had to wade into the water to retrieve one of the stray boats (we didn't tell our parents about that). Occasionally we used the horse tank at the barn to sail the boats, which was not as much fun as going to the creek. Since I was the only one of the kids with a pony, they often came to our house to ride "Happy." The girls favored riding the pony to playing in the creek.

Christmas was full of excitement that started when Dad, my sister, and I went to the timber to cut a cedar tree. Sometimes we remembered a nice tree from when we were mushroom hunting, and other times we had to search to find the right tree. Christmas Eve was always at Grandmother's house in Rosendale. I could hardly wait to eat and open the gifts so we could get to bed and wait for Santa. There were times I was awake and downstairs before 4:00 am, only to be sent back to bed until everyone was awake. It seemed forever before my sister was up. Attending church and being in church programs, especially at Christmas and Easter, are very much a part of my childhood memories. The two weeks at Vacation Bible School was also an enjoyable time. The last 2 years I was in VBS, three of us rode our bicycles the 2 ½ miles to attend.

It was common for friends or relatives to call on Sunday morning to say they were coming over for dinner after church. Many Sunday afternoons were enjoyed with my parents and uncle and aunt driving the country roads of Northwest Missouri. A picnic lunch was sometimes packed so we could stop and eat at a nice spot along the road. Gasoline prices before the war were less than 19 cents a gallon and even after the war, the price stayed at 19.9 cents for years. An afternoon drive in the country was an inexpensive pastime that many people used to enjoy.

I stayed in Savannah with Dad's Aunt Mary when Mother and Dad went shopping. Grandpa lived there with his sister and had a little shop in back where he and I made things from wood. That may be when I became interested in woodworking. The house was next to the lumberyard and on the other side of the lumberyard was the railroad. I was fascinated watching the steam engines go by. There was a long, steep grade on the railroad between St. Joseph and Rea, which made the engines, pull down and belch clouds of smoke. If the train had a heavy load, the wheels would slip as they came up the steep grade south of Savannah. I can still remember the sound of the wheels slipping and the engine starting all over with a slow chug, chug, chug, gradually picking up speed. As the train built up speed, the wheels would slip again, and again. Savannah also had an interurban line (a single car) that operated on a rail between Savannah and St. Joseph. The tracks ran in front of Aunt Mary's house on Main Street, down to the Cancer Sanatorium and on to St. Joseph.

On the farm, Dad had a 50-gallon barrel, built on wheels, that was used to mix "slop" for the hogs. Slop consisted of water, skim milk, shorts (ground meal), tankage, table scraps, and peelings. Mother saw me at the barrel one day and asked what I was doing. I told her I was baptizing some kittens. Lucky for the kittens, she saw me in time to save them. As I got older, I was given the job of helping feed the livestock, pets, and chickens, as well as gathering the eggs. I didn't like gathering the eggs if a hen was sitting on the nest because snakes sometimes crawled under the hen to eat the eggs. Dad never drank anything with alcohol but kept whiskey in the sheep shed for newly born lambs that were weak. My cousin and I found the bottle, caught a rooster, and gave it whiskey. The whiskey made the rooster crow as if it was early morning.

When I was in the first grade of school, I rode home on the second bus,

Maurice, Beverly, and Kay Fothergill on Maurice's pony, Happy

which meant I had to wait at the school until the bus returned from its first route. I played around the swing several evenings, getting the legs of my bib-overalls wet and was warned not to come home with wet clothes again. The next evening I did as I was told and did not play at the swing but instead went down over a little bank in back of the school to a large pool of water. I don't know why, but I stepped in the water and dropped up to my waist in the lagoon system for the school. I knew the trouble I would be in after the long, wet, and smelly ride home. The school fenced in the lagoon shortly after that.

As a kid, I enjoyed watching the men butcher, thresh grain, put up hay, and shear sheep. On butchering day at our farm, Dad was out long before daylight building a big fire in the barn lot. He had piled the wood up the evening before so he could get water boiling early in the large cast iron kettles. Hot water was used to scald the hide of the hogs so the hair could be removed easier. It was usually cold at butchering time but I didn't mind. Butchering involved four or five neighbors working together to butcher several hogs. While the men were outside slaughtering the hogs, the women were cleaning the head, tongue, liver, heart, and other internal organs as well as cleaning and scraping the small intestines so they could be used as casings to stuff the sausage. The sides of meat were cut up later after they had a chance to cool. The scraps of fat, some with little pieces of meat, were cooked and then squeezed through the lard press to make lard. I liked eating the hot cracklings after the liquid fat had been squeezed out. The cast iron kettles were not only used to cook the fat but were used later to make homemade lye soap, cook corn to make hominy, boil dirty garments, and many other farm uses.

When I was 7 or 8 years old, Dad let me ride Happy to carry water to the men working in the fields. Three or four jugs with straps were hooked over the saddle horn and taken to the field. The jugs were either crock jugs or glass jugs wrapped in burlap to help keep the water cool. Everything was great until two of the jugs hit together and one of them broke. The broken jug belonged to a neighbor and I was really worried about telling him what had happened but I knew I had no choice. He was not mad about the broken jug and I felt much better. There were no bathrooms in the farm homes so the men washed up for lunch at the well (using a "wash pan"). Dad's Uncle George had a barrel fastened to the cross arms of the windmill with a sprinkler head in the bottom. The barrel was filled with water each morning and by evening; the water was warm for a shower.

Northwest Missouri was very dry in the late 1930s. Farms had no ponds at that time and many of the wells were running dry, our farm being no exception. Even though water in the creeks had stopped running, there was one spot on our farm where the creek bottom

476

continued to stay muddy. Dad dug a deep hole at that spot and sunk a 50-gallon barrel with the ends cut out. In a short time, the barrel filled with water so it could be dipped out and hauled to the barn for the livestock.

I never did mind doing chores but I was disappointed if I couldn't get in the house in time to hear "Jack Armstrong the All American Boy." During the war, Jack Benny broadcast his radio show from the St. Joseph Auditorium. A blood drive was held a few weeks before the broadcast and everyone donating blood received a free pass. My parents both donated blood and received passes. I am not sure how I was able to go but I went with them to see and hear the broadcast.

I have memories of Saturday night in Rosendale when most of the farmers sold their cream and eggs and bought groceries. Rankin's Produce and Hardware Store bought produce and sold feed and hardware. While the cream was being tested and the eggs were being candled (a method of checking to see if the eggs were fresh by placing them over a light) most everyone went to the free "picture show."

Sunday, December 7, 1941 is remembered very well. We were in the kitchen when the announcement came over the radio that Pearl Harbor had been bombed and we were at war. It wasn't long until many things were either rationed or hard to get (meat, sugar, flour, butter, material, gasoline, tires). Since we lived on a farm, had a garden, and raised our own meat it wasn't as bad for us as some that lived in the city. Even at that we had to cut back, substituted, or did without. Mother made dresses for herself and for my sister but material was hard to buy. Feed companies soon started putting chicken feed in printed sacks. Mother usually went with Dad to buy feed so she could select a print pattern she liked and to get enough sacks for the items she wanted to make. The women sometimes took their sacks to the neighborhood Women's Club Meeting where they traded sacks for a print they liked better. Even though gasoline was rationed Dad was able to manage because he had an allotment for the tractor. At school we had scrap paper drives, scrap iron drives, and even collected and dried milkweed pods. The fluffy portion attached to the milkweed seeds was used to fill life preservers during the war. Savings stamps and bonds were sold

at school and it became a contest to see who could fill their stamp book first.

After Germany started bombing England, one of our cousins living there inquired about sending their children to the U.S. until the war was over. I remember my parents having discussions with Dad's brothers about the children coming. As I remember they answered that it would be all right, but the children were not sent. I was never sure why they didn't come until just a few years ago when I located some of the cousins in England while I was working on family genealogy. In one of my letters I mentioned that I remembered someone in England asking to send their children to the U.S. during the war. I received an answer that she remembered her parents talking about sending her and her brother over but decided against it because the risk of the ship being sunk was too high.

I grew up at a time when working was expected and accepted, without any question. I never once had the feeling of being abused. With only a few exceptions, my childhood memories are good and I don't know of very many things I would want to change.

Mom Would Always Grab Her Pipe for the Cellar
By Bessie C. Hainline of Elmo, Missouri
Born 1930

In 1931, my father Albert and mother Bessie (Johnson) Kerns and 14 children moved from Blanchard, Iowa, to Elmo, Missouri. We put our furniture in the boxcar of a Wabash train for a distance of around 9 miles. I was one year old.

We lived in the section house the railroad owned. Dad was the section foreman so it was very low rent. Two more children were born in Elmo, making 16 children. There were nine boys, seven girls. Many years later they let Dad and Mom live there free. They just had to keep taxes paid up each year on the house. Five of the boys were bachelors, so they lived there also until the house was torn down.

In 1938 or 1940, my sister Ella Mae and I got into a little mischief. It was her fault because she was older. Dad and Mom fed every hobo that walked the tracks. Dad had a line of credit at Joy's grocery store. If he

Bessie's dad, Albert R. Kerns

had the money, he would pay for what we got instead of putting it on credit. Dad sent Ella Mae and I to the store to get a loaf of bread and a pound of bologna to feed one of the hoboes. We got the bread and bologna and put it on Dad's credit, then spent the money at Shoney's drug store that had ice cream, etc.

Got home, and Dad said, "Where is the change?" Ella Mae said, "We lost it." Dad said, "Where did you lose it?" Well, we said, "In between Shoney's and Walter's hardware store." Dad took us up to the vacant lot. We

Mary, Ella Mae, Helen, and Bessie

all three were on our knees looking for money that wasn't there. Dad said, "Girls, let's go home." On Sunday morning, we had extra people for dinner. After dinner, Dad called Ella Mae and I in the kitchen. He introduced us to the company. Our father said, "I want to introduce my girls, Frank and Jesse James. "

We were taught a good lesson. We remembered this all our lives. Out of sixteen, four are still living: myself, sisters Ella Mae and Helen, and brother Albert.

Dad really watched out for all of us when the weather was bad. He would sit on a chair by the kitchen door and watch the clouds and wind. When he thought it was needed, we went to the cellar. The cellar was where we kept our canning, along with a bin full of potatoes. We children sat on the potato bins, as it was usually full. Mom had her own special chair. In the cellar was a shovel and pick in case the cellar caved in. After herding, mostly younger boys, and girls, the older boys wouldn't go any more. Mom would always grab her pipe, and long green tobacco, and wooden matches. Dad would say we will get blown away while you are getting your pipe.

Every so often, Dad would open the cellar door to peek out to see what was going on. Dad had a good awareness of storms. He would always know when it was time to go to the cellar or when to leave the cellar.

Working with My Dad
By Patsy Cox of Cameron, Missouri
Born 1938

My dad was a very loving and caring man. He was dedicated to making a good living for his family and leaving the land better than when he came to it. He worked from sunup to sundown, and was a leader in many organizations, yet he took the time to listen to me.

I enjoyed working with my dad on the farm more than inside the house. He taught me to operate the tractor at a very early age. I cultivated corn, being careful to stay between the rows and not plow the corn plants out of the ground. I harrowed the disked ground to help level and smooth the clods.

One of my earliest efforts was when I drove the tractor and hay wagon as men loaded shocks of wheat onto the wagon to

478

be taken to the thrashing machine. My dad owned a Farmall tractor. One day my uncle brought his Ford tractor. The problem was that the throttle on the Ford worked opposite that of the Farmall. So when I was slowing down to cross over a small ditch, I went faster instead of slowing and my Granddad that was on the top of the shocks was tossed off the wagon. He was not injured.

One time when I was about twelve, my dad was putting hay bales into the hayloft. The opening for inserting the hay bales was on the north side of the barn. I was on the little B Farmall tractor on the south side of the barn. A cable was attached to the tractor supported by and stretching across the rafters to the hayforks on the north side. Men on the north side would load the bales onto the hayforks, and then I was to back the tractor, which lifted the hay bales up and across the loft to the proper dropping place. Someone in the loft would trip a lever to loose them and then I was to drive forward to lower the hayforks and to lift another load until the wagon was empty. Then another wagon was in line to unload more hay.

After two days of sitting in the sun wearing my shorts and driving the tractor back and forth, the fronts of my thighs were sunburned pretty badly. Mother convinced me to stay in the house the next day to recover from the burn. I was sure I would be all right the next day and resumed my position still wearing shorts. This time I was burned so badly I could hardly walk. I managed to painfully walk up the stairs that evening. I could not lay with my legs straight, so my sister rolled a blanket and put it under my knees so as they were flexed slightly. She then laid a cold wet towel across my thighs to cool the heat of the burn.

One time my dad asked my sister and me to cut cockle burrs in the cornfield and he would pay us. We were overjoyed at the thought of earning some money. Needless to say, it was not an easy job to walk every row of corn to chop out the cockle burrs, so we decided to skip a few rows. Daddy never knew until we told him years later. He said he wondered why there were still so many cockle burrs.

When I was in my mid-teens, my dad told me I could have the proceeds of one litter of pigs if I would do all the feeding and care of them. I had to get up early to feed and water them, and then return to the house to wash and change my clothes to go to school. The first sow to have her pigs had more pigs than any of the others. When they were big enough to take to market my dad deducted the cost of the feed and any other expenses, yet I made a good profit.

Daddy didn't like to milk the cows but mother did. She wanted the milk to cook with and to drink. We had a cream separator, which separated the cream from the milk. It had to be washed and put together carefully or it wouldn't work. Some of the cream was churned in a Daisey Churn to make butter. Some was kept in the icebox and taken to town on Saturday evening to sell along with the extra eggs.

One summer my sister and I decided we wanted to learn to milk. It was difficult so the next summer we conveniently forgot how. Mother evidently didn't mind for she never said anything about us milking again.

When I was a very small child I was flogged by a rooster, therefore I had no liking for chickens. When I was asked to gather the eggs, I would lay a stick on the neck of the hen and fling her out of the nest by the tail. Then I disposed of the broken eggs and brought the rest into the house.

Our entertainment was board games, puzzles, and I loved to help my brother put together model cars and planes. Saturday nights were fun. As a small child when Dad was finished with his work, we went to town. Mother gathered her eggs and cream to sell and then pay for her groceries, and then she sat in the grocery store to visit with the other ladies. Daddy went to the pool hall, and we went to the movie to watch Tom Mix, The Lone Ranger, Gene Autry, Roy Rogers, and the like. It cost us 50 cents to get in, and to buy a snack and drink. These were the good old days. When the movie was over, we went to the grocery store, and Mother would send us to get Daddy. We were not allowed to enter the pool hall, so we stood outside until we got his attention. When his game was finished we left, picked up Mom, and went home.

My life began in the little farm house of my parents, with the assistance of a family friend. I was the first-born at home; my brother, the third, was born breech and died before the completion of his birth. Because my mother believed that if she had been in the hospital they might have been able to have saved her son, she insisted that she go to the hospital for the birth of the following three children she would have.

Our first mode of transportation was our two horses and a wagon. We would ride to the little town of Coffey to buy feed. Mother allowed my sister and I to pick out the feed sacks for our dresses.

Shortly before I was to begin school, we moved to another house. This house was close to my father's family and only a quarter of a mile from the school. We also housed the teacher, Mr. Nickerson, and his wife in one room of our house. On weekends, they went to their own home.

I loved this old man and his wife and worked very hard to impress him by learning the alphabet and numbers very quickly. I enjoyed school so much that I would go to school early, before he arrived. One day I sat on the step for a long time and wondered why he was not coming. I finally became tired of waiting and walked the quarter mile home to find out it was Saturday. Another time, there was about three inches of new snow on the ground. I decided to drag my feet to make a path for Mr. Nickerson. In a little while, I decided it would be funny to make a crooked path, so I drug my feet from one side of the road to the other, back and forth. I thought it was funny, but I don't remember if he ever commented on it.

In March of my third year of school, we moved again, but I continued going to the same school. My dad took me by tractor across the field to the highway and to the timber on the opposite side, of which I was to meet my cousins. They were to show me the way through the timber to school. We were late, my cousins had already gone, and I had

Patsy Klindt in the early 1950s

to find my way across the creek and through the timber. I was very frightened. To this day, I don't remember ever walking through timber with my cousins.

The teacher that I loved became ill and couldn't teach any longer. He moved back to his home in Bethany. The young man who replaced him was very different. Where Mr. Nickerson allowed us to play in a creek off the school grounds at lunchtime, the young man would not allow us off the school ground and we all had to play football, girls, as well as the boys. I hated this.

I had a crush on an older boy and thought the young female teacher was partial to him. In my jealousy, I wrote her name and his name on the wall of the outhouse. I was found out and had to scrub the words.

In my sixth grade, the community to the west decided to hire a teacher and open the school building for the area children. There I finished grade school. I had to walk a mile to the highway to catch the school bus and ride several miles to high school.

This was the last move my parents made. The house was a large colonial with two main rooms downstairs, and a smaller room to the back. My sister and I slept in an equally large room upstairs and my brother slept in a smaller room.

This house was cold all the winter, but they all were. Mother would stuff rags in the cracks around the windows, but many times, we would awake with snow blown in to the inside of the window. We had a wood-burning stove in the kitchen and large double burner oil stove in the living room. My sister and I would stand in front of this stove until it felt as though our flannel gown would burn, then we ran upstairs, jumped into our twin bed, draw our knees up into our gown until the bed was warm. Then we could stretch out and sleep.

We had no electricity, telephone, or plumbing until I was a senior in high school. Our daily chores were to fill the kerosene lamps, and carry cut wood into the porch so it would remain dry. We had an 'outhouse' at the far north side of the yard and used Sears and Wards catalogs to cleanse ourselves.

The barn was leaning to the north and the previous owner had attached a cable from the barn to a large oak tree. One evening as Mother had gone to get the milk cows, my sister and I were playing on the hay wagon parked under the cable. We were tall enough that we could reach the cable and swing on it. As we played and screamed, having so much fun, our mother came running, out of breath and shouted, "What's wrong?" Because of our screaming, she thought we were hurt. We weren't punished but told to stop our screaming.

One year my siblings and I woke up thinking it was morning and went downstairs to open our Christmas gifts. Mother and Daddy had just barely gotten out of the room, it was 10 PM. Thereafter we were not allowed to get up until 6 AM. We took an alarm clock to bed with us to make sure we were up by six. We never got more than one gift apiece, plus there was always a large paper sack of nuts, another of candy, another of fruit, and a coconut for each of us.

More Family Time
By Carmeta F. (Hopkins) Angle of King City, Missouri
Born 1933

I was born in a small farmhouse north of Albany, MO, in Gentry County, in November 1933. I am one of five children, one older brother and sister and one brother and sister younger. Times were pretty hard for families then. We had no electricity or running water so everything we did was by hand. Our lights were kerosene lamps and lanterns, which had to be filled and cleaned daily.

Yes, the outdoor outhouses and chambers was a must. Not handy but needed.

I was five years old when I started to school in the first grade. There was a one room school for all eight grades and one teacher. My older brother and sister and I walked one and one half mile to and from school. My older brother helped keep coal in the large stove in the corner of the schoolhouse, where we could put our wet boots and gloves to dry when it was snowy. We didn't have any canceled snow days. We always had school. No, I didn't get any school spankings, maybe a talking to sometimes, which hurt as bad as the spanking.

Not very often did we have a radio program. Sometimes we could hear Lone Ranger and Grand Ole Opry till the battery got low, which was borrowed from the old Model A we had. It had to be cranked. Oh yes, then there were the party line telephones, about everyone had one. So every jingle of telephone everyone was listening. So your conversations were short at times. Saturday night baths were had in winter by a wood heating stove: one side froze the other one burned so it was a fast bath.

Our first wringer washer was heaven sent and ran off a kerosene motor. When using a tub and washboard for years anything easier was appreciated.

Most of our clothes were homemade by Mom from flour and feed sacks, which some mothers could trade colors and have different garments so not all looked alike. Saturday movies were only if there was a free one out side where the folks sold eggs and cream.

My brother's first car had a rumble seat, which was nice, only living on a country road, no grease or blacktop, was a dusty, dusty mess. We didn't use it much, only for short trips.

Yes, all had chores to do that were old enough. When we got home from school, we always changed out of our school clothes and got work done. We helped carry milk from the barn to the house to be separated so milk was in one can and cream in another. But you keep spouts in place. There was no cream in the milk that went back out to the barn for pig food.

There were not too many homemade toys. Some toys were made out of spools, dolls made out of old stockings, and a wooden cow from a smooth board.

Iceboxes were a luxury to have. If not, a chunk of ice wrapped in blankets and put in a tub then put in the cellar where all the canned foods were kept. Later there were rotary telephones in some homes, which was quite different from party line telephones. As

481

I got older and out of grade school at age 12, I stayed some with a neighbor to help with her housework as she had some surgery done and needed help. After I got old enough I went to work in a cap factory making baseball caps. I worked there till I got married at 21. After two years, I had two girls and stayed home with them and babysat other people's children and did washing and ironing, until the girls were in school, then I started working outside the home. Often when they were out of school, they were on their own. I worked in a doctor's office and a nursing home.

Some of the other duties and chores we were involved in included when Dad planted cane for some food supply. When it was ripe and ready, the leaves had to be stripped off then the top cut off. After this was completed, it had to be cut off at ground level with a corn knife, one stalk at a time. I was careful never to let it touch the ground and get it in the dirt. We carried it to the wagon and stacked it evenly. Then it was taken to my uncle's place where he had a sorghum mill. He went through all the steps, putting the juice in a big vessel type cooker with a fire under it and stood and watched it very closely not to overcook it. This made it dark and strong and made several cans of molasses. This was used to make lots of molasses cakes, cookies, syrup for pancakes and biscuits, and candy. This all had to be done before cold weather. Sometimes my uncle would keep a can of molasses to pay for his work.

Dad, my older brother, and a friend would also go out in timber or old farmhouses not lived in to get the honeybee's honey and large clear pieces of honeycomb. You could put it in clean white cloth or such and squeeze out honey. It always had to be real cold for this. The remaining left in the big container was placed in a cold area. When we needed more honey we very carefully got more honeycomb, checking to make sure no bees were eaten. This also took care of buying sugar at the store.

At age 41, I went to get my G.E.D. diploma and enrolled in Nurses' school and got my L.P.N. I continued to work in health care for several years. A job I really enjoyed was as a school nurse at a small school of grade school children. It was a great job. My husband then passed away so I moved closer to my children, and then worked a few more years in a retirement home for people who needed care and couldn't be left alone. Then I had to retire because of health reasons. I miss working.

Some days when the snow and roads get bad I feel lucky to be in and wonder about my children and grandchildren out on the snowy roads.

I have two daughters, two granddaughters, and one grandson dead, and I have 5 great-grandchildren, 3 boys and 2 girls.

Yes, I remember the war when Pearl Harbor was attacked on Dec. 7, 1941. There were a lot of friends and relatives lost to the conflict. Coffee, sugar, and gas were rationed. Each person in a home had a book of stamps and when they were used up, until next month sometimes was hard. Even if you had money, nylon stockings or any nylon products were not available. It was all sent to make parachutes and things for the war service. We also had iron drives. You could go and find old farm equipment no longer usable as any iron product was needed. You made a pile and once a month someone from the township or county would come pick it up to send and be melted down to be reused for war equipment. It was a time when we all tried to help and work together. Most had more family time together. No TV, cell phones, or computers to distract us, even if we could have afforded one.

Good old days are gone and I only think of them in the past. It would be very hard for people nowadays to tolerate the ups and downs we had. Just lots of memories.

Always on Saturday
By Marjorie Packard of Cameron, Missouri
Born 1929

I have great and wonderful memories of midcentury Cameron, MO. Cameron is a typical farm town in Northwestern Missouri. In 1940 when I was 11 years old, it was very different than now. We lived on a farm 3 miles south of town. Our home was on a steep hill with the road slanting down in both directions. Of course, these roads were not graveled!

My mother and dad were hard-working people. They were young, energetic, neighborly, and independent. All week they worked hard without the convenience of

Marjorie's parents, Archie and Clara Goodrich with Marjorie

electricity, refrigeration, or indoor plumbing. There were no tractors, automatic milking machines, or fancy equipment.

Saturday was a special day in our family. No matter what the weather, we always went to town. In spring and summer when chores, milking, and farm work were "caught up," it was late when we started out but in winter, we went earlier in the day.

Daddy had a nice 30-something Model A Ford. It served us well for many years. When the weather was bad, he put on tire chains.

Fresh bathed and dressed up in our best, we piled into the car. He would start the motor and step on the gas. We rolled out of the driveway down the hill at full speed. It was great going until we reached the bottom! There in those bad days, we sunk in the deep mud or soft snow drifts up to the hubs. Dad would "gun" the motor and rock back and forth several times until we gained a few inches. Many times, he would get out and push the car with the motor running. Often he would have to dig us out until we reached higher ground. I remember complaining loudly about cold feet when we were stuck in the snow.

The road to the Catholic cemetery a couple miles south of town was graveled. We were happy to get to that place. Grandma and Grandpa Armstrong lived on a small farm just across the road from the cemetery. They never did own a vehicle. Horses were good enough for Grandpa! We usually picked them up on our way to town.

The folks always took eggs and cream and maybe chickens to sell at Chad Nichol's poultry house. They used that money to buy groceries and supplies. Sometimes I got a dime or a quarter. I could go to the picture show for a dime.

Friday and Saturday the Ritz Theater ran a double feature—a cowboy show, a black and white B movie, some cartoons, and a serial such as "Jungle Girl." The previews of coming events lured us back next week.

Mother and Grandma bought groceries at one of the four or five grocery stores on 3rd Street, Hyde's, I think. They would hold your order until you picked it up later. Then it was on to Plain Price to look at fabric (piece goods), notions, shoes, or underwear—Plain Price had everything!

As kids we weren't afraid to walk up or down 3rd Street, in groups or alone. No one would bother us. When I had some money, I loved to go to our dime store, Mattingly Bros. They had a big glass case at the front, loaded with candy of all kinds. You could buy it by the piece or by the pound. They had a variety of 5-cent candy bars and 1-cent bubble gum. The other counters were filled with wonderful stuff: makeup, nail polish, lipstick, all in beautiful colors. They also had Blue Waltz perfume, sparkly jewelry, and toys. After much looking, I usually bought a paper doll book to cut out or some trinket (marked Made in Japan).

The men usually just stood around visiting about neighbors, the weather, or the crops. They might gather at Connel's Hardware on the corner of 3rd and Walnut.

Third Street was much different then than now. It was an exciting place. The stores stayed open late in good weather, maybe until 11 or 12 or until people were leaving. There was a retail store in every building and all the parking places were taken. Cars could go either way, up or down the street.

The town was full of people visiting and shopping and having a good time.

I have wonderful memories of those Saturdays in Cameron. They were special to our family. Rain or shine, we always went to town on Saturday.

In and Around Trenton, MO
By Reginald Werner Robertson of
Wheatland, Missouri
Born 1930

I guess I started remembering things at an early age for my first encounter at age of four. I remember taking my mom's (Georgia) iron apart to see what made it get hot. Well needless to say, she wasn't a bit happy and told me if I didn't get it back together before Dad (Reginald "Reggie) got home from work that something else would be hot and it wouldn't be the iron.

At age 6, I started into the Reams country school, with one teacher, one room, and grades 1st through 6th. I usually rode my bike on our gravel road with a neighbor boy.

Dale was an animal lover and he always had some kind of critter and tried to bring some to school when he could. Such was Sammy the squirrel, but Sammy met his demise when on the way to school, he came out of Dale's pocket and the back wheel ran over him. In the winter when the potbelly stove was a-going and the teacher was at the blackboard, Dale would hop up and throw a few rifle shells in the stove to liven things up some. To my knowledge nobody got shot.

Normally we had about 8 to 10 kids in the school and that proved to be great enough

Reginald's mom, Georgia Robertson with her children, Werner and Zora Bell

challenge for the teacher. Recess time was playing Tag or Annie Over where we threw a ball over the schoolhouse to see who could catch it as it came over, or tormenting the girls.

When I was in 4th grade, we lived on a small farm, only 30 acres, and I contracted Scarlet Fever at school and was really sick. We were quarantined but Dr. Cullers would come to the house to see me till I was better. Dad used to visit and would come down after dark to see me and Mom and one night Mom turned out the lights and Dad ended up in the basement he had dug out. Yes, Dad decided we needed a basement so he jacked the whole house up and proceeded to dig out all the dirt, one shovel at a time, and wheeled out the dirt.

I was happy that I had a sister now and she was getting old enough to play with. We had a Red Radio wagon and a tricycle and when the wheels wore out on one we transferred them to the other and I am not sure we were ever able to buy new wheels. But we put a lot of miles on both.

It was only a mile to walk to school, and Mom didn't want us to ride double on my bike on the main road. When we got home from school, we would get our chores done, usually of feeding the chickens, gathering the eggs, or what else that was on the list, and then plant ourselves in front of the old Atwater Kent radio to listen to Jack Armstrong, Captain Midnight, The Shadow, Fibber Mc Gee and Molly, and Jack Benny.

My grandfather Robertson lived the next house up the road and when he went to town with his team of horses and steel wheeled wagon he would call to see if I would like to go along which I usually did. The ride was so rough on that gravel road it almost shook your teeth loose, but fun. Grandpa didn't drive but Grandma did in her new Buick. Grandma grew strawberries and made jams and jellies and fresh butter, and eggs she sold to folks in the town of Trenton.

Grandma and Grandpa Robertson moved to Missouri from North Platte, Nebraska, where they had settled after coming to this county from Perth, Scotland. Their farm bordered the farm owned by Buffalo Bill Cody. They became good friends and Buffalo Bill gave them several Indian articles such as a Chief's headdress that I loved to try on every time at Grandma's, a complete Indian maiden's dress, and moccasins all with bead work. My aunt Jean sold them to a collector much to my sorrow.

Sis and I loved to go to town on Saturday to the theater for 2 western shows with one of these: Hop-a-long Cassidy, Lone Ranger, Zorro, Gene Autry, or Roy Rogers, with cartoon for the sum of 10 cents and 5 cents for popcorn.

I remember the Sunday of December 7, 1941, and hearing President Roosevelt announce that Pearl Harbor had been attacked and that "Day Would Live In Infamy." A scary time for a youngster. Dad was never called up to serve but my uncle was and his outfit was in the Pacific Islands.

After 6th grade I was headed to town to the 7th grade at the Central Jr. High where I went for one year and then to the Trenton High School. I remember the Jr. High was across the street from the bakery and the air really smelled good of fresh baked bread.

There was a small auto parts store across from the school and one day I noticed a help wanted sign in the window so in I went and got my first job in town dusting shelves, putting stock away, and sweeping and cleaning the toilet. Not my favorite but you've got to start somewhere. During my school years, I had several different jobs including working at grocery stores, drug stores, and farming.

High school was fun. I learned to play clarinet and was in the band, was a cheerleader, and gave all the girls a chance. You might say an equal opportunity young man. After school, I got a job working at the Plaza Hotel first as a bellhop and worked my way up to desk clerk. Once we had a rep from Tucker Motors come to stay at the hotel while he was in the area trying to set up dealerships. Well let me tell you that was a car that was before its time, no wonder the Big 3 wanted it gone. I and everybody who worked at the hotel had to inspect the Tucker he was driving with so many new innovations that no other car manufacturer hadn't even thought of. Well the Plaza Hotel was a good job, teaching responsibility and respect along with an adult education. We had a place downtown called Meeker's where a lot of the teenagers hung out to talk and in back was a very small room with a jukebox and dance floor and you could swing your girlfriend a few times to your favorite song.

Reginald's grandfather, Alexander Robertson with Werner in 1932

Dad was a hard worker; he worked in town for the Ford dealer as a mechanic and body and fender man, then came home after work and fired up the old steel-wheeled Fordson tractor and work in the fields till dark and the manifold on the tractor would be cherry red when he came in. That 40 acres was right alongside of an old railroad track. The only train was sort of a Tooner Ville Trolley between small towns to the east of Trenton. When I heard the train coming if I could I would run up to the bridge to wave at the engineer.

One time I went over to get Mr. Horn's rifle and knocked on the door and he yelled come on in so I did and got the surprise of my life, for there was his teenage daughter Nettie in the old washtub bathing, she didn't seem to be embarrassed, but I sure was.

Once I was cleaning out a small shed in the barn lot and my mare, Star, kept coming and looking in while I was inside. Well that afternoon we went into town and when we got home, I went out to do chores but couldn't find her anywhere. After I checked all the gates I headed to the house and walked by the shed I had been cleaning out earlier and just happened to look through the door and all I saw was legs so I walked over and there inside was Star and after she had got inside somehow she had got to her feet and there she was stuck inside up against the rafters. The dilemma was

485

Werner and his sister, Zora Belle

there was no way to get her out but saw the front of the shed out so that's what I did and then tried to explain to Dad what happened.

Before I graduated from High School I talked Dad into building me a motor bike out of my original bike and by golly he did and it was a great motorized bike, powered with a gas engine from an old Maytag washing machine. Well, I rode that bike everywhere and the mileage was wonderful: 25 miles on a pint of gas and a fill up at the gas station was 3 cents and if the hills were too much for the engine I could pedal to help. I was the only kid in the town that had a motorized bike. After the bike was my first car and it was a dandy, cost me $50, a 1929 Ford Model A with rumble seat. This car was in need of TLC when I got it, but little by little Dad helped me fix it up to a great car with a rebuilt engine, new paint job, and a renewed interior that I was proud of. You see my dad had been a mechanic all his life.

In the winter sometimes it would get so cold in the winter that to get the car started Dad had to jack up a rear wheel and even build a small fire under the oil pan to get the engine started. My, the progress that has been made.

My grandpa and grandma Wickizer lived on a small farm in North MO. It was great fun to go to visit them because I got to see my cousin Tommy as we were just a year apart in age. Grandpa had an old mare called Mead and that poor old horse took off every time

we came towards her with a bridle. It was old Mead's colt Star that I was given.

As you can imagine two young boys could get on Grandma's nerves so she made up some cock-in-bull story about some old man who used to live in the old ruins up on the hill that buried a treasure no one had found. We grabbed a shovel and were off to find our fortune. Well as you can guess we didn't find anything but we sure moved a lot of dirt almost as if the place had been bombed and Grandma had some peace and quiet for a little while.

Grandma and Grandpa used to go shopping for groceries in a little town called Modena, not much there but a grocery store, gas station, church, dry goods store, and a garage/blacksmiths shop.

Tommy's mother Aunt Mary loved to play the piano and she played by ear and we would all gather around and sing while she played. Yes that was some of our entertainment.

After High School and one year at Jr. College my buddy Jack talked me into joining the Air Force so that's what we did. I gave four years to my country and proud of it. It was 1950 during the Korean War, I was sent from Carswell AFB., Ft. Worth, Texas to Sidi Slimane, French Morocco, North Africa (the sandbox, as it was called) for my overseas duty just 30 days after I got married to my one and only. Whoopee!

Hard work, yes, but we weren't bored as kids, we were busy and we respected and loved our family, friends, and neighbors, and knew the value of things including money, for if we wanted something bad enough we worked for it.

Memories of being Raised on a Farm
By William Brosi of Easton, Missouri
Born 1944

I feel fortunate to have grown up on a small farm in the Northwestern part of Missouri after World War II, seeing the changing times over the years of my life.

My dad had a team of horses he called Kate and Tops. My grandfather's team was named Prince and Barney. I drove that team making hay. My dad didn't use his horses much anymore as he had a 1937 A John Deere tractor. So he sold the team of horses. I was very young when he put me on the tractor. He started his boys early in life working with machinery and never thought much about the danger it could bring. He must have had confidence in our ability. To this day, I have and own the '37 A tractor.

I have seen the changing ways of farming since after that time. Dad had a few stock cows, sheep, hogs, milk cows with veal calves, and chickens. I recall putting up hay loose with a hay loader, then pulling it into the hayloft with a grab fork on to the track down the center of the barn to drop it any part of the center of the barn that was built around the year 1951. One year, after nine loads of loose alfalfa hay that was not quite cured or green yet, that about burnt the barn down. The next year was when a new square hay baler was purchased. From them on we humped bales into the barn and humped it out in the winter. Seemed that was when winters were winters with a lot of snow!

We ground a lot of feed for the chickens, hogs, and cows, along with a lot of corn-shocked fodder. All that extra work is now replaced by big machinery and big round hay balers. I had scooped a lot of ear corn. Grinding that ear of corn made good feed for feeder calves. I remember seeing a sow or hog eat the kernels of corn off the cob, holding the ear down with her front foot. That has always stuck in my mind.

We milked a few Holstein cows, and separated the milk to cream and fed the skim milk to the hogs. Carrying five-gallon buckets down to the hog lot and granary, going through a small gate not making a noise. If they heard that gate squeal a little they knew what to expect. I was almost too young to remember when Dad would mix the skim milk with some ground feed and make a slop. The hogs did well on that. They would be big and fat. When butchering, you wanted fat for the lard. Now the hogs need to be lean for the pork processing plant.

During the summer, my mother raised a lot of chickens, getting the chicks in the spring. She bought several straight runs that would be enough roosters to be butchered, and then so many that would be layers. When the roosters were big enough to butcher, she would do two on a Saturday: one to put in the freezer and the other for Sunday dinner. After getting home from church, she would hurry to prepare the Sunday dinner of fried chicken, mashed potatoes and gravy, and a vegetable and a Jell-O salad of some kind. Fried potatoes were at every evening meal. We ate good! Mom took pride and care of her chickens. She sold eggs to buy staples and things she couldn't raise, along with the cream that was separated.

One evening before the sun set and as the chickens were taking their time going to the chicken house to roost for the night, I was walking around with my BB gun to pass the time. It had been shot enough to be somewhat weak. This old laying hen was ahead of me. I was thinking I would make her jump by shooting her. If I hit her in the neck, she would really jump. I shot! Hitting her, yes, in the neck. She flipped and flopped about 4-5 times as well as my heart! I survived but she didn't!

Scared, I gathered up the dead chicken, looking around to see if anyone was watching. I crept around the machinery shed, down past the granary to the ditch to dispose of my unfortunate bird. I don't recall if I slept that night, but I must have as when you work hard on a farm, you're tired. I never mentioned that incident for a long time, until the time my brother and myself were home on military leave, before he went to Viet Nam. We were talking about things one evening and I thought it was time to confess my accidental experience, now that I was 21 and old enough not to get a licking. Looking back, if only I had confessed to killing one of Mom's best laying hens, and with her help to butcher it, we could have had a big chicken and noodle meal the next day.

There were several buildings on the farm and each one had its purpose for the animals and machinery. We were raised to put everything under a roof. Take care of your tools and things you worked with. Observing the construction of some of the buildings that Grandpa and my dad put together was amazing for that period of time. All the concrete foundations that were formed and mixed by hand! The most used building on an everyday basis was the washhouse built at least 100 years ago. When Grandpa built it, it was constructed and finished as good as any house! Ten feet of the east end was the smokehouse where cured hams were hung along with other butchered meat during that time of the year. There was a wood stove in the main part with a fire almost every day to heat water to wash the cream separator 7 days a week. Mom washed clothes every Monday, carrying water in and carrying it out. "Love, honor, and carry water" is where that terminology came from. She hung the washed clothes on the clothesline to dry, even in the winter trying to get them dried. Many times they were frozen stiff. We also bathed there. When we worked up or processed butchered hogs and beefs and chickens, it was a place to come in to get warmed up during the cold days from doing outside chores. The attic of the washhouse, where they stored unused items that now are collectible or antiques was called the washhouse garret. How many people have heard that name for an attic?

The building that got abused was the outhouse. It took a terrible beating almost every time my brother went in and settled down. A dirt clod or rock would be thrown, hitting it with a big ka-thug! Dirt clods were thrown the most, as they would break up with more of a splattering sound.

I was blessed and am thankful to have been raised in the country on a small farm. To have served my country and return to a home that my parents provided to come back to! To have memories of being raised on a farm! God bless America!

Not So Complicated As Today
By Carol Wood of St. Joseph, Missouri
Born 1938

I grew up on a farm in Northwest Missouri, just south of the small town of Stanberry. We had a battery radio to listen to; this was before TV was ever heard of. We didn't have electricity until I was 12. This was in the early 1950s. It was a big undertaking when the REA came thru the countryside.

I went to a one-room country school named Beggs. We started first grade, as we didn't have kindergarten in those days. It was 1 1/2 miles by road to the school but I generally walked through the fields and pastures and it was only 1/2 mile. My brother and sister were several years older so I went to grade school by myself. When they were in school, they had ponies to ride but I was in the modern age so I rode a bike when weather permitted. When I walked through a neighbor's pasture

Carol (Maxwell) Wood

there were always cattle there, but they never did bother me. Our neighbor was always out in the barnyard doing chores when I walked to school each morning. It was years later that I figured out, he wasn't just doing his chores, he was making sure I wasn't bothered by his livestock.

One year we had only 12 children in school. Another girl named Carole went all 12 years of school with me. Most of the time we were the only two in the same grade. The year we entered high school, the country school closed. Everyone was bused to Stanberry to school. Entering high school was a big step. From a class of two to a class with 25 students was a big step. I walked 1/4 mile to meet the bus each day.

In winter, we wore jeans under our dresses to keep warm. In those days, girls weren't allowed to wear any kind of jeans or slacks to school. The first thing you would do when you got off the bus, was rush to the bathroom and get your jeans off and get to your locker before anyone could see you.

We did not have indoor plumbing except for a pump in the kitchen that Mother could pump water from a cistern into a sink. That was a great thing for her. Before that, she carried water from a well outside. We had no bathroom until later years when we had a tub. That was big for us, as you carried water to the tub, then when you were finished it could drain out. Before that, you always had to carry water to the tub, and then dump it out.

Our outhouse was in the chicken yard. We always seem to have an old rooster that would trap me in the outhouse. I've spent many times running to the main yard from an old rooster. Chickens were always around the barnyard too. On Saturday night, we always hurried to get chores done so we could go into town. Saturday night was the time you got to see your friends and do the weekly shopping. One Saturday I was chased by an old rooster. I turned and threw a rock at him and hit him in the head and killed him instantly. Needless to say, I had to dress him for Sunday dinner before I could go to town.

Another thing we had in the country was telephone party lines. There were usually 6 to 9 people on the same line. Everyone had their own ring. There was a switchboard in town that all calls came through. There was an operator who directed all calls. You might have two short rings for your call; someone else had 1 long ring. You could listen in anytime you heard the phone ring. You generally knew that someone was listening whenever you received a call. It happened that my friend, Carole, and I were on the same party line. Whenever some boy would call, after the conversation was over and he'd hung up, whoever had received the call would say, "Carol are you there?" then we would carry on our conversation about what had just taken place. To our knowledge, the boys were never aware of what took place.

After graduating from high school, I left the farm and moved to the city of St Joseph to attend business college. That was a big move for a country girl in the '50s. I wasn't alone as two friends moved to the city with me. We lived at the YWCA for a few months. The YWCA rented rooms to young single girls and it was a good place to live as we had a housemother to supervise us and also had to sign in and out each time we left.

I later worked in a bank and met my future husband in 1958. We've been married over 54 years, raised 3 children, and live in the same house we purchased 52 years ago.

I still think back to those days of growing up in the country. It was a quiet time and not so complicated as things are today.

Dancing Down 275(59) Highway at Midnight
By Glen H. Brown of Mound City, Missouri
Born 1932

Why do we like to reminisce about the mundane experiences that were commonplace growing up?

Remembering the late 1940s, there was an episode when the M. C. High School replaced the window shades and left the old cords behind that were handy for knot tying exercises. A hangman's noose was of particular interest. While heading down the hill toward town, a dead rat was found along the street. Perfect for hanging practice. The street sign at 5th and State gave great viewing advantage. Unfortunately, that was the address of the Lee Browning liquor store, whose owners were having differences with a group from down the bluff road. Threats were implied and the local paper thought it worth reporting. Impressions and imaginations do mysterious things. How were we to know?

During those years my dad, George Brown (the mechanic not the horse trader) had an auto repair shop east of the Davis Creek Bridge on 4th Street. Dad's cousin, Buckshot Wilson, was demonstrating his new gold-plated show pistol one hot summer day in the shop. Well, an old man and his wife were camped in an Airstream camper between our shop and Dutch Cardinell's gas station. They were sitting in the shade relaxing when Buckshot fired his trusty 44! Took a lot of coaxing to calm the old folks down.

Aufy Shipman was one of the more colorful persons for me during those years. I remember calling him Arfy; it just seems an "r" fit better. In those days, it was common for a lot of people to have a "nick" name. Arfy was a poor man's tractor mechanic. He didn't have a shop so my dad let him do his thing in our shop. Arfy had three tools he did all his work with: an 18" screw driver, 12" crescent wrench, and a 2 1b. hammer. Once during Christmas break he was repairing the differential on a school bus, he drove and inadvertently forgot to put a jack under it while removing the support "U" bolts on the axle. When the last nut came off, the spring snapped down just missing his head. All you know what broke out and caused pandemonium among the loafers: Tom Fogg, Dwight Loucks, and August Young, who happened to be gossiping around our heating stove.

On another occasion, Arfy was working on a Massyharris tractor belonging to John Buckles. He was overhauling the transmission and was checking it out with the engine running while he stood on the floor operating the clutch and gearshift by hand. Evidently, the fork that moves one of the gears wasn't in its groove putting the gear in but not taking it out. When Arfy let the clutch out thinking it was in neutral he didn't know it was in gear! The tractor took off with Arfy chasing after it. This was late evening, we were in the shop. Arfy couldn't get on the tractor so he tried to hit the push-button switch with a broom handle. The front end of the tractor went out the back door; the back wheels climbed about 8" off the floor then fell back several times until the battery fell out and shut the engine off. I was packing the wheel bearings on Dr. D.C. Perry's Packard when this happened and it took me 30 minutes to find the bearing after all the excitement.

Spectator sports weren't as popular when I was young so we were forced to be more imaginative. Lazy summer days on occasion were ideal for cruising the country roads in my 1925 Model "T" Ford touring car with a case of Getz on ice from the ice plant packed in an old wooden nail keg in the back seat. Just 3 or 4 of us exploring the dirt roads. Gas was 20 cents a gallon, you were incommunicado, no radio or cell phones. Available land phones consisted of the Independent line or the Farmers line. Some businesses had both that were crank operated oak boxes that were usually wall mounted. All calls went through an operator, fascinating!

Our nights out would be considered limited by today's standards. Square dancing peaked our interest if we could find one and had transportation. Honky- Tonkin for the older ones usually started at the It'll-Do in Oregon, then move to the New Dell in Savannah and if we were really wound up we might make it to the Frog Hop in St. Joe. Dancing in the middle of 275(59) highway on the way home at midnight would be out of the question now, but, oh, happy days!

I Regretted Having Such a Smart Mouth!
By Donna Carter of Gilman City, Missouri
Born 1933

I am 79 years of age and have lived in Northwest Missouri my entire life. I was born on a farm in Harrison County and grew up with parents, siblings, and a wonderful grandmother. Never being able to have children, she took my mother and her sister into her home and raised them as her own. Their parents had divorced due to my grandfather's problem with alcohol. When my parents married, Grandma invited them to live with her and my dad would farm the land.

I started school at age five, at a one-room country school in the small village of Blue Ridge. I was the only person in first grade and there were two in second grade. Since Grandma had taught me to count to 10, and read from the Primer and the "Dick and Jane" book, the teacher put me in second grade. I graduated from Bethany High School at age 16.

Outhouses were the common thing in those days. At school, there were two outhouses: one for girls, one for boys. At home, we were quite modern with a "three holer" and a sidewalk leading to the privy!

My dad was a farmer, so cattle and hogs were always around, and the desire to learn to milk was strong (although I later wondered why).

We had a sow that refused to stay in a pen. If the gate leaned even a bit, that old girl could climb over it and be out.

Dad liked to hunt and fish, so with chores done early we would head for the river. We had a two-burner camp stove and Mother would take potatoes to fry. Lunchmeat (bologna) was a real treat, but we usually had it to eat. We would set the trotlines, eat supper, and then "run" the lines to see if we had any fish. The fish were channel catfish or blue cat. If there were lots of fish on the lines, we would rebait the hooks, sleep awhile on the sand bar, put the wet clothes back on, and get more fish.

Being a girl didn't prevent me from

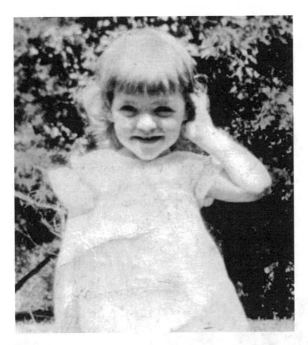
Donna Carter at age 3

fieldwork. My first job in the field was making hay with a team of horses and a sulky rake. I was twelve years old at the time, but now I would be hard pressed to handle that task.

We had one horse that preferred to pull alone. Living on a dirt road, we sometimes had to go to town when it was very muddy. If we got stuck on the half mile between home and the gravel road, I would walk back home, get the horse, and ride it to where the car was mired down. If "Buster" could see the car, he would try to turn around and go home. We also used him to pull hay in the barn. The hayrack would be on the side of the barn where the "hay door" was open. Dad would set the hayfork in the loose hay; I would be on the other side of the barn, with the horse hitched to a rope that ran through the barn on a pulley. Dad would tell me when to lead the horse and would yell when I was to stop. Now, aren't big round bales better than that?

I recall a wringer washer salesman coming to demonstrate a washer. It had a gasoline engine and with your foot, you pushed a starter pedal. Grandma decided we needed it, so the purchase was made. That was quite a change, because laundry was done on a washboard prior to that time.

I really liked horses and one day I decided to see if I could ride a horse through the door and into the barn (a rather narrow door). I lay down on the horse's back, head on his neck, and legs straight along his back. Fortunately, all went well. My parents never knew of this escapade.

We had a wooden icebox and kept ice in it during the heat of summer. A large dishpan was kept under the area where the ice was stored to catch water as the ice melted. If the pan wasn't emptied regularly, there would be a mess to clean up.

An aunt and uncle lived in Oklahoma and it was decided we would pay them a visit. We started in late evening, a poor decision. Kansas City presented a problem! By some miracle, we finally arrived in Tryon, OK. The car we traveled in burned lots of oil. We started with a 5-gallon can of oil and I have memories of stopping beside the road and Dad adding oil.

Grandma made most of my dresses. I did have "hand me down" dresses from an older cousin. Girls certainly didn't wear jeans or slacks in those days!

I didn't get many spankings, but one I remember quite well. Mother told me that if I didn't quit some naughty thing I was doing, she would give me a spanking. I replied, "You will have to catch me first." I ran around the house and Mother went around the other way and met me. I regretted having such a smart mouth!

When I was attending country school, we had a teacher that didn't always get to school on time. One day all the kids were there and the older boys had started a fire in the heating stove. Someone had the bright idea to put the fire out (by pouring water on it) and hide in the outhouses. Of course, smoke poured out the chimney and we were caught.

It has been fun and quite interesting to recall things that took place when I was growing up.

Fast Sleds and Pregnant Mares in 1961
By Gary Morris of Oregon, Missouri
Born 1947

The year 1961 in Northwest Missouri, was a year of deep snow, fast sleds, and pregnant mares. It was a good year.

I was an eighth grader and while life on the farm was good, it was also hard. I never realized it was hard at the time and if anyone had it much better than my family, well, I guess I just wasn't aware of it. Oh sure, I knew that some of the kids in town (town was five miles down the creek road and had a population of about 435) had better bikes and clothes. Shoot, some of them even had transistor radios taped onto their bikes. My chores included splitting kindling wood, gathering corn cobs to start the fire with in the winter, slopping hogs, carrying water, and when I got older, milking 2 to 4 cows morning and night. Before we could milk them though, my siblings and I had to go to whichever pasture they were in and bring them to the barn. They spent the night in the barnyard (that's what all the books called it but we called it the "cow lot" and usually just "lot" for short) and then after morning milking we would take them back to pasture. Of course, my dad usually did that part when the school year was in session. But most of the farm kids I knew had chores to do and even those few that I knew who lived in town, usually worked odd jobs such as "walking beans" or mowing yards and cemeteries. So we were taught at an early age to work and have responsibilities, a trait that seems to be lacking today. As we got older and stronger, we helped farmers gather their baled hay from the fields and placed it in their barns. For that we got anywhere from $0.75/hr. to $1/hr. That doesn't sound like much but at that time gas was only about 23 cents/gallon and when I was in high school I could "run all over" for a buck or two.

Gary Morris sleigh riding in 1961

Before I got to that "milestone" stage in my life, however, there was Kimsey. Kimsey was the one room school where I and my 4 siblings began and ended our elementary education; all except my youngest sister, Ruthie. She had to finish her elementary years in town because Kimsey closed after my eighth grade graduation. We had a different teacher nearly every year, seven during my tenure. These brave men and women had to teach classes from 1st grade thru 8th. Most years there were

no students in all 8 grades depending on who had moved into the district or out, and often older more advanced pupils would help the teacher by listening to younger students read or give their spelling lessons. I went all 8 years with only one other girl, Rosalie, in my grade and we went on through high school together too. In fact we were editor and assistant editor on our yearbook our senior year. I think that in my 8th grade, the last year for Kimsey there were two 8th graders, one 7th grader, one 6th grader, and two 3rd graders for a total of only six kids but I remember an enrollment when I was younger of as high as 13 kids. Those were fun times. It was 1/2 mile to school from my house and while I walked most days, there were times in the winter when I took my sled and times in the spring or summer when I took my bike. Kimsey was mainly downhill from our farm so going was easy but coming home was a drag, pun intended!

In the winter of 1961 we had a heavy snow and the temperature was so variable that when it finally did get really cold, there was a crust thick enough that I could "sleigh ride" on top of the snow without the sled's runners going through. I walked out to the end of our driveway and the snow was level with the top of the hood of the old Nash Rambler and I wouldn't even break through. Man, I could fly all over the farm and through the neighbor's alfalfa field to school. I went places I never had been able to go before and it was really cool until you hit a soft spot and a runner went through the crust. This happened once in Terhune's field on the way to school and I had my younger cousin on top of me when it happened. The sled came to a sudden stop and we kind of slid along sledless, so to speak. His weight forced my cheek down into the crusty snow and when we got to school I was bleeding a little. This sort of startled our teacher but was probably a topic at supper time with her husband and I'm sure it didn't create the stir it would in today's world. Sleigh riding was something we all did at recess with the littler kids stacked up on top us older ones. Those were the days of runner type sleds and you could actually guide them around a curve unlike the coaster or saucers kids use today. Oh we had coasters too, but they were usually fashioned from sun visors off junked cars or something of that nature.

I was proud that my sled was the fastest one in school. It was of low profile, long in design and even had a steering knob mounted on one of the steering handles. It was very fast; until six of us guys decided to load onto it beginning with an 8th grader on bottom, then a 7th grader, couple of 5th or 6th graders, and then me and one little kid on top. We went down the hill okay but Junior caught his neck on a small willow tree when we crashed and the overloaded sled runners were sprung so badly that the sled was never any good again. I always regretted that ride. We had never heard of Guinness' Book of World records then; we were just being boys. Junior was unscathed too and never missed any school from the "wreck."

There were other misadventures at Kimsey that revolved around sleds. We sometimes would get so far over the next hill when the coasting was good, that we could not hear the bell signaling recess was over, (or so we said). We would all suffer for that a couple of days if the teacher had to put on his or her boots and come yell at us. The same thing would happen when we chose to let our sleds down a 7 foot drop into the floor of a 5 foot pipe culvert that ran diagonally under the county road and our school driveway. This culvert was accessible by climbing down the huge bolts and nuts that held the culvert sections together and letting the sled down by its pull rope to the waiting kid below. There was a ribbon of ice in the floor of the culvert about 2 feet wide and you could really fly down the flow line and out onto Kimsey Creek when the weather was cold enough. You just had to make sure the coast was clear and no kid was walking back upstream pulling his sled behind when you cut it loose because there was no room for two and no stopping. I recall my dad telling of a time when he was coon hunting late at night with his hounds and fell through the ice on that creek. He was wet up to his knees so he went into the basement of Kimsey School to dry off by the furnace, forgetting that the school marm was spending the winter nights upstairs. Rumor has it that she was about scared out of her wits. I was too young to remember it but I have no reason to believe my dad would make it up.

Spring time found us playing Kick the Can, Handy Over, Softball, or a variety of games we had made up. If no one wanted to play any of those games, there was always swinging or teeter totter. I have had dreams of that school, and I could still smell the water that was pumped from the cistern and kept in a large crock container with a push button on the side. It was not offensive, just unique. Every kid had his own cup hanging nearby. Plastic hadn't been around all that long and there were mostly tin cups hanging on the nails. Each morning a teacher-appointed kid would get the water from the hand pump over the cistern. About once a week a selected volunteer would take the chalkboard erasers outside and "dust" them by pounding them on the concrete sidewalk.

Once a farmer's horses got out of the pasture and took up residence around our school. There must have been 5 or 6 of them and some of the older boys would ride them around and then jump off if they started into a trot because they had no bridle or halter to control them with. But I was only a 2nd or 3rd grader then and was not as brave as the older boys. Once while being excused to go to the outdoor restroom, several horses were between me and the privy so I found a large oak tree to get behind but I reported to the rest of the gang how I had to push the ponies out of the way to get into the john. A few days later the farmer repaired his fence and came and got his horses. That was a sad day.

Town kids were envious of Kimsey kids. Our school year ran September to April and theirs went until May so we got an extra month vacation and we made sure we rubbed it in at every opportunity. Sometimes I would go into town at those times we were out and visit a buddy while in class to see what city schools were like. They had organized Jr. High basketball that we could not have at Kimsey, and as far as I could tell that was the only thing I really missed out on. I don't think "town kids" got to sit around with their feet over the floor register drying out their socks while they had reading class. Once a mouse fell down on the furnace under that huge grate and made an awful stink so we got to go home early. Some-forward thinking soul decided maybe a crayon dropped onto the furnace would get the same results and tried it a week or two after the mouse. It worked once, but only once.

Pie Suppers were the high light of the school year at Kimsey. Neighbors would come from all around to watch us kids perform in some sort of skit or play and then enjoy an hour or two of socializing while polishing off chili and pie. I never knew a farm mom who couldn't cook up a storm although I suppose they existed. While the grownups were visiting, we kids would go outside to the playground. There were no outdoor lights and how we kept from getting hurt worse than the usual scrapes and bruises we endured is anybody's guess.

Spring arrived as usual in 1961 and I think everyone was ready for it. Soon the smell of budding trees and Mayflowers and the sound of croaking frogs in the pond convinced us spring really was upon us. And oh, yes, my 22 year old mare? She presented me with the prettiest little filly colt you ever saw. Yes sir; 1961 was a good year!

Howe (Longjohn) Shanks
By Dick Couldry of St. Joseph, Missouri
Born 1943

Rattlesnake and permanent wave solution. Huh! What in the world, do they have in common? Howe Shanks my grandpa that's what. These are but two of the many stories that my mom has told me over the years about Grandpa. A book of humorous tales about his hunting, fishing, trapping, and moonshining wait to be written.

As the story goes, one day the boys were playing down by the tobacco barn when they came across a large rattlesnake. Being careful not to be beaten they picked up several tobacco stakes and began beating the snake to death. Being so outnumbered the poor snake didn't have a chance. Once they were sure the poor outnumbered snake was dead, the boys picked it up with one of the stakes and began teasing the girls with it. Needless to say, the girls were running around screaming hysterically.

Finally, one of the boys came up with the idea of playing a joke on Grandpa by putting the snake in the floorboard of his old army truck, then hide in the barn and watch all the fun. And then jump out and laugh at him for getting scared by the rattler. Knowing that Grandpa was going to be leaving soon to go hunting with several other neighbors, they carefully took the dead rattler and coiled it up on the floorboard of the truck on the driver side. Then they all ran to the tobacco barn to wait and watch to see Grandpa get scared by the unwanted passenger. Soon Grandpa came out of the house carrying his shotgun and a sack with some sandwiches. The girls started giggling and the boys told them to be quiet or they would ruin all the fun. Grandpa opened the door and immediately saw the unwanted passenger without hesitation, down to the ground fell the sandwiches and up went the shotgun, "Boom!" This sound had not been part of the great plan because now there was a gaping hole in the floorboard and a sorrowfully mutilated rattler. "Damn," yelled Grandpa, "How did that rattler get in my truck, and look at the hole in my floorboard!"

Needless to say, the smiles on our faces quickly changed to fear at the thought that Grandpa would find out that it was all a joke and no longer a joke. They quietly watched as Grandpa picked up the poor rattler with the barrel of his shotgun and was going to throw it away. But then they heard him say, "I better put the snake in the back of the truck to show the boys or they wouldn't believe me about how that gaping hole got in the floorboard of my truck." Needless to say, the true story of the ratter was never revealed. And thereafter Grandpa always cracked the door to the truck to take a peek before getting in.

Grandpa was a skillful coon hunter and coon dog trainer. He would hunt the little bandit-faced critters for food and their pelts. At season's end, he would sell all his pelts to the furriers that came around each season.

Some neighbors had come by to pick up Grandpa Drum, Lead, and Old Blue, his three best coondogs, to go coonhunting. It would be well into the morning before his return. Just so happens that day the girls had pooled all their money and caught a ride into town with a neighbor lady to buy a bottle of permanent wave lotion. It was the rage at that time. So that night the girls got a bucket and mixed the solution together and gave each other a heaping soaking of the magical beautifier solution. Once they had all been beautified they had a little of the magical brew still left. Not wanting to waste it, they thought they would poor it into a bottle and keep it for future use. They looked all over for a bottle to put the wonder brew in and the only thing that they could find was Grandpa's whiskey jug in the cabinet and it only had a couple of swallows left in it so they thought, well, we will pour out this little amount of whiskey and put their precious solution in it for future beautifying. So they carefully poured the rest of the magical brew being careful as to not spill a drop into the old whiskey jug. Then they placed the jug back up in the cabinet and they would tell Grandpa in the morning what they had done. So off to bed the girls went. It was very cold and wet that night and very late when Grandpa came home from a successful hunt. There was no electricity in the house and Grandpa didn't want to light a lantern and wake anyone. The house was heated by one big old potbelly stove. He went over and put some more wood in the old pot belly stove and stood there and warmed himself for a while and then thought, "Boy a good shot of the old brew" would really warm up his innards. You can see where this is going, right?

Well on with the story. He walked over to the cabinet and reached up and grabbed his old jug and reared his head back and raised the jug high into the air and placed it against his mouth and took a big swig of his natural body warmer. "Aghh!" screamed Grandpa as he flung the jug into the air and against the old potbelly stove breaking it into several pieces. He staggered around gasping for air and banging into the kitchen table, waking everyone up. Grandma ran to his side yelling, "Howe, what is the matter? Are you ok?" Still unable to speak and gasping trying to get air in his lungs, Grandpa yelled out in a squeaky voice "Bad whiskey! Bad whiskey." Grandma got a dipper full of water from the water pail and finally got Grandpa to drink it and settle down. By now, all the kids were down in the kitchen. The girls figured out what had happened. The girls looked at each other and were afraid to explain what they had done. Finally, Grandpa was breathing ok but for several days, he had one of the rawest throats that he had ever had. As the girls went back

to the bedroom, they asked themselves if they should go ahead and tell Grandpa about the wave lotion. The consensus was unanimous. It was the bad whiskey, Grandpa said so.

Ice Storm Winter of 1936-37
By Sidney M. Miner of Chillicothe, Missouri
Born 1928

The storm started in late December 1936, with a slow rain in freezing temperatures; it began as a slow mist changing to sprinkling and freezing. This went on for 3-4 days increasing in rain to sleet with temperatures going down. This covered an area in Caldwell, Carroll, and Livingston County, Missouri. I am not sure how much further it may have gone. One morning in January of 37, my dad came to our bedroom and said, "Get up boys, we have a problem". I and my brother got out of bed, looked out the window to see the countryside covered in 3-4 inches of ice. I was about 8 years old; my brother was 12 or 13.

There was stock in the barn and Dad and my older brother went to milk the cows. It was very difficult to get to the barn, which was about 200 yards from the house, not sure, how many times they fell getting there. They held on to the fence until they got to the barn, getting back to the house with a bucket of milk was even more difficult. I don't think all of the milk made it.   After we ate breakfast, Dad decided we should get all the hatchets and shovels we could find and chop a path from the barn to the well at the house. We would then lead each animal to the well for water.

At that time, we had about 6-7 milk cows and 4 horses that had to be watered. This was soon after the Big Depression, and we could not afford to lose one animal, not even one little pig. I don't remember what we did about the hogs. The chickens were in the henhouse, but they had to be fed and taken water.

After a few days of this, we fell into some sort of routine. However, there was another problem coming up, that being, what about flour, etc. Well, my uncle who lived about a mile north, called and said he was going to go to Hale, about 5 miles away and get a few items, so he and my older brother skated to Hale, out across the field pulling a small sled and tied a few things on the sled. As you can see, this was no easy task, to get over a fence or cross a ditch, but had to be done. The skates would clamp onto the sole of your shoe, not easy on shoes.

There was no traffic on the road. I cannot remember how long it was before we seen any kind of car or truck on the road. At that point, during the Depression years, there were not a lot of cars to be on the road. I don't remember how long we were out of school. We went to a one-room school about a half mile from home. I think we were out for about 3-4 weeks. I was in the third grade. All grades, 1-8 were taught. I do not remember where the teacher lived. I think about a mile from the school, and am not sure, but think she walked to school.

While we were out of school, we spent most of our time helping with the stock and chipping ice, so we could walk to different buildings. And then, we would get in some sled riding, which was a lot of fun, because on the ice you could go for a long way depending on how good the hill was.

We did not lose any stock, however, I understand that some stock did slip and break bones, so were destroyed. I never heard how much damage to buildings, or how many stock was lost. After about a week, we were able to get the stock out of the barn by covering the holding lot with hay, so they could get around and then in a few days they would have the ice broke up to where they could get around. As I remember, this went on for about 6 weeks, and I must admit, I was glad when we were able to get some firm ground to walk on.

Lightning Strike

I was about 17 years old in 1945, working on a farm in Livingston County, Missouri, south of Avalon about 2 miles. It was late in the day, time to milk the cows and raining pretty hard and quite a bit of lightning. I first had to find the cows and bring them into the barn. I was on a slight hill looking for any sign of cows. All of a sudden, it felt like someone had come up behind me and hit me on the head with a board. I, or the strike put my head down and I saw sparks fly from every metal button on my clothes, and my overshoes. I fell to the ground, or perhaps was knocked to the ground, looked around, and then got up slowly, at which time a large clap of thunder came, which I guess scared me, and I fell to the ground again, and stayed there for a few minutes. When I had regained my strength or composure, I rose to my feet, but was not sure what I was supposed to be doing, so I went to the barn and stood there for a while, but could not quite understand what to do next. The lady at the house came looking for me and asked if I was all right. I said I was, but I guess she knew I wasn't, because she told me to quit for the day, and I went home. The next day, we, the owner and I, went to the spot where I was hit to look for any signs of other strikes. We found a big locust tree that had been split, and about 30 feet of fence that was gone. We thought I must have been the third or fourth item that was hit. I had my rubber overshoes on, or I would not be telling this story, and I have been a little afraid of lightning ever since.

Index A (Hometown)

Betty Henderson	Cameron	Missouri	216
Dorothy Mattox	Cameron	Missouri	405
MaryAnn McCurdy	Cameron	Missouri	55
Mary A. Morton	Cameron	Missouri	183
Marjorie Packard	Cameron	Missouri	482
Gene Simmons	Cameron	Missouri	187
Ivala L. Taylor	Cameron	Missouri	278
Donna Wilcox	Cameron	Missouri	236
Carolyn S. Hughes	Carrollton	Missouri	443
C. R. "Bob" Lock	Carrollton	Missouri	50
Raejean Overholtzer	Carrollton	Missouri	103
Bettie Lee Sawatzky	Carrollton	Missouri	472
Sylvia M. Eads	Castle	Missouri	314
Alice Nathan	Chatham	Illinois	286
Herbert Boude	Chillicothe	Missouri	83
Barbara Boehner Cook	Chillicothe	Missouri	465
Iona D. Coult	Chillicothe	Missouri	397
Connie Dow	Chillicothe	Missouri	141
Lois Jones	Chillicothe	Missouri	121
Ruby Lamp	Chillicothe	Missouri	261
Goldie E. Little	Chillicothe	Missouri	269
Sidney M. Miner	Chillicothe	Missouri	495
Phyllis F. Peniston	Chillicothe	Missouri	22
Rhonda Riggins	Chillicothe	Missouri	31
Sharon Condron Spainhour	Chillicothe	Missouri	81
Patty Stevens	Chillicothe	Missouri	144
Paula Wilson	Chillicothe	Missouri	468
Virginia Cruth	Clearmont	Missouri	372
Dean Fitzgerald	Columbia	Missouri	181
Rowena Smith	Columbia	Missouri	168
Betty Walch	Cottonwood	Arizona	79
Joseph E. Sullenger	Darlington	Missouri	208
Ethel Ann Williams	Darlington	Missouri	157
Marie E. Bird	Dearborn	Missouri	347
Lu Durham	Dearborn	Missouri	392
Barbara J. Farris	Dearborn	Missouri	474
Virginia Golden	Dearborn	Missouri	237
Lou Anna Williams	Dearborn	Missouri	238
Ramona Cowger	DeKalb	Missouri	430
Brenda Bennett	Dodge City	Kansas	151
Nina L. Adkinson	Eagleville	Missouri	415
William Brosi	Easton	Missouri	486
Stephen B. Givens	Easton	Missouri	176
Mrs. Howard Jackson	Easton	Missouri	182
Betty Williams	Edgerton	Missouri	256
Karen Farrell	Effingham	Kansas	370
Oleda Cooper	El Dorado	Kansas	473
Bessie C. Hainline	Elmo	Missouri	477
Dorothy Essig	Excelsior Springs	Missouri	274
Adalaye Terry-Vaughn	Excelsior Springs	Missouri	58
Eunice Rader	Fairfax	Missouri	377
Beverley (Barton) Slemp	Fairfax	Missouri	403
Lorena Stevens	Fairfax	Missouri	387
John E. Wolfe	Faucett	Missouri	374

Joyce Mendenhall	Fayetteville	Arkansas	308
Barbara Taylor Graves	Forsyth	Missouri	40
Vincent L. Scott	Freeport	Texas	251
Lois Carter	Gallatin	Missouri	32
Julie Coffman	Gallatin	Missouri	401
Bonnie Place	Gallatin	Missouri	126
Donna Carter	Gilman City	Missouri	490
Lyle M. Harrison	Gilman City	Missouri	102
Linda Milligan	Gilman City	Missouri	150
Jo Coleman	Gladstone	Missouri	83
Joyce Sherman Comfort	Gladstone	Missouri	78
Vaden Hopkins	Gladstone	Missouri	244
Neal Wharton Lawhon	Gladstone	Missouri	274
Duane Taylor	Gladstone	Missouri	262
Patricia Farris	Gower	Missouri	165
Wardie B. Hines	Gower	Missouri	146
C. Max Randal	Grand Rapids	Missouri	363
Martha (Rinehart) Groom	Grant City	Missouri	344
Carol Moriarty Parman	Grant City	Missouri	69
Doyle H. Parman	Grant City	Missouri	307
Mary M. Roach	Grant City	Missouri	275
Frances J. Heman	Green Castle	Missouri	406
Ruth Pierce	Hamilton	Missouri	197
Robert Shaney	Hamilton	Missouri	278
Donna J. Perry	Helena	Missouri	402
Gladys Reiman	Helena	Montana	36
Pauline Blanton	Hiawatha	Kansas	107
Gladys Anderson	Holt	Missouri	434
Priscilla Faulkner	Holt	Missouri	280
Norman Provow	Holt	Missouri	279
Judith Bailey Hoyt	Independence	Missouri	365
David S. McComas	Independence	Missouri	88
Louise M. Harris	Jameson	Missouri	472
Gene Prindle	Jameson	Missouri	354
Lois Prindle	Jameson	Missouri	390
Mary M. Bontrager	Jamesport	Missouri	418
Iris Boyle	Jamesport	Missouri	265
Stan Peery	Jamesport	Missouri	248
Cora Miller Ropp	Jamesport	Missouri	110
Christy D. Schrock	Jamesport	Missouri	166
Clara Soverns	Kansas	Kansas	121
Carolyn Abbott	Kansas City	Missouri	117
Mildred Irene Adkison	Kansas City	Missouri	282
Shirley Averett	Kansas City	Missouri	305
Marilyn N. Brown	Kansas City	Missouri	277
Sherry J. Brown	Kansas City	Missouri	440
Ruth Chinn	Kansas City	Kansas	171
Esther Dauma	Kansas City	Missouri	389
Neal R. Dawson	Kansas City	Missouri	214
John Delameter	Kansas City	Missouri	205
John A. Dillingham	Kansas City	Missouri	100
Max Field	Kansas City	Missouri	191
Nancy Gloth	Kansas City	Missouri	119
Thelma C. Harrold	Kansas City	Missouri	284

Clark Israel	Kansas City	Missouri	85
Carolyn Sue (Hathaway) Jones	Kansas City	Missouri	448
Donna Kitterman	Kansas City	Missouri	54
Linda Wilson Mangels	Kansas City	Missouri	195
Dorothy J. McLaughlin	Kansas City	Missouri	248
Billie Frances Mosley	Kansas City	Kansas	74
Betty Reavis	Kansas City	Missouri	386
Nita Waterman	Kansas City	Missouri	299
Virginia Whitmore	Kansas City	Missouri	27
Ruth (Massey) Cave	Kearney	Missouri	426
Marilyn A. Reed	Kearney	Missouri	167
Pat Stamper	Kearney	Missouri	149
Charles M. Turner	Kearney	Missouri	445
Mary Weldon	Kidder	Missouri	210
Carmeta F. (Hopkins) Angle	King City	Missouri	481
Romey Clayton Davis	King City	Missouri	87
Lester Estill	King City	Missouri	250
Jo Ella (DeFreece) Gilbert	King City	Missouri	232
Pat Hall	King City	Missouri	364
Larry Sealey	King City	Missouri	184
Mary Ann Willis	King City	Missouri	175
Wilma J. Woods	Kingston	Missouri	45
Tom Stegman	Lathrop	Missouri	120
Carolyn Cavender Lloyd Buck	Lawson	Missouri	137
Bonnie Carroll	Lawson	Missouri	352
Rexena Petree	Lawson	Missouri	150
Athel McIntosh	Lebanon	Missouri	388
Anna Egli-Maynard	Lee's Summit	Missouri	324
Edmund L. Miller	Lee's Summit	Missouri	66
Shirley Edwards Otis	Lee's Summit	Missouri	275
Patsy Pendergraph	Lee's Summit	Missouri	405
Janet F. Andes	Liberty	Missouri	46
Darrell Bashford	Liberty	Missouri	364
Nadine Gatterman Baugher	Liberty	Missouri	375
Betty Boettcher	Liberty	Missouri	366
Norma I. Bush	Liberty	Missouri	276
Ramona Fuenfhausen	Liberty	Missouri	129
Wilbur T. Hill	Liberty	Missouri	144
Nancy Styhl	Liberty	Missouri	376
Emma Jane Summers	Liberty	Missouri	411
Lila Weatherford	Liberty	Missouri	444
John Pope	Little Rock	Arkansas	128
Judy Wallace	Los Lunas	New Mexico	314
Eileen Schaeffer Dozier	Lowry City	Missouri	163
Marj Locker	Ludlow	Missouri	339
Clifford Webb	Ludlow	Missouri	339
Lettie Siddens	Marceline	Missouri	419
James Gerry Ferguson	Maryville	Missouri	30
Jessie Marie (Long) Jones-Smith	Maryville	Missouri	233
Ermel Joslin	Maryville	Missouri	198
Sandy Messner	Maryville	Missouri	52
Christine K. Punzo	Maryville	Missouri	316
Don Shamberger	Maryville	Missouri	229
Delores Sloan	Maryville	Missouri	103

Gene Steinmeyer	Maryville	Missouri	123
Bonnie Swalley	Maryville	Missouri	424
Vada Wooten	Maryville	Missouri	153
Lucille Zimmerman	Maryville	Missouri	293
John D. Eggleston, Sr.	Maysville	Missouri	151
Charlene Cashatt	Mesa	Arizona	407
Richard Barrett	Mound City	Missouri	351
Glen H. Brown	Mound City	Missouri	489
Maurice Fothergill	Mound City	Missouri	475
Julie Gilland	Mound City	Missouri	368
Dolores J. Huiatt	Mound City	Missouri	472
Robert Smith	Mound City	Missouri	355
Marie Wheeler	Mound City	Missouri	291
Maurice C. Wheeler	Mound City	Missouri	303
Twilla Hughes Yandell	Mound City	Missouri	413
Maurice W. Carter	Murfreesboro	Tennessee	24
Ida Mae Shultz	Newport	North Carolina	91
Bonnie (Sherwood) Allwood	Norborne	Missouri	334
Arthur T. Enss	Norborne	Missouri	199
Mildred Koontz	Norborne	Missouri	377
Alice Rosalie Riley	Norborne	Missouri	63
Bonnie Keyserling	Odessa	Missouri	37
Marilyn Maun	Odessa	Missouri	461
Virginia Province	Olathe	Kansas	145
Gary Morris	Oregon	Missouri	491
Old Bud Neiderhouse	Oregon	Missouri	109
Anna Lou Webster	Oregon	Missouri	321
Timothy D. Duncan	Orrick	Missouri	212
Imogene Clark	Osborn	Missouri	205
Peggy Moore	Overland Park	Kansas	201
William D. Huffman	Palmyra	Missouri	427
Earnest Johnson	Pasadena	Maryland	287
Lavena Lowrey	Pattonsburg	Missouri	302
Janet M. Preston	Perry	Kansas	320
Juanita Phillips Gibson	Pharr	Texas	138
L. E. "Drifter" Place	Phoenix	Arizona	431
Marjorie J. Roush	Pickering	Missouri	404
L' Berta Shelton	Pinehurst	North Carolina	240
Marsha Dale	Platte City	Missouri	241
Dorothy Donnelli	Platte City	Missouri	31
Richard C. Edwards	Platte City	Missouri	284
Betty Lutes Hoskins	Platte City	Missouri	445
Linda Lintner	Platte City	Missouri	255
Bonnie Livingston	Platte City	Missouri	239
Kay Jean Pierpoint	Platte City	Missouri	394
Connie Rawlings	Platte City	Missouri	211
Terry Barnett	Plattsburg	Missouri	384
Jean E. Beery	Plattsburg	Missouri	266
Catherine Henley	Plattsburg	Missouri	196
M. Patricia Luckenbill	Plattsburg	Missouri	186
Patricia J. Rix	Plattsburg	Missouri	229
Judith A. Wood	Plattsburg	Missouri	184
V. M. Wood	Plattsburg	Missouri	381
Colonel Philip K. Moore	Pleasant Hill	Missouri	101

Jeanie (Garner)Moore	Pleasant Hill	Missouri	310
Roger Hunt	Pocahontas	Iowa	120
George Lee, Sr.	Portland	Oregon	337
Glen Easter	Princeton	Missouri	73
Edna Goodknight	Princeton	Missouri	183
Frankie Haggard	Princeton	Missouri	363
Pearl L. Heck	Princeton	Missouri	192
Marian Moore	Princeton	Missouri	457
Peggy L. James	Ravenwood	Missouri	449
Buford Weddle	Ravenwood	Missouri	319
Neal Carpenter	Raytown	Missouri	27
Lawrence J. Jones	Raytown	Missouri	148
Dixie L. Swafford	Rayville	Missouri	325
Geraldene Pittenger	Reynoldsburg	Ohio	47
Judith Dunwoodie	Richmond	Missouri	462
Norma Edson	Richmond	Missouri	203
Virgil "Junior" Lee Johnson, Jr.	Richmond	Missouri	134
Mary Lou Leslie	Richmond	Missouri	363
Virginia Miller	Richmond	Missouri	382
Juanita Sherwood	Richmond	Missouri	38
Ed Chamberlin	Ridgeway	Missouri	193
Wanda Geyer Findley	Ridgeway	Missouri	36
Norma Jean (Benson) Medlin	Ridgeway	Missouri	162
Bonnie D. Harville	Robertsdale	Alabama	222
Donald Daugherty	Rock Port	Missouri	395
Martha Smith	Rock Port	Missouri	388
Dawn Blair	Rosendale	Missouri	306
Carolyn Sawyers Tulloch	San Jose	California	84
Diana Arn	Savannah	Missouri	392
Sylva Bowman	Savannah	Missouri	113
Lora Ellen Crowley	Savannah	Missouri	376
Ruthanna Ezzell	Savannah	Missouri	352
Adeline Flint	Savannah	Missouri	444
Walter Maris	Savannah	Missouri	118
Marilyn Moran	Savannah	Missouri	296
Marguerite Smith	Savannah	Missouri	328
Keith Stanton	Savannah	Missouri	115
Everett Dale Thompson	Savannah	Missouri	261
Donald Vilven	Savannah	Missouri	65
Shirley Peterson	Shelbyville	Missouri	399
Deborah Dilks	Sibley	Missouri	262
Pastor James F. "Jim" Broker	Skidmore	Missouri	459
Karen Jones	Skidmore	Missouri	29
Sharon Aring	Smithville	Missouri	375
Don Foster	Smithville	Missouri	285
Randell McCloud	Spickard	Missouri	268
Larry Pollard	Spickard	Missouri	54
Mary Waldron Greene	Springfield	Missouri	70
Ruth Carol Trotter Proffitt	Springfield	Missouri	207
Mary Ann (Hughs) Allen	St. Charles	Missouri	306
William H. Davis	St. Johns	Florida	152
Neal E. Arnold	St. Joseph	Missouri	252
Sandra Kay Ashler	St. Joseph	Missouri	353
Norma Louise Barnes	St. Joseph	Missouri	435

Nancy R. Belcher	St. Joseph	Missouri	143
Ethel Bledsoe	St. Joseph	Missouri	362
Helen M. Brock	St. Joseph	Missouri	197
Nancy Browne	St. Joseph	Missouri	350
Margie Buescher	St. Joseph	Missouri	360
John Buhman	St. Joseph	Missouri	20
Dick Couldry	St. Joseph	Missouri	494
Sharon Curren	St. Joseph	Missouri	428
Richard Drozd	St. Joseph	Missouri	76
Richard Eisenberg	St. Joseph	Missouri	111
Jean Farthing	St. Joseph	Missouri	156
Mary Jane Fields	St. Joseph	Missouri	437
Larry Flinchpaugh	St. Joseph	Missouri	60
Helen Patricia Fountain	St. Joseph	Missouri	100
Florence Fries	St. Joseph	Missouri	33
Paula A. Gibson	St. Joseph	Missouri	147
Julia Hautzenroeder	St. Joseph	Missouri	107
Bonnie Hoecker	St. Joseph	Missouri	307
Patricia A. Jones	St. Joseph	Missouri	250
Carolyn S. Kiner	St. Joseph	Missouri	429
Doug Kingery	St. Joseph	Missouri	425
Janice Lathrop	St. Joseph	Missouri	297
Ronald Lathrop	St. Joseph	Missouri	237
Virginia Luikart	St. Joseph	Missouri	402
Neva Lyons	St. Joseph	Missouri	385
Verba Massey	St. Joseph	Missouri	378
Carole McClellan	St. Joseph	Missouri	196
Connie S. Merriott	St. Joseph	Missouri	151
Maxine Deatherage Monroe	St. Joseph	Missouri	204
Huston E. Myers	St. Joseph	Missouri	97
Buddy Nigh	St. Joseph	Missouri	105
Eileen Oyler	St. Joseph	Missouri	114
Billie Paden	St. Joseph	Missouri	113
Emma F. Patterson	St. Joseph	Missouri	376
Maxine Pew	St. Joseph	Missouri	386
Katherine M. Rhodes	St. Joseph	Missouri	226
Margaret McCush Roberts	St. Joseph	Missouri	155
Mildred D. Roberts	St. Joseph	Missouri	166
Joanna Jackson Shaw	St. Joseph	Missouri	44
Linda Shoots	St. Joseph	Missouri	145
Carl Spillman	St. Joseph	Missouri	195
Norman O. Steidel	St. Joseph	Missouri	290
Glennrose Gann Steward	St. Joseph	Missouri	156
Robert Stinson	St. Joseph	Missouri	143
Darlene Y. Terry	St. Joseph	Missouri	144
J. Peter Thielen	St. Joseph	Missouri	57
Donna L. Thomas	St. Joseph	Missouri	380
Nancy Thompson	St. Joseph	Missouri	380
Helen Walters	St. Joseph	Missouri	124
Nancy Ann Webster	St. Joseph	Missouri	219
Dixie Lee Leffler Wilkinson	St. Joseph	Missouri	179
Carol Wood	St. Joseph	Missouri	488
Louise Wilkerson Cummins	Stanberry	Missouri	144
Kathleen Eckard	Stanberry	Missouri	410

Irene Ellis	Stanberry	Missouri	267
Laurel Evans	Stanberry	Missouri	309
Warren James	Stanberry	Missouri	150
Lester E. Pierce	Stanberry	Missouri	161
Duane Stuart	Stanberry	Missouri	265
Roy D. Stuart	Stanberry	Missouri	423
Ken White	Stockton	Missouri	215
Philip R. Clark	Tarkio	Missouri	276
Duane Clement	Tarkio	Missouri	466
Sherry Clement	Tarkio	Missouri	25
Beverly L. Gibbons	Tarkio	Missouri	195
Mildred M. Hurst	Tarkio	Missouri	455
Jack Mehaffey	Tarkio	Missouri	275
Deloris (Tyler)Reeves	Tarkio	Missouri	322
Mary Eulalah Adwell	Tempe	Arizona	41
Joanne Kline	Traverse City	Michigan	422
Marian Campbell	Trenton	Missouri	173
Lucille Fletcher	Trenton	Missouri	403
Doris Griffin	Trenton	Missouri	149
Mary Foland Holt	Trenton	Missouri	101
Rick Mason	Trenton	Missouri	114
Janice L. Miller	Trenton	Missouri	271
Betty Smith	Trenton	Missouri	358
Betty Taul	Trenton	Missouri	433
Dorothy Taul	Trenton	Missouri	373
Rebecca Ann Howe Taylor	Trenton	Missouri	258
Sherry Miller	Trimble	Missouri	34
Linda Kay Guy	Troy	Kansas	453
John W. Hutchcraft	Union Star	Missouri	18
Lorraine S. Walter	Waldport	Oregon	274
Melville Booher Davis	Washington Center	Missouri	345
Jenny Beutler	Watson	Missouri	412
Kay Gibson	Watson	Missouri	127
James Nicks	Watson	Missouri	30
Marolynn Shafer	Waukee	Iowa	387
Beverly Clinkingbeard	Westboro	Missouri	49
Lyllis Vette	Westboro	Missouri	451
Ruby Allen	Weston	Missouri	391
Nancy Hope Chitty	Weston	Missouri	74
Elaine Grame	Weston	Missouri	438
Melissa Kimball	Weston	Missouri	115
Frances Berryman Munsterman	Weston	Missouri	146
Dorothea Scott Payne	Weston	Missouri	408
Reginald Werner Robertson	Wheatland	Missouri	484
Juanita Waters	Williamsburg	Kentucky	177
Dr. Harold E. Hayden	Worth	Missouri	213
Wanda Pierson Hayden	Worth	Missouri	217
Jerry Kincannon	Zebulon	North Carolina	253

Index B (Year of Birth)

Geraldene Pittenger	1923	47
Eunice Rader	1923	377
Judy Wallace	1923	314
Richard Barrett	1924	351
Margie Buescher	1924	360
Norma I. Bush	1924	276
Charles G. Cotton	1924	281
Betty O'Connor Curtis	1924	201
Betty Henderson	1924	216
Bonnie Hoecker	1924	307
Lawrence J. Jones	1924	148
Lavena Lowrey	1924	302
Christine K. Punzo	1924	316
Ida Mae Shultz	1924	91
Betty Taul	1924	433
Ruby Allen	1925	391
Neal Carpenter	1925	27
Lucille Fletcher	1925	403
John Pope	1925	128
Robert Shaney	1925	278
Keith Stanton	1925	115
Lila Weatherford	1925	444
Marian Campbell	1926	173
Irene Ellis	1926	267
Neva Everly	1926	122
Florence Flanary	1926	357
Edna Goodknight	1926	183
Warren James	1926	150
Verba Massey	1926	378
Emma F. Patterson	1926	376
Phyllis F. Peniston	1926	22
Lois Pauline (Clark) Peterson	1926	313
Bonnie Place	1926	126
Christy D. Schrock	1926	166
Marolynn Shafer	1926	387
L' Berta Shelton	1926	240
Lettie Siddens	1926	419
Gene Simmons	1926	187
Carolyn Abbott	1927	117
V. Cooper	1927	329
Iona D. Coult	1927	397
Laurel Evans	1927	309
Florence Fries	1927	33
Juanita Phillips Gibson	1927	138
Pearl L. Heck	1927	192
William D. Huffman	1927	427
C. R. "Bob" Lock	1927	50
Marilyn A. Reed	1927	167
Mary M. Roach	1927	275
Juanita Sherwood	1927	38
V. M. Wood	1927	381
Susie L. Berry	1928	249
Maurice W. Carter	1928	24
Mary Jane Fields	1928	437

Dean Fitzgerald	1928	181
Darlene Holliday	1928	279
Dolores J. Huiatt	1928	472
Sidney M. Miner	1928	495
James D. Parman	1928	249
C. Max Randal	1928	363
Beverley (Barton) Slemp	1928	403
Delores Sloan	1928	103
Lorena Stevens	1928	387
Anna Lou Webster	1928	321
Ruthanna Ezzell	1929	352
Joanne Kline	1929	422
George Lee, Sr.	1929	337
Dorothy Mattox	1929	405
Marian Moore	1929	457
Eileen Oyler	1929	114
Marjorie Packard	1929	482
Betty Smith	1929	358
Adalaye Terry-Vaughn	1929	58
Buford Weddle	1929	319
Ken White	1929	215
Connie Yates	1929	190
Betty Boettcher	1930	366
Iris Boyle	1930	265
Anna Egli-Maynard	1930	324
Bessie C. Hainline	1930	477
Athel McIntosh	1930	388
Reginald Werner Robertson	1930	484
Juanita Waters	1930	177
Virginia Whitmore	1930	27
Mary Ann Willis	1930	175
Vada Wooten	1930	153
Nina L. Adkinson	1931	415
Darrell Bashford	1931	364
Nancy R. Belcher	1931	143
Philip R. Clark	1931	276
Joyce Sherman Comfort	1931	78
Kathleen Eckard	1931	410
Jessie Marie (Long) Jones-Smith	1931	233
Ruby Lamp	1931	261
Neal Wharton Lawhon	1931	274
Neva Lyons	1931	385
Randell McCloud	1931	268
Patricia J. Rix	1931	229
Robert Stinson	1931	143
Lyllis Vette	1931	451
William F. Yates	1931	283
Jean E. Beery	1932	266
Joyce A. Bell	1932	332
Glen H. Brown	1932	489
Nancy Browne	1932	350
Elaine Flint Bullock	1932	182
Martha Burks	1932	159
Ramona Cowger	1932	430

Virginia Cruth	1932	372
Norma Edson	1932	203
Bonnie D. Harville	1932	222
Dr. Harold E. Hayden	1932	213
Betty Lutes Hoskins	1932	445
Ermel Joslin	1932	198
Darline Kussmann	1932	288
Bonnie Livingston	1932	239
Marilyn Maun	1932	461
Dorothea Scott Payne	1932	408
Deloris (Tyler)Reeves	1932	322
Carolyn Sawyers Tulloch	1932	84
Mary Weldon	1932	210
Carmeta F. (Hopkins) Angle	1933	481
Bonnie Carroll	1933	352
Donna Carter	1933	490
Lois Carter	1933	32
Charlene Cashatt	1933	407
William R. Clark	1933	224
Oleda Cooper	1933	473
Patricia Farris	1933	165
Don Foster	1933	285
Maurice Fothergill	1933	475
Martha (Rinehart) Groom	1933	344
Carolyn S. Hughes	1933	443
Roger Hunt	1933	120
Stan Peery	1933	248
Marilou Perris	1933	17
Donna J. Perry	1933	402
Mildred D. Roberts	1933	166
Martha Smith	1933	388
Donald Vilven	1933	65
Maurice C. Wheeler	1933	303
Mary Ann (Hughs) Allen	1934	306
Anna L. Clark	1934	447
Louise Wilkerson Cummins	1934	144
Max Field	1934	191
Helen Patricia Fountain	1934	100
Ramona Fuenfhausen	1934	129
M. Patricia Luckenbill	1934	186
Peggy Moore	1934	201
Mary A. Morton	1934	183
Rexena Petree	1934	150
Betty Reavis	1934	386
Norman O. Steidel	1934	290
Beverly Stevens	1934	379
Glennrose Gann Steward	1934	156
Ron Wray	1934	317
Norma Appleman	1935	274
Pauline Blanton	1935	107
Betty J. Clement	1935	311
Barbara Boehner Cook	1935	465
Wanda Geyer Findley	1935	36
Judith Bailey Hoyt	1935	365

Mildred M. Hurst	1935	455
Carolyn S. Kiner	1935	429
Norma Jean (Benson) Medlin	1935	162
Norman Provow	1935	279
Rebecca Ann Howe Taylor	1935	258
Marie Wheeler	1935	291
Twilla Hughes Yandell	1935	413
Sherry J. Brown	1936	440
Wanda Pierson Hayden	1936	217
Walter Maris	1936	118
Carole McClellan	1936	196
Huston E. Myers	1936	97
Buddy Nigh	1936	105
Gene Prindle	1936	354
Marjorie J. Roush	1936	404
Ron Searcy	1936	350
Don Shamberger	1936	229
Tom Stegman	1936	120
Emma Jane Summers	1936	411
Darlene Y. Terry	1936	144
Donna Wilcox	1936	236
Ed Coles	1937	125
Virginia Golden	1937	237
Frances J. Heman	1937	406
Mary Foland Holt	1937	101
Goldie E. Little	1937	269
MaryAnn McCurdy	1937	55
Colonel Philip K. Moore	1937	101
Patty Stevens	1937	144
John E. Wolfe	1937	374
Wilma J. Woods	1937	45
Bonnie (Sherwood) Allwood	1938	334
Beverly Clinkingbeard	1938	49
Patsy Cox	1938	478
Eileen Schaeffer Dozier	1938	163
Dorothy Essig	1938	274
Priscilla Faulkner	1938	280
Jo Ella (DeFreece) Gilbert	1938	232
Lois Jones	1938	121
Janice Lathrop	1938	297
Mary Lou Leslie	1938	363
Doyle H. Parman	1938	307
Kay Jean Pierpoint	1938	394
Rowena Smith	1938	168
Nancy Ann Webster	1938	219
Carol Wood	1938	488
Evelyn Anderson	1939	95
Dawn Blair	1939	306
Pastor James F. "Jim" Broker	1939	459
Marilyn N. Brown	1939	277
Barbara A. Butler	1939	312
Duane Clement	1939	466
John A. Dillingham	1939	100
Arthur T.Enss	1939	199

Barbara Taylor Graves	1939	40
Ruby Hawkins	1939	169
Earnest Johnson	1939	287
Edmund L. Miller	1939	66
James Mills	1939	243
Marilyn Moran	1939	296
Ruth Pierce	1939	197
Duane Stuart	1939	265
J. PeterThielen	1939	57
Janet F. Andes	1940	46
Sandra Kay Ashler	1940	353
GeorgeBowles	1940	270
Carolyn Cavender Lloyd Buck	1940	137
Dorothy Donnelli	1940	31
Carolyn Sue (Hathaway) Jones	1940	448
BonnieKeyserling	1940	37
Old Bud Neiderhouse	1940	109
Janet M. Preston	1940	320
Cora Miller Ropp	1940	110
Carl Spillman	1940	195
Bonnie Swalley	1940	424
Lucille Zimmerman	1940	293
Sharon Aring	1941	375
Marie E. Bird	1941	347
Judith Dunwoodie	1941	462
John W. Hutchcraft	1941	18
Virginia Miller	1941	382
Jeanie (Garner) Moore	1941	310
Patsy Pendergraph	1941	405
Ruth Carol Trotter Proffitt	1941	207
Katherine M. Rhodes	1941	226
Margaret McCush Roberts	1941	155
Larry Sealey	1941	184
Joanna Jackson Shaw	1941	44
Donna L. Thomas	1941	380
Nita Waterman	1941	299
Dixie Lee Leffler Wilkinson	1941	179
Shirley Averett	1942	305
Patricia A. Jones	1942	250
Connie S. Merriott	1942	151
Alice Rosalie Riley	1942	63
Nancy Styhl	1942	376
Everett Dale Thompson	1942	261
Betty Walch	1942	79
Ethel Ann Williams	1942	157
Carol Kay Wolf	1942	378
Judith A. Wood	1942	184
Una Buck	1943	307
Ed Chamberlin	1943	193
Nancy Hope Chitty	1943	74
Dick Couldry	1943	494
Donald Daugherty	1943	395
John Delameter	1943	205
Richard Eisenberg	1943	111

Kay Gibson	1943	127
Ronald Lathrop	1943	237
Janice L. Miller	1943	271
Linda Milligan	1943	150
Connie Rawlings	1943	211
Joyce Ridge	1943	318
Lorraine S. Walter	1943	274
Jenny Beutler	1944	412
William Brosi	1944	486
Georgia Corbin	1944	401
Esther Dauma	1944	389
Richard Drozd	1944	76
Paula A. Gibson	1944	147
Elaine Grame	1944	438
Donna Kitterman	1944	54
Sherry Clement	1945	25
Sharon Curren	1945	428
Melville Booher Davis	1945	345
Jean Farthing	1945	156
L. E. "Drifter" Place	1945	431
Paula Wilson	1945	468
Herbert Boude	1946	83
Jo Coleman	1946	83
Glen Easter	1946	73
Nancy Gloth	1946	119
Lyle M. Harrison	1946	102
Virgil "Junior" Lee Johnson, Jr.	1946	134
Shirley Peterson	1946	399
Diana Arn	1947	392
Connie Dow	1947	141
Adeline Flint	1947	444
Russell L. Gienapp	1947	470
Karen Jones	1947	29
Joyce Mendenhall	1947	308
Gary Morris	1947	491
Donna Keever Pitts	1947	260
Charles M. Turner	1947	445
Helen Walters	1947	124
Barbara J. Farris	1948	474
James Gerry Ferguson	1948	30
Rick Folsom	1948	342
Mary Waldron Greene	1948	70
David S. McComas	1948	88
James Nicks	1948	30
Dixie L. Swafford	1948	325
Duane Taylor	1948	262
Betty Williams	1948	256
Timothy D. Duncan	1949	212
Richard C. Edwards	1949	284
Stephen B. Givens	1949	176
Doug Kingery	1949	425
Frances Berryman Munsterman	1949	146
Larry Pollard	1949	54
Rhonda Riggins	1949	31

Linda Shoots	1949	145
Sharon Condron Spainhour	1949	81
Dorothy Taul	1949	373
Mary M. Bontrager	1950	418
Joyce Ann Coffman	1950	133
Marsha Dale	1951	241
Deborah Dilks	1951	262
Peggy L. James	1951	449
Linda Lintner	1951	255
Rebecca Jean (Berry) McGregor	1951	93
Sherry Miller	1951	34
Joseph E. Sullenger	1951	208
Terry Barnett	1953	384
Melissa Kimball	1953	115
Alice Nathan	1953	286
Raejean Overholtzer	1953	103
Pat Stamper	1953	149
Sandy Messner	1954	52
Linda Wilson Mangels	1956	195
Karen Farrell	1957	370
Marj Locker	1958	339
Nancy Thompson	1958	380
Brenda Bennett	1959	151
Linda Kay Guy	1965	453
Julie Coffman	1969	401
Neal E. Arnold	Unknown	252
Delbert Beechy	Unknown	131
Helen M. Brock	Unknown	197
Imogene Clark	Unknown	205
Lora Ellen Crowley	Unknown	376
Romey Clayton Davis	Unknown	87
Larry Flinchpaugh	Unknown	60
Beverly L. Gibbons	Unknown	195
Pat Hall	Unknown	364
Catherine Henley	Unknown	196
Clark Israel	Unknown	85
Mrs. Howard Jackson	Unknown	182
Lila Kidney	Unknown	472
Jerry Kincannon	Unknown	253
Mildred Koontz	Unknown	377
Rick Mason	Unknown	114
Shirley Edwards Otis	Unknown	275
Carol Moriarty Parman	Unknown	69
Bill Prindle	Unknown	389
Lois Prindle	Unknown	390
Wilford Prindle	Unknown	23
Bettie Lee Sawatzky	Unknown	472
Marguerite Smith	Unknown	328
Clara Soverns	Unknown	121
Gene Steinmeyer	Unknown	123